Volume 3

The Human Odyssey

From Modern Times to Our Contemporary Era

Edited by Mary Beth Klee, John Cribb, and John Holdren

Contributing Writers

Tamim Ansary
Roger Bruns
Robin Currie
Rebecca Jones
James Lynch
Mara Rockliff
Michael Stanford

Academic Reviewers

John Breihan *Loyola College*
Benjamin Elman *Princeton University*
Sheldon Garon *Princeton University*
Patricia Herlihy *Brown University*
Morton Keller *Brandeis University*
Michael Rubin *The American Enterprise Institute for Public Policy Research*
Luther Spoehr *Brown University*
Sheldon Stern *Former Historian, John F. Kennedy Presidential Library*
Edward Woodfin *Converse College*

Staff for This Volume

Lisa Dimaio Iekel *Project Manager and Production Manager*
Jeff Burridge *Text Editor*
Kay McCarthy *Associate Text Editor*
Suzanne Montazer *Art Director*
Jayoung Cho *Senior Designer*
Charlotte Fullerton *Illustrations Editor*
Lee Horton *Illustrations Researcher*
Jean Stringer *Rights Specialist*
Betsy Woodman *Research Editor*
Martin Walz *Map Editor*
Martha Sencindiver *Indexer*
Patricia Pearson *Teaching Specialist*
Ashley Young *Clean Reader*
Connie Moy *Quality Control Manager*

Bror Saxberg *Chief Learning Officer*
John Holdren *Senior Vice President for Content and Curriculum*
Mary Desrosiers *Senior Vice President for Product Development*
Maria Szalay *Vice President for Product Development*
Tom DiGiovanni *Senior Director of Instructional Design*
Kim Barcas *Creative Director*
John Agnone *Director of Publications*
Charles Kogod *Director of Media and IP Management*
Jeff Burridge *Managing Editor*
Corey Maender *Senior Project Manager*
Candee Wilson *Online Project Manager*

About K12 Inc.

Founded in 1999, K12 Inc. is an elementary and secondary school service combining rich academic content with powerful technology. K12 serves students in a variety of education settings, both public and private, including school classrooms, virtual charter schools, home schools, and tutoring centers. K12 currently provides comprehensive curricular offerings in the following subjects: Language Arts/English, History, Math, Science, Visual Arts, and Music. The K12 curriculum blends high quality offline materials with innovative online resources, including interactive lessons, teacher guides, and tools for planning and assessment. For more information, call 1-888-YOUR K12 or visit www.K12.com.

Volume 3

The Human Odyssey

From Modern Times to Our Contemporary Era

Edited by Mary Beth Klee, John Cribb, and John Holdren

K12

Cover Images

Front cover and title page:
Top: U.S. astronaut Joseph R. Tanner helps build the International Space Station, 2006
Bottom: Canadian soldiers train for battle in France during World War I, 1916

These two images—one of a modern marvel, the other of a modern catastrophe—recall the heights and depths of the human odyssey during the contemporary era. In the photo at top, Joseph R. Tanner is floating more than 200 miles above the earth's surface as he works on the International Space Station. The space shuttle *Atlantis* carried Tanner and his fellow astronauts to the station. The bottom photo was taken during World War I, one of the most disastrous wars in history. Canadian soldiers in northern France practice scrambling out of a trench, known as going "over the top," to attack enemy trench lines. Much of the fighting in World War I bogged down into such trench warfare.

Back cover top: Alexander Graham Bell sends his voice across more than 800 miles of wire as he makes the first telephone call from New York to Chicago in 1892. Bell invented the telephone in 1876.

Back cover bottom: Kenyan environmental and political activist Wangari Maathai receives congratulations via cell phone after winning the Nobel Peace Prize in 2004. Throughout the world, cellular technology has brought phone service to remote areas where telephone lines would be difficult and expensive to install.

978-1-60153-018-9

Library of Congress Control Number: 2004007909

Printed by Quad Graphics, Versailles, KY, USA, May 2018

Contents

Part 2 The Cataclysm (1914–1946)

Part 3 Nuclear Stakes in a Shrinking World (1947–the present)

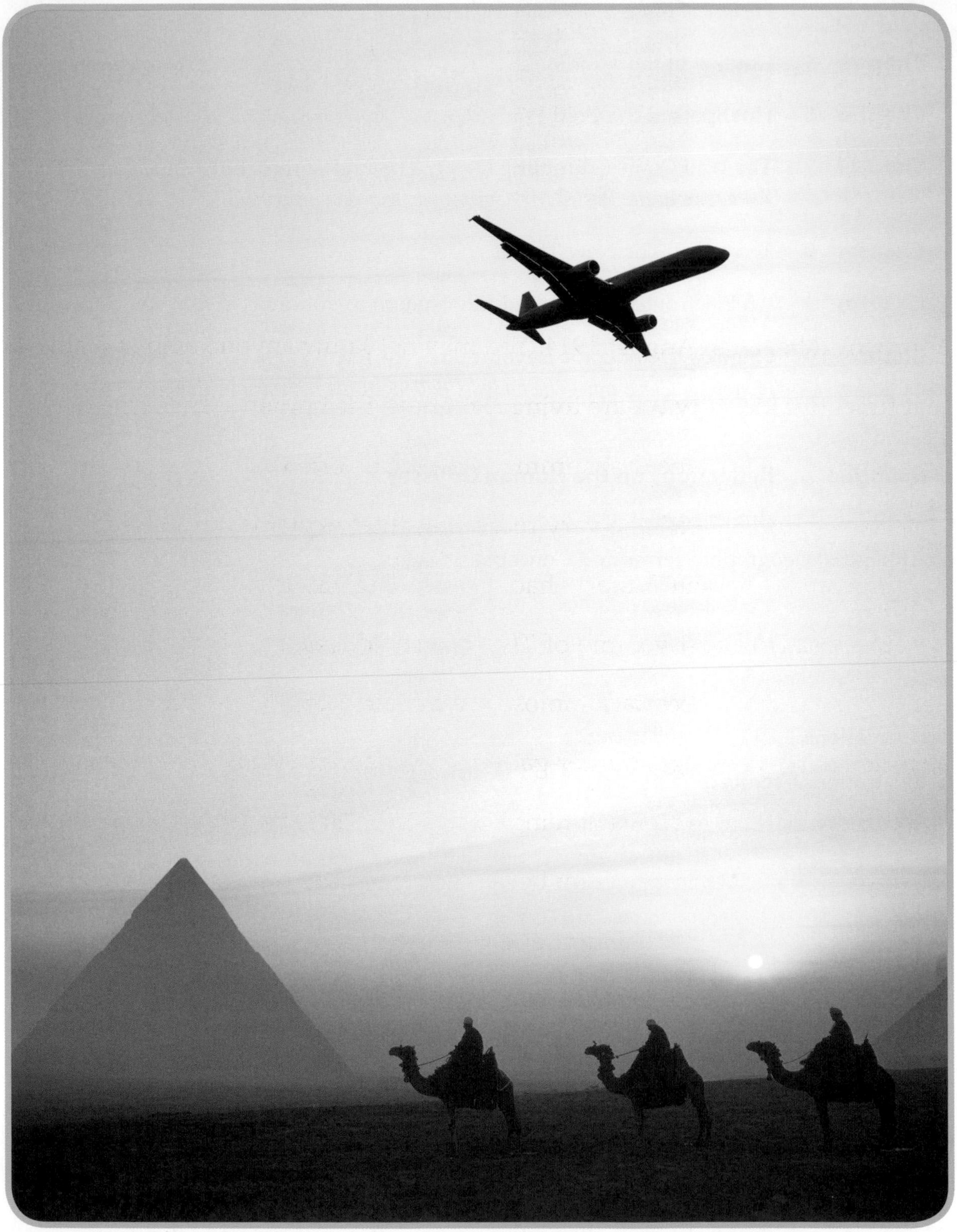

A modern jetliner soars over ancient Egyptian pyramids, suggesting how our contemporary era is part of a human odyssey that links us to distant times and places, and takes new forms each day. (photo montage)

Your History, Your World

Your world began in August 1914. You may not know anyone who was alive at that time. But the story we are living right now, the human story of the twenty-first century, took shape that summer. Historians often call it the beginning of "the contemporary era," the very recent past that explains our present.

Of course, human history had been going on long, long before 1914. If you've read the first volume of *The Human Odyssey*, you know that our human journey goes back almost two million years. More than fifteen thousand years ago, hunter-gatherers wandered at the edge of ice sheets, and etched charcoal portraits of reindeer and bulls on cave walls. They fashioned tools, such as needles made from bone, and cleavers and arrowheads of stone.

An *odyssey* is a long and adventurous journey.

Over time, those early men and women used their ingenuity to do less hunting and more farming. They channeled water from rivers to irrigate fields. In time, they grew more crops than they needed to survive. This surplus of food was a great leap forward for humanity. It meant that some people could now devote themselves to other work besides hunting or farming — they could build or bake or make pottery or do other specialized jobs.

When you have a *surplus*, you have more than you need of something.

Ancient Egyptian scribes toil beneath hieroglyphic symbols.

The Renaissance: A Rebirth of Classical Ideals

The word *Renaissance* means "rebirth." This time in Europe, from the late fourteenth to early seventeenth centuries, was in part a rebirth of classical ideals of beauty in art and architecture. *Classical* here means "from ancient Greek and Roman times." Renaissance artists such as Leonardo da Vinci, Michelangelo, and Raphael created drawings, paintings, and sculptures that breathed new life into classical ideals of beauty. Michelangelo's 14-foot-tall statue of David, carved from a single block of marble, revives classical ideals of grace and form, while embodying the Renaissance spirit of nobility, daring, and confidence.

Michelangelo completed the *David* in 1504.

About five thousand years ago, human beings took another great step forward when they developed writing. On clay tablets or on pyramid walls, scribes told how people worked and harvested, who ruled them, and what gods they worshipped. With writing, humans could easily pass on knowledge. They began building cities. Soon they built awe-inspiring civilizations. You can still see the remains of what these early people built — for example, Sumerian ziggurats, Egyptian pyramids, Hebrew and Greek temples, Indian baths, and Chinese city walls.

These different peoples developed complex ideas about how to live a good life, how to govern themselves, and what laws they should follow. In their monuments, their writings, and their art, they recorded their beliefs about their gods or God.

These civilizations that flourished thousands of years ago often developed in splendid isolation. For all that they knew of each other's existence, most might as well have been on different planets. The ancient Egyptians didn't know about the Chinese. The ancient Greeks hadn't heard of the Olmecs, nor had the Olmecs heard of the Greeks. Tenth-century Vikings sailing the seas didn't know about Anasazi cliff-dwellers in America's southwest. Australian aborigines had never heard of African chieftains.

In the second volume of *The Human Odyssey*, we saw how our modern world began to take shape when human beings from different parts of the globe began to discover each other. These encounters between cultures and civilizations really took off when European mariners figured out how to build sleek, lightweight ships. Curious about their world and eager to make a profit, Europeans set out to explore the globe and establish colonies in many lands. Soon, peoples from different hemispheres met, and often clashed. Spanish conquistadors fought Aztec warriors. English colonists took land from North American Woodland peoples. Arab traders and European merchants bought African slaves.

These encounters between different civilizations changed the world forever. Suddenly, the world's continents and their peoples were linked in various ways — by trade, conquest, and settlement. Our world became a little smaller.

The energy that drove Europeans to explore far-off lands was part of the spirit of the Renaissance

(REH-nuh-sahns), a period of great European cultural achievement from the late fourteenth to early seventeenth centuries. It was a time marked by curiosity about the here and now, and a new confidence in human potential and achievement. Many historians see the beginnings of our modern world in the Renaissance. Indeed, one defining feature of the modern world is the spread of European civilization that began in Renaissance times.

Of course, during the long span of the fifteenth to seventeenth centuries, Europe was not the only place where great things were happening. Civilizations beyond Europe also flourished. While Portuguese explorers probed the African coast, the Inca in Peru built a vast system of roads, as well as Machu Picchu, an extraordinary city high in the Andes mountains. While English colonists were settling in Massachusetts Bay, India's Mughal emperor put the finishing touches on the Taj Mahal, a breathtakingly beautiful memorial to his dead wife. While French navigators explored Canadian lakes and rivers, Chinese rulers busily dictated laws from their newly completed Forbidden City, and sent warriors on horseback to patrol along the seemingly endless Great Wall, built to keep out invaders from the north. Still, the biggest changes during this time — changes that brought civilizations and cultures into contact and launched our modern world — were driven by European confidence, curiosity, and profit-seeking.

In the 1600s, as Europeans continued to explore and colonize far-off lands, many European thinkers looked closely at the physical world and made great strides in understanding the workings of nature. In Italy, for example, Galileo Galilei designed a telescope and studied the night sky. He confirmed that the Earth moves around the sun, and not, as people had long believed, vice versa. In England, Isaac Newton developed ground-breaking ideas in astronomy, mathematics, and physics. As scholars learned more and more through careful observation and experimentation, a Scientific Revolution began to change the way people thought and lived. Many thinkers grew confident that the physical world operated according to predictable "laws of nature." They became convinced they could use their powers of reasoning to discover those laws of nature.

At about the same time, political philosophers, such as England's John Locke, believed that human reason could also perceive natural laws about human society and human rights. Locke thought that people have natural rights to life, liberty, and property, and that governments must protect these rights. Across the Atlantic, England's American colonists agreed. In 1776, the thirteen American colonies declared independence from England. This radical step, the colonists said, was necessary to defend their rights to "life, liberty,

India's Taj Mahal, built in the 1630s, is one of the most striking examples of Muslim architecture in the world.

Locomotives, like this British one from 1899, helped reshape the world during the Industrial Revolution.

and the pursuit of happiness." European kings and queens grew more alarmed when the American Revolution sparked a wave of democratic uprisings in Europe and South America.

Another kind of revolution — an Industrial Revolution — was starting to change the way many people lived and worked. In the early 1700s, British inventors experimented with power-driven machinery and developed new mechanical looms and pumps that made it possible to produce more goods faster than ever before. By 1870, England churned out more cloth, thread, iron, and steel than any other nation. New means of transportation, such as steamships and locomotives, and new means of communication, such as the telegraph and the telephone, caused the world to shrink even more.

Which brings us to the summer of 1914. In August, human engineering and effort combined to link two oceans that had been separated by continents for millennia. When the Panama Canal opened on August 15, ships could travel easily from the Atlantic to the Pacific Ocean. For the first time, steamships from Europe did not have to circle the entire South American continent before heading west to China or Japan. Large vessels from California could cut right through the narrow Isthmus of Panama and continue on their way east to New York City. This shortened their trips by months. The Panama Canal, with its massive concrete locks, swinging steel gates, and fifteen hundred electric motors, filled people with a surge of pride. Human ingenuity had overcome one of the great challenges of nature. This was 1914! This was progress!

Millennia is the plural of millennium, a period of 1,000 years.

Why then did no one come to celebrate the canal's opening? Because something else happened in August 1914: the beginning of the First World War. What exactly does that phrase mean, a "world war"? To understand, keep in mind that war has had a long and grim role in human history.

War has been part of the human condition for as long as human beings have walked the planet. Sumerian city-states battled each other. Ancient Egyptians fought the Nubians and Hittites. The ancient Persians attacked the ancient Greeks. Greek city-states fought each other so often that they resolved to declare a truce every four years in order to hold the Olympic Games. Chinese warlords routinely attacked each other and then the Mongols. The Mongols waged war on anyone to their south and west. Arab tribes went to war against other Arabs, and then pushed into non-Muslim lands. European Christians launched wars against Muslims in the Crusades, and then they fought each other for thirty long years. The Aztecs conquered and enslaved their neighbors. Some African tribes battled each other and sold their captives into slavery.

The fact is, in 1914, war was not new anywhere in the world. But the war that began in August 1914 was different. It started in Europe with an assassination, and soon it raged on five seas and two continents. It engaged peoples from all over the globe. It killed millions — *millions*.

This unprecedented and expansive conflict marks the beginning of our era, the contemporary era, a time in which the long march of

Help with Pronunciation

In this book you will encounter words that may be new to you. To help you pronounce those words, we have respelled them to show how you say them. For example, the word *Renaissance* is respelled as (REH-nuh-sahns). The capital letters indicate which syllable to accent. For a closer look at how to pronounce the respelled words, see the Pronunciation Guide on page 408.

human progress has taken unexpected turns, some for the better, some for the worse. When the twentieth century began, most people in the Western world greeted it with optimistic hopes for human progress. People anticipated a healthier, more prosperous, better fed, better educated, better governed, and better connected world. They looked forward to such wonders as air travel. Some even dreamed of space travel.

Today, a century later, science and technology have made giant strides. Smallpox and other diseases that once killed thousands have been eliminated or are on the wane. The world's food supply has grown enormously. Human beings have set foot on the moon. Communication is instantaneous with television, computers, the Internet, and cell phones. People are better clothed and better fed than ever before. More people than ever enjoy the benefits of liberty. More nations are led by democratic governments, and more people exercise hard-won freedoms of thought, action, and speech.

But all that progress has come at a huge cost in lives lost, nations destroyed, and havoc wreaked. The scientific progress of the twentieth century has resulted not just in antibiotics but also in nuclear weapons that can destroy the planet, as well as pollutants that are gradually endangering the environment. Technological progress—in electronics, chemicals, and arms—has made it possible for dictators and demagogues to control, spy upon, and sometimes wipe out large numbers of their peoples.

A *demagogue* is someone who stirs up people's prejudices and makes false claims and promises in order to gain power.

The world community has grown ever more closely linked, but at the start of the twenty-first century, it remains a community of nearly two hundred independent nation-states. Each nation makes its own choices and sets its own priorities. International organizations officially proclaim common ideals of freedom, equality, and human dignity, but many people, and some leaders in key places, reject these ideals.

Much of the best and worst of our times emerged simultaneously and in ways hard to separate. In Part 1 of this book, we'll start by looking back at events leading up to 1914. Then we'll move to our contemporary era and focus on the cataclysmic events of the first part of the twentieth century, including two world wars and the Great Depression. We'll then turn to examine some staggering problems and astounding accomplishments of the twentieth century's second half.

This book is mostly about the contemporary era, the world into which you were born and will live out your lives. It's your history, and your world. A wise leader once said, "We study the past in order to commit ourselves to the future." In this book, we're looking back, but we're really talking about your future.

What's "Western"?

To historians, *Western* civilization refers not to a direction but to ideas and values inherited from the ancient Greeks and Hebrews, and generally shared in Europe and the Americas. Western civilization is sometimes contrasted with Eastern civilization, made up of the shared ideas of India, China, Japan, and other countries.

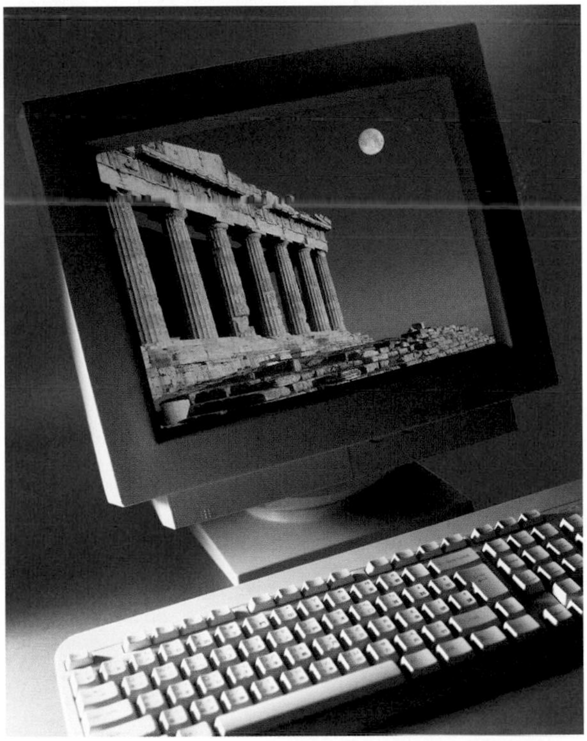

A new way to see the ancient Parthenon (photo montage)

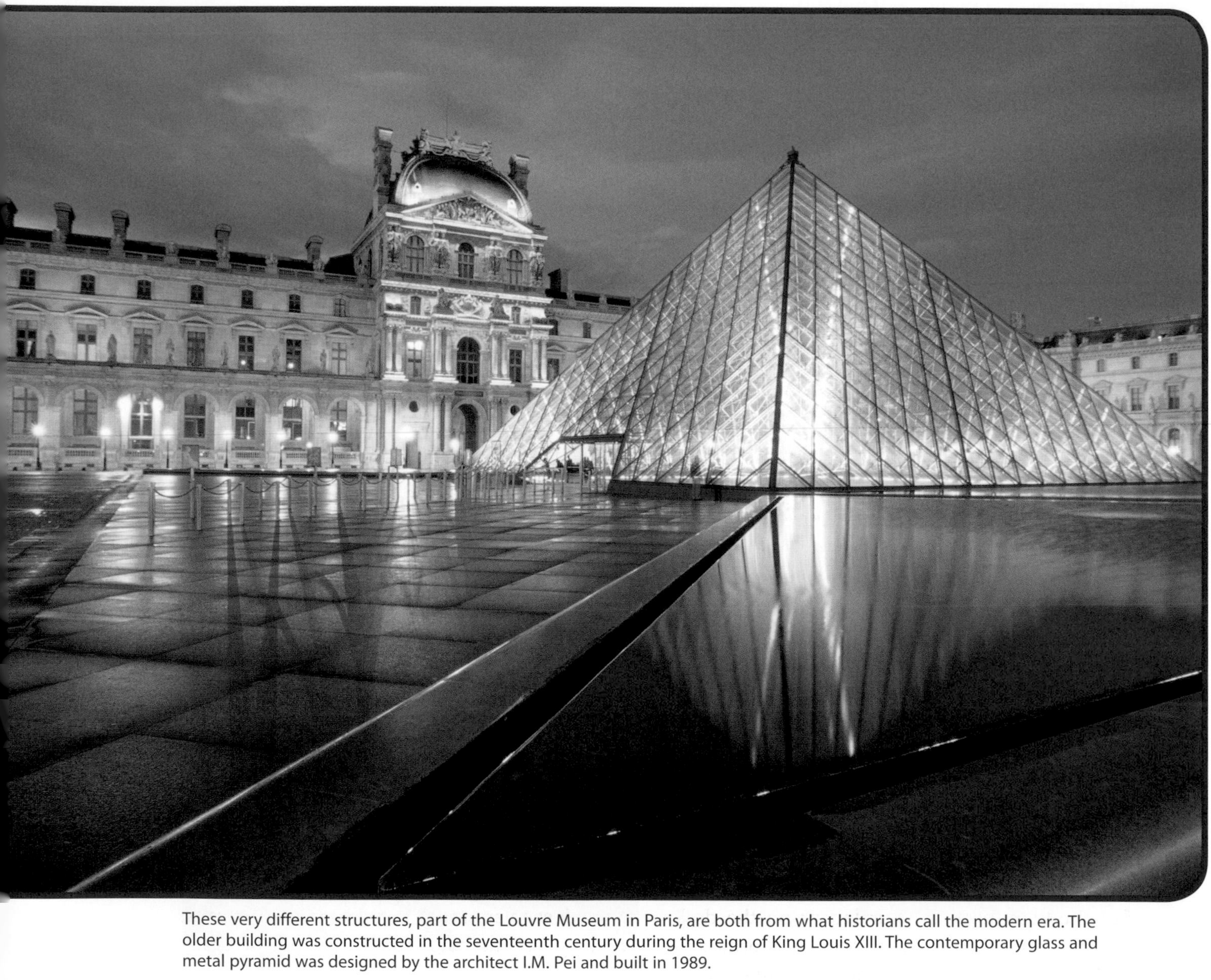

These very different structures, part of the Louvre Museum in Paris, are both from what historians call the modern era. The older building was constructed in the seventeenth century during the reign of King Louis XIII. The contemporary glass and metal pyramid was designed by the architect I.M. Pei and built in 1989.

From Modern to Contemporary

Here's something you should know about modern history: The closer you get to the present, the harder it is to figure out what's most important. It's especially hard when you approach contemporary times. We'll talk about why in a minute, but first let's review some terms. *Modern history* is the story of roughly the last six hundred years, beginning with the Renaissance and coming right up to the present. *Contemporary history* is part of modern history — the most recent part. Historians disagree a little about when our contemporary era began. Some say 1900, but most agree that it's no later than 1914, with the start of the First World War.

People sometimes say "modern times" when they really mean the "contemporary era." In this book, we're focusing mostly on the contemporary era, the main lines of what's important from 1914 to the present.

Why is it so hard for us to see what's important in our contemporary era? Because we're in the middle of it. We have little or no distance from it. Pick up this book and hold a page right up to your nose. The letters turn into a blur. Put the book back in your lap or on the desk and the letters come into focus as words and sentences. History is like that — we need a little distance from events in order for them to come into focus and make sense.

Or think of it this way: History is like an ocean, and we twenty-first-century human beings are swimming in one of its many bays. Even on a calm day, when the wind is still and it's easy to keep our heads above the water, we can only see so much — a blinking lighthouse in the distance, or a few gray homes along the shore. But bobbing along in the water, we can't see very much or very far. If it's stormy, we may see nothing but the splash of spray in our faces.

Distance — which is like the passage of time in history — will help us see more. Imagine floating in a hot air balloon over the bay. From above, you see the familiar landmarks: the lighthouse and the homes you know well. But now you see something you never knew existed: a gleaming white bridge going from the island to the mainland.

Whether you're looking down at a calm sea or breaking waves, the distance lets you see how it all fits together. For the first time you see the many twists and turns in the coastline. From above you see where the bay reaches the ocean, and you understand why the lighthouse was built where it was. Now that you're not in the water but looking down on it from above, you've got a better view. It helps you see things whole; it puts things in perspective.

In the first part of this book, we're trying to get some perspective. Before we jump into the bay and start paddling around in the contemporary era, we want to take a look from a distance. We will start by going back to the late eighteenth and nineteenth centuries. That perspective will help us see the rushing current of the twentieth century more clearly.

When We Started Speeding Up

History is the story of change over time — both how things have changed and how they have remained the same. In the contemporary era, the pace of change has been very rapid indeed. That's something new. Until 1800, for most people in most parts of the world, the general rhythms of life remained largely the same from one day to the next. The world people left at the moment of their death was very much like the world into which they were born.

But in the late eighteenth and the nineteenth centuries, revolutionary events sped up the pace of change. Kings and emperors could no longer be confident they would be making all the decisions. Peasants and farmers no longer expected they would die near the fields where they had been born. Many would become city-folks and earn their living with tools their fathers and mothers had never known. Beginning in the West, and then spreading across the world, there was a growing sense that the one thing you could expect of life was not sameness but change.

The second volume of *The Human Odyssey* told how those big changes came about and shaped our modern world. Democratic revolutions got a lot more people involved in governing. The Industrial Revolution moved many people from country to city and dramatically increased production of various goods, from cloth to rifles. A technological revolution made urban life both more bearable (for example, through better lighting and public transportation) and more complex (for example, by making cities more crowded than ever before).

In the first part of this book, we'll review how those revolutionary developments set the stage for the calamities and triumphs of the twentieth century. We'll look at how the American and French Revolutions influenced the world long after they ended. We'll recall how the Industrial Revolution changed the way people worked and lived, and further spurred democratic change.

We'll see how a "Second Industrial Revolution" generated more wealth, more products, and more problems. We'll meet some businessmen and thinkers who tried to figure out how to improve life in this new urban, industrial world. We'll see how ordinary people tried to adapt to these changes. We'll take a closer look at nineteenth-century Germany, Japan, and China to see how these nation-states were growing, interacting, and positioning themselves for the future.

Steam pumps helped power the Second Industrial Revolution.

Well-to-do Germans show off their automobiles in 1900. Within two decades, automobiles would transform daily life.

One big change we'll examine is the rise of *popular nationalism*—that is, the growing feeling, among ordinary peoples across the globe, of attachment to their specific nation, of pride in their homeland. As citizens gained more rights in the 1800s, they participated more in their national governments. Their sense of loyalty broadened from their town or local parish to their country. Whether they were British, German, French, American, or Japanese, they hoped their nation would have the finest cities, the most productive factories, the best railroads, the fastest ships, the strongest army and navy.

In the nineteenth century, some nations began to compete to establish the biggest global empire. The British took an early lead, building an empire so large that, as people said, "the sun never set" upon the British Empire. The French, Germans, Italians, Japanese, and Americans didn't want to be left behind. We'll examine this new imperialism and see how the ambitions of powerful industrial nations played out in many parts of the world, especially in China, which had the world's largest population.

Finally, in our look back at how major changes of the eighteenth and nineteenth centuries paved the way for our contemporary world, we'll review how technology changed at an almost dizzying pace. Electric lights illuminated dark city streets. Electric current powered new street cars, factories, and homes. Telegraph cables made it possible to transmit news instantly across a continent or across oceans from one continent to another. Gasoline-powered automobiles zipped by horse-drawn carriages, leaving them in a haze of fumes and dust.

Life was changing fast, and for the most part, people thought it was changing for the better. Optimistically—some might say, naively—they believed that human reason and ingenuity guaranteed progress.

How did all this change and apparent progress lead to the appalling chain of events that, in the summer of 1914, triggered the most terrible war the world had ever known? Keep that question in mind as we look back to the eighteenth and nineteenth centuries. In those centuries we find the ideas and events that led to the cataclysmic beginning of our contemporary era.

The Gleaners, painted in 1857 by the French artist Jean-François Millet, depicts the centuries-old activity of picking up grains left behind after a harvest. Yet even as Millet painted, massive changes were causing millions of Europeans to move from the countryside to cities, bringing an end to age-old ways of life.

The World Transformed: Two Kinds of Revolution

Plowing, planting, hoeing, harvesting. In 1775, that's what most people did, day after day, month after month, year after year. Nearly all of the world's inhabitants were farmers. Here and there, craftsmen, shopkeepers, merchants, and shipbuilders worked in scattered cities and towns. But most people worked the land, seldom leaving their farms or villages. They expected each day to be pretty much the same as the day before.

In 1775, almost all these people were ruled by kings, queens, or wealthy landowning lords. Aristocracy—government by a small privileged class—was widespread, while democracy was nowhere to be found. The idea of democracy—government by the people—had been born long ago in ancient Greece. It had been tried in republican Rome, and it worked in limited ways in Renaissance Florence and in Commonwealth England. But those days were gone.

A *republic* is a form of government in which citizens elect representatives to make laws and govern on their behalf.

And yet, even as people went about their mostly unchanging daily lives, the world in 1775 stood on the verge of massive change. The coming years would unleash a wave of democratic revolutions. Many nations would throw out their kings, queens, and emperors, as the people clamored for self-rule. Another kind of revolution, an industrial revolution, would push millions of people from farms in the quiet countryside to factories in growing cities. In time, farmers would become the minority, and nations would turn to manufacturing in pursuit of new wealth.

You know the story of these democratic and industrial revolutions if you've read the previous volume in *The Human Odyssey* series. The following pages briefly summarize high points of this tumultuous time, so critical to the shaping of the modern world.

What's a Commonwealth?

The term *commonwealth* comes from the old word *weal*, which meant "well-being." Thus a commonwealth is a state or nation governed for the common good of its people. Commonwealth England lasted from 1649 to 1660.

Harbinger of Change: The American Revolution

"The welfare of America is intimately connected with the happiness of all mankind."

The words of a proud American? No. They were written by a young French aristocrat, the Marquis de Lafayette (mahr-KEE duh lah-fee-ET). Lafayette had been born into a noble family and inherited a great fortune. He was part of the ruling class. But he lived at a time when many people in France and elsewhere were beginning to ask: Why should so few people rule so many? Why should people obey kings and nobles, especially those who show no respect for their subjects? Don't ordinary people have rights? Why shouldn't they rule themselves?

Marquis is a title of French nobility, like "count."

While such questions fueled heated discussions among Lafayette and others in Europe, in faraway North America they sparked a revolution. In July 1776, thirteen British colonies declared independence from England and established the United States of America. Thomas Jefferson gave fresh and forceful expression to ideas that had been circulating among liberty-loving Englishmen for years. In phrases shocking to any monarch's ears, the Declaration of Independence asserted that "all men are created equal, that they are endowed by their Creator with certain unalienable rights, that among these are life, liberty, and the pursuit of happiness." The declaration insisted that governments exist for the benefit of the people, not rulers, and that the people should decide how to govern themselves.

Across Europe, rulers, philosophers, and adventurers turned their eyes toward this democratic revolution. The Marquis de Lafayette did more than look; he leaped into the struggle. The Frenchman thought the fight might bring him glory and adventure. But he also yearned to aid the cause of liberty. "As soon as I knew of this quarrel," he wrote, "my heart was committed to it and I thought only of joining my colors to it."

Against his family's wishes, 19-year-old Lafayette bought a ship, sailed to America, and volunteered to serve without pay. He served as an aide to George Washington and soon became a close friend of the American leader.

Lafayette endured the long winter at Valley Forge, where the hungry, half-naked soldiers slept on the frozen ground. Later, when he received command of some troops, he equipped them at his own expense.

English Liberty in Action

Since 1215, when a group of noblemen forced King John to sign the Magna Carta, the English had taken steps to limit the power of their monarch (usually a king). Englishmen created a governing body called Parliament to help make laws. The Parliament was divided into two chambers. One chamber, the House of Lords, represented the nobles, while the other, the House of Commons, represented the common people. The English believed that kings should rule, but that all people should have some representation in government.

In the mid-1700s, Britain's North American colonists were loyal British subjects, proud of their heritage of liberty and of the basic rights they enjoyed as Englishmen, such as the right to trial by jury. Each of the thirteen colonies had its own assembly that made its own laws. The king appointed some colonial governors, but mostly he let the colonists govern themselves. Merchant ships from England and America crisscrossed the Atlantic, keeping up a brisk trade.

That changed in the 1760s. After a long war against France, fought partly on American soil to protect the colonies, the Parliament in London tried to pay for the costs by placing new taxes on the colonists. The colonists protested that they had no representatives in Parliament. "No taxation without representation!" they cried. Some of the colonists began calling their king a tyrant. Others began to ask why a distant island should rule a continent three thousand miles away. In large part, it was English ideas of rights and liberty that spurred the American colonists to take arms against England.

George Washington confers with the Marquis de Lafayette at Valley Forge, Pennsylvania, during the American Revolutionary War. The French nobleman was devoted to the cause of liberty in both Europe and the New World.

During the war, Lafayette returned to France to urge his king to help the colonists in their fight against France's old enemy, Britain. The French king, Louis XVI, agreed to send ships, troops, and arms — the French, after all, were always glad to help bring down the British. Lafayette sailed back to America and took to the field against British General Cornwallis.

In 1781, with the help of a French fleet, the Americans, led by George Washington, trapped Cornwallis at Yorktown, Virginia, and forced him to surrender. Lafayette was there with Washington as the British soldiers filed out of their trenches to give up their arms. Tradition has it that a British band played a tune called "The World Turned Upside Down."

A few years later, in 1787, Washington and other leaders of the new United States met in Philadelphia to lay the foundations of the new American government. Guided by James Madison, they wrote a Constitution that specified how the government of the new republic should operate. This would be a nation governed by the people, as the Constitution boldly declared in its opening words: "We the People of the United States, in order to form a more perfect union…."

The Bill of Rights, quickly appended to the Constitution, spelled out basic rights of the American people, such as the rights to free speech and freedom of the press — rights that the government could not take away.

The U.S. Constitution and the Spread of Democracy

The United States Constitution is the oldest written national constitution in effect today and one of the most imitated political documents in the world. As democracy spread around the world, revolutionaries overseas examined the U.S. Constitution for inspiration and ideas. During the early nineteenth century, when Spain's colonists in Latin America declared independence, they used the U.S. Constitution as one model for their new constitutions. From Venezuela, Argentina, and Chile to Switzerland, Liberia, Australia, and Japan, countries around the world have designed their own constitutions based in part on the U.S. Constitution.

The American Revolution introduced a daring democratic experiment in government by the people. It also showed that colonies did not have to remain colonies forever, that they might be entitled to independence. Soon the democratic experiment spread back to the continent that had provided the ideas behind the American struggle for liberty. But in Europe, democratic revolution followed a different path.

Liberty, Equality, Fraternity: The French Revolution

When Lafayette returned to France, he was celebrated as the "Hero of Two Worlds." To many in France, he had become a symbol of the ideas that had inspired revolution in America — ideas about freedom, equality, and self-government. Now, many Frenchmen hoped those same ideas would soon bring changes at home.

Lafayette loved to spend time with Thomas Jefferson, Benjamin Franklin, and other Americans who came to France as representatives of the new United States. He hung a copy of the Declaration of Independence on his wall, but left an empty space beside it. He hoped someday to fill that space with a similar French document — a declaration of rights for the French people.

Lafayette wanted the French people to rule themselves as the Americans were doing. He hoped for a constitutional monarchy in France. The French, he said, should still have a king, but the king should obey a written constitution and respect the people's rights.

Lafayette, an American Name

Grateful Americans viewed the Marquis de Lafayette as one of the heroes of the Revolution. After the war, they began naming towns after him, from Fayetteville, North Carolina, to Lafayette, California. Over the decades, more than 600 towns, cities, counties, mountains, rivers, lakes, schools, and naval ships have been named after the Frenchman who fought so hard for American independence.

Why was it so important to have a constitution? A constitution, the basic law of the land, specifies the rules by which a country is governed and defines the power of each branch of government. When Lafayette returned to France, the French had no constitution, and there were few limits on the king's power. An effective constitution, however, could limit the power of the king and guarantee the people's basic rights.

Such concerns meant little to Louis XVI, the king of France. He was an absolute monarch — he governed with nearly unlimited power. He spent his days hunting on the sprawling grounds of his palace at Versailles (vuhr-SIY). He dined at sumptuous banquets, surrounded by groveling courtiers and well-fed nobles. Meanwhile, many of the common people in France had barely enough to eat.

Louis XVI didn't worry about the peasants' hunger, but he did worry about his nation's debts. France had spent a lot in fighting the British in two wars. The nation was almost bankrupt.

In 1789, Louis called a meeting of the Estates-General, a group that had not met in 175 years. The Estates-General included deputies representing various classes — the nobles, the clergy, and the common people of France.

Louis had one reason for convening the Estates-General — he needed money. To get it, he wanted to impose new taxes on the people. Although he ruled with *almost* unlimited power, he could not impose new taxes without calling together the Estates-General. But the Estates-General did not give the king what he wanted. Instead of getting new tax money, he soon found that he had a revolution on his hands.

The deputies formed a new group called the National Assembly. At a meeting of the Assembly, Lafayette presented a draft of the Declaration of the Rights of Man and of the Citizen, which he had written with Thomas Jefferson's help. It was, he hoped, a model for a government by the people of France. "Men are born and remain free and equal in rights," it declared. The queen of France called Lafayette a traitor to his class, but he stuck to his belief in the dignity of all people and in their ability to govern themselves.

While the National Assembly debated the Declaration of Rights, some eight thousand

Parisians attacked the Bastille, an ancient fortress and symbol of royal authority. The French Revolution had begun. The cry "Liberty, Equality, Fraternity!" rang through the streets.

Lafayette became the head of the National Guard. He tried to keep order, hoping that Louis XVI would see that he needed to give more power to his own people.

But things did not go as Lafayette had hoped. Radicals began to take control of the revolution. They were not content to accept a constitutional monarchy — instead, they wanted no more kings or nobles. They arrested the royal family and began flinging aristocrats into prison. They ordered the arrest of Lafayette — after all, he was a nobleman. When Lafayette tried to slip over the border, he was arrested and spent the next five years in prison.

France was now a republic, governed by the people's representatives. But it was a troubled republic. Revolutionaries put Louis XVI on trial. They declared the king guilty of "crimes against the Revolution" and sent him to death on the guillotine (GIH-luh-teen). During the bloody years known as the Reign of Terror, tens of thousands of people lost their heads on the guillotine. Carts rumbled through the streets of Paris carrying "enemies of the Revolution" to their executions. No one seemed safe.

When Lafayette finally got out of prison, a new figure was rising to power in France. Napoleon Bonaparte, a brilliant general, promised that he would restore order and preserve the people's freedoms.

Lafayette did not trust Napoleon. He feared the general would become a tyrant. When the two met, Lafayette advised Napoleon to work for the people's rights. "They expect it from you, and it is for you to give it to them," Lafayette said.

Lafayette's fears turned out to be justified. Napoleon craved power and glory. He had himself crowned emperor and launched a war to dominate Europe. Everywhere his armies marched, he promised the people freedom from the rule of kings.

"The peoples of Germany, the peoples of France, of Italy, of Spain all desire equality," Napoleon declared. Across Europe he swept away old governments ruled by dukes, princes, and other nobles. In their place, he introduced constitutions and legal systems in which all were equal in the eyes of the law. All, that is, except the Emperor Napoleon.

The French Revolution began on July 14, 1789, when Parisians stormed the Bastille, a symbol of royal authority.

Napoleon's wars and words influenced people as far away as Latin America. They were inspired by the ideas that Napoleon (despite his self-glorifying actions) said he stood for — liberty, equality, and rule by law. Spain's colonists in South America declared independence and fought to win their freedom. They tried to establish new republics and began a long struggle toward democracy.

Two July Celebrations

In the United States, July 4 is Independence Day, a national holiday on which Americans celebrate the birth of their nation. In France, July 14 is a national holiday commonly known as Bastille Day. On this day, the French commemorate the storming of the Bastille on July 14, 1789, the symbolic beginning of the modern French nation.

Napoleon's army met defeat at last at the battle of Waterloo. With the once-mighty emperor exiled to a tiny island in the South Atlantic, the monarchs of Europe tried to make sure that such a revolution would never happen again. They put a king back on the French throne, who promptly stamped out many of the liberties that Lafayette and others had fought for. All over Europe, monarchs tightened their grip on power and hoped that the great storm had passed. "The Concert of Europe," as these revolution-hating kings were called, wanted to eliminate any trace of democracy from their lands. But, as you will see in later chapters, these democratic ideas would soon spring forth with renewed power.

Britain Launches the Industrial Revolution

In 1776, the same year the Americans declared their independence, a crowd gathered at a coal mine near Birmingham, England, to see a new machine. It was a steam-driven pump, designed to remove water from underground springs flowing deep in the mine. For years, miners had used crude steam-driven pumps to remove water from mines. But this new pump, its Scottish inventor claimed, was better. Its steam engine was much more efficient, he said, and would not break down as often.

As the crowd watched, an engineer pulled levers and opened valves on the huge machine. The engine thundered to life, and the giant pump began to plunge up and down. In less than an hour, the machine had done its work, clearing water that had stood 57 feet deep in the mine. The crowd cheered the machine's inventor, James Watt.

Watt's steam engine helped launch the Industrial Revolution. In just a few years, steam engines would power machines in factories all across Britain. As Watt's partner, Matthew Boulton, wrote, "The people in London, Manchester, and Birmingham are steam mill mad."

The Industrial Revolution, which began in Britain's textile industry, eventually transformed the making of many goods from handmade to machine-made. For centuries, weavers had made cloth by hand. In the eighteenth century, inventors devised new machines to speed up the weaving process. But these machines — powered by waterwheels, horses, or human muscles — could only do so much. When James Watt's efficient steam engine was adapted to run the new textile machines, British textile factories began to produce more cloth than ever.

Steam-powered looms fill an early nineteenth-century mill in Halifax, England. British textile mills like this one, which often employed women and children, launched the Industrial Revolution.

The Industrial Revolution spread quickly as Watt and other inventors installed steam engines in factories that made everything from buttons to cannons. Britain rapidly became the world's leading industrial nation. Factories sprang up across Europe and in America as well.

The Industrial Revolution was launched not only by new machines, such as Watt's efficient steam engine, but also by new ideas. Watt's fellow Scot, Adam Smith, came up with a new way of thinking about how goods and services are produced, distributed, and consumed.

In that remarkable year of 1776, Smith published a book called *The Wealth of Nations*. In this book Smith argued that governments should not try to control most business decisions. Instead, said Smith, governments should let the natural forces of the economy work. He believed that buying and selling should be guided by human self-interest — for example, businesses that desire to make money (and what business doesn't?) should produce the goods that people most want to buy. Competition, thought Smith, would make businesses more efficient and help keep prices down. To make wealth grow, he said, governments should keep their hands off business and allow people to make deals, start companies, and take risks when they saw opportunities.

As government officials began to follow Adam Smith's advice, British businessmen prospered even more. Workers, however, often suffered from the government's hands-off policies. The government did little or nothing to control business owners who were more concerned about their own profits than the health and safety of the workers.

New Forms of Transportation and Communication

The Industrial Revolution spread largely because of a simultaneous revolution in transportation and communication. Beginning in the late eighteenth century, inventors thought up new ways for goods and information to move quickly over long distances.

For centuries, a journey on the roads of Europe meant struggling along paths full of boulders, tree stumps, holes, and puddles. Another Scot, John McAdam, developed a way to build roadbeds with foundations of crushed rock that drained well. On these new roads, wagons and carriages could move faster and farther.

Manufactured goods also began to move more quickly by water. Builders dug canals so that barges could carry products along these manmade waterways. It didn't take long for the steam engine to take to the water. Inventors such as the American Robert Fulton figured out ways to make the engines turn paddles to propel boats. Steamships began carrying goods up and down rivers, and eventually across oceans.

Other inventors applied the technology of steam engines to land transportation. An Englishman named George Stephenson became the "Father of the Railroad" when he built a steam-powered engine to pull wagons along wooden rails. Next came bigger locomotives and iron tracks. Soon, in Europe and the Americas, trains were pulling freight and passengers across hundreds of miles of track at the then-brisk speeds of up to 20 miles an hour.

Just as the railroad made transportation faster, so Samuel Morse's telegraph made communication faster. The telegraph enabled people to send messages quickly from city to city, even from country to country. In 1866, people in Britain and North America could use an underwater cable to telegraph each other across the Atlantic. A few years later, a person in California could telegraph someone in India.

New Wealth, New Problems, New Demands for Power

The Industrial Revolution dramatically changed the way people lived. In industrial nations, many people left the farms where their families had lived for generations and moved to cities to work in the new factories. The Western world was changing from an agricultural society to an urban and industrial one.

Industrialization brought the rise of a new class of powerful businessmen, the captains of industry. The men who owned the factories and railroads were just as rich, and often much richer, than the nobles and landowners of previous centuries.

A nineteenth-century Welsh copper foundry fouls the air.

For many people, the Industrial Revolution improved the standard of living and created new opportunities. They found jobs managing the offices, stores, factories, and other businesses in the cities. These people formed a new and growing social group, a middle class with enough wealth to buy the shirts, hats, chairs, watches, and toys produced in steam-powered factories.

But in these dark, noisy, foul-smelling factories, men, women, and children spent long hours toiling at dangerous machines. They trudged home through soot-clogged air, past waste yards of ashes and coal, to filthy, overcrowded apartments. For them, the great transformations of the Industrial Revolution meant little more than an unending round of poverty, toil, and suffering.

These social changes led to new demands for political change. Rich factory owners who controlled much of their nations' wealth wanted more influence in running their governments. Members of the growing middle class called for changes to improve their own lives. They demanded representation in legislatures and parliaments.

Reformers pressed for changes that would improve the working and living conditions of factory workers. They called for new regulations to restrict long work hours and make factories cleaner, safer places. They began to demand that the working class have a voice in government. Not surprisingly, those demands erupted first in Britain, but the new clamor for political participation soon spread.

The Spread of Representative Government

For 15 years after the fall of Napoleon, the monarchs of Europe had tried to snuff out democratic reform. Then, in 1830, another democratic uprising flared in France. King Charles X had tried to strengthen his grip on the country, clamping down on the press and dissolving the elected legislature. So Parisians took to the streets. At the center of the uprising was the old revolutionary, Lafayette. Revolutions soon broke out in other European nations. While they failed to achieve the democratic changes Lafayette longed for, he maintained his belief in human dignity and the natural rights of all people. "I was always of a hopeful nature, and hope is far from abandoning me," he said.

Lafayette was right not to give up hope. In 1848, another wave of democratic uprisings swept Europe. In Paris, citizens again poured into the streets to protest restricted voting rights, government corruption, and poor economic conditions. Government troops turned their weapons against the citizens. The people quickly built barricades out of paving stones, carts, old furniture, and whatever else they could find. As the fighting raged on, the king fled the country, and France once again proclaimed itself a republic.

Revolutions quickly spread across Europe. In Vienna, capital of Austria's Habsburg Empire and home to the young emperor Franz Josef, students and workers rioted for a new constitution and greater liberties. Revolutionaries in Hungary, which was part of the Austrian empire, demanded greater freedom and more rights. Italian states rose up against their rulers. In some German states, peasants burned the manor houses of the nobility, while workers destroyed machines and factories they believed had cost them their jobs.

The *Habsburg* in *Habsburg Empire* refers to the ruling family of Austria.

The tidal wave of revolutions in 1848 quickly crested, then just as quickly receded. In France, the people chose Napoleon Bonaparte's nephew, Louis Napoleon Bonaparte, as the president of their Second Republic. He soon moved to crush the protests of French workers and impose controls on the press. A few years later, he declared himself Emperor Napoleon III. Elsewhere in Europe, other monarchs used armed force to put down the revolts of the people.

Yet for a while in 1848, the ruling class of Europe felt the world shaking beneath its feet. Monarchs, aristocrats, and the wealthy elite saw their power and privilege under attack. As one Frenchwoman of the time wrote, aristocratic society felt a "terror incomparable to anything since the invasion of Rome by the barbarians."

The *elite* (ay-LEET) are those who enjoy the highest status or special privileges in a society.

A Barricade of the 1848 Revolution

A Page from the Past

Les Misérables, *which means* The Miserable Ones, *is a novel by the French author Victor Hugo. One of the most famous books of the nineteenth century, it follows the lives of several characters in the decades following the Napoleonic wars. In the following passage, the author describes a street barricade erected during the 1848 Revolution in a neighborhood of Paris called the Faubourg Saint-Antoine (foh-BOOR san an-TWAHN). Hugo based his description on his own memories of street barricades he had seen during that revolt.*

The barricade Saint-Antoine was monstrous; it was three stories high and seven hundred feet long.... Merely from seeing it, you felt in the Faubourg the immense agonizing suffering which had reached the extreme moment when

Government troops storm a street barricade in Paris during the 1848 Revolution.

distress rushes into catastrophe. Of what was this barricade made? Of the ruins of three six-story houses, torn down for the purpose, said some. Of the prodigy of all passions, said others. It had the woeful aspect of all the works of hatred: Ruin. You might say: who built that? You might also say: who destroyed that? ...Here! that door! that grating! that shed! that casement! that broken furnace! that cracked pot! Bring all! throw on all! push, roll, dig, dismantle, overturn, tear down all!...

You saw there, in a chaos full of despair, rafters from roofs, patches from garrets with their wallpaper, window sashes with all their glass planted in the rubbish, awaiting artillery, chimneys torn down, wardrobes, tables, benches, a howling topsy-turvy, and those thousand beggarly things, the refuse even of the mendicant, which contain at once fury and nothingness. One would have said that it was the tatters of a people, tatters of wood, of iron, of bronze, of stone, and that the Faubourg Saint-Antoine had swept them there to its door by one colossal sweep of the broom, making of its misery its barricade....

A *mendicant* is a beggar.

The barricade Saint-Antoine made a weapon of everything; all that civil war can throw at the head of society came from it.... It threw up to the clouds an inexpressible clamor; at certain moments defying the army, it covered itself with multitude and with tempest; a mob of flaming heads crowned it; a swarming filled it; its crest was thorny with muskets, with swords, with clubs, with axes, with pikes, with bayonettes; a huge red flag fluttered in the wind; there were heard cries of command, songs of attack, the roll of the drum, the sobs of women, and the dark wild laughter of the starving. It was huge and living; and, as from the back of an electric beast there came from it the crackling of thunders. The spirit of revolution covered with its cloud that summit whereon growled this voice of the people which is like the voice of God.

Power to the People?

By 1875, about a century after Lafayette had taken up arms for liberty and James Watt had built his steam engine, the Western world was undergoing a dramatic transformation.

The Industrial Revolution had driven people from farms and villages into factories and cities. It created new industry, new wealth, and new problems. It fueled new demands for political power, not only by the rich owners of industry, but by the millions of poor laborers who formed the backbone of the Industrial Revolution.

The democratic revolutions that spread across Europe in 1830 and 1848 did not sweep away the continent's monarchies, but they did send a powerful message. Ideas about natural rights, equality, liberty, and human dignity had taken hold. Ordinary people — factory workers, shopkeepers, office managers, dock laborers — demanded some control over their own lives.

Monarchs and aristocrats found themselves out of step with the times, forming what the French called "l'Ancien Régime" (lahn-syan ray-ZHEEM), a term that came to mean "the old order, the old way of ruling." The new order compelled the old rulers to pay more attention to the demands of the people and deal with the people's elected representatives. Monarchs found their powers increasingly limited by new constitutions. As the powers of the kings declined, the rights and privileges of the people, such as the right to vote, gradually grew — but often only as the result of violent struggle.

In the hundred years following 1775, the world hurtled through more dramatic change than it had seen in any previous century. It was no longer the case that every year resembled the previous year in the lives of ordinary people. There was more movement, more change, some would say more opportunity, others more insecurity. And still more change was on the way.

Slavery in the Industrial Age

Even in the midst of growing demands for natural rights and liberty, slavery remained a persistent and terrible fact. At the end of the eighteenth century, three-quarters of the world's population lived in bondage of some sort. There were unpaid farm laborers in Asia, serfs in Russia, African slaves in the Islamic empires of North Africa and the Middle East, and African slaves in mines or on plantations in the Americas.

Around 1800, the Industrial Revolution increased the demand for slaves in some parts of the world. Because English textile mills could weave more and more cloth, they required more and more cotton, most of which they imported from America. To pick the cotton, which was back-breaking work, American plantation owners used more slaves.

In the 1700s, England dominated the transatlantic slave trade. But around 1800, the British took the lead in the growing movement to abolish slavery. Volume 2 of *The Human Odyssey* recounted the efforts of William Wilberforce and other abolitionists. In Parliament and in one British town after another, these abolitionists campaigned tirelessly to expose the evils of slavery. In 1807, the British Parliament abolished the slave trade in the British West Indies. In 1833, Parliament outlawed slavery in all British colonies.

Elsewhere, change came slowly. In 1808, the United States prohibited the importation of more slaves, but slavery in the United States lasted until the end of the Civil War in 1865. In some lands, slavery was not outlawed until well into the twentieth century.

Visitors flock to the Palace of Electricity at the Paris Exposition of 1900. The Exposition showcased the achievements of the Second Industrial Revolution, in which electricity and steel transformed the lives of millions of people.

Meeting the Challenge of Change

In 1900, a great exhibition in Paris showcased the technological achievements of the nineteenth century. Enthusiastic visitors saw signs of progress even before they entered the exhibition halls. The Eiffel Tower, 11 years new, soared high above the city skyline. On the banks of the Seine (sen), the elegant Gare d'Orsay (gair dor-SAY), the city's first electrified railway terminal, opened its doors. Arriving at the exposition, fifty million visitors flocked to see a steel crane that could lift 45-ton weights into the air, a steam locomotive capable of pulling a 200-ton load at a breathtaking 75 miles per hour, and an amazing moving staircase called an "escalator."

Many of these marvels were housed in the awe-inspiring Palace of Electricity. Five thousand light bulbs bathed the palace in light. Beneath its halls, the mere flick of a switch unleashed up to 40,000 horsepower to drive all the machines on display.

Just a half century earlier, London had hosted the Crystal Palace Exhibition, the world's first industrial fair. The British were proud of the early lead they had taken in the new industrial world. But compared to the Paris Exposition of 1900, the Crystal Palace show seemed positively old-fashioned. What had happened in just five decades to make such progress possible?

A Second Industrial Revolution

The wonders in Paris were part of a second great wave of industrial growth in the Western world. It began about 1875 and lasted into the early part of the twentieth century. It is often called the Second Industrial Revolution. The first Industrial Revolution had been based largely on one material, iron, which was used to make everything from machine parts and pipes to railroad tracks and bridges. But the Second Industrial Revolution employed a different material — steel.

In the mid-1800s, inventors came up with new methods for producing steel in large quantities. Manufacturers and builders preferred steel to iron because it was lighter, stronger, and more flexible. Railroads, bridges, and soaring structures like the Eiffel Tower were built of steel. Steel was used to make more precise and powerful machines that mass-produced goods more easily than ever before. A flood of cheap products — from screws and bolts to buttons and bicycles — poured from the factories of industrial nations.

During the first Industrial Revolution, a single kind of energy, steam power, had been used to drive the engines in factories, ships, and trains. During the Second Industrial Revolution, inventors found new energy sources in electricity and petroleum.

Electricity brought light to people's homes. It led to new methods of communication, like the telegraph and telephone. It powered factories and new forms of transportation, like the electric streetcar. Meanwhile, fuels produced from petroleum made possible a whole new way of getting around — the automobile.

Cities aglow with streetlights. Skyscrapers pushing up toward the clouds. Elegant theaters showing motion pictures. Phonographs playing recorded music. Huge steamships skimming the oceans. All these wonders of the Second Industrial Revolution enabled people to do more, make more, and go faster than ever before. Such advances fueled dreams of unlimited progress — surely, many people thought, mankind could use technology to solve one problem after another.

Others observed that despite technological advances, some problems were not getting solved. In fact, they seemed to be getting worse. Bigger factories led to more people working long hours for low wages. Growing cities meant more people living in crowded, filthy tenements. The gap between rich and poor seemed to grow wider and wider.

By the end of the nineteenth century, it was clear that progress had its problems. Industrial workers, the urban poor, and city-dwellers cried out for improvements in their living and working conditions.

"Lost and Doomed Are the Cities"

The economic system that had made the Industrial Revolution possible was capitalism. In a capitalist economy, individuals own property and make most of the decisions about how to use it. Adam Smith, you recall, argued that government should keep out of the way and let the natural forces of the economy work. Each person, said Smith, should make decisions based on his or her own self-interest.

But in the new industrial economy, the self-interest of business owners had little in common with the best interests of workers. During the nineteenth century, many poor people had flocked from the countryside to cities for jobs. But the jobs they found offered only hardship, danger, long hours, and low wages. Men, women, and even children toiled long hours — up to 16 hours a day — in factories that the English poet William Blake described as "dark Satanic mills."

Danger lurked everywhere in the factories. Tired workers risked mangling a limb in clanking gears, axles, and blades. To a factory owner, an injured or sick worker was a useless worker to be readily replaced from among the masses of job-seekers flooding into the cities.

For many workers in 1900, conditions at home were worse than in the factory. Home was an overcrowded tenement building in a neighborhood filled with disease, filth, and crime. With so many new workers arriving in the cities, landlords squeezed as many people into the tenements as they could. In Vienna in 1912, most working class families had, on average, less living space than inmates in prisons. Those who lived in attics set out buckets to catch the rain, and those in cellars used old umbrellas to deflect the constant drips. Outside, they used the gutters along the streets as sewers and garbage dumps.

In most large cities in the first half of the nineteenth century, deaths outnumbered births. One writer calculated precise figures to prove that Paris, without the constant influx of people from the countryside, would disappear within 550 years. As the German poet Rainer Maria Rilke declared in 1905, "Lost and doomed are the cities, and their short spell seeps away."

What to Do?

As the twentieth century began, the wretched state of the cities led one British writer to claim, "No civilization can be healthy or stable that is built on such a mass of stunted human lives."

Politicians, reformers, and clergy knew that something had to be done.

Because the Industrial Revolution began in Britain, the British confronted these problems earlier than other nations. By the mid-nineteenth century, Parliament passed the Factory Acts, which limited the workday in most textile mills to nine hours for children under 13, and ten hours for women. Neighborhoods became a bit safer and cleaner, as new police officers known as "bobbies" began patrolling London's streets. New sewers carried waste away to where the Thames emptied into the sea, thus helping reduce disease.

The British government also passed laws to help the poorest of people. These Poor Laws established places called workhouses where the poor were sometimes sent to live and do whatever work was given to them. But the workhouses were often dirty, crime-ridden places. As Charles Dickens observed of the workhouses in *A Christmas Carol*, "Many can't go there; and many would rather die."

While governments tried to solve problems brought on by industrialization, too often their efforts did little good. Even when governments did pass new laws, many factory owners simply ignored them. Despite reforms, the gap between rich and poor city-dwellers widened to a great chasm. By 1897 in Great Britain, two-thirds of the national income was in the hands of less than one-eighth of the population. In London alone there were 100,000 paupers and 70,000 homeless people.

Some people began to believe that drastic situations required drastic measures. A growing number of thinkers challenged the capitalist system itself. Instead, they proposed *socialism,* an economic and political system in which the government controls property and the distribution of income. In a socialist system, community ownership replaces private ownership, and government control replaces individual self-interest and the free play of market forces. When these ideas emerged in the early 1800s, no countries rushed to adopt socialist principles. But as problems grew, so did the hopes of many that socialism would replace the capitalist order.

A young laborer at her station in a Vermont cotton mill

Robert Owen: Utopian Socialist

Robert Owen, a successful businessman from Wales, saw what the Industrial Revolution was doing to workers, and it sickened him. Long hours and grim working and living conditions turned men into brutes, he concluded. So in 1799, when Owen and his business partners bought the New Lanark textile mills in Scotland, he took bold steps. Owen prohibited labor for children under 10. He set up schools for the young. He built better housing for the mill workers.

As New Lanark thrived, Owen decided that he wanted to create a small experimental community based on the socialist ideals of cooperation and group effort. In 1825, he bought land in Indiana and started the "New Harmony" community. New Harmony was to be a *utopia*—a perfect society. Owen wanted all the workers to share in the labor and profits. But harmony did not prevail. Residents quarreled over how things should be run, and the experiment failed after a few years.

Although Owen's vision of a socialist utopia did not succeed, his hope of creating better conditions for laborers endured.

Karl Marx and Class Struggle

In 1900, many socialists were inspired by the works of an exiled German writer who had been calling for change since mid-century. Karl Marx, born in Prussia in 1818, witnessed firsthand the misery brought on by the rapid industrialization of his homeland. He became a journalist and wrote many articles criticizing the government, condemning the powerful, and calling for the overthrow of capitalism.

Marx predicted that a coming revolution would replace capitalism with a kind of socialism called communism. A communist society, as Marx imagined it, would be one in which "class distinctions have disappeared" and "all production has been

The Communist Manifesto

A Page from the Past

The Communist Manifesto, *which Karl Marx and Friedrich Engels published in 1848, became one of the most influential documents of modern times. Marx and Engels wrote that society is always divided into classes that struggle against each other. They predicted that the working class, which they called the proletariat (PROH-luh-TEHR-ee-uht), would eventually overthrow the bourgeoisie (bourzh-wah-ZEE), the class that owns and runs businesses.*

The history of all hitherto existing society is the history of class struggles. Freeman and slave, patrician and plebeian, lord and serf, guild-master and journeyman, in a word, oppressor and oppressed, stood in constant opposition

A *patrician* is someone born into a high-ranking or noble family.

A *plebeian* is a commoner.

Karl Marx (holding paper) and Friedrich Engels (next to Marx) proofread a German newspaper that they edited. Together, they wrote *The Communist Manifesto*, which predicted that communism would eventually replace capitalism.

concentrated in the hands of a vast association of the whole nation" — in other words, the state owns all resources, the government distributes the abundant goods, and — at least in Marx's vision — all citizens would share in the common wealth.

In 1848, the year many revolutions broke out across Europe, Marx and his friend Friedrich Engels published a pamphlet called *The Communist Manifesto*. They argued that the problems of capitalism would bring economic and social collapse in Europe and North America. In a post-capitalist society, said Marx and Engels, all citizens would have a chance to share society's wealth equally. But such sharing would not come easily. The rich, Marx knew, would not give up their wealth and power without a struggle.

to one another, carried on an uninterrupted, now hidden, now open fight, that each time ended either in a revolutionary reconstitution of society at large, or in the common ruin of the contending classes.... In ancient Rome we have patricians, knights, plebeians, slaves; in the Middle Ages, feudal lords, vassals, guild-masters, journeymen, apprentices, serfs....

The modern bourgeois society that has sprouted from the ruins of feudal society has not done away with class antagonisms. It has but established new classes, new conditions of oppression, new forms of struggle in place of the old ones. Our epoch (EH-puhk), the epoch of the bourgeoisie, possesses, however, this distinctive feature: it has simplified the class antagonisms. Society as a whole is more and more splitting up into two great hostile camps, into two great classes directly facing each other — bourgeoisie and proletariat....

With the development of industry the proletariat not only increases in number; it becomes concentrated in greater masses, its strength grows and it feels that strength more.... The collisions between individual workmen and individual bourgeois take more and more the character of collisions between two classes....

Of all the classes that stand face to face with the bourgeoisie today, the proletariat alone is a really revolutionary class.... The proletariat, the lowest stratum of our present society, cannot stir, cannot raise itself up, without the whole...of official society being sprung into the air....

The development of modern industry, therefore, cuts from under its feet the very foundation on which the bourgeoisie produces and appropriates products. What the bourgeoisie therefore produces, above all, are its own grave-diggers. Its fall and the victory of the proletariat are equally inevitable.

Feudalism was a medieval system in which lords granted land to *vassals*, who in turn owed loyalty and military service to their lords.

Serfs were peasants who were obliged to remain on the land of their lord and pay him with labor and rents.

The Communist Manifesto predicted an unavoidable war between "two great hostile camps…two great classes directly facing each other—bourgeoisie and proletariat." By the *bourgeoisie*, Marx and Engels meant factory owners, bankers, merchants, and the ruling classes. The *proletariat* included the "working men of all countries." The two groups were on a collision course. "Let the ruling classes tremble," declared *The Communist Manifesto*. "The proletarians have nothing to lose but their chains."

After the 1848 revolutions failed, the rulers of Europe were determined to stamp out radical movements. Marx fled the continent for London, where he could more safely develop his radical ideas.

Britain at that time was known as the "workshop of the world." In factory towns and crowded cities, Marx saw the misery of the laborers in stark contrast to the fabulous wealth of their capitalist bosses. He spent hours in the British Museum in London, thinking, studying, and writing. Over the course of 10 years, he produced a 2,500-page work called *Das Kapital*, criticizing the capitalist system. In this book, Marx described what he believed were historical forces shaping the inevitable decline of capitalist society as a result of the struggle between the classes. He predicted a series of revolutions by workers that would eventually topple the capitalist system and replace it with a "dictatorship of the proletariat." In the resulting truly communist society, wealth would be equally shared. History, Marx was sure, was on his side.

The Paris Commune

From our present-day perspective, we can see that things have not turned out as Marx predicted. For one thing, the Industrial Revolution did not produce two opposed classes but instead many new groups, each with its own interests. But back in 1871, events in France persuaded many that Marx might have a clear grasp of historical realities.

In 1870, France and Germany fought a bitter war known as the Franco-Prussian War. France's Emperor Napoleon III (Napoleon Bonaparte's nephew) imagined it would be a quick victory for France. After all, his troops had the latest rifles and military equipment. But the Germans had more troops and were better organized. Soon they were bearing down on Paris. For four months, the Parisians withstood a relentless pounding of artillery. In the end, however, Napoleon III surrendered and agreed to Germany's harsh terms for peace, including a triumphal procession of the German victors into the city of Paris.

Even before the war, Parisians had felt anger and resentment toward their government. After the war's humiliating end, as the citizens of Paris watched German troops leaving the capital, they decided to make the city a self-governing commune to improve the lot of the working people. In municipal elections in March 1871, Parisians elected republican and socialist leaders known as the Communards. They toppled a statue of Napoleon Bonaparte from its pedestal. They discarded the Revolution's tricolor flag and flew instead the socialist red flag.

In France, a *commune* is an administrative district, somewhat like a county.

Working-class Parisians, armed and angry, were now in charge. The Paris Commune passed laws allowing workers to take over some factories and turn them into cooperatives. It prohibited work at night for Paris bakers. The Communards also formed a Committee of Public Safety. The committee rounded up and imprisoned those considered sympathetic to monarchy or hostile to workers. Some were shot. The committee's actions—indeed its very name—brought back dark memories of the French Revolution's Reign of Terror.

A *cooperative* is a business owned and controlled by its workers.

All over Europe, the ruling elite trembled at what they saw as "the red tide" of socialism. Karl Marx, writing at his desk in the British Museum, was delighted by the events in Paris. He believed that the Paris Commune confirmed his ideas—at last, he thought, the "dictatorship of the proletariat" had come about.

If so, it didn't last long. Within a brief two months, the French government dashed hopes of a countrywide revolt when it sent troops marching into Paris. The Communards resisted. They executed hostages and burned stately old public buildings to the ground. But the troops stamped out the Paris Commune with brutal ferocity, killing some 20,000 citizens in a single week.

Marx drew his own conclusions. He criticized the Communard leaders for trying to work within the framework of democratic government when instead, Marx said, they should have utterly smashed the old capitalist system. The leaders of Europe noted his words. Was this, they wondered, what they could expect from future socialist uprisings? Would a communist revolution transform Europe—perhaps violently?

Social Democrats and Labor Unions

Europe's socialists were deeply influenced by Karl Marx, but not all agreed with the German philosopher. Many argued that a violent overthrow of capitalism was not the only means to bring about social change. Instead of dismantling the capitalist system, they wanted to reform it. The way to do that, they said, was to elect socialists to government offices who could then use their power to redistribute wealth.

These Social Democrats were a diverse group of reformers. Some were less concerned about making laws than about gaining power. Some thought the key to change lay in organizing the workers. Still others came to agree with Marx and reject all participation in what they called "bourgeois government."

Though their personalities, aims, and philosophies were different, Social Democratic Parties were forming all across Europe in the late nineteenth century. They made members of the ruling class very nervous—partly because during this time, Social Democrats were actively organizing labor unions.

Labor unions were organizations of workers who banded together for higher wages, better working conditions, and a shorter workday. Earlier governments had banned such associations of workers. They believed that labor unions, also called trade unions, posed a threat to the capitalist system. Now, in country after country, governments gave way to workers' demands and lifted their bans against labor unions.

Unions formed in all kinds of industries and trades. Of course the owners of factories, mills, and mines all resisted. But workers came to realize the huge power they possessed if they acted as one. Instead of individual workers negotiating with an employer, workers bargained collectively. If this did not get them what they wanted, they could put even more pressure on industrialists by

Keir Hardie and Christian Socialism

In late nineteenth-century Britain, the Social Democrats were led by Keir Hardie (kir HAHR-dee). Hardie, who had started mining coal at age 10, was a self-educated man. He read Marx's writings and disagreed with some of his ideas. He described himself as a "Christian socialist," one whose socialism was inspired by the Gospels. Hardie worked to organize a Labour Party. He hoped that as workers gained more seats in Parliament, they would find legislative solutions to growing problems. In *From Serfdom to Socialism* (1907), Hardie wrote:

> This generation has grown up ignorant of the fact that socialism is as old as the human race. When civilization dawned upon the world, primitive man was living his rude communistic life, sharing all things in common with every member of the tribe.... The peoples who have carved their names most deeply on the tables of human story all set out on their conquering career as communists, and their downward path begins with the day when they finally turned away from it and began to gather personal possessions.

Keir Hardie addresses a supportive crowd in London.

going on strike—by refusing to work, and thus bringing a business to a grinding halt.

Unions struck in factories, in mines, and in steel mills. Sometimes the strikes turned bloody when workers and guards hired by owners took up arms against each other. Sometimes owners broke the strikes, and workers gained nothing.

Going on Strike

In 1899, angry workers went on strike at Le Creusot (luh kruh-ZOH), a huge French steel works. The factory managers had promised to raise the workers' pay but cut it instead. Management ignored the union and ridiculed their complaints. Company spies identified workers who complained, and managers quickly fired them. Soon, the workers' anger boiled over. "Away with the factory police! Long live proletarian solidarity!" shouted the strikers. Near the end of a 90-day strike, 9,000 men and women prepared to march on Paris, but the organizers of the strike stopped them. They had persuaded the French government to get involved, and in the end, the factory owners met the workers' demands.

French steelworkers, demanding better pay, march at Le Creusot in 1899.

Sometimes the unions won the changes they demanded. By 1900, strikes were becoming the preferred strategy of the unions. In that year alone, six European countries saw some 4,000 strikes involving 800,000 workers.

In Europe and North America, thousands of workers rushed to join unions. In Britain in 1894, one and a half million workers were union members. By 1914, the number rocketed to more than four million. In Germany, union membership showed similar gains. Newly confident workers saw that they gained strength through solidarity. The labor unions gave workers a way to wield some power of their own.

The Welfare State

The Social Democratic Party organized in nearly every industrialized European nation, spreading ideas about workers' rights and sharing wealth. One leader strongly opposed such ideas—Germany's iron-willed chancellor, Otto von Bismarck.

In Germany, the *chancellor* is the leader of government, similar to the prime minister in Great Britain.

If you read Volume 2 of *The Human Odyssey*, you've met Otto von Bismarck, the brilliant politician and masterful statesman who forged the German states into one nation led by a king or "kaiser" (KIY-zur). Bismarck was the man behind the 1870 war in which Germany defeated and humiliated the French people. As you'll read in the next chapter, Bismarck promoted rapid industrialization in the new German nation, turning it into an economic and military powerhouse.

In Germany as elsewhere, with industrial growth came many social problems and discontent among working people. And with the discontent came the rise of socialism in Germany, much to the horror of Bismarck, who was from an aristocratic family.

Bismarck regarded socialists as dangerous revolutionaries and took rapid steps to put down the efforts of men he considered little more than "robbers and thieves." A few years after his victorious army had defeated France, he turned on Germany's Social Democrats. He persuaded the German parliament to ban the party for a time. But Bismarck realized that this would not be enough. He saw that he would have to lure

German workers away from radical political parties. So in the 1880s, he took the first steps to set up what would become a welfare state, a state in which the government assumes large responsibility for people's financial needs.

Bismarck introduced accident insurance for workers, which provided money to workers injured in the workplace. He also established insurance for the elderly, which gave government support to those who could no longer work. Despite these steps, and much to Bismarck's frustration, more and more Germans joined the ranks of the Social Democrats.

Other European leaders followed Bismarck's example in promoting government involvement in social programs. In Britain during the early 1900s, David Lloyd George and the governing Liberal Party tried methods similar to those Bismarck had used in Germany. Determined to "lift the shadow of the workhouse from the homes of the poor," Lloyd George and his government pushed reforms that improved the conditions of British workers. He introduced old age pensions, which guaranteed an income to people who were too old to work. He granted benefits to workers who became unemployed. And he provided government funds to help the sick and infirm.

A *pension* is an income that someone receives after retiring from a job.

But in Britain, too, the workers kept pushing far ahead of the national leaders in demanding change. Eventually, Lloyd George's Liberal Party lost power to a new Labour Party. Supported by the ever-growing trade unions, the Labour Party became the voice of workers and others who hoped Britain would become a true welfare state.

A Different Idea in the United States

To help solve social problems, Europeans turned to their governments much more readily than Americans. Why? Because of Europe's past. For centuries in Europe, kings and the ruling class considered themselves in charge of protecting the people. During the Middle Ages, for example, a lord's castle walls offered peasants protection from invading armies. In Europe, both revolutionaries and traditionalists tended to think that governments should take charge and manage social and economic problems.

In the United States, however, people were suspicious of strong government. From the time of their Revolution, Americans believed that power concentrated in government was a threat to liberty. As most Americans saw it, the main function of government was to protect natural rights more than to bring about certain social goals. Because they were wary of a powerful government, Americans tended to think that individuals should take care of themselves.

Similarly, in matters of philanthropy, while Europeans tended to favor government-run programs, Americans emphasized individual action. For example, Andrew Carnegie, who made millions in steel, emphasized the responsibility of wealthy individuals to use their fortunes for the common good. Upon his death, he left nearly 350 million dollars to charity.

An Uncertain Future

By 1910, governments in the industrialized nations of Europe were making serious efforts to improve the lives of the poor. They had seen how social and economic tensions could erupt into revolution. To prevent such violent change, they introduced laws to protect workers from the effects of accidents, sickness, old age, and unemployment. Industrialists were coming to realize that they could no longer treat workers as mere commodities in the manufacturing process. City planners were trying to solve the worst urban problems.

But was it enough? For socialists and communists, it was not. They saw in the rise of labor a fulfillment of Marx's predictions about the great struggle between the classes. And they took heart, hoping for the "dictatorship of the proletariat" that Marx had predicted.

Workers operate gigantic machinery in a steel plant at Essen, Germany, about 1900. By the turn of the twentieth century, Germany rivaled Britain as an industrial power. By 1910, Germany produced twice as much steel as Britain.

Powerhouse in Europe: Germany Rising

"The workshop of the world"—that's what people called Great Britain, the land where the Industrial Revolution began. Until the late nineteenth century, textile mills, railroads, and factories made Britain the most highly industrialized country on earth.

But when the Second Industrial Revolution sped up the pace of change, Britain found itself challenged by rivals across Europe and North America. The United States, recovering from its Civil War, had enormous natural resources, ambitious businessmen, and inventive geniuses like Thomas Edison and the Wright brothers.

The British faced other competition closer to home. One European country emerged to challenge Britain for the title of Europe's economic and industrial powerhouse—Germany.

Germany Unites to Compete

Germany had to come from far behind to catch up with Britain as an industrial power. Through the first part of the nineteenth century, Germany was mostly a land of fields and farmers. It was not even a unified nation, but instead a number of small states ruled by various kings, princes, and dukes, who often quarreled and fought with each other.

But by the mid-nineteenth century, these German states were swept up in the powerful worldwide current of nationalism. *Nationalism* is a strong sense of attachment or belonging to one's own country. It can be a bond that holds people together, for better or worse.

Early in the nineteenth century, Napoleon triggered a wave of nationalism in many regions. When his French troops marched into German lands, people who once felt only local loyalties began instead to think of themselves as "Germans." A shared sense of opposition to Napoleon united these once-divided peoples. After all, they spoke the same language and shared much of the same culture and history.

In the 1860s, Otto von Bismarck rose to power in Prussia, the strongest German state. Bismarck was determined to forge Germany into a unified nation. He drew the smaller states together into an alliance under the leadership of Prussia. In 1870, the allied German states invaded and defeated France. After this brief Franco-Prussian War, Bismarck declared the birth of a new, united German Empire. The king of Prussia, Wilhelm I, became the emperor of Germany and was given the title of kaiser. Wilhelm I appointed Bismarck to be

The title *kaiser*—the German word for "Caesar"—was meant to recall the power of the great emperors of ancient Roman times.

Germany, c. 1871

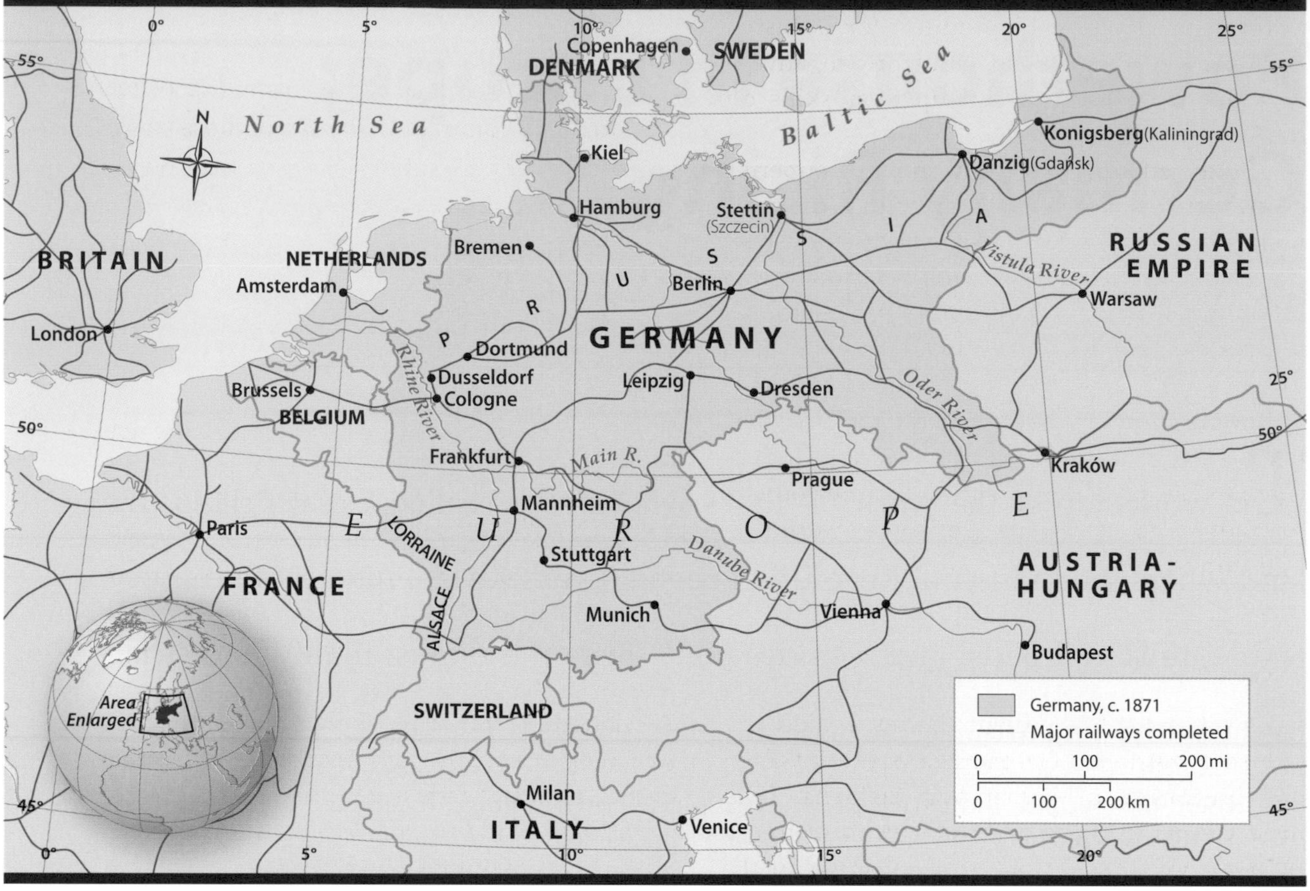

Bayer Leads the Chemical Industry

German technical schools led the development of a new chemical industry that specialized first in making dyes for cloth, and then in producing medical products. Friedrich Bayer, a German inventor, came up with a way to manufacture an indigo-colored dye from coal tar. In 1863, he started his own company, and soon Germany was exporting millions of dollars worth of dyes. Another German chemist wondered if coal tar might also be a source for medical preparations. Dr. Felix Hoffmann invented a drug he called "aspirin," which Bayer's company began to sell in 1899. Eventually people in many countries were buying Bayer's aspirin pills to relieve a variety of aches and pains.

his chancellor—the most powerful official in the new nation. Because of his strength and ruthlessness, people called Bismarck the "Iron Chancellor."

Bismarck wanted to do more than unify Germany. He was determined to turn his nation into an industrial power that could compete with Great Britain and the increasingly prosperous United States. To get money for new factories, he forced the defeated French to pay huge penalties. At the same time, Germany took over the French provinces of Alsace (al-SAS) and Lorraine (luh-RAYN), which were rich in the iron ore needed to make steel.

The abbreviation *c.* before a date stands for the Latin *circa*, meaning "about," indicating the date is approximate.

French money and land helped fuel German industrial development. So did the example of Britain, which had industrialized first. The Germans followed the British model and built textile mills, steel mills, and railroads. The Germans introduced an educational innovation when the government set up technical schools across the country. These schools trained German students to do scientific research that prepared them to develop new ideas and products for industry. Britain had no such schools; in Britain, inventors and technicians picked up their skills on the job.

By the end of the 1800s, Germany's superior system of technical education helped the new nation catch up with Britain as an industrial power. In the early 1870s, when Germany was becoming unified, Britain produced twice as much steel as Germany. By 1910, the tables had turned — Germany produced twice as much steel as Britain. German dominance in the production of steel, the main material of the Second Industrial Revolution, shows just how far the country had advanced to become the new powerhouse in Europe.

Werner von Siemens: Inventor and Businessman

One of the most important figures behind the industrialization of Germany was the inventor and businessman Werner von Siemens. Like most Germans in the early nineteenth century, Siemens grew up on a farm. He was one of 14 children. Werner's brother Carl came up with an invention that helped make the Second Industrial Revolution possible. He developed a way to make steel in a gas furnace, so that the metal could be produced in much larger quantities than before.

It was Werner, however, who became even better known, not only for his many inventions, but also for building an industrial empire that stretched across the globe. As a boy, Siemens showed a strong interest in science and technology. He hoped to go to a university and become an engineer, but his parents had no money to send him. Instead, he became an army officer so he could attend the army's school of engineering.

Once, an officer friend of Siemens challenged another officer to a duel, and asked Siemens to act as his second. But dueling was against the law, and Siemens was sentenced to six months in prison for participating. While in prison, he passed the time by conducting scientific experiments. After only a month, Siemens received an unexpected pardon. He begged to be left in his cell to finish his experiments! He was disappointed when the head of the prison insisted that he leave.

A *second* is a person who stands by to assist one of the combatants in a duel.

Gutta What?

Gutta-percha is a type of evergreen tree found in southeast Asia. It is also the name of the creamy latex that comes from the sap of those trees. The latex, a rubbery substance that is both durable and pliable, turned out to be an excellent electrical insulator. Siemens used it to sheathe electrical cables.

During the early 1840s, while Siemens was in the army, an American inventor, Samuel Morse, developed the telegraph. Fascinated by this new technology, Siemens started working to improve it. He came up with a new kind of telegraph, though it would not prove as successful as Morse's. More important, Siemens figured out a way to insulate underground telegraph wires, using a rubberlike substance called gutta-percha.

In order to market his inventions, Siemens started his own telegraph company. The German government hired his firm to lay a telegraph line stretching from Berlin, Germany's capital city, to Frankfurt. Encouraged by his success, Siemens decided to leave the army and go into business full-time. He hired his brothers to help him run the business.

The Siemens brothers soon expanded their operations beyond Germany, opening branches in Britain and Russia. In the 1870s, the company succeeded in laying a telegraph cable along the bottom of the Atlantic Ocean, stretching from Ireland to North America. Siemens' insulator, gutta-percha, proved invaluable, because unlike earlier materials used for insulating wires, it was not devoured by marine plants or animals.

While running his huge and growing business, Siemens kept on inventing. He developed

Siemens dynamos, like this one, generated electricity and helped turn Germany into an industrial powerhouse.

a steam-powered dynamo, a machine that generated electricity, and made it possible to produce large amounts of electricity more cheaply than before. After Thomas Edison invented the electric lightbulb in 1879, Siemens helped bring this new technology to Germany. Soon Siemens's dynamos were generating electricity to light thousands of German homes and the streets of cities like Berlin.

Siemens became more and more interested in ways that electricity could improve people's lives. He built the first practical electric locomotive, as well as some of the first electric streetcars. By the beginning of the twentieth century, streetcars attached to overhead electrical wires were transporting people to work in most major European cities.

Siemens was not only an innovator in technology but also in business. Far more than most employers of his time, he believed in taking care of his workers. He once wrote to his brother Carl, "The money earned would burn like a red-hot iron in my hand if I did not give the faithful employees their expected share." He shared profits with his workers, set up a pension fund for them, and required them to work only eight and a half hours a day at a time when many employers demanded much longer shifts.

By the time he retired, Siemens was both wealthy and widely respected. In old age, Siemens wrote his autobiography, in which he remarked, "My life was beautiful, because it consisted of successful labor and useful work."

"My Field Is the World": Albert Ballin

By doing business in countries as far away as Russia and the United States, Werner von Siemens helped turn Germany into one of the world's great economic powers. Another German who played a central part in this transformation was a businessman named Albert Ballin (AHL-buhrt BAHL-een).

When he was growing up, Ballin's family had so little money that he had to drop out of school to help his father's business. His father ran an

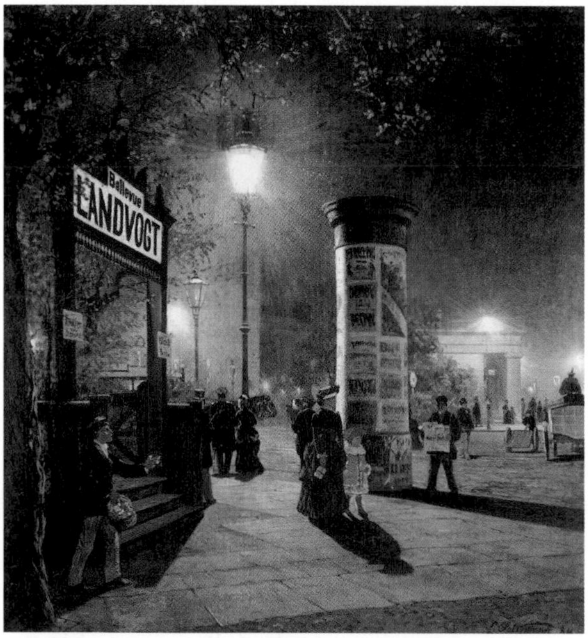

In the late nineteenth century, Werner von Siemens helped bring electric lights to the streets of Berlin.

agency that booked passage to the United States for German immigrants. After his father died, Albert took over the business. He developed it into an independent shipping company that cut costs by carrying passengers one way and cargo on the return trip.

Ballin's ingenuity impressed the owners of a shipping company called the Hamburg-America Line, which was founded in the 1840s to transport freight and passengers between the United States and the port of Hamburg in Germany. In 1886, they hired Ballin, and he soon became the company's managing director. The motto of the Hamburg-America Line was "My Field Is the World." Under Ballin, the company lived up to its motto, sending ships not just across the Atlantic but around the globe.

A voyage across the ocean was, in Ballin's time, generally an exhausting, uncomfortable journey. Ballin asked: Why should that be so? Ballin's fleet introduced some of the world's first luxury liners, cruise ships with gilded staircases and reception halls full of palm trees, designed so that people could travel in style — at least, those rich enough to afford it.

But the most profitable ships in Hamburg-America's fleet were the simpler vessels designed to carry freight. Under Ballin, the company sent ships to trade with countries as far away as China. As the nineteenth century gave way to the twentieth, the Hamburg-America Line could boast of being the largest steamship company in the world.

Ballin's success led to a friendship with Germany's kaiser (at the time, Wilhelm II, whom you'll meet later). The kaiser admired the entrepreneur and enjoyed the company of wealthy businessmen. But many members of the German nobility muttered against the friendship — not because Ballin was a businessman but because he was a Jew. Anti-Semitism — prejudice against Jews — was an ancient and powerful prejudice in Germany, especially among the country's aristocrats. No matter how rich and successful Ballin became, he would never be fully accepted in the highest ranks of German society.

An *entrepreneur* is someone who operates a new business and assumes the risks of such a venture. The term comes from an old French word that means "to undertake."

Berlin: Capital of Change

If there was a capital of the Second Industrial Revolution, it was Berlin, Germany's capital city. After Germany became unified in 1871, Berlin swelled with government officials. Entrepreneurs like Werner von Siemens located their companies in Berlin because they wanted to do business with the government, and because they could hire skilled scientists and engineers from the city's new technical schools. As more factories opened in Berlin, people from all over the country poured in, hoping to find work. Between 1880 and 1914, the city's population exploded.

At first there was not enough room for all these newcomers. Working-class people of the city lived in miserable, overcrowded tenements called "rental barracks." When they left the tenements, it was only to work brutally long hours

Gottlieb Daimler and the Revolution in Transportation

In the middle of the 1800s, a Belgian mechanic invented the internal combustion engine, a new kind of engine powered by gasoline. In 1885, a German inventor named Gottlieb Daimler (GAHT-leeb DIYM-lur) came up with a better, smaller model of the internal combustion engine. He mounted it on a bicycle, creating what he called a "Riding Carriage," or what we call a motorcycle.

In 1889, Daimler attached his engine to a four-wheeled vehicle. Many historians say that this was the first automobile. Others credit the invention of the auto to another German engineer of the time, Karl Benz. Everyone agrees, however, that between them the two Germans—Daimler and Benz—started the automotive revolution. Each inventor set up his own company. Later these merged into a single company that today is best known for making the Mercedes-Benz, one of the world's finest cars. (Mercedes was the name of a daughter of a friend of Daimler.)

In 1913, Berlin saw nonstop construction. Autos and electric trolleys filled busy streets.

in the city's factories. They lived in constant fear that sickness or injury would cause them to lose their jobs.

In an effort to improve their lives, workers began to organize into unions. Some even joined radical political parties calling for revolution. As you read in the last chapter, Bismarck grew alarmed by these signs of unrest and convinced the government to come up with programs to protect workers' welfare. The German government teamed up with employers to provide workers with health insurance and pensions.

Kaiser Wilhelm wanted Berlin to become a grand capital city, like Paris or London. He ordered the building of a new parliament building and a new cathedral. At the same time, he had streets widened and lined with monuments celebrating Germany's past victories in war.

Meanwhile, new technology helped solve some of the problems of the booming metropolis. Electric lighting made streets safer. Electric trolley cars designed by the Siemens company whisked people to work. Berliners, impressed that their city used so much electricity, began to refer to their capital as "Elektropolis" — the Electric City. When city planners saw that the streets were becoming too crowded with trolleys and horse-drawn carriages, they built an underground railroad — what we call a subway. After it opened in 1902, Berliners grew used to clattering along through tunnels deep beneath the earth.

In 1896, Berlin prepared to show itself off to the world by hosting the Berlin Trade Exhibition. Kaiser Wilhelm knew that "Berlin is not Paris," but he wanted to display his nation's strengths. Giant cranes and hissing steam engines competed for attention with an electric Wurst machine that could turn 4,000 swine a year into salami and sausage.

When the American writer Mark Twain visited Berlin, he observed, "It is a new city, the newest I have ever seen. Chicago would seem venerable beside it." In other words, even a city as new and bustling as Chicago seemed ancient and stodgy compared to the hectic swirl of Berlin. To many visitors, and to the proud Berliners themselves, Berlin seemed the most modern city in the world.

An Army and Navy on the Rise

Automobiles and trolley cars were not the only products of the Second Industrial Revolution in Germany. Kaiser Wilhelm ordered a massive military buildup, harnessing technology to create terrible new machines of war.

When Bismarck became chancellor of the German state of Prussia in 1862, he proclaimed, "The great questions of our day are not decided through speeches and majority votes...but through iron and blood." Bismarck reorganized the Prussian army so that troops would be led by highly trained professional officers. Every man in Prussia was required to serve in the army for three years. Bismarck saw to it that Prussian troops were armed with a new weapon, the needle gun, which could fire five times a minute. Prussian generals learned how to use railroads to move troops rapidly into position. It was this efficient, well-organized Prussian army that so easily defeated France in 1870.

After the Franco-Prussian War, when Prussia united with the smaller German states to form the new nation of Germany, Bismarck charted a less warlike path for his country.

"A strong Germany wishes to be left in peace and develop peacefully," he said. Bismarck believed that the nation's new power and status could best be protected through diplomacy. He devoted much of his attention to building alliances with other powerful countries, such as Austria-Hungary, against potentially hostile nations. Yet Bismarck also believed that Germany needed a strong military to protect itself from other European powers. As he pointed out, "One does not attack someone whose dagger is loose in the sheath"—in other words, someone who is armed and ready to strike back.

Diplomacy is the practice of conducting negotiations between groups or countries.

Bismarck served as chancellor of Germany for two decades. In 1888, a new kaiser, Wilhelm II, came to the throne. This Wilhelm resented Bismarck's authority and influence, and he soon forced the aging Iron Chancellor to resign.

Wilhelm II was a vain, boastful man, used to having things his own way. He once declared, "He who is against me I shall crush." Behind the bluster lay deep insecurity. An injury at birth had left him with a withered left arm, a defect that doctors tried to correct with braces and even electric shock treatments. As he later recalled, "The only result was that I was in a painful way, greatly tortured." As a boy, his sense of balance was so bad he could not ride a horse without help. But a prince was expected to be a good rider, so when he was eight years old, his tutor placed him on a horse without stirrups. The tearful child fell off again and again, and each time the tutor placed him back in the saddle. He finally learned to ride, but his withered arm and youthful humiliations left emotional scars he carried the rest of his life.

Kaiser Wilhelm II strikes a pose in one of the many military uniforms he loved to show off.

Wilhelm's grandmother was Queen Victoria of England, and he often visited Britain. He longed to become an important figure on the world stage, like his British relatives. He became fascinated with the proud British navy, whose ships ruled the waves. "There awoke in me," he wrote, "the will to build ships of my own like these some day, and when I was grown up to possess as fine a navy as the English."

The young prince felt right at home when he entered the German army. "The officer corps provided me with joy and happiness and contentment on earth," he said. He loved military pomp and ceremony. His closets were filled with some two hundred uniforms. He delighted in war games, though he insisted that his side always win.

When Wilhelm became kaiser, he was determined to present himself as a bold German warrior who would expand his nation's power. Germany, he declared, must have its "place in the sun" among the world's greatest nations. Under the rule of Wilhelm II, the German army grew. Scientists and engineers were encouraged to develop new weapons, including huge cannons that hurled shells for miles, guns that shot enormous flames, and poison gas that could choke enemy troops to death.

In the late 1890s, the kaiser and his admirals began a ship-building program designed to rival Britain's huge fleet. He believed that only with such a navy could Germany become a true world power.

The German dreadnought *Ostfriesland*

Alarmed by the sight of a growing navy just across the North Sea, the British started building bigger battleships of their own. They soon created a fearsome kind of warship called the dreadnought. Each of these huge, fast, heavily armored ships carried 10 gigantic guns designed to sink any smaller ship that opposed it. In response, the Germans produced their own dreadnoughts. By 1914, the British fleet included 22 of these monstrous warships, the German fleet 15.

German Nationalism on the Rise

As German industry and the German military grew, something else grew with them: German nationalism.

In the late nineteenth and early twentieth centuries, nationalism changed from a feeling that "my country is a wonderful place" to the belief that "my country is better than other countries, and whatever my country does is right." This new self-glorifying kind of nationalism took hold in much of the Western world, and it led to heated rivalries among nations.

Nowhere was this strident new nationalism more pronounced than in Germany. German counts and princes made toasts to "the greater Germany." The Kaiser gave speeches about "the greatness of our Fatherland." He urged schools to "produce nationally-minded young Germans." He boasted that "the Berlin school of sculpture is at a level which even the Renaissance could not possibly have surpassed." Newspapers ran articles assuring readers that Germany was destined to be a leader of nations. A professor at Berlin University summed up the thoughts of many German nationalists: "The more powerful state is the better state, its people are the better people, its culture is a superior culture."

Such nationalism often went hand-in-hand with militarism—the glorification of military might. Leaders of some industrial nations believed that the use of force was ultimately the most effective way to solve international problems. Again, militarism was nowhere more evident than in Germany. Kaiser Wilhelm II told German soldiers that "the tasks that the old Roman Empire...was unable to accomplish, the new German Empire is in a position to fulfill. The means that make this possible is our army." A German general wrote that war "is not only a necessary element in the life of the people, but also an indispensable factor in culture, indeed the highest expression of the strength and life of truly cultured peoples."

When German soldiers marched off to crush France in the Franco-Prussian War of 1870, they marched to a song called "The Watch on the Rhine." It was a song that would echo across Europe and beyond in the coming century.

The *Rhine* is one of the longest and most important rivers in Europe. Much of the river flows through Germany.

A voice resounds like thunder-peal,
'Mid dashing waves and clang of steel:
The Rhine, the Rhine, the German Rhine!
Who guards today my stream divine?

Patriotism vs. Nationalism

Patriotism and nationalism are related, but not the same. *Patriotism* means love of country. A patriot is someone who is devoted to his or her country, looks after its interests, and wants to help make it a good place. *Nationalism*, on the other hand, has come to mean glorifying one's own nation over all other countries, even at the expense of other countries. Nationalism became a dangerous force in the late nineteenth century.

Chorus: *Dear Fatherland, no danger thine;*
Firm stand thy sons to watch the Rhine!

They stand, a hundred thousand strong,
Quick to avenge their country's wrong;
With filial love their bosoms swell,
They'll guard the sacred landmark well!

The dead of an heroic race
From heaven look down and meet this gaze;
He swears with dauntless heart, "O Rhine,
Be German as this breast of mine!"

Surging Forward

As the twentieth century dawned, Germans proudly celebrated their country's growth to power and prosperity. While factory workers continued to struggle with low wages and poor working conditions, middle and upper class Germans basked in the prosperity the Second Industrial Revolution had brought them. Like most educated Europeans, they believed that advancing technology would eventually solve the problems and conflicts in their society. And surely, they told themselves, Germany's modern army and growing navy made the young empire a true world power.

In a speech delivered in 1902, Kaiser Wilhelm II looked at his nation's recent achievements with pride and gazed into the future with confidence. "Broad and wide flows the river of our science and research," he said. "There is no work in the domain of new research which has not been composed in our language, and no thought springs from science which has not been tried out here first and been adopted by other nations afterwards. And this is the world empire after which Germany is striving."

Launching the Lusitania

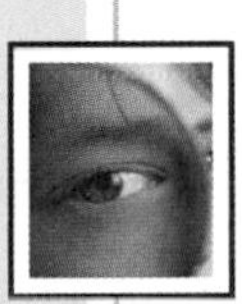

Historical Close-up

The spirit of the Second Industrial Revolution — pride in huge projects, dreams of unlimited progress, enthusiastic nationalism — took to the seas around the turn of the twentieth century. Shipping companies in Britain, Germany, and the United States competed to design gigantic luxury liners that could cross oceans in days. Albert Ballin turned Germany's Hamburg-America Line into the world's largest steamship company. In Britain, where industrialists were not accustomed to being left behind, the directors of the famous Cunard Line scrambled to build bigger, faster floating palaces.

Great Britain was embarrassed. Worse — humiliated. Bad enough that back in 1897, Germany had captured from the British Cunard Line the coveted Blue Riband, the trophy for the fastest transatlantic crossing, and had held it without challenge ever since. Doubly bad that Britain's White Star Line had recently been gobbled up by a giant shipping company owned by the unbelievably wealthy American banker J. P. Morgan. Now, on top of everything, a Cunard ship had broken down in the middle of the Atlantic Ocean, floating helplessly until one of Morgan's steamers came to the rescue, towing it to shore.

A *conglomerate* is a huge corporation doing business in several different fields.

The message wasn't lost on anybody, least of all the British press. The newspapers were full of questions. Would the Cunard Line, once Britain's pride, also be taken over by a powerful foreign conglomerate? Or would the British government step in to save the day?

Stung, the government quickly responded with a loan of 2.6 million pounds. Cunard's mission: to build a pair of purely British ocean liners, the biggest, grandest, and *fastest* in the world.

The first of the twin ships was named the *Lusitania,* but everyone called her Big Lucy. Big Lucy was much larger than any ship that had ever been built: 787 feet long, 87 feet wide, and displacing 31,550 gross tons. The metal rivets alone — four million to hold the hull together — weighed 500 tons. Mammoth steam turbines powered the ship, driven by more than three million blades that required 65,000 gallons of water a minute to stay cool. Her 27 boilers and 192 furnaces burned a thousand tons of coal a day.

Of course, there was more to Lucy than machinery. The *Lusitania* was to be a luxury ship, seven decks high, built to rival the finest hotels of Europe, with every modern convenience from an elevator to electric fans. Thousands of workers labored for more than a year to fit her out. They laid nearly 300 miles of electric cable and installed state-of-the-art dishwashers and refrigerators. They adorned the ship with the finest woods from ancient forests, and with skillfully wrought bronze and iron. They lugged in heavy hand-carved oak tables and chairs. They hung silk draperies, folded linen, polished silverware, and checked and rechecked every detail down to the last bar of soap.

At last, the ship was ready to launch. On the summer afternoon of the *Lusitania*'s first sea test, crowds gathered along the dock, admiring the four towering 75-foot smokestacks and the huge propellers. A lucky few with invitations climbed aboard — fashionable ladies in their fitted jackets and long skirts, important-looking gentlemen with bowler hats and gold-tipped canes. Filled with pride at their part in this historic occasion, they leaned on the rail and watched the crowd grow smaller as the liner headed out into the open sea. They were on the greatest ship afloat, the liner that would win back the Blue Riband and restore Britain to what they saw as its rightful place at the head of the industrialized nations.

Then a tremor ran along the keel. It started as a barely noticeable vibration, but as the ship gained speed, the stern began shaking violently. The decks rattled. As frightened passengers clung to the rail, the captain shouted orders, and Big Lucy slowly turned and headed back to port.

It was a devastating setback. The ship had to be pulled into dry dock. The entire stern was gutted, and then shored up with anything the Cunard architects could think of—brackets, arches, columns—until finally the tremor was under control.

Reinforced and hastily redecorated, Big Lucy was ready for her maiden voyage. First, however, the ship was thrown open to the public. Twenty thousand people streamed on board over the next four days, eager to see this modern marvel of a floating palace. Dazzled and delighted, they toured through the seven decks, gasping at each new sight: elegant salons furnished with marble fireplaces, thick carpets, and sparkling chandeliers; first-class cabins with silver-plated bathroom fixtures; an open-air "sidewalk café" complete with wicker chairs and palm trees; and every kind of newfangled gadget, from an ice-cream maker to a boot-cleaning machine.

Indoors, it was easy to forget that you were on a ship. The first-class dining room, two stories high and topped by an enormous gilded dome, was designed

The *Lusitania*, pride of Britain's Cunard Line, boasted this open-air "sidewalk café," elegant salons, and lavish cabins. The vessel's builders were determined to make it the biggest, fastest, most luxurious ship afloat.

in the style of the French king Louis XVI. First-class passengers enjoyed a smoking room boasting a stained-glass ceiling and walls paneled with Italian walnut. Those who preferred fresh air could relax in lounge chairs on the deck, or, if it was raining, stroll under the covered promenade.

The wealthiest passengers, if they so wished, could cross the Atlantic in comfort and style without ever leaving their cabins. For a one-way fare of $4,000 (at a time when a typical weekly wage was about $20), they could occupy a Regal Suite: two bedrooms and a bathroom, private parlor, dining room, and pantry, all in sophisticated styles ranging from French Renaissance to English Country.

While the gilt and glitter of the first-class sections of the *Lusitania* astonished and amazed, many of those who toured the ship may have been equally impressed by the second and third classes. With their mahogany washstands and soft woolen curtains, the spacious second-class cabins lived up to Cunard's boast that its second class equaled first class on any other ship. Stewardesses brought second-class passengers tea in their cabins and served

The *Lusitania* waits at dock in New York Harbor in 1907. Huge crowds flocked to see the ship's luxurious interior. Although the British built the *Lusitania*, Americans shared in its glory as a symbol of industrial progress.

them breakfast in bed. Even third class was surprisingly comfortable, with its six-berth cabins instead of dormitory-style open berths.

On September 7, 1907, the *Lusitania* left port at last, bound for New York City. Two hundred thousand people gathered to witness the departure. They stood on the dock, cheering and waving their hats and handkerchiefs, while on board the ship's band struck up a tune. Then, as all the other ships in the harbor blasted their steam whistles in salute, Big Lucy headed out.

The ship was well-stocked with plenty of food. Meals in first class were the fanciest, naturally, but on the *Lusitania* even the third-class fare was delicious. By the time they reached New York, the passengers and crew had breakfasted on two tons of bacon and ham and 40,000 eggs, dined on 25,000 pounds of meat and 4,000 pounds of fish, consumed 1,000 pineapples and 500 pounds of grapes, and downed 4,000 pounds of coffee along with 500 gallons of fresh cream.

One thing, however, even Cunard could not arrange to perfection — the weather. Rain and fog prevented Big Lucy from making the Atlantic crossing at her maximum speed. The German record remained unbroken.

Despite this disappointment, the arrival in New York Harbor was a triumph. Americans thrilled to the newest, the biggest, the best, and the *Lusitania* was all of these. To the thousands thronging the shore, the approaching ship looked like a floating skyscraper. Once it docked, sightseers swarmed to get a firsthand look at the gorgeous interiors.

"Just now," wrote one American newspaper, "the man who came over in the *Lusitania* takes precedence of the one whose ancestors came over in the *Mayflower*." Never mind that Lucy was a British ship; everyone shared in her glory. She stood for the heights of industrial progress: distance conquered, nations linked in peace and progress.

A few weeks after its first voyage, the *Lusitania* made the Atlantic crossing again. This time, the weather was fine. Cheered on by the eager passengers, the crew worked night and day to keep the speed up to just under 24 knots. Four days, nineteen hours, and fifty-two minutes after leaving England, the ship reached port, breaking the world record. The Blue Riband was Britain's once again, and Big Lucy had proved herself the biggest, most beautiful, and *fastest* ship in the world.

A train chugs past Western-style buildings while ships from Western nations ride at anchor in the harbor in this print from the late nineteenth century, which depicts the Japanese city of Yokohama. At the time, Japan was the one Asian nation that made vigorous attempts to turn itself into a modern industrial powerhouse.

A New Powerhouse in Asia: Meiji Japan

Factories, telegraph lines, railroads, steamships, electric trams, automobiles — in less than a century, the Industrial Revolution changed the face of Europe and North America. While England led this wave of change, other nations, like Germany and the United States, were quickly catching up.

By 1900, Germany produced more steel and more electrical products than England. The United States had booming oil and steel industries of its own, not to mention more railroad track than any other Western nation.

The industrialized Western nations sought raw materials like coal, iron, and rubber for their growing industries. They also wanted overseas markets to buy their manufactured goods. They sent steamships abroad in search of both. In parts of Africa and Asia, they found what they were looking for.

Would the Industrial Revolution take root in other lands? For years, much of Africa and Asia remained unindustrialized. But one Asian country actively responded to the Western challenge. Japan, an island nation in the Pacific, decided to beat the West at its own game. In the space of fifty years, Japan transformed itself from a feudal kingdom, ruled by the shogun (SHOH-guhn) and defended by his samurai (SA-muh-riy), into a modern industrial nation.

Shogun was the title of the military ruler of Japan from the late twelfth century to the mid-nineteenth century.

Samurai were professional Japanese warriors who served Japanese feudal lords.

Perry Comes to Call

One bright July day in 1853, the people of Uraga (ou-RAH-gah), a Japanese fishing village, watched in awe as four huge, black-hulled ships entered the bay. Two of these ships were enormous three-masted sailing vessels. They were being towed swiftly against the wind by two monstrous black ocean liners belching soot. The Japanese, who had never seen steamships before, were alarmed by the sight of these "giant dragons puffing smoke." Messengers hurried to the city of Edo (EH-doh), where the shogun ruled, to warn of "alien ships of fire."

In reality, the terrified villagers were looking at a squadron of the United States Navy. Its commander, Commodore Matthew Perry, had been sent to persuade Japan to trade with the United States.

For more than two centuries, Japan had traded very cautiously with Western nations. In the 1540s, European traders and missionaries had started coming to Japan. As merchants sold guns and other goods to rival warlords, missionaries converted many Japanese to Christianity. Then, in the early seventeenth century, a powerful

From the President to the Shogun

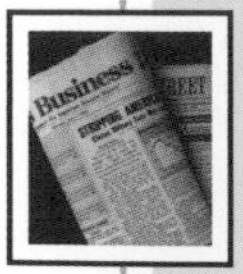

A Page from the Past

Here is part of the letter that President Millard Fillmore sent in 1853, by way of Commodore Perry, to the Tokugawa shogun of Japan. The president's tone is friendly, but when he mentions that American steamships "can go from California to Japan in eighteen days"—a remarkably fast voyage at that time—he is conveying a subtle threat, in effect, "If you say 'No,' our navy could be at your shores to help you change your mind—and quickly."

GREAT AND GOOD FRIEND: I send you this public letter by Commodore Matthew C. Perry, an officer of the highest rank in the navy of the United States, and commander of the squadron now visiting your imperial majesty's dominions.... I have no other object in sending him to Japan but to propose to your imperial majesty that the United States and Japan should live in friendship and have commercial intercourse with each other....

The United States of America reach from ocean to ocean, and our Territory of Oregon and State of California lie directly opposite to the dominions of your imperial majesty. Our steamships can go from California to Japan in eighteen days.

Our great State of California produces about sixty millions of dollars in gold every year, besides silver, quicksilver, precious stones, and many other valuable articles. Japan is also a rich and fertile country, and produces many very valuable articles. Your imperial majesty's subjects are skilled in many of the arts. I am

A *dynasty* is a group or family that rules for a time.

A *shogunate* is a Japanese dynasty.

dynasty known as the Tokugawa (toh-kou-GAH-wah) shogunate began to rule Japan. The Tokugawa worried that European traders and rulers would try to tamper with Japan's affairs, and perhaps even threaten the shogun's rule.

In the 1630s, the Tokugawa shogun took extreme steps to seclude Japan from foreign influence. He closed all but one port to foreigners. He decreed that any Japanese who tried to leave the country would be put to death. He also ordered the death of many Japanese who had converted to the foreign religion of Christianity.

The shogun, however, did not want to be ignorant of developments beyond Japan's borders. So he permitted a few Dutch and Chinese ships to bring foreign goods to the country each year, insisting that they trade only at the port of Nagasaki (nah-gah-SAH-kee), hundreds of miles from the capital. The shogun allowed Japanese scholars to study books brought by the Dutch on subjects such as astronomy and anatomy.

Indeed, in the Tokugawa era, Japanese society was one of the most literate on earth at the time. It was also one of the most urbanized—the Japanese city of Edo was larger than London or Paris. For the most part, however, the shogun remained wary of influences from London, Paris, or other foreign cities, and Japan shielded itself from the outside world.

In the 1850s, the United States began to look at Japan with new interest. American merchants, who were trading with China and other Asian lands, were eager to trade with Japan.

desirous that our two countries should trade with each other, for the benefit both of Japan and the United States.

We know that the ancient laws of your imperial majesty's government do not allow of foreign trade, except with the Chinese and the Dutch; but as the state of the world changes and new governments are formed, it seems to be wise, from time to time, to make new laws....

Commodore Perry is also directed by me to represent to your imperial majesty that we understand there is a great abundance of coal and provisions in the Empire of Japan. Our steamships, in crossing the great ocean, burn a great deal of coal, and it is not convenient to bring it all the way from America. We wish that our steamships and other vessels should be allowed to stop in Japan and supply themselves with coal, provisions, and water. They will pay for them in money, or anything else your imperial majesty's subjects may prefer.... We are very desirous of this.

These are the only objects for which I have sent Commodore Perry... friendship, commerce, and a supply of coal and provisions.

Your good friend,
Millard Fillmore

Also, Japan's islands would provide a convenient location where American whaling vessels could restock and American naval ships could refuel.

The president of the United States, Millard Fillmore, wrote a letter for Commodore Perry to deliver to the Japanese shogun. In this letter, Fillmore asked that American steamships, "in crossing the great ocean,...be allowed to stop in Japan and supply themselves with coal, provisions, and water." And, he suggested, wouldn't trade between the two countries be good for all involved?

When he arrived in Japan, Commodore Perry refused to deliver the letter to minor officials who tried to board his ship. He negotiated until a representative of the Tokugawa shogun himself accepted the document. Then Perry sailed away, giving the Japanese some time to decide on their response.

Commodore Matthew Perry arrives in Japan in 1853, demanding that the Japanese open their country to trade.

But Americans had no intention of taking "no" for an answer. Commodore Perry returned the following year with an even larger squadron of heavily armed ships — nine of them.

Japan's leaders realized that their sword-wielding samurai were no match for Western ships, cannon, and rifles. They also knew that their neighbors, the Chinese, had just been crushed by the British in a series of wars. So they reluctantly agreed to open their country to more trade.

The United States and other Western nations insisted that Japan's rulers sign trade treaties that did not treat Japan as an equal partner. For example, the treaties required Japan to maintain low tariffs on goods imported from the West. The treaties also stated that Westerners residing in Japan were not subject to Japanese law.

A *tariff* is a tax imposed by a government on imported or exported goods.

Soon the ships of America and Europe were entering Japan's ports, stocking up on coal, food, and water, and buying tea and silkworms. Japan's proud isolation came to an end.

The humiliated shogun realized that he'd better learn more about what his nation was up against. He decided to send two delegations to the West, one to the United States in 1860 and another to Europe in 1862.

A Samurai in San Francisco

In both these missions to the West, Japan was represented by Fukuzawa Yukichi (fou-kou-ZAH-wah yoo-KEE-chee), the son of a samurai. Fukuzawa had grown up amidst polished swords, lacquered suits of armor, and the crested helmets of the samurai class. He carried two swords suspended from his belt, as befit a man of samurai rank.

In Japan, the proper order of names is "last name, first name." Thus, in *Fukuzawa Yukichi*, *Fukuzawa* is the family name and *Yukichi* is the first name.

Fukuzawa had a keen mind and was an avid student of language. He had learned Dutch and then used a Dutch-English dictionary to teach himself English. His first trip to San Francisco in 1860 changed his life and the life of Japan.

In America, Fukuzawa admired everything from the elegant horse-drawn carriages to the thundering railroads. He delighted in new ideas and inventions, and was eager to have his picture taken by one of the amazing new cameras. He was photographed dressed in an elaborate, traditional samurai outfit, complete with full skirts and double swords suspended from his belt.

Fukuzawa Yukichi poses with a young American girl.

The next day he broke with all tradition. He had himself photographed in simple garb beside a 15-year-old American girl, the photographer's daughter. This was, as Fukuzawa knew, a startlingly unconventional gesture, because at the time most Japanese men socialized with women only in highly regulated circumstances. The photograph, which has become one of the most famous in Japanese history, was Fukuzawa's way of saying, "You see? We can break with the old ways. We can be modern."

After the trip to San Francisco and the 1862 mission to Europe, Fukuzawa returned to his homeland with new ideas. He wrote a book called *Conditions in the West*, in which he argued that Japan must go the way of the West and make a bold leap from feudal ways to the modern age. Some Japanese heartily agreed with Fukuzawa's argument. Others, however, strongly disagreed, and a few even tried to kill him for his beliefs.

By this time, many Japanese noblemen had lost respect for their shogun. They believed that if the shogun could be bullied by the United States or any European power, then the country needed a more powerful government. A civil war broke out, which ended in 1868 with the defeat of the shogun's forces. The victorious rebels announced that they were restoring rule by the emperor, who in recent times had been just a figurehead with no real power.

The Meiji Look West

The emperor, a boy of 15 named Mutsuhito (mout-sou-HEE-toh), was brought from Kyoto, the ancient imperial capital in the west, to Edo. Edo, which had been home to the shogun, was promptly renamed Tokyo (TOH-kee-yoh), a name that means "Eastern Capital."

Japanese officials declared the reign of Emperor Mutsuhito as the beginning of a new period in their country's history, which they called Meiji (MAY-jee), meaning "Enlightened Rule." The 1868 restoration of the emperor as the governor of Japan is known as the Meiji Restoration. Mutsuhito is remembered as the Meiji Emperor, and the long period of his reign (1868–1912) is known as the Meiji Era.

While powerful Japanese officials restored the emperor to his throne, they did not go back to all the ancient ways. Instead, they wanted to move forward. They had resented Japan's weakness in the face of Western power. So in 1868 the new emperor proclaimed, "Knowledge shall be sought throughout the world so as to strengthen the foundations of imperial rule."

Under Meiji rule, Japan set out to abandon its feudal past and modernize. No longer would Japan be divided into rigid classes of samurai, farmer, artisan, and merchant. When Fukuzawa heard of this new policy, he was delighted. As he later recalled, "I at once renounced my rank as samurai and gave up wearing the two swords."

In 1871, another group of Japanese officials set off on a year-long tour of Europe and the United States. Fukuzawa was ill and could not join them. The Japanese delegation traveled from a land of fishing villages and rice paddies to cities full of factories, telegraph poles, steamships, and locomotives. The officials toured shipyards and iron foundries. They visited paper plants, cotton mills, and coal mines.

Everywhere they went, the Japanese officials took notes on what they saw. In England, the Japanese visited courts and prisons. They also examined British workhouses and concluded that in London, the poor were worse off than in Japan. The Japanese visitors were puzzled when they saw gas workers on strike—to the Japanese, the workers seemed well paid. After visiting Western schools, one mission member wrote, "Nothing has more urgency for us than schools.... Our people are no different from the Americans or Europeans of today; it is all a matter of education or lack of education."

Another Japanese official admiringly observed that "most of the countries in Europe...abound in wealth and power." He also noted that the industrialization that had brought such wealth and power happened quickly—"it has taken scarcely forty years to produce such conditions." The message was clear—if Japan wanted to, it could catch up to the West, and quickly.

The Meiji government decided to respond to Western dominance not by isolating itself but by rapidly modernizing. The Japanese embraced the slogan "Prosperous Nation, Strong Military," and set out to become as wealthy and powerful as Europe and the United States.

Japanese officials depart Yokohama in 1871 on a year-long tour of Europe and the United States.

Taking Action

Emperor Mutsuhito's government began to invest heavily in the latest means of communication and transportation. In 1870, a telegraph started operating between Tokyo and the city of Yokohama (YOH-koh-HAH-mah). In 1872, the Japanese opened their first railway, and within 35 years they laid 5,000 miles of track, knitting together the major cities.

The Meiji government encouraged the growth of trade and industry by setting up a modern banking system and investing in industry. The government bought coal mines and invested in textile mills, cement factories, and shipyards. When these ventures failed, the government decided to sell the businesses to private companies run by Japanese businessmen who had studied Western methods of manufacturing.

Soon the smokestacks of factories towered over the countryside. The Japanese constructed a huge steel mill and started building their own steamships. Japan industrialized so successfully that by the end of the Meiji era, more than 80 percent of the country's exports consisted of manufactured goods rather than raw materials.

As Japan modernized, leading officials understood that a modern economy relied on an educated workforce. For years, Fukuzawa Yukichi had been calling for more and better

The Encouragement of Learning

A Page from the Past

Fukuzawa Yukichi remains one of the most important figures in modern Japanese history. His bust stands prominently in front of Keio University in Tokyo, and his face is on Japan's 10,000 yen note. In this excerpt from The Encouragement of Learning (1872), *Fukuzawa discusses education and Japan's progress since the Meiji Restoration. Do any of his ideas sound familiar?*

When men are born, Heaven's idea is that all men should be equal to all other men without distinction of high and low or noble and mean.... However, taking a wide view of this human world, we find wise and ignorant men, rich men and poor men, men of importance and men of little consequence.... Why should all this be?... [Nowadays] the distinction between the wise and the foolish comes from whether they have studied or not.... Only those who strive for learning and are capable of reasoning will become men of rank and riches while those without learning will become poor and lowly.

Learning does not mean knowing strange words or reading old, difficult literature or enjoying poems and writing verses and such accomplishments, which are of no real use in the world. These accomplishments give much pleasure to the human mind...but one's best efforts should be given to real learning that is near to men's everyday use — for instance,... the composition of letters, bookkeeping, the abacus, the use of scales. Advancing farther there will be many subjects to be taken up: geography...the study of nature...history...economics...ethics.

education for the people of Japan. He started an influential newspaper to spread modern ideas, including his repeated arguments for public education. Fukuzawa himself founded a university in Tokyo.

Soon the Meiji government ordered that schools be built in most Japanese towns and villages. By 1900, the great majority of Japan's children were educated at least through the elementary level. Like European schools, Japan's schools taught not only reading and writing but also strong loyalty to their nation. Every student had to memorize a pledge that commanded, "Should an emergency arise, offer yourselves

Mitsubishi: From Coal to Cars and Electronics

Some of the large family-owned businesses that began around the time of the Meiji Restoration are still important today. For example, in the 1870s the Mitsubishi company got its start in shipping. The company's ambitious leaders quickly moved on to coal mining, shipbuilding, and producing steel, glass, and aircraft. Today, the Mitsubishi group of companies is best known for manufacturing automobiles and electronics.

For the study of these subjects one should read the translations of Western books. In writing, one may let the Japanese alphabet suffice in most cases....

Since the return of Imperial rule, Japan's system of government has come to be much changed. Externally she associates with the world under international law; internally, she guides the plain people to take family names and to go on horseback *(see below)*, which one may consider the finest act of all times. One may say that the movement to make the four classes—samurai, farmer, artisan, and merchant—equal has been placed on a firm footing.

Therefore, henceforth among the people of Japan there will be no such thing as the rank to which a man is born. Only by his ability and the position he holds will a man's rank be determined....

Note: In the Tokugawa era, before the Meiji came to power, class barriers in Japan were strong. Common people had only first names and no surnames. Only nobles and samurai were allowed to ride horses. The Meiji changed both of these customs.

The Japanese 10,000 yen note features a portrait of Fukuzawa Yukichi.

Coeval means of the same age or time period.

courageously to the State; and thus guard and maintain the prosperity of Our Imperial Throne coeval with heaven and earth." In this way, the Japanese school system was designed to produce not only industrious workers, but also loyal subjects.

A New Fighting Force and a Plan for Empire

While visiting the West, Japanese officials had met with leaders such as Germany's Otto von Bismarck. Impressed by Bismarck's reorganization of the Prussian army, the Meiji set out to build a Japanese army organized on modern principles. Instead of the colorful robes of the samurai, soldiers would wear standard uniforms. They would fight with rifles and machine guns rather than swords. And, like German soldiers, most Japanese soldiers would be drafted to serve for a period of three years.

As a model for their navy, Japan turned to Great Britain, which had the largest navy in the world. Japanese naval officers studied in Britain, and the ships of the Japanese navy were built in European shipyards.

Imperialism is the policy by which one nation controls another country or territory, often one that is far away.

By the 1880s, Japan's Meiji leaders watched with alarm as Europeans embarked on a new campaign of imperialism. European nations wanted raw materials for their factories, markets for their manufactured goods, and fueling stations for their naval vessels. Britain, France, Belgium, Portugal, Germany, the Netherlands, and other European nations carved up Africa among them, taking cotton, copper, diamonds, rubber, and other materials, and shipping them back to Europe.

Japan built a powerful, modern navy, which it used to begin building an empire.

But what most worried the Japanese was Western imperialism in Asia. The British, French, Dutch, and others controlled vast parts of Asia. The Japanese wondered: Will we be next?

They continued to build up their army and navy. And they began to feel a strong sense of national pride. One influential Japanese writer, Tokutomi Soho (toh-kou-toh-mee SOH-hoh), angrily denounced "the scorn of the white people" — the European imperialists — while proudly declaring Japan to be "the most progressive, developed, civilized, and powerful nation in the Orient."

Orient is an old term for "east." From the Middle Ages to the nineteenth century, Westerners referred to all lands east of Jerusalem as "the Orient."

It was not long before Japan's rapid industrial growth fueled the same appetite for raw materials that spurred the industrialized European nations. Between 1890 and 1910, as Japan's trade and prosperity increased, the country's population shot up by more than 20 percent. The densely populated nation needed more coal, more iron, and more rice. And it wanted someone to buy its many manufactured wares.

Japan's western neighbor, Korea, had what Japan wanted. Korea, at this time a poor country with a weak government, had natural resources like iron and coal. Japan's government worried that the little country might be taken over by an imperialist power like Russia or Britain, or even by China. When China sent troops to Korea, it was too much for the Japanese. They believed that the Korean peninsula — jutting out from the Asian mainland just across the Sea of Japan — was, as newspapers at the time called it, a "dagger pointed at the heart of Japan."

In 1894, Japan sent troops to Korea, supposedly to protect it. This action provoked a war with China, the largest nation in eastern Asia. In the Sino-Japanese War, no one expected the

The prefix *Sino-* means "Chinese."

Meiji Japan in the Early 1900s

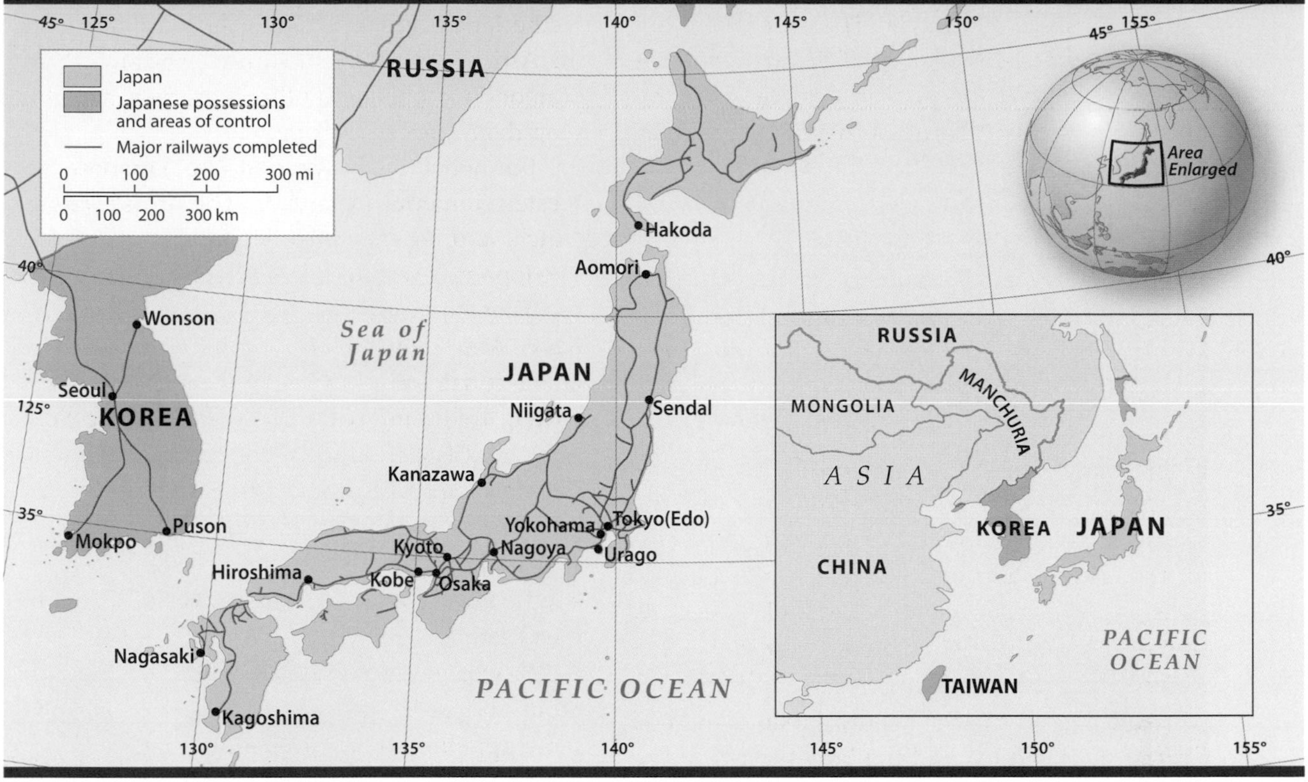

little island nation to defeat its much larger neighbor. But in a contest lasting less than a year, the well-coordinated forces of Japan trounced the poorly organized Chinese army and navy. In response to the victory, Fukuzawa wrote, "I could hardly refrain from rising up in delight."

Japan proceeded to dominate Korea. The Japanese also demanded that China turn over the island of Taiwan to Japan. And Meiji leaders pressed for rights to Manchuria, a province in the north of China. Startled Europeans and Americans watched as Japan showed its strength in modern weaponry, warfare, and imperial bullying.

A great surge of nationalist feeling swept through Japan. The writer Tokutomi declared that Japan's victory had proved "civilization is not a monopoly of the white man." Japan, he boasted, had "a character suitable for great achievements in the world." A nation that had wanted to defend itself against Western imperialism now set out on an imperialist path of its own.

The End of the Samurai

By the time of the Meiji Restoration, most samurai were no longer fearsome warriors, as they had been during Japan's Middle Ages. The Meiji push to modernize Japan threatened the samurai's remaining privileges. Under the Meiji, a new legal system made all people subject to the same laws, regardless of class. Japan's new army relied on drafted soldiers, not sword-wielding samurai. The Meiji government even forbade the samurai to wear their swords in public.

Some samurai, like Fukuzawa Yukichi, were delighted with these changes, and they helped modernize Japan by working as writers, teachers, or civil servants. But other samurai felt injured and insulted by the Meiji reforms. Some rebelled against the government. The emperor's forces crushed them, and their leader committed suicide. So ended the era of the samurai as Japan's noble warriors.

This 1898 French cartoon shows imperialist rulers dividing China among themselves as a Chinese man protests. Britain's Queen Victoria, Germany's Kaiser Wilhelm, Russia's Tsar Nicholas, and Japan's Emperor Mutsuhito are joined by "Marianna," a symbol of the French republic. Like many political cartoons, this one exaggerates the characters' features.

Imperialism in Action: The Scramble for Asia

When telling the story of the nineteenth and twentieth centuries, historians use terms like *industrialism, nationalism,* and *imperialism.* These "-isms" are a kind of shorthand — a single term can sum up thousands of specific people, events, causes, and effects. The advantage of such terms is that they provide convenient categories in which to organize a multitude of events. The disadvantage is that they hide the faces of individual people, the contours of particular landscapes, the sights and sounds of specific events. Even though "-isms" blur over specific people, places, and events, such terms do convey an important point—that over the course of time, the specific actions of many people combine into larger trends.

The late nineteenth century was an age of nationalism — a time when people in industrializing nations felt deeply devoted to their own countries. They also felt competitive toward other nations. This competitiveness sometimes took the form of imperialism, as nations raced to see which could take over the most lands and build the biggest empire.

In the late nineteenth century, imperialism was not new. Thousands of years before, Egyptians, Persians, and Greeks had all taken over other lands. In the 1500s and 1600s, imperialism motivated Spain, Britain, France, and Portugal to colonize North and South America.

In the late 1800s and early 1900s, industrial nations ventured overseas to claim distant land, resources, and markets. European nations led this "New Imperialism," gobbling up territories and resources in Africa and Asia.

The country that had industrialized first and fastest, Great Britain, led the European drive for colonies and built the largest empire. Other European nations—France, Germany, Belgium, the Netherlands, Italy—joined the competition for overseas territories. Non-European nations got into the act as well. Japan, eager to copy the ways of the West, took part in the global land grab. Even the United States, itself a former colony, acquired a few overseas territories.

One of the motivations behind imperialism was industrialization. The industrial nations wanted resources such as coal to power their railroads and rubber to make tires. They wanted markets where people in distant lands could buy their manufactured goods. They wanted fueling stations for their naval vessels. And, without a doubt, the industrial nations wanted power. They wanted the power to take distant resources for their own, to rule faraway lands, to determine how people in these lands should live, even to specify what religion they should follow. Westerners justified their actions by telling themselves that they were bringing "civilization" to "backward" peoples.

In the second volume of *The Human Odyssey*, we looked at the course of imperialism in Africa, where Europeans divided up almost the entire continent by 1900. Now let's examine what happened in Asia, especially in China.

Darwin and Imperialism

The industrialized nations competed to control the biggest empire. This competition was fueled by new ideas in science, growing out of the work of the British naturalist, Charles Darwin. In 1859, Darwin published *On the Origin of Species by Means of Natural Selection*. Darwin observed that in a world of limited resources, species compete to survive. He concluded that species with useful traits live longer and have more offspring—and are thus more likely to survive—than species without those useful traits. For example, on an island where the plants produce many hard seeds, the species of birds most likely to survive will be those that have developed short, strong beaks capable of cracking hard seeds.

Other writers took Darwin's ideas about natural selection and applied them to human society. In their view, life was a struggle in which individuals—or nations—must compete for limited resources. These ideas, which came to be known as "social Darwinism," could be summed up in the phrase, "survival of the fittest." Which nations would survive? Only the fittest. And which were those? The ones with the most factories, the biggest cities, the strongest armies, the most resources—and, therefore, the most colonies. Such social Darwinist thinking spurred nations to compete ever more fiercely to build the biggest empire.

The Asian Grab

Because Great Britain was the first nation to industrialize, it had a head start in the race for colonies. By the mid-1800s, Britain had built a vast empire that stretched from Canada to Australia. The British navy, the largest in the world, so dominated the oceans that a popular song boasted, "Britannia Rules the Waves." By 1897, when Queen Victoria celebrated 60 years on the throne with her Diamond Jubilee, the British could truthfully proclaim, as newspapers bragged, that "the sun never set" on their empire. The little island nation had the largest empire in the world, ruling nearly *one quarter* of the land surface of the globe.

At least as early as the seventeenth century, the British had made inroads into Asia, where the British East India Company (whose tea was dumped in Boston Harbor in 1773) did business in the Indian cities of Calcutta, Madras, and Bombay. In the 1850s, Great Britain came to rule most of India. Queen Victoria proudly proclaimed India as the brightest "jewel in the crown" of the British Empire. Other Asian "jewels" in Britain's crown included Ceylon, Singapore, and Burma.

Other nations scrambled to keep up with Britain. The French took over most of Indochina in Southeast Asia. Germany established a colony in East Africa and staked a claim in the Pacific, taking some islands in Indonesia. Russia, also trying hard to industrialize, reached for colonies in Central Asia and gained footholds in Turkey and Persia. The United States acquired the Philippines and annexed Hawaii. And, as you've seen, Japan, newly modernized, turned an imperialistic eye on Korea and then Taiwan.

Indochina is the name for the eastern half of a long peninsula southeast of China. It includes modern Vietnam, Cambodia, and Laos.

Imperialism in Asia, c. 1914

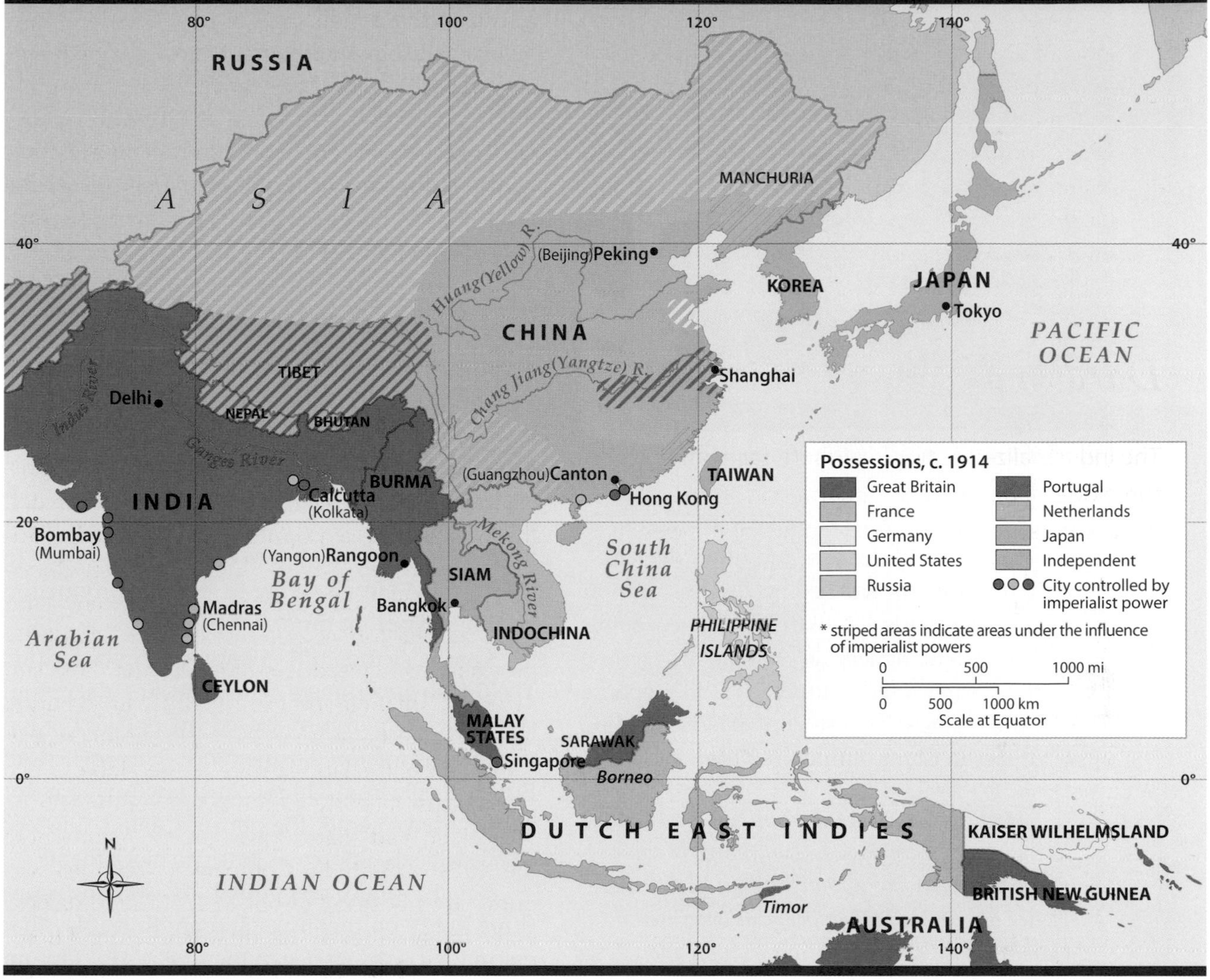

Old China Meets the New West

What about China, the land of Confucius, the Great Wall, and the Forbidden City? China wanted to be left alone. But the great Asian giant, with its natural resources and vast potential markets, was a tempting target for imperialist ambitions.

Around 1800, China was ruled by the Manchu, a people from north of China who established a dynasty called the Qing (ching). The Manchus, who were closely related to the Mongols, had invaded China in the 1640s. Even two hundred years later, many Chinese people still considered them foreigners and resented their rule.

Like other dynasties before them, the Qing limited Chinese contact with outsiders. The Manchu court tolerated some foreigners, such as the Jesuit missionaries who were in charge of the dynasty's Astronomy Bureau. The rulers of the Celestial Kingdom, as the Manchu authorities called themselves, allowed foreigners to use just one port, Canton. There Europeans could exchange silver and a few other goods in return for tea, silk, and porcelain from Chinese merchants.

Jesuits are members of an order of Catholic priests called the Society of Jesus, founded in 1540. They did missionary work around the globe in the sixteenth century.

King George III of Great Britain sent a royal ambassador to China to discuss trade opportunities with Emperor Qianlong (chee-UHN-LOUNG). The ambassador soon learned that the Manchu emperor was acquainted with Western culture and accomplishments. Indeed, Jesuit architects had designed the emperor's

Emperor Qianlong limited contact with outsiders.

residence. Its glamorous rooms were filled with European clocks, telescopes, and other devices.

Still, the emperor showed no desire to import more European goods. He, like most Chinese of this time, regarded foreigners as "barbarians" whose civilizations were inferior to China's. In response to the British king's request for expanded trading opportunities in China, Emperor Qianlong wrote:

> *I have no use for your country's goods. Our Celestial Kingdom possesses all things in abundance and wants for nothing within its frontiers. Hence there is no need to bring in the wares of barbarians to exchange for our own products. But since tea, silk, and porcelain, products of the Celestial Kingdom, are absolute necessities for the peoples of Europe and for you yourself, the limited trade hitherto permitted in my province of Canton will continue. Mindful of the distant loneliness of your island separated from the world by desert wastes of sea, I pardon your understandable ignorance of the customs of the Celestial Kingdom. Tremble at my orders and obey.*

There is no record of whether King George III trembled at the emperor's orders.

The Opium Wars

By the 1830s, tensions mounted between China and Britain as British traders sold something they knew many Chinese people wanted, even if their government did not—opium. Opium was a drug made from poppies grown in Britain's colony of India. It was used in traditional Chinese medicine as a pain killer, but Europeans encouraged the Chinese masses to smoke it. Eventually millions of Chinese became addicted to opium, and British traders made enormous profits.

The Chinese government declared opium illegal. British traders just ignored the law and bribed port authorities to allow the drug into the country. Finally, however, a public official named Lin Zexu (dzeh-SHOO) set out to stop the sale of opium.

Lin Zexu was a concerned and honest man who refused to accept bribes. In 1839, he destroyed every trace of opium he could find, and then sent a letter to Britain's Queen Victoria denouncing the "class of evil foreigners that makes opium and brings it for sale, tempting fools to destroy themselves merely in order to reap profit." He asked her to stop the production and sale of opium immediately. (See page 70.)

Queen Victoria did not appreciate the lecture. The British government refused to stop the opium shipments. Lin, in turn, closed the port of Canton to all British ships. Furthermore, he expelled all British people from China. When English merchant vessels tried to enter the port of Canton, Lin sent small sailboats, known as junks, to block them.

Great Britain responded by sending gunships to fire on the junks and anything else that got in their way. So began the first of two Opium Wars between China and Great Britain.

China's junks were no match for the powerful British navy. Eventually the Chinese were forced to surrender. China signed a humiliating treaty that exempted British citizens from Chinese law and gave Great Britain five duty-free ports, as well as special trading privileges that included the freedom to continue shipping opium to China. The treaty also gave Britain a new colony in China, Hong Kong.

> Nations often place taxes, called *duties*, on merchandise arriving from other countries. Duty-free merchandise is free of such taxes.

Soon afterward, China was pressured to sign similar treaties with the United States and France. These forced agreements with industrial powers came to be known by the Chinese people as "unequal treaties." The treaties opened more ports to Western ships and more land to Christian missionaries. Many Chinese worried that their country was losing its culture to greedy foreigners.

Lin Zexu, banished after the humiliating Opium Wars, was among the first to urge China to modernize or risk further defeats. He wrote letters to Chinese government officials, urging them to adopt the technologies, weapons, and methods of warfare that the Western industrial nations had used against China. Without such changes, he warned, China could not defend itself.

Despite the defeats of the Opium Wars, most Chinese officials ignored the disgraced Lin. They asked themselves: Why should China take lessons from the West? Many worried that railroads, factories, telephone lines, and other attempts at modernization would disturb the imperial ancestors, throw people out of work, and create even more dependence on foreigners. Instead, they insisted that China must move forward by building on its historic strengths, not those of the West.

China's Lesson to Japan

In the late nineteenth century, Japan industrialized rapidly, partly because its leaders had seen what happened to China when it refused to modernize. In 1872, Fukuzawa Yukichi cautioned that Japan should not react like the "the Chinese who thinks there is no nation in the world except his own, and whenever he meets some foreigners, he calls them barbarians as if they were beasts walking on four legs, despises them, and detests them, and simply endeavors to keep them out, never thinking of the real strength of his own country, with the result that he is subjected to humiliation by those 'barbarians.'"

The British warship *Nemesis* fires on Chinese junks during the First Opium War in 1841. According to an eyewitness, it took the *Nemesis* barely three and a half hours to destroy 11 junks. Western military power rapidly overwhelmed the Chinese. They soon signed humiliating treaties that gave Western nations special trading privileges.

Lin Zexu Writes to Queen Victoria

A Page from the Past

In 1839, Lin Zexu wrote to Britain's Queen Victoria reminding her that China had outlawed the sale of opium and demanding that she stop British traders from selling the drug in his country. In his letter, Lin Zexu followed the Chinese practice of his time in referring to foreigners as "barbarians."

We find that your country is [far from China]. Yet there are barbarian ships that strive to come here for trade for the purpose of making a great profit. The wealth of China is used to profit the barbarians; that is to say, the great profit made by barbarians is all taken from the rightful share of China. By what right do they then in return use the poisonous drug [opium] to injure the Chinese people?… Let us ask, where is your conscience? I have heard that the smoking of opium is very strictly forbidden by your country; that is because the harm caused by opium is clearly understood. Since it is not permitted to do harm to your own country, then even less should you let it be passed on to the harm of other countries….

Suppose a man of another country comes to England to trade, he still has to obey the English laws; how much more should he obey in China the laws of the Celestial Dynasty?

Now we have set up regulations governing the Chinese people. He who sells opium shall receive the death penalty and he who smokes it also the death penalty. Now consider this: If the barbarians do not bring opium, then how can the Chinese people resell it and how can they smoke it? The fact is that the wicked barbarians beguile the Chinese people into a death trap…. Therefore, in the new regulations, in regard to those barbarians who bring opium to China, the [death] penalty is fixed….

The barbarian merchants of your country, if they wish to do business for a prolonged period, are required to obey our statutes respectfully and to cut off permanently the source of opium…. May you, O [Queen], check your wicked and sift your vicious people before they come to China, in order to guarantee the peace of your nation, to show further the sincerity of your politeness and submissiveness, and to let the two countries enjoy together the blessings of peace.

To *check* means, in this usage, to restrain, stop, or block.

Self-Strengthening (and Self-Destruction)

In the mid-nineteenth century, as China's population soared, some Chinese leaders began to pursue a process they called "self-strengthening." Their idea was to borrow only bits and pieces of Western science and technology—just enough, they reasoned, to allow the Chinese to use Western machines and weapons, but without adopting Western ideas and values. The trouble was, only a few officials truly understood this philosophy and tried to make it work. Most just pretended to follow the philosophy.

A *dowager* is a widow who receives either a title or property from her dead husband.

One of the biggest pretenders was the Empress Dowager Cixi (SEE-she), a conniving woman who rose to power after her husband, the emperor, died in 1861. For years the Manchu empress ruled China in the name of her son, who was only five years old when he ascended the throne. She had a bamboo screen set up behind the throne. Sitting behind the screen, she could discreetly tell the boy what to say and do.

The boy emperor died in his teens, but the Empress Dowager stayed in control by placing the imperial crown on the head of her sister's son, a three-year-old boy named Guangxu (gwahng-SHOO). Making herself his legal guardian, Cixi resumed her place behind the bamboo screen.

The Empress Dowager pretended to support efforts to modernize China. Through her nephew, she approved funds to improve the Chinese navy. But Cixi secretly arranged to use those funds to build something more important to her—a luxurious summer palace to replace the one that British and French troops had burned in 1860.

Located in Beijing, the renovated palace was surrounded by lush gardens and marble statues, graceful rainbow-arch bridges, and cooling fountains. The empress could enjoy tea on her two-tiered Marble Boat, which boasted colorful glass windows and appeared to float effortlessly on Kunming Lake. At dinnertime, the empress drank from her jade cup and ate with golden chopsticks as she picked among the delicacies on

The powerful Chinese Empress Dowager Cixi

China's Growing Population

Since ancient times, China had been the most populous land in the world. In the nineteenth century, China's population soared, despite the effects of misrule and imperialism. In 1800, China had 300 million people. In 1850, the population was just over 400 million—more than the populations of all the nations of Europe put together—and rising rapidly. One great challenge the country faced was to feed the ever-increasing population.

her plate. Inside the palace kitchens, 128 cooks worked to prepare 150 different dishes at a single meal. Outside, Chinese peasants hoped they had enough rice to last through the coming winter.

Japan Strikes

In the previous chapter, you learned how Japan's rapid industrial growth sparked imperialist ambitions in its leaders. In 1894, Japan joined the scramble for control of Chinese territory. Japan set its eyes on Korea, which had long been dominated by China.

Japan's motives for imperial conquest were the same as those of the Europeans. Japan, a small island nation, needed coal to power its factories, markets for its products, and more rice to feed its people. Korea had much that Japan needed. But who would control Korea—Japan or China? To answer that, the two countries went to war.

You've learned how the Japanese had little trouble winning the Sino-Japanese War. The Chinese thought they would win easily, but China's military was both unprepared and undersupplied. Many Chinese officers found they had no artillery shells. Some discovered they had been supplied with shells filled with sand rather than gunpowder. That's partly because the Empress Cixi had used funds meant for artillery shells to build her summer palace.

China's defeat was probably the biggest humiliation it had experienced in an already humiliating century. Japan had long been a little sister to China, smaller and less advanced. Now great, big China was forced to sign a treaty that recognized little Japan's victory, and gave the Japanese the Chinese island of Taiwan.

The Japanese also forced China to make huge payments in silver. Defeated and near desperation, Chinese officials turned to Europe for help. The Europeans helped China recover some territory it had lost to Japan, but in return they demanded even more trading rights and territories. Germany, Russia, France, and Great Britain each established what they called "spheres of influence" in China—regions in which an industrialized nation exercised control and often enjoyed special economic privileges and trade opportunities. The Europeans spoke of "carving up the Chinese melon." The Chinese city of Shanghai (shang-HIY) became the Asian banking center for the European powers. Shanghai's business district soon began to look like a European city, with gas lighting on its broad boulevards.

One More Try at Reform

In the face of the humiliating loss to Japan and the division of China into European spheres of influence, Emperor Guangxu, now 27, decided it was time to restore China's self-respect.

In the summer of 1898, Guangxu set to work on "One Hundred Days of Reform." He issued 40 decrees designed to turn China into a modern, constitutional state, similar to Meiji Japan. Among other things, the reforms took some power away from the monarchy and created local assemblies, a national parliamentary government, and a public school system.

The changes horrified the Empress Dowager. From her summer palace, she engineered a coup d'etat (koo day-TAH). Some of Emperor Guangxu's young advisers fled the country, but the Empress Cixi executed the six she caught. She let the young emperor live, but banished him to an island in the palace lake.

A *coup d'etat* is the overthrow of a government by force. The French term means a blow or sudden strike against the state.

As the twentieth century approached, China was weak and crippled. As if the foreign manipulations and poor leadership were not bad enough, natural disaster added to China's misery. Drought led to famine, which left millions of people desperately poor and hungry. Many of China's suffering people grew angrier every day. They directed some of their anger at the Empress Dowager, but most at the foreigners who, most Chinese people believed, had brought nothing but trouble.

The Boxer Rebellion

In China's provinces, several groups met secretly to plan how to drive the foreigners from their country. One of these secret societies was known as the Boxers, because the martial arts movements in their religious rituals resembled shadow boxing.

The Boxers opposed both the Empress Dowager and the influence of foreigners. Their motto was "Overcome the Qing, wipe out the foreigners"—which was like saying the same thing twice, since the Boxers, like most Chinese, regarded the Qing as foreigners. But when the Empress Dowager saw how the peasants supported the Boxers, she cannily decided to support them, too. So the Boxers changed their motto to "Support the Qing, wipe out the foreigners."

Like many Chinese people, the Boxers were angriest at the foreigners they knew best—the Protestant and Catholic missionaries who lived among them and wanted to change their religion and their customs. Pearl S. Buck, a novelist who grew up in China as a child of American missionaries, remembered how other children avoided her or called her "little foreign devil."

In the long, hot summer of 1900, the Boxers rose up in a rage, killing missionaries, diplomats, journalists, and thousands of Chinese Christians. Although the industrialized nations that had carved up China were more inclined to compete than cooperate, they came together to put down the Boxer Rebellion. Six European nations, plus the United States and Japan, quickly rallied to send a rescue force that crushed the Boxers.

With foreign armies in the provinces, even the Empress Dowager could see the need for change. Over the next few years, she announced a series of reforms in the military, financial, and educational institutions of China. She even announced a plan to bring constitutional government to China. But it was too late.

China—one of the largest nations in the world, and once the center of one of the most advanced civilizations on earth—was in ruins. Most of its citizens were uneducated and desperately poor, living in huts made of bamboo or sun-dried brick, with paper-covered windows.

German cavalry arrive in Beijing to put down the Boxer Rebellion. The Boxers, angry at foreign domination of China, rose up in 1900. The rebellion was short lived. Several Western nations, plus Japan, quickly crushed the uprising.

They had no reason to trust either their imperial rulers or their foreign occupiers. Forty million people found their comfort in the haze of opium.

The Fight for Manchuria

After cooperating to crush the Boxers, the industrialized nations went back to competing for Chinese land and resources. Both Russia and Japan sought to control Manchuria, a province in northern China. The Russians were building the Trans-Siberian Railway, a six-thousand-mile railroad from Moscow to a Russian port on the Sea of Japan. They wanted to control Manchuria in order to protect their railroads. Japan wanted Manchuria for its coal and rice. The Japanese also thought that controlling Manchuria would ensure their control of Korea.

In 1905, the Japanese, flush with confidence after defeating the Chinese in the Sino-Japanese War, decided to gamble on defeating the Russians for control of Manchuria. Fighting the Russians on the Manchurian plains, the Japanese troops made little headway. But Japan had more success at sea. Japan's modern navy, which included ships captured from the Chinese, easily sank Russia's vessels.

At the turn of the twentieth century, most Chinese were uneducated and desperately poor.

To the Western world's surprise, the Japanese defeated the Russians in the Russo-Japanese War. In a peace treaty brokered by the United States, Japan gained ports in Manchuria that had belonged to Russia, but the Russians were allowed to keep their railroad. Japan hungrily eyed the rest of Manchuria.

At the turn of the century, a Chinese leader summed up what appeared to be the fate of China: "The rest of mankind are the carving knife…while we are the fish and the meat." Industrialized nations claimed spheres of influence, ports, trading privileges, and Chinese territory. Only a few Chinese people continued to hope for a strong, independent China.

The Birth of a Republic

Through the disasters and humiliations of the nineteenth century, some Chinese realized that not all their country's problems could be blamed on foreigners. They believed that a corrupt, feeble Manchu government was responsible for many troubles. Sun Yat-sen (soun yaht-sen) was one who reached that conclusion—and decided to do something about it.

You might remember Sun Yat-sen from Volume 2 of *The Human Odyssey*. The son of a humble peasant family, he traveled as a laborer to Hawaii and Hong Kong, where he managed to obtain a good education in schools set up by Christian missionaries. Eventually he became a physician. He also became a convert to Christianity and picked up many Western political ideas. When Sun returned to China, he was dismayed to see his country becoming "not the colony of one nation, but of all." He urged the Chinese to adopt democratic ways of government, and he encouraged nationalist pride.

In 1894, Sun Yat-sen formed the Revive China Society. Its members vowed to expel the Manchus and establish a republic. The next year Sun helped lead a revolt against the Manchus. But the uprising failed, and he fled the country.

He traveled the world for the next 16 years, seeking support for a republican revolution in China.

By 1911, both the Empress Dowager and her banished nephew were dead, leaving yet another five-year-old boy on the throne. This boy was to be the last emperor of China, because in that year a revolution finally toppled the Qing dynasty.

Sun Yat-sen learned of the uprising when he opened a newspaper while having breakfast in a restaurant in Denver, Colorado. At once he began to make his way home to China, where the people greeted him as a hero of the revolution. On January 1, 1912, he took office as the first president of the Republic of China.

The new president recognized the harm imperialism had done to China, but he also realized that his country could learn from the very nations that had carved China like a melon. He wanted the Chinese people to adopt some Western political principles, such as government by the people. His plan was to blend one of the world's oldest cultures with much that was valuable from the West—as he put it, to "choose the good fruit" of modern civilization and "reject the bad." Sun Yat-sen's term as president turned out to be short-lived, but he is still known as "the father of the revolution."

Sun Yat-sen wanted China to be a republic. He helped free China from domination by imperial powers.

China would face many problems in the years ahead, but the revolution showed that China and her many people were ready for change. After a century of domination by imperial powers, the Chinese were learning the importance of modernization. And their humiliation and suffering reinforced their longstanding tendency to be wary of foreigners.

Sensing coming disaster, German artist Ludwig Meidner painted *Apocalyptic Landscape* in 1913. At that time, when many people in Western nations were optimistic about modern-day progress, Meidner wrote that he was haunted by visions in which "many graves and burned cities writhed across the plains."

Igniting the Powder Keg

The year is 1913. In a dark, dingy studio in the city of Berlin, a young German artist, Ludwig Meidner (LUHD-wig MIYD-nehr), paints at night by gaslight. He works feverishly, squinting through the flickering haze as he jabs the brush onto the canvas. From the strokes of brown, black, blue, and gray emerges the vision of a nightmare, a catastrophe, a spectacle of suffering and death and apocalyptic ruin.

Apocalyptic means forecasting terrible disaster.

What compelled Meidner to paint crumbling buildings and exploding landscapes at a time when many others were celebrating the triumphs of modern-day progress?

In many Western nations, the year 1914 dawned with a bright sense of promise. The industrial and democratic revolutions that had launched the nineteenth century appeared to hold out the prospect of greater wealth and liberty in the twentieth. Factories hummed and ships weighed anchor for foreign ports. More people were taking part in the political life of their countries, helping to make laws and important decisions.

In the United States, the Ford Motor Company announced an eight-hour work day and a wage of five dollars a day, a generous salary for that time. In Europe, Norwegian women celebrated their newly won right to vote. In China, leaders of the new republican government announced they would join the Universal Postal Union, connecting their mail service to the rest of the world. Many world leaders were making plans to attend the official August opening of the Panama Canal, which linked the Atlantic and Pacific Oceans.

Yet all was not sunny and bright — dark clouds loomed on the horizon, portents of conflicts to come. Tensions mounted as the industrialized nations competed to see which country could build the most productive factories, the richest colonies, the most powerful military. Germany raced Britain to build more battleships. France rushed to match the size of Germany's huge army. Britain, France, Germany, and Russia — as well as Japan and the United States — scrambled to dominate overseas territories.

Where would this race for arms and territory lead? Some statesmen feared that the clashing ambitions of industrialized nations would trigger what one British diplomat called a "long-dreaded European war."

Europe on the Eve of World War I, c. 1912

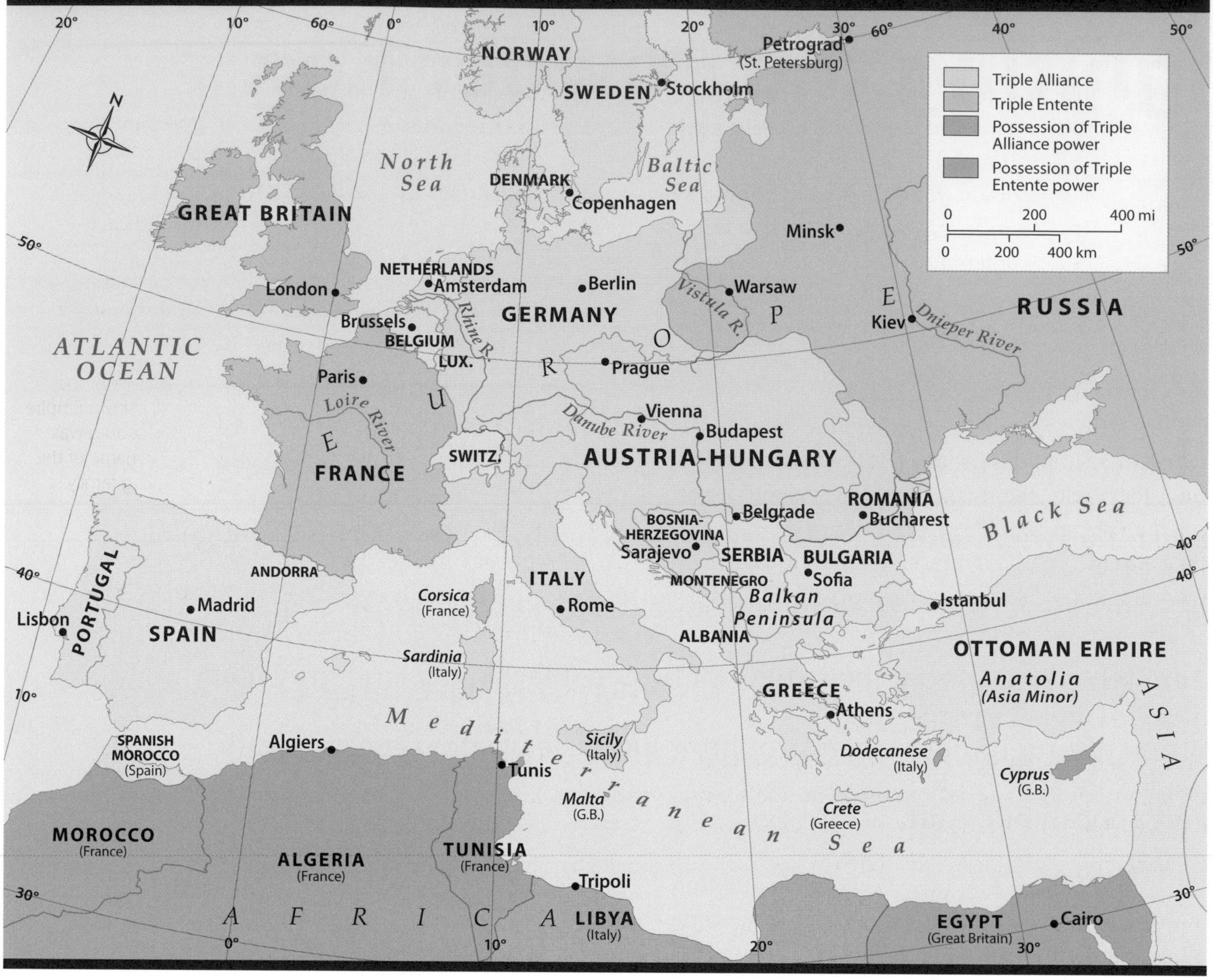

While statesmen debated politics and policies, artists like Ludwig Meidner were haunted by visions of catastrophe and devastation. Artists, said the poet Ezra Pound, are "the antennae of the race" — meaning that, for the human race, artists pick up signals before they become clear to others. In Meidner's case, the signals all warned of impending doom and destruction.

Fragile Alliances

For more than four decades, Europe's industrialized nations had been building their armies and weapons, yet still managed to keep the peace. How did they avoid going to war against each other? In part, through a system of military alliances. Nations entered into agreements with other nations that said, in effect, "If your enemies attack you, I will come to your aid. And if my enemies attack me, you will come to my aid." Through such alliances, the European powers hoped to protect themselves and discourage each other from launching a major war.

The German Chancellor Otto von Bismarck was a master of this strategy of keeping the peace by building alliances. In 1879, to strengthen Germany's security, he made an alliance with Austria-Hungary. Each empire pledged to fight for the other if attacked by Russia. A few years later, Italy joined the agreement, which became known as the Triple Alliance. Germany, Austria-Hungary, and Italy, the three members of the Triple Alliance, pledged that if any member were drawn into a war with two or more countries, the other members would come to its aid.

The French were alarmed by neighboring Germany's military buildup and by the Triple Alliance. So France formed its own alliance with Russia. The two nations agreed to mobilize their troops if any nation in the Triple Alliance mobilized, and to help each other if attacked by Germany.

To *mobilize* troops means to assemble them and get them ready for war.

An *entente* is an understanding between two or more nations.

Britain, troubled by the buildup of the German navy, decided it had better seek potential allies. Britain, France, and Russia reached an informal understanding to support each other. This agreement was known as the Triple Entente (ahn-TAHNT).

By 1907, Europe's great powers lay divided into two camps: on one side, the Triple Alliance, and on the other side, the Triple Entente. These complicated alliances helped maintain a fragile peace. But they also meant that if one nation went to war, all of them might find themselves in a fight.

The Balkan Peninsula: The Powder Keg of Europe

You've seen that a self-glorifying sense of nationalism, an almost aggressive pride in one's country, led the industrialized nations to compete in establishing global empires. Each tried to outdo the other in colonizing other lands.

In time, however, the people in those colonies developed nationalist feelings of their own. Motivated both by resentment against their foreign rulers and pride in their own countries, colonists all over the world demanded freedom from imperial rule. If you've read the second volume of *The Human Odyssey*, then you know how Mohandas Gandhi led the people of India in a movement for independence from the British Empire. You also learned how Sun Yat-sen helped China in its revolution to throw out various foreign rulers.

In the southeast corner of Europe lay another hotbed of nationalism, in a region known as the Balkan Peninsula, or "the Balkans" for short. *Balkan* is a Turkish word meaning "mountain," and an apt name for a peninsula covered with several mountain ranges.

For centuries, most of the Balkan Peninsula had been ruled by the Ottoman Empire, an Islamic empire with its home in Asia Minor. During the sixteenth and seventeenth centuries, the Ottoman Empire had been one of the most powerful empires in the world. But as European nations industrialized and grew strong, the Ottoman Empire grew weak.

Asia Minor is a large peninsula also called Anatolia.

At the outset of the twentieth century, two other empires sought to control the Balkan Peninsula. One was Russia, ruled by Tsar Nicholas II. The other was Austria-Hungary, ruled by Emperor Franz Josef.

Austria-Hungary is also known as the Austro-Hungarian Empire or the Habsburg Empire. Habsburg was the name of the ruling family.

The people of the Balkan Peninsula, which was divided into several small states, wanted to rule themselves. The long years under Ottoman rule had already stirred feelings of nationalism in the Balkans. More than once, revolutionaries in the Balkan states had fought for independence from the Ottoman Empire. The people of the Balkans were not willing to sit back and watch as new foreign rulers tried to take control of the peninsula.

Serbia was one of the states that made the Balkans such a hotbed of nationalism. The Serbs were part of a larger ethnic group known as the Slavs, who lived throughout eastern Europe. Serbia had won its independence from the Ottoman Empire in 1878, but Austria-Hungary, Serbia's northern neighbor, eyed the region greedily.

An *ethnic group* is a group of people who share a common language and culture.

What Is "Balkanization"?

In the early twentieth century, the Balkan Peninsula was divided into a handful of small states, often at odds with each other. These states were populated by several different ethnic groups that did not always get along. The division of the peninsula into several countries gave rise to the term *Balkanization*, which has come to mean a fragmentation into small, often hostile, parts.

A 1912 political cartoon from the British magazine *Punch* illustrates the Balkan troubles reaching the boiling point.

The Serbs were enraged when, in that same year, Austria-Hungary occupied neighboring Bosnia-Herzegovina (BAHZ-nee-uh HERT-se-gaw-VEE-nah). The Serbs had hoped to make Bosnia-Herzegovina, where many Slavs also lived, part of a larger Serbian kingdom. Likewise, many Slavs in Bosnia-Herzegovina longed to be part of a larger Serbia and free from Austrian control.

Such tensions earned the Balkans the nickname "the Powder Keg of Europe." Germany's sharp-eyed Chancellor Bismarck looked at the explosive situation and predicted that "some damned thing in the Balkans" was likely to plunge Europe into its next major war.

The Powder Keg Explodes

In the summer of 1914, tensions ran high in the Balkans — even the slightest spark might ignite the Powder Keg of Europe. That spark came in August when the Archduke Franz Ferdinand, heir to the Habsburg throne in Austria, paid an official visit to Sarajevo (sar-uh-YAY-voh), the capital of Bosnia.

The archduke had been warned that there might be trouble from Bosnian nationalists who were desperate to free their land from Austro-Hungarian rule. But he decided to make the trip anyway. On June 28, 1914, as the archduke's open car drove down a street in Sarajevo, a young Bosnian jumped aboard and shot Franz Ferdinand and his wife, killing them both.

News of the assassination raced over telegraph and telephone wires. Austrian officials believed that Serbia's government had been involved in the plot to kill the archduke. To Emperor Franz Joseph and his advisors, the assassination presented the perfect excuse to crush Serbia and put an end to the Slavic independence movements at the edge of the Austro-Hungarian Empire.

But Austria-Hungary faced one very big problem — Russia. This giant empire, home to many Slavic peoples, might spring to defend Serbia against any takeover attempt by Austria-Hungary. Austrian officials checked

The assassination of Franz Ferdinand and his wife Sophie was the spark that plunged the great powers of Europe into war.

with German leaders to see if they could count on Germany's support. Kaiser Wilhelm II — the kaiser who had fired Bismarck — encouraged his Austro-Hungarian ally to move against Serbia. He sent assurances that if Russia entered the fight, Germany would be at Austria's side. And then the kaiser boarded his imperial yacht for a three-week summer cruise.

Urged on by the Germans, the Austrians declared war on Serbia. Russia's leader, Tsar Nicholas II, felt tremendous pressure to come to Serbia's aid. He exchanged urgent telegrams with his cousin, Kaiser Wilhelm II. "I beg you," Nicholas telegrammed Wilhelm, "in the name of our old friendship to do what you can to stop your allies from going too far."

Wilhelm, who suddenly realized that urging the Austrians to crush Serbia might be a bad idea, wired the tsar: "I am exerting my utmost influence to induce the Austrians to arrive at a satisfactory understanding with you."

But these last-minute efforts by the tsar and the kaiser to avoid a catastrophe came too late. Too many people had been whipped into a frenzy for war, and too many generals were ready to fight. The tsar's generals convinced him to send troops not just to the Austro-Hungarian border with Russia, but to the German border as well. They did not trust the kaiser. Meanwhile, Wilhelm's generals convinced him that it was best to attack Russia before Russia had the chance to strike first.

Events rushed forward. The system of alliances that Europeans had counted on to keep the peace became a horrible trap. Russia mobilized for a fight with Austria-Hungary. That brought Germany, Austria-Hungary's ally in the Triple Alliance, into the war. France called up troops to support Russia, its ally in the Triple Entente. Germany declared war on France, as German troops began a march toward Paris by way of Belgium. Britain responded by declaring war on Germany.

In a matter of weeks, the great powers of Europe had plunged into war. On one side were Germany and Austria-Hungary, and eventually the Ottoman Empire. On the other side were Britain, France, and Russia.

Where would this long-dreaded conflict lead? The British foreign secretary, Sir Edward Grey, had forebodings as he gazed at the street lights outside his office. "The lamps are going out all over Europe," he told a friend. "We shall not see them lit again in our lifetime."

"All aboard for Berlin! And what fun we'll have there!" Such shouts were typical in 1914 as trainloads of soldiers pulled out of Paris train stations, bound for what most thought would be a quick fight. But the Great War turned out to be a four-year disaster that left millions dead.

The Great War

A short and glorious war. That's what many Europeans expected in 1914. After all, almost every European conflict since 1871 had ended in a matter of weeks. Why not this one as well? "We'll cut them in half!" one Allied general predicted just before the war began. "All aboard for Berlin! And what fun we'll have there!" shouted a workman to the crowd at a train station in Paris. The fighting, one German politician believed, would be a "ringing opening chord for an immortal song of sacrifice, loyalty, and heroism."

The brief heroic song, however, turned into a discordant symphony of horror, carnage, and destruction. The Allied Powers of France, Russia, and Britain faced off against the Central Powers of Germany, Austria-Hungary, and, eventually, the empire of the Ottoman Turks. The fighting spread from Europe to the Middle East and Africa, spanned the high seas, and lasted four years. It drew in such distant nations as Japan, and involved troops from remote colonies like Senegal, New Zealand, and India.

By the time the war was over, more than nine million soldiers were dead. Four empires lay in ruins. The high hopes and confidence of the previous century turned to despair.

The war that raged from 1914 to 1918 is called World War I, to distinguish it from a second catastrophic war that came later in the twentieth century. Of course, those who lived through World War I could not foresee future conflicts. They only knew the world had never seen warfare on such a vast scale. They gave the disastrous war another name—the Great War.

"Home by Christmas"

In the summer of 1914, the assassination of the Archduke Ferdinand triggered a rapid chain of events. Millions of soldiers mobilized. Local townsfolk cheered the soldiers on. Young women threw flowers. Schoolboys clapped and cheered. Older men regretted that their chance to fight had long since passed. Even mothers watched with pride. "You'll be home by Christmas," they called to the troops.

Everyone agreed—a few months, an easy victory, and the boys would be marching home again. Rousing newspaper editorials reprinted a line in Latin from the ancient Roman poet Horace: *Dulce et decorum est pro patria mori*— "It is sweet and right to die for your country." The noble sentiment inspired thoughts of glory — for surely, in this war, there would be little dying and much glory. It would all be over so quickly.

Each of the great powers found reasons for confidence. After their loss to Germany in 1871, the French had built massive barricades on their eastern border. Certainly, they thought, no attacker could ever take fortress towns such as Verdun (vuhr-DUHN). The British felt sure their Royal Navy — the biggest, most powerful navy in the world — would easily destroy the German fleet and choke the German economy by blockading German ports. The overall strategy seemed simple: France would attack Germany from the west, while Russia attacked from the east. Then Russia, after quickly overwhelming Germany, would turn to deliver a lethal blow to the Austrians. Simple — quick — easy.

How World War I Started

Here are the main incidents in the rapid-fire chain of events that led to the beginning of World War I in 1914:

August 1—Germany sees Russian troops mobilizing and declares war on Russia; France orders a general mobilization.

August 3—Germany declares war on France.

August 4—Germany invades Belgium; Britain, alarmed by the invasion of a neutral country, declares war on Germany.

August 5—Austria-Hungary declares war on Russia.

August 23—Japan declares war on Germany and begins to occupy German colonies in China and the Pacific.

The Germans had their own plan for a quick victory. They had the most powerful army in Europe, with more than two million troops ready to fight. The Germans planned to deliver a swift knockout punch to France and then, with their Austrian allies, dash east to deal with the Russians, who usually took a long time to get their army ready.

Yes, it would be a short war. Everyone thought so. The boys would be "home by Christmas."

The War Widens on Two Fronts

The long-anticipated fighting began on August 4, 1914, when a million German troops surged west into Belgium. Belgium was not their target — it was just a way to get to France without having to encounter the strong defenses the French had built on their border with Germany. Belgium, which lay between northeast France and Germany, had few defenses. German generals reasoned that their troops could march quickly through Belgium and then storm south into France and capture Paris. That done, they could move quickly by train back to Germany and arrive at the border with Russia before the Russians could put their boots on.

The Germans charged into Belgium expecting little resistance. But the Belgians fought back. They cut communication lines, sabotaged roads, and blew up railway tunnels and bridges. The British, who had promised to protect Belgium, rushed to the small country's aid.

Together, the Belgian and British forces slowed the Germans. But the Germans struck back hard. They shocked everyone when they burned the Belgian university town of Louvain to the ground, including its medieval library and priceless manuscripts. As German troops pushed south, they shot hundreds of Belgian civilians who dared to resist the invasion. British and French newspapers denounced the "barbarism" of troops they likened to "the Huns." Americans, and many Germans as well, were shocked to see the Germans — from the land of Gutenberg and Goethe (GUR-tuh) — as book-burners and foes to civilization.

The *Huns* were horse-mounted tribes from Central Asia that invaded Europe beginning in the fourth century.

Gutenberg (died c. 1468) invented a way of printing with moveable type, which made books more widely available.

Goethe (1749–1832) was a world-renowned writer and philosopher.

World War I, 1914–1918

Allies
Central Powers
Neutral nations
Greatest extent of Central Powers invasion, 1918
Trench line
Armistice line
Major battles
0 200 400 mi
0 200 400 km
WESTERN FRONT BATTLES
GREAT BRITAIN
English Channel
NETH.
GERMANY
Louvain
BELGIUM
LUX.
Somme (1916)
FRANCE
Verdun (1916)
Seine R.
Paris
Marne (1914,1918)
NORWAY
Oslo
SWEDEN
Helsinki
Petrograd (St. Petersburg)
Stockholm
Volga R.
DEC. 1917
Moscow
Jutland (1916)
North Sea
DENMARK
Copenhagen
Baltic Sea
RUSSIA
GREAT BRITAIN
Lusitania Sinking (1915)
Minsk
London
NETHERLANDS
Berlin
GERMANY
Warsaw
Kiev
Eastern Front
1918
Area enlarged above left
1914
BELGIUM
LUX.
Rhine R.
Dnieper R.
ATLANTIC OCEAN
Paris
NOV. 1918
Prague
Loire R.
Western Front
Danube R.
Vienna
FRANCE
SWITZ.
AUSTRIA-HUNGARY
ROMANIA
Black Sea
E U R O P E
Sarajevo
ANDORRA
SERBIA
PORTUGAL
Madrid
Corsica (France)
ITALY
MONTENEGRO
BULGARIA
ARMENIA
Lisbon
SPAIN
Rome
ALBANIA
Istanbul
Gallipoli(1915)
Sardinia (Italy)
OTTOMAN EMPIRE
Anatolia (Asia Minor)
SPANISH MOROCCO (Spain)
Algiers
GREECE
Athens
ASIA
Mediterranean Sea
Sicily (Italy)
Tunis
ALGERIA (France)
TUNISIA (France)
Malta (G.B.)
Cyprus (G.B.)
MOROCCO (France)
AFRICA
Crete (Greece)
ARABIA
Cairo
Nile R.
LIBYA (Italy)
EGYPT (Great Britain)
ALASKA (U.S.)
CANADA
UNITED STATES
HAITI
CUBA
BR. HOND.
HONDURAS
GUATEMALA
NICARAGUA
COSTA RICA
PANAMA
BRITISH GUIANA
FRENCH GUIANA
BRAZIL
NETH.
BELGIUM
GREAT BRITAIN
FRANCE
PORTUGAL
ITALY
MOROCCO
TUNISIA
GAMBIA
PORT. GUINEA
SIERRA LEONE
LIBERIA
GOLD COAST
NIGERIA
KAMERUN
FR. EQ. AFRICA
BELGIAN CONGO
ANGOLA
GERMAN S.W. AFRICA
N. RHODESIA
BECHUANALAND
ALGERIA
FR. W. AFRICA
TOGO
LIBYA
EGYPT
UNION OF SOUTH AFRICA
GERMANY
AUSTRIA-HUNGARY
MONTENEGRO
SERBIA
ROMANIA
BULGARIA
GREECE
OTTOMAN EMPIRE
RUSSIA
CHINA
NEPAL
BHUTAN
KOREA
JAPAN
FORMOSA
ERITREA
INDIA
FR. SOM.
BR. SOM.
SIAM
ITALIAN SOM.
ANGLO-EGYPTIAN SUDAN
UGANDA
BR. EAST AFRICA
GERMAN EAST AFRICA
MADAGASCAR
NYASALAND
PORT. EAST AFRICA
S. RHODESIA
FRENCH INDOCHINA
PHILIPPINES
SARAWAK
KAISER WILHELMS-LAND
MALAY STATES
PAPUA
AUSTRALIA
NEW ZEALAND

The twentieth century's First World War combined old and new as cavalry divisions on horseback faced off against heavy artillery. In this painting, British forces desperately try to hold back German troops advancing through Belgium.

Slowed but not stopped, the Germans pushed south into France, on course for Paris. Despite French and British resistance, by the end of September German soldiers were only two days' march from the capital city. So far, the German strategy — quick maneuvering to defeat France — seemed to be working.

But then, the French and British forces rallied, confronting the Germans at the Marne River. In early September, two million soldiers fought a colossal battle, and the Allied forces pushed the Germans into retreat. As the Germans fell back, both sides dug long trenches and unrolled spools of barbed wire. By year's end, two parallel, opposing lines of entrenchments stretched some 450 miles, from the North Sea to Switzerland.

That line became known as the Western Front. For nearly four bloody years, the two sides bogged down on the Western Front. To almost everyone's surprise, the anticipated "short and glorious" war turned into a long, gory deadlock.

Meanwhile, fighting erupted east of Germany in a vast area that came to be known as the Eastern Front. Russian troops had mobilized more quickly than the Germans thought possible. Without maps or effective reconnaissance, two Russian armies thrust deeply into a region of forests and marshy lakes in eastern Germany. The Germans drove the Russians back. In two opening battles, the Russians suffered almost 250,000 casualties.

In war, *reconnaissance* means scouting ahead to survey enemy territory.

The *casualties* of war include the dead, wounded, captured, and missing.

Russia fared better against the Austrians, winning victories that threatened to knock the Austrians out of the war. For the most part, however, the war along the Eastern Front, as on the Western Front, ground down into a stalemate. No longer was there talk of troops home by Christmas.

Horror in the Trenches

Trench warfare on the Western Front came to define World War I. It began with foxholes, scraped from the earth by exhausted soldiers. Soon both sides were developing mazes of underground shelters and communication trenches leading to hospitals, supply dumps, and railroads. On the front lines, in the firing trenches, French and British soldiers peered over earthen mounds and sandbags. They stared across "no-man's-land," a few hundred yards of bombed-out earth between them and the Germans.

Life in the filthy, narrow trenches was agony, even when there was no fighting. Rainwater collected in the trench bottoms. "The weather is miserable and we often spend days on end knee-deep in water," reported a young corporal in the German army, Adolf Hitler (about whom you'll read much more later in this book). Another soldier wrote, "The men slept in mud, washed in mud, ate mud, and dreamed mud." Fresh food was always a rumor away. The air stank from human waste and decomposing bodies. Lice infested the men's hair and clothing, and rats scurried at their feet.

But the miserable monotony of waiting in the trenches was bliss compared to the horror of trench warfare itself. Soldiers seldom saw the enemy they were fighting. Each side unleashed powerful artillery barrages that hurled shells up to 75 miles. In the trenches, the men crouched and prayed that the shells would not find them. The shells, hollow cases containing explosives, ranged from the size of a fist to the size of a man, and they caused more destruction and death than any other weapon in the war. "Shells of all calibers kept raining on our sector," one French soldier wrote. "The trenches disappeared, filled with earth…the air was unbreathable. Our blinded, wounded, crawling, and shouting soldiers kept falling on top of us and died splashing us with blood. It was living hell."

Artillery includes any guns too large to be fired from the hand or shoulder.

The *caliber* of an artillery shell is its diameter.

When the generals gave the order to attack, the soldiers scrambled out of their trenches — they called it going "over the top" — and made a dash

The Christmas Truce

Many troops on the Western Front celebrated the 1914 Christmas holiday within earshot of the enemy. On Christmas Eve, the Germans placed Christmas trees adorned with candles above their trenches, then called out, "English soldiers! English soldiers! Happy Christmas!" Some began to sing *Silent Night*.

Across the darkness came more sounds of singing, as the British responded with their own hymns. Some men even leapt out of the trenches to shake hands with their enemies and take photos to send home. For a brief time, an unofficial truce reigned on the Western Front. By the New Year, however, both sides were back at war.

Canadian soldiers in northern France practice scrambling out of a trench, known as going "over the top," to attack enemy trench lines. Much fighting in the Great War, especially on the Western Front, bogged down into trench warfare.

Two U.S. soldiers make their way through plumes of smoke. Troops on both sides relied on masks to protect them from poison gas, one of the horrors of trench warfare.

Deadly Firepower

The Industrial Revolution made World War I the most deadly in history. It was the first war in which actual firepower killed more soldiers than disease. Long-range rifles were supplemented by new machine guns that could fire up to 600 rounds per minute. Larger guns were accurate to six or seven miles, and some huge artillery shot as far as 75 miles. In World War I, on average, five thousand men died each day for four years, most from shellfire.

The British developed an armored, gun-carrying, tracked vehicle known as a "land battleship," or what we call a tank. Tanks could crush barbed wire and cross trench lines, impervious to machine-gun bullets. Early tanks were clumsy vehicles and often broke down. They did not play a big role in World War I, but they represented a major technical advance and would become important in later warfare.

toward the enemy trenches. The chances of making it alive across no-man's-land were not good. Trees had been blasted away, leaving no cover. Buried land mines lay waiting, and barbed wire snaked across the broken fields. Machine guns fired from enemy trenches could mow down whole lines of advancing soldiers. When the battles were over, as the survivors crept back to their trenches, stretcher-bearers scurried into no-man's-land to try to retrieve the wounded.

Each side tried to invent weapons that would end the trench warfare stalemate. In April 1915, the Germans introduced a new weapon — chlorine gas. This poison crept like a stealthy fog across the trenches. It could choke a man to death in minutes. Later in the war, the Germans launched attacks with mustard gas, which blinded people and burned the skin. Soon both sides developed and used poison gas. Factories began to churn out gas masks. When troops in the trenches saw a gas cloud approaching, they hurried to don clumsy gas masks and hoped the winds would push the terror some other way.

Verdun and Somme: "Hell cannot be so terrible."

In early 1916, the Germans tried to break the stalemate on the Western Front by launching a devastating artillery assault on the French city of Verdun. The French had declared they would defend the ancient fortress town at all costs. Knowing this, the Germans decided to target Verdun. Here, said one German general, "the forces of France will bleed to death."

Twenty million artillery shells fell on Verdun in four months. French artillery responded in kind. Week after week, the soldiers lived with the deafening roar of cannon. The shells turned forests into fields of matchsticks and, eventually, an empty, cratered moonscape. When rains came, the muddy battlefield was clogged with corpses.

By the end of June 1916, the number of men killed or wounded at Verdun had passed 400,000. In his diary, a French lieutenant, who was eventually killed by an artillery shell, wrote, "Humanity is mad. It must be mad to do what it is doing. What a massacre! What scenes of horror and carnage! I cannot find words to translate my

Dulce et Decorum Est

One of the most horrible new weapons of World War I was poison gas. A British officer named Wilfred Owen wrote a poem titled Dulce et Decorum Est *about a soldier caught in a gas attack and transported to a field hospital in a cart. The poem's title is from the Latin motto that was so popular before the war:* Dulce et decorum est pro patria mori—*"It is sweet and right to die for your country."*

A Page from the Past

Bent double, like old beggars under sacks,
Knock-kneed, coughing like hags, we cursed through sludge,
Till on the haunting flares we turned our backs
And towards our distant rest began to trudge.
Men marched asleep. Many had lost their boots
But limped on, blood-shod. All went lame; all blind;
Drunk with fatigue; deaf even to the hoots
Of tired, outstripped Five-Nines that dropped behind.

Five-nines were explosive shells, so-named because their caliber was 5.9 inches.

Gas! Gas! Quick, boys!—An ecstasy of fumbling,
Fitting the clumsy helmets just in time;
But someone still was yelling out and stumbling,
And flound'ring like a man in fire or lime...
Dim, through the misty panes and thick green light,
As under a green sea, I saw him drowning.
In all my dreams, before my helpless sight,
He plunges at me, guttering, choking, drowning.

If in some smothering dreams you too could pace
Behind the wagon that we flung him in,
And watch the white eyes writhing in his face,
His hanging face, like a devil's sick of sin;
If you could hear, at every jolt, the blood
Come gargling from the froth-corrupted lungs,
Obscene as cancer, bitter as the cud
Of vile, incurable sores on innocent tongues,
My friend, you would not tell with such high zest
To children ardent for some desperate glory,
The old Lie; Dulce et Decorum est
Pro patria mori.

German soldiers face French artillery fire at the Battle of Verdun. Millions of explosions turned the land near Verdun into a cratered moonscape.

impressions. Hell cannot be so terrible. Men are mad!" But the French held the line.

In the summer, to ease the pressure on Verdun and break through the German lines, the British launched an attack along the Somme (sahm) River. Nearly 2,000 artillery guns unleashed a week-long barrage to destroy the German positions and blast away the barbed wire that blocked no-man's-land in front of their trenches. In the hour before the infantry advanced, 60 shells per second pounded the German positions. The bombardment could be heard 300 miles away in London.

On that summer morning along the Somme, thousands of young British soldiers went "over the top," clambering from their trenches along 18 miles of the Western Front. Almost shoulder to shoulder, they stepped out across no-man's-land. Gunfire erupted from the German lines. "I heard the 'patter, patter' of machine guns in the distance," a British sergeant recalled. "By the time I'd gone another ten yards, I seemed to be on my own. Then I was hit myself."

Soldier after soldier fell to the ground, dead or wounded. In a few hours, 20,000 British soldiers died, and another 40,000 were wounded. Only a few reached the enemy trenches. The first day at the Somme was the bloodiest of the war. And still the fighting went on. By October, at least a million men had been killed or wounded at that deadly site.

There would be no breakthrough on the Western Front. The grind of the war continued. The American novelist F. Scott Fitzgerald summed up the futility of it all. One of his characters reflects, "See that little stream—we could walk to it in two minutes. It took the British a whole month to walk to it, a whole empire walking very slowly, dying in front and pushing forward behind. And another empire walked very slowly backward a few inches a day, leaving the dead like a million bloody rugs."

The Eastern Front and Challenges for the Ottomans

The Eastern Front, the scene of Russia's life-and-death struggle, was much longer than the Western Front. In August 1914, German forces dealt advancing Russians a hard defeat. When the Ottoman Empire decided to join the Central Powers in October 1914, Russia's situation became desperate.

In 1915, German and Austrian armies drove the Russians 300 miles back into their own territory, taking more than a million prisoners and killing or wounding as many more. Russia's leader, Tsar Nicholas, decided to take personal command of the army. He proceeded to make a series of spectacularly stupid decisions that cost his nation many thousands of lives. (You'll learn more about this in the next chapter.) Many wondered how long the ill-equipped, ill-fed Russian army could go on.

The British tried to come to the aid of Russia by opening up another front in the south against the Ottoman Turks. The British sent troops to the Gallipoli Peninsula on the western shores of Turkey's Dardanelles strait. The Gallipoli expedition failed, but it led some Italians to believe that the Allies could win the war.

Italy, which had stayed out of the fight, now joined the Allies, hoping to grab territory from Austria and the Ottoman Empire as they fell. It launched a series of attacks against the Austrians in the Alps, opening another long battlefront.

The Armenian Massacre

In this long, terrible war, one region, Armenia, suffered an especially horrifying tragedy. Situated in a remote part of eastern Asia Minor, Armenia was ruled by the Ottoman Empire. The Armenians, who were Christians, had long endured persecution under the rule of the Ottoman Turks, who were Muslim. The Armenians hoped that a Russian victory over the Ottoman Empire would help secure the independence they had long sought from the Turks.

In the spring of 1915, the Ottomans accused the Armenians of cooperating with the Russians. The Ottomans used this as an excuse to execute tens of thousands of Armenian men and boys. Ottoman troops plundered Armenian villages, raped thousands of women, and then began the systematic deportation of women, children, and the elderly. These Armenians were herded onto trains, taken to a desert region, and left to walk to their deaths, usually of starvation. In all, more than a million Armenians, about half of the Armenian population, perished. "There are," lamented an Armenian poet, "no words in the dictionaries to describe the hideousness of the terrors."

To *deport* someone is to send that person out of the country.

Today, historians looking back at the massacre of the Armenians in 1915 sometimes refer to the tragedy as the Armenian Genocide. *Genocide* is the deliberate and systematic destruction of a racial, political, religious, or cultural group.

Many historians see the Ottoman's actions against the Armenians as the first genocide in a century marked by further acts of official mass murder. The term *genocide* was first used in 1944 to describe Nazi actions against the Jews in World War II (about which you'll read more in a later chapter). The term had not been invented in 1915, but at that time a troubled American diplomat in Istanbul warned the U.S. State Department: "It appears that a campaign of race extermination is in progress."

Lawrence of Arabia

It was not only the Armenians who sought independence from the rule of the Ottoman Turks. Other peoples, including many Arabs, also wanted freedom from the Ottoman Empire.

When the Great War began, the Ottoman Empire included Egypt, Arabia, and Syria. The people in these lands, though Muslim, had long resented Turkish rule. One man who recognized this deep resentment was Thomas Edward Lawrence, a British archaeologist who had spent much time studying the region. He saw that many Arabs were eager to fight the Ottomans.

The Ottoman Turks

The Turks are an ethnic group that migrated west from Central Asia in the early Middle Ages. They settled in Asia Minor and parts of southeastern Europe, and converted to Islam. In the thirteenth century, a group of these Turkish tribes united under the leader Osman, and fought to rule all of Asia Minor. The Ottoman Turks (Ottoman refers to Osman) created a vast and powerful Islamic empire in the 1500s and 1600s.

Lawrence, who had lost two brothers on the Western Front, wanted to see the war end. He thought he could hasten the end by helping to bring down the Ottoman Empire. So he set out to enlist the Arabs as allies of the British in the fight against the Ottoman Turks.

From Cairo, the capital of Egypt, Lawrence helped organize an Arabian revolt. He helped stir up nationalistic fervor throughout the Arabian Peninsula. Soon Arab units were disrupting Ottoman supply trains by mining bridges and railways.

Lawrence of Arabia, as he became known, was hailed as a hero, though he paid a high personal cost. He was captured and brutally tortured before he managed to escape. His efforts, however, gained the British a new ally in their struggle against the Ottomans and fueled Arab hopes for independence.

War at Sea

Before the Great War began, Great Britain and Germany had raced to build up their navies. In May 1916, their warships met off the coast of Denmark in the Battle of Jutland, the greatest sea battle of the war.

For two days, huge dreadnoughts, cruisers, and destroyers pounded away at each other. More than two dozen ships were destroyed. Both sides claimed victory, and both suffered high casualties. Although the British lost twice as many sailors as the Germans, the Battle of Jutland left the British navy in control of European waters. Now the British fleet could enforce its blockade of Germany's

North Sea ports, making it difficult for food and help to reach the Central Powers.

Still, the Germans had another deadly new weapon for the war at sea—submarines called U-boats. The "U" stood for *untersee*, German for "undersea." For several decades, the navies of industrialized nations had experimented with submarines as weapons. But World War I was the first war in which submarines played a significant role.

To sailors and passengers aboard ships, U-boats brought terror from the deep. Prowling the sea lanes, lurking just beneath the surface, a submarine could launch a torpedo and destroy a ship before the crew even knew that an attack was coming.

At the beginning of the war, in response to the British blockade of German ports, Germany announced a submarine blockade of Britain. U-boats began to torpedo vessels in waters around Britain, including neutral cargo ships. In 1915, they sank at least two passenger ships that they suspected of carrying munitions. The U-boats even torpedoed ships that tried to come to the rescue of survivors in the water. Such acts, like the attack on civilians in Belgium, seemed to defy the old rules of "civilized" war.

The Sinking of the *Lusitania*

On May 1, 1915, the *Lusitania*, the pride of Britain's Cunard Steamship Line, sailed from New York Harbor for its home port in Liverpool, England. Most of the tourists and businessmen aboard the luxurious British ocean liner looked forward to the voyage.

Some, however, were nervous. The German embassy had placed an ad in newspapers declaring, "Travelers intending to embark on the Atlantic voyage are reminded that a state of war exists between Germany and her allies and Great Britain.... Vessels flying the flag of Great Britain...are liable to destruction." But surely, most people thought, the Germans wouldn't attack an ocean liner carrying civilian passengers.

For six days, the *Lusitania* steamed across the Atlantic without incident. Then, as passengers gathered on deck to watch the Irish coast approach, a German U-boat sent a torpedo slamming into the ship's hull. The splendid *Lusitania* sank in 18 minutes, taking 1,198 people, including 128 Americans, to their deaths.

The sinking of the passenger ship *Lusitania* infuriated Americans and made them more willing to enter the Great War.

The sinking of the *Lusitania* turned many Americans against Germany. Up to this time, the United States had managed to stay out of the Great War. But when German torpedoes destroyed the *Lusitania*, many Americans began to think the time had come for their country to enter the war against the Central Powers.

War in the Skies

In the spring of 1915, German airships called zeppelins crossed the North Sea to bomb London and the east coast of England. Zeppelins created alarm among the British people, but only limited damage. They proved vulnerable to antiaircraft guns and fighter planes. Later in the war, the Germans used zeppelins only for scouting missions.

Another new technology, however, became a deadly instrument of warfare—the airplane. World War I broke out only about a decade after the Wright brothers made their first flight at Kitty Hawk, North Carolina. At first, both the Allied and Central Powers used planes to scout the positions of enemy armies. On these early flights, pilots occasionally leaned out of their cockpits to shoot at each other with pistols. But by 1916, squadrons of fighter planes outfitted with machine guns were battling each other for control of the skies.

Daring pilots known as aces made the clouds their battlefields. Their swirling dogfights with enemy planes made them heroes in the newspaper pages. Unlike the warfare in the trenches below, the war in the air seemed an arena for individual maneuver and daring. Even though the aces were fighting with new kinds of weapons, their battles seemed a throwback to a time when valiant warriors pitted their skills against each other in duels to the death.

Of all the fliers who took to the skies during World War I, none achieved greater fame than Germany's Manfred von Richthofen (rihkt-HOH-fuhn)—known, for the color of his warplane, as "the Red Baron." Von Richthofen became the most successful fighter pilot of the war, with more than 80 confirmed air combat victories.

On April 21, 1918, in a dogfight high above the Somme River while in pursuit of a British plane, von Richthofen met his death. Another British pilot shot at him from behind, while Allied troops on the ground fired from below. One of the bullets found his chest. The Red Baron managed to land his plane in territory controlled by Australian soldiers, but he died soon after. Old notions of chivalry had not entirely vanished: The next day, officers from Britain's Royal Air Force served as pallbearers at the Red Baron's funeral, and at his graveside an Australian guard of honor fired a salute to the fallen ace.

Total War

In 1914, most Europeans had expected a short war with few casualties. By 1916, as the war dragged on, leaders on both sides stubbornly refused to seek a truce even in the face of nightmarish death and destruction. To seek peace, they thought, would be unpatriotic and weak. They stubbornly resolved to keep fighting till the bitter end.

World War I escalated into the first "total war," a war in which the opposed nations used virtually every resource they possessed to keep up the fight, involving every citizen in the effort. The Allies enlisted not just their own citizens on the home front, but many people from their dominions and colonies as well. Hundreds of thousands of Australians, Canadians, Irish, and New Zealanders fought in Europe and the Middle East. Soldiers from British and French possessions in Africa and Asia took up arms—Indians, Senegalese, Algerians, Moroccans, South Africans, and others. The conflict, mostly European at first, grew into a true world war.

Dominions were self-governing nations in the British Empire.

Determined to fight to the bitter end, European governments took charge of many aspects of their nations' economies. They turned whole industries — steel, rubber, munitions — to war production. Government leaders in Britain, France, and Germany

The *munitions* industry produces bombs, grenades, rifles, ammunition, and the like.

The War of Emotions: Propaganda

As the fighting dragged on and casualties mounted, public enthusiasm for the war faded. To build support for the struggle, leaders used propaganda—biased information designed to rouse emotions.

Much wartime propaganda fueled hatred of the enemy. In Britain's new cinema industry, newsreel announcers described the Germans who carried out bombing raids on London as "baby-killers." German propaganda portrayed the Allies in similar terms, blaming the British blockade for a sharp increase in infant mortality.

Propaganda posters on both sides showed heroic soldiers defending the homeland against the enemy. Posters became recruiting tools. The English poster pictured here shows a mother and her daughter, who represent the women of Britain, telling their men to go to war.

British recruiting poster urges men to join the war effort.

brought union leaders and businessmen into the planning. Soon government agencies in both the Allied and Central powers were setting prices, determining wages, rationing food, and deciding which industries would get what resources.

Rationing is the planned distribution of something (such as food) in short supply.

Planned economies — economies largely planned and controlled by governments — temporarily replaced free market capitalism in Europe. The Germans did this most effectively, rationing food to meet the growing challenge of the British blockade, and even requiring that civilians work in specific industries.

The Great War and Women's Suffrage

In the late nineteenth and early twentieth centuries, educated women throughout the West worked for suffrage, the right to vote. If you read Volume 2 of *The Human Odyssey*, you met reformers such as Susan B. Anthony in America and Emmeline Pankhurst in Britain, who made speeches, organized conferences, led marches, and even chained themselves to lampposts.

By 1914, Finland, Norway, Australia, New Zealand, and a few American states had granted women the right to vote, but in most places women still weren't welcomed at the ballot box.

The Great War helped turn the tide for the suffrage movement in the West. During the war, millions of women went to work in jobs usually done by men. Reformers insisted that if women could take on such jobs, then surely they should be allowed to vote.

During the war and shortly afterward, Western governments began to recognize women's enormous contributions to the war effort by granting the right to vote. Britain, Sweden, Germany, Poland, Hungary, Austria, Czechoslovakia, and Canada all approved woman suffrage. In 1920, the 19th Amendment to the U.S. Constitution gave American women the right to vote. In France and Italy, women had to wait until the mid-1940s to cast their ballots.

Women's Changing Roles

Societies changed dramatically during World War I, especially for women. Many women who had never worked outside the home took jobs in banking, commerce, and industry. Whereas only a small number of women held clerical jobs before the war, millions entered the workforce between 1914 and 1918. In Britain alone, more than 1.3 million women took new jobs or worked outside the home for the first time.

As men perished on the Western Front, women worked to support their families. They collected train tickets and ran elevators. They worked as bank tellers, telephone operators, and shopkeepers. Above all, they worked in heavy industry and in munitions factories. Nearly 40 percent of workers in Germany's major munitions plant were women.

With women at work, the mills, factories, mines, and furnaces of Europe greatly increased production. Women enabled factories in France to produce six times more explosives than they had before women entered the workforce.

War pushed women to take on tasks once reserved for men. This change led to a growing belief among women in the Western world that they could support themselves and contribute to their nations' economies outside as well as inside the home.

Grim Prospects

By 1917, the Allies faced grim realities. German submarines attacked ships heading to and from Britain in an attempt to starve the island nation into surrender. Meanwhile, mutinies broke out in the French army.

Perhaps worst of all for the Allies, Russia seemed on the verge of collapse. The huge country had suffered some of the war's worst blows, with at least 1.7 million soldiers dead by 1917, another 5 million wounded, and about 2.5 million taken prisoner. Revolution was erupting in the tsar's empire.

Would the crippled Russian forces be able to carry on? The prospects did not look hopeful.

All Quiet on the Western Front

Erich Maria Remarque, a German veteran of World War I, published All Quiet on the Western Front *in 1929. Many people consider the work one of the greatest war novels of all time. Although the book is fiction, Remarque drew on his wartime experiences to paint a detailed and realistic depiction of the horrors of trench warfare.*

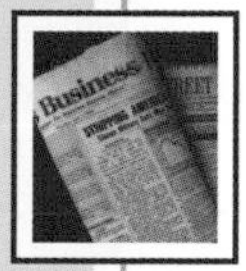

A Page from the Past

We wake up in the middle of the night. The earth booms. Heavy fire is falling on us. We crouch into corners. We distinguish shells of every calibre.... The dugout heaves, the night roars and flashes. We look at each other in the momentary flashes of light, and with pale faces and pressed lips shake our heads.... When a shell lands in the trench we note how the hollow, furious blast is like a blow from the paw of a raging beast of prey....

Slowly the grey light trickles into the post and pales the flashes of the shells. Morning is come. The explosion of mines mingles with the gunfire. That is the most dementing convulsion of all. The whole region where they go up becomes one grave....

The attack does not come, but the bombardment continues. We are gradually benumbed. Hardly a man speaks. We cannot make ourselves understood.

Our trench is almost gone. At many places it is only eighteen inches high, it is broken by holes, and craters, and mountains of earth. A shell lands square in front of our post. At once it is dark. We are buried and must dig ourselves out....

Towards morning, while it is still dark, there is some excitement. Through the entrance rushes in a swarm of fleeing rats that try to storm the walls. Torches light up the confusion. Everyone yells and curses and slaughters. The madness and despair of many hours unloads itself in this outburst. Faces are distorted, arms strike out, the beasts scream; we just stop in time to avoid attacking one another....

Night again. We are deadened by the strain — a deadly tension that scrapes along one's spine like a gapped knife. Our legs refuse to move, our hands tremble, our bodies are a thin skin stretched painfully over repressed madness, over an almost irresistible, bursting roar. We have neither flesh nor muscles any longer, we dare not look at one another for fear of some incalculable thing. So we shut our teeth — it will end — it will end — perhaps we will come through.

Vladimir Lenin, leader of the Russian Revolution, urges his countrymen forward in this dramatic Russian poster from 1924. In 1917, Lenin, a devoted Marxist, helped start an uprising that toppled the tsar from his throne and turned Russia into a communist nation. Red, so prominent in this poster, was the color associated with communism.

Revolution in Russia

On a street in a city in Russia, a crowd gathered. Restless, hungry, and angry, they grumbled their approval as a speaker shouted, "What do you get from war? Only wounds, starvation, and death!"

In early 1917, Russia was on the verge of collapse. Millions of Russians lay dead on frozen battlefields or maimed in hospitals that lacked medical supplies. Millions more were starving. As a hard winter set in, hungry rioters clamored for bread while mobs stormed government buildings. "Anarchy reigns in the capital," one official reported. "Government is paralyzed."

It was clear to everyone, including the leaders of both the Allied and Central Powers, that Russia was in crisis.

Russia Struggles to Modernize

While Russia suffered terrible losses in the Great War, the nation's crisis had deep roots, going back many centuries. The war magnified a conflict between Russia's long feudal past and its recent efforts to enter the modern era.

It was not until the late 1800s that Russia began to industrialize in earnest. This vast empire, straddling two continents, was rich in natural resources and had an enormous population. But only in the quarter-century before the outbreak of war did businessmen begin to build modern factories. Then railroads and telegraph wires began to connect cities like St. Petersburg and Moscow, which ballooned in size. Workers embarked on the construction of the Trans-Siberian Railroad, which would become the longest rail line in the world. By 1900, Russia had become one of the world's leading producers of oil. In the production of iron and steel, it ranked behind only the United States, Germany, and Britain.

As the twentieth century approached, Russia's industrial progress was matched by its cultural achievements. Universities in Moscow and St. Petersburg attracted growing numbers of students. Not only in Russia, but also throughout Europe and the United States, people read the novels of Leo Tolstoy, such as *War and Peace* and *Anna Karenina*. They listened to symphonies by Peter Tchaikovsky and thrilled to his ballets, including *Swan Lake* and *The Nutcracker*. In Russia's cities, people discussed the possibility of a written constitution and an elected legislature—both of which, until recently, seemed unthinkable in a land long ruled by iron-fisted tsars.

Yet despite these changes and hopes, Russia suffered from a stark division between rich and poor. At the top of society was a tiny class of nobles who held most of the land in Russia. Many owned estates so vast they rivaled small countries.

For three centuries, Russia had been led by tsars from the Romanov (ROH-muh-nahf) family. In the years leading up to World War I, Tsar Nicholas II held the throne. He ruled with his nervous and unpopular German-born wife, Alexandra, a granddaughter of Britain's Queen Victoria. Nicholas was a weak but stubborn man, jealously attached to his royal privileges. Like previous tsars, he treated the empire as his private possession, never doubting his right to absolute rule and never suspecting that he would be the last of the Romanovs.

The privileges enjoyed by the small minority of Russian nobles rested on the backs of the vast majority of the people at the bottom of Russian society, the peasants who did the farm work. Through most of the nineteenth century, these peasants were serfs, tied to the land and enjoying few rights. Noblemen considered the serfs little more than part of their estates. Although technically serfs were not slaves, they owed labor to their masters. The masters, in turn, allowed the serfs to use the land to grow just enough to support themselves.

Although Russia legally abolished serfdom in 1861, this did little to improve the lives of the peasants. By 1900, peasants made up 80 percent of Russia's 129 million people. They lived in shacks and spoke Russian, while the tsar and the richest nobles lived in luxurious homes or glittering palaces, where they preferred to speak French.

Thus, as the twentieth century began, Russia was a rapidly modernizing country still burdened by its feudal past. A new class of business and industrial leaders was emerging. Many peasants were leaving the countryside for factory work in cities. But millions of suffering peasants continued to work on the estates held by rich nobles, while the powerful tsar resisted efforts to limit his authority. Change met resistance to change, and the friction generated social unrest.

Marxist Revolutionaries

By 1900, signs of unrest flared in the capital city of St. Petersburg, in Moscow, and in other cities. Students schemed to overturn the old order. Workers shouted demands for change. Citizens openly criticized Tsar Nicholas.

Indeed, in turn-of-the-century Russia, you could find anti-tsarist groups on every corner. There were anarchists who wanted no government at all. There were liberals who wanted a constitutional democracy. There were socialists who wanted a powerful state running the economy. And there were a growing number of revolutionaries who considered themselves "Marxists." They called for communism, the system envisioned by the German philosopher Karl Marx. They looked forward to the revolt of workers against owners that Marx had predicted. They shared Marx's vision of a classless society in which all means of production — factories, equipment, railroads — belong to the people as a whole.

An *anarchist* is someone who rejects any ruling authority or established order.

Lenin Leads the Cause

One of the most devoted Marxists was Vladimir Lenin (VLAD-uh-mihr LEN-in). His real name was Vladimir Ilyich Ulyanov, but Russian revolutionaries commonly took "revolutionary" aliases. Lenin had grown up in middle-class comfort. He was an avid reader and a curious boy who spent much time alone and had few friends. When Lenin was 17, his brother was hanged for plotting against the tsar. This tragedy turned Lenin's thoughts to revolution.

The young man found his life's mission when he discovered the works of Karl Marx. From then on, Lenin spent every waking moment working for his cherished cause — a communist revolution.

The world has rarely seen a more forceful, opinionated, or dogmatic personality than Vladimir Lenin. A stocky, bald man, Lenin had absolute certainty in his own ideas and no tolerance for differences of opinion. Anyone who disagreed with him was his enemy. He wrote and spoke in blunt, clear, graceless language, which nonetheless had the power to plant his vision of communism in the hearts and minds of angry workers.

As a young man, Lenin became the leader of a Social Democratic revolutionary group. In 1895, Russian authorities arrested him and later exiled him to Siberia, the northern region of Russia where winters are bitterly cold. There he had three years to think and write.

By the time he was released from exile, Lenin had decided that a small party of full-time, professional revolutionaries would be most effective in bringing about change, because they could act with unity and secrecy. So in 1903, he picked a fight that split the Social Democrats in two. Lenin's faction was called the Bolsheviks (BOHL-shuh-viks), which means "majority," even though it was actually quite a small and secretive group. The rival faction was called the Mensheviks (MEN-shuh-viks) — oddly, a word that means "minority," even though they were the larger group.

A *faction* is a group at odds with other groups.

Lenin surrounded himself with loyal followers. One was a tough, quiet, and ruthless young disciple, Joseph Stalin (STAH-luhn). Stalin's adopted name meant "Man of Steel." Another towering revolutionary, however, had ideas of his own, and he nearly equaled Lenin in arrogant self-confidence. This man, born Lev Davidovich Bronshtein, once stole a passport from a prison guard named Leon Trotsky (TRAHT-skee) and used it to escape Russia just ahead of the tsar's police. He lived the rest of his life as Leon Trotsky.

A fiery speaker and brilliant writer, Trotsky started out as a Menshevik, but he later joined the Bolsheviks. He never challenged Lenin for the top spot, but eventually secured a place as the clear number two of the Bolshevik Party.

Lenin, Trotsky, and other revolutionaries were taken by surprise in 1905, when unrest in Russia suddenly turned to actual revolt. Russia was losing a war to Japan, which struck a blow to Russian pride. Unemployment rose during the war. Discontented students and workers blamed Tsar Nicholas. One Sunday, thousands of workers and their families poured into the streets of St. Petersburg, carrying a petition asking the tsar for economic improvements and democratic change. The tsar's troops responded by shooting hundreds of them.

"Bloody Sunday" enraged Russian workers and set off a wave of strikes. All across the country, workers began setting up councils known as "soviets" (SOH-vee-etz) to lead their struggle. Peasants, soldiers, and students also joined these soviets, or formed their own. At last Tsar Nicholas yielded to pressure and created an elected

The Marxist-Leninist Doctrine

By the time he forged the Bolshevik Party, Lenin had developed his own brand of Marxism. In 1902, he presented his new ideas in a famous pamphlet titled "What Is to Be Done?" Marx had predicted that in the course of time, historical forces would bring about a workers' revolution. Lenin said revolutionaries should not wait for history to take its course. Instead, they should form a disciplined party of "professional revolutionists" who could operate in secret, combat the police, and seize power on behalf of the industrial working class, the class Marx called the "proletariat." In 1902, Russia didn't have a large proletarian class. But Lenin said that once his revolutionary party took power, it would build factories that would enlarge the proletariat, who would then forge a classless communist society.

January 9, 1905, was known as "Bloody Sunday" after the tsar's troops shot hundreds of workers who had gathered at the Winter Palace in St. Petersburg to demand reform.

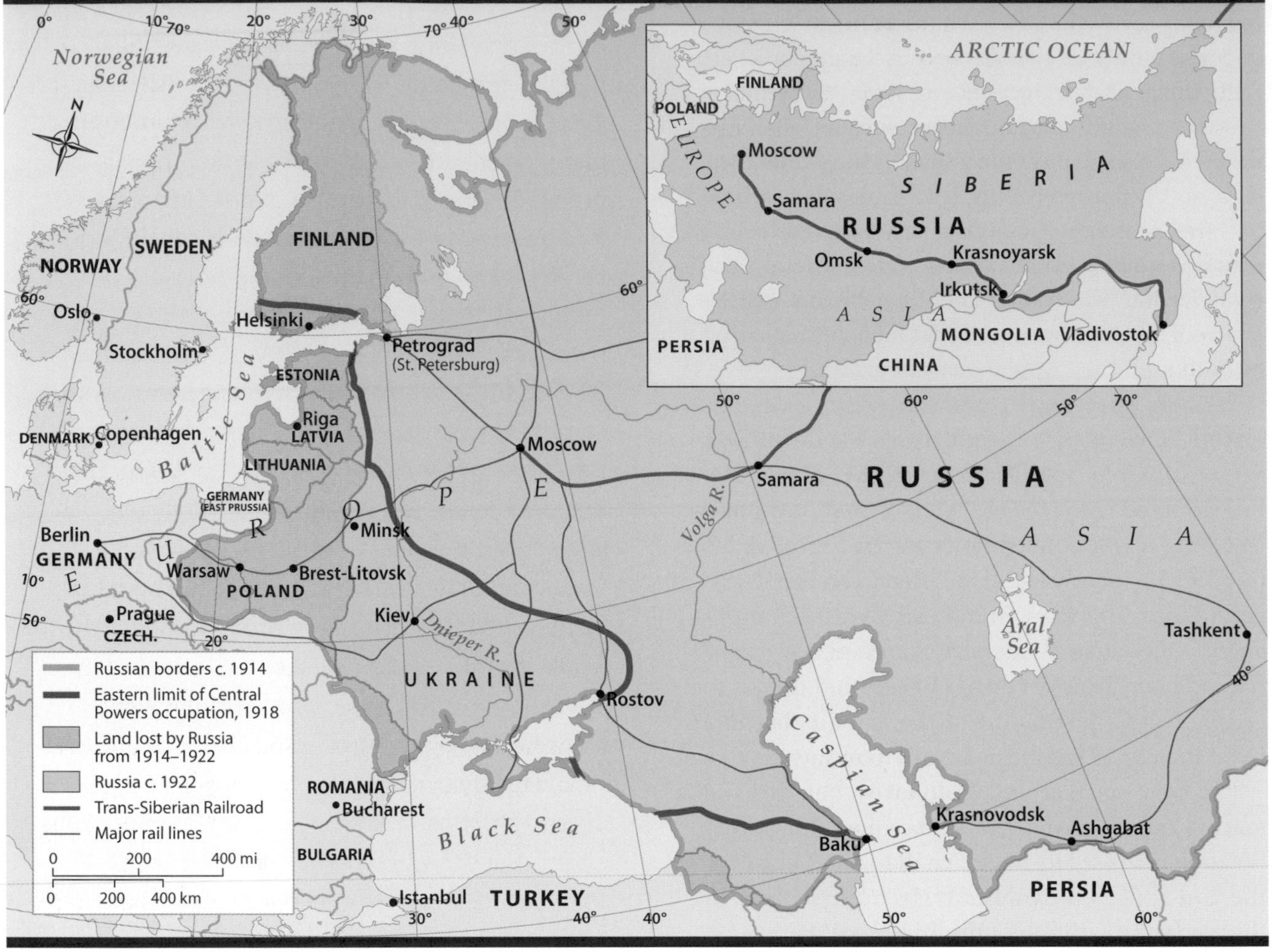

Russia Before and After the Revolution

parliament called the Duma (DOO-muh) — but he then refused to cooperate with it.

The revolution of 1905 looked like a failure. More and more soviets were organized, but the tsar's secret police hunted down the leading revolutionaries and sent them to prison or into exile. Stalin ended up in Siberia. Lenin and Trotsky fled from Russia. They spent years wandering from city to city, writing, arguing, and planning.

War Leads to Revolution

By the second decade of the twentieth century, Russia had already been shaken by tremors of revolution. The disastrous consequences of Russia's entry into the Great War triggered complete social upheaval.

Russian armies suffered from little food, poor equipment, and many terrible generals. The worst generals even wanted their men to fight with bayonets — against machine guns — because they thought it showed more gallantry. In 1915, Tsar Nicholas insisted on taking charge of military affairs, though he had almost no military talent or experience. While Russian troops managed to win most of their battles against the Austrians, they were regularly defeated by the Germans. The Germans poured into Poland and parts of Ukraine, both considered Russian territory. By the end of 1915, some five million men had been killed, wounded, taken prisoner, or simply gone missing — and the end wasn't in sight.

As Russian troops suffered on the battlefields, so did the people back home. Many went jobless and hungry as factories in St. Petersburg and Moscow shut down for lack of fuel. Grain and other foods were scarce in inland cities. There was no general shortage of either fuel or food — it's just that neither could get to the cities because the trains were being used to move troops and wartime supplies. Instead of bringing wheat and oil, the trains that steamed from the front to Moscow, the hub of the railroad system, often carried wounded soldiers who needed shelter, medical care, and food — all of which were in short supply.

Amid the misery of World War I, the ruling elite of Russia went on living a life of tea parties and lavish balls. They seemed unwilling or unable to recognize that their world was falling apart around them.

As World War I ground Russia to bits, the soviets — the workers' councils — organized ever more ferocious demonstrations. In early 1917, crowds of women, mostly textile workers, poured into the streets of the Russian capital, whose name had been changed from St. Petersburg to Petrograd (PE-truh-graht). The crowds chanted "Peace and bread! Peace and bread!"

At the beginning of the Great War, Russian leaders decided to rename their capital city, replacing the German "-burg" with the Russian "-grad," changing St. Petersburg to Petrograd.

Tsar Nicholas II had learned nothing from Bloody Sunday. He dispatched troops to crush the demonstrations. But this time, instead of shooting anyone, the soldiers joined the mobs. The tsar realized he had lost control. In March 1917, he did the unthinkable — he gave up the Russian throne. Thus ended the first act in the great drama of the Russian Revolution.

Rasputin's Strange Power

Even before Russia entered World War I, the royal court of Nicholas and Alexandra was shaken by a family crisis. The young son of the tsar and tsarina was seriously ill. He suffered from hemophilia, a disease that prevents clotting of the blood. The doctors were at a loss—what could be done to help the boy?

A call went out for Rasputin (ra-SPYOOT-uhn), a self-proclaimed holy man with a dirty beard, hypnotic eyes, and a reputation for healing powers. Rasputin came, and whatever he did comforted the boy. The grateful tsarina came to idolize Rasputin. Around Alexandra, Rasputin acted like a holy mystic; but once outside the royal court, he lived a depraved life, devoted to fulfilling his sensual pleasures.

During the war, when Tsar Nicholas left the palace to take charge of troops on the front, Alexandra funneled money to Rasputin and let him decide who should be appointed to high government positions. Thus, in a strange way, Rasputin wielded tremendous power in Russia—until 1916, when a group of noblemen, fearing he would bring shame and ruin on the monarchy, murdered him.

Lenin Returns

It looked as if revolutionaries had succeeded at last. But who were the victors? And what sort of government should Russia have? No one knew, since so many differing forces had opposed the tsar. The elected representatives in the Duma, whom the tsar had ignored, hastily assembled a Provisional Government to run the country. They made plans for a big meeting in the fall, at which elected delegates would gather to write a constitution and chart Russia's future.

Provisional means temporary. A provisional government is one set up to serve until a permanent government can be put in place.

Far away in Switzerland, the exiled Lenin spotted his moment. How could he get back to his homeland across all of Germany, the country

Women in Petrograd demanded "Peace and bread!" in March 1917. The rally marked the first organized women's march in Russia.

at war with Russia? It looked impossible, but Lenin got some powerful help. The German government gave him money, a railroad carriage, and all the guards he needed to get safely to Finland. From there, Lenin could easily enter Russia. Why did the Germans help Lenin? Because they liked the idea of revolutionary chaos in the country they were trying to conquer.

At this time, Leon Trotsky was in New York City, living in a small apartment in the Bronx. He too rushed back to Russia, where he took charge of the biggest workers' group, the Petrograd Soviet. This group wielded as much power as the Provisional Government, and for many months it wasn't clear who was really in charge of Russia.

When one of the tsar's former generals led a revolt, the Provisional Government gave thousands of guns to the workers of Petrograd to fight the general and his troops. Most of the arms ended up in the hands of the Bolsheviks, setting the stage for the second act in the Russian Revolution.

In the early hours of November 7, 1917, Bolshevik guards led by Trotsky seized key bridges and government buildings throughout the capital. When morning came, Lenin announced that the Petrograd Soviet had taken charge. Since Bolsheviks controlled this soviet, it was actually Lenin and his allies who were now in control. Within weeks, Lenin dissolved the Petrograd Soviet and began to rule directly in the name of Russia's workers, soldiers, and peasants.

A Humiliating Treaty

When the Bolsheviks took power, German armies were marching toward the Russian capital. Lenin thought German communists might remove this threat by leading a revolution in Germany to overthrow the kaiser's government. Lenin firmly believed in the unity of the world's working class. He reasoned that a German communist state would never wage war on a Russian communist nation. He sent Trotsky to tie up the Germans in peace talks until the German revolution broke out.

But no revolution broke out in Germany. The talks crumbled, and the German army surged to within a hundred miles of Petrograd.

Lenin hastily moved his capital to Moscow, where he was forced to make peace on any terms he could. He signed a treaty that gave Germany huge chunks of Russia, including more than a quarter of its best farmland, one-sixth of its population, much of its industry, and most of its coal and iron. Russia was now out of the Great War.

This humiliating treaty crippled Russia, but it left Lenin free to launch his communist program. He declared that all land, all banks, all mines, and all factories now belonged to the state. Under the Communist Party, as the Bolsheviks now called themselves, peasants were forbidden to sell their crops. Instead, Lenin ordered them to give all that they produced to the government.

Revolutionary Terror

Other revolutionary groups, such as the Mensheviks, bitterly disagreed with Lenin's measures. Lenin did not like disagreement. He assembled a police force called the Cheka (CHEH-kah) to hunt down his opponents. Cheka officers had authority to arrest and execute anyone they considered dangerous. As Lenin put it, "You surely don't think we're going to come out the victors if we don't use the harshest kind of revolutionary terror?"

No one knows how many thousands of people the Cheka killed between 1918 and 1920. The casualties included the former Tsar Nicholas II and his entire family—even the children and a pet dog—all of whom were murdered in a house where they had been imprisoned.

Russia slipped further into chaos. Gangs of bandits roamed the land. Various ethnic groups began fighting for independence. Generals who supported the murdered tsar began gathering armies at the fringes of the former empire. These forces came to be known as "Whites," in contrast to the Bolsheviks, who had long been called "Reds."

The Communists put Trotsky in charge of fighting the Whites. In less than a year, Trotsky built an army of almost three million troops. Over the next two years, the Reds and the Whites fought one of history's most savage civil wars. In a nation already devastated by the Great War, millions were killed, and still millions more died of starvation and disease.

The Whites got some help from other countries, such as Britain, but Trotsky's army was

Tsar Nicholas II, Tsarina Alexandra, and their children sit for a portrait in 1913. Five years later, during the Russian Revolution, the Bolsheviks killed the royal family to ensure that Nicholas and his heirs could never regain the throne.

far bigger and more unified. By late 1920, the Reds routed the Whites. The Bolsheviks were in charge of a Russia reduced to rubble.

A Dictatorship Is Born

With power firmly in hand, Lenin took on the Herculean task of rebuilding the country. He declared that national groups within the old Russian empire had the right to form independent republics, so long as they were socialist republics controlled by workers' soviets. Thus, the country forged by Lenin's Communist Party took a long and awkward name—the Union of Soviet Socialist Republics (USSR).

The republics within the Union of Soviet Socialist Republics turned out to be anything but independent. All of the soviets were really controlled by Lenin's Communist Party. Government administrators across the new country had to follow orders from local Communist Party officials. Within the party, all officials reported to higher officials and received orders from above.

All but the most trivial decisions flowed from a Central Committee in Moscow, the capital of the new country. Within this central core, power was concentrated in the hands of a small ruling group called the Politburo (PAH-lut-byour-oh). This inner circle included Stalin, the so-called man of steel, and Leon Trotsky, creator of the Red Army. Ultimately, however, at the center of this centralized system, one dictator held absolute power—Chairman Vladimir Lenin.

In order to run the new communist state, Lenin sought to control many aspects of people's lives, including their religious beliefs. Years before, Karl Marx had described religion as "the

From Russia to USSR

Russian revolutionaries renamed their nation the Union of Soviet Socialist Republics. English-speaking people in the West often shortened the name to the Soviet Union or the USSR. Many people continued to refer to the powerful communist country as Russia, despite the fact that the USSR included millions of non-Russians, such as Finns, Latvians, Lithuanians, Ukrainians, Poles, Tatars, and Turkic peoples, among many others.

Vladimir Lenin (right of center) is depicted in this painting as a hero of the people after overthrowing the tsar's government and establishing a communist state. But Lenin also founded a dictatorship that sought to control the lives of the very people he claimed to have freed from tyranny. The red banners of Bolshevism fly behind him.

opium of the people." He meant that religion, like a drug, offered people an escape from the struggles and challenges of life. Lenin agreed.

Lenin distrusted the Russian Orthodox Church. He thought that for many centuries, tsars and nobles had used the church as a tool to keep power. Lenin ordered the government to seize church property. His Communist Party launched a campaign to turn people against religion. The government imprisoned many priests and sentenced more than a thousand to death. It outlawed religious instruction for children. The Communist Party adopted atheism—the belief that there is no God—as an official policy. In Lenin's dictatorship, which demanded complete loyalty to the state, there was no room for faith in God or freedom of religion.

Lenin and his fellow Bolsheviks saw the Russian Revolution as merely the first step in a larger drama. They expected their communist revolution to spread across Europe and the world. They fervently believed that this worldwide revolution would launch a golden age. They saw it as their duty to spread communism abroad. Such beliefs made Europe's weary sovereigns very nervous. Americans also watched uneasily.

Lenin's aspirations for worldwide communism, which he passed on to succeeding generations, made the Russian Revolution of 1917 a crucial event not just in Russian history but in the history of the world. The revolution eventually affected every other nation in some way, and helped shape the course of the twentieth century.

Lenin Predicts a Worldwide Revolution

A Page from the Past

Lenin believed it was only a matter of time before workers around the world would rise up and overthrow their capitalist or "bourgeois" masters. In March 1919, he addressed the First Congress of the Communist International, an organization of communist leaders from several countries. In attendance were representatives of groups such as the Spartacus League, a Marxist faction of the German Social Democratic party. Here are some of Lenin's remarks.

Comrades, our gathering has great historic significance.... The bourgeois are terror-stricken at the growing workers' revolutionary movement. This is understandable... since the imperialist war inevitably favors the workers' revolutionary movement, and... the world revolution is beginning and growing in intensity everywhere.

All that is needed is to find the practical form to enable the proletariat to establish its rule. Such a form is the Soviet system with the dictatorship of the proletariat.... A practical form of dictatorship has been found by the working people. The mass of workers now understand it thanks to Soviet power in Russia, thanks to the Spartacus League in Germany and to similar organizations in other countries. All this shows that a revolutionary form of the dictatorship of the proletariat has been found, that the proletariat is now able to exercise its rule.

Comrades... it is especially important to note that in other countries, too, the latest form of the workers' movement is asserting itself and getting the upper hand.... Even though the bourgeoisie are still raging, even though they may kill thousands more workers, victory will be ours, the victory of the worldwide Communist revolution is assured....

No matter how the bourgeoisie of the whole world rage, how much they deport or jail or even kill Spartacists and Bolsheviks—all this will no longer help. It will only serve to enlighten the masses, help rid them of the old bourgeois-democratic prejudices and steel them in the struggle. The victory of the proletarian revolution on a world scale is assured. The founding of an international Soviet republic is on the way.

A rifle and helmet mark the grave of a French soldier on a battlefield at Verdun. After four years of fighting, the Great War finally ended, but only after millions had died and much of Europe had suffered almost unimaginable destruction. Peace had come, but it was a peace that left many with a deep sense of anger and loss.

War's End and a Troubled Peace

When Russia, exhausted and humiliated, signed a peace treaty with Germany, the Great War ended on much of the Eastern Front. Now Germany was free to shift masses of troops to the Western Front. Confident German generals were sure they could hammer their way through the weary French and British lines.

The Germans knew they had to move quickly. Yes, the Allied Powers had lost Russia, but they had gained a new and powerful partner—the United States.

"Lafayette, We Are Here!"

Since 1914, the United States had kept its distance from the war. Most Americans saw it as a nasty European fight—why should they get involved? Great Britain and France put pressure on the United States to join the Allies, but Americans remained neutral. President Woodrow Wilson had even won re-election in 1916 on the slogan, "He Kept Us Out of War."

But Americans found it hard to remain neutral as they heard reports of atrocities like the burning of the Belgian town of Louvain. Americans were especially angered when a German submarine fired torpedoes into the *Lusitania*. Among those who died when the great ship sank were more than a hundred U.S. citizens.

Initially, the Germans apologized for the *Lusitania* disaster and agreed to stop such attacks. But in early 1917, the Germans announced they would resume unrestricted submarine warfare. They proceeded to sink American cargo ships.

President Wilson realized that the United States could not avoid a conflict that was spreading to engulf so much of the world. On April 2, 1917, he went before Congress and asked it to declare war on Germany. Wilson was surprised when the congressmen responded by erupting into cheers. Back at the White House, he remarked to an aide that it was strange that people should cheer for war. Then he put his head on a table and wept.

Soon American troops were on their way to Europe. On July 4, 1917, energetic, fresh-faced U.S. soldiers paraded through Paris on their way to the tomb of the French patriot, the Marquis de Lafayette. Lafayette, you recall, had fought for the United States during the Revolutionary War, and now Americans were coming to the aid of France. "Lafayette, we are here!" declared a U.S. officer at Lafayette's tomb.

Wilson's High Ideals

President Wilson did not join the war just to defeat the Germans. He felt he had a higher aim. He believed America was waging war for the good of mankind. In urging Congress to declare war, Wilson said that "the world must be made safe for democracy." By early 1918, Wilson, confident of an Allied victory, was already thinking ahead to what would happen after the fighting ended. He was thinking about a peace treaty that, he hoped, might rid the world of such catastrophic wars.

Let's find out more about this idealist, this intellectual, this man determined to change the world.

Woodrow Wilson was born the son of a Presbyterian minister. He spent his childhood in the southern part of the United States, where his family moved from church to church. From his father he learned how to think clearly, write precisely, and speak persuasively. His father also gave him a strong sense of right and wrong that guided him throughout his life.

His earliest memory, Wilson said, was of "standing at my father's gateway in Augusta, Georgia, when I was four years old, and hearing someone pass and say that Mr. Lincoln was elected and there was to be war." As he grew up, he witnessed the struggles of Southerners during and after the Civil War, and he never forgot how desperate and bitter a defeated people could feel.

President Woodrow Wilson hoped to find a way to forge a lasting peace in the wake of the Great War.

Wilson grew up to be a serious, studious young man. Most of his friends thought he would become a minister, like his father and grandfather. But politics and government fascinated him. He became a professor of political science. Later he became president of Princeton University in New Jersey. In 1910, he ran for governor of New Jersey, and he won. In 1912, he was elected president of the United States.

As president, Wilson was a reformer, often on the side of the underdog. He encouraged Congress to pass laws to help struggling farmers and to end child labor. He set up the Federal Trade Commission to stop unfair business practices. These ideals of justice and fairness also shaped Wilson's thinking about how to bring the Great War to an end.

When President Wilson took his nation into war, he was determined that Americans would not shed blood on European soil just to save a few kings and emperors. He wanted to create a different kind of world, one in which ambitious or arrogant monarchs could not lead their nations into yet more bloodshed. On January 8, 1918, while the war still raged in Europe, President Wilson stood before the U.S. Congress again and presented a program to end the conflict and solve some of the problems that had triggered the fighting.

Wilson's Fourteen Points

Wilson approached his task with a missionary's zeal. He had lofty goals — some would say unrealistic ones. "What we demand in this war," he told Congress, "is that the world be made fit and safe to live in; and particularly that it be made safe for every peace-loving nation which, like our own, wishes to live its own life, determine its own institutions, be assured of justice and fair dealings by the other peoples of the world, as against force and selfish aggression."

Wilson then proceeded to list fourteen principles that would help remake Europe after the war. His Fourteen Points, as they are known, called for justice, not revenge. Wilson wanted the

President Wilson's Fourteen Points

A Page from the Past

In his Fourteen Points, President Woodrow Wilson laid out his idealistic plan for lasting peace in a postwar world.

I. Open covenants of peace...no private international understandings of any kind, but diplomacy shall proceed always frankly and in the public view...

A *covenant* is a formal and binding agreement between two or more parties.

II. Absolute freedom of navigation upon the seas, outside territorial waters, alike in peace and in war...

III. The removal, so far as possible, of all economic barriers and the establishment of an equality of trade conditions among all the nations...

IV. Adequate guarantees given and taken that national armaments will be reduced to the lowest point consistent with domestic safety...

V. A free, open-minded, and absolutely impartial adjustment of all colonial claims...

VI. The evacuation of all Russian territory and...a sincere welcome into the society of free nations under institutions of her own choosing...

In this context, to *evacuate* means to withdraw foreign military forces.

VII. Belgium...must be evacuated and restored, without any attempt to limit the sovereignty which she enjoys in common with all other free nations...

VIII. All French territory should be freed and the invaded portions restored...

IX. A readjustment of the frontiers of Italy should be effected along clearly recognizable lines of nationality...

X. The peoples of Austria-Hungary, whose place among the nations we wish to see safeguarded and assured, should be accorded the freest opportunity of autonomous development...

Autonomous means self-governing.

XI. Romania, Serbia, and Montenegro should be evacuated, occupied territories restored...

XII. Nationalities which are now under Turkish rule should be assured an undoubted security of life and an absolutely unmolested opportunity of autonomous development...

Unmolested means free from disturbance or interference.

XIII. An independent Polish state should be erected which should include the territories inhabited by indisputably Polish populations...

XIV. A general association of nations must be formed...for the purpose of affording mutual guarantees of political independence and territorial integrity to great and small States alike....

victors of the Great War to be generous toward defeated countries. A generous peace, he hoped, would save the world from bitterness that might become the seed for future wars.

Under the Fourteen Points, Wilson stressed *self-determination*. He said the people of Poland, Romania, Serbia, Turkey, and many other lands should determine their own fate. Wilson hoped that self-determination would end the old imperialist system in which powerful industrial nations grabbed and ruled overseas colonies.

The Fourteen Points also included principles to help avoid tensions between nations. Wilson called for an end to secret treaties between countries. He urged freedom of the seas and removal of barriers to trade. He called for nations to reduce their stockpiles of arms and weapons. He said that disputes over colonies must be resolved fairly, taking into account the wishes of colonized peoples.

Finally, the Fourteen Points proposed creating a new organization made of countries throughout the world. This League of Nations would have one major goal—to help keep peace. Wilson hoped that in the League of Nations, members could solve their differences through discussions and votes rather than armed conflict. He also hoped the League's members would pledge to defend any member attacked by another nation. He reasoned that even a very powerful country would hesitate to attack another if it knew it would face the united opposition of the League of Nations.

What If?

In 1918, after Russia surrendered and dropped out of the war, German troops that had been fighting on the Eastern Front moved to the Western Front to battle the British and French. But German generals left a million troops on the Eastern Front to occupy and expand their newly acquired territory in Russia. Consider this: What if the Germans had chosen to move more troops to the Western Front? Could they have defeated the Allied armies there and gone on to win the war? We'll never know.

Wilson believed that out of the Great War's widespread destruction, something good could come—a lasting peace and the spread of freedom. "We are fighting for the liberty, the self-government, and the undictated development of all peoples," he declared. "No people must be forced under sovereignty under which it does not wish to live."

To have *sovereignty* over people is to have supreme power over them.

High ideals indeed—and ones that would not be welcomed by embittered Europeans and disillusioned Americans.

The War's End

Even as Wilson sent American troops to Europe and laid out his vision for the future, German armies were rushing toward the Western Front. Germany's military leaders gambled on one last-ditch attempt to break the stalemate in the trenches. They had reason for hope: More than half a million new German troops were arriving from the east. In March 1918, German generals combined the fresh troops, artillery, and poison gas to launch what they hoped would be a devastating final offensive in France.

They almost succeeded. The assault pushed British and French troops back. But Germany suffered terrible casualties during this advance. And there would be no more reinforcements to come.

French and British forces also suffered tremendous casualties, but they managed to regroup. British factories were churning out thousands of trucks and new lightweight tanks. They figured out how to coordinate their infantry, artillery, tanks, and air support to repel the Germans.

And the Allies could now count on American help. Hundreds of thousands of U.S. soldiers were arriving in Europe every month. By the fall of 1918, an overwhelming two million Americans had joined the Allied ranks. Said one French officer, "Life was coming in floods to reanimate the dying body of France."

By August, Germany's massive offensive had collapsed. Now it was the Allies' turn to launch assaults on the German trenches. Thousands of Germans surrendered. The long stalemate on the Western Front finally came to an end.

Meanwhile, to the south, the Italians finally defeated an Austrian army weakened by mass desertions. In Palestine and Syria, British forces triumphed over the Ottomans.

In the fall of 1918, both the German kaiser and the Austrian emperor faced uprisings among their hungry people. The British had blockaded German ports, causing a shortage of food in Germany and Austria. Angry crowds in Berlin and Vienna rioted to demand food and to protest the ongoing fighting. One Austrian official warned, "If the monarchs of the Central Powers cannot make peace in the coming months, it will be made for them by their peoples." The kaiser and emperor worried that something like Russia's Bolshevik Revolution might be erupting in their own empires.

They had reason to worry. Allied forces had not yet crossed the German border, but the city of Munich was in turmoil. Revolution threatened to break out all across Germany. Workers openly expressed admiration for the Bolsheviks and formed workers' councils, modeled on Russian soviets, to take over many duties of government. Workers also went on strike demanding peace. Mobs roamed the streets.

On November 9, 1918, Kaiser Wilhelm abdicated the German throne. A new republican government took power. Some generals of the German army, which still held its defensive positions in France, wanted to fight on. Many German soldiers opposed surrender. But the new government called for a truce.

When a monarch *abdicates the throne*, he formally gives up his power to rule.

On the morning of November 11, 1918, the war came to an end. Representatives of France, Britain, and Germany gathered in a train car outside the French town of Rethondes (ruh-TOHND) and signed an armistice. It demanded that Germany leave the territories it occupied, surrender its arms, and allow Allied powers to patrol the Rhineland, the land in western Germany along the banks of the Rhine, bordering France.

An *armistice* is a truce that brings an end to fighting, before the official signing of a peace treaty.

At the eleventh hour on the eleventh day of the eleventh month of 1918, the guns finally fell silent on the Western Front.

British and French soldiers rejoiced at the news — at last, they could leave behind the horrors of the trenches. Many German soldiers, however,

At the eleventh hour on the eleventh day of the eleventh month of 1918, an armistice finally brought the Great War to an end. All along the Allied trenches, soldiers celebrated and wept for joy.

Soldiers blinded by mustard gas move past the bodies of dead comrades in this painting by the American artist John Singer Sargent. Some 9 million soldiers died during the Great War, and 21 million were wounded. It is not known how many millions of civilians died.

felt betrayed by the armistice. Even though they had been steadily retreating, they did not believe they had been defeated by the Allies. Many felt they had been stabbed in the back by their own government. "Firing has ceased," a German general told his troops. "Undefeated . . . you are terminating the war in enemy country."

A corporal in the German army, Adolf Hitler, could hardly believe that Germany had lost the war. He had served as a "runner" carrying messages along the front lines, and had twice won the Iron Cross, a military medal for bravery. He was in a hospital, recovering from the effects of a British gas attack, when he heard the news of his country's surrender. "I tottered and groped my way back to the ward," he later recalled, "threw myself on my bunk, and dug my burning head into my blanket and pillow." Like many Germans, he was consumed by rage and a desire for revenge.

The "Glorious Dead"

The world had never experienced a conflict like the Great War. About 9 million combatants perished, far more than in all the wars during the previous hundred years. About 21 million soldiers were wounded. No one knows how many civilians died of disease, hunger, and other war-related causes. Some historians believe as many noncombatants died as soldiers.

Germany and Russia suffered the most casualties, each with about 1.7 million dead in battle. France lost almost as many, from a smaller population. Nearly half of all French men between the ages of 20 and 35 at the start of the war were dead or wounded by the war's end.

Britain and its empire lost nearly a million men. Once powerful Austria-Hungary lost more than a million. More than half a million Italians died, and perhaps 325,000 Turks, their exact numbers never counted. The United States, which had joined the fighting late, suffered much lighter losses. Still, almost 120,000 American soldiers died.

The numbers are appalling but abstract. How is it possible to comprehend loss on such a scale? Consider that in some villages, all the able-bodied young men volunteered to fight alongside their hometown friends — and often they died together, sometimes in a single battle on a single day. For the women, children, and elderly left behind, waiting for the men to come home, there would be no reunions.

Two years after the armistice, the remains of an unidentified soldier were returned to Britain from a battlefield on the Western Front. The British buried the remains with full military honors at Westminster Abbey in London. Within a week, more than a million Britons came to pay their respects at the Tomb of the Unknown Soldier.

King George V asked the nation to come to a standstill for two minutes every November 11 at precisely 11 a.m. to remember the moment of the armistice. "All locomotion should cease," requested the king, "so that, in perfect stillness, the thoughts of everyone may be concentrated on reverent remembrance of the glorious dead." Across Britain, people inscribed their war memorials with this verse, still repeated today at memorial services throughout Britain and its former colonies:

They shall not grow old,
as we that are left grow old:
Age shall not weary them,
nor the years condemn.
At the going down of the sun
and in the morning
We will remember them.

November 11: A Day to Remember

For a while after the Great War, the people of Britain referred to November 11 as Armistice Day. Today they know it as Remembrance Day. In the United States, November 11 is called Veterans Day.

The Cost of Total War

In addition to the staggering human losses, the face of Europe was scarred and bruised by the war. In France and Belgium, as armies advanced and retreated, they wrecked farms, villages, and towns. Artillery fire destroyed bridges, railroad tracks, roads, factories, and homes. Many villages close

By the time the Great War ended, many French towns and villages were ruined. France was one of the war's victorious nations, but because much of the fighting had taken place on its soil, France suffered far more destruction than neighboring Germany, one of the war's losers, where little fighting took place.

The Allied leaders gather at Versailles (from left to right: British Prime Minister David Lloyd George, Italian Prime Minister Vittorio Orlando, French Premier Georges Clemenceau, and U.S. President Woodrow Wilson).

to the front lines were wiped out. Whole stretches of the Western Front — pounded by shells, gouged by trenches, exposed to poison gas — were reduced to barren wastelands. In the winter after the war, starvation stalked much of Europe.

For Britain and Germany, the cost of waging total war added up to about 60 percent of each country's economic output. By 1918, the fighting cost about $10 million *an hour*. To pay for it all, governments had raised taxes. When that wasn't enough, they borrowed money. Nations ran up huge debts, mostly to the United States.

The U.S. economy thrived during the war as Americans sold food and weapons to the combatants. In Europe, however, the fighting devastated business and trade. Many European companies went out of business, and thousands of returning soldiers could not find jobs. After the war, European businessmen discovered that former customers in Latin America and Asia no longer needed their goods. People in those markets had grown used to doing without European products or had started buying them from other sources, such as the United States.

For the Allies in Europe, the cost of victory was almost complete ruin. When it came time for the victors to forge a peace settlement, the leaders of France knew whom to blame — Germany.

Versailles: A Punitive Peace

Two months after the armistice, the Allies assembled at Versailles (vuhr-SIY), a lavish royal palace built around 1700 by France's "Sun King," Louis XIV. Their purpose was to agree to the terms of a lasting peace.

Delegates arrived from around the world, representing the 32 victorious nations. The Japanese, who had supported the Allies, sat at the negotiating table. They had become an important power, commanding the third largest navy in the world. India and China also sent delegations. Real decision-making power, however, lay with France, Britain, and the United States.

At this meeting to decide the fate of the defeated Central Powers, one group was conspicuous by its absence — the Central Powers. They were not invited.

Woodrow Wilson arrived in Europe to a hero's welcome. Parisians greeted him with, according to some, the largest crowd in France's history. To the continent's war-weary people, he seemed a savior, a man who might create a new and better world.

But Wilson's idealism did not stop France from wanting to punish Germany. Only 48 years before, the French had suffered a humiliating loss to the Germans in the Franco-Prussian War. Now, after another and even deadlier German onslaught, the French had triumphed, but at the cost of a generation of their youth.

The prime minister of France, Georges Clemenceau (zhorzh kleh-mahn-SOH), was determined to cripple Germany and make it incapable of striking again. "For the catastrophe of 1914," Clemenceau bluntly stated, "the Germans are responsible." He proposed harsh terms for France's historic enemy. He called for Germany to make huge financial payments, called reparations, to cover the costs of the war. He also demanded the disarmament of Germany's military, and that French troops be stationed in the German Rhineland.

While Clemenceau longed to punish Germany, Woodrow Wilson sought a generous peace. In Wilson's eyes, the United States had fought not to save France but "to redeem the world and make it fit for free men like ourselves to live in."

He argued for a peace based on his Fourteen Points and their promise of self-determination. This war, he said, had been fought so that the world could "be made safe for democracy." His proposals would break apart old empires. But, Wilson argued, they offered the best chance of helping the Germans — themselves bitter, angry, and vengeful — accept their defeat and get on with their lives.

Clemenceau, known as "the Tiger," had no intention of helping Germany in any way. "God was satisfied with Ten Commandments," he reportedly sneered, "Wilson gives us fourteen."

Between Clemenceau and Wilson stood Britain's prime minister, David Lloyd George. He had just won an election on the promise in a campaign slogan, "Make Germany Pay!" But Lloyd George was a practical leader. Behind the scenes, he tried to find a compromise between the French and American positions.

In the end, the Treaty of Versailles included many of France's demands. It included a "war guilt" clause that blamed Germany for the war. The treaty stripped Germany of its overseas colonies and many regions along its borders. It also demanded that Germany pay large reparations.

But the Treaty of Versailles also included some things that Wilson wanted. It partly incorporated his idea of national self-determination, the belief that nations should rule themselves. And it stated that the Allies would set up the League of Nations that Wilson so badly wanted.

Wilson agreed to many French demands in order to save his idea of the League. He was certain that such an organization could help solve many problems. After signing the treaty, he wrote to his wife, "Well, it is finished, and, as no one is satisfied, it makes me hope we have made a just peace; but it is all in the lap of the gods."

Redrawing the Map

The Treaty of Versailles changed the map of Europe. The Allies' peace terms dramatically altered political boundaries in eastern and central Europe. To make sense of these changes, refer to the map on page 116 as you read the following:

- The empire of Austria-Hungary was split into new independent states: Austria, Hungary, and Czechoslovakia, as well as a kingdom of Serbs, Croats, and Slovenes that eventually became Yugoslavia, "the land of the southern Slavs."
- A restored nation of Poland emerged from territory previously controlled by Germany, Russia, and Austria-Hungary.
- The Ottoman Empire was reduced to Istanbul and a small part of Asia Minor.
- Greece occupied the western part of Asia Minor.

Wherever the Allies drew new borders, many people protested that they had been left on the wrong side of the line. Many Germans and Hungarians found themselves ruled by Italians, Poles, Czechs, or Romanians. In all, more than 20 million people in eastern and central Europe

A French political cartoon shows (left to right) David Lloyd George, Georges Clemenceau, and Woodrow Wilson surveying a "new world" created by the Treaty of Versailles.

Europe After World War I, c. 1923

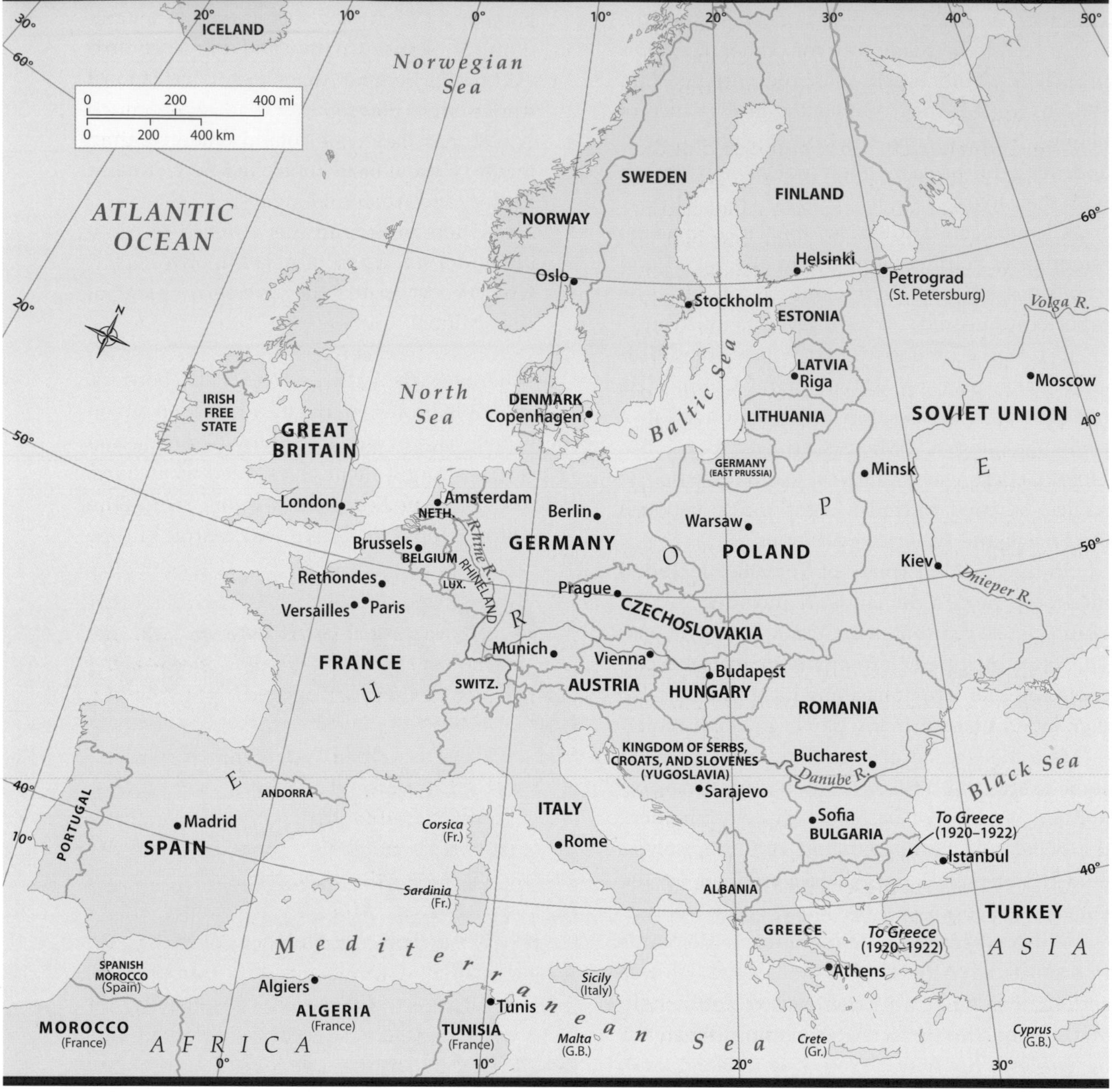

lived as minorities in nations to which they felt no allegiance. Many of those people had fought in the Great War out of feelings of nationalism and a desire for self-determination. Their anger over the new postwar borders sowed seeds for future conflicts.

Beyond Europe, many of the Arabs who had fought against the Ottomans failed to win their freedom immediately after the war. Instead, they found themselves living in territories called mandates. These mandates were administered by Britain and France, which were supposed to prepare them for self-government. As you'll learn in a later chapter, the Arab people living in these mandates resented this arrangement and longed for independence.

Meanwhile, in southern and eastern Africa, the British took over what had been German colonies. In western Africa, former German possessions went to the French. These changes also sowed seeds of resentment.

German Response to the Treaty

As you've seen, the Treaty of Versailles was the result of a compromise among the conflicting views of different Allies. At no time in the working out of this compromise did the Central Powers have any say.

The Germans, bitter and humiliated at their defeat, saw nothing just about the Treaty of Versailles. They complained that the Allies had not included them in the treaty talks, but had just showed them the finished product and told them to sign it. According to one British diplomat, when the representatives of the victorious powers were all seated at the signing ceremony, "the German delegates were brought in; they passed close to me; they looked like prisoners brought in for sentence...."

The terms dictated by the Treaty of Versailles made many Germans feel anything but peaceful. Indeed, they seethed with vengeful anger and looked forward to the chance to strike back in another war. As a German general told one of his countrymen, "Since we Germans were summoned to Versailles and the Allies did not come to Berlin, we can easily play down at home the extent of our military defeat. We should be grateful to the Allies for this oversight. Thanks to it, we'll be able one day to resume and conclude this war. I'll make it my business to see that we shall then be in a position to make up once and for all for all of our present misfortunes. In the final battle we shall be the victors."

American Isolationism

By 1920, the Great War had been over for more than a year. And yet in many ways peace had not yet come.

The wreckage of war left people in Europe with a deep sense of anger, loss, and failure. Disputes over power and territory often erupted into violence. Across the continent, governments faced coups, plots, and threats of revolution.

In the United States, Americans felt more disillusioned than triumphant. Americans opened their newspapers and saw pictures of the death and devastation. They saw young men coming home with missing arms and legs, or with lungs ruined by gas attacks. The veterans told horrifying stories of fighting on the front. People asked: What had it all been for?

President Wilson had said the United States had gone to war to make the world "safe for democracy." But many Americans found it hard to believe that the fighting had done much good. As far as they were concerned, the United States would have been better off staying out of Europe's problems and wars.

Americans were ready to get on with their own lives and with the business of their own country. They wanted to put the quarreling nations of Europe out of mind. Even though the United States had become one of the world's leading economic powers, with American businesses thriving in markets around the globe, the American people embraced *isolationism*, a policy of withdrawal from world affairs.

Woodrow Wilson still hoped that his League of Nations could help make a better world. He traveled the country, giving speech after speech, trying to convince his countrymen that the League was a good idea. But most citizens met his appeals with skeptical stares. As the president pushed himself in his campaign for the League of Nations, his health, which had never been good, failed. He suffered a massive stroke.

The U.S. Senate reflected popular opinion and refused to ratify the Treaty of Versailles. But more than popular opinion swayed the Senate — party politics were also at work. When President Wilson, who was a Democrat, had gone to Versailles to negotiate peace, he had taken only fellow Democrats with him. Republican senators — who were in the majority in Congress — refused to support the Treaty of Versailles. This meant the United States, now one of the leading powers in the world, would not join the League of Nations. Without the United States, the League was doomed to failure.

Although his health was shattered, Wilson vowed to fight on for his dream. But it was clear his time had passed. He left the presidency knowing that he had helped pull the world through the Great War, but also fearing that more bloodshed lay ahead. "What the Germans used were toys compared with what they would use in the next war," he worried.

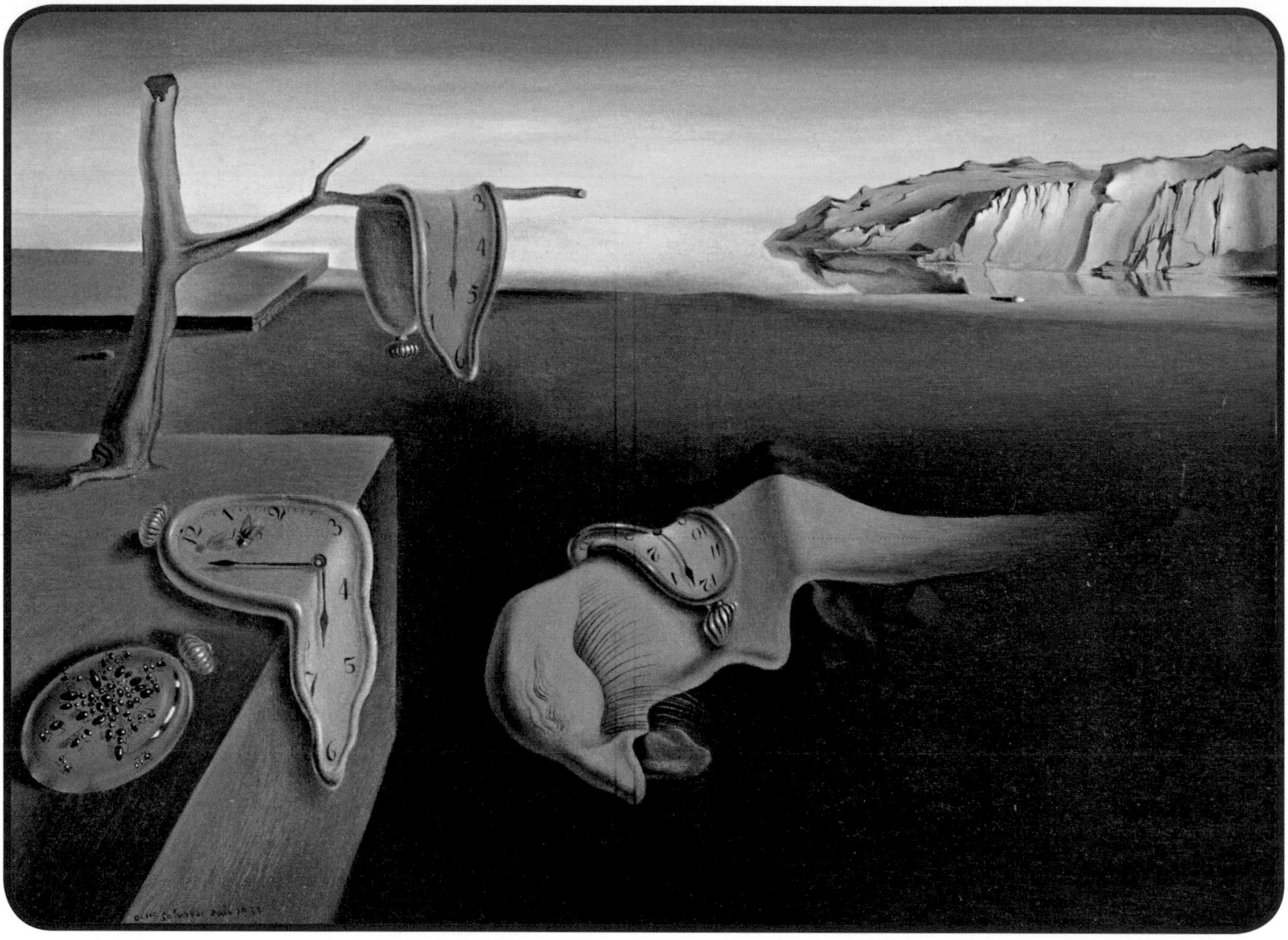

Surrealist Salvador Dalí painted *The Persistence of Memory* in 1931. The Spanish artist often distorted familiar objects like watches, and placed them in dreamlike or nightmarish settings. Dalí's upside-down face can be seen in profile under the watch. Following the Great War, many artists, like Dalí, searched for new meaning in an uncertain world.

Terrible Uncertainty: Art and Belief After the War

Day by day, month by month, year by year, the death count of the Great War increased into the millions. Even this, however, paled before the fatal power of an influenza epidemic. This disease, which raged across six continents in 1918 and 1919, was a *pandemic*, an epidemic that spread worldwide. It killed between 50 million and 100 million people, causing even more deaths than the Great War itself.

The figures were staggering: 20 million dead in India, uncounted millions in China, half a million dead in the United States, more than 400,000 in France, 250,000 in Japan, 200,000 in Britain, 12,000 in Australia, whole villages wiped out in Alaska and Africa. Steam shovels dug mass graves to bury the dead.

First the Great War, and now this awful pandemic—what was the world coming to?

The French poet Paul Valery said this about the decades after World War I: "The storm has died away and still we are restless, uneasy, as if the storm were about to break. Almost all the affairs of men remain in a terrible uncertainty."

In the industrialized Western world, the twentieth century had dawned with such optimism and confidence. But since 1914, so many horrible things had happened that people wondered whether it was possible to influence, let alone control, the course of human events. Reason seemed to play a questionable role in human affairs, and progress seemed far from certain.

In the years leading up to World War I, some artists had already begun to question the direction of human history. Turn back to page 76 to take another look at the *Apocalyptic Landscape* painted by Ludwig Meidner. This landscape is far from a pleasant rural scene; it's more like a nightmare in paint. It was painted in 1913, on the eve of the Great War. Meidner seemed to be sensing the tremors warning of a great catastrophe to come. His style, known as Expressionism, shows the world filtered though his emotions—in this case, anxiety, sorrow, terror.

In this chapter, we'll examine how some artists, composers, and writers—just before and after the Great War—explored creative paths that led in new directions, sometimes startling, sometimes disturbing.

Art and Reality: Dada Mocks "Lovely Idiocies"

In the early years of the twentieth century, some artists radically redefined the relation between art and reality. Pablo Picasso and Wassily Kandinsky

Cut with the Dada Kitchen Knife through the Last Weimar Beer-Belly Cultural Epoch by the German Dadaist artist Hannah Höch, 1919

Many Manifestos

The Dadaists were fond of issuing manifestos—assertive public declarations of their opinions. Dada manifestos were full of provocative, outrageous statements. In his January 1921 manifesto, Tristan Tzara wrote:

> If you have serious ideas about life,
> If you make artistic discoveries
> and if all of a sudden your head
> begins to crackle with laughter,
> If you find all your ideas useless and
> ridiculous, know that
> *IT IS DADA BEGINNING TO SPEAK TO YOU*

A Dada manifesto issued in 1918 in Germany ended by proclaiming, "To be against this manifesto is to be a Dadaist!"

(presented in the second volume of *The Human Odyssey*) rejected the longstanding idea that art should mirror nature. Indeed, in Picasso's Cubist paintings, it was as though he held a shattered mirror up to nature, breaking reality into an array of sharp-edged fragments. Kandinsky's abstract pictures were full of bold colors and strange shapes, with little if any resemblance to anything existing in reality. (See page 122.)

After the war, in response to a world in which the old certainties seemed lost or shattered, many artists altered, questioned, or simply abandoned reality in their works. One group of artists asked, "What is reality?" and answered, in effect, "Sheer idiocy and chaos." In the words of Tristan Tzara, one of the founders of the artistic movement called Dada, "[Dada] says to you: There is Humanity and the lovely idiocies which have made it happy to this advanced age."

The Dadaists looked at the ruins of World War I and responded with a bitter laugh. If this is what modern civilization has brought us, they thought, then the best thing art can do is undermine, subvert, and mock everything about modern civilization, including art itself.

Dada was a kind of anti-art. In a typical Dada gesture, in response to a call for works to be exhibited in an art show, the French artist Marcel Duchamp submitted a work titled *Fountain*. It was a porcelain urinal, signed by the artist, but under the name "R. Mutt." The organizers of the show chose not to exhibit Duchamp's *Fountain*.

Surrealism Taps the Unconscious

In its eagerness to tear down all that had been art, Dada could only go so far. But out of the impulses behind Dada there emerged another artistic movement more intent on shaping a new vision. This movement was called Surrealism.

The term *Surrealism* was coined in 1924 by a French poet, André Breton (breh-TAWN), as a shortened form of "super realism." Surrealist writers and artists tried to explore what they thought was the deeper reality of the unconscious mind.

The Surrealists were influenced by the theories of the Austrian physician Sigmund Freud, a pioneer in the field of psychology. Freud said that human behavior is not always a matter of conscious, rational choice. He believed that the human mind has different parts. With the conscious mind, the reasonable and reasoning part, we think and solve problems. But, said Freud, another part of the mind—the unconscious—is filled with powerful instincts and strong urges that shape our actions, even though we are not aware of their power.

Surrealist writers and artists wanted to tap the unconscious mind for access to what they thought was a deeper, truer reality. In a 1924 "Manifesto of Surrealism," Breton rejected reason, which he and others believed had led civilization into the madness of war. Breton wrote that the Surrealist artist aimed "to express…the actual functioning of thought…in the absence of any control exercised by reason, exempt from any aesthetic or moral concern."

What would a Surrealist poem sound like? Consider how one of Breton's poems begins: "The timetable of hollow flowers and prominent cheekbones invites us to leave volcanic salt shakers for birdbaths. On a red checkerboard napkin the days of the year are arranged. The air is no longer as pure, the road no longer as wide as the famous bugle."

What would a Surrealist painting look like? Consider the work of Salvador Dalí. Dalí read Freud's work on the unconscious mind and on dreams. He read Breton's poems. He said he wanted his work to be like "handmade color photography of concrete irrationality." In his Surrealist paintings, familiar objects like clocks and cranes are meticulously rendered, but sometimes distorted, and often placed in unreal settings, both dreamlike and nightmarish. In *The Persistence of Memory*, pocket watches hang limply in an eerie landscape. The painting is like a glimpse into the realm of dreams and the unconscious. (See page 118.)

"Things Fall Apart"

In 1920, the Irish poet William Butler Yeats published words that can be read as, in part, a response to the terrible uncertainties of the twentieth century. In these lines from "The Second Coming," Yeats presents a dark vision of a chaotic world with little prospect of hope:

Things fall apart; the center cannot hold;
Mere anarchy is loosed upon the world,
The blood-dimmed tide is loosed,
and everywhere
The ceremony of innocence is drowned;
The best lack all conviction, while the worst
Are full of passionate intensity.

James Joyce and the Stream of Consciousness

While Breton, Dalí, and other Surrealists tapped their unconscious minds for dreamlike images, some writers tried to chart the flow of the mind in a technique called stream of consciousness. The Irish novelist James Joyce took the technique of stream of consciousness to new lengths in fiction.

Joyce's most famous novel, *Ulysses*, published in 1922, is set in the city of Dublin. It follows three central characters through a single day. Joyce structured the novel to parallel the narrative of the *Odyssey*, Homer's great epic poem from ancient Greece. The ancient myth provides an underlying framework for Joyce's experiments with language.

In *Ulysses*, as one critic put it, Joyce used words to capture "the mind of man in all its apparent inconsequence and confusion, its mixture of memory of the past and attention to the present, of things thought, things imagined, things felt and things experienced in the subconscious." *Ulysses* ends with many pages of one character's unpunctuated and uninterrupted thoughts:

> ...frseeeeeeeefronnnng train somewhere whistling the strength those engines have in them like big giants and the water rolling all over and out them all sides like the end of Loves old sweetsonnnng the poor men that have to be out all night from their wives and families in those roasting engines....

James Joyce became one of the most influential writers of the twentieth century. His example encouraged other writers to experiment with language and push the boundaries of storytelling into new literary forms.

After attending a concert of Arnold Schoenberg's music, artist Wassily Kandinsky painted *Impression III (Concert)*. Kandinsky often thought of his painting as having rhythm and mood, like music. He once compared painting to the music of a piano: "Color is the key. The eye is the hammer. The soul is the piano, with many strings."

Rethinking Music: Stravinsky and Schoenberg

Some music historians like to say that modern music began in Paris in 1913 with the premiere of a ballet called *The Rite of Spring*. The music for the ballet was composed by the Russian composer Igor Stravinsky. When the audience first heard the music — by turns eerie, harsh, fierce, wild, pounding, like an eruption in sound of dark, irrational forces — some hissed and booed. When they saw the dancers leaping jerkily in response to the music's violent rhythms, some shouted and whistled. Fistfights broke out in the crowd.

Although many in that first audience rejected Stravinsky's *The Rite of Spring*, the music strongly influenced other modern composers. And in time, people learned not just to accept but to enjoy Stravinsky's music. (Indeed, in 1940, the American filmmaker Walt Disney used *The Rite of Spring* as one of the major works in his animated film, *Fantasia*.)

The musical innovations of another modern composer, Arnold Schoenberg (SHUHRN-buhrg), have not achieved the same popular acceptance, although they did influence other composers. Schoenberg had grown up in Vienna, Austria, a city sometimes called the capital of classical music. During their careers, the greatest classical composers — Haydn, Mozart, Beethoven, and Schubert — had all worked in Vienna, composing, conducting, or performing. Vienna also welcomed Johannes Brahms, the composer who carried on the tradition of Beethoven.

At first Schoenberg was strongly influenced by the style of Brahms. But he began to explore strange new harmonies in his music. Audiences accustomed to the flowing melodies of Mozart and Schubert were put off by Schoenberg's compositions. His music became increasingly *atonal* (ay-TOH-nuhl), which means it had no key, and was not centered on any specific musical tone.

While it is difficult to convey in words what music "sounds like," the painter Wassily Kandinsky rendered his vision of Schoenberg's music in *Impression III (Concert)*, which he painted after attending a concert of Schoenberg's music. Kandinsky and Schoenberg (who himself painted) exchanged many letters in which they discussed their ideas about art.

After serving briefly in the Austrian army in World War I, Schoenberg went back to composing. He developed a method of composition called twelve-tone music, which worked through a careful arrangement of notes in numerical patterns. The method is also known as serialism, because the music is based on a special series of interrelated tones.

To many music lovers, twelve-tone music sounded discordant. But other composers, who were Schoenberg's devoted students, saw it as genius. The music of Schoenberg and his followers is sometimes referred to as the Second Viennese School.

Between the Second Viennese School and the music of earlier composers associated with Vienna, there is a stark contrast worth noting. These earlier composers — Haydn, Mozart, Beethoven — all wrote music that was widely enjoyed in its time. Large crowds flocked to hear a new Mozart opera or the latest symphony by Beethoven. Their music was popular music — it was sung at home and hummed by people in the streets. In contrast, the atonal and twelve-tone works of Schoenberg and his followers have never attracted a wide audience. Their highly abstract, intellectual schemes appealed to some other musicians, but left the average listener puzzled. The challenging complexity of this modern music — indeed, of much modern art — shrank the audience for such art. As the public turned to more popular culture, many modern artists found themselves addressing each other and a relatively small group of scholars.

America's Roaring Twenties

In Europe, the Great War left behind death, destruction, and poverty. In the United States, it was a different story. The United States had been spared the physical ruin of the war and enjoyed an economic boom in the decade that followed.

In the Roaring Twenties, so named because the U.S. economy "roared," Americans switched on their radios — the newest form of entertainment — and listened to swinging jazz music. Many took to the streets in automobiles, which had become more affordable as they rolled off Henry Ford's assembly lines. Crowds bought tickets for the movie theaters, where silent film stars like Charlie Chaplin kept audiences laughing. When the "talkies" — movies with sound — began in the late 1920s, even more Americans fell in love with the movies.

In the wake of the Great War, the standards of American social decorum and moral life changed. Young ladies once constrained by corsets and chaperones became flappers who dared to show their legs, bob their hair, and drive

A flapper and her friend do the Charleston, a lively dance of the Roaring Twenties featured on a 1926 *Life* magazine cover.

automobiles by themselves. Young men took off in flying machines and danced to ragtime music. The spirit of the times is captured in these lyrics by the American songwriter Cole Porter:

> *In olden days a glimpse of stocking*
> *Was looked on as something shocking,*
> *But now, God knows,*
> *Anything goes.*

The Jazz Age

The Roaring Twenties in America are also known as the Jazz Age. The name comes from the vibrant new American music that got its start in the cultural melting pot of New Orleans. There, African American musicians mixed African rhythms with European musical traditions, marching band music, the jaunty swing of ragtime, and more. As these musicians migrated north to Chicago, New York, Saint Louis, and other cities, they took jazz with them.

Jazz became the music of choice for the postwar young generation. They danced to it in nightclubs and listened to it on the radio and on phonograph records. As the popularity of jazz grew, so did outcries against the new music. One professor described jazz as "an irritation of the nerves of hearing, a sensual teasing of the strings of physical passion." A New York newspaper warned that because of jazz, "Moral disaster is coming to hundreds of young American girls."

Blues singer Mamie Smith and her Jazz Hounds were one of the popular bands of the Jazz Age.

That didn't stop people from lining up to get into the Cotton Club in Harlem, a largely African American section of New York City. There, in the late 1920s, crowds danced to the music of Duke Ellington's band. In the segregated club, the crowds were white; the musicians were black.

In European cities, especially Paris, some African American musicians found less racial tension and division. They settled in Europe and brought jazz with them. It wasn't long before this distinctively American music became popular on the international scene. Jazz influenced the work of major European composers, such as Igor Stravinsky and Maurice Ravel. In America, the songwriter and composer George Gershwin merged jazz techniques with classical forms in a piano concerto that has become a modern favorite, *Rhapsody in Blue*.

The Lost Generation

For some, the glittering festivities of the Roaring Twenties had a desperate edge, like an attempt to drown the sorrows of the past decade in a binge of frantic partying. Many of the young American soldiers who had gone off to fight in the Great War returned home bitter and disillusioned. They had lived through poison gas, muddy trenches, and the death of friends. They had longed for the safe familiarity of home, but once back, they felt like strangers in a strange land. They asked themselves: Did their sacrifice have any meaning? What was the point of it? What was the point of anything?

Such questions haunted a young American writer named Ernest Hemingway. He had served as a Red Cross ambulance driver in the war. Only a few weeks after arriving in Europe, Hemingway was seriously wounded by a mortar shell that killed one soldier and blew the legs off another.

After the war, Hemingway returned to America. Like others back from the war, he felt uncomfortable and out of place—the war had changed him, but home remained relatively unchanged. Hemingway, an aspiring writer, took a job with a newspaper that sent him to Paris as a correspondent. There he joined a growing group of expatriate artists and writers.

An *expatriate* is someone who has willingly left his or her own country to live in a foreign land.

With his new bride, Hemingway settled in a cheap apartment in the part of Paris called the Left Bank.He filed reports for his newspaper and worked on writing his first stories. He often visited Gertrude Stein, an American writer whose home in Paris served as a hub for artists and writers. It was Stein who once said to her young visitor, "All of you young people who served in the war, you are all a lost generation."

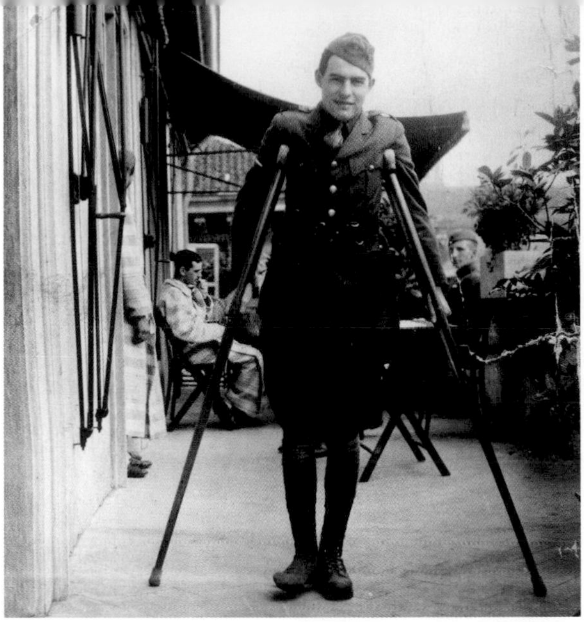

Ernest Hemingway recovered from war wounds and became part of "the Lost Generation" that survived the Great War.

"Soldier's Home"

A Page from the Past

Ernest Hemingway developed a prose style for which he has become well known: direct, understated, terse, powerful. You can see this style at work in one of his early stories, "Soldier's Home." In the excerpt below, Hemingway describes a young solider named Krebs, who returns from the fighting in Europe to his small-town home in Oklahoma. Hemingway's description of Krebs captures the disillusionment and alienation felt by many returning soldiers.

At first Krebs…did not want to talk about the war at all. Later he felt the need to talk but no one wanted to hear about it. His town had heard too many atrocity stories to be thrilled by actualities. Krebs found that to be listened to at all he had to lie, and after he had done this twice he, too, had a reaction against the war and against talking about it. A distaste for everything that had happened to him in the war set in because of the lies he had told….

Krebs acquired the nausea in regard to experience that is the result of untruth or exaggeration, and when he occasionally met another man who had really been a soldier and they talked a few minutes in the dressing room at a dance he fell into the easy pose of the old soldier among other soldiers: that he had been badly, sickeningly frightened all the time. In this way he lost everything….

He did not want to tell any more lies. It wasn't worth it.

He did not want any consequences. He did not want any consequences ever again. He wanted to live along without consequences.

Hemingway pretended to dislike the label, but he and other writers of his generation — including F. Scott Fitzgerald, Ezra Pound, John Dos Passos, and Hart Crane — understood what Stein meant. They had been changed by the war. The values they had grown up with seemed empty in the postwar world.

In an epigraph to his first novel, *The Sun Also Rises*, published in 1926, Hemingway quoted Stein's words. In so doing, he fixed a name to the generation that had survived the war only to confront the terrible uncertainties that followed — the Lost Generation.

Challenges to Christianity

For many people, the postwar sense of uncertainty fueled doubts about the Christian faith, which had long shaped the lives of many in the Western world.

Even before the Great War, Christianity had faced several challenges, especially in Europe. During the Industrial Revolution, masses of people had moved from villages to cities. In leaving their villages, they left behind churches that had been centers of community life, involved in the lives of individuals from baptism to burial. In the hectic, crowded cities of Europe, however, churches had a difficult time meeting the needs of rapidly growing urban populations. Religion became less important in the lives of many Europeans.

The destruction of the Great War brought more disillusionment about religion. If this is what the world is coming to, many Europeans thought, then what good is religion doing for humanity? Middle class workers found more relief in new forms of entertainment, such as listening to the radio or going to a movie, than in attending church.

Scientists continued to make findings that did not accord with many traditional Christian beliefs. As scientists explained the workings of nature, they offered rational explanations for phenomena once considered miraculous. Charles Darwin's theories, in particular, sparked strong opposition from some religious leaders. His theories seemed to undermine the idea of divine creation. If natural selection was responsible for the creation and destruction of species, what role did that leave for God?

Some modern philosophers raised more doubts. Karl Marx had called religion the "opium of the people." In the late nineteenth century, another German philosopher, Friedrich Nietzsche (NEE-chee), waged a vigorous campaign against religion in general and Christianity in particular. (He also criticized traditional morality and most of Western philosophy from the Greeks onward.) Nietzsche, an atheist, claimed, "God is dead." For Nietzsche, this meant that the idea of God no longer had any moral authority in the modern world. Nietzsche saw Christianity as a religion for the weak, for those without sufficient power and will to forge their own values.

Sigmund Freud, the pioneer of psychology, said that religion is something invented by mankind to fulfill a need. "Religion is an illusion and it derives its strength from the fact that it falls within our instinctual desires," Freud wrote.

In 1922, T.S. Eliot, an American expatriate poet living in England, published a poem called "The Waste Land." The poem depicts a postwar world that is emotionally exhausted and spiritually desolate, lacking hope or faith. In this excerpt, Eliot describes a dry, barren physical landscape that suggests his vision of the modern world as a spiritual wasteland:

What are the roots that clutch,
what branches grow
Out of this stony rubbish? Son of man,
You cannot say, or guess, for you know only
A heap of broken images, where the sun beats,
And the dead tree gives no shelter,
the cricket no relief,
And the dry stone no sound of water.

Eliot himself held on to his religious beliefs. Millions of Europeans, however, decided that they could lead their lives without the daily influence of Christianity. Church attendance in Europe declined as many people could no longer find in Christianity the answers they sought in a fragmented postwar world.

An Age of Doubt

In history, certain periods and decades take on an emotional life of their own. For example, historians often refer to the optimistic years of the late nineteenth and early twentieth century in Europe as *la Belle Epoque* or "the Beautiful Age," a time when art, architecture, and innovation seemed to blend harmoniously. But for many artists and intellectuals, the time following World War I is remembered as a time of doubt, uncertainty, and despair.

So much had been lost. Did individual choice matter? Did human reason play any role in the affairs of men? Were dark, unconscious realities the greater reality? As the 1930s unfolded, those questions seemed ever more pressing.

Alexander Fleming's Miracle Drug

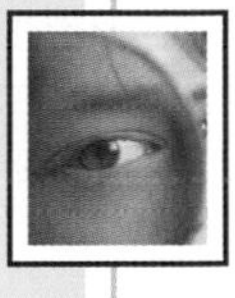

Historical Close-up

Despite the sense of uncertainty that characterized the years following the Great War, there were some tremendous advances in the areas of science and technology. The theories of Albert Einstein (about whom you'll read more later) led scientists to revise the way they viewed the workings of the universe. Astronomers such as Edward Hubble looked into the eyepieces of huge new telescopes and discovered remote galaxies. The American physicist Robert Goddard, as well as scientists in Germany and the USSR, experimented with small rockets. Improving technologies brought airplanes that crossed oceans and radios that broadcast music, ball games, adventure shows, and other kinds of entertainment.

In medicine, one of the most important advances was the development of antibiotics, miracle drugs that saved millions of lives. Penicillin was the first antibiotic. Before it, even a minor illness or injury — a sore throat or scratch on the arm — could lead to death. The work of a persistent Scottish doctor named Alexander Fleming changed all that.

In 1906, Alexander Fleming, a young doctor from Scotland, took a job in the inoculation department at St. Mary's Hospital in London. With other researchers, he studied diseases and developed vaccines. When troops started marching across Europe at the beginning of the Great War, Fleming left the hospital to join the Royal Army Medical Corps, where he was assigned to a wound treatment and research center.

During the war, Fleming saw firsthand what military doctors had known for ages — that more soldiers died of disease than from the wounds they received on the battlefield. About half died from infections that began in relatively minor wounds. Even though doctors tried to clean the wounds with disinfectants, this treatment did little good for injured soldiers who had been lying in muddy trenches for days. By the time the soldiers reached a field hospital, their wounds — mixed with dirt, shrapnel, and bits of clothing — had become so infected that amputation was often the only treatment possible. Otherwise, a dangerous infection could spread through their bodies and kill them.

Scottish doctor Alexander Fleming was the first to discover the benefits of penicillin.

Determined to find a way to stop so many deaths, Fleming set up a makeshift laboratory. Peering through his microscope, he studied the bacterial cells that were causing infections.

Of the trillions of bacteria in the human body, most are helpful — for example, they aid digestion or help build capillaries that move blood through the intestines. But a tiny minority of bacteria can cause infections, which can make even a harmless-looking scratch turn fatal.

How could these infections be prevented? Fleming kept trying to answer this life-and-death question when, after the war, he returned to St. Mary's Hospital.

It was an exciting time to be a medical researcher. Recent discoveries made it possible to see inside the human body with X rays, and to understand the role of vitamins in preventing such diseases as rickets and scurvy.

One fall day in 1928, while working quietly in his lab, Fleming noticed a dirty Petri dish in which he had been growing bacteria. Green mold was growing in the contaminated dish.

There was nothing astonishing about this — unwashed, dirty dishes often get moldy — but one odd detail caught Fleming's eye. He noticed the moldy area showed no signs of the yellow bacteria.

Setting aside all other work, Fleming cut off a tiny piece of the mold, put it in a tube of sterilized broth, and began testing it. He found that, even when diluted six hundred times, his "mold juice" could kill bacterial cells. Yet it did not damage cells in the human body.

There are thousands of different molds, and Fleming didn't know which one was in his mold juice. So he took the juice to a specialist who identified the mold as *penicillium rubrum*. Fleming decided to stop calling his concoction "mold juice" and name it *penicillin*.

Fleming presented his findings at a medical conference, but none of the other doctors there showed much interest. Even the researchers who worked with Fleming refused to believe that penicillin could improve the body's natural defenses against infection.

Still, Fleming continued his experiments. He found that penicillin killed a wide range of disease-causing microbes without damaging healthy cells. But he couldn't figure out a way to grow and purify enough penicillin to be reliably useful. He asked several chemists for help, but they were stumped, too.

Meanwhile, men, women, and children continued to die of infections. One of the most feared diseases was pneumonia. Pneumonia often started out as a sore throat, cough, or chill, but then quickly turned into a deadly inflammation of the lungs. It killed millions of people around the world every year.

Fleming felt sure his penicillin could cure pneumonia and other infections if someone could only figure out how to extract and purify the active ingredient. Finally, in 1939, at a conference in New York, he was cheered by news of American researchers who were studying penicillin.

After he returned to England, Fleming learned of some Oxford University researchers who had found a way to purify and stabilize a penicillin that was thousands of times stronger than his original "mold juice." He stopped by to congratulate them. They were surprised. He had been working in obscurity for so long they thought he was dead! But Fleming was elated to find that other scientists recognized the promise of penicillin and were making progress in their research.

With another war threatening Europe, the Oxford researchers completed their work in the United States. The penicillin they developed soon became known as a "miracle drug." It was the first in a class of drugs known as *antibiotics*, which can stop the growth of a wide range of bacteria.

Finally, with penicillin, sore throats and stray scratches would no longer carry the same threat of developing into fatal infections. The twentieth century saw many other medical advances, but the development of antibiotics was one of the most important, saving millions of lives and increasing life expectancy for almost everyone on the planet.

Arab nationalists attend the Paris Peace Conference in 1918. Prince Faisal, later king of Iraq, stands in front; Colonel T.E. Lawrence (Lawrence of Arabia) stands second from right in the center row.

Growing Nationalism in the Middle East

Nationalism — you've heard the term many times. Nationalism, the strong sense of attachment or belonging to one's own country, is more than an idea, more than a feeling. It goes beyond patriotism; it gets bound up with people's hopes and dreams — hopes for freedom, dreams of ruling themselves in a land of their own. It can become a powerful force, at times creative, at times destructive.

Nationalism was on the rise in the late nineteenth and early twentieth centuries. Nationalism fueled competition between European nations. It energized Meiji Japan. And it sparked unrest in the Balkan Peninsula — unrest that ignited the Great War.

During World War I, nationalism remained a powerful force, especially in lands that had long been ruled by foreign powers. Nationalists in Asia, Africa, and Europe fought to free themselves from the grip of the aging Austro-Hungarian and Ottoman empires. By the end of the war, some succeeded: For example, Czechoslovakia, Hungary, and Poland won their independence.

Nationalists in the Middle East had similar hopes. During the Great War, they fought alongside the British and French to help defeat Ottoman rulers who had long dominated much of the Middle East. They hoped that after the war, their homelands would become self-governing nations.

But the victorious European nations, which had long-standing interests in the Middle East, had other plans. The old imperial powers of Great Britain and France decided they should be in charge of running the affairs of many Middle Eastern lands. Thus, for the first time in hundreds of years, many of these Muslim kingdoms came under direct European rule. Such an arrangement did not end the ambitions of Middle Eastern nationalists. On the contrary, it made them all the more determined to succeed.

New Mandates in the Middle East

The *Middle East* — a label coined by an American naval historian — is not a precise term. It generally refers to a geographic region that includes northeast Africa and southwest Asia. On a map, the arc of the Middle East swings from Egypt through the Arabian Peninsula, then up through the Fertile Crescent into Iran (ih-RAHN) and Asia Minor.

We think of the Middle East as a single region because for centuries most of its peoples have shared a common culture. Many of the region's inhabitants speak Arabic. But the people

Other Nationalist Movements in the Middle East

Throughout the Middle East during the 1920s and 1930s, there were many more nationalist uprisings, such as one against the British in Iraq in 1920, and one against the French in Syria in 1925. In each case, Britain and France granted more rights to their mandates. Sometimes they even granted independence, but they kept their armed forces ready to intervene. Iraq, for example, gained independence in 1932 under King Faisal.

identity from the time of Greek conquest by Alexander the Great and Roman conquest by Julius Caesar. Husayn believed that Britain's presence in Egypt was a new phase of this Western component of Egypt's identity.

Taha Husayn hoped his countrymen could benefit from this latest Western influence. He called for "Egyptian education to be firmly based on a certain harmony between these three elements." Many new leaders shared this vision of Egyptian national identity. They thought Egypt could build on the glory of its ancient past and be grounded in Islam while integrating Western learning and adopting the principle of separation of church and state in government.

Others in Egypt disagreed. In 1928, an Egyptian teacher named Hasan al-Banna (hah-SAHN ahl-bahn-NAH) formed an organization called the Muslim Brotherhood. Al-Banna denounced not only Western influence but also anyone who did not follow the Muslim faith as he defined it. He thought all governments should follow strict Islamic law.

Secular means relating to worldly concerns rather than religious concerns.

Members of the Muslim Brotherhood rejected the constitution that Egypt had adopted just five years before. They did not want a nation influenced by Western ideas and values. They denounced the idea of a secular nation that separates church and state. They called for a government run according to Shari'ah, the Islamic legal and moral code. Muslim peoples, they said, should accept nothing less than complete Islamic rule.

The start of the Muslim Brotherhood marked the rise of a new movement in the Arab world called Islamism. Islamists believed that Muslim teaching and law should guide all parts of Islamic society.

Islamism attracted many followers in Muslim lands that had experienced rapid change from their contact with the non-Muslim, industrialized West. Islamists longed for a pure Islamic state, which they thought would restore harmony to their lands. Islamists were often at odds with the new nationalist movements that accepted the principle of separation of church and state.

Not just in Egypt but throughout the Middle East, nationalism and Islamism were growing responses to foreign domination.

Ibn Saud Unites Arabia

On the Arabian Peninsula, other events strengthened the Islamist movement. Before the war, the peninsula had been divided into different kingdoms, some of which were independent and some of which were under Ottoman rule. The interior and eastern sections were ruled by an independent and increasingly powerful family called the House of Saud. The western section, which was home to Islam's two holiest cities, Mecca and Medina, was ruled by the Ottomans. They appointed Sharif Hussein (shahr-EEF hoo-SAYN), an Arabian noble, as ruler since his family claimed descent from the Prophet Muhammad.

Although the Ottomans had put Sharif Hussein in charge, he felt no obligation to them. In World War I, Hussein cooperated with the British and French, hoping to oust the Ottomans entirely. For his help, he fully expected to be named "King of the Arabs" when the fighting ended. He envisioned himself at the head of a great independent empire that would include Egypt, Syria, and Jordan. Instead, at the war's end, he had to content himself with his part of the Arabian Peninsula, although his sons became kings of Iraq and Jordan.

The annual pilgrimage to Mecca draws crowds around the Kaaba, a sacred shrine. Muslims are supposed to journey to Mecca and visit the Kaaba at least once before they die.

In his own realm, Sharif Hussein was in for a rude awakening. For years, the rival Saud family had been building their armies and expanding their territory. The House of Saud also gained the support of many Arabs by aiding an Islamic religious movement known as Wahhabism (wah-HAH-bih-zuhm).

Wahhabism urged strict observance of Islamic law. Wahhabists believed that outside influences had corrupted the Islamic faith. They thought that Muslims should model their society on the way people had lived more than 1,000 years earlier. They considered themselves warriors for the "true" Islam. They sometimes destroyed places they considered to be false shrines. They even killed fellow Muslims who did not meet their standards of Islamic purity.

The Wahhabist tribal leader Ibn Saud hungrily eyed Sharif Hussein's kingdom. He wanted it because it contained the holy sites of Mecca and Medina. When Sharif Hussein declared that Wahhabi pilgrims could not visit the Muslim holy sites, Ibn Saud saw an excuse for action. His long military preparation paid off. He caught Sharif Hussein by surprise. Hussein believed that no one would ever challenge a member of Muhammad's own family, but Ibn Saud did just that, and he won a quick victory.

By 1926, the Wahhabist House of Saud controlled the Arabian Peninsula. Ibn Saud announced he would protect the holy sites for all Muslims. Six years later, in 1932, Ibn Saud named the lands under his control the Kingdom of Saudi Arabia. He molded Saudi Arabia into a Muslim state, governed by strict adherence to Muslim law. Unlike Egypt, Saudi Arabia would have no secular constitution.

Wahhabist tribal leader Ibn Saud won control of the Arabian Peninsula and founded the Kingdom of Saudi Arabia.

Mustafa Kemal Leads Turkey to Independence

In one part of the Middle East, nationalists founded a country free of Western control but friendly to many Western traditions and ideas. That country, Turkey, lay in the heart of the old Ottoman Empire. The determined nationalist who led Turkey to independence was Mustafa Kemal (MOO-stah-fah keh-MAHL). He defeated European armies who wanted to divide the country, and then almost single-handedly forged a modern republic.

Mustafa Kemal had grown up in Salonika, a port city in northern Greece, which was part of the Ottoman Empire. His father insisted that his son go to one of the new secular schools to acquaint him with European thinking and learning. Kemal later went to Istanbul to study at the Ottoman War College. There he distinguished himself as a superb student and an independent thinker.

At the War College, many young Turkish cadets chafed under the rule of the sultan, whom they believed to be weak and corrupt. They wanted a strong, honest government, and they worried the sultan could not lead Turkey forward.

Sultan is a title given to some Muslim rulers. The ruler of the Ottoman Empire was a sultan.

Although the cadets were forbidden to read anything but official textbooks, many secretly read works about the French Revolution and its Declaration of Human Rights. Mustafa Kemal and some friends started an underground newspaper calling for the sultan's overthrow. But all this went on behind the scenes. In 1905, Kemal graduated as a captain and was considered a promising young officer.

During World War I, Kemal led the Ottoman forces that defeated an attempted Allied invasion of Turkey at Gallipoli, near Istanbul, the capital city of the Ottoman Empire. He became a national hero, and grateful Turks pronounced him "the Savior of Istanbul."

Kemal might have saved Istanbul, but the Allies won the war. In 1918, British, French, and Italian troops set up a military administration in Istanbul. The Greeks, Turkey's historic enemy, occupied parts of Asia Minor.

Mustafa Kemal was sickened by his country's decline. He was disgusted when the sultan signed a treaty with the Allies that shrank the once-grand Ottoman Empire to the city of Istanbul and only a small part of Asia Minor.

In May 1919, the defeated sultan ordered Mustafa Kemal to northern Asia Minor to put down a rebellion. Instead, Kemal began organizing a nationalist movement to resist the Allied occupation. He declared that the sultan was nothing more than a prisoner of the Allies. He told cheering throngs that he, Mustafa Kemal, would lead his countrymen to independence. With his nationalist allies, Kemal organized a provisional (that is, temporary) government with its capital in the city of Ankara. This new government's Grand National Assembly elected Kemal president.

Over the next three years, through both war and negotiation, Kemal and his nationalist forces overthrew the sultan, drove Greek and French forces from Asia Minor, and negotiated a new peace treaty with the Allies. In 1923, the war-weary Allies recognized Turkey as a sovereign nation and independent republic. The new nation covered most of Asia Minor and a small portion of southeastern Europe.

Ataturk Transforms a Nation

Mustafa Kemal looked upon his newly independent nation and declared, "The civilized world is far ahead of us. We have no choice but to catch up." He worried that a traditional Islamic nation would not be able to compete in an industrial world dominated by the West. So he took immediate steps to transform Turkish life.

Some of those steps were symbolic. Most Turks had only one name, a given name. ("Mustafa" was a nickname that Kemal had acquired early in his life.) Kemal ordered all Turks to choose a family name in addition to their given name. Turkey's Grand National Assembly awarded their new leader his new name. They named him Ataturk, meaning "Father of the Turks." From then on, Mustafa Kemal was known as Kemal Ataturk, and usually just Ataturk.

In the 1920s and 1930s, Ataturk's new government took one revolutionary step after another. It changed the alphabet from Arabic letters to Latin letters similar to those used in the West.

It created a public education system that taught students in the Turkish language, and it prohibited most traditional Islamic schools. The Turkish government also worked to limit the influence of Muslim clergymen. The Assembly decided that Islamic law would not be the basis of government, but that Turkey would be a secular nation with a constitution separating church and state.

The *Gregorian* calendar is named after the sixteenth-century pope who made it the official standard.

Ataturk convinced his nation to adopt the Gregorian calendar used by most of the Western world. Turks had been using the Muslim lunar calendar, which dated years since Muhammad's flight from Mecca to Medina. The Gregorian calendar dated years from Christ's birth. With one stroke of the government's pen, 1344 became 1925.

Ataturk also urged Turks to dress more like Westerners. He insisted that "internationally accepted civilized dress suits us, too." The government prohibited men from wearing turbans and the traditional, flat-topped head covering called the fez. It required top hats and tails for ceremonial occasions. Ataturk himself discouraged women from wearing the veil used in many Muslim countries. "Let them show their faces to the world, and see it with their eyes," he said. "Don't be afraid. Change is essential."

Under Ataturk's government, women gained new rights. The Assembly forbade the old Muslim practice of marriage to more than one woman. It gave women equal inheritance rights, in contrast to earlier laws that allowed women to receive only half a man's share. Women gained the right to enter institutions of higher learning. Turkey awarded women the right to vote in parliamentary elections in 1934, 14 years after the United States, and a decade before France. In 1935, Turkish voters elected 17 women as delegates to the Grand National Assembly.

Ataturk pushed hard to bring Turkey's economy into the industrial age. Most Turks were

Turkish leader Mustafa Kemal, known as Ataturk, urged his countrymen to embrace many Western ideas and customs, such as Western clothing, which he referred to as "international dress." Under his leadership, Turkey also adopted the Western alphabet and calendar, a constitution that recognized the separation of church and state, and greater rights for women.

farmers. Ataturk's government set up a model farm not far from the capital to show the latest techniques and modern equipment. New state banks increased loans for agriculture. Ataturk used government power and funding to build railroads and expand electric service. The state also set up factories to produce textiles, glass, and steel.

Ataturk's changes sometimes brought resistance. In 1925, Muslim Kurds in southern Turkey led a revolt to overthrow the "godless government" and restore Islamic law. Ataturk dispatched troops and declared martial law. The Turkish Assembly gave him the power to close down any organization or publication he deemed subversive. Ataturk issued orders to shut down newspapers and disband opposition political parties. Journalists were jailed and sternly warned against treason. Some members of the Muslim Brotherhood received death sentences.

Muslim Women and the Veil

For centuries, many Muslim women have worn either a full-face veil, leaving only the eyes exposed or, in modern times, a headscarf known as the hijab. The headscarf typically covers the hair, ears, and neck. In some Muslim nations, such as Saudi Arabia and Iran, all women are required to wear the hijab. Muslims still debate whether such dress is required by their faith.

In many parts of the Muslim world, women wear a headscarf known as the hijab.

Until his death in 1938, Ataturk pushed for a strong, independent Turkey. He insisted that Turkey's best hope for success in the modern world was as a secular nation. At his death in 1938, the grief-stricken Turks proclaimed him "Eternal Leader."

Reza Khan: Independence for Iran

In the 1920s, another Middle Eastern nation embarked on a nationalist and secular path. Turkey's neighbor to the southeast, Iran — or, as the Europeans called it, Persia — was an independent but weak nation at the end of World War I. Foreign powers had been interfering in Persia for centuries. Russian troops invaded in the nineteenth century, and in 1917 the Russian Revolution spilled over the border into Iran. Some communists hoped that Iran would become a new "soviet" for the USSR. The British had their eyes on Iran's oil reserves. Meanwhile, the country lapsed into chaos under the rule of an ineffective shah.

Shah is the title for the traditional ruler, or king, of Iran.

A fiercely nationalist Iranian military officer, Reza Khan (RIH-zuh kahn), decided his nation must resist foreign domination and become a strong independent state. In 1921, he marched troops into Tehran and took over the capital city. He sent the shah away on a long vacation in Europe, and then proceeded to take over as head of the government. For the next 20 years, Reza Khan controlled his nation's destiny.

Reza Khan thought that, like Turkey, his nation should become a modern, secular republic. But Iran's clergymen did not share his vision. They were appalled that Ataturk had shrunk the role of the clergy. They objected to Ataturk's insistence on republican rule. If Iran were to become a modern republic, then what role would be left for the imams and the mullahs? These clergymen were powerful figures in societies governed by Islamic law. They did not like the idea of losing their power and influence.

In Islam, an *imam* is a religious leader.

A *mullah* is an Islamic religious teacher.

Reza Khan decided to meet them halfway. He would not proclaim his nation a republic. It would be a monarchy, and he would become its new shah.

Nationalist leader Reza Khan declared Iran a constitutional monarchy, made himself shah (or king), and took the name Reza Shah Pahlavi. He ruled for more than two decades.

But he would keep an eye on the clergymen. He wanted to reduce their influence in government.

The new shah attempted to foster national pride by recalling the glory of the ancient Persian Empire. Long before Muhammad's time, Persia had been a major power. For his new dynasty, Reza Khan chose the name Pahlavi (PAH-luh-vee), which was an old name for the Persian language. As shah, he was known as Reza Shah Pahlavi. From now on, the Persian language of Farsi—not Arabic, Turkish, or Kurdish, all of which were spoken in Iran—would be Iran's official language. And because the Farsi word for Persia was "Iran," the nation's name was officially changed to Iran in 1935.

Iran Expands and Modernizes

Reza Shah believed that the key to independence was military strength. He immediately set about building up the army. He required all young men to enlist. The shah then used his large force to conquer rivals and expand Iran's territory.

Under Reza Shah, Iran modernized its transportation and education systems. The government built many new highways and roads. By the end of the 1930s, a new trans-Iranian railway connected Iran from the Persian Gulf to the Caspian Sea. It was a fabulous feat of engineering over tough terrain. The cost of transporting goods fell, which spurred the economy.

Like Ataturk, the shah closed many religious schools and made education a public responsibility. The new state-run schools taught loyalty and patriotism. The shah also thought Iran's capital needed a first-rate university. In 1934, the University of Tehran opened, and it soon started admitting women.

As in Turkey, women in Iran gained important rights and access to education. The shah himself discouraged use of the veil and even outlawed it in 1936. Reza Shah was infuriated when an imam denounced women who did not wear the veil. His armored car pulled up to the mosque of the offending preacher, and the shah personally hauled the imam off to jail. (Later, as you'll learn, Iranian women lost many of these rights and freedoms.)

Like Ataturk in Turkey, Reza Shah in Iran held enormous power and used it to stamp out dissent. And many did object to the changes the shah demanded. They violently protested against his insistence on Western-style dress in public buildings. They bitterly complained against his decree that Iranians adopt family surnames.

While the shah encouraged modernization and even "Westernization," he opposed foreign influence in his nation's affairs. Through the 1920s and 1930s, the powerful shah worked to minimize British profits, and maximize Iranian, in the oil fields. To diminish Russian influence, he outlawed the Communist Party.

Purifying a Language

The Persian language called Farsi was the native language of about half of Iran's large and diverse population. Reza Shah Pahlavi set up the Academy of Persian Language and Literature, one of whose official and practically impossible tasks was to get rid of all Farsi words of Arabic origin.

In the 1920s, European Jews increasingly settled Palestine as part of a movement known as Zionism. Like many others who relocated to Palestine, these Jewish colonists left automobiles and much modern technology behind as they established new homes in the land of their ancestors.

Palestine and the Zionist Movement

In the years following the Great War, the Middle East saw the rise of a different type of nationalist movement — the movement for a Jewish homeland in Palestine.

Palestine is a small strip of land bordering the eastern shore of the Mediterranean Sea. Palestine's location — at the point where Africa and Asia come together, just a short distance across the Mediterranean from Europe — has long made it a place where different cultures have met, sometimes peacefully, sometimes violently.

While Palestine is a small region, it is hugely important to the followers of three major religions — Judaism, Christianity, and Islam. For Jews, it is the "promised land" where Moses led the Hebrews. To Christians, it is important as the land of Jesus' birth and death. According to a widespread belief among many Muslims, it was from Palestine that Muhammad's spirit traveled to heaven. For these reasons, Palestine is often referred to as the Holy Land.

In the late 1800s and early 1900s, Arabs from the land now called Syria made up most of Palestine's population. Some of those Arabs were Christians, but most were Muslim. Most Jews in Palestine lived in and around cities like Jerusalem, and even constituted a majority in Jerusalem through much of this time.

In the late eighteenth century, European Jews began buying land in Palestine and moving there in greater numbers. They started a movement called Zionism, which aimed at establishing a Jewish state in Palestine. The word *Zion* refers to a hill in Jerusalem, where in ancient times the Israelite King David ruled, and where his son Solomon built his kingdom's holy temple.

Why did the Zionists choose Palestine as the site for a Jewish state? Not only because they considered it the Holy Land, but also because they considered it the Jewish people's ancestral homeland. They remembered that centuries before, a Jewish state had thrived there until the Romans forced most Jews out of the region.

One strong motivation behind the Zionist movement was nationalism — the Jews, like many other peoples, wanted their own state. Another motivation for Zionism was the long history of oppression of Jews. During the late nineteenth and early twentieth centuries, anti-Jewish sentiment was on the rise in Europe. Many people accused Jewish intellectuals of spreading dangerous ideas. They resented wealthy Jewish businessmen like Albert Ballin, director of Germany's Hamburg-America Line, or like the Rothschild family of bankers in France.

Sometimes the prejudice against Jews turned violent. Waves of *pogroms* — organized massacres of Jews — swept parts of Russia and Poland. Faced with such oppression, Zionists worked to establish a state in Palestine where Jews from all over the world might find refuge.

The Jews' desire for their own state received support from the British. In 1917, British Foreign Secretary Arthur Balfour issued the Balfour Declaration, which supported "a national home for the Jewish people," while also insisting that the "rights of existing non-Jewish communities in Palestine" be fully respected.

After World War I, Palestine became a mandate of Great Britain. Hopeful Zionists encouraged more Jews to move into the area. By 1922, Jews made up just over 10 percent of Palestine's population.

Lingering Tensions in the Middle East

As more Jewish immigrants arrived in Palestine hoping to establish a Jewish nation, some Arabs in the region grew alarmed. For centuries, Palestine had been inhabited mostly by Muslims, and they considered it sacred land. Arab nationalists opposed the idea of a Jewish nation and looked forward instead to an independent Palestine governed by Islamic law.

While many Arabs opposed Zionism, a few expressed support. In 1919, King Faisal of Iraq wrote, "We Arabs, especially the educated among us, look with the deepest sympathy on the Zionist movement." In the king's opinion, Zionist proposals for a Jewish state in Palestine were "moderate and proper."

Few people shared King Faisal's vision. Tensions rose in Palestine as various forces began to collide — Jewish nationalism, Arab nationalism, growing Islamism, fervent devotion to the Holy Land, age-old prejudices, and anger at old imperialist powers. As you'll read in later chapters, these tensions would give rise to bitterness and violence for decades to come.

Adolf Hitler, Nazi Germany's leader, ascends stairs at Buckeburg, Germany, to address a rally in 1934. Nazi storm troopers line his path with banners carrying the swastika, the symbol of the Nazi Party. Hitler was one of a number of ruthless dictators who rose to power in Europe during the 1920s and 1930s, a time when many people longed for strong leaders.

The Great Depression and the Rise of Dictators

In 1920, the poet William Butler Yeats wrote that "the worst are full of passionate intensity." He was not trying to predict the future, but his words describe all too well what would happen in the coming decades.

In Europe in the 1920s and 1930s, disillusioned survivors of the Great War struggled to rebuild their lives amid shattered economies and uncertainties about the future. More than anything else, they wanted security and a release from fear. Their desire was so strong that many willingly traded freedom for security. They put their destinies into the hands of leaders who promised to bring the stability and prosperity that people so desperately wanted. Because they did, some of history's worst dictators took charge in Russia, Italy, and Germany.

Europe in the Wake of War

In the Treaty of Versailles, the victorious Allies pinned all the blame for World War I on Germany. They set punishing terms intended to prevent any more German aggression. They forced Germany to disarm by giving up most of its weapons, including its dreadnoughts and air force. They limited the Germans to an army of 100,000 men—a mere fraction of its former strength.

Germany lost all the territory it had gained from Russia. France reclaimed the region of Alsace Lorraine (which it had lost to Germany in 1871). Soon afterward, France occupied part of the German Rhineland, a region rich in coal and iron. The Allies also ordered Germany to pay large reparations every year.

The Germans had no intention of paying such reparations. German leaders told their countrymen that the terms imposed on them were too severe. They said that paying the reparations would mean crippling the nation. Restless, resentful Germans still wondered why their country had lost the war.

The German government made things worse by printing new German marks to deal with rising prices and to support striking workers in French-occupied areas. It printed so much new money that the marks were soon worth little more than wastepaper. By late 1923, a single U.S. dollar could be traded for four *trillion* marks. In German restaurants, people grimly joked that they could get a cheaper meal by eating fast, because the price was rising as they chewed. Some government officials even asked to be paid in potatoes instead of cash.

The *mark* was the basic unit of German money, just as the dollar is the basic unit of U.S. money.

Even though France was one of the victors of the Great War, it was worse off than Germany. The most destructive battles had been fought in France, so the country had more rebuilding to do than any other. It had borrowed heavily from the United States during the war, and now

Stalin ordered millions of peasants, such as these women, onto huge collective farms where they became, in effect, slave laborers for the Soviet communist regime. Stalin hoped that such "collectivization" would improve the Soviet Union's food production. Those who refused to cooperate were exiled to Siberia—a punishment that often meant death.

potential rival, into exile, and later had him murdered in Mexico. By 1928, Stalin reigned supreme as the Soviet Union's dictator.

Stalin was driven by one goal — to make communism victorious, first in Russia and then elsewhere. The first step, as he saw it, was to transform the Soviet Union into an industrial power. The country was still devastated from the fighting of World War I. Stalin faced a choice. He could focus the hungry people's energies either on building factories or on growing food. He chose the factories. He decided his people must starve, if necessary.

Beginning in 1929, Stalin's troops herded some twenty million peasants into cities to work in factories. Many others were ordered onto huge "collective farms" that covered thousands of acres. The Communist Party planners hoped that these collective farms would be more efficient than millions of tiny farms. They reasoned that peasants could pool their labor and use modern equipment, such as tractors, to produce more food, which the state could use to feed factory workers.

Many peasants who owned their own land and livestock resisted this drastic plan. Rather than comply, they slaughtered their own farm animals, destroyed their own tools, and burned their own crops. Stalin declared that these troublesome peasants, who mainly lived in the fertile Ukraine, were capitalists who "must be eliminated as a class."

Any peasant caught eating his own produce was imprisoned or shot. Those who rebelled against "collectivization" were marched to Siberia.

Stalin Targets the Church

Stalin, like Lenin, was hostile to religion in general and the Russian Orthodox Church in particular. He closed and demolished churches in peasant villages, continued the persecution of priests, and used a Communist Party organization called The League of the Militant Godless to promote atheism. The League sponsored competitions to determine which group of peasants could produce more—religious peasants who had priests bless their land, or "godless peasants" who used scientific techniques. The results, of course, were a foregone conclusion.

It has been estimated that perhaps fifteen million people were thus deported, and that about three million—mostly children—died along the way. The survivors ended up in brutal prison camps where many more died.

Totalitarian Rule in the Soviet Union

Millions of peasants were, in effect, slaves on the Soviet Union's collective farms. Still, they could not produce enough food. Famine spread across much of the USSR. In the Ukraine, once the bread basket of eastern Europe, people ended up eating rats and earthworms. In 1932 and 1933, about five million people in the Ukraine died of hunger.

Some Communists quietly questioned Stalin's program, but none dared do so in public. Stalin tolerated no dissent and kept his eyes open for anyone who might challenge his leadership.

At a Communist Party meeting in 1934, one popular party official named Sergei Kirov (syir-GYAY KYEE-ruhf) gave an eloquent speech praising Stalin. But Stalin noticed that Kirov received more applause than he. An assassin soon shot Kirov on the street.

Stalin, who probably ordered the killing, exploited the murder to increase his power. He claimed that Kirov's killing revealed a vast conspiracy against the state. To meet the crisis, Stalin demanded the power to arrest anyone he deemed a threat, to try people in secret, and to execute them if he saw fit.

Stalin got his new powers and used them to undertake a so-called purge of the Communist Party. He arrested any rivals, including close comrades from the revolutionary days. He had them tortured until they agreed to confess to treasonous crimes in open court. Then he had them killed. Stalin himself signed execution orders sending hundreds of thousands of people to their deaths.

Stalin had become a totalitarian ruler, a dictator exercising almost total control over the state and the lives of its people. Across the huge country, his Communist Party told farmers and factory workers exactly what it expected them to produce.

By the 1930s, Stalin's brutal plan to create an industrial nation seemed to be succeeding. The Soviet Union was becoming an industrial powerhouse, producing steel, cars, tractors, and military goods.

Throughout the horrors, Stalin's power increased because he had mastered the art of propaganda. Government-controlled newspapers portrayed the dictator as a warm family man, the father of his people. This was a lie. But those not directly affected by Stalin's evil tactics were willing to close their eyes. At least Stalin was moving the country forward, they told themselves.

Totalitarianism

Totalitarianism is a form of government that controls almost every aspect of people's lives, including political, economic, cultural, religious, and social activities. Totalitarian regimes are often headed by dictators with absolute power. In order to keep power, totalitarian governments try to bind their people in some shared effort, such as war. Or they may try to unify the people through fear or hatred of something, such as a foreign enemy. Totalitarian governments are quick to stamp out anyone or anything that opposes them, and often maintain secret police forces to root out dissenters. They often try to manipulate the information their citizens get through government-controlled newspaper, radio, and television.

Mussolini's Fascism

Elsewhere in Europe, a kind of totalitarianism called fascism (FA-shi-zuhm) was taking root. In the 1930s, fascist governments glorified the nation above all else. They insisted that all citizens put the interests of the state ahead of their individual interests.

Fascism comes from the Latin *fasces*, a ceremonial bundle of rods wrapped around an ax, carried by officials in ancient Rome as a symbol of state power and strength through unity.

Fascist thinking grew out of feelings of nationalism that had swept Europe in the decades leading up to World War I. After the chaos of the war, people desperately longed for order,

Benito Mussolini marches with his thuggish Blackshirts at a demonstration in Rome in 1922.

stability, and something to believe in. Power-hungry leaders channeled the people's desperation into the idea of devotion to their state. Nationalism, taken to an extreme, rotted into fascism.

Modern Europe's first fascist dictator was the Italian Benito Mussolini (MOO-soh-LEE-nee). The son of a blacksmith, Mussolini had fought for the Italian army during World War I and attained the rank of corporal. After the war, Italy, like other European countries, suffered from economic depression and social unrest. Mussolini saw his chance. He extolled the glories of ancient Rome and organized discouraged Italians into the Nationalist Fascist Party.

Mussolini's Fascists were political gangsters. Dressed in black shirts, they carried clubs and bats, which they used to beat up anyone they disliked. They especially hated socialists and communists, whom they blamed for Italy's economic troubles. Across Italy, discontented workers had gone on strike and started riots. Many Italians feared that their country, like Russia, would plunge into communist revolution. Mussolini and his Fascist Party played on such fears to gain power. They attacked striking workers, trade union offices, and anyone who seemed to have Bolshevist sympathies. They promised to revive Italy's economy and protect the nation from revolutionary terror.

Communism vs. Fascism

Communist and fascist governments resemble each other in some ways. In both, a dictator often rules. Both suppress opposition and claim that individual liberties must be sacrificed for the greater good of society. Both tend toward totalitarian control of people's lives. But their economic policies are different, and so are their larger goals.

In a communist society, the government directs the economy and owns most or all of the land, factories, and other resources that contribute to the economy. In theory, workers control the production of goods and share property. The stated goal of communism is a world in which social classes disappear and all people are treated equally. That's the theory—in reality, leaders of communist nations usually have far more material goods and privileges than the workers, who lack both wealth and freedom.

A fascist government allows individuals to own property and businesses, but it maintains strict control over economic activity, and makes sure that private businesses serve the government's goals. Fascism glorifies the nation and its leaders, and calls on citizens to put the interests of the nation above individual interests. Fascist regimes often use war as a way to expand and strengthen the state. They reject the idea of equality for all. On the contrary, fascists often persecute minorities, and claim that their own national group is superior to others and therefore destined to rule.

Italy at this time was a constitutional monarchy with a shaky parliamentary system. In 1921, by bullying voters, the Fascist Party won a few seats in parliament. The next year, Mussolini issued an ultimatum: "Either the government of the country must be given peaceably to the *Fascisti*, or we will take it by force." Tens of thousands of Blackshirts, as they were known, poured into the capital in what Fascists called the "March on Rome." Cheering crowds lined the roads to greet them. The king hastily appointed Mussolini as prime minister.

Mussolini soon declared himself *Il Duce* (il DOO-chay). The words mean "the Leader," but Mussolini was really a dictator. To unify the Italian people, he demanded extreme devotion to the state. This meant extreme devotion to the leader who represented the power of the state, Il Duce, Mussolini himself.

Mussolini brought order to Italy, but at a great cost. With utter contempt for democracy, he threw out the parliamentary system and established the Fascists as the single party in power. He outlawed all other political parties and declared trade unions illegal. He suppressed all rights to free speech. He used spies and secret police to intimidate anyone who might object to his rule.

Mussolini, a savvy politician, carefully picked his partners. Although he had snuffed out parliament, he let the king, whom the people liked, remain on the throne. He cooperated with the Catholic Church and persuaded the pope to recognize the authority of the Fascist dictatorship. He worked closely with businessmen and industrialists. Unlike communists, fascists believed in an economy built on private ownership.

Mussolini's Militarism

Mussolini used militarism — the glorification of military might — to rally his followers and divert their attention from continuing social problems. He championed war as an ennobling cause. "Fascism," he wrote, "believes neither in the possibility nor the utility of perpetual peace. War alone... puts the stamp of nobility upon the peoples who have courage to meet it."

Mussolini pushed Italy into war by stirring up old resentments against Ethiopia. Italy had tried to colonize this African country in the 1880s, but the Ethiopians had fought fiercely and defeated the Italians. In 1935, however, when Mussolini ordered an invasion of Ethiopia, the Ethiopian troops could not survive against Italian air strikes and poison gas.

Almost 400,000 people gathered in Rome to hear a triumphant Mussolini boast of Italy's victory. Colonizing Ethiopia was, for Mussolini, part of his dream of reviving the ancient Roman Empire — once the most powerful in the world — in modern Italy.

Hitler's Early Years

Fascism quickly spread beyond Italy throughout Europe. Mussolini's ideas appealed to a young, willing believer named Adolf Hitler.

A lonely and secretive man from a small town in Austria, Hitler never finished high school, but he did have some talent as an artist. In 1907, he moved to Vienna and tried to enroll at the Academy of Fine Arts, where he failed the entrance exam twice. He soon came to dislike Vienna's ethnic diversity — he felt there were too many Slavs and too many Jews.

In 1913, Hitler moved to Munich, Germany. When the Great War broke out, he tried to enlist in the Austrian army, which rejected him as physically unfit for service. The Germans, however, accepted him as a volunteer in their infantry. Henceforth, Germany became his adopted homeland. Hitler threw himself into the war effort. In the Great War, he survived gas attacks and twice won the Iron Cross for bravery.

Germany's defeat made Hitler bitter and angry. He lashed out against the politicians who had surrendered, for he believed Germany had been on the verge of winning the war. Soon, encouraged by Army commanders, Hitler took over a tiny political party. He renamed it the *Nationalsozialistische Deutsche Arbeiterpartei* — the National Socialist German Workers Party, or Nazi (NAHT-see) Party for short. He quickly attracted thousands of followers by playing upon their sense of frustration with the Weimar government.

In 1923, with inflation soaring and the ranks of his Nazi supporters growing, Hitler sensed the time was right to start a revolution against the Weimar government. He led a band of Nazis into a political meeting in a beer hall and seized three government officials. "The National Revolution has begun," he screamed. The next day, however, the police arrested him, and Hitler went to prison.

Mein Kampf and Anti-Semitism

Hitler served only nine months of a five-year sentence. While behind bars, he began writing his memoir, *Mein Kampf* (miyn KAHMPF), which means "My Struggle." The book set forth Hitler's philosophy — if one can use that word for the vile stew of ideas he put on paper.

Whereas Karl Marx had seen class conflict as the driving force of history, Hitler said it was race. He claimed that the Germans were members of a so-called Aryan (AIR-ee-uhn) race, a master race destined to rule humanity.

In *Mein Kampf,* Hitler expounded the self-glorifying myth that civilization grew out of the Aryan conquest and enslavement of "inferior" races. He wrote:

> The Aryan alone...laid the groundwork and erected the walls of every great structure in human culture.... It was not by mere chance that the first forms of civilization arose there where the Aryan came into contact with inferior races...and forced them to obey his command. The members of the inferior race became the first mechanical tools in the service of a growing civilization.... As a conqueror, [the Aryan] subjugated inferior races and turned their physical powers into organized channels under his own leadership, forcing them to follow his will and purpose....

Hitler directed his most intense racial hatred against the Jews. "The Jew," he wrote, "offers the most striking contrast to the Aryan." Anti-Semitism, hatred of the Jews, had a long history in Europe, particularly in Germany. Hitler stoked the fires of that prejudice. He blamed the Jews for all Germany's troubles. Pages of *Mein Kampf* are filled with disgusting rants like this: "[The Jew] is and remains a parasite...[that] spreads over wider and wider areas according as some favorable area attracts him. The effect produced by his presence is also like that of the vampire; for wherever he established himself the people who grant him hospitality are bound to be bled to death sooner or later."

Hitler told Germans that it was their "sacred mission" to maintain racial purity. The German people, he said, must "occupy themselves not merely with the breeding of dogs, horses, and cats but also with care for the purity of their own blood." For Hitler, it was not enough to maintain the purity of the Aryan race; he also called for the elimination of what he viewed as inferior races. The elimination of the Jews, he wrote, "must necessarily be a bloody process."

Hitler as *Führer*

Hitler saw himself as the leader of a new and pure Aryan race. He promised to lead Germans to glory by conquering new territories and giving them *lebensraum* (LAY-bens-rowm) — "living space." He believed they would find much of this

Anti-Semitism—Where the Word Came From

Anti-Semitism means hatred of or prejudice against Jews. The term was coined in 1879 by the German writer Wilhelm Marr, who wrote an angry pamphlet claiming that Jews (such as Albert Ballin, president of the Hamburg-America steamship company) were trying to take over Germany. Marr's term *anti-Semitism* was inaccurate. A Semite is a person who speaks any one of several related languages, such as Hebrew, Arabic, or Assyrian. Arabs and many non-Jews are Semites. Nonetheless, a century later, we still use the term *anti-Semitism* to mean prejudice against Jews.

"living space" by conquering Russia, home of the Slavs — an "inferior" race in Hitler's eyes.

In part, Hitler wanted to conquer Russia because it was the home of communism, a philosophy he detested. He despised the thought of revolution by "inferior" peoples. He viewed communists as "a mob of loafers, deserters, political place-hunters, and Jewish dilettantes." In *Mein Kampf,* Hitler warned that "if the Marxist teaching were to be accepted as the foundation of the life of the universe, it would lead to the disappearance of all order that is conceivable to the human mind."

A dilettante is one who carelessly dabbles in various pursuits.

During the 1930s, as the Great Depression hit Germany hard, Hitler's lunatic ranting began to appeal to many Germans. As wages shrank and prices climbed, millions lost their jobs. Hitler offered an explanation of the country's woes and an enemy to blame — the Jews. "If a people is to become free," Hitler exhorted, "it needs hate, hate, and once again hate." And most of all, in Hitler's twisted view, hate of the Jews.

With their message of anti-Semitism and promise of a glorious future for the Aryan race, Nazi candidates began winning elections. By 1932, they held 38 percent of the seats in the Reichstag, the German parliament.

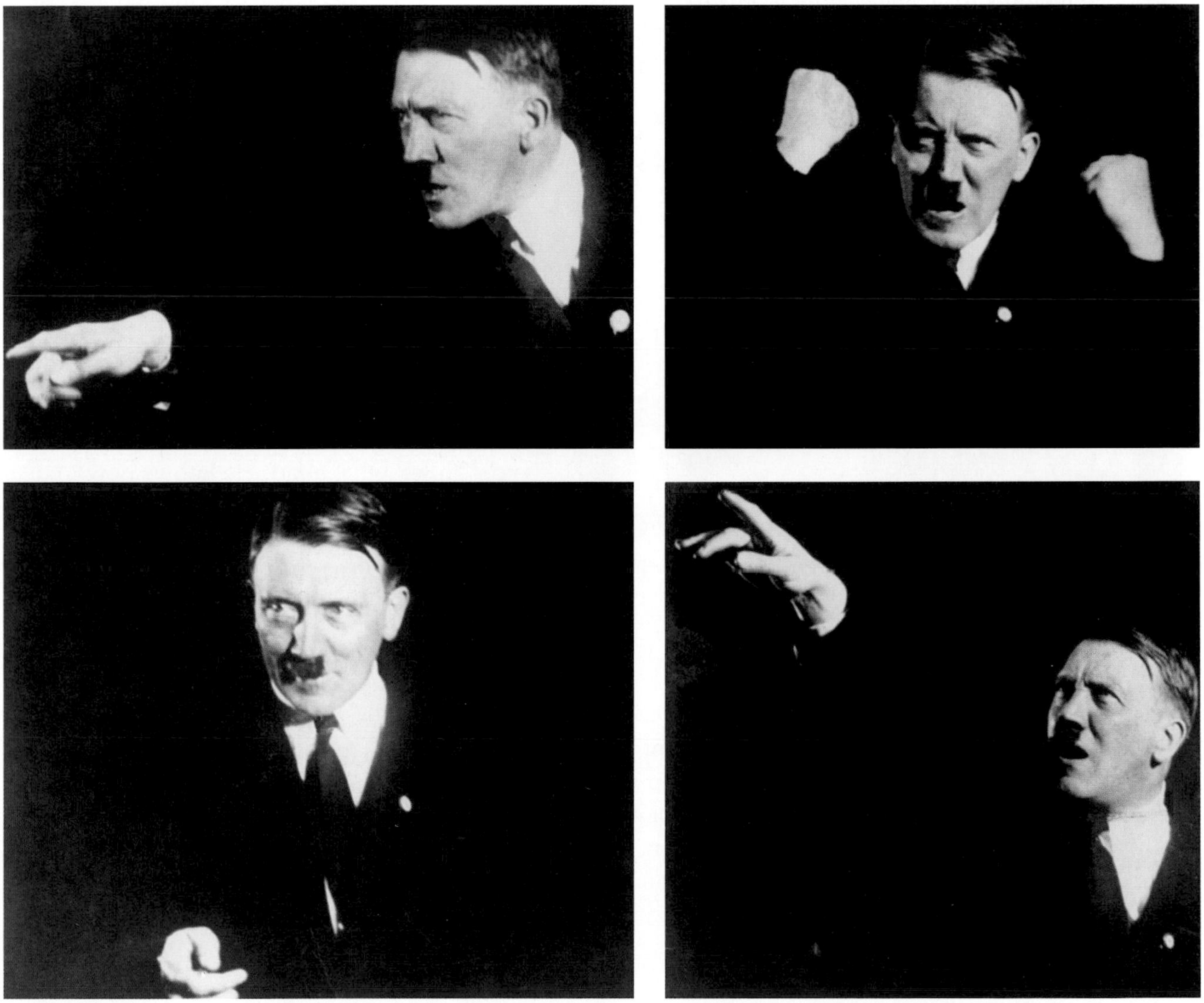

Adolf Hitler roused German audiences by launching into tirades in which he extolled the glories of the "Aryan" race and blamed the Jews for Germany's economic woes. He promised Germans that he would lead them to greatness through conquest.

The Hitler Youth

Hitler encouraged loyalty to Nazi Germany, and to its führer, by setting up paramilitary organizations for young people of the so-called Aryan race. Boys 14 to 18 had to join the Hitler Youth. Its members wore uniforms, learned about Nazi Party beliefs, built up their physical strength, and practiced for war through exercises such as throwing mock grenades and crawling under barbed wire. Girls 14 to 18 had to join the League of German Maidens, which encouraged activities such as camping, playing sports, and preparing to be housewives while learning Nazi doctrine. Some youth groups even taught members to spy on their own families and report any anti-Nazi talk they overheard.

Hitler Youth rally on National Socialist (or Nazi) Party Day in Nuremberg, Germany, 1933

Germany's aging president appointed Hitler as his chancellor. When Germany's president died, Hitler folded the presidency into his own office and claimed for himself the new title of *führer* (FYUR-uhr), which meant, simply, "leader." Like the leaders of Russia and Italy, the führer of Germany would soon become a totalitarian dictator.

Nazis in Charge

Hitler and his Nazi Party had risen to power through legitimate, democratic means—by winning elections and gaining seats in the parliament. But this was much too slow a method for the ambitious führer. In 1933, he saw an opportunity to bypass the democratic process. Someone, probably acting on Hitler's orders, set fire to the Reichstag building. Hitler blamed the communists and warned of a threat to state security. To meet this supposed danger, he claimed he needed the power to arrest any communist or socialist he deemed a threat. With this power, Hitler, like Stalin in the USSR, began to wipe out every possible challenge to his rule.

One man Hitler came to view as a severe challenge was Ernst Röhm (room). Röhm was a former army officer whom Hitler had put in charge of building a paramilitary force called the SA, which stood for *Sturmabteilung* (shturm-ap-TIY-loung), or "Storm Division." As the SA expanded to twenty times the size of Germany's official army, Röhm grew more popular than Hitler himself.

A *paramilitary group* is a group of citizens trained and organized in military fashion.

On June 30, 1934, a date the Nazis called "The Night of the Long Knives," Hitler ordered his agents to arrest and shoot SA leaders. The führer himself oversaw the execution of Röhm. Hitler claimed he was crushing a conspiracy "against the German people." To deal with future threats, he demanded the power to arrest and execute anyone he wanted. When Stalin heard this, he said, "Hitler, what a lad! He knows how to deal with political opponents."

From *Kristallnacht* to Concentration Camps

Hitler rallied the German people by playing upon their fears and keeping them focused on the Jews as a scapegoat. Each year he was in power, he imposed greater hardships on Germany's Jewish population. He stripped Jews of citizenship rights, removed them from public offices, seized many Jewish families' possessions, and outlawed marriage between Jews and non-Jews.

A *scapegoat* is a person or group that bears the blame for the faults or misdeeds of others.

One terrible night in November 1938, Hitler sent Nazis on a rampage through the streets, destroying Jewish-owned stores and beating or killing any Jews they found. Hitler called this

Kristallnacht (kris-TAHL-nackt), "The Night of Broken Glass." Many Germans approved. Many others didn't but were too frightened to protest.

They had good cause to be frightened. The Nazis now had a secret police network that rivaled Stalin's. It was staffed by more than 100,000 spies in Germany. The Nazis also set up prison camps, not for criminals but for people who did not share Hitler's views.

The secret police began to round up thousands of people — communists, socialists, journalists, and others — and detain them without trial in the prison camps. The Nazis claimed that detaining such "undesirables" was for the greater good of the Nazi state. In reality, it was a convenient, brutal way for Hitler to get rid of his political enemies or anyone else he did not like.

For prisoners in these camps, which came to be known as concentration camps, there was little chance of ever leaving. Upon arrival, they were stripped and had their heads shaved. They were dressed in rough clothing, herded into bleak barracks, and given minimal rations. Then they were relentlessly worked to death. As you'll read in a later chapter, Hitler's concentration camps would become even more ghastly for many more people.

A German synagogue (Jewish place of worship) lies in ruins after *Kristallnacht*, "The Night of the Broken Glass." On that night of November 9–10, 1938, Hitler's troops ransacked thousands of Jewish synagogues, businesses, and homes.

Franco and the Spanish Civil War

In the 1930s, a decade of widespread economic hardship and political turmoil, one ruthless dictator after the next surged to power.

Like other countries, Spain was shaken by strikes, violent protests, and assassinations. In 1936, General Francisco Franco quickly mustered an army and moved to seize power.

A brutal civil war erupted. On one side were Franco's forces, called the Nationalists. On the other side were the Republicans, those who supported Spain's recently elected socialist government.

The Nationalists received help from Hitler and Mussolini. These dictators sent money, weapons, and troops to Franco, whom they considered a fellow fascist.

The Republicans received equipment and supplies from the Soviet Union's Stalin. The Republicans were also aided by the International Brigade, an army of 60,000 idealistic volunteers from many countries who wanted to stop the would-be dictator Franco.

Germany and the Soviet Union used the Spanish Civil War to test new tanks, aircraft, and other weapons. German planes experimented with dropping bombs on cities. Both sides executed thousands of civilians. As many as 800,000 people died in the war, which turned out to be a dress rehearsal for a far more ghastly, widespread conflict.

After three years of fighting, the Republican forces could no longer hold out. The Spanish Civil War ended in 1939, with the victorious Franco established as the fascist dictator of Spain. Franco ruled Spain until his death in 1975.

This Spanish Civil War poster urges Spaniards to join the battle against Franco's Nationalist army with the words "First win the war! Less empty talk!" The red color symbolizes communism. Franco ultimately won the war and became the fascist dictator of Spain.

Militarism and Dictatorship in Japan

As fascism spread in Europe, militarism reared its ugly head in Asia, in the island nation of Japan.

Earlier you learned how, in the late nineteenth century, Japan worked hard to transform itself into a modern, industrialized nation. During this time, known as the Meiji Era, Japan set out to become as wealthy and powerful as Europe and the United States. The Japanese embraced the slogan "Prosperous Nation, Strong Military," and they achieved both. But like Europe and the United States, Japan suffered during the Great Depression of the 1930s. With its scant farmland, limited resources, and exploding population, Japan plunged into economic crisis.

Some Japanese began to blame the West for the country's problems. They preached hatred of democracy, of communism, of capitalism, of all things Western.

Many Japanese also blamed their own government. Military leaders saw the widespread public discontent with Japan's parliament, called the *Diet*, as an opportunity to seize more power. Some officers plotted to attack the Diet,

Japanese infantry and cavalry troops enter Nanking, China, through a triple-arched gateway. After the fall of the city to Japan in late 1937, Japanese soldiers went on a rampage raping and killing thousands of Chinese, a tragedy that came to be known as "the rape of Nanking."

assassinate political leaders, and set up a military dictatorship. Although they did not go through with their plot, various military groups did carry out attacks against government officials.

Like the fascists in Europe, Japan's militarists had imperialist ambitions. They dreamed of controlling Manchuria, a province in northeast China with rich deposits of coal and iron. In 1931, the Japanese army ignored the wishes of the Diet and seized Manchuria. The army quickly set up its own government to rule the province. Some Japanese officials protested the invasion, but imperialist groups threatened them and intimidated them into silence.

During the next few years, Japanese forces conquered much of the Chinese coast. In the city of Nanjing, also known as Nanking, Japanese troops raped and slaughtered many thousands of civilians. Many victims were burned or beheaded in what came to be called "the rape of Nanking."

By this time, Japanese military leaders had gained enough power to control the government. Civilian rule ended in Japan for all practical purposes. Some admirals and generals began to talk of forging a new Japanese empire that would dominate much of Asia. In the years to come, these military leaders would transform Japanese society into a machine preparing for war.

German tanks roll into Poland in 1939 as German soldiers look on. The lightning speed of Nazi tanks and troops ensured an easy victory against the Poles. The German invasion of Poland marked the beginning of World War II, the most horrific war in history.

A Second World War Begins

Hitler. Mussolini. Stalin. In the 1930s, these three totalitarian leaders held much of Europe in their grip. All three bitterly resented the losses their countries suffered during the Great War. All three led frustrated and angry populations, many of whom were ready and willing to take up arms.

Halfway around the world, the military leaders of Japan, the most industrialized Asian nation, turned their country into a war machine. They boasted of forging a glorious Japanese empire.

The major actors were in place. The stage was set for global disaster.

In 1939, World War II began. This Second World War was clearly the unfinished business of the first. Germany, Italy, and Japan each sought to right what they considered the wrongs inflicted by World War I. They began by embarking on conquest. They ended by plunging the world into death and destruction that surpassed even the staggering losses of World War I.

Japan and Italy Test the League's Limits

You recall that after the Great War, Woodrow Wilson convinced victorious nations to establish the League of Nations. Wilson thought the League could help prevent wars, especially another world war. He hoped that every nation would join the League and work to resolve their differences peacefully. But the League's prospects for success dimmed when the United States chose not to join it. Those nations that did join often argued about what the League should do. The actions of aggressive fascist regimes soon revealed the ineffectiveness of the League.

In 1931, when Japanese troops marched into Manchuria, the League of Nations protested. Japan responded by simply quitting the League and occupying the coal-rich region in northern China. During the next few years, as Japan conquered large areas of eastern China and slaughtered thousands in Nanking, the League was powerless to stop the aggression.

In 1935, when Mussolini launched an invasion of Ethiopia, Italy and Ethiopia were both members of the League of Nations. The Ethiopian emperor, Haile Selassie (HIY-lee suh-LA-see), delivered an emotional speech to a meeting of the League, in which he declared, "Should it happen that a strong government finds it may with impunity destroy a weak people, then the hour strikes for that weak people to appeal to the League of Nations.... I ask the fifty-two nations, who have given the Ethiopian people a promise to help them in their resistance to the aggressor, what are they willing to do for Ethiopia?"

Ethiopian troops, shown here, were poorly armed and no match for Mussolini's army when it invaded Ethiopia in 1935.

The League of Nations issued declarations critical of Italy, and it forbade the importation of some Italian goods. But these were largely symbolic actions with no real effect. Once again, the League's inability to stop hostilities revealed its ineffectiveness as a peacekeeping body.

Hitler's Third Reich

In Germany, Hitler, having proclaimed himself führer, proceeded to ignore the Treaty of Versailles. He said his nation bore no guilt for the Great War and would pay no further reparations. In 1933, he withdrew Germany from the League of Nations. Two years later, he defiantly announced that Germany would rearm, a move forbidden by the Versailles treaty.

Why the Third *Reich?*

The German word for "empire" is *Reich*. Hitler said two great German empires preceded his own. He considered the Holy Roman Empire from medieval days the first German empire, and the second empire the time of the kaisers from 1871 to 1918.

Factories that had stood idle during the Depression started cranking out ammunition, bombers, and tanks called *panzers* in German. To build the German army, Hitler renewed the practice of conscription, drafting men for required military service. Hitler announced that he was establishing a "Third Reich" (riyk), or Third Empire, that would last a thousand years and outshine all previous German empires.

Hitler was not above seeking allies. In 1936, he and Mussolini formed an alliance known as the Rome-Berlin Axis. They chose the name "Axis" to suggest that all of Europe revolved around a line running between those two capitals. Japan soon entered into an agreement with Germany. Together, Germany, Italy, and Japan formed the Axis Powers.

Gaining "Living Space"

One of Hitler's major objectives was to gain *lebensraum*, the "living space" he claimed the Aryan race deserved. To gain "living space," German troops marched into the Rhineland in 1936. Under the Treaty of Versailles, this region was supposed to act as a buffer between France and Germany, and German troops were forbidden to enter it.

When Hitler sent his armies into the Rhineland, France and Britain protested, but they did nothing more. Both nations were preoccupied with the economic crisis at home brought on by the Depression. Neither wanted to risk a fight. "Above all, no war," one French newspaper pleaded.

If other European powers had stood up to Hitler, then perhaps he would have backed down. But when no other country moved to stop him, the führer's confidence soared. The German people applauded his boldness. With his popularity at home rising, and with foreign leaders showing no signs of resisting German expansion, Hitler laid plans to gain more lebensraum. Shortly after his troops marched into the Rhineland, the führer stood on a balcony in Berlin and watched thousands of brown-shirted storm troopers parade by. As they marched they sang, "For today we own Germany and tomorrow the entire world."

Storm troopers were the soldiers in Hitler's Storm Division, or SA.

Two years later, Hitler again violated the Treaty of Versailles. He ordered his army into Austria and announced that he was annexing it to the German Reich. The leaders of France and Britain protested but took no action to safeguard Austria's independence. After all, they reasoned, many Austrians supported union with Germany. So, France and Britain watched as the Third Reich grew. (The United States did not even consider getting involved because at this time Americans saw Hitler as Europe's problem.)

When a country *annexes* a territory, it adds that territory to its domain.

Later in 1938, Hitler threatened to invade Czechoslovakia (cheh-kuh-sloh-VAH-kee-uh). Czechoslovakia was one of the new nations created at the end of World War I when the victorious Allies redrew the map of Europe. The northwestern part of Czechoslovakia, called the Sudetenland, bordered Germany and was inhabited by millions of German-speaking people. Hitler demanded that this region be turned over to Germany. Czech leaders said no. They called on France for help.

British Prime Minister Neville Chamberlain and Adolf Hitler shake hands at the 1938 Munich Conference. Chamberlain fooled himself into believing he had appeased Hitler.

The Policy of Appeasement

As tensions mounted, European nations seemed to be heading into another catastrophic conflict. Some leaders saw war as the only way to stop Hitler. Others argued for peace at any price.

In September 1938, leaders of France, Britain, Germany, and Italy met in Munich, Germany. The British prime minister, Neville Chamberlain, negotiated face-to-face with Hitler. Chamberlain, the son of a businessman and well known politician, believed all differences could be negotiated. He assumed that Hitler was a fundamentally reasonable man who would be willing to compromise. When the führer said he would be satisfied with taking just the German-speaking parts of Czechoslovakia, Chamberlain and the French premier agreed. They gave in to Hitler's demands, hoping the fascist dictator would cause no more trouble.

The French and British pursued a policy of *appeasement*—giving in to an aggressor nation's demands in the hope of preventing war. In the 1930s, British and French diplomats saw appeasement as their best hope to preserve peace, even if it meant allowing Germany to seize the German-speaking areas of Czechoslovakia.

Prime Minister Chamberlain flew home to a hero's welcome, happily claiming that he had secured "peace for our time." Others disagreed. A member of the British Parliament, Winston Churchill, addressed the House of Commons and issued this warning:

> We are in the presence of a disaster of the first magnitude which has befallen Great Britain and France.... We have sustained a total and unmitigated defeat.... This is only the beginning of the reckoning. This is only the first sip, the first foretaste of a bitter cup which will be proffered to us year by year unless by a supreme recovery of moral health and martial vigor, we arise again and take our stand for freedom as in the olden time.

Appeasement Fails and War Begins

In his speech, Churchill had warned that "Czechoslovakia will be engulfed in the Nazi regime." His warning proved true.

Hitler was not interested in peace. He had already marched into the Rhineland and annexed

Axis Surge in Europe and North Africa

Allied and Allied-controlled nations
Axis and Axis-controlled nations
Farthest extent of Axis military occupation, Nov. 1942
Nations neutral during most of war
Land annexed by Germany
Boundary of Germany, 1933
Russian advances
Axis advances
Major battles
0 200 400 mi
0 200 400 km
GERMAN ANNEXATIONS c. 1939
GERMANY (EAST PRUSSIA)
NETH.
Berlin
POLAND
Warsaw
BELGIUM
GERMANY
RHINELAND
LUX.
SUDETENLAND
Prague
CZECHOSLOVAKIA
FRANCE
Munich
Vienna
Budapest
SWITZ.
AUSTRIA
HUNGARY
ITALY
Norwegian Sea
North Sea
Baltic Sea
ATLANTIC OCEAN
English Channel
NORWAY
SWEDEN
FINLAND
Oslo
Stockholm
Helsinki
Leningrad (St. Petersburg)
ESTONIA
LATVIA
Riga
LITHUANIA
DENMARK
Copenhagen
Glasgow
Belfast
IRISH FREE STATE
GREAT BRITAIN
Battle of Britain 1940–1941
Coventry
London
Dunkirk
Amsterdam
NETH.
Brussels
BELGIUM
LUX.
Rethondes
Paris
Maginot Line
FRANCE
Vichy
VICHY FRANCE
Berlin
GERMANY
GERMANY (EAST PRUSSIA)
Rhine R.
Prague
Munich
SWITZ.
Vienna
AUSTRIA
SLOVAKIA
Budapest
HUNGARY
Warsaw
POLAND
Minsk
Moscow 1941
SOVIET UNION
Kiev
Dnieper R.
Stalingrad (Volgograd)
Volga R.
E U R O P E
ROMANIA
Bucharest
Danube R.
Black Sea
YUGOSLAVIA
Sarajevo
Sofia
BULGARIA
Istanbul
ALBANIA
GREECE
Athens
TURKEY
ASIA
PORTUGAL
SPAIN
Madrid
ANDORRA
Corsica (Fr.)
ITALY
Rome
Sardinia (Fr.)
Mediterranean Sea
Sicily (Italy)
Malta (G.B.)
Crete (Gr.)
Cyprus (G.B.)
SYRIA (Fr.)
LEBANON (Fr.)
PALESTINE (G.B.)
TRANS-JORDAN (G.B.)
Suez Canal
SPANISH MOROCCO (Spain)
Algiers
Tunis
MOROCCO (France)
ALGERIA (France)
TUNISIA (France)
Tripoli
El Alamein 1942
SAUDI ARABIA
LIBYA (Italy)
EGYPT (Great Britain)
Nile R.
Red Sea
AFRICA
FRENCH WEST AFRICA (France)
FRENCH EQUATORIAL AFRICA (France)
ANGLO-EGYPTIAN SUDAN (Great Britain)
1939
1940
1941
SWEDEN
FINLAND
NORWAY
GERMANY
SOVIET UNION
GREAT BRITAIN
POLAND
IRELAND
HUNGARY
SWITZERLAND
ROMANIA
FRANCE
BULGARIA
SPAIN
ITALY
TURKEY
PORTUGAL
LIBYA
EGYPT
SAUDI ARABIA
FRENCH WEST AFRICA
ETHIOPIA
ANGOLA
MOZAMBIQUE

Austria. Since he had met no opposition, he saw his European foes as spineless. So in March 1939, to the shock of Chamberlain and those who had advocated appeasement, Hitler's troops seized the rest of Czechoslovakia. Once again, in the face of Hitler's aggression, the French and the British stood aside. Churchill's prediction became reality: "Silent, mournful, abandoned, broken, Czechoslovakia recedes into the darkness...."

British and French officials turned to their old ally from World War I, Russia—that is, the Soviet Union. They wanted Stalin to join them in opposing Hitler. But while Stalin negotiated with Britain and France, he was also holding talks with Hitler's representatives. In August 1939, Europe was astounded when Stalin signed a treaty with Hitler. In this treaty, often called the Nazi-Soviet Nonaggression Pact, the Nazis and Communists set aside their mutual loathing and agreed not to go to war with each other. They also secretly agreed to divide the independent nation of Poland between them.

On September 1, 1939, Hitler attacked Poland—more living space for the master race, he argued. Shortly afterward, he issued a command that further confirmed his ruthless nature—he ordered the "mercy killing" of all incurably ill patients in German hospitals. In the führer's twisted mind, a master race should not be encumbered by invalids.

As Nazi forces pounded east, the British and French abandoned their failed policy of appeasement. On September 3, 1939, some 21 years after the Great War had ended, both nations declared war on Germany. World War II was underway.

Blitzkrieg: Lightning War

The Second World War would be unlike the first. In World War I, armies had fought for weeks to gain inches of ground on the Western Front. Hitler, who had spent time in the trenches, was determined to avoid that defensive stalemate. The führer had modern tanks, planes, trains, and trucks that could move armies more quickly and with greater firepower than before.

The Germans unleashed a new kind of warfare called *blitzkrieg* (BLITS-kreeg) or "lightning war," which involved surprise attacks and quickly overwhelming the enemy with massive force. The ill-equipped Polish army was the first to experience the speed and surprise of German blitzkrieg. The Poles expected to fight a defensive war along their nation's borders. But the Germans grouped their speedy tanks together and rolled over Polish defenses. Skimming just above the trees, Nazi planes bombed Polish soldiers. Behind the tanks and planes, German infantrymen kept up the attack. It took only a month for the Germans to sweep across Poland.

In response to the aggressive acts of the Axis Powers, France and Great Britain banded together to form the Allied Powers. In the years ahead, several other nations joined the Allied effort.

"Another Munich"

Eventually, everyone could see that British Prime Minister Chamberlain and the French diplomats made a huge mistake when they decided to appease Hitler at the Munich Conference in 1938. "Another Munich" and "another 1938" have become phrases that mean making the wrong choice by giving in to an aggressor nation.

Stalin Swallows the Baltic States

As part of their nonaggression pact, Hitler and Stalin had agreed to divide Poland between them. Only a couple of weeks after Hitler launched his blitzkrieg from the west, Stalin sent Soviet troops into Poland from the east. Tens of thousands of Polish troops surrendered to Russian forces.

Stalin then moved quickly to take over countries to the north of Poland. He met little resistance when he annexed Estonia, Latvia, and Lithuania, three countries known as the Baltic States because they lie near the Baltic Sea.

But another northern country, Finland, surprised Stalin by putting up a fierce fight. The Finns, though greatly outnumbered, knew how to maneuver in the snow-covered winter landscape. They skied into battle while Soviet troops bogged down in snowdrifts. In the end, however, the Soviets overwhelmed the Finns. Stalin threw almost a million soldiers and a thousand tanks into the fight, and the Finns were forced to surrender.

Scandinavia is the region of northern Europe occupied by Denmark, Sweden, and Norway.

In April 1940, Hitler launched another blitzkrieg into Finland's Scandinavian neighbors, Denmark and Norway. Little Denmark surrendered immediately, and Norway two months later. Hitler's control of these lands provided a strategic location from which the Nazis could attack England.

The Fall of France

In the spring of 1940, nearly all the news was bad for the Allies. German air bombardments pummeled the Netherlands and Belgium into submission. In May, Belgium surrendered unconditionally. In northern Europe, refugees fleeing occupied lands clogged the roads while hundreds of thousands of British and French troops, sent to defend Belgium, retreated toward the sea.

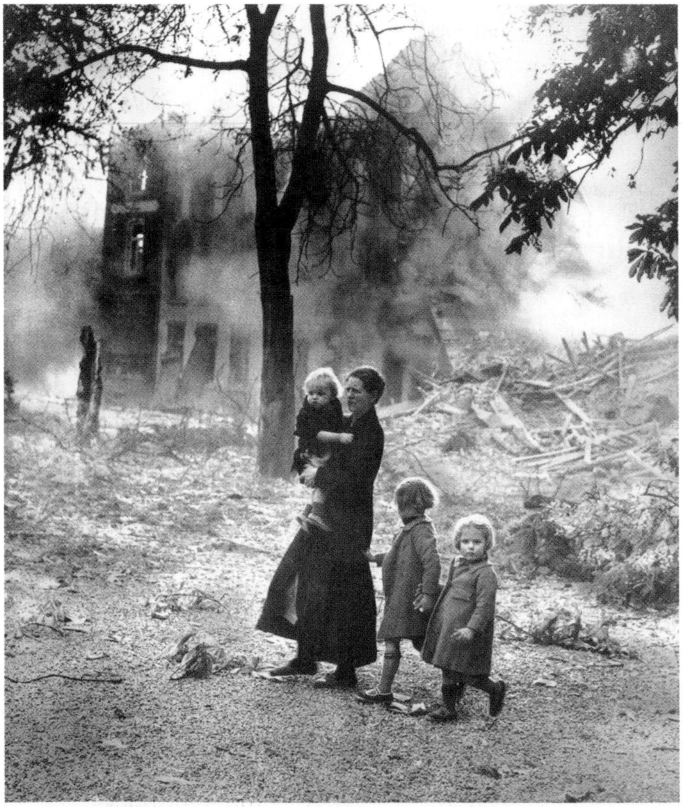

A Belgian mother and her children, left homeless by the 1940 German blitzkrieg against their nation, wander past rubble in search of shelter.

Soon the Allied forces had their backs to the English Channel at the French port of Dunkirk. As the Germans closed in around them, the British government sounded an urgent call for help across southern England: Anyone with any kind of seagoing boat should set sail for Dunkirk to help rescue the stranded soldiers.

Hundreds of ships — Royal Navy vessels, tugboats, motorboats, fishing boats, paddle steamers, yachts — set out for Dunkirk. While German and British warplanes fought overhead, the makeshift armada ferried soldiers across the Channel to safety, then turned around and headed back to France to pick up more desperate troops. The Miracle of Dunkirk, as the operation came to be known, saved more than 300,000 men from death or capture on the beaches.

There would be no such miracle for France. The French military had spent years building a long series of fortifications, bunkers, and underground barracks for thousands of soldiers along the border with Germany. They were certain that this strong line of defense, named the Maginot (MA-zhuh-no) Line, could repel a German attack. But by moving through Belgium, Hitler's army swept around the northern end of the Maginot Line and flooded into France.

On June 14, 1940, the Nazi army reached Paris, and the French government surrendered unconditionally. Parisians wept while German trucks rumbled through their streets.

Hitler remembered that at the end of World War I, German generals had signed a humiliating armistice in a railroad car in Rethondes, France. Now the führer insisted that the French surrender in the very same railroad car. Hitler himself attended the surrender. He arrived wearing one of his prized possessions — the Iron Cross medal he had won in the First World War.

French Collaboration and Resistance

After the fall of Paris, the French set up a new government in the town of Vichy (VIH-shee) in central France. The Vichy government soon began to cooperate with the Nazis, running the country as the Germans saw fit. French officials in the Vichy government arrested people suspected of anti-Nazi activities. They prevented

French people from leaving the country. They passed anti-Semitic laws, and helped pay for the costs of maintaining German troops in France. The name *Vichy* came to represent collaboration with Hitler's regime.

In wartime, a *collaborator* is someone who helps his own country's enemies or assists an occupying force.

Many in France were appalled at the Vichy government. Thousands joined a movement called the Resistance, which fought the Nazi occupation. Working in secrecy, Resistance members relayed information about German operations to the Allies, published underground newspapers, and helped Allied prisoners of war escape. Armed groups of Resistance fighters disrupted German operations by attacking garrisons, derailing trains, cutting telephone wires, destroying bridges, and blowing up ammunition depots.

The Nazis sometimes responded by rounding up French hostages and killing them. They hoped the executions would discourage Resistance activity. But the Resistance fought on, determined to assault the Germans as much as they could until the Allies could liberate their country.

Churchill: "Blood, Toil, Tears, and Sweat"

On May 10, 1940—the same day the Nazis invaded the Netherlands and Belgium on their way to France—the British replaced their prime minister. Neville Chamberlain, who had advocated appeasement of Hitler, stepped aside for Winston Churchill.

Churchill proved to be one of the greatest statesmen of all time. He knew war from firsthand experience. As a young correspondent for British newspapers in the 1890s, he had reported the news while bullets whistled past him in Cuba and India. As an army officer in the Sudan, he had taken part in one of the British army's last major cavalry charges. During the Boer War in southern Africa, he had escaped from a prisoner of war camp.

At the outset of World War I, "Winnie" had commanded the Royal Navy as First Lord of the Admiralty. By the middle of the war, he was leading a battalion of infantry on the Western Front. Between the wars, Churchill, a talented artist, painted and wrote a four-volume history of World War I, or "the World Crisis," as he called it. While a member of Parliament in the 1930s, he saw the danger of Hitler's rise to power and urged Britain to prepare to fight the führer.

Some called Churchill a warmonger. Only after Germany invaded Poland did the British understand that he was right. Now, at age 65, he was their prime minister. He later wrote, "I felt... that all my past life had been but a preparation for this hour and for this trial."

In May 1940, as the Germans smashed through the Netherlands on their way to Belgium and France, Churchill addressed the British Parliament. He said:

> I have nothing to offer but blood, toil, tears, and sweat.... You ask, what is our policy? I can say: It is to wage war, by sea, land and air, with all our might and with all the strength that God can give us; to wage war against a monstrous tyranny, never surpassed in the dark, lamentable catalogue of human crime. That is our policy.... What is our aim?... It is victory, victory at all costs, in spite of all terror, victory however long and hard... for without victory there is no survival.

The Battle of Britain

As of June 1940, Hitler ruled Germany, Austria, Czechoslovakia, Poland, Denmark, Norway, Belgium, and much of France. And still his forces marched on.

Across the English Channel, the British stood alone against Hitler. "The Battle of France is over," Winston Churchill told Parliament. "I expect that the Battle of Britain is about to begin." Churchill rallied his countrymen: "Let us therefore brace ourselves to our duty, and so bear ourselves that if the British Empire and its Commonwealth last for a thousand years, men will still say, 'This was their finest hour.'"

In the summer of 1940, over the skies of southern England, the Battle of Britain began. Hitler sent his air force, the Luftwaffe (LOOFT-vah-fuh), to pound the British into surrender. He believed that if his planes could eliminate Britain's Royal Air Force (RAF), then his army and navy could mount a successful invasion of the

Smoke from burning buildings wreathes the dome of St. Paul's Cathedral after a German air raid on London.

The Enigma Machine

Thanks to some daring spies and brilliant mathematicians, British military planners were able to keep one step ahead of the Germans throughout much of World War II. The German military used an encryption machine, called Enigma, to send and receive coded messages. Since Enigma constantly changed codes, the Germans considered the messages it sent unbreakable. But just before the start of the war, Polish code-breakers gave Britain one of the Enigma machines, along with decoding techniques. British mathematicians were then able to crack German codes.

Allied code-breakers deciphered thousands of German military messages. The intelligence they gathered helped the Allies anticipate Luftwaffe bombing missions and track German submarines. The Germans never realized that the Allies had broken their Enigma codes. Many historians believe the code-breaking shortened the war.

island nation. The massive air campaign launched against Britain, a first in the history of warfare, would not prove as easy as Hitler imagined.

The Germans first attacked British air force bases. Through July and August, when German planes appeared, British pilots dashed to their waiting Hurricane and Spitfire fighter planes. Civilians on the ground held their breath as British and German airmen fought dogfights high above them. They watched in horror when burning planes, with trails of smoke behind them, crashed to the ground or plunged into the English Channel.

The Germans had many more planes than the British. But the British Spitfires proved more than a match for the finest German planes. The British had two other advantages. They had broken some of Germany's secret codes, so they could decipher German radio transmissions about oncoming attacks. And the British had radar. This recent invention used radio waves to detect incoming enemy planes.

For a month, the Luftwaffe launched raid after raid on British air bases, ports, and docks. To meet the German onslaught, RAF pilots took to the skies, with some pilots flying up to seven missions per day. On August 15, 1940, the Luftwaffe sent hundreds of planes to bomb targets in northeast and southern England. But the RAF held its own, inflicting heavy losses on the Germans. On August 20, Churchill said in tribute to the fallen RAF pilots, "Never in the field of human conflict was so much owed by so many to so few."

The Germans decided to expand their air war and bomb cities such as London, Coventry, Glasgow, and Belfast. Desperate British parents put thousands of children on trains and sent them to stay with relatives in the country, where it was safer. When air-raid sirens wailed, Londoners scurried into cellars, backyard shelters, and subway stations, where they huddled while explosions tore through the city overhead. When the all-clear siren sounded, they emerged to see which homes, schools, stores, and factories had been bombed into rubble. After every attack, rescue workers searched the ruins of buildings for survivors, as Londoners picked through the wreckage of their homes.

Often, a shout went up from the street: "There's Winnie!" Crowds quickly gathered to see their prime minister striding among them, inspecting the ruins in London's East End, where many of the city's poor lived. Bowler hat on his head and cigar between his teeth, Churchill defied air-raid sirens as he paced through the worst-hit sites, inspecting the damage, listening to the locals, and offering words of encouragement.

Everywhere he went, Churchill flashed the V-for-victory sign with two fingers. The prime minister came to symbolize Britain's defiant resistance.

As he exhorted his people to action, Churchill, whose mother was American, kept up a steady correspondence with U.S. President Franklin Roosevelt, urging the United States to join the Allies. Roosevelt was sympathetic, but Americans did not want to enter another European war. Churchill reasoned that if Britain could hold out, the United States would eventually join the fight to defeat Nazism. The prime minister warned: "If we fail, then the whole world, including the United States, including all that we have known and cared for, will sink into the abyss of a new Dark Age...."

Winston Churchill flashes a victory sign. The prime minister—who once famously said, "Never give in, never, never, never."—inspired his nation during its darkest hours.

Churchill never sugar-coated the sacrifice required of his countrymen. "We shall defend our island, whatever the cost may be," he told the British people. "We shall fight on the beaches, we shall fight on the landing grounds, we shall fight in the fields and in the streets, we shall fight in the hills; we shall never surrender."

After months of devastating aerial attacks, Hitler found he could not bomb Britain into submission. By late 1940, the worst of the Battle of Britain was over. But the war was far from over. In fact, it was spreading.

Mussolini Attacks, Hitler Helps

When the Germans pressed into France, Italy's dictator, Benito Mussolini, claimed territory there as well. Later, as Hitler focused on the Battle of Britain, Mussolini turned his attention to North Africa. Hoping for an easy victory, he ordered troops based in the Italian colony of Libya to invade British-held Egypt.

Why fight over Egypt? Because control of Egypt meant control of the Suez Canal, an important waterway linking the Mediterranean and Red Seas. The Suez Canal also gave access to oil reserves in the Middle East.

Italian forces pushed into Egypt. But the British struck back. Although the British had fewer troops, they had better tanks. These tanks were much improved from the first armored vehicles used in World War I. They were faster, more maneuverable, more reliable, and more destructive. In a series of battles, the British pushed back the Italians and captured well over 100,000 prisoners.

As Mussolini's forces faltered, Hitler sent help in the form of a tank force commanded by General Erwin Rommel. British and German forces pushed each other back and forth. German news reports celebrated Rommel's victories and nicknamed him the "Desert Fox."

Next, Mussolini decided to attack Greece. The Greeks routed the Italian invaders, driving them out in short order. Again, Hitler had to send German troops to help the Italians.

"Barbarossa": Hitler Turns on Stalin

In 1939, Hitler and Stalin had signed a nonaggression treaty. But Hitler was no prisoner to his promises. The pact was Hitler's way of temporarily avoiding conflict with the Soviet Union while focusing his power on other goals. Hitler knew that eventually he would fight the Soviet Union, since both he and Stalin were determined to dominate eastern Europe. Moreover, Hitler maintained a deep hatred of Bolshevism. And he continued to view the Slavic people as an "inferior" race, destined to provide living space and labor for their Aryan masters.

In June 1941, Hitler launched his invasion of the Soviet Union, called Operation Barbarossa after a medieval German emperor. More than three million German troops poured into Russian territory. The attack forced Stalin to join the war on the side of the Allies.

Nazi armies sped across the steppes of western Russia, the flat terrain ideal for their fast-moving tanks, trucks, and motorcycle outriders. As the Russian army retreated, its troops pursued a "scorched earth" policy, just as they had in the early 1800s when Napoleon invaded Russia. In falling back, the Soviet troops destroyed crops, bridges, railroad tracks, and telephone wires so they would not fall into enemy hands.

Hundreds of thousands of Russian troops became prisoners of war. The Nazis, who considered them inferior Slavs, showed no mercy. More than half the Russian soldiers died of starvation or disease as the Germans marched them toward prisoner of war camps.

On their relentless drive east across a 2,000-mile front, the Germans cut off the city of Leningrad from the rest of the country. The citizens of Leningrad endured a siege that lasted 872 days. On many of those days, the Germans bombarded the city for more than nine hours at a time. During lulls in the barrage, families searched for firewood, food, and water. Nearing starvation, they ate any food they could lay their hands on — dogs, cats, crows, mice. Their drinking water came from the city's river and canals, where many dead bodies floated. In all, about a

A German panzer convoy storms through a Russian town in late 1941. Hitler broke his nonaggression pact with Stalin that year, and ordered more than three million Nazi troops into the Soviet Union in an invasion called Operation Barbarossa. The attack forced the Soviets to join Britain and the other Allies in the fight against the Axis Powers.

million people, a third of Leningrad's population, died during the siege.

Hitler ordered his forces toward Moscow, the capital of the Soviet Union. Some patrols got so close to Moscow that they could see the spires of the Kremlin, the ancient fortress at the heart of the capital. But as the frigid Russian winter set in, German troops began to suffer. Their generals had been so sure of a quick victory that they had provided no winter clothes for their men. Soldiers' fingers and toes turned black from frostbite. The temperature plummeted, and thousands froze to death in their trenches.

Napoleon in Russia

History sometimes seems to repeat itself. As the winter of 1941–42 arrived, more than one Nazi general must have recalled what happened to Napoleon Bonaparte, who in 1812 invaded Russia with 600,000 troops. The French emperor had anticipated a quick victory. His forces pushed all the way to Moscow. But winter caught the invaders low on supplies, and Napoleon was forced to order a westward retreat. His hungry army was barely able to march. Men and horses froze in the snow or died of starvation. Soldiers deserted by the hundreds. The Russians killed or captured those who fell behind. By the time Napoleon's army reached Paris, there were barely 40,000 troops left.

FDR and the Arsenal of Democracy

In England, Winston Churchill read reports that the German assault against Russia had stalled. He took heart that Hitler now had to fight on two fronts. And again, he urged President Roosevelt to join the war.

Franklin Delano Roosevelt had faced many struggles in his life. He had been a vigorous and healthy man, with an active career in politics, when in 1921, at age 39, he was struck by polio. The crippling disease left Roosevelt paralyzed from the waist down. As he slowly recovered, he made up his mind that he would not let the disease slow him down. For several hours each day, he built up his muscles with swimming and other exercises. He strapped steel braces onto his legs and hobbled on crutches, trying over and over without success to walk to the end of his long driveway. Roosevelt never again walked without aid, but he made himself strong enough to reenter public life.

In 1928, FDR, as he was known, won the governorship of New York. Then in 1932, in the depths of the Great Depression, he ran for and won the presidency of the United States. His leadership during the Depression led Americans to elect him to a record third term in 1940. They admired his spirit and abilities, and they wanted him to keep them out of war.

Privately, Roosevelt disagreed with his countrymen about the war. He believed that the United States would have to fight or risk a world ruled by Hitler. Roosevelt began building up the American army and sent 50 aging U.S. destroyers to the British. Several months later, the United States began a program for selling arms to the Allies known as Lend-Lease. It allowed the U.S. government not only to sell but to lend or lease armaments to any nation deemed "vital to the defense of the United States."

U.S. factories began turning out tanks, planes, and guns, and shipping them to Britain. The

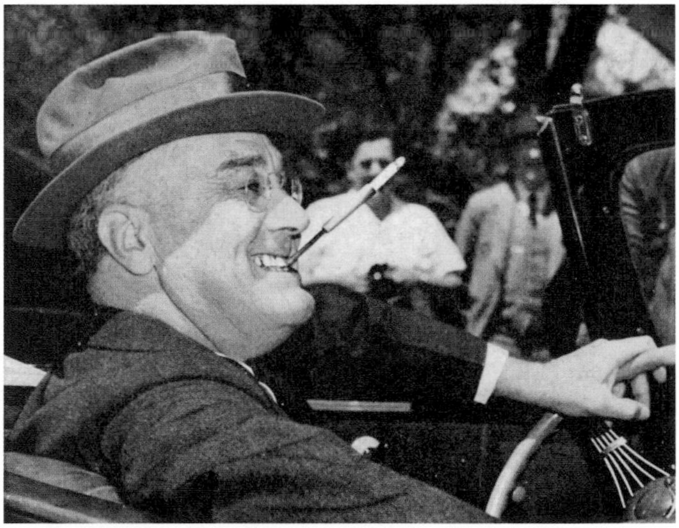

Americans admired FDR's confidence and optimistic spirit, but wanted him to keep them out of war.

An *arsenal* is a factory that makes weapons or a place where arms are stored.

president told Americans, "We must be the great arsenal of democracy." America was not yet at war. But by using its industrial might to arm countries fighting the Axis Powers, it was edging into battle.

In September 1940, the United States began its first peacetime draft. Some Americans were furious to see the direction that Roosevelt was heading. They protested that the U.S. government needed to concentrate on helping the country recover from the lingering effects of the Great Depression, not on war in Europe. At a protest in New York, one banner read, "We want work over here, not death over there."

By late 1941, hundreds of U.S. supply ships were steaming across the Atlantic carrying war supplies to Britain. German submarines torpedoed the supply ships when they could. Many Americans believed the submarine attacks would provoke the United States to enter the war.

But it was a catastrophe in the Pacific Ocean that brought World War II to the United States.

Pearl Harbor: Day of Infamy

Like the red sun on its national flag, Japan was on the rise in Asia. By the beginning of World War II, the island country had been industrializing for nearly 70 years. Japanese factories produced steel and textiles, while Japanese shipyards launched ships that sailed for ports around the world. Tokyo, the capital, bustled with seven million people.

Yet Japan's success brought problems. The population was growing, but land was limited. Japan had fewer natural resources than larger countries. It looked to other Pacific nations for raw materials such as oil, rubber, and metals.

Japanese military leaders, who controlled much of the government, had spent years building up the army and the navy. By the time World War II began, Japanese troops occupied Korea, Taiwan, and parts of mainland China.

In 1940, after the outbreak of the war, Japan joined Germany and Italy as an Axis Power. Japan's military leaders had visions of a grand empire that would cover much of Southeast Asia and the islands of the South Pacific.

In the middle of that domain lay the Philippine Islands. At this time, the Philippines were an American territory. Thousands of U.S. troops were stationed in military bases on the islands. The Japanese leaders calculated that it was only a matter of time before America entered the war. They decided that their best weapon against the United States was surprise.

Six huge Japanese aircraft carriers, loaded with dive bombers and escorted by battleships and destroyers, set course for Hawaii. Their target—Pearl Harbor, home of the U.S. Navy's Pacific Fleet.

Sunday, December 7, 1941, began as a peaceful morning at Pearl Harbor. American battleships floated at their moorings. At the airfield, U.S. planes sat on the ground, wingtip to wingtip. Many of the soldiers and sailors were getting ready for church.

Just before eight o'clock, a buzz in the sky broke the morning stillness. A swarm of warplanes dropped out of the clouds. At first the sailors thought they must be U.S. planes on a training exercise. But warning sirens began to wail, and the planes, with the red sun painted on their wings, screamed toward the harbor. The Japanese had caught the Americans completely off guard.

Explosion after explosion rocked the navy base as sailors ran for cover. Some reached their antiaircraft guns and began shooting, but it was too late. Ships burst into fireballs as bombs tore into their hulls. A 1,760-pound bomb ripped through the deck of the USS *Arizona*. Minutes later the colossal battleship split in two and sank to the harbor's bottom, taking more than a thousand crewmen with her.

When the Japanese planes headed back to their carriers, they had destroyed two battleships and damaged six others. They also left behind the wrecks of several smaller vessels. The remains of nearly two hundred U.S. planes littered the ground. Almost 2,500 servicemen were dead.

President Roosevelt was stunned by the news. The next day, he traveled to Capitol Hill, where he grimly addressed a joint session of Congress. His speech was broadcast by radio around the country to sixty million Americans.

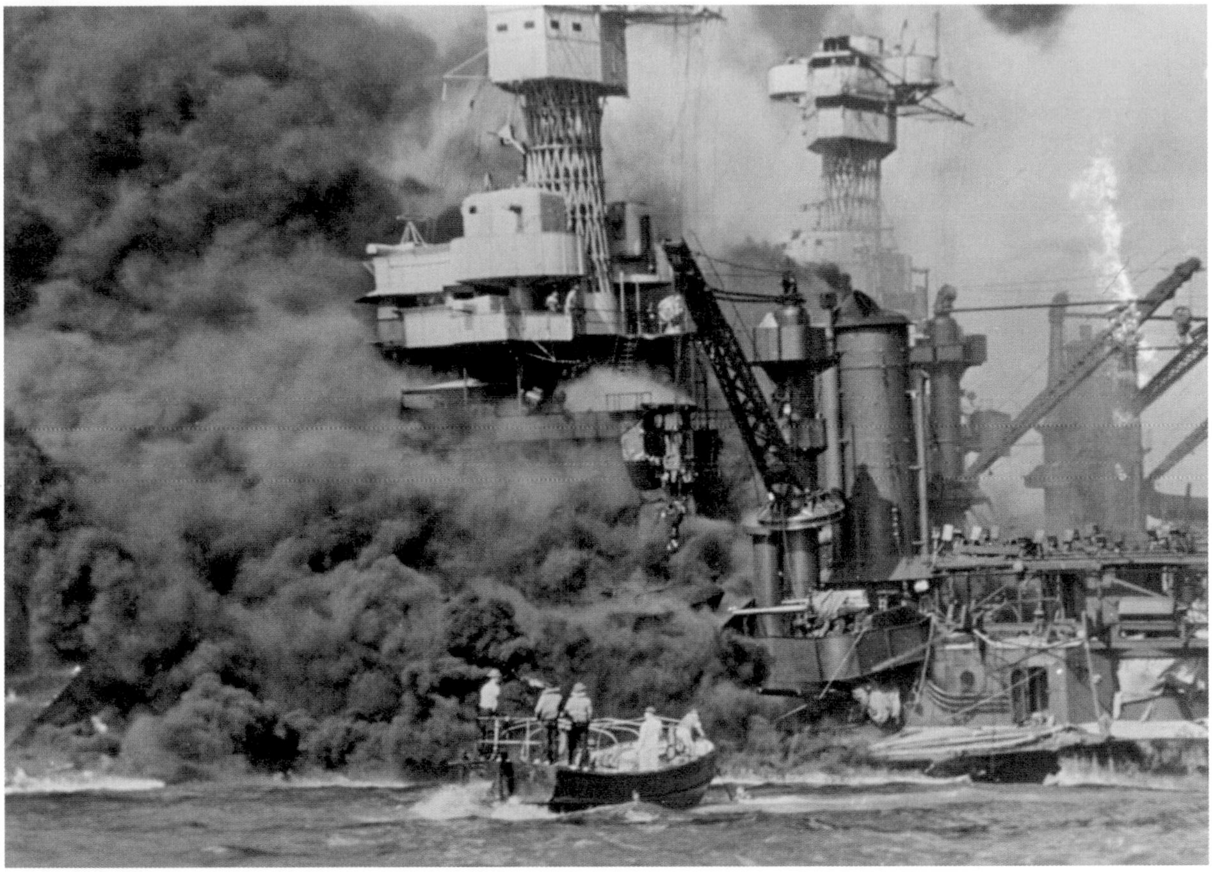

At Pearl Harbor, sailors in a small boat rescue survivors alongside the battleship USS *West Virginia*, which was torpedoed during the Japanese surprise raid on December 7, 1941. The next day, President Roosevelt asked Congress for a declaration of war against Japan, and the United States joined the Allies in the fight against the Axis Powers.

Roosevelt had strapped on his steel braces and walked with painful slowness into the chamber on the arm of his son. He gripped the lectern firmly with both hands.

"Yesterday, December 7, 1941—a date which will live in infamy," he began, "the United States of America was suddenly and deliberately attacked by naval and air forces of the empire of Japan."

When the president asked Congress for a declaration of war against Japan, Congress overwhelmingly approved it. Three days later, Japan's Axis partners, Germany and Italy, declared war on the United States. The United States, in turn, joined the Allies in the fight against the Axis Powers. World War II now stretched around the globe.

The Philippines Fall

Ten hours after the attack on Pearl Harbor, Japanese bombers also struck U.S. air bases in the Philippine Islands.

Within days, Japanese troops landed in the Philippines. A few weeks later they occupied Manila, the capital, without opposition. American and Filipino forces, under the command of General Douglas MacArthur, had moved west to the Bataan (buh-TAN) Peninsula.

After three months of fighting, General MacArthur was ordered to a command post in Australia. As he left, he vowed to the troops, "I shall return."

In April 1942, Japanese forces took the Bataan Peninsula. About 70,000 American and Filipino prisoners, already hungry and exhausted, were forced to march more than sixty miles to a prison camp.

On the Bataan Death March, as it has become known, the Japanese treated their prisoners with brutal cruelty. Prisoners were starved and beaten. Those who could not go on were killed with a swift thrust of a bayonet. Some were forced to dig their own graves and then buried alive.

Axis Surge in Asia and the Pacific

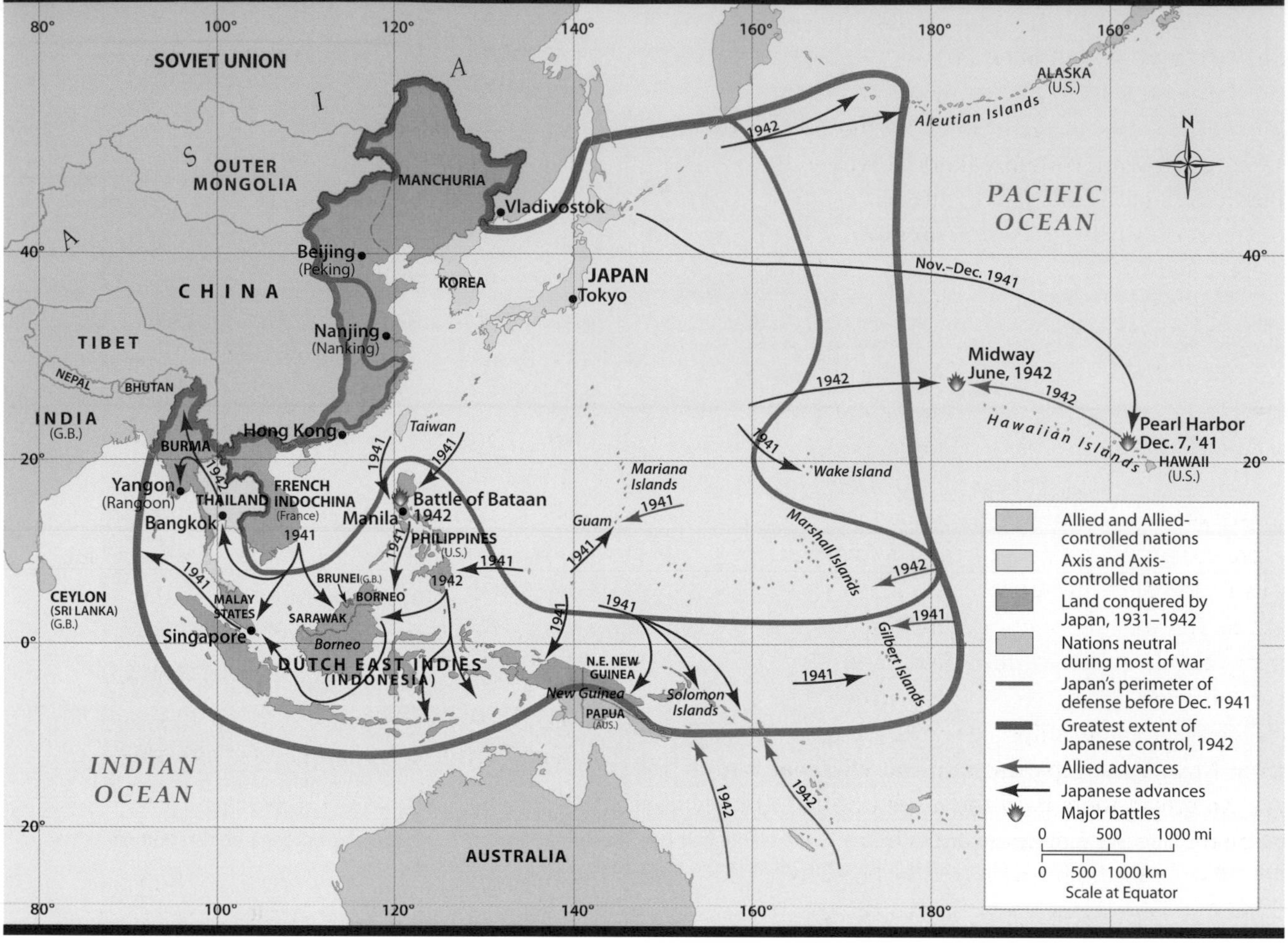

As the Japanese took over, they imprisoned thousands of American, British, Australian, and Canadian civilians living in the Philippines. The Santo Tomas internment camp in Manila held the largest body of American civilians captured in U.S. history. For the first five months of internment, the Japanese assumed no responsibility for feeding their prisoners. Filipinos outside the camp sent food over the wall to the captured men, women, and children within. As the war dragged on, many of the interned civilians died of hunger, overcrowding, and disease.

To *intern* people is to confine them, especially in wartime.

In the months following Pearl Harbor, Japan's army and navy launched assaults across thousands of miles of land and water. Japanese troops seized the island of Guam, a U.S. possession, and the British colony of Hong Kong. They pushed into mainland China, battling both Chinese government and communist armies. Japanese forces stunned the Allies by marching across the Malay Peninsula and capturing Singapore, a British stronghold and naval base. They conquered Indonesia, invaded New Guinea, and threatened Australia. They occupied Burma and seemed ready to attack India. By early 1942, it looked as though the Japanese would soon fulfill their ambition to rule a vast Asian empire.

On to Midway

Some Japanese military leaders believed the American people would not have the stomach for a long, hard fight in the Pacific. But the surprise attack on Pearl Harbor united Americans in support of war. Even the Japanese admiral who had planned the raid reportedly told his fellow naval officers, "I fear that we have only succeeded in waking a sleeping giant."

Luckily for the United States, none of its aircraft carriers had been at Pearl Harbor when the Japanese attacked. Within months, the U.S. Pacific Fleet was regrouping. In the spring of 1942, American code-breakers discovered that Japan's warships planned to attack the U.S. naval outpost of Midway Island, about 1,500 miles west of Hawaii.

In their Pacific Fleet, the Americans had fewer ships than the Japanese force steaming toward Midway. But this time the Americans had the advantage of surprise. U.S. commanders ordered an attack on the approaching Japanese ships.

American pilots roared off their carriers to strike the first blow. As they drew near the Japanese ships, they met heavy antiaircraft fire. About 150 planes were shot down. But those that made it through pounded the Japanese ships with bombs. Within minutes, three Japanese carriers were in flames, and a fourth sank later, along with other ships. The rest limped away from Midway. A Japanese admiral who watched the American fliers paid them the ultimate compliment: "These men are samurai."

The Americans had won the battle of Midway. But the war was just half over. And it was going to get much worse.

Civilian Internees in the War

Both the Axis and Allied powers imprisoned civilians during the war. As they conquered territories, the Germans, Japanese, and Italians interned civilians from Allied nations, often in prison camps where the conditions were wretched and the treatment cruel. Great Britain, Canada, and the United States also put civilians in special camps, where the treatment was generally at least humane and prisoners never lacked for basic necessities.

Great Britain arrested tens of thousands of German and Italian civilians in England. Canadians interned more than 20,000 people of Japanese descent, most of whom were Canadian citizens. The United States interned 120,000 inhabitants of Japanese descent—of these, 65 percent were American citizens. The Allied nations set up such camps because they worried these civilians might aid the enemy. But the roundup of Japanese Americans and Japanese Canadians is remembered with shame in North America. Many who were interned received reparations decades after the close of the war.

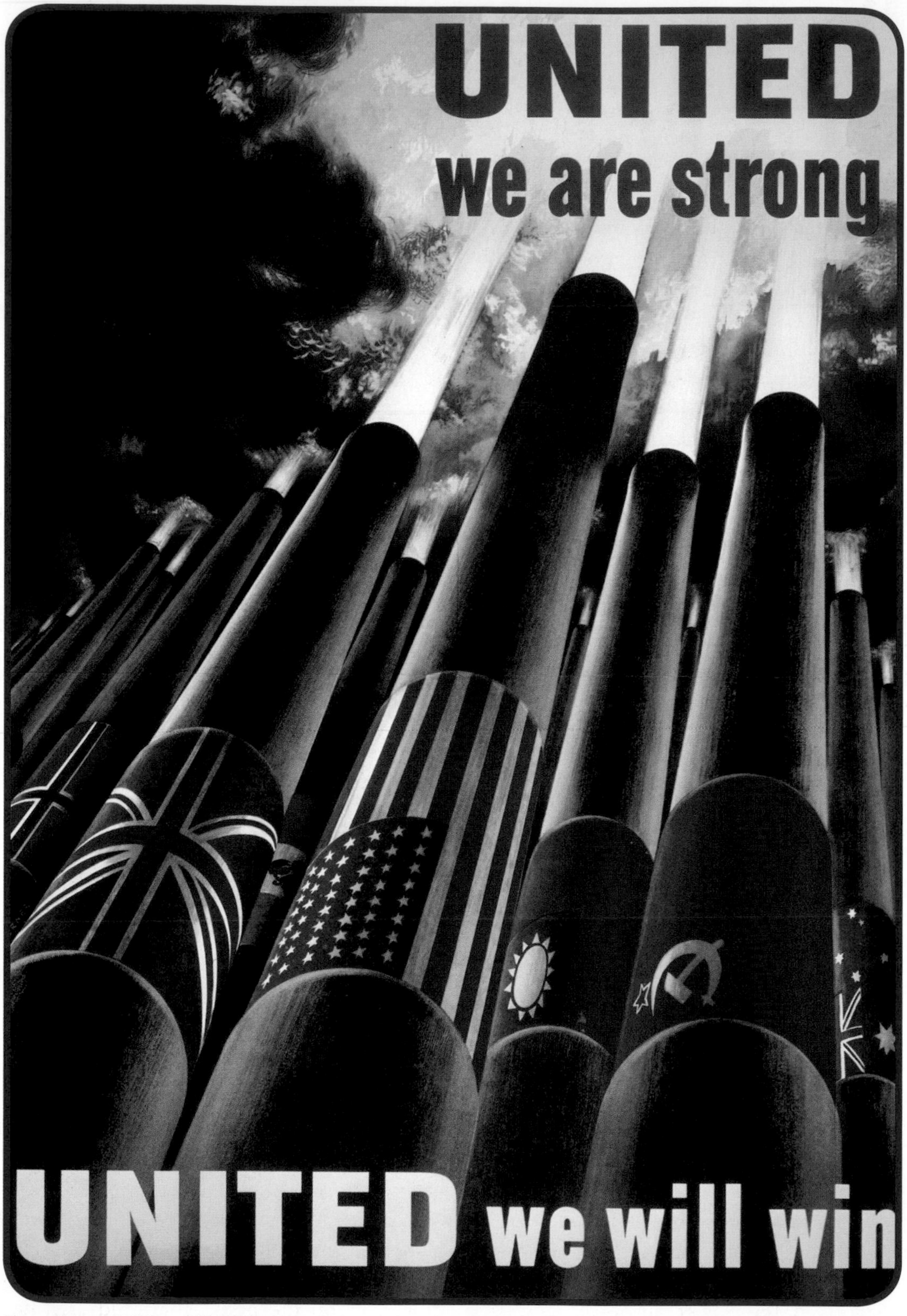

Flags of several Allies of World War II encircle cannons in a poster designed to inspire Americans during the fight against the Axis Powers. Represented are (left to right) Norway, the United Kingdom, the United States, China, the Soviet Union, and Australia.

Allied Victory and the Shape of Evil

At the close of 1942, a reasonable person might have concluded that most of the world would soon be ruled by fascist dictators. Hitler dominated the European continent, and German troops were pressing deep into Soviet territory. Mussolini's Italian troops had invaded Egypt, and when Hitler supplied reinforcements, the Axis Powers proceeded to pound the British forces there. In the Pacific, Japan held not only the Philippines, but also large parts of China and the former French and British colonies of Vietnam, Malaya, Singapore, Burma, and Indonesia. Though the Japanese had suffered a severe blow at Midway, they were far from beaten.

After 1942, however, the Allies slowly turned the tide of war, first on the Eastern Front, then in the Mediterranean, and finally with an invasion of northern Europe. In this chapter, we'll see how the Allies achieved victory over the Axis. We'll also examine the terrible price paid by many of the war's victims. The closing years of World War II reveal the height of human courage and ingenuity, as well as the depths of human evil.

Stalin Holds the Eastern Front

As you read in the previous chapter, when Hitler's forces invaded the Soviet Union in June 1941, the Nazis caught the Soviets by surprise. A blitzkrieg assault devastated the Soviet air force. German troops quickly pushed east, capturing Kiev, laying siege to Leningrad, and bombing Moscow. But by January 1942, an ally came to Russia's aid — the harsh, frigid winter. With the help of "General Winter," as they called their natural ally, the Russian army successfully drove the Germans from Moscow.

Hitler wanted to stay on the offensive. By the summer of 1942, he had a new objective — the industrial port city of Stalingrad (now Volgograd) along the Volga River. If the Nazi troops took Stalingrad, Hitler reasoned, the Axis could cut off Russia's oil supply, which moved through the city. Hitler also knew that the defeat of *Stalingrad* — named after the USSR's leader — would be a severe psychological blow for the Russians.

Stalin knew that, too. When German troops closed in on the bomb-shattered city, he gave the Soviet defenders a single order: "Not one step backward!"

Allied Victory in Europe and North Africa

Norwegian Sea
ATLANTIC OCEAN
NORWAY
SWEDEN
FINLAND
Oslo
Helsinki
Leningrad (St. Petersburg)
Stockholm
ESTONIA
LATVIA
Riga
LITHUANIA
Moscow
SOVIET UNION
North Sea
DENMARK
Copenhagen
Baltic Sea
IRISH FREE STATE
GREAT BRITAIN
London
Amsterdam
NETH.
Berlin
Potsdam
GERMANY (EAST PRUSSIA)
Minsk
Warsaw
POLAND
English Channel
Calais
D-day Normandy (June 6,1944)
BELGIUM
LUX.
Cologne
Leipzig
Dresden
Prague
AUSCHWITZ
Kiev
Dnieper R.
Stalingrad (Volgograd) (1942–43)
Paris
Rhine R.
Nuremberg
GERMANY
Battle of the Bulge Ardennes (1944–45)
DACHAU
Munich
SLOVAKIA
HUNGARY
Budapest
Vienna
AUSTRIA
SWITZ.
FRANCE
ROMANIA
Bucharest
YUGOSLAVIA
Danube R.
Yalta
Black Sea
ITALY
Sarajevo
Sofia
BULGARIA
ANDORRA
PORTUGAL
Madrid
SPAIN
Corsica (Fr.)
Rome
Istanbul
ALBANIA
Sardinia (Fr.)
TURKEY
ASIA
GREECE
Athens
SPANISH MOROCCO (Spain)
Algiers
Tunis
Sicily
SYRIA (Fr.)
Malta (G.B.)
Cyprus (G.B.)
LEBANON (Fr.)
MOROCCO (France)
Crete (Gr.)
Mediterranean Sea
TUNISIA (France)
Tripoli
PALESTINE (G.B.)
TRANS-JORDAN (G.B.)
El Alamein (1942)
ALGERIA (France)
Suez Canal
Cairo
SAUDI ARABIA
EGYPT (Great Britain)
AFRICA
LIBYA (Italy)
Nile R.
Red Sea
Volga R.
EUROPE
1942
1943
1944
1945
Allied and Allied-controlled nations
Axis and Axis-controlled nations
Farthest extent of Axis military occupation, Nov. 1942
Nations neutral during most of war
Meeting of Western and Soviet forces at end of WWII
Allied advances
Major battles
Concentration camps
0 200 400 mi
0 200 400 km
PACIFIC THEATER
USSR
MANCHURIA
UPPER MONGOLIA
CHINA
TIBET
JAPAN
KOREA
INDIA
BURMA
FRENCH INDOCHINA
THAILAND
HAWAII
DUTCH EAST INDIES
N.E. NEW GUINEA
PAPUA
AUSTRALIA
NEW ZEALAND
ALASKA
CANADA
UNITED STATES
MEXICO
CUBA
COLOMBIA
BRAZIL
BOLIVIA
ARGENTINA
GREENLAND
NORWAY
SWEDEN
FINLAND
GERMANY
GREAT BRITAIN
IRELAND
SWITZERLAND
FRANCE
SPAIN
ITALY
USSR
POLAND
HUNGARY
ROMANIA
BULGARIA
TURKEY
EUROPEAN THEATER
LIBYA
EGYPT
SAUDI ARABIA
FRENCH WEST AFRICA
ETHIOPIA
KENYA
FRENCH EQUATORIAL AFRICA
ANGOLA
SOUTHWEST AFRICA
MOZAMBIQUE
SOUTH AFRICA

The Battle of Stalingrad

The 199-day Battle of Stalingrad was the bloodiest battle in human history. The Germans initially won the city. The Soviets took it back. The two sides often fought in hand-to-hand combat from building to building, on rooftops, on staircases, and in cellars. Soviet soldiers tied grenades to their bodies and threw themselves under German tanks. A German soldier wrote that "the Russians are defending themselves with insane stubbornness." Another said, "Stalingrad is no longer a town. By day it is an enormous cloud of burning, blinding smoke... a vast furnace lit by the reflection of flames."

Time was on the side of the Russians. German supplies were running low, and another brutal winter was setting in. When the Volga froze in November, Russian soldiers were able to push supplies across it by night. The Red Army managed to encircle the German troops and starve them into defeat. Hitler ordered his troops to fight on, but the last surrendered in February 1943.

The Battle of Stalingrad proved the turning point in the war on the Eastern Front. In the following months, the Russians and Germans clashed repeatedly, but the Soviets, inspired by the desire to save "Mother Russia," drove Hitler's army back toward Germany.

At the close of the Battle of Stalingrad, perhaps 800,000 Axis troops had lost their lives. More than a million Soviet soldiers lay dead. An unknown number of civilians perished in Stalingrad. As one soldier observed, distances in the Soviet Union were no longer measured in meters, but in corpses. By some estimates, the battle cost two million lives in all. And there was much more fighting to come.

The Allied Ranks

At the outset of World War II, Britain and France were the chief powers of the Allied nations. As the war spread, nearly fifty countries joined the Allied ranks. The Soviet Union and the United States were the most powerful countries to join Britain and France. The long list of Allies also included large nations such as Australia, Canada, and China, as well as smaller ones such as Liberia, El Salvador, and Panama.

Russian soldiers advance across a field of rubble during the Battle of Stalingrad. The Soviet army managed to turn back Hitler's attacking forces, but before it was over, the battle cost perhaps two million lives and destroyed the city.

British tanks advance across desert sands near El Alamein, Egypt, in 1942. The German general Erwin Rommel—known as the Desert Fox—tried to overrun Egypt, but British and American forces managed to drive him back.

From North Africa to Italy

As his battered army struggled to drive the German invaders out of the Soviet Union, Stalin pressured Churchill and Roosevelt to launch an Allied invasion of Europe from England. This would open a second battle front, thus pressuring the Germans to move their troops from Russia to the west. The British and the Americans agreed on the need for an invasion, but the British wanted more time to prepare the attack. And Churchill first wanted to take care of business in North Africa, especially in Egypt, where for decades Britain had protected its interests in the Suez Canal.

When Italy's Fascist dictator, Benito Mussolini, sent his troops into Egypt, he was so certain of victory that he selected a white stallion to ride during a triumphal entry into Cairo. He never took that ride, however, because the British managed to push back the Italian forces. That's when Hitler sent Rommel, the Desert Fox. With his tanks and troops, Rommel took a key port city in Libya, and then advanced into Egypt as far as the village of El Alamein (el a-luh-MAYN).

In October 1942, British forces under General Bernard Montgomery, known as "Monty," unleashed air strikes, infantry charges, and the power of more than a thousand tanks against Rommel's troops. Rommel resisted for over a week but soon had to retreat to the west.

Waiting for him were more than 100,000 Allied troops, mostly Americans, under the command of an American general, Dwight D. Eisenhower. After months of fighting, Rommel and his troops found themselves squeezed between the forces of Eisenhower and Montgomery.

The British and Americans proceeded to finish the job of clearing North Africa of Axis troops. Then they crossed the Mediterranean and began inching their way up the Italian peninsula — Mussolini's homeland. The people of Italy decided they had had enough of war. In July 1943, they overthrew Mussolini. The Germans propped him up in a puppet government in the north, but now the defense of Italy was up to the Germans. They made sure that the Allied march up the Italian peninsula was a slow and bloody struggle.

A *puppet government* is one that is heavily influenced or controlled by a foreign nation.

Who Were the Egyptians For?

Many Egyptians and Arab nationalists hoped for an Axis victory in World War II. They sympathized with Hitler and Mussolini because they resented the British and French, who for decades had dominated much of the Middle East. Hitler's anti-Semitism also appealed to them. Arab nationalists hoped that a defeat of the Allies would bring greater independence for Middle Eastern states.

Planning for D–day

By January 1944, the Allied high command focused on launching the all-important invasion of northern Europe from England. They planned to move a huge force of men and machinery across the English Channel, and then liberate western Europe and defeat the Nazis.

The man responsible for making the invasion a success was U.S. General Eisenhower, who had commanded the operation that helped defeat Rommel in Africa. "Ike," as he was known, was a mild-mannered Midwesterner with an extraordinary talent for organizing armies. Now his job was to organize the invasion of the century. There were countless problems to solve and questions to answer. How many men should attack? Which divisions? How many warships and naval vessels? What about tanks? Which planes? How many paratroopers? What kind of landing craft? Where would they invade?

Eisenhower knew he could count on the enormous American industrial machine. In 1944, assembly-line workers in the United States toiled around the clock to manufacture tanks, armored cars, warplanes, guns, and ammunition. Ships carried weapons and hundreds of thousands of American soldiers across the Atlantic—a voyage that had become somewhat safer since the British and Americans enjoyed more success in sinking German U-boats.

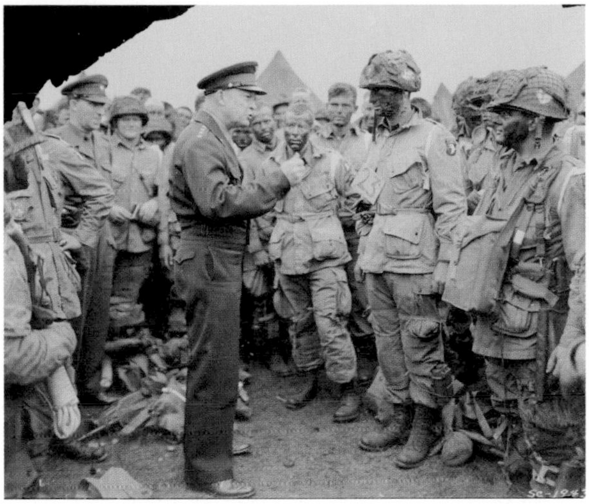

General Dwight D. Eisenhower meets with U.S. troops just before the Allies' D–day invasion of northern Europe.

The ships unloaded in Britain, where Eisenhower was gathering his invasion force. One big question Eisenhower faced was where to make the crossing from England. Most people thought the invasion would take place at the French port of Calais (ka-LAY), where the English Channel is narrowest. Ike fooled the Germans into thinking a huge Allied army was amassing across the Channel from Calais. He even equipped this

Women work on the nose cones of A-20 attack bombers at the Douglas Aviation Company in Long Beach, California. During the war, millions of American women joined the labor force, often working in factories to help produce military supplies.

Why D–day?

During World War II, the term *D–day* was used by military planners to designate any secret date for a military campaign. June 6, 1944, was one of many D–days, but this major assault is the most famous D–day in history.

shadow army with inflatable tanks and fake landing craft, and filled the airwaves with misleading radio messages.

Meanwhile, the *real* invasion force gathered farther west along Britain's coast and prepared to strike the French region of Normandy. The size of the initial force was enormous: close to 160,000 Allied troops, about 13,000 aircraft, 1,500 tanks, and 6,500 sea vessels, which included dozens of warships and 4,000 custom-designed landing craft.

Eisenhower tirelessly encouraged his troops. He visited crews on ships, climbed into the cockpits of warplanes, observed tank maneuvers, and took target practice with the infantry. "This operation is being planned as a success," he declared. "We cannot afford to fail."

By early June 1944, the troops, mostly British, American, and Canadian, were ready to embark. "The mighty host was as tense as a coiled spring," Eisenhower later remembered, "and indeed that is exactly what it was — a great human spring, coiled for the moment when its energy would be released and it would vault the English Channel in the greatest amphibious assault ever attempted."

An *amphibious assault* is one in which seaborne forces come ashore to attack enemy-held terrain.

The surprise invasion had a code name — D–day. On June 6, 1944, the tides and weather were rough, but Eisenhower gave the order: "OK, let's go."

American troops wade ashore on Omaha Beach during the D–day landings of June 6, 1944. The Allied invasion of Normandy met stiff resistance but drove the Germans inland.

From D–day to Paris

Under cover of darkness, the great Allied armada started across the English Channel toward five Normandy beaches, code named Omaha, Utah, Sword, Gold, and Juno. For most of the American troops, this would be their first combat. They were, said one of Ike's officers, "as green as growing corn."

When the fleet got within range of the French coastline, huge guns aboard the Allied warships began to pound the German defenses, while transport planes dropped paratroopers behind enemy positions. Allied soldiers, laden with 60-pound packs, clambered from the ships into flat-bottomed landing craft. Seasick and scared, they waited until the landing craft ran close to shore. As steel doors fell forward, the troops jumped into the water. Some struggled and drowned from the sheer weight of their packs, but most pushed as quickly as they could for the beach.

Although the Allies took the Germans by surprise, they still met heavy gunfire from the hills beyond the beaches. On Omaha Beach, which the Americans assaulted, 90 percent of the men in some units were killed or wounded.

Despite the awful losses, Eisenhower's painstaking preparations began to pay off. More and more landing craft arrived. In 24 hours, some 156,000 troops came ashore in Normandy. Tanks, trucks, and jeeps began rolling up the beaches. By day's end, all five landing sites were secured.

In the next three weeks, the Allies landed more than a million men, nearly 200,000 vehicles, and 600,000 tons of supplies. Mile by mile, the attacking forces fought their way inland. German troops fought them at every step.

The Allies advanced toward Paris. As they converged on the city, Hitler ordered his generals to burn the French capital to the ground. Fortunately, the generals hesitated. On August 25, Allied troops liberated Paris, and grateful Parisians lined the streets to cheer them on.

British, American, French, and Canadian forces now drove east toward Germany's great natural defense, the Rhine River. Meanwhile, Russian troops pressed west toward Germany.

Discovering the Unthinkable: The Holocaust

As Allied troops liberated German-occupied territories and began to push into Germany itself, they discovered a horror that defied imagination.

The advancing soldiers came across prison camps surrounded by walls, fences, barbed wire, and guard towers. Entering the camps, they were stunned to find men, women, and children so thin and sick that they looked almost like skeletons. In some places, the Allies found thousands of bodies and pieces of human remains. Battle-hardened troops wept at the sight of corpses littering the muddy ground or piled into giant pits.

What had happened? For years, the Allies had heard reports that the Nazis were arresting Jews, communists, Slavs, people with physical or mental disabilities, and others considered "inferior." But few people outside of German-occupied areas could imagine — or were willing to recognize — the terrible crimes that Hitler's regime was committing. Now, as the Allies pushed toward Berlin, they discovered the full scope of the Nazis' brutality — a campaign of carefully planned mass murder known as the Holocaust.

A holocaust is complete destruction, especially by fire. The term *the Holocaust* refers to the mass slaughter of Europe's Jews and others by the Nazis.

German soldiers round up Jews in Warsaw, Poland, in 1943. As Allied armies pushed closer to Germany, they came across camps where Hitler's regime had imprisoned and killed Jews and others designated as "inferior" by the Nazis. The Nazi campaign of mass murder, known as the Holocaust, stands as one of the most horrible tragedies in history.

Nazis forced Jews to wear Star of David badges. *Juif* means "Jew" in French.

Named for a king of ancient Israel, the six-pointed Star of David, also called the Shield of David, is a widespread symbol of Judaism, the religion of the Jews.

You learned that Hitler used anti-Semitism—hatred of Jews—to rally the German people and gain power. He believed that Germans were a master "Aryan" race, whose troubles could be blamed on the Jews. When the German army conquered lands where millions of Jews lived, the Nazis forced them to wear yellow Star of David badges so they could be easily identified. Following on the heels of the German army as it drove into the Soviet Union and other countries, specially trained death squads sought out those marked with yellow stars.

The death squads murdered perhaps a million Jews, as well as socialists, Communist Party members, and others that Hitler viewed as troublemakers or as "inferior." Sometimes the Nazis forced their victims to dig trenches, and then shot them so the bodies tumbled into the shallow mass graves. Sometimes they killed people by hanging them, burying them alive, or packing them into sealed vans and suffocating them with fumes from the engine exhaust.

For Hitler, none of this was enough. He was determined to reach, as he put it, "the Final Solution to the Jewish Question"—the killing of *all* the Jews in Europe.

To achieve his "Final Solution," Hitler needed a more systematic way to commit genocide. For that, he turned to his growing network of concentration camps.

As you learned, soon after coming to power in Germany, Hitler began to set up prison camps for socialists, communists, and others who opposed Nazi views. The first of these concentration camps was built in 1933 near the town of Dachau (DAH-kow). In the following years, Hitler ordered more concentration camps built throughout Germany and in countries the Nazis conquered. As Nazi armies marched across Europe, they forced thousands of Jews and others onto trains, which hauled the captives, like cattle, to concentration camps.

The prisoners often spent days packed into the freight cars without food or water. Many died before reaching their destinations. Those who did reach the camps often became slave laborers, forced to mine coal or work at factories that made guns, airplanes, cement, fuel, or other products needed for the war.

Many prisoners lived only a few weeks or months. They died of overwork, starvation, or one of the diseases that frequently swept through the camps. The Nazis usually killed those who could not work fast enough.

The Ghettos

In many cities, the Nazis rounded up Jews and herded them into neighborhoods known as ghettos, sealed off from the outside world by high walls or fences, barbed wire, and patrolling guards. There were about 400 Jewish ghettos in Poland alone. The biggest was in Warsaw, Poland, where about 500,000 Jews were isolated in overcrowded, unsanitary conditions. At first the ghettos were intended to keep Jews separate from so-called Aryans, Hitler's "master race." Later, the Nazis used the ghettos as places to hold Jews until they could be shipped to concentration camps.

The Death Camps

By late 1942, the Nazis had constructed six special concentration camps in German-occupied Poland. They came to be known as death camps. Hitler had them built for one purpose—to kill. The most notorious of the death camps was at Auschwitz (OWSH-vihts), in southern Poland.

At Auschwitz, trains pulled straight into the camp so the prisoners, mostly Jews, could be quickly unloaded and sorted. Guards immediately divided new arrivals into two groups—those capable of slave labor, and those not.

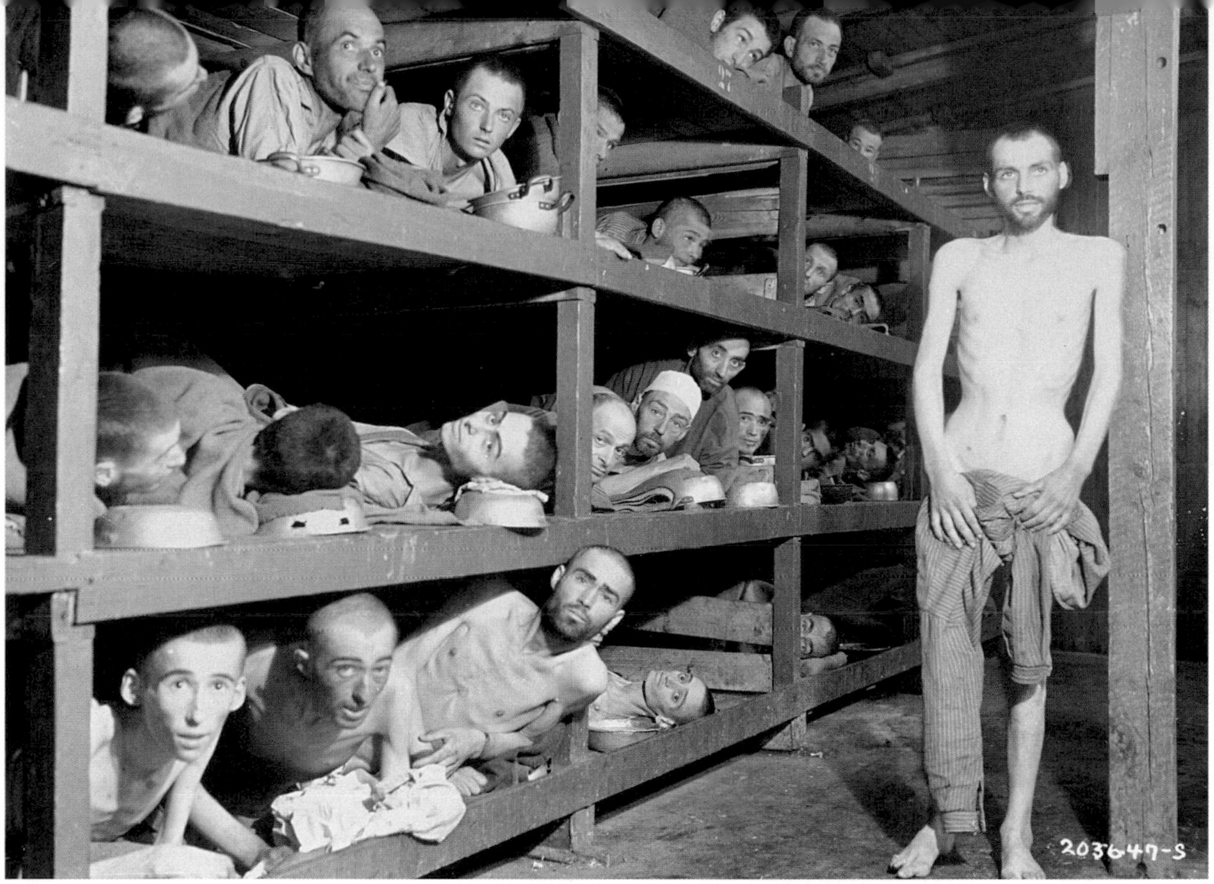

Survivors of the Buchenwald Concentration Camp in Germany stare out from wooden bunks in their barracks shortly after U.S. troops arrived in April 1945. The Nazis worked to death or executed millions in such camps.

Those chosen to be laborers were put into striped uniforms and tattooed on the left arm with a registration number. Then they were marched off to work in factories or mines. Their fate was extermination through work. They labored eleven hours a day. Guards used whips, sticks, and their fists on those unable to keep up the pace. By the end of 1943, at least half a million slave laborers died of exhaustion and starvation at Auschwitz.

Those designated as unfit for work when they arrived at Auschwitz — including the sick, the elderly, pregnant women, and children under 16 — met a much swifter death. Guards ordered them to undress and herded them into large underground chambers, where the prisoners were told they would shower. But the shower rooms were actually gas chambers. When the guards could squeeze no more people inside, they sealed the airtight metal doors and released poison gas, killing everyone. Afterward, prison workers removed rings from fingers and extracted gold fillings from the teeth of the dead.

At first, Auschwitz officials buried bodies in mass graves in a nearby meadow. But as the corpses piled up, the Nazis needed another way to dispose of the human remains. Hitler's engineers designed crematoriums that could burn 2,000 bodies at a time. When the crematoriums were at work, gray smoke clouded the sky over the camp.

Officials at Auschwitz and other camps used some prisoners as guinea pigs in brutal medical experiments. Doctors injected bacteria into prisoners' bone marrow. They exposed inmates to intense cold, extreme pressure, drowning, burning, starvation, electric shock, and different types of poisons to see how the human body reacted before death.

Even as Hitler's armies began to retreat toward Germany, the Nazis continued to send "undesirables" to the death camps. Jews from Italy, Austria, Greece, and Hungary were transported to Auschwitz. During the summer of 1944, the camp gassed and burned thousands of people a day. Before the war's end, an estimated two million people were murdered at Auschwitz alone.

In all, the Holocaust claimed the lives of perhaps eleven million people, including about six million Jews — two-thirds of the Jews in Europe.

Allied Victory in Europe

Throughout the summer and fall of 1944, and into the winter, the Allies closed in on Germany. The Soviets approached from the east, and the British, Americans, and other forces from the west. German troops were fighting now to defend "the Fatherland." When forced to give ground, they blew up bridges and destroyed railroads to slow the Allied advance.

In December 1944, Hitler made a desperate attempt to turn back the oncoming tide of troops. He ordered his generals to launch an assault on a thinly held American line in the Ardennes (ahr-DEN) Forest in Belgium. Some 200,000 German soldiers and 600 tanks rammed into the Allied front. They caught the Americans by surprise and forced them back, creating a huge bulge in their lines. In the Battle of the Bulge, as the fight came to be known, 19,000 American troops were killed. The American line bent, but did not break. After two weeks of fighting, the Allies managed to rally and halt the German attack. Soon they were pushing forward again, smashing through German defenses.

Bombers pounded Germany's industrial and commercial centers — American bombers by day, British by night — with no regard for civilian versus military casualties. The Allies dropped hundreds of tons of bombs on the city of Dresden, setting off a firestorm that could be seen 200 miles away. Bombs fell on Hamburg, Berlin, Cologne, Leipzig, and other cities, reducing block after block to rubble.

As the Soviet army approached Warsaw, the Poles took heart and revolted against their German occupiers. They expected the Soviet troops to come to their aid. But Stalin despised the Poles and had plans to dominate their country after the war. He held his army outside of Warsaw and waited for the Germans to crush the revolt. Hitler's troops burned and dynamited most of the city. The Nazis killed as many as 250,000 Poles, and sent hundreds of thousands more to concentration camps. Only then did the Soviet army move in to capture the ruins of Warsaw. The Poles would long remember this betrayal.

By the spring of 1945, Americans advancing from the west and Soviets fighting from the east finally met at the Elbe River south of Berlin. They swapped rations and vodka, congratulating their colleagues in arms.

Meanwhile, other Soviet troops closed in on Germany's capital, Berlin, where Adolf Hitler hid in a fortified bunker fifty feet underground. In desperation, he continued to issue impossible orders to units that no longer existed.

Hitler knew that the Russians were pushing closer to his bunker. He also learned that his Axis partner, Mussolini, was dead, shot by his own people. Before the Russians could capture him, the führer sat at a table and shot himself with a pistol.

Seven days later, on May 7, 1945, Germany surrendered. The Allies celebrated the next day as V-E Day — Victory in Europe Day. In London, New York, Moscow, Paris, and cities throughout the world, people cried, hugged, and danced in the streets. Churchill called it "the signal for the greatest outburst of joy in the history of mankind."

A statue atop Dresden's town hall overlooks miles of ruins. Allied bombers pounded the German city, setting off a firestorm that destroyed thousands of buildings.

The aircraft carrier USS *Hornet* fights off a kamikaze attack in the Pacific. As depicted in this painting, a single kamikaze plane loaded with bombs could destroy an entire ship if it got past defending fighter planes and antiaircraft guns.

The Allies' Pacific Push

The war in Europe was over, but fighting in the Pacific continued.

Since the Battle of Midway, the United States had pursued a strategy of "island hopping," moving toward Japan by taking one island at a time. On more than a hundred Japanese-occupied islands, American troops fought their way ashore, often suffering heavy losses. For example, more than a thousand Americans died taking a tiny island called Tarawa (tuh-RAH-wuh), and nearly five thousand Japanese died defending it.

The Americans realized they could not afford to fight for every Japanese-occupied island. So they leapfrogged some, bypassing the Japanese garrisons and leaving them, as one U.S. admiral put it, to "wither on the vine."

As the Americans edged ever closer to their homeland, Japanese fliers began to use a new form of air warfare—suicide attacks by pilots known as kamikaze (kah-mih-KAH-zee), which means "Divine Wind." Kamikazes turned their bomb-filled planes into weapons and deliberately crashed them into American vessels. By giving up his own life, a single kamikaze pilot could kill hundreds of Americans and destroy a whole ship.

Japanese fliers launched a bold attack on U.S. forces attempting to retake the Philippine Islands. As you've read, General Douglas MacArthur was the American commander in the Philippines at the start of the war. When the Japanese captured the islands, MacArthur made his famous promise to the people of the Philippines: "I shall return." He became the commander of U.S. operations in the Pacific, and by late 1944, his forces were poised to take back the Philippines.

As the U.S. ships approached the islands, more than 400 kamikaze pilots flew out to meet them. They drove their planes straight at the American vessels, sinking and damaging several. But MacArthur made good on his promise to return. In October 1944, he landed on the Philippine island of Leyte (LAY-tee). By February, his troops were pressing into Manila, to the cheers of both Filipinos and Allied civilians imprisoned in the city.

U.S. troops continued to hop from island to island. After brutal fighting, they captured Iwo Jima (EE-woh JEE-mah), about 700 miles from Tokyo. They moved on to take Okinawa (oh-kee-NAH-wah), a stepping stone to the major islands of Japan. On that small island, the Japanese lost nearly 70,000 soldiers, and the Americans more than 12,000.

Soon American pilots were taking off from airstrips on Pacific islands and bombing Japan itself. These raids reduced Japanese cities to ruins. Allied victory over Japan was no longer in doubt. But as the grim losses in taking each island had proven, the Japanese were willing to fight to the last man.

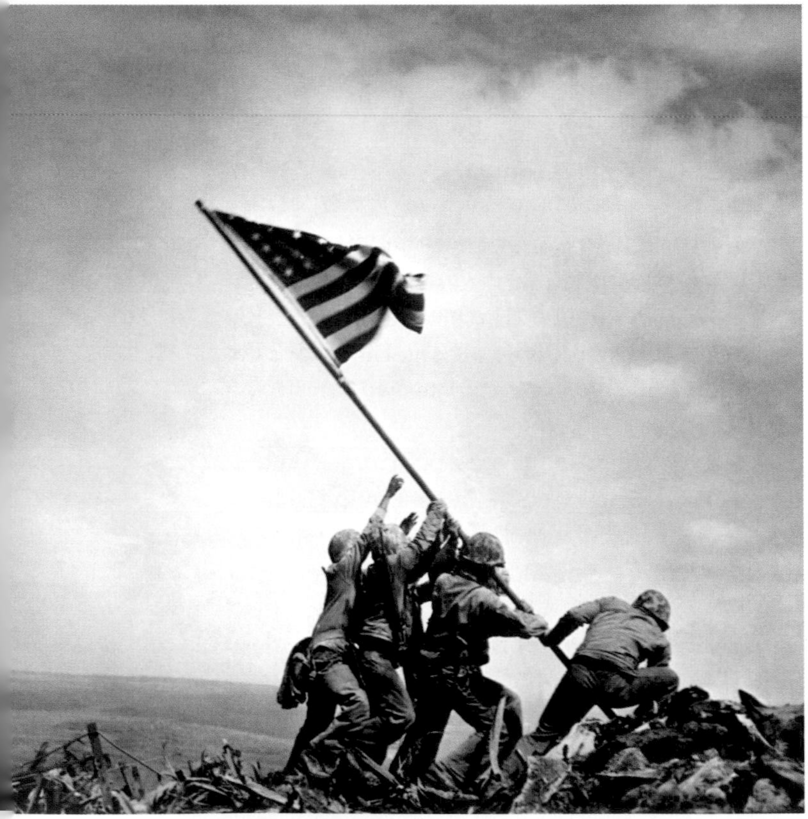

Soldiers raise the American flag on the island of Iwo Jima. Some 6,800 Americans died capturing the island's eight square miles; 21,000 Japanese died defending it.

General Douglas MacArthur and his staff wade ashore in the Philippines, making good on the general's promise: "I shall return."

The Manhattan Project

Island hopping brought the Allies close to Japan. The next logical step would be to invade Japan itself. Some U.S. military officials predicted that half a million American soldiers would die in an invasion of the Japanese homeland. Everyone agreed that even more Japanese would perish. But by the summer of 1945, American scientists offered President Harry Truman an alternative.

Even before the outbreak of the war, scientists had been exploring the structure of atoms and speculating about the possibility of splitting an atom's nucleus. They were building on the insights of Albert Einstein, a great German-born physicist. (You'll read more about Einstein at the end of this chapter.) Einstein's revolutionary theories, and his famous formula $E=mc^2$ (energy equals mass times the speed of light squared), led scientists to understand that the process of nuclear fission — splitting the nucleus of an atom — could set off a chain reaction capable of unleashing a huge amount of energy. Perhaps this energy could be used to light whole cities. Or perhaps it could be used to create a weapon, an atomic bomb of almost unimaginable destructive power.

While Einstein did not have a bomb in mind when he developed his theories, he immediately understood when his fellow scientists explained their destructive potential. Other physicists who had fled from fascist regimes in Europe urged Einstein to put the matter before the president. In 1939, Einstein was living in the United States because he was of Jewish descent and no longer allowed to

Allied Victory in Asia and the Pacific

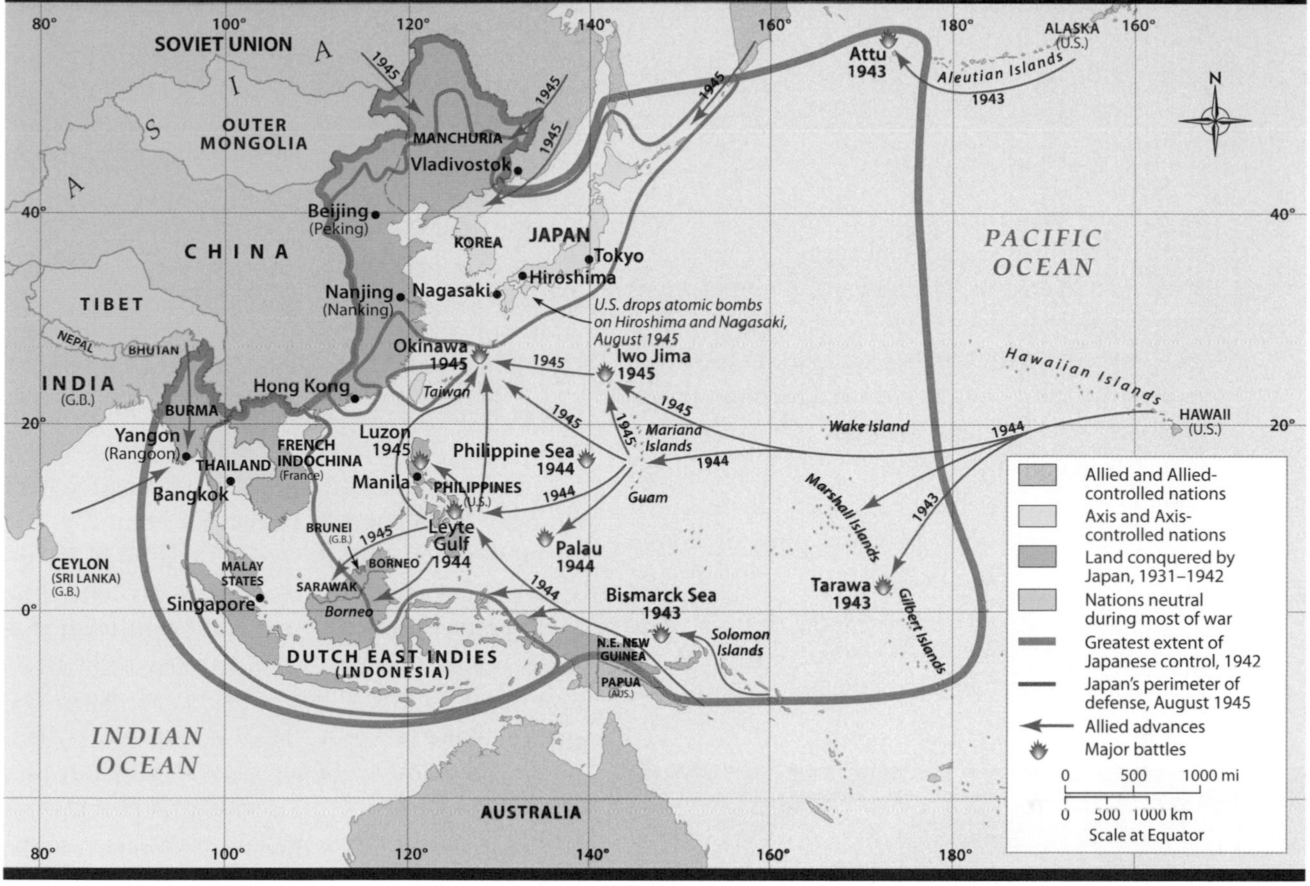

teach at his German university. He wrote to Franklin Roosevelt, warning the president that the Nazis were already working to build an atomic bomb, and urging that the United States do the same. Einstein and his fellow physicists believed the United States should hurry to develop an atomic bomb before Hitler because they knew that once Hitler had the bomb, he would not hesitate to use it.

President Roosevelt authorized the start of a top-secret research program that grew to include eminent scientists from other Allied nations. The program was code-named the Manhattan Project. Led by an American scientist named J. Robert Oppenheimer, the Manhattan Project's researchers set to work at secret locations across the country, even under a football stadium in Chicago. Eventually some 120,000 men and women were working on the project. Their goal—to win the race to develop an atomic bomb.

In July 1945, about three years after the Manhattan Project began, scientists successfully detonated an experimental atomic bomb at a remote location in the New Mexico desert. By this time, the Germans had surrendered and Hitler was dead. President Roosevelt, who had set the Manhattan Project in motion, was also dead. Harry Truman, the new president of the United States, had to decide if the United States would use the bomb against the Japanese.

From FDR to Truman

Franklin Delano Roosevelt, the popular American president who had led the United States through the Depression and most of World War II, died on April 12, 1945, at age 63. Elected to an unprecedented fourth term, Roosevelt's spirit was as strong as ever, but his health had been poor. He was succeeded by his vice president, Harry S. Truman.

Dropping the Bomb and Victory in Japan

Truman, who had led troops in World War I, understood how costly an invasion of Japan would be. Japan's military leaders, recalling old samurai traditions that forbade surrender, were determined to continue the fight, even in the face of inevitable defeat. Japanese civilians had endured terrible punishment from U.S. bombers, but the nation showed no signs of giving in. Japanese workers built tunnels where people could take refuge when bombs fell, and housewives trained to fight invaders with bamboo spears. Japanese soldiers and civilians alike prepared themselves with the slogan, "A hundred million will die together for the emperor and the nation!"

Truman concluded that dropping an atomic bomb on Japan could bring the war in the Pacific to a swift end. Some American officials, and even some of the scientists who had worked on the Manhattan Project, opposed the idea of using the bomb. They believed that the Allies could defeat Japan without using such a terrible weapon. Truman knew that dropping an atomic bomb would kill thousands of Japanese civilians and cause horrific destruction. But he believed that it would cost far fewer lives, Japanese and American, than an invasion of Japan. He wrote a short note to his secretary of war: "Release when ready but not sooner than August 2."

A nuclear bomb sends a column of smoke rising more than 60,000 feet into the air over the Japanese port of Nagasaki.

On August 6, 1945, an American pilot steered his B-29 bomber, the *Enola Gay,* toward the Japanese port city of Hiroshima (heer-uh-SHEE-mah). On board the plane sat a single atomic bomb. It looked like a long, black trash can with fins, but it contained the equivalent of 15,000 tons of dynamite. Once over Hiroshima, the pilot dropped the bomb and turned for home.

A brilliant flash gave way to a huge mushroom cloud that bloomed over the city. The explosion unleashed an expanding fireball that flattened five miles of downtown Hiroshima and instantly killed almost 80,000 civilians. The nuclear blast left many more people maimed or hideously burned, while others fell victim to a new, more gradual killer — radiation poisoning.

The Japanese government did not surrender. Three days later, another U.S. plane dropped a second atomic bomb on the city of Nagasaki (nah-gah-SAH-kee), destroying the heart of the city and killing or injuring another 80,000 people.

On August 14, Japan's Emperor Hirohito addressed his people by radio. Japanese citizens listened to the broadcast with heads bowed and tears in their eyes. It was the first time they had ever heard their emperor's voice. He announced that his government had agreed to unconditional surrender.

The surrender ceremony took place in Tokyo Bay, on board the battleship *Missouri,* the flagship of the U.S. Pacific Fleet. General MacArthur stood on the ship's deck and watched as Japanese officials signed the official surrender. Behind him gathered the signers for all the Allied nations that had fought the Japanese. The war was finally over.

In Allied nations around the world, exuberant crowds celebrated V-J Day — Victory in Japan Day. In New York City, two million people flooded into Times Square, where soldiers and sailors embraced passing young women in what one serviceman called the "kissingest day in history."

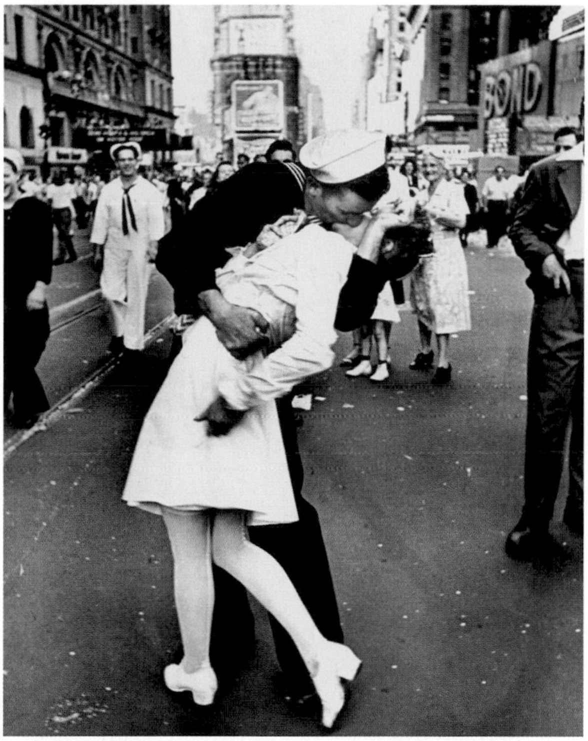

A jubilant sailor kisses a nurse in New York City's Times Square as crowds celebrate the Allies' victory over Japan.

In Pearl Harbor, flares and searchlights illuminated the night sky as the U.S. sailors cried tears of joy at the thought that they could finally go home.

Yet behind the celebrations stood all the horror of the last six years.

The Legacy of World War II

Exactly six years and one day after Hitler's invasion of Poland, World War II was over. But that peace had come at a terrible price. World War II caused more death and destruction than any other war in history. Some 17 million soldiers died in battle. No one knows for sure how many civilians perished from disease, starvation, bombings, and Hitler's mass murders. The total number of soldiers and civilians killed likely topped 60 million.

When the war ended, cities across much of Europe and Asia lay in ruins. Millions of civilians were left hungry and homeless.

Two industrial powers, Germany and Japan, lay crippled. Britain still had its empire, but was battered and exhausted. The United States and the Soviet Union emerged from the war as two military giants, poised to dominate the postwar world, but starting out in very different conditions.

American factories had produced many of the weapons and supplies needed for Allied victory. The United States, which saw no fighting on its mainland, ended the war with a booming economy that constituted nearly 50 percent of the world's wealth. The U.S. emerged from the war as the richest, most powerful nation in the world.

The Soviet Union, by contrast, suffered much more from the fighting. In the western part of the country, the war had destroyed nearly 5 million homes and obliterated thousands of towns and villages. Some 25 million Soviets were dead. More Soviets were killed in the defense of Stalingrad alone than Americans in the whole war.

Yet the Soviet Union still covered more territory than any other nation in the world. Its huge army was battered but intact. Soviet troops controlled much of Eastern Europe. The United States and Britain quickly began to fear that Joseph Stalin had no intention of giving up the territory his Red Army had seized from Axis Powers.

World War II left in its destructive wake another legacy, perhaps the most terrible of all. For the first time in history, there existed a weapon that could wipe out entire nations. Before the United States dropped atomic bombs on Hiroshima and Nagasaki, President Truman had informed Joseph Stalin about the new weapon. The Soviet leader was unfazed by the news. His spies had already told him that American scientists were at work on the bomb. The dictator took comfort in the fact that his own scientists were not far behind.

A woman's back shows patterns of clothes burned onto her skin by the nuclear blast at Hiroshima.

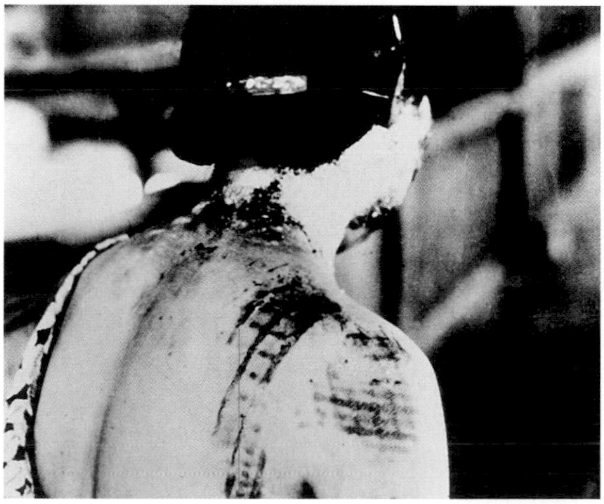

The Genius of Albert Einstein

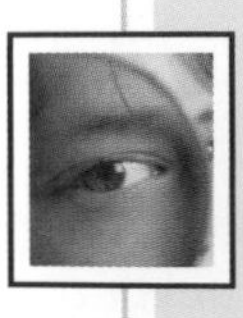

Historical Close-up

As you've read, Albert Einstein was the physicist who wrote to President Roosevelt during World War II, warning that the United States must not let Adolf Hitler become the first to possess a nuclear bomb. Why was the American president willing to listen to this scientist from Germany? Let's pause to learn more about this remarkable man's life and why his work has made his name synonymous with genius.

As a little boy in Germany, Albert Einstein didn't seem particularly bright at school. When his father asked Albert's headmaster what profession the boy should take up, the headmaster replied, "It doesn't matter; he'll never make a success of anything."

Yet many people today agree that Albert Einstein had the greatest scientific mind of the twentieth century.

Even as a boy of five, when young Albert first used a compass, he was fascinated by invisible forces. What made the compass needle move? At 16, he was deeply curious about light. If you could run fast enough to keep up with a beam of light, he wondered, what would it look like?

Einstein dropped out of his German military high school, but he graduated from a Swiss technical university. He excelled in mathematics and wanted to pursue an academic career. At the university, however, Einstein had regularly cut classes to pursue his own studies, so his professors did not give him good recommendations. No university hired him. Instead, in 1902, he took a job as a clerk in the Swiss patent office.

Every afternoon, when he finished reviewing patent applications, he would turn to his own work. He bounced ideas off friends who shared his passion for mathematical speculation. With pencil and paper, he scratched calculations that would change the way scientists understand the world.

In 1905, which has become known as his "miracle year," Einstein, age 26, sent a series of papers to a respected scientific publication. He politely asked the editors to publish the articles "if there is room." Yes, there was room — and the articles quickly aroused worldwide interest among scientists.

One of the articles explored the nature of light. Einstein showed that light consists not only of waves, as physicists already knew, but also of packets of energy, which he called "light quanta," and which we now call "photons." In other papers, Einstein explored the idea that matter is made up of small particles in constant motion.

In another article, titled "On the Electrodynamics of Moving Bodies," Einstein presented his theory of relativity. He theorized that under certain circumstances, time and space are not absolute, but can change relative to each other. He predicted that the closer we get to the speed of light—186,000 miles per second—the more time seems to slow down. There's no way to test this since no vehicle can travel at the speed of light. But years after Einstein put forth his theory, physicists were able to confirm Einstein's predictions by performing delicate tests with very precise timepieces called atomic clocks. Einstein's theory of relativity reshaped the scientific understanding of the relation between space and time.

In another paper published in that amazing year of 1905, Einstein followed up on his earlier thinking about the relation between matter and energy. He realized that matter—even the tiniest particle—is teeming with energy. He expressed the relationship between energy and matter in a simple, elegant equation, $E=mc^2$, which means, "Energy equals mass multiplied by the speed of light squared." Later, Einstein explained his equation in these words: "It followed from the special theory of relativity that mass and energy are both but different manifestations of the same thing.... Furthermore, the equation...showed that very small amounts of mass may be converted into a very large amount of energy and vice versa."

At first, Einstein's theories remained beautiful abstractions, discussed by scientists, but untested and unproven. One of the strange predictions of his relativity theory was that a ray of light passing near a massive object, such as our sun, would not travel in a straight line but would bend slightly. He proposed that this prediction be tested during an upcoming solar eclipse.

In May 1919, less than a year after the end of World War I and about a decade after Einstein had first put forth his theories of relativity, British scientists traveled to an island near West Africa, the best location for viewing the eclipse. They managed to capture images from which they could take precise measurements of the light's angle. Einstein was right — the angle of the light shifted precisely as he had predicted.

Newspapers reported the experiments confirming Einstein's theories. The *Times* of London blazed this headline: "Revolution in Science — New Theory of the Universe — Newton's Ideas Overthrown — Momentous Pronouncement — Space 'Warped.'" Most people did not understand the details of Einstein's work — the math was incredibly advanced, the ideas highly abstract. But they did understand that something exciting, important, and even a little unsettling was going on in the world of science — that space, time, and energy were not what they had long been assumed to be.

In 1921, Einstein was awarded the Nobel Prize for Physics. The German physicist leapt from obscurity to celebrity. For the next decade and more, he traveled far and wide on several lecture tours. He was interviewed, photographed, and applauded wherever he went. His name became synonymous with intellectual brilliance — to say, "That guy's a real Einstein" meant "He's a genius."

World War I appalled Einstein, who considered himself a pacifist. When other German intellectuals publicly defended Germany's actions, Einstein took a stand against the war. "My attitude," he said, "is not derived from any intellectual theory but is based on my deepest antipathy to every kind of cruelty and hatred."

As Hitler rose to power in Germany, Einstein worked with others in the Jewish community to oppose fascism. Growing anti-Semitism in Germany led him to support Zionist causes. Despite the fact that Einstein headed a major research institute in Berlin, the Nazis responded by denouncing Einstein's work as "Jewish physics." The threat was clear. Einstein left Germany in 1932, never to return. He joined the Institute for Advanced Study in Princeton, New Jersey, and became an American citizen. He regularly spoke in support of many causes that opposed fascism or sought justice for the oppressed.

In the 1930s, German scientists, building on the revelations of Einstein's equation, $E=mc^2$, showed that splitting a uranium atom resulted in the release

Albert Einstein, depicted in this portrait, changed the way scientists view the universe. The great physicist's theories also led to the development of the nuclear bomb.

of extraordinary amounts of energy. Einstein was horrified that his insights might be turned into a massively destructive weapon. Some scientists in the United States worried that the Germans now had a head start on building an atomic bomb. They asked Einstein, who had enormous prestige, to bring the issue to Franklin Roosevelt's attention.

In 1939, Einstein sent a letter to President Franklin Roosevelt, telling him of the potential for a weapon and urging that the United States quickly begin experimental work to develop such weaponry before the Germans. The president authorized research that led to the Manhattan Project, which developed the bombs dropped on Hiroshima and Nagasaki.

While Einstein's colleagues worked on the Manhattan Project, Einstein himself did not. Because Einstein had actively supported pacifist and socialist causes, U.S. government officials did not trust him enough to involve him in a top-secret project.

Soon after the Japanese surrendered, Einstein spoke out for control of the terrible potential of atomic power. "We scientists," he said, "whose tragic destiny it has been to help make the methods of annihilation ever more gruesome and more effective, must consider it our solemn and transcendent duty to do all in our power in preventing these weapons from being used."

To the end of his days, it remained Einstein's goal, as he put it, "to assure that the results of our scientific thinking may be a blessing to mankind, and not a curse."

A 1947 poster suggests the hope that the United Nations, established after World War II, might grow to become a world body that would help keep a lasting peace and prevent more terrible wars. *Nations Unies* means "United Nations" in French.

Securing the Peace, Uniting the Nations

Early in 1945, even before World War II ended, confident Allied leaders began to plan the shape of a postwar world. Although troops were still fighting, victory was in sight as Allied forces moved into Germany — Soviet armies from the east, and American and British forces, along with French troops, from the west. It was only a matter of time before Germany fell.

Barely three decades had passed since Germany had fallen at the end of World War I — only to rise again, angry and embittered, seeking vengeance on the powers that had imposed the harsh terms of the Treaty of Versailles. Now, with World War II drawing to a close, Allied leaders remembered the utter failure of the settlements following World War I. Instead of bringing peace, the Treaty of Versailles and other measures had deepened existing hatreds and led to even worse devastation and bloodshed.

Could the world avoid that mistake again? Could another global war be prevented? Could a lasting peace be achieved when, even among the Allied Powers, there were deep rifts and tense differences?

The Big Three at Yalta

In February 1945, President Franklin Roosevelt, Prime Minister Winston Churchill, and Premier Josef Stalin met at Yalta, a resort on the Black Sea. Their purpose was to discuss the future of Europe and the world after the war. Since their countries had led the fight against the Axis Powers, these three leaders were often called the Big Three. Big Two might have been more accurate, for the war had left Great Britain battered and weakened. The Soviet Union was even more ravaged, but the vast nation possessed enormous resources that gave it the potential to emerge from the war as the most powerful country in Europe.

At Yalta, the Big Three met as allies. But in the back of their minds, they knew the alliance might not last. Among their many differences, the sharpest was this: The United States and Britain were democracies that embraced capitalism, while the Soviet Union was a communist dictatorship. The U.S. and Britain hoped for greater democracy throughout Europe, while Stalin hoped to spread his nation's communist influence, particularly in Eastern Europe. Both camps suspected that once Germany was beaten, they would no longer be allies but rivals, or even enemies.

To prevent a clash, the Big Three agreed in principle to divide Germany and Europe after the

The Big Three—Winston Churchill, Franklin Roosevelt, and Joseph Stalin—meet at Yalta in February 1945 to discuss the future of Europe and the world after World War II.

war. Eastern Europe, including the eastern part of Germany, would fall under Soviet control, since Soviet troops occupied that territory. The United States and its allies would decide the fate of western Europe. That was the general agreement. The Big Three decided to sort out the details at a later meeting, to be held in Potsdam, Germany.

The Potsdam Conference

Before the Potsdam Conference convened in July 1945, Franklin Roosevelt died. The new U.S. president, Harry S. Truman, took his place in the Big Three. Truman soon found that he would have to face Stalin without Churchill's help, because in the midst of the Potsdam Conference, British voters replaced Churchill with a new prime minister, Clement Attlee. (Although the British cheered Churchill as a war leader, they thought the opposition Labor Party offered a better set of social and economic programs for postwar England.)

Truman and Attlee arrived at Potsdam concerned about what Stalin had been doing. Back at Yalta, Stalin had made vague promises about giving democracy a chance in Eastern Europe. But in the Soviet-occupied countries, he seemed determined to set up communist governments that he could control.

Nevertheless, at the Potsdam Conference, Truman, Attlee, and Stalin began trying to resolve issues that had been put off at Yalta. Right away, they disagreed about war reparations. How much should Germany be forced to pay?

Stalin insisted that the Germans pay huge reparations. The British and Americans thought that was a bad idea. They believed that demands for large reparations after World War I had led to German bitterness and helped cause World War II. But Stalin kept pointing out that his country had suffered terrible destruction from the German invasion. He was determined that the Soviet Union be paid as much as possible. In the end, Stalin got many of the reparations he demanded.

Seeking Just Punishment

As the war moved toward its conclusion, the Allies also had to decide how to treat the defeated Nazis. Should they inflict harsh punishments on German leaders? Some thought so, especially after the Allied armies found the Nazi concentration camps with their mountains of corpses, starving survivors, and hideous gas chambers. For such atrocities, someone had to be held responsible. Some officials urged hunting down Nazis and hanging them on the spot.

Truman wanted to pursue a different course, one that Roosevelt had favored. He believed that the individuals responsible for the war should be identified, charged with specific crimes, and brought to justice through legal means. Truman wanted to affirm the rule of law.

But under what law could Nazi leaders be charged? No international legal system existed. How could people of one sovereign nation convict the leaders of another? Could people be convicted of crimes that were not defined as crimes by any legal authority at the time they were committed?

Moreover, which leaders should be put on trial? Many Nazi leaders were dead. Hitler and two of his top lieutenants, Goebbels and Himmler, had committed suicide. Of the führer's inner circle, only Hermann Göring (GUR-ing), Hitler's deputy, had been captured alive. But the Allies had arrested other high-ranking Nazi leaders, such as Joachim Von Ribbentrop, Germany's foreign minister; Albert Speer, Hitler's fawning architect; and Alfred Rosenberg, who wrote unreadable volumes of Nazi philosophy. How could such men be brought to justice?

The Allies decided to establish a special court, an International Military Tribunal, representing many nations. They appointed prosecutors and chose the German city of Nuremberg as a trial site. They also defined the crimes for which the Nazis would be tried. "Crimes against peace" included plotting and starting an unprovoked war of aggression against another country. "War crimes" included acts such as sending prisoners of war to slave labor camps. "Crimes against humanity" included murder, enslavement, and inhumane acts against civilians — acts so awful that they could never be considered legal in any country, anywhere.

The Nazi leaders were astounded to learn they would be tried for such crimes. Most said they were not responsible. They said they had not personally committed any atrocities, but had just followed orders handed down by Hitler and others.

Men who *had* personally committed atrocities were also in custody, such as concentration camp guards who had pushed children into gas chambers with their own hands. During the trials, a psychologist interviewed some of these men and found them strangely ordinary. After a day's "work" at the camps, they went home to have dinner with their families, play with their pets, and tinker at their hobbies. Like their superior officers, they said they were just following orders.

Hitler's deputy, Hermann Göring, takes the oath in the witness box at the Nuremberg War Crimes Trials. His jokes about the Holocaust and lack of remorse horrified judges.

The Nuremberg prosecutors wanted to punish not only the guards and others who carried out the orders to commit atrocities, but also the leaders who planned the atrocities and gave the orders.

The Nuremberg Trials

The first of 13 trials at Nuremberg ran for nearly a year, from November 1945 to October 1946. They focused on the most important Nazi leaders.

The prosecutors had plenty of evidence to support their case because the Nazis had kept detailed records of their crimes and conversations. The Allies found hundreds of tons of records stored in mines, tunnels, and castles across Europe. Presented in open court, these documents proved beyond all doubt that the Nazis were guilty of unprovoked aggression, unprecedented atrocities, and an attempt to exterminate all Jewish people with their "Final Solution."

The prosecutors also put death camp survivors on the stand to tell their stories. Witnesses told of German guards calmly shooting prisoners until their trigger fingers tired, then stopping for a cigarette and a bite to eat. They told of camp officials blandly ordering thousands of innocent people to their deaths, and then going off to enjoy an evening at the opera.

When a film of the atrocities was shown in court, the accused Nazis sat pale and stunned. In the light of day, among civilized people, they could not believe what they had done. Only Göring, a man with a jovial manner and a hideous charm, showed no remorse. He smiled at the gruesome stories or acted bored.

In the first year of the Nuremberg Trials, 12 of 22 men on trial were convicted and sentenced to death by hanging. Hitler's architect and friend, Albert Speer, was not among those sentenced to death. Even though he had used thousands of slave laborers in his monumental building projects, he claimed ignorance of the atrocities. He received a 20-year prison sentence instead of death. Göring escaped punishment another way — he committed suicide before he could be hung.

During the war, these two American civilians were interned in the Philippines by the Japanese. Mistreating prisoners was one of the crimes addressed at the Tokyo Trials.

The Tokyo Trials

Meanwhile, a similar trial was taking place in Tokyo. Although the Japanese had not attempted Nazi-style genocide during the war, the Tokyo Trials did expose many acts of brutality. The Japanese military had used biological weapons against Chinese civilians. In prison camps, prisoners of war were often beaten, murdered, and mutilated. Some accounts put the death rate in Japanese camps at seven times higher than it was in German and Italian prisoner of war camps.

Emperor Hirohito, who had ruled Japan during the war and had full knowledge of these atrocities, was never charged with war crimes. But 25 military and government leaders were tried and convicted. Seven were executed.

The Tokyo Trials added weight to the judgments at Nuremberg. Together, the two trials demonstrated that the leaders of nations were accountable to the world and subject to laws that crossed international boundaries.

The Nations United?

Before World War II ended, Allied leaders met to plan an international organization that would work to prevent war, promote cooperation among countries, and help settle international disputes. If those goals sound familiar, it's because after World War I, the League of Nations had adopted similar goals. But this new organization — to be called the United Nations (UN) — was intended to succeed where the League had failed.

The League of Nations failed in part because the United States refused to join it. To prevent that from happening again, President Roosevelt convened a meeting in August 1944 at Dumbarton Oaks, an estate in Washington, D.C. There, delegates from the Soviet Union, the United States, Great Britain, and China hammered out a structure for the new international peacekeeping organization.

After Franklin Roosevelt died, Harry Truman continued the push to create the United Nations. In the summer of 1945, the United States hosted an international conference in San Francisco. Fifty nations sent representatives, and they filled

The Structure of the United Nations

The basic plan agreed on at Dumbarton Oaks remains in place at the UN to this day. The United Nations is divided into two chambers. One chamber, the General Assembly, includes delegates from all the member nations. Each nation, big or small, has one vote. The General Assembly democratically discusses and decides important matters.

The other chamber is the Security Council. Originally, there were five permanent members of the Security Council—China, Great Britain, France, the Soviet Union, and the United States—plus six nonpermanent members with two-year terms. Today, 15 countries sit in the Security Council but only five—the People's Republic of China, Great Britain, France, Russia, and the United States—have permanent seats. Any one of the permanent members of the Security Council can veto decisions made by the rest of the Council.

Flags of member nations fly at the United Nations headquarters in New York City. The General Assembly meets in the low building with the sloping roof, at left. The taller building houses staff offices.

in the plan sketched at Dumbarton Oaks. On October 24, 1945, the United Nations was born. The first meeting was scheduled for January of the following year in London.

Human Rights for All

President Truman asked Roosevelt's widow, Eleanor, to join the first U.S. delegation to the United Nations. It was a bold choice. Eleanor Roosevelt had earned tremendous admiration in the United States for her work on behalf of the poor and oppressed, but she had never held a political office. She had no direct experience in international affairs, though she had been a behind-the-scenes advisor in her husband's foreign policy decisions. She also brought the prestige of the Roosevelt name to the American delegation.

Mrs. Roosevelt shared her late husband's vision of a United Nations. She wondered if she was up to the task, since she had no official experience in foreign diplomacy, but she accepted the appointment.

In its first year, the United Nations set up a Human Rights Commission. Its job was to help prevent atrocities such as those the Nazis had committed. To achieve this mission, the commission decided to begin by drawing the world's attention to countries that violated people's rights.

But the mission raised a question: What rights belonged to all humans? Where, for example, could one draw the line between the rights of a government over its citizens and the rights of citizens against their government?

Such questions had been addressed in earlier documents you know about. In 1776, the Declaration of Independence declared that all people are born with "certain unalienable rights, [and] that among these are life, liberty, and the pursuit of happiness." In 1789, the French National Assembly drafted a similar Declaration of the Rights of Man and of the Citizen. Eleanor Roosevelt's husband had spoken of "four freedoms" worth fighting for: freedom of expression, freedom of worship, freedom from want, and freedom from fear.

The fledgling United Nations wanted a more complete declaration of rights that everyone

Eleanor Roosevelt holds the Universal Declaration of Human Rights, which she helped draft.

could embrace, regardless of culture or country. The General Assembly appointed a committee to draft such a statement. The committee elected Mrs. Roosevelt as its chairman.

Drafting the Universal Declaration of Human Rights

The committee was a brilliant and diverse collection of people — a French legal scholar, a Lebanese philosophy professor, a Pulitzer Prize–winning journalist from the Philippines, an outspoken advocate of women's rights in India, and several more. Mrs. Roosevelt was in charge of keeping them all working toward a single unified statement. She knew that the group's members did not agree on key questions. For example, which was more important, political freedom or economic equality? Individual rights or the rights of whole groups, such as national minorities?

Because enormous cultural differences separated her committee members, Mrs. Roosevelt hosted informal dinners where they could get to know each other. Much progress took place at these gatherings. Mrs. Roosevelt's warmth, good humor, and stamina helped the group turn tangled arguments into a coherent set of principles.

The finished statement, the Universal Declaration of Human Rights, took a bold stand on individual rights. It called for freedom of expression, for human dignity, and for safety from torture and false imprisonment. It also insisted on the rights to work, to rest, and to have food, clothing, housing, and medical care.

On December 10, 1948, the United Nations adopted the Universal Declaration of Human Rights. Some argued with the specific rights the document listed. And of course the statement itself did not make the world a just place. But it did take a dramatic stand on rights and freedoms — especially dramatic in contrast to the wartime years just past, during which so many rights and freedoms had been so flagrantly violated.

The Universal Declaration of Human Rights

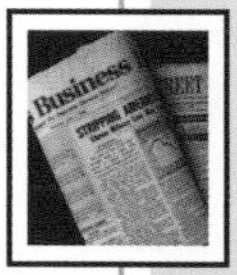

A Page from the Past

On December 10, 1948, the United Nations adopted the Universal Declaration of Human Rights "as a common standard of achievement for all peoples and all nations." Here are some of the rights set forth in the 30 articles of the Declaration.

Article 1. All human beings are born free and equal in dignity and rights. They are endowed with reason and conscience and should act towards one another in a spirit of brotherhood.

Article 2. Everyone is entitled to all the rights and freedoms set forth in this Declaration, without distinction of any kind, such as race, color, sex, language, religion, political or other opinion, national or social origin, property, birth or other status....

Article 3. Everyone has the right to life, liberty and security of person.

Article 4. No one shall be held in slavery or servitude; slavery and the slave trade shall be prohibited in all their forms.

Article 5. No one shall be subjected to torture or to cruel, inhuman or degrading treatment or punishment.

Article 7. All are equal before the law and are entitled without any discrimination to equal protection of the law….

Article 10. Everyone is entitled in full equality to a fair and public hearing by an independent and impartial tribunal, in the determination of his rights and obligations and of any criminal charge against him.

Article 13. (1) Everyone has the right to freedom of movement and residence within the borders of each state.

(2) Everyone has the right to leave any country, including his own, and to return to his country.

Article 17. Everyone has the right to own property alone as well as in association with others.

Article 18. Everyone has the right to freedom of thought, conscience and religion….

Article 19. Everyone has the right to freedom of opinion and expression….

Article 21. Everyone has the right to take part in the government of his country, directly or through freely chosen representatives…. The will of the people shall be the basis of the authority of government….

Article 23. Everyone has the right to work, to free choice of employment, to just and favorable conditions of work and to protection against unemployment….

Article 24. Everyone has the right to rest and leisure, including reasonable limitation of working hours and periodic holidays with pay.

Article 25. Everyone has the right to a standard of living adequate for the health and well-being of himself and of his family, including food, clothing, housing and medical care and necessary social services….

Article 26. Everyone has the right to education. Education shall be free, at least in the elementary and fundamental stages….

Article 29. …Everyone has duties to the community in which alone the free and full development of his personality is possible….

The State of Israel Is Born

As the Allies examined Nazi records, and as the Nuremberg Trials proceeded, more evidence of the horrors of the Holocaust came to light.

By the war's end, Hitler's "Final Solution" had caused the murder of six million Jews — two-thirds of all the Jews in Europe. Many of the Jewish survivors were determined to leave Europe. Of those who wanted to leave, many hoped to immigrate to Palestine. Their desires fueled Zionism, the movement to establish a Jewish state in Palestine.

As you've read, the Zionist movement began in the 1800s, when European Jews began moving to Palestine. Zionists considered Palestine their ancestral home. But the area was by no means empty. An Arab population had lived there for centuries.

During World War I, British foreign secretary David Balfour had declared British support for a national Jewish homeland in Palestine, as long as it didn't violate the rights of non-Jewish people in the area. After World War I, when Great Britain was in charge of Palestine, Arabs and Jews competed to enlarge their rights and territories.

In the 1920s and 1930s, as Nazism gained strength, Jewish refugees fled central Europe and tried to find new homes in other countries. Often, they were turned away. Some found themselves at sea in leaky boats, looking for any place to land. Palestine was one place where they could find refuge. Before World War II, the Jewish population in Palestine increased dramatically, though Arabs still formed the majority.

After the war, Britain decided to let the United Nations deal with the challenges in the area. Zionist leaders urged the UN to support the idea of an independent Jewish nation in Palestine. The proposal sparked tremendous controversy. Arabs fiercely opposed it, in part because Palestinian Arabs wanted to establish their own state in the region.

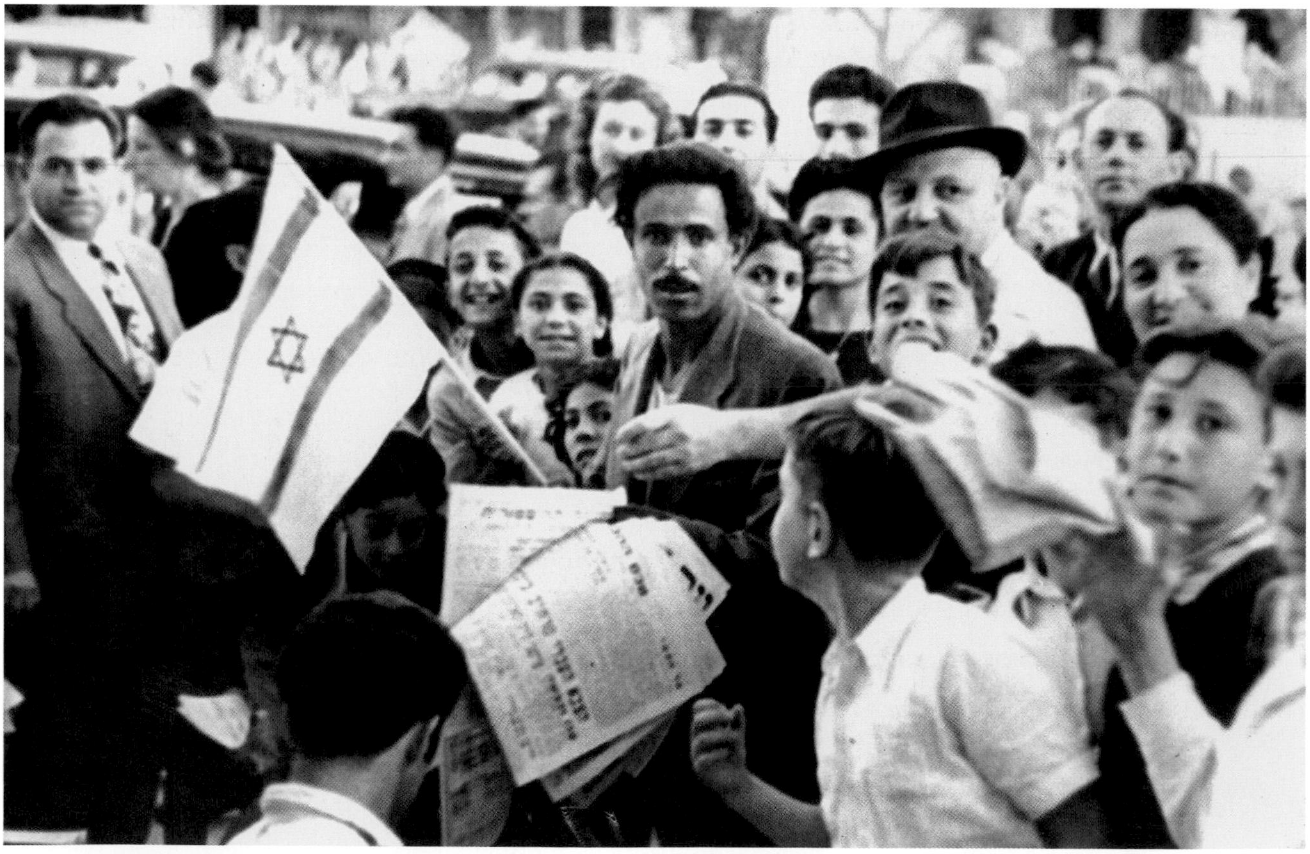

A crowd gathers in Tel Aviv in May 1948 to celebrate the proclamation of the new state of Israel. Jews in the Middle East rejoiced, but Arab Palestinians viewed the Zionists as Western invaders who were taking Arab lands.

The United Nations General Assembly voted to partition the disputed region into two countries, one Arab and the other Jewish. The Arab nation would be called Palestine. The Jewish nation would be called Israel. The United States first supported, and then opposed, and finally came back to supporting the creation of the state of Israel. In May 1948, Israel officially became a nation.

Jews in the Middle East rejoiced—at last, they had their own state. Arab Palestinians, on the other hand, were furious at the decision. In their view, the Zionists were Western invaders who were robbing Arabs of their lands.

Some viewed the action of the United Nations as an example of how the organization could solve thorny international problems. Others predicted that the decision to partition Palestine would lead to bloodshed for decades to come.

New Tensions

Shortly before the end of World War II, in the meeting at Yalta, the United States and the Soviet Union had managed to reach agreement. At the war's end, both nations sat on the Security Council of the new United Nations. But new tensions were pitting these great powers and former allies against each other.

As Churchill, Truman, and other Western leaders had suspected, Stalin had no intention of giving democracy a chance in Eastern Europe. In the Soviet-occupied countries of Bulgaria, Romania, Hungary, Czechoslovakia, and Poland, the Soviet dictator was ready to use any means, including force, to make sure that Communist Party governments took over those countries.

Meanwhile, elsewhere in the world, colonized peoples began to rebel against their European rulers. Independence movements stirred in India, Indochina, and parts of Africa. It seemed only a matter of time before European powers would have to give up their rule of foreign lands.

As these colonized nations gained independence, would they become democracies allied to the United States, or would they join Stalin's Communist camp? Could the great powers settle their differences through peaceful means? Or were they headed toward yet another world war?

Barbwire and cinder blocks stretch before the Brandenburg Gate, a famous Berlin landmark. In 1961, East Germany's communist government suddenly erected the barrier to keep East Germans from moving to the western, democratic part of the city. The wire was later replaced with the Berlin Wall, perhaps the most infamous symbol of the Cold War.

The Cold War Begins: Rebuilding Amid Deepening Divisions

Scarcely had World War II ended when a rift split the victorious Allies. Soviet leaders suspected the United States and Great Britain of trying to dominate the world on behalf of Western capitalists. U.S. leaders believed the Soviet Union was trying to forge a worldwide communist society ruled by a totalitarian dictatorship. The distrust grew into a rivalry that threatened the planet.

Joseph Stalin, the Soviet dictator, took steps to widen the divide between his regime and his former allies. He imposed rigid censorship to keep out Western ideas. By 1946, the Soviets were refusing to allow most Western goods into the USSR or into Soviet-controlled nations in Eastern Europe.

Britain's Winston Churchill described this division between the former allies as "an iron curtain" descending across Europe. On one side of this Iron Curtain, he said, lay the Western nations, with their ideals of freedom and self-determination, and with their dynamic exchange of goods and ideas. On the other side lay the Soviet Union and Eastern European countries such as Poland, Hungary, Czechoslovakia, and Romania, where people lived with little if any freedom under the thumb of oppressive governments. Churchill said that these nations lay in "the Soviet sphere," and that they were all under "a very high and in some cases increasing measure of control from Moscow," the Soviet capital.

Churchill further charged that communists were working to drag more nations behind the Iron Curtain. Around the world, said Churchill, communists were trying to undermine legitimate governments and set up puppet regimes favorable to Moscow. Churchill wondered: Would the West let the communists get away with it? Had Britain and America eliminated a monster like Hitler only to elevate Stalin?

Why a "Cold War"?

Since the Western powers and the Soviets were so hostile to each other, why didn't they plunge into a bloody war? Because after World War II — which ended with the United States dropping two horrifyingly deadly atomic bombs — the stakes of war had increased dramatically.

In 1949, the Soviet Union exploded an atomic bomb of its own. American scientists responded by building a hydrogen bomb a thousand times more powerful than the one that had annihilated Hiroshima. In 1952, when scientists tested the first H-bomb on an uninhabited island in the

The United States tested the first hydrogen bomb in 1952 in the South Pacific. The Soviet Union had the H-bomb by 1955.

Pacific, they were stunned to find that it utterly destroyed the island and spread deadly radiation for hundreds of miles.

Such doomsday weapons made war a much riskier proposition. Two countries armed with H-bombs might not only destroy each other but devastate much of the planet as well.

This chilling fact resulted in a tense forty-year standoff known as the Cold War, a long confrontation of arms and ideas that spanned the globe and pitted East against West. It was called "cold" because the real adversaries, the Soviet Union and the United States, never directly fought each other. There were battles and bloodshed, but in other countries, where people allied themselves with one side or the other. Both the Soviet Union and the United States supplied their allies with money, weapons, and sometimes troops.

Kennan Urges Containment

One night in early 1946, an American diplomat in Moscow sat down to write a telegram to his home office in Washington, D.C. George Kennan, a shy intellectual, hoped to help his bosses better understand the puzzling actions of the USSR. The Soviets had been among the victors in World War II, so why did they continue to act as if they were under siege? As Kennan set out to analyze Soviet motivations, his telegram expanded to more than 5,000 words—words that precisely expressed what many had been vaguely feeling.

The Soviet Union's leaders, Kennan wrote, had a view of the world rooted in the "traditional and instinctive Russian sense of insecurity." Russia had suffered numerous invasions—by Napoleon in 1812, and by German and other forces during both world wars in the twentieth century. Now, as Kennan explained it, Soviet leaders were motivated by an extreme fear of future invasions.

Soviet leaders, said Kennan, were also motivated by a determination to destroy capitalism—an evil system, according to Marxist beliefs. The Soviets regarded Western democracies, which were capitalist nations, as a menace to their communist system and as a threat to their power. Therefore, as Kennan explained, Soviet leaders would subvert democratic governments and support communist or anti-Western revolutionary movements wherever they could.

To *subvert* a government is to undermine or overturn it.

Kennan said that the West should pursue a policy of *containment*—that is, preventing the expansion of communism. How could Western nations contain communism? By strengthening noncommunist countries, especially those bordering the Soviet Union. By doing this, Kennan argued, the West could build a bulwark of democratic states strong enough to resist any attempted communist takeover.

The Truman Doctrine

Kennan's ideas were soon put to the test by a crisis in the eastern Mediterranean. A civil war broke out in Greece. There, communist-led rebels were waging war against the noncommunist government. Nearby, a communist insurgency also threatened Turkey.

An *insurgency* is a revolt against a government. It is like a revolution but not as widespread.

Amid this unrest, the Soviet Union moved troops to the Turkish border. It threatened to invade both Turkey and Greece, countries too weak on their own to resist the Soviets. Turkey and Greece had been receiving emergency aid

Europe During the Cold War, c. 1950

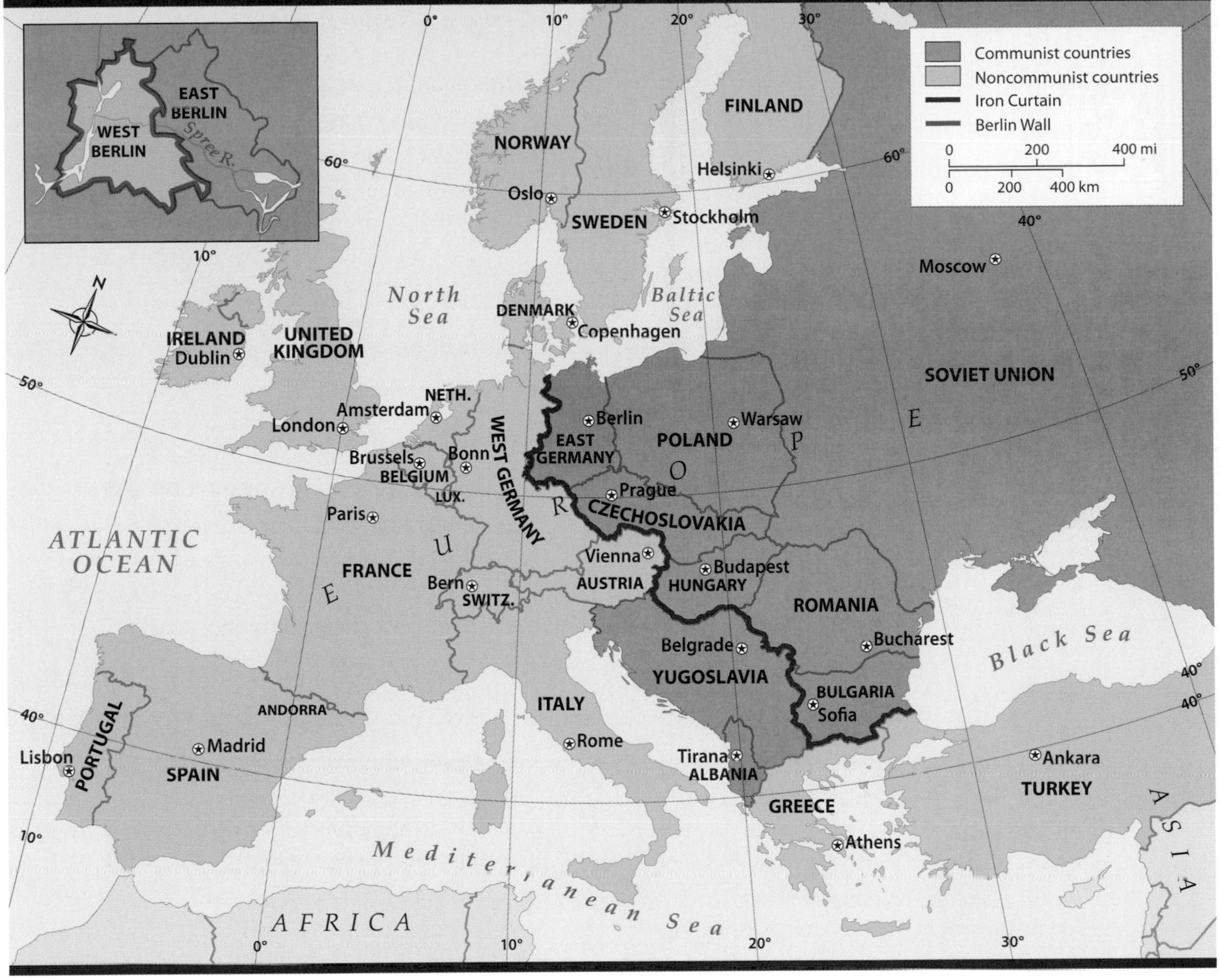

from Great Britain, but the British informed President Truman that they could no longer afford to provide that aid.

What was the United States to do? Until 1917, the United States had stayed out of European conflicts. But faced with the potential expansion of communism into Turkey and Greece, President Truman said that the United States could not stand aside. In a speech to Congress in 1947, Truman said that in the wake of World War II, American security depended on containing the Soviets. The president asked Congress for money to support Greece and Turkey. He also declared that henceforth the United States must "support free peoples who are resisting attempted subjugation by armed minorities or by outside pressures."

The president's policy, known as the Truman Doctrine, committed the United States to the containment of communism wherever it threatened to spread. It meant that the United States would try to halt the expansion of Soviet influence. Some objected to Truman's plan. They believed that the problems in Greece and Turkey could be solved through diplomatic means at the United Nations. Others, remembering World War II, still thought of the Soviet Union as an ally, not a hostile power that had to be contained.

Truman, however, was firmly resolved to stop communism, while Stalin was single-mindedly determined to spread it. The Cold War was underway.

The Truman Doctrine

A Page from the Past

On March 12, 1947, President Harry S. Truman addressed the United States Congress. He asked Congress to approve aid to Greece and Turkey, which were under threat from communist forces. He also articulated a policy that has become known as the Truman Doctrine. Here are some excerpts from that speech.

We shall not realize our objectives... unless we are willing to help free peoples to maintain their free institutions and their national integrity against aggressive movements that seek to impose upon them totalitarian regimes. This is no more than a frank recognition that totalitarian regimes imposed on free peoples, by direct or indirect aggression, undermine the foundations of international peace and hence the security of the United States.

...At the present moment in world history nearly every nation must choose between alternative ways of life. The choice is too often not a free one.

One way of life is based upon the will of the majority, and is distinguished by free institutions, representative government, free elections, guarantees of individual liberty, freedom of speech and religion, and freedom from political oppression.

The second way of life is based upon the will of a minority forcibly imposed upon the majority. It relies upon terror and oppression, a controlled press and radio, fixed elections, and the suppression of personal freedoms.

I believe that it must be the policy of the United States to support free peoples who are resisting attempted subjugation by armed minorities or by outside pressures.

...The seeds of totalitarian regimes are nurtured by misery and want. They spread and grow in the evil soil of poverty and strife. They reach their full growth when the hope of a people for a better life has died. We must keep that hope alive.

The free peoples of the world look to us for support in maintaining their freedoms.

If we falter in our leadership, we may endanger the peace of the world — and we shall surely endanger the welfare of our own nation.

President Harry S. Truman

The Eastern Bloc vs. the West

To understand the Cold War, you need to understand the terms used to refer to the opposing sides. After World War II, the main opponents in the Cold War, the United States and the Soviet Union, were often referred to as the world's two *superpowers*. A superpower is a country that has the ability to influence events and project its military and economic might throughout the globe.

The Soviet Union and its Cold War allies in Eastern Europe were referred to as the Eastern Bloc. The term was also used to describe Soviet allies elsewhere in the world, including nations far from Eastern Europe. Many Eastern Bloc governments were communist regimes, manipulated or controlled by the USSR. In nations such as Poland, Romania, and Bulgaria, people had little freedom under the rule of tyrannical governments. The Eastern Bloc nations under Soviet sway were sometimes called "satellites" of the Soviet Union.

The United States and its allies were sometimes referred to as the Western Bloc, but more often as "Western nations" or simply "the West." The Western nations—such as Great Britain and France—were anticommunist. Many, but not all, were democracies committed to ideals of freedom of expression, self-determination, and individual liberty. Some allies of the West, such as Spain under Franco, were dictatorships. The United States put up with these dictators, and sometimes even aided them, because they were opposed to communism.

Throughout the Cold War, the Eastern Bloc and the West distrusted each other. Each group was anxious to defend its interests and expand its influence. Each side built up arms, spied on the other, and accused the other of aggression. But of course the two sides had very different goals and values.

The Marshall Plan: Rebuilding Europe

One of the Cold War's superpowers, the United States, undertook a plan designed to achieve a political goal through a humanitarian effort. The goal was to contain communism. The effort was to rebuild Europe—a massive effort, since after World War II much of the continent lay in ruins.

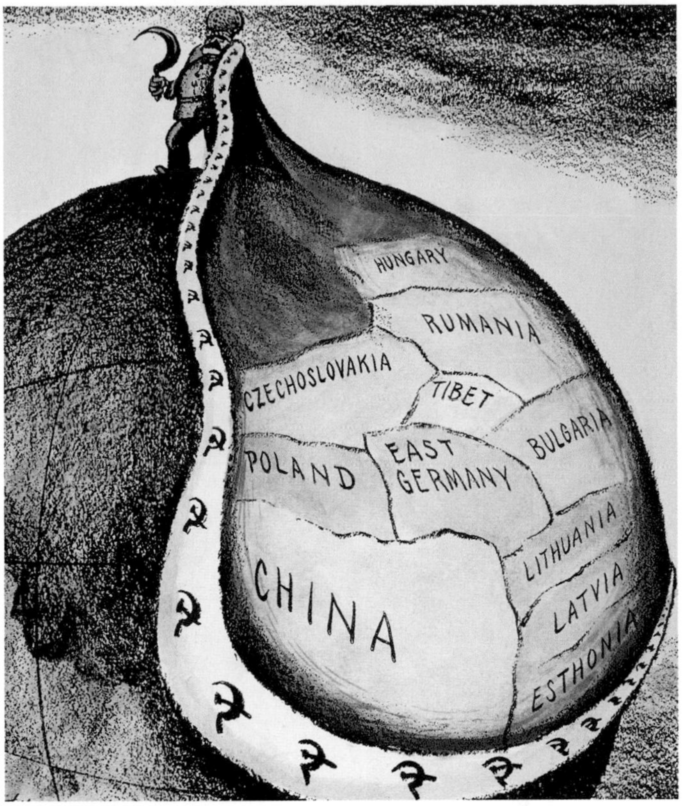

As this 1951 political cartoon indicates, the Soviet Union dominated much of Eastern Europe and Asia. Soviet satellite states and allies came to be known as the Eastern Bloc.

To the Soviets, a ruined Europe seemed fertile ground for the spread of communism. As Stalin surveyed postwar Europe, he saw several economies on the verge of collapse. He knew that the resulting poverty, chaos, and despair could lead to the kind of turmoil that had enabled the Bolsheviks to seize power in Russia back in 1917.

Truman also knew that poverty and chaos could lead desperate people to embrace communism, and he was determined to prevent that outcome. So he and his advisors developed an innovative plan for rebuilding the war-torn continent. They called it the European Recovery Program.

On June 5, 1947, Truman's secretary of state, George Marshall, revealed the plan in a speech at Harvard University. Marshall had been the army's chief of staff during World War II, in charge of organizing and planning much of the U.S. war effort. Winston Churchill had once called him the "organizer of victory."

Under the Marshall Plan, the United States offered massive aid to help rebuild war-torn Europe.

The Motives of the Marshall Plan

The Marshall Plan was, in part, a humanitarian act by the United States—in dollars spent, it was one of the most generous acts in history. Many Americans believed it was essential to help war-ravaged Europe get back on its feet.

The Marshall Plan was also an attempt to learn from past disasters. Truman, Marshall, and other U.S. leaders recognized that World War II had sprung out of the poverty and chaos sown by the postwar settlements of World War I. They believed that by reviving the world economy they could prevent the rise of more dictators.

Finally, the Marshall Plan was a calculated effort to promote Western interests and values. The United States hoped that the infusion of dollars would support capitalist economies (including its own), strengthen democratic governments, keep communism at bay, and build strong trading partners for businesses.

Even though the United States had just spent billions on war, Marshall now suggested that it spend billions more on peace. Marshall laid out the case for spending American dollars to help rebuild a Europe ruined by war. The money would help purchase machinery, modernize factories, repair railroads, and reconstruct cities.

Marshall proposed that the United States extend this aid not just to its allies but also to its former enemies. He proposed to help rebuild all of Europe, including the Soviet Union and its satellites.

The British foreign secretary called the plan "a lifeline to sinking men." Almost immediately it came to be known not by its official name, the European Recovery Program, but as the Marshall Plan, after the man who proposed it.

Stalin quickly rejected any aid from the Marshall Plan. He thought that the United States would use its dollars to take over the economies of the countries it helped, strip them of resources, and reduce their people to low-paid employees of American companies. He also believed that taking help from Western capitalists would be a sign of failure for the communist system. Stalin refused to allow Eastern Bloc nations under his control to accept any aid, a bitter disappointment to countries such as Poland and Czechoslovakia.

Czechoslovakia was the only Soviet satellite that still enjoyed some independence. The Czech foreign minister, Jan Masaryk, spoke publicly of wanting to learn more about the Marshall Plan. But the communists put an end to such talk by seizing full control of Czechoslovakia. Two weeks later, Masaryk was found dead on the sidewalk in front of his house. Official reports said he had committed suicide.

The Marshall Plan went into operation in the summer of 1947. Over the course of four years, several Western European nations received about $13 billion in aid that included dollars, food, fuel, machinery, and technical assistance from U.S. businessmen and engineers. The aid helped rebuild cities, factories, and economies with equipment and supplies bought mostly from American companies. By 1960, Western Europe had recovered, and businesses in Europe and America prospered.

German children living in West Berlin stand atop building rubble and cheer a U.S. cargo plane. During the Berlin Airlift of 1948–49, thousands of such flights brought food, fuel, and other supplies to desperate West Berliners after Joseph Stalin blockaded their portion of the city in an attempt to gain control of it.

The Berlin Airlift

While Western Europe began to rebuild with the help of the Marshall Plan, Stalin continued to strengthen his hold on Eastern Bloc nations. One spot behind the Iron Curtain remained beyond Stalin's control—a portion of the city of Berlin, the historic capital of Germany.

At the end of World War II, Germany was a fractured land. The four wartime Allies—Great Britain, France, the United States, and the Soviet Union—had temporarily divided the country into four zones, with each of the Allies occupying and controlling a zone. On the western side of the country, the British, French, and Americans planned to merge their zones and create a single new democratic German state. But Stalin kept a firm grip on the eastern side of Germany. He hoped to see all of Germany fall under communist rule.

When the Allies partitioned Germany into four zones, they partitioned the capital city of Berlin as well. Berlin lay 200 miles within eastern Germany, in the zone controlled by the Soviets. The Soviets controlled East Berlin, while the United States, Great Britain, and France controlled West Berlin.

The Western democracies saw West Berlin as a powerful symbol of their refusal to give in to Soviet aggression. They kept a stream of trucks and trains flowing to West Berlin to supply its people with food, fuel, and other necessities. But to reach West Berlin, those supplies had to travel through Soviet-controlled East Germany.

In June 1948, Stalin ordered that all supplies coming into West Berlin by road, rail, or water be stopped. Cutting off the supplies meant that West Berliners would soon face starvation. Stalin hoped that by blockading the city, he could force the United States and its allies to give up their part of Berlin, thus transforming the city into a unified capital city under Soviet control.

Truman decided that he could not afford to let the free portion of Berlin fall into Stalin's totalitarian grip. He countered with an ambitious mission to rescue West Berlin without declaring war on the Soviet Union.

In this rescue mission, known as the Berlin Airlift, thousands of huge cargo planes carried food, fuel, and other needed supplies into the city. Stalin could have shot the planes down, but he knew that such action might cause the United States to respond with nuclear bombs. So he did not challenge the airlift.

During the Berlin Airlift, Allied planes landed as often as every four minutes in West Berlin. Over the course of 15 months, more than 277,000 flights delivered some 2.3 million tons of supplies to the blockaded city. In May 1949, Stalin realized that his attempt to strangle the western portion of the city into submission had failed. He backed down and lifted the blockade.

In that same year, Germany itself was divided into two countries. The western side of the nation became the Federal Republic of Germany, often called West Germany, with the city of Bonn as its capital. Its citizens enjoyed free elections, freedom of speech, and other rights recognized by many governments throughout the West.

The eastern side of Germany became the German Democratic Republic, often called East Germany, with East Berlin as its capital. Despite its name, East Germany was far from democratic. The Communist Party controlled the government, which took its directions from the Soviet Union. There were no free elections. Those who criticized communism ran the risk of being imprisoned or whisked away, never to be seen again.

As Winston Churchill had feared, the Iron Curtain seemed to be turning into a permanent barrier, trapping millions of people behind it.

The North Atlantic Treaty Organization

At its worst point, the Berlin crisis looked like it might spark a new war. But Stalin's fear of America's atomic bombs — which, at the time, only the United States had — made him back down from a fight. Truman knew the Soviets were working to build atomic weapons. And he knew that when they succeeded, they would be less willing to back down. In preparation for that day, the president began talking with several Western European nations about forming a military alliance.

In 1949, the North Atlantic Treaty Organization (NATO) was born. Its 12 member nations agreed that if one of them was attacked, the others would come to its defense. It was the first time the United States had joined a military alliance during a time of peace.

The Soviet Union and its Eastern Bloc satellites eventually responded by signing their own mutual defense treaty, called the Warsaw Pact. To some observers, this new system of military alliances was a frightful reminder of the alliances that European nations formed in the years leading to World War I. They wondered if the world was starting down a road toward yet another catastrophic conflict.

Cold War Alliances

The North Atlantic Treaty Organization and the Warsaw Pact were the two main military alliances formed during the Cold War. Each alliance was designed to discourage an attack by enemy forces.

North Atlantic Treaty Organization (NATO): Established in 1949 to deter a Soviet attack on a member nation. Original members: Belgium, Canada, Denmark, France, Iceland, Italy, Luxembourg, the Netherlands, Norway, Portugal, the United Kingdom, and the United States.

Warsaw Pact: Established in 1955 as a Soviet-led military alliance in response to NATO. Members: Albania, Bulgaria, Czechoslovakia, East Germany, Hungary, Poland, Romania, and the Soviet Union. (Ended in 1991)

Japan Rebuilds and Reforms

As Europe revived, Japan was rebuilding as well. Because the United States had beaten Japan without Soviet help, Stalin had no part in settling Japan's fate. In fact, a single American played a dominant role in the restoration of Japan — General Douglas MacArthur, commander of all U.S. military forces in the Pacific.

MacArthur was a larger-than-life figure, both admired and loathed. He could be stubborn, arrogant, and vain, but he was also a born leader. During World War II, when MacArthur was forced to abandon the Philippine Islands, he promised "I shall return" — a promise he kept when, later in the war, U.S. forces under his command retook the Philippines.

After the war ended, MacArthur became commander of the occupation forces in Japan. He saw the job as an opportunity to bring long-needed reforms to the island nation, and he used his power to transform the country.

During the nineteenth century, you recall, Meiji Japan had set out to reform its economic, military, political, and educational institutions along Western lines. But in the 1930s, military leaders with imperialist ambitions gained control of the

This photo of U.S. General Douglas MacArthur and Emperor Hirohito was the general's way of showing the Japanese people exactly who was in charge of postwar Japan.

government and led Japan into World War II. After the war, MacArthur and his advisors set about changing Japan's course once again. They were determined that this time, it would become a democratic, capitalist, and peaceful nation.

MacArthur started by disarming five million Japanese soldiers. Then he created a new constitution for Japan. A group of army and navy officers drafted one in six days, using a book about world constitutions as a reference. This new constitution set up a parliamentary government like that of Great Britain. It guaranteed individual civil liberties like those in the U.S. Bill of Rights. It gave women the vote and others rights. Under the new constitution, Japan gave up its right to make war and maintain a military.

Japan's parliament is called the *Diet.*

MacArthur also succeeded in putting the country's highest-ranking wartime military leaders on trial for war crimes. All were convicted and most sentenced to life imprisonment. Emperor Hirohito did not face trial. MacArthur knew that most Japanese revered their emperor, and the general wanted to keep the people on his side. So he avoided holding Hirohito responsible for Japan's war crimes, even though the emperor had been fully aware of them.

MacArthur did, however, strip Hirohito of political power and make him announce that he was a human being, not, as Japanese tradition dictated, a god. MacArthur also had a photo taken of himself with the emperor, and made sure it was widely distributed. The image of the general towering over the emperor was MacArthur's way of dramatically showing who was in charge.

As in Europe, the United States did not rebuild Japan entirely for unselfish reasons. The Cold War had reconfigured the world so quickly that the United States needed a stable, friendly Japan to stand as an ally against communism. The West had a special need for an ally in East Asia because a worrisome new communist power had emerged there — China.

China: Communism and Mao's Early Years

To make sense of the emergence of communism in China, we need to step back about forty years. In 1911, Chinese revolutionaries overthrew the last Qing emperor, ending a dynasty that had ruled for more than two centuries. As you know, Sun Yat-Sen became the provisional president of the new Republic of China. His party, the Kuomintang (KWO-mihn-tahng), also known as the Nationalist Party, set out to unify and modernize China, and to end the long domination of the country by foreigners.

But the collapse of the old empire left a fragmented country. Sun Yat-Sen soon gave up the presidency, and warlords began battling to control various parts of China. As the warlords fought, China's intellectuals argued about the fate of their country. Some supported the Kuomintang's desire to forge a modern, democratic China. Some longed to return to older ways. And some hoped to see China embrace the doctrines of Marx and Lenin and become a communist nation.

Out of the fledgling communist movement in China emerged a leader who would become one of the most powerful men in the world — Mao Zedong (MOW zuh-DOUNG). Mao was born in

Refugees crawl across the shattered remains of a bridge as they flee south to escape advancing Chinese Communist troops. China entered the Korean War in late 1950.

War gave Japan the push it needed to help its economy prosper.

To head the UN forces, the Security Council approved General Douglas MacArthur. MacArthur proceeded to organize one of the most daring maneuvers in modern military history. He gathered 261 ships, the largest invasion fleet since D–day, and landed troops in South Korea at the city of Inchon (IHN-chuhn), a place supposedly invulnerable to such attack because high cliffs bordered the ocean. Taking the North Koreans by surprise from behind, MacArthur drove them out of Seoul and herded them north.

As UN troops pushed north, they drove up the Korean peninsula, in some places coming close to the Yalu River, North Korea's border with China. But MacArthur was unaware that Mao Zedong had decided to come to the aid of the Korean communists. The Chinese leaders saw MacArthur's advance into North Korea as an invasion of a communist land by a Western army, and thus as a threat to China itself. Urged on by Stalin, China sent hundreds of thousands of troops into the war.

The army fighting against MacArthur suddenly tripled. The Chinese forced the overwhelmed UN troops to retreat, and then retreat some more, until they were cornered and fighting for their lives.

The fighting dragged on. The United States possessed nuclear weapons but dared not use them, for behind North Korea stood China, and behind China loomed the Soviet Union, which now had its own atomic bombs. When MacArthur publicly criticized Truman's handling of the conflict in Korea, the president fired the general. The Korean War ground to a stalemate in which both sides suffered terrible casualties without gaining an inch of territory.

Stalin's Death and the War's End

There is no telling how long the war in Korea might have lasted had it not been for mysterious events that took place in March 1953 at Stalin's villa just outside Moscow. Stalin was there with his inner circle of advisors. These men had come to realize they were never safe around the Soviet dictator. No one was too high ranking or too trusted to escape his suspicion, and no one he suspected of disloyalty lived very long. After all, Stalin had recently said, "I don't even trust myself."

On the morning of March 1, Stalin's bodyguards found him in his bedroom unable to speak. Official reports said he died of a stroke four days later. Many historians think he was poisoned, possibly by his chief spy, Lavrenti Beria (BAIR-ee-uh). Beria, along with two others, took Stalin's place after his death.

Stalin had insisted that the Chinese continue the fight in Korea, but Beria believed that the war had gone on long enough and approved a cease-fire. On July 27, 1953, an armistice brought an end to the Korean War. It wasn't a peace treaty, for nothing was settled, but at least the fighting stopped.

More than three million people were dead or missing, and millions more left homeless. North Korea remained a communist nation, its people living under totalitarian rule. South Korea remained a capitalist nation aligned with the Western democracies.

From Stalin to Khrushchev

In Moscow, meanwhile, a Soviet Communist Party official named Nikita Khrushchev (nih-KEE-tuh kroosh-CHEHF) was elected the party's General Secretary. On the surface, Khrushchev seemed a likeable man with a sense of humor. But he had been a Stalin henchman in the 1920s, and beneath his cheerful exterior lay plenty of ruthless cunning. Khrushchev arranged to have Lavrenti Beria arrested, convicted of being a Western agent, and shot. By 1956, Khrushchev had emerged as the USSR's dominant leader.

Khrushchev was devoted to communist ideals. He believed that the only way for communism to move forward was to admit past errors.

As leader of the USSR, Nikita Khrushchev shocked many by admitting publicly that Stalin had committed grievous crimes. Yet Khrushchev kept a tight grip on the Soviet empire.

Stalin's Legacy

Without doubt, Joseph Stalin was one of the most brutal and murderous dictators in history. During his reign of terror, which lasted from 1929 to 1953, he ordered millions of his countrymen to be killed or sent to labor camps. He deliberately starved millions more. The Soviet leader tolerated no challenge to his authority. He planted his secret police throughout the communist world behind the Iron Curtain, and those who opposed him were often jailed or executed, or simply disappeared. Stalin bullied satellite nations and dispatched troops to crush all resistance to his rule. He robbed his own people of their freedom and trampled on their human rights. His style of government—iron-fisted rule by terror in the name of communist ideals—came to be known as Stalinism.

At a meeting of the Soviet Communist Party, he announced that Stalin had committed grievous crimes, including the executions of hundreds of thousands of people for "anti-Soviet activities." The meeting's delegates were shocked. They knew about Stalin's atrocities but didn't want to admit them to the world. In parts of the Eastern Bloc, however, Khrushchev's words awakened hope. Leaders of some Soviet satellites thought they might now have more freedom to run their states without interference from Moscow.

It would take more than speeches to change the dictatorial brutality built into the Soviet Union. When the Polish Communist Party installed a new leader without Khrushchev's approval, the General Secretary flew into a rage and threatened to send Soviet troops into Poland. In the autumn of 1956, when Hungarians poured into the streets of their cities to demand more freedom, Khrushchev sent tanks into Hungary to crush the rebellion. The Hungarians suffered some 20,000 casualties, including about 2,500 deaths.

Western leaders protested but did not intervene to repel Soviet troops from Hungary. Their

In 1956, students in Hungary staged protests to demand more freedom, and Hungary's government announced that it would withdraw from the Warsaw Pact. Nikita Khrushchev responded quickly. Soviet tanks rolled through the Hungarian capital of Budapest, and the Red Army crushed the anticommunist uprising.

policy was to "contain" communism, to prevent its spread. But Hungary was a communist country before Khrushchev sent tanks rolling into Budapest, the country's capital. Western leaders rationalized that Khrushchev's show of force did not represent a spread of communism. While Western nations did offer help to many thousands of Hungarian refugees, they chose not to risk war with the Soviet Union.

The Berlin Wall

Five years after Soviet troops stamped out revolution in Hungary, one of the most infamous and hated symbols of the Cold War took shape in the city of Berlin.

By this time, Berlin was a tale of two cities. West Berlin, which lay deep inside East Germany, was a pocket of freedom behind the Iron Curtain. Since the end of World War II, it had been protected by Britain, France, and the United States. Most of the wreckage of war had disappeared. In its place stood prosperous, busy streets lined with office buildings, shops, cafés, hotels, and theaters.

In contrast, East Berlin was a drab city full of empty storefronts and buildings scarred by World War II. Refrigerators, washing machines, and cars — fairly common in West Berlin — were luxuries possessed by only a few top Communist Party officials in East Berlin. Worst of all, East Berliners had few political freedoms.

East Berliners did have one cherished liberty. Since the war, they had been allowed access to the city's western sector, where many friends and family members lived. It was easy to walk into West Berlin and never go back to the communist East. The East German and Soviet governments watched as, year after year, hundreds of thousands of East Germans did just that. They fled to the West through West Berlin, seeking freedom and economic opportunity. Many were young, skilled, and educated.

In the early morning hours of August 13, 1961, soldiers of the East German army quietly moved up to the boundary between the eastern and western sectors of the divided city. Some began driving long metal stakes into the ground while others unrolled spools of barbwire. By daybreak the crude barricade was complete. East Berliners suddenly found themselves cut off from West Berlin. Within days, the barbwire fence was replaced by a concrete barrier guarded by mines, machine guns, and soldiers with orders to shoot anyone attempting to cross the Berlin Wall.

The East German government had acted, with Soviet approval, out of a sense of desperation. By the time the Berlin Wall went up, more than two and a half million of its citizens had already fled to the West. Khrushchev admitted that the "East German economy would have collapsed if we hadn't done something soon against the mass flight."

The world watched anxiously to see how the United States would respond. The new U.S. president, John F. Kennedy, quickly mobilized military reserve units and reinforced the brigade of American troops in West Berlin. His actions sent a clear signal that the United States was prepared to use force to defend the surrounded city. It soon became evident, however, that he was not prepared to risk war with the Soviet Union by demolishing the Berlin Wall. The president decided that, in this case, he could tolerate the situation. "It's not a very nice solution," he said, "but a wall is a hell of a lot better than a war."

The Cold War Continues

As the 1960s began, the Cold War showed no signs of easing. Behind the Iron Curtain, millions of people lived under totalitarian governments they neither chose nor supported. Much of the world remained aligned into two opposing camps, one side backed by the communist Soviet Union, the other side by the democratic United States.

Each superpower remained suspicious of the other and anxious to advance its own influence. And each possessed nuclear weapons capable of apocalyptic destruction. It was a world divided and on the brink.

A woman ventures a peek through a hole in the Berlin Wall. Thousands of guards patrolled the wall on the communist side, ready to arrest or shoot anyone trying to cross into West Berlin.

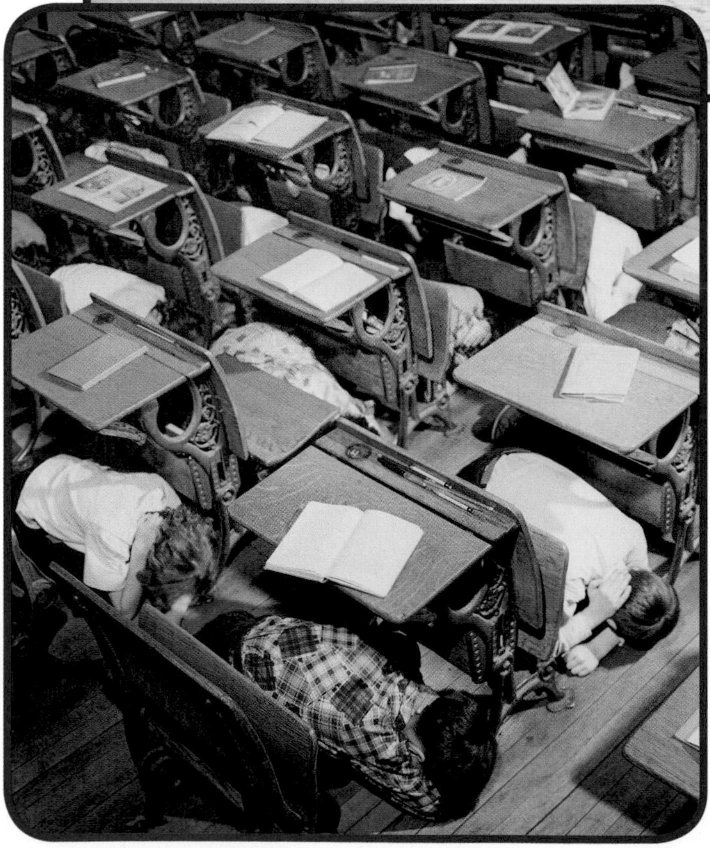

During the Cold War, much of the world was divided into two opposing camps—communist and noncommunist. The United States and the Soviet Union developed vast arsenals of nuclear weapons. People on both sides wondered if they were living on the brink of a third world war, one that would end in nuclear holocaust.

Above: An armored vehicle pulls a missile through Moscow's Red Square as part of a parade in 1962. Left: American schoolchildren take part in a "duck-and-cover" drill in which they practice what to do during a nuclear attack.

A World Divided and on the Brink

During the two decades following World War II, communism made bold advances around the world. In 1949, Mao Zedong led China, the world's most populous nation, into the communist camp. In Korea, the Chinese Communists fought United Nations forces, led by the United States, to a standstill. Less than six years later, a revolutionary leader brought communism to the Western Hemisphere — indeed, right to the doorstep of the United States — in Cuba, an island nation only 90 miles from southern Florida.

In this chapter, we'll examine Cold War tensions at a time when communism seemed to be spreading around the globe. We'll also see how the world came perilously close to nuclear war.

Mao's "Great Leap Forward"

After the victory of his Chinese Communist forces, Mao Zedong ruled a country of over half a billion people — nearly a quarter of the world's population. China was an overwhelmingly rural country, where most people tried to make a living by farming. But a small minority of landlords owned a large proportion of the land, while the majority of poor peasants barely scraped by.

To win the allegiance of peasants, Mao launched an ambitious program of land reform. His government seized almost half the land in China and redistributed it to landless peasants. At the same time, Communist Party officials encouraged peasants to attack their former landlords. Hundreds of thousands of landlords and their relatives were killed.

Not surprisingly, Mao formed a strong alliance with the other communist colossus, the Soviet Union. The Soviet dictator, Stalin, poured aid into China. Soviet advisors helped the Chinese plan an economy based on the Soviet model, emphasizing rapid industrialization. Within a few years, the output of Chinese factories doubled.

With Soviet help, China gradually began to modernize — for example, people in some areas enjoyed electricity and running water. But the pace of change was not fast enough to please Mao. Early in 1958, he declared, "Now we must start a technological revolution so that we may overtake Britain in fifteen or more years." It was a breathtaking ambition — to overtake one of the most industrialized countries on earth in so short

Mao Zedong chats with steel factory workers in 1959. During the Great Leap Forward, China's communist leaders tried to force the country to increase industrial output.

a time. Mao had always yearned to see a radical transformation of Chinese society. Years of absolute power only increased his impatience to achieve that goal.

But how was China to become a great industrial power almost overnight? It lacked the capital to invest in enough modern factories and machines. Mao knew that for all China's poverty, it was rich in one thing — people. He decided that the government would mobilize the vast manpower of China, forcing the people to work far harder than they ever had. He called this new campaign the "Great Leap Forward."

In an attempt to increase food production, Mao ordered millions of peasants into communes where they grew rice and other crops. The effort failed, and many people starved.

Communist officials traveled around the country, exhorting workers with the slogan "More, faster, better, cheaper." They ordered factories to speed up production, and then speed it up even more. Frightened managers drove both their machines and their workers to the point of breakdown. Tens of thousands lost their lives in accidents caused by overwork and faulty machinery.

Knowing that steel is vital to modern industry, Mao decreed that China would double its steel production in a single year. Since China's steel mills could not possibly meet this goal, he ordered people all over China to build "backyard furnaces." Peasants who had almost nothing were forced to melt down anything they owned made of metal — tools, pots and pans, even hair ornaments and door hinges. But the metal produced by these furnaces hardly deserved to be called steel and proved almost useless.

Mao also demanded a dramatic increase in food production. China needed huge quantities of grain both to feed the workers in the new factories and to export to the Soviet Union in exchange for heavy machinery. Mao's government ordered almost the whole rural population into gigantic communes consisting of 5,000 or more households. Inhabitants of a commune were forbidden to leave it. They had to give up all of their private property and labor in the communal fields. In an attempt to meet the government's demands for ever-larger harvests, commune officials drove the workers mercilessly. Thus, a communist government claiming to rule in the name of the workers effectively turned those workers into slaves.

The commune system turned out to be an inefficient way to work the land. Harvests were poor. Officials were terrified to admit that they couldn't meet production goals, so they lied and claimed bountiful harvests. Meanwhile, to pay the costs of industrialization, the government sent more and more grain abroad.

Soon there wasn't enough food to feed the people who were growing it. Desperate peasants ate whatever they could scavenge — corncobs, apricot pits, tree bark. Weaker people — especially children — simply starved to death.

Mao's Great Leap Forward had been intended to turn China into a powerful and prosperous nation. Instead it brought about the greatest man-made famine in human history. By the time Mao ended the campaign in the early 1960s, at least 20 million people had died of starvation, perhaps many more.

China Breaks with the Soviets

From the time of the Communist takeover in 1949, China had considered the Soviet Union its most important supporter and ally. The Soviets had made loans to the Chinese and sent experts to help them construct factories. They also sent military advisors to help them build their armed forces. Soviet technical experts even helped the Chinese develop a nuclear bomb.

But the relationship between the two Communist powers began to change in 1953 with the death of the Soviet leader, Joseph Stalin. A few years after Stalin's death, his successor, Nikita Khrushchev, gave a speech condemning Stalin as a tyrant who had committed many crimes. Khrushchev also accused Stalin of making himself almost an object of worship in the Soviet Union, glorifying himself above the communist cause.

When Mao learned of this speech, he was angry at Khrushchev. As a dictator, Mao had much in common with Stalin. Like Stalin, he accepted the deaths of millions of his countrymen as the necessary price for the pursuit of his goals. Furthermore, Mao had worked hard to glorify himself to the Chinese people. China's Communists revered him as the "Great Helmsman." A volume called *Quotations from Chairman Mao* — known as the "little red book" — was distributed to millions throughout China.

This photo, believed to be a propaganda piece made from a collection of photos, was used to rally support for Mao Zedong. The people are all holding copies of *Quotations from Chairman Mao*, a book that millions of Chinese students, workers, soldiers, and others read in order to show their loyalty to the communist regime.

Mao was just as angry when Khrushchev called for "peaceful coexistence" with the United States and other capitalist nations. Khrushchev argued that there was no need to wage war on capitalist nations to spread communism. He predicted that capitalist systems would eventually collapse under the weight of their own corruption and unfairness. Until that time, said the Soviet premier, communist and capitalist nations might as well live and let live.

Mao rejected Khrushchev's views. The Chinese leader believed that communists should battle fiercely against capitalism—even at the risk of nuclear war. In 1957, Mao told a gathering of communist leaders that he would welcome a new world war, even if it killed half the people on earth, because "imperialism would be razed to the ground and the whole world would become socialist." To Khrushchev, such talk sounded dangerous, even mad.

Megalomania is a mental illness that causes a person to fantasize that he or she is all-powerful.

Khrushchev considered Mao a megalomaniac. For his part, Mao dismissed Khrushchev as timid and cowardly. He believed that the Soviet leader had betrayed the spirit of Marx and Lenin by arguing that the transition to a communist world could come about slowly and peacefully rather than quickly and violently. For Mao, the communes of the Great Leap Forward, where private property had been abolished, proved that a communist society could be achieved almost overnight. But Khrushchev criticized the Great Leap Forward campaign as reckless and ineffective.

Tensions between the Soviet Union and China came to a head in 1960. In that year, the newspaper of the Chinese Communist Party publicly attacked the Soviets for their policy of peaceful coexistence. In response, the Soviets withdrew all of the experts and advisors that they had sent to help the Chinese. The close alliance between the world's two great communist powers came to an end.

Mao Launches the Cultural Revolution

By the early 1960s, Mao realized that the Great Leap Forward had been a failure. He reluctantly accepted the advice of officials who urged him to reduce the size of the communes. He grudgingly allowed peasants to grow food for themselves on their own plots of land. Soon agricultural production rose. The famine ended, and life seemed to be gradually improving for the Chinese people.

But within a few years, Mao again grew dissatisfied with the pace of change. He decided that many people in his government were not true communists but had been infected by Khrushchev-style moderate views. In 1966, he set out to rid the country of such thought by launching a radical new campaign called the "Great Proletarian Cultural Revolution."

With the Cultural Revolution, Mao sought to uproot any traces of capitalism and Western influence in China. Even more radically, he was determined to destroy the traditional culture of China itself—its ancient art, religion, and philosophy. Mao hoped that by destroying the "Four Olds"—old thought, old culture, old customs, and old habits—the spirit of communist revolution might be renewed.

To carry out the Cultural Revolution, Mao created a new group, the Red Guards. This group consisted almost entirely of teenagers, both high school and college students. Born around the time of the Communist victory in China, they had been raised to believe in Mao as an all-wise, infallible leader. Now they pledged their absolute loyalty to him.

All Red Guards were supposed to carry and memorize Chairman Mao's "little red book" of quotations. One famous saying asserted, "A revolution is not a dinner party...it cannot be so refined, so leisurely and gentle.... A revolution is an insurrection, an act of violence." Another quotation declared, "Every Communist must grasp the truth, 'Political power grows out of the barrel of a gun.'"

Sayings like these primed the Red Guards for their work of destruction. At a mass rally in Beijing, one of their leaders cried, "We will smash the old world to smithereens!" Throughout China, young people shouted, "We will smash whoever opposes Chairman Mao!"

Among the first victims were teachers and professors—the men and women who passed on China's traditional culture and values. All over China, Red Guards turned on their teachers. They dragged them out of their classrooms and humiliated them, forcing them to kneel in front of jeering crowds with dunce caps on their heads. Often, they beat them. In Beijing, Red Guards beat a school's headmistress to death, using wooden sticks studded with nails.

Mao ordered the closing of all the schools and colleges in China. The government gave the Red Guards free railway passes so that they could travel easily. Everywhere they went, Mao's young shock troops beat and humiliated teachers, low-level officials, and others they suspected of not being true communists. They murdered thousands, and drove thousands more to commit suicide out of shame and despair.

Many who escaped the beatings and torture were sent to the countryside to be "reeducated" through backbreaking labor. Some of China's most prominent scholars and scientists were put to work shoveling pig manure and cleaning latrines.

The Red Guards hated all signs of luxury and Western influence. One of their victims remembered: "They smashed flower and curio shops because they said only the rich had the money to spend on such frivolities.... Because they did not think a socialist man should sit on a sofa, all sofas became taboo. Other things, such as innerspring mattresses, silk, velvet, [and] cosmetics... were all tossed onto the streets to be carted away or burnt."

No one was permitted to wear Western clothes like long skirts or blue jeans. The Red Guards themselves, male and female, wore identical green uniforms with red armbands on their shirtsleeves.

Chaos in Communist China

Violence increased as the Red Guards carried out Mao's campaign against culture. They burst into people's homes to seize books and paintings. To escape being beaten or tortured, many citizens burned their own books and artworks.

Red Guards destroyed museum exhibits. They even wrecked the home of Confucius, the greatest of ancient Chinese philosophers, whom Mao had declared the enemy of communism. Mao himself ordered the destruction of many historical monuments. He wanted almost nothing left standing that could remind the Chinese of their pre-communist past.

But by the end of 1967, Mao became concerned that if he allowed the chaos to continue, it might rage completely out of control. So he summoned Red Guard leaders to a meeting and ordered them to restrain themselves. Mao did not officially call a halt to the Cultural Revolution, but after 1967 the violence died down.

Still, two years of madness had caused incalculable losses to the country. Hundreds of thousands of people died, and millions more had their lives disrupted. A generation of Chinese students lost the chance for an education, and some of China's greatest historical treasures had been obliterated. The Cultural Revolution — the ultimate symbol of Mao's fanatical brand of communism — was in many ways a great leap backward.

This 1966 Chinese poster demonstrated how Red Guards would deal with anyone deemed to be an "enemy of the people" during the Cultural Revolution.

Soviet Premier Nikita Khrushchev and U.S. President John F. Kennedy met for talks in Vienna, Austria, in 1961. Khrushchev tried to intimidate the young president by banging his fist on the table and declaring, "I want peace, but if you want war that is your problem."

Khrushchev and Kennedy

In June 1961, the newly inaugurated president of the United States, John F. Kennedy, met in Vienna, Austria, with the leader of the Soviet Union, Nikita Khrushchev. The two most powerful leaders in the world were, in almost every way, utterly different. Some of these differences were easy to see. Kennedy was only 44 — the youngest man ever elected president of the United States — while Khrushchev was 67. The tall, handsome Kennedy towered over the short, plump Khrushchev. (A British diplomat once described the Russian leader as a "little bull.")

But the differences between the two men went well beyond age and appearance. Khrushchev had grown up poor and left school at an early age. He worked in factories before rising to prominence in the Communist Party. By contrast, Kennedy had been born into a wealthy family and educated at some of the finest schools in the United States. A witty speaker, he came across as polished and sophisticated. The very unpolished Khrushchev displayed a crude sense of humor and was given to displays of temper. Once, at a meeting of the United Nations, when a diplomat criticized the Soviet Union, Khrushchev took off his shoe and banged it furiously on the table in front of him.

When they met in Vienna, Khrushchev and Kennedy spent two days talking about the state of the world. They debated whether communism was destined to overcome capitalism. They spent many hours discussing trouble spots such as Germany, and especially Berlin, tensely divided into Western and Soviet zones.

The Soviet leader considered the young American president "inexperienced" and "immature." In their talks, Khrushchev tried to bully Kennedy. When the president criticized the Soviet Union for intervening in the affairs of other countries, Khrushchev angrily accused him of hypocrisy. The United States, too, he pointed out, had military forces all over the world. It was the

Americans, he declared, who had "delusions of grandeur," thinking they were so rich and powerful that they could "afford not to recognize the rights of others."

After the talks, Kennedy told a journalist, "I never met a man like this. [I] talked about how a nuclear exchange would kill seventy million people in ten minutes and he just looked at me as if to say, 'So what?'"

In truth, Khrushchev's behavior was mostly bluster, an act designed to put down the young president. He wanted to avoid nuclear war as much as any Western leader, especially since the Soviet nuclear arsenal was much smaller than that of the United States. At the same time, he was a tough dictator and a committed Marxist, determined to advance the cause of communism both at home and abroad.

Just two months after meeting with Kennedy, Khrushchev allowed the East Germans to build the Berlin Wall to keep people from crossing into West Berlin, where they hoped to find freedom and prosperity. The Soviet premier watched to see how the American president would respond. When Kennedy took no real action, Khrushchev assumed that the American president must indeed be timid and indecisive.

Castro's Cuba

While the Soviet Union and China were the two largest, most powerful communist nations in the world, they weren't the only ones President Kennedy had to worry about. By the time Kennedy took office in 1961, communism had come to America's doorstep — to the Caribbean island of Cuba. The government there was in the hands

A World Divided

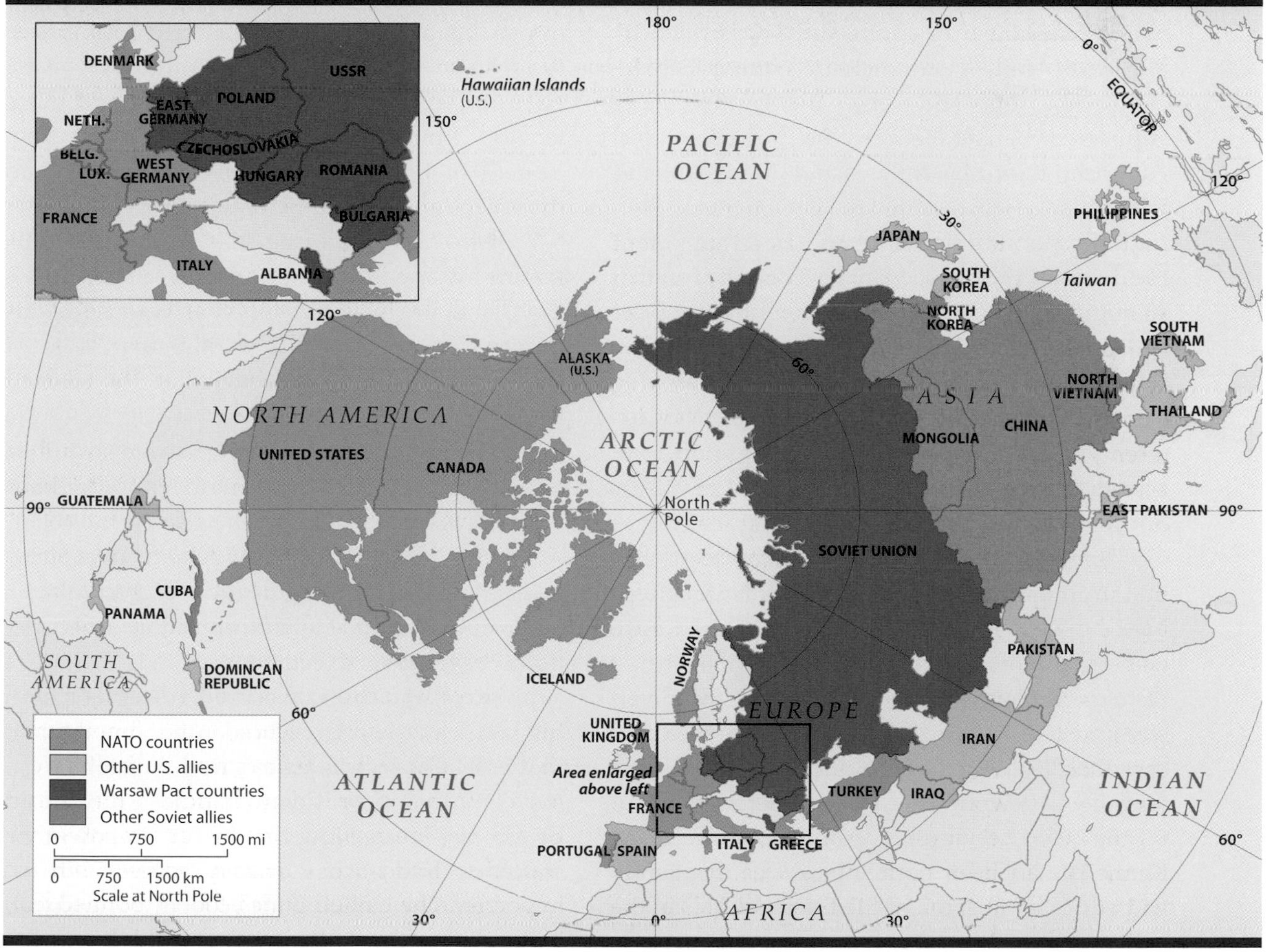

of a strong-willed, determined dictator named Fidel Castro.

Castro was born in Cuba in 1927. His father was from Spain, which had ruled Cuba for nearly 400 years, and he had come to the island as a draftee in the Spanish army. Castro's father later settled down in Cuba and became a prosperous landowner.

Cuba became independent of Spain in 1898, after the Spanish-American War. The United States, which had played a big part in helping Cuba gain independence, established a naval base in Cuba at Guantanamo Bay. Americans largely controlled affairs on the island until the 1930s. By the 1950s, half of Cuba's sugar exports went to the United States. Sugar was by far the island's most important product — so important that a saying ran, "No sugar, no country."

Arable land is land good for growing crops.

American companies invested heavily in Cuba. They owned most of the island's arable land, as well as 90 percent of its utilities and 50 percent of its railroads.

In Fidel Castro's youth, Cuba was ruled by a corrupt and brutal dictator named Fulgencio Batista (buh-TEE-stuh). The United States supported Batista because he helped protect American interests on the island. Many Cubans, including Castro, resented the United States, both for its economic dominance and for its support of the dictator. They especially resented the fact that so many Americans grew rich by doing business in Cuba while much of the island's population remained poor, with little hope of improving their lives. Only 40 percent of Cuban children went to school. In the countryside, hundreds of thousands of poor farm workers lived in rickety houses without electricity or running water.

These facts of Cuban life — poverty-stricken and dominated by a dictator with American backing — weighed on the mind of Fidel Castro as he grew into a passionate young man with a taste for violence. Although he went to university and received degrees in law, Castro became convinced that the only solution to Cuba's problems lay in revolution.

In 1953, he joined a group of rebels in an attack on a Cuban army barracks. Sentenced to prison for his role in the attack, he gave a fiery courtroom speech. Pouring contempt on the "miserable tyrant" Batista, Castro claimed to be fighting in the name of Cuba's poor. He ended his speech with the ringing sentences, "Condemn me. It does not matter. History will absolve me."

Communist Revolution in Cuba

Castro was released after serving two years of his sentence. His time in prison had made him even more committed to the overthrow of Batista. In 1956, he led a small group of armed followers into a jungle-covered mountain range in southeastern Cuba. Here, they formed a guerrilla band that became known as *los barbudos* (the bearded ones) because the men lacked water and soap for shaving.

From their refuge in the mountains, Castro's men staged hit-and-run attacks on Batista's soldiers. Many Cubans — especially the poor — took Castro's side in this fight. They looked at him as a sort of Robin Hood — a bandit chieftain fighting an unjust tyrant while he tried to improve the lives of the poor. Over the next two years, Castro's forces grew. He seized more and more territory from the government. Finally, on New Year's Day, 1959, the capital city of Havana fell to the rebels, and Batista fled the country.

Castro made himself leader of Cuba. His regime introduced health care and schools across the island. He was also popular because of his proven courage and his spellbinding style of speaking. One reporter noted that "he seemed to weave a hypnotic net over his listeners." He always sported a beard and appeared in public wearing green military fatigues to remind Cubans of his days as the commander of *los barbudos*.

Although Castro had fought to overthrow a dictator, he had no intention of becoming a democratic leader. He did not allow free elections. Instead, he executed hundreds of Batista supporters, and threw those who disagreed with his policies into prison. It soon became evident that Fidel Castro was Cuba's new dictator.

For a long time, Castro had been influenced by Marxist ideas. Now that he was in power, he started to build a communist system, with the government controlling the economy. The Cuban

Fidel Castro (center) led a rebel army that in 1959 forced the U.S.-backed dictator Fulgencio Batista to flee Cuba. Castro then set up a repressive communist dictatorship. His government seized the property of many companies in Cuba, including those owned by Americans. Castro's actions and close relationship with the USSR alarmed U.S. government officials.

government confiscated all major companies, starting with those owned by Americans. Such actions won Castro the friendship of the most powerful communist state, the Soviet Union, which promised economic and military aid.

The Bay of Pigs

The leaders of the United States were alarmed to see communism establishing a foothold in the Western Hemisphere, especially one so near the U.S. coast. Soon after taking office, President Kennedy gave the go-ahead to implement a secret plan for an invasion of Cuba.

The invasion force would not include U.S. soldiers, since a direct U.S. attack against Castro might provoke the Soviet Union to respond. Instead, the invaders would consist of 1,500 Cubans who had fled Castro's dictatorship, and who had been armed and trained by the United States. Kennedy hoped that the amphibious assault would inspire the rest of the Cuban people to rise up and overthrow Castro.

In April 1961, the small army of Cuban exiles landed on the island's coast at a place called the Bay of Pigs. At once everything began to go wrong. The United States had promised to support the attack with its air force, but at the last minute Kennedy changed his mind out of fear that it might expose the U.S. role. Castro sent Soviet-made tanks against the invaders, who managed to drive only a quarter mile inland. After three days of fighting, the invaders were killed or captured.

The Bay of Pigs disaster humiliated Kennedy and the United States. The attack caused no uprising against Castro. On the contrary, most Cubans rallied around their leader, who had seemingly defeated the mighty "Colossus to the North."

The Cuban Missile Crisis

The Soviet leader, Nikita Khrushchev, was impressed by Castro's successful defiance of the United States. Khrushchev decided the Soviet Union should give Cuba its full support. By doing so, the Soviets could help spread Marxism in America's backyard, as the saying went, and increase their prestige as the leaders of the communist world.

Khrushchev also reasoned that supporting Cuba would help equalize the "balance of power" between the United States and the Soviet Union. The Americans possessed many more nuclear weapons than the Soviets. They even had missiles pointing at the Soviet Union from the neighboring country of Turkey. Now Khrushchev decided to "throw a hedgehog down Uncle Sam's pants," as he put it. He would station his own nuclear missiles in Cuba — a country only 90 miles from the United States.

In October 1962, President Kennedy's advisors brought him an alarming report. An American spy plane flying 70,000 feet above Cuba had photographed nuclear missile sites under construction in Cuba. The construction was just days away from completion. When finished, the sites would be able to launch nuclear missiles that could hit cities in the United States.

Kennedy was stunned and horrified. He quickly began a series of almost nonstop meetings with his top military leaders and statesmen. They all realized that once the missile sites were finished, the Soviet Union would be able to strike the United States with little or no warning.

Some of Kennedy's advisors urged him to bomb the missile sites before they were ready for use. Some argued that he should also invade Cuba by air and sea. Others warned that an attack on the island could prompt the Soviets to seize West Berlin. It might well start a nuclear war. Some urged Kennedy to avoid confrontation and give diplomacy a chance.

Kennedy realized that he had little time for diplomacy. He believed that if the United

In the autumn of 1962, U.S. military planes flying over Cuba took a series of photographs that indicated new military construction and the presence of Soviet technicians. By October, U.S. experts confirmed that the Soviets and Cubans were building missile launch sites. This photo was taken by a Lockheed U-2 spy plane on November 1, 1962.

States appeared weak in the face of this threat, it would encourage a Soviet arms buildup in the Western Hemisphere. But the young commander in chief also distrusted the top military men who urged an attack. He had served in the navy in World War II, and had become convinced that war between the superpowers, especially nuclear war, would be catastrophic.

The U.S. Constitution identifies the president as *commander in chief* of the armed forces.

Faced with few options and potentially catastrophic consequences, the president chose another course. He ordered a naval blockade of Cuba, to keep more weapons from reaching the island, and to pressure the Soviets to dismantle the existing missile sites. He realized that if his strategy failed, he might soon be leading his country into a third world war.

On the Brink of Nuclear War

On October 22, 1962, Kennedy made a television address telling the nation and the world about the Soviet missiles in Cuba, and about the American naval blockade. He announced that all ships approaching the island would be stopped and searched to make sure they carried no weapons that could be used to attack another nation. "I call upon Chairman Khrushchev to halt and eliminate this clandestine, reckless, and provocative threat to world peace," Kennedy said. He also declared that the use of Soviet nuclear weapons anywhere in the Western Hemisphere would lead to a retaliatory attack on the Soviet Union.

Clandestine means done in a secretive, hidden way.

Nikita Khrushchev responded that a naval blockade of Cuba was "an act of aggression" and a violation of international law. He cautioned that if U.S. Navy vessels tried to stop Soviet ships at sea, Soviet subs might sink them. The USSR would not start a nuclear war, he warned, but "if the U.S. insists on war, we'll all meet together in hell."

In New York, American and Soviet ambassadors to the United Nations exchanged angry words. The American ambassador demanded, "Do you, Ambassador Zorin, deny that the USSR has placed and is placing missile sites in Cuba? Yes or no?" When the Soviet official refused to answer directly, the American showed the Security Council photographs of the missile sites. "We know the facts and so do you, sir," he insisted. The Soviet ambassador ridiculed the photographs.

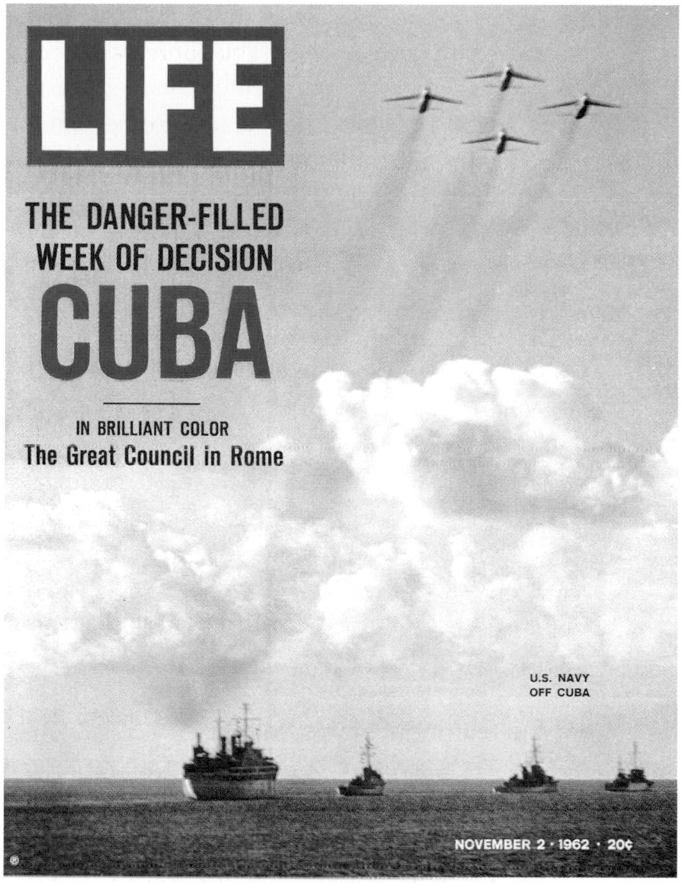

This 1962 *Life* magazine cover shows part of the U.S. naval blockade off the coast of Cuba. For a week in October, the world's two superpowers seemed headed toward war.

As the crisis deepened, Americans stocked up on food and emergency supplies, and formed long lines at gas stations. Schools held air-raid drills, during which children hid under their desks—as if that would do any good during a nuclear attack. Millions of city dwellers, fearing they lived in a nuclear target, left their homes and fled to other parts of the country.

People around the world held their breath and waited to see if Soviet ships would challenge the American blockade. Some ships were reported to have stopped dead in the water, or to have turned back from Cuba. A Soviet tanker approached the island. A U.S. Navy ship stopped the tanker, searched it, determined that it carried only oil, and let it pass.

Meanwhile, U.S. and Soviet officials exchanged urgent messages. The Soviets reminded the Americans that the United States had put missiles in Turkey aimed at the Soviet Union. Could they not understand that the Soviets felt just as threatened by the American missiles? But Kennedy stuck to his demand—the Cuban missiles had to go.

At the end of October, the Soviets backed down. They agreed to remove their missiles from Cuba in exchange for an end to the blockade and an American pledge not to invade the island. The American secretary of state commented, "We were eyeball to eyeball, and I think the other fellow blinked." But Khrushchev gained something he wanted, too. Kennedy had secretly agreed to withdraw U.S. missiles from Turkey.

The tense standoff between the superpowers in the Cuban Missile Crisis had an unexpected result. It led to a thaw in relations between the United States and the Soviet Union. Frightened by their journey to the nuclear brink, the two nations began talks aimed at limiting the use of nuclear weapons.

The world has never again come so close to a nuclear conflagration. Of those two weeks in October 1962, one historian has said, "The Cuban Missile Crisis was the most dangerous event in human history."

"I am a Berliner"

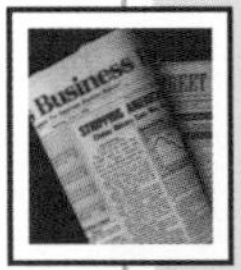

A Page from the Past

On June 26, 1963, eight months after the Cuban Missile Crisis, John F. Kennedy traveled to West Berlin and stood before the Berlin Wall, a grim symbol of the divide between communist and democratic nations. In the shadow of the wall, he gave a speech proclaiming support for the struggle of West Berliners to maintain an island of freedom within communist East Germany. The crowd roared its approval when he declared "Ich bin ein Berliner" — *I am a Berliner.*

Civis Romanus sum is a Latin phrase meaning "I am a Roman citizen."

Two thousand years ago, the proudest boast was "*civis Romanus sum.*" Today, in the world of freedom, the proudest boast is "*Ich bin ein Berliner.*"

I appreciate my interpreter translating my German!

There are many people in the world who really don't understand, or say they don't, what is the great issue between the free world and the Communist world. Let them come to Berlin. There are some who say that communism is the wave of the future. Let them come to Berlin. And there are some who say in Europe and elsewhere we can work with the Communists. Let them come to Berlin. And there are even a few who say that it is true that communism is an evil system, but it permits us to make economic progress. *Lass sie nach Berlin kommen*. Let them come to Berlin.

Freedom has many difficulties and democracy is not perfect, but we have never had to put a wall up to keep our people in, to prevent them

Enthusiastic Berliners greet President John F. Kennedy in June 1963. Kennedy traveled to West Berlin to deliver a message of defiance to the Soviet and East German governments. In his famous speech, he declared that the Berlin Wall was "the most obvious and vivid demonstration of the failures of the Communist system, for all the world to see."

from leaving us.... [The Berlin Wall is] an offense not only against history but an offense against humanity, separating families, dividing husbands and wives and brothers and sisters, and dividing a people who wish to be joined together....

Freedom is indivisible, and when one man is enslaved, all are not free. When all are free, then we can look forward to that day when this city will be joined as one and this country and this great Continent of Europe in a peaceful and hopeful globe. When that day finally comes, as it will, the people of West Berlin can take sober satisfaction in the fact that they were in the front lines for almost two decades.

All free men, wherever they may live, are citizens of Berlin, and, therefore, as a free man, I take pride in the words "*Ich bin ein Berliner*."

Edwin "Buzz" Aldrin walks on the lunar surface on July 20, 1969, during the *Apollo 11* mission to the moon. Fellow astronaut Neil Armstrong, the first man to set foot on the moon, took the picture. The historic *Apollo 11* voyage was the product of remarkable scientific advances in the postwar years—and the product of a space race between the United States and the USSR.

Looking Up and Away: Scientific Advances in the Postwar Years

The atomic bombs that ended World War II in the Pacific, as well as the hydrogen bombs built during the Cold War, were made possible by advances in science. Yet during the 1950s and 1960s, even as the Soviet Union and United States came dangerously close to nuclear catastrophe, other scientific breakthroughs improved communication, saved lives, and ultimately drew the people of the world closer together. Some of these advances came out of the Cold War rivalry, while others were the result of determined individuals making up their minds to solve vexing problems.

In this chapter, we'll describe some technological leaps made in the quarter century following World War II. It was an era that gave us television, satellites, and computers. It witnessed medical advances, a "Green Revolution" that dramatically increased food production, and a space race that put men on the moon.

Inventing TV

You probably know Thomas Edison as the man who gave the world the electric lightbulb, Alexander Graham Bell as the inventor of the telephone, and Guglielmo Marconi as the father of the radio. But what about one of the most popular inventions in history — television? Who invented TV?

No one single name comes to mind for the simple reason that no single person invented it. Dozens of scientists working all over the world, often in fierce competition, helped develop TV.

Many historians trace the beginning of television to an alert English telegraph operator named Joseph May. One day in 1872, May heard a strange hum coming from his telegraph receiver. He noticed that the noise disappeared when he blocked the sunlight from a nearby window. May assumed, correctly, that the wires in his equipment were converting light into electricity.

When May shared news of his discovery, scientists theorized that images carried by light might be captured and transmitted over telegraph wires. But they couldn't figure out how to turn their theories into machines that worked.

Decades later, during the years leading up to World War I, a young Russian engineering

Television—Seeing Far

The word *television* comes from the Greek word *tele*, meaning "far," plus *vision*, which comes from the Latin word *videre*, "to see." So *television* means "to see far."

student named Vladimir Zworykin (ZWOR-ih-kin) pondered the problem. While demonstrations against Tsar Nicholas flared in the streets, Zworykin studied at the St. Petersburg Institute of Technology, where he helped a professor work on a primitive television system. Later, during the Bolshevik Revolution, when the professor disappeared, Zworykin decided to emigrate to the United States before he too was carted away.

Zworykin ended up in Pittsburgh, Pennsylvania, working for the Westinghouse Electric Corporation, which had pioneered the development of radio. He wanted to return to the television experiments he had begun with his professor in St. Petersburg, but Westinghouse officials weren't interested. So Zworykin experimented with television at night. He often worked into the early morning hours, until company guards told him to go home.

Zworykin's night work produced several patents, including one for the iconoscope, a camera tube that produced pictures by scanning images electronically, and another for the kinescope, which reproduced those scanned images on a picture tube. The images were blurry and just one-inch wide. But together these inventions formed a complete, though crude, television system.

Westinghouse executives weren't impressed. They couldn't imagine television ever being as popular as radio. Who would want to watch fuzzy images on a one-inch screen?

Zworykin found a believer in a fellow Russian immigrant, David Sarnoff, general manager of Westinghouse's sister company, the Radio Corporation of America (RCA). In 1929, Sarnoff arranged to have Zworykin transferred to RCA, where he could devote himself to working on his television.

Russian émigré Vladimir Zworykin, shown here in about 1951 when he worked for RCA, is credited as one of the inventors of television.

Zworykin or Farnsworth?

What happened next is a little unclear. Not long after he started working for RCA, Zworykin visited the lab of an American inventor named Philo Farnsworth. A couple of years earlier, Farnsworth had developed a device that transmitted a simple televised image—a straight line. By 1929, Farnsworth was transmitting images of people. After visiting Farnsworth's labs, Zworykin returned to RCA, and soon RCA introduced its first TVs. Did Zworykin take ideas from Farnsworth?

Years of lawsuits followed, with both Farnsworth and RCA claiming credit for inventing television. The U.S. Patent Office eventually sided with Farnsworth, but he lost other legal battles with RCA, and several years passed before the company paid him any money for his work.

Some claim that Farnsworth deserves the title of "inventor of TV." For example, in 1999 *Time* magazine named him one of the 100 most influential people of the twentieth century for his work in developing television.

What's on TV?

Thanks to the work of Farnsworth, Zworykin, and others, TV pictures became larger and clearer. But David Sarnoff — RCA's president, and the man who had hired Zworykin — knew that before people would buy televisions, there would have to be programs that they would want to watch. In 1939, he introduced television to the American public by broadcasting programs from the World's Fair in New York City, including a telecast of President Franklin D. Roosevelt opening the fair.

Sarnoff hoped to broadcast a lineup of television programs in 1941, but World War II interrupted his plans. Westinghouse, RCA, and other companies around the world dropped everything to manufacture equipment for the war effort. After the war, RCA and its radio subsidiary, the National Broadcasting Company (NBC), launched network TV programs such as *The Kraft Television Theater*, which featured different dramas every week, and *Kukla, Fran and Ollie,* a popular show that featured puppets.

Even though most people did not own television sets in the late 1940s, they were curious about the invention. They often stood outside store windows and watched the black-and-white images moving on the screens. Others gathered around boxy TV sets in their neighbors' living rooms. The glow of a television screen worked almost like an ancient campfire drawing people together.

As television sets became cheaper, more and more people bought them, particularly in the United States, where the economy was booming. In 1946, about 7,000 American homes had televisions; by 1950, there were 10 million TV sets in the United States. By the end of the 1950s, 90 percent of American households owned a television, and most families spent their evenings watching it.

National networks and local stations turned popular radio shows into TV programs — variety shows, soap operas, comedies, westerns, and sporting events. Now viewers could *see* what they had once only been able to hear. They laughed at comedienne Lucille Ball's predicaments on *I Love Lucy,* thrilled to western adventures on *Gunsmoke,* and cheered for their favorite baseball teams, all from the comfort of their living rooms.

By the end of the 1950s, nine out of ten American homes boasted a television set, and families often gathered around it to watch the latest shows, including comedies, sporting events, and westerns.

People also turned to television for news and educational programs, though network officials quickly learned that gimmicks helped lure viewers. When NBC started a morning news and information program called *Today,* only a few viewers watched. But when the network brought in a chimpanzee to cohost the show, *Today* instantly became one of the most popular programs on television.

Variety Shows and Soap Operas

In television's early years, variety shows and soap operas were favorites of many viewers. Variety shows such as *The Ed Sullivan Show* featured a variety of entertainment—singing, dancing, short comedy sketches, juggling, and more—that the whole family could enjoy. Soap operas, which began in the era of radio, were so named because soap companies, such as Procter & Gamble, often sponsored the shows.

The World Tunes In

As Europe recovered from World War II, people in Britain, France, West Germany, and other countries also began buying television sets. European countries developed their own television networks, which were mostly controlled or funded by national governments. In England, the British Broadcasting Corporation (BBC) quickly became one of the world's most watched networks. In 1953, the BBC helped usher in the age of television when it broadcast the coronation of young Queen Elizabeth II. Some twenty-two million TV viewers watched the ceremonies.

Even as television spread through Europe and beyond, people around the world often tuned in to American TV programs, which American networks sold at low prices to overseas broadcasters. From Spain to Japan, viewers enjoyed Hollywood westerns and comedies. These shows were so popular that some countries established rules limiting American TV programs to open time for other shows.

Near the end of his life, Vladimir Zworykin looked in dismay at the collection of shows that filled television screens. He had hoped that TV would serve mainly to help educate people. Instead, he believed, most broadcasts were trivial and unproductive. "I hate what they've done to my child," he said of television. "I would never let my own children watch it."

Despite Zworykin's dismay, television at its best could open a window on the world. As it spread from country to country, viewers could see how distant people lived and what foreign lands looked like. Documentaries showed images of explorers navigating the Nile River in Egypt, musicians performing in New York's Carnegie Hall, or Olympic athletes competing in Mexico City. News programs showed history as it unfolded, even if it was happening thousands of miles away.

Even comedies like *Ozzie and Harriet* were windows into a different world for many people. They made Americans laugh, but in other parts of the world, they showed people a squeaky clean picture of how some middle-class Americans lived: what amazing kitchen devices they owned, what kind of living room furniture they had, and how easily they moved from place to place in their big, comfortable cars. This vision of America as a land of plenty created new hopes, new resentments, and new expectations worldwide.

Despite many mediocre programs, television did live up to its name—it helped people "see far." Not since the printing press had one invention done so much to expand and change people's horizons.

The Computer Revolution Begins

World War II may have delayed the development of home television sets, but it boosted other inventions. One of the most important was the computer.

During the war, a British mathematician named Alan Turing led the design of an early computing machine that allowed British intelligence officers to break secet German military codes created by the Enigma machine. Early computers were huge, clunky machines that performed calculations and processed information electronically.

After the war, the invention of transistors—tiny devices that control the flow of electric current—and the development of other miniature electronic equipment allowed computers to become smaller, quicker, and more reliable. Nevertheless, in the 1950s and 1960s, a "small" computer was still big enough to fill a room. It would take another generation to create personal computers for homes and offices.

In the 1950s and 1960s, giant computers were marvels of their time—yet a machine like this one had less computational power than one of today's laptop computers.

To the Stars and Back

After World War II, companies that had been building bombers started building new passenger jets for commercial airlines. By the late 1950s, travelers could board a four-engine jetliner and fly between Europe and the United States. In the next decade, passenger air travel literally took off, dramatically decreasing the time it took to reach distant parts of the globe.

With American companies like Boeing building bigger and faster aircraft, the United States took the technological lead in air travel. For this reason, Americans were caught off guard by a dramatic announcement. On the evening of October 4, 1957, TV and radio news programs broadcast a strange sound — a deep "beep-beep-beep" that newscasters identified as coming from *Sputnik*, a 184-pound artificial satellite sent into space by the Soviet Union.

When they first heard news of *Sputnik*, people around the world instinctively looked up. Sure enough, if they looked up at the right moment (especially through binoculars), they could see *Sputnik* as a dot of light crossing the night sky. The small silver satellite — about the size of a large beach ball — orbited earth every 96 minutes.

The launch of *Sputnik* gave Americans a jolt, exactly as Nikita Khrushchev, the Soviet premier, intended. He had planned this triumph in time for the fortieth anniversary of the Bolshevik Revolution in November 1957. The success of the Soviet satellite started a new phase of the Cold War, a space race between the Soviet Union and the United States.

Many Americans were upset that the USSR had beaten them into space. After all, an American, Robert Goddard, had invented the world's first liquid-fuel rocket. Even Wernher von Braun (VEHR-nuhr von brown), a brilliant scientist who had developed rockets for Germany during World War II, was now an American citizen and one of the leaders in the U.S. rocket program. Why, then, was *Russia* the first country to send a satellite into space? More important, what did this mean for American security?

The United States had a satellite program of its own in the works, but before the first American satellite could be launched, the Soviets sent up *Sputnik II*, nicknamed "Muttnik" because it carried the first space traveler, a dog named Laika (LIYK-uh). Laika survived the launch and orbit, but when the satellite's cooling system failed, she died of overheating.

That setback did not discourage the Russians. They now had two satellites orbiting the

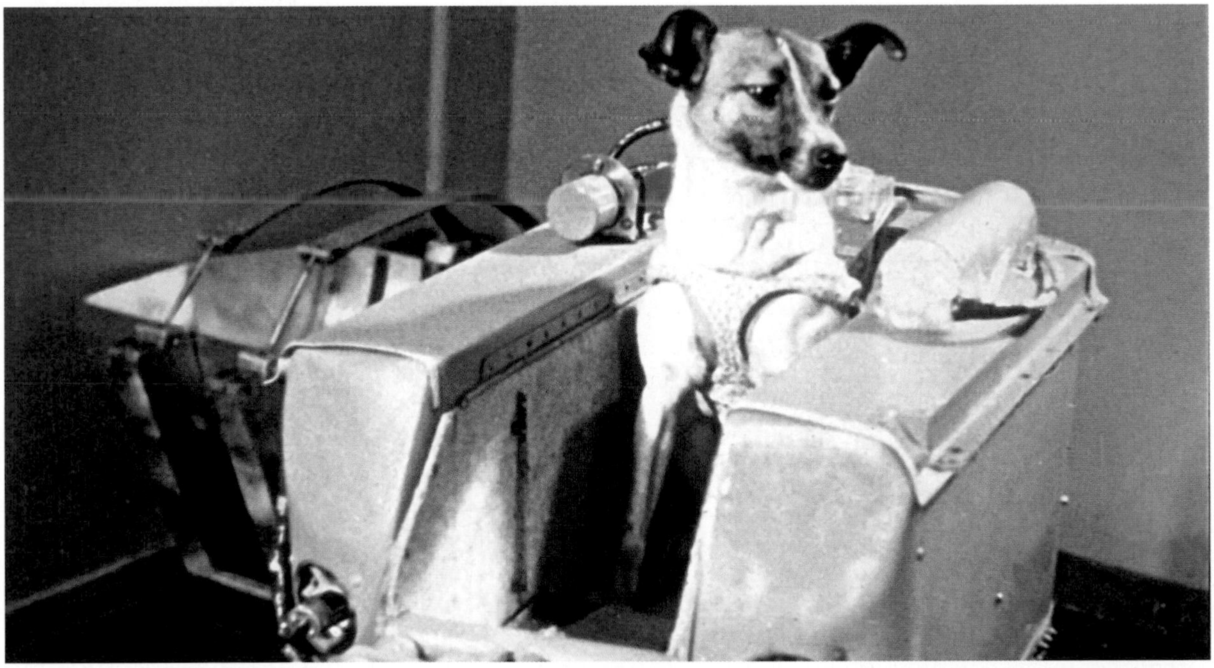

In 1957 a dog named Laika became the first living creature in outer space when she blasted off aboard a Russian rocket. Laika died of overheating when *Sputnik II*'s cooling system failed. She helped pave the way for humans to venture into space, but her death sparked a lively debate about animal rights.

earth. The Americans remained stuck on the ground and rushing to catch up.

In December 1957, the United States attempted to launch a 70-foot rocket with a grapefruit-size satellite perched on top. As the world watched on television, the rocket burst into flames and collapsed. The tiny satellite fell to the ground and rolled away. Newspapers dubbed the American effort "Flopnik" and "Kaputnik."

The U.S. space program finally achieved a successful launch on the evening of January 31, 1958, when the satellite *Explorer* entered orbit. Less than a year later, President Dwight D. Eisenhower announced the formation of the National Aeronautics and Space Administration (NASA), a government agency he hoped would help the United States take the lead in the space race. The U.S. government also sponsored new science and engineering programs in schools. Educators worried about "what Ivan knows that Johnny doesn't know."

At every stage of the space race, however, the Soviets seemed to be pulling ahead. NASA managed to send two monkeys, Ham and Enos, into space—they survived the journey. But the Russians did NASA one better by sending the first human into space. On April 12, 1961, cosmonaut Yuri Gagarin (guh-GAHR-in) became the first person in space when he orbited the earth in a flight that lasted one hour and forty-eight minutes. When he returned, he boasted, "Now let the other countries try to catch us!"

In April 1961, Russian cosmonaut Yuri Gagarin became the first human to travel into space. His spacecraft *Vostok I* orbited as high as 203 miles above the earth.

What Is a Satellite?

A satellite is any object that continuously orbits the earth or another body in space. Some satellites, such as earth's moon, are known as natural satellites. Others, built on earth and launched into space, are known as artificial satellites.

Since 1957, more than forty countries have launched artificial satellites. In the early years of the twenty-first century, about three thousand satellites were orbiting the earth, gathering information about the weather, carrying telephone calls, monitoring crops, and assisting in the navigation of ships.

Some artificial satellites also take photographs and transmit radio signals for military communication, which is one reason why Americans were so nervous about the Soviet Union's early satellites during the Cold War.

A few weeks later, Alan Shepard became the first American to travel into space. But his trip was much shorter, just fifteen minutes, and he did not orbit the earth. To many, the United States was clearly behind in the space race.

Shooting for the Moon

When the young and energetic John F. Kennedy became president in 1961, he had no intention of staying in second place. He asked NASA officials what part of the space race Americans stood the best chance of winning. Their answer—landing a crew of astronauts on the moon.

President Kennedy immediately embraced the idea. On May 25, 1961, he told Congress, "I believe that this nation should commit itself to achieving the goal, before this decade is out, of landing a man on the moon and returning him safely to earth. No single space project in this period will be more impressive to mankind, or more important for the long-range exploration of space, and none will be so difficult or expensive to accomplish."

The president, still smarting over the defeat of U.S. forces at the Bay of Pigs in Cuba a month before, may have been looking for a way to restore national confidence. The moon landing appealed to his imagination and competitiveness. It seemed, as he put it, to be a way of "embarking on a sea of new knowledge."

Some people questioned how putting a man on the moon would contribute to the long-range exploration of space. They said that NASA could learn just as much from cheaper, safer unmanned flights. Kennedy stood firm. The United States would go to the moon, he said, "because that challenge is one that we are willing to accept, one we are unwilling to postpone, and one which we intend to win."

NASA undertook the Apollo program to develop the skills and equipment needed for a moon landing. If everything went just right, NASA scientists figured they could fulfill President Kennedy's promise and put a man on the moon before 1970.

But everything did not go right. The spacecraft for the first mission, *Apollo 1*, had so many technical problems that its commander, Virgil "Gus" Grissom, hung a lemon on it while it was being assembled.

NASA tested the *Apollo 1* capsule in January 1967. Grissom and two other astronauts, Edward White and Roger Chaffee, were locked inside, just as if it were a real launch, and the capsule was pressurized with oxygen. The astronauts had been in the capsule for five hours when a piece of exposed wiring near Grissom's seat produced a tiny electrical arc. The spark caused the oxygen-filled capsule to burst into flames. The astronauts were trapped. All three died before they could be rescued.

Critics cried out that the Apollo program was not only a waste of money but also of lives. Many Americans, however, took heart from something Gus Grissom had said a week before his death: "We are in a risky business, and we hope that if anything happens to us, it will not delay the program. The conquest of space is worth the risk of life."

"One Giant Leap for Mankind"

NASA officials took two years to assess what had gone wrong with *Apollo 1*. Engineers made 1,300 changes—including one that provided the space capsule with an escape hatch that opened easily—before U.S. astronauts returned to space.

A series of successful flights took American astronauts closer and closer to the moon, and finally into the moon's orbit. By mid-1969, NASA was ready to try a moon landing with the *Apollo 11* mission.

On July 16, 1969, three astronauts—Neil Armstrong, Edwin "Buzz" Aldrin, and Michael

A *Saturn V* rocket lifts off from Florida's Kennedy Space Center on July 16, 1969, carrying *Apollo 11* astronauts Neil Armstrong, Michael Collins, and Edwin Aldrin to the moon.

Collins — boarded the spacecraft *Columbia*. It took three days traveling at 24,000 miles per hour to reach the moon's orbit. Computers on earth helped guide the spacecraft on its journey.

Once *Columbia* was in the moon's orbit, Armstrong and Aldrin boarded a small lunar landing module called the *Eagle*. They left Collins and the *Columbia* orbiting the moon while they descended to the surface.

With Armstrong at the controls, the *Eagle* glided past NASA's planned landing spot near the moon's Sea of Tranquility. The terrain was rocky, and Armstrong had to look for a smooth spot to land. Finally, with just a few seconds of landing fuel left, he brought the *Eagle* down in a clearing near a small crater.

"Houston," he radioed back to the Texas flight center, "Tranquility Base here. The *Eagle* has landed." It was July 20, 1969.

Six hours later, with more than a billion people around the world watching on television, Armstrong climbed down a ladder and stepped onto the moon's surface. "That's one small step for a man," he said, "one giant leap for mankind."

A few minutes later, Aldrin joined Armstrong on the moon's surface. They planted an American flag, conducted some experiments, gathered moon rocks, and gazed back at earth.

After two hours and twenty-one minutes of exploration, the two astronauts returned to the *Eagle*. Several hours later, when they fired rockets that lifted them back into orbit, they left behind the first human footprints on the face of the moon.

The United States had won the race to the moon — what did it mean? In terms of the Cold War, the moon landing boosted American pride. But the event was something more, not only for Americans but also for millions of people around the world, of various nationalities, who watched the grainy televised images of Neil Armstrong stepping onto the lunar surface, or heard his words on their radios. It was a moment of optimism and hope in a century that had been marked by violence and upheaval. It was a nearly unimaginable

Edwin "Buzz" Aldrin, the second man to step onto the moon's surface after Neil Armstrong, poses beside a U.S. flag that he and Armstrong planted. Because there is no wind on the airless moon, a stiff wire holds the flag out from its pole. With the planting of the flag, the United States won the race to the moon, a victory in the Cold War with the Soviet Union.

If left undisturbed by human activity, the first footprints on the moon will remain for perhaps a million years, since there is no wind or water there to erode them away.

triumph of human ingenuity and daring. The successful voyage to the moon was a reminder that human beings are capable of solving enormous problems and making age-old dreams come true. It proved, as President Kennedy had said, that "man in his quest for knowledge and progress is determined and cannot be deterred."

What Precisely Did Armstrong Say?

"That's one small step for a man, one giant leap for mankind." Those are the words that Neil Armstrong planned to say as he stepped onto the moon's surface. Yet millions of television viewers heard him say, "That's one small step for man, one giant leap for mankind." Without that one-letter word, *a*, before the word *man*, the phrase seemed repetitious, like saying, "That's one small step for mankind, one giant leap for mankind."

Had Neil Armstrong botched his words as he set foot on the moon? Perhaps not. A recent computer analysis of NASA recordings indicates that Armstrong may have indeed uttered "a." Using sophisticated software to examine the audio file, an Australian computer programmer found evidence that the syllable was spoken but lost in the transmission to earth. If that analysis is correct, modern technology has rescued one of the most famous phrases in history.

Starting a Green Revolution

The triumphant spirit of the Apollo moon landing led some to ask: If we can put a man on the moon, can't we solve some problems that affect millions of people here at home?

At least one of those problems was evident even from outer space. Looking down from their orbit around earth, astronauts could see parts of the planet lush with green forests and crops that fed whole nations. But other parts were dusty, brown, and parched — regions where crops grew poorly or not at all, and where many people went hungry every year.

Famine, and the threat of famine, have hung over people through the ages. Over and over, nations have gone to war and millions of people have died in the effort to secure a steady and safe supply of food. At the end of World War II, widespread famine had seemed almost certain as rising birth rates produced more mouths to feed. In the 1960s, a best-selling book predicted that worldwide starvation was just a few years away.

A worldwide famine did *not* occur, thanks in large part to an American plant breeder named Norman Borlaug (BOR-lahg). He taught farmers around the world how to increase their yields — that is, how to grow more grain on the same amount of land.

Borlaug grew up on an Iowa farm during the Great Depression, when severe droughts parched the earth and turned farms into swirling clouds of dust. Even as a boy, he noticed that farmers who used modern techniques, such as fertilization and irrigation, had better yields than those who relied on the whims of nature.

Borlaug decided to devote his life to teaching farmers how to use modern methods that would allow them to grow more food. He joined a program aimed at teaching modern agricultural methods to Mexican farmers. Farms in Mexico were producing so little grain that the country had to import wheat and corn from other nations.

Borlaug's first efforts backfired. He told farmers to douse wheat plants with fertilizer to make

Dr. Norman Borlaug's Green Revolution helped increase the world's food supply during the postwar decades.

How Green Was the Green Revolution?

Today the word *green* is often associated not with increased crop yields but with environmentalists who work to protect the earth from harmful effects of human activities. Some environmentalists have criticized Norman Borlaug and others for encouraging techniques that use artificial fertilizers, which can damage the environment.

Borlaug agreed that natural fertilizers from the by-products of animals would be better. But he pointed out that farmers in poor countries did not have enough animals to produce enough fertilizer for all the crops they needed to grow.

It was more important, Borlaug thought, to use the means available, including artificial fertilizers, to help feed starving people. Borlaug said that if his critics "lived just one month amid the misery of the developing world, as I have for fifty years, they'd be crying out for tractors and fertilizers and irrigation canals."

This tension between feeding people and protecting the environment is a reminder that solutions to problems sometimes create their own sets of new problems.

them grow taller and fuller. The wheat stalks grew so tall and bushy that they toppled over and rotted on the ground.

Borlaug solved that problem by using his knowledge of plant genetics to develop shorter, fuller wheat stalks. He also showed farmers how to irrigate their fields and properly fertilize their plants. The resulting crops produced more than enough grain to feed the people of Mexico, and farmers were soon exporting the surplus to other countries.

This was the beginning of what came to be known as the Green Revolution, the widespread use of modern agricultural techniques to increase the world's food supply and thus reduce the threat of famine. Borlaug traveled the world advocating his methods—irrigate farms, fertilize crops, and breed new plants to maximize grain production. He concentrated on wheat, rice, and corn because these crops could provide the most food per acre.

Using the methods Borlaug advocated, many poor countries where people often died of starvation began to produce enough food to feed their populations. Under Borlaug's guidance, Pakistan increased its wheat production from 3.4 million tons annually to 18 million tons. India went from 11 million tons to 60 million. In both countries, the increased grain production averted mass starvations. By some estimates, the agricultural methods spread by the Green Revolution helped save the lives of a billion people.

The Defeat of Polio

While agricultural scientists sparked a Green Revolution, medical researchers made great advances in the field of health care. Picking up on the work of Alexander Fleming and others, scientists developed scores of antibiotics to treat infectious diseases, as well as new drugs to treat disorders such as diabetes and heart disease. New vaccines helped prevent the spread of viral diseases such as measles and polio.

Polio was one of the most feared diseases of the twentieth century. It struck without warning, killing some of its victims and paralyzing others, leaving them confined to wheelchairs, leg braces, and iron lungs for the rest of their lives. Although people of all ages could contract polio—Franklin

A nurse prepares students in Pittsburgh, Pennsylvania, to receive polio vaccine shots in 1954 as part of a nationwide test of the vaccine. Research by Dr. Jonas Salk and others helped protect hundreds of millions against polio.

Delano Roosevelt was stricken when he was 39 — it often seemed to target children, especially in the warm summer months. Indeed, the disease was sometimes called "infantile paralysis."

For a long time, no one understood how polio spread. Everyone was afraid of it. The fear of catching polio kept families away from beaches and swimming pools in the summer.

In 1948, an American researcher named Jonas Salk identified three types of the polio virus in his lab at the University of Pittsburgh. He eventually developed a vaccine that he tested on himself, his wife, their children, and other volunteers. They all developed antibodies that protected them against the disease.

In 1954, the National Foundation for Infantile Paralysis — now called the March of Dimes Foundation — began a nationwide test of Salk's vaccine. Nearly two million schoolchildren lined up for injections. The vaccine proved to be 80 to 90 percent effective in preventing polio.

Over the next four years, doctors and nurses administered some 450 million doses of the polio vaccine. The dreaded disease began to disappear from much of the world. Thus, even as twentieth-century science had brought terrible weapons of war such as mustard gas and the atomic bomb, it was also helping people live longer, healthier lives.

How Vaccines Work

A vaccine usually consists of dead or weakened disease-producing microorganisms administered into the body through an injection (a shot) or other means. The body responds by producing antibodies to build up your immunity to the disease. Today, vaccines can protect you against many diseases, including chicken pox, mumps, and tetanus.

A New Pop Culture: The Beatles and the "Global Village"

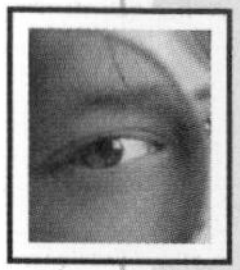

Historical Close-up

In the decades after World War II, technologies such as television, satellites, radio, and movies made it possible to broadcast images and sounds instantly around the world. People in different hemispheres could listen to the same music, see the same shows, share the same slang, and adopt the same styles of clothing. The United States, with its booming economy, exported rock and roll, Hollywood movies, Coca-Cola, and much else that became popular all over the globe. Other countries also helped create a popular culture that crossed boundaries and became increasingly international. In the 1960s, one British rock band took the world's airwaves by storm.

On a chilly February day in 1964, Pan Am flight 101, the *Yankee Clipper*, lifted off the runway from London's Heathrow Airport. On board were four young men from Liverpool—John Lennon, Paul McCartney, George Harrison, and Ringo Starr. Their band, the Beatles, was wildly popular all over Europe. Everywhere they went, the "Fab Four" found themselves mobbed by screaming, sobbing, fainting teenage fans—a phenomenon the British tabloids referred to as "Beatlemania."

In Britain, *tabloids* are newspapers that feature lurid stories about violence, crime, and celebrity gossip.

Police struggle to hold back young Beatles fans in London. Such "Beatlemania" spread across continents in the 1960s, a sign of a new global pop culture.

Now the lads were on their way to the United States for an appearance on one of America's favorite television programs, *The Ed Sullivan Show*. As they watched England shrink rapidly below the wings of the American plane, they wondered if their spectacular success would follow them across the Atlantic. It was George, "the quiet one," who put it into words: "They've got everything over there," he said. "What do they want *us* for?"

To a generation of Europeans growing up in the years after World War II, America — prosperous, booming, technologically advanced — seemed to have, well... *everything*. Flashy cars. Eye shadow. Instant cake mix. Marilyn Monroe. Electric can openers. Donald Duck. Jukeboxes. Drive-in movies. Kentucky Fried Chicken.

While Germany, France, and Britain struggled to get up and running again after a devastating war, the United States had its foot pressed firmly on the accelerator. American factories, no longer needing to make tanks and guns, unleashed a steady stream of consumer goods such as TVs and dishwashers. On the radio, presidential speeches gave way to catchy tunes with titles such as "Swingin' on a Star" and "In the Cool, Cool, Cool of the Evening." And the fledgling television industry, which had ground to a halt after Pearl Harbor, now shifted into overdrive, entertaining a growing audience with fare such as *Howdy Doody, The Adventures of Ozzie and Harriet*, and, of course, *The Ed Sullivan Show*.

These bright, appealing images of the American way of life splashed across the screens of Europe like a vision from another world. Gleaming supermarkets filled with tidy cans and boxes in endless mass-produced rows. Kitchens crammed with futuristic appliances that did all the work. Living rooms where happy families lounged in front of their very own TV sets. Clean-cut boys and pretty girls in ponytails and bobby socks, strolling across the manicured lawns of a modern suburb or cruising in Chevrolets to order shakes and fries from a waitress on roller skates.

Intellectuals railed against the tidal wave of American popular (or "pop") culture. They said it was brainless, superficial, materialistic, and childishly vulgar. It promised endless pleasure but delivered, as one British critic charged, nothing but "cheap gum-chewing pert glibness." How could Europeans — heirs to the high culture of Shakespeare, Michelangelo, da Vinci, and Beethoven — let themselves be sucked in by sugary soft drinks, bubbly teen idols, and slick magazines filled with gossipy fluff?

But young Europeans couldn't get enough. In Paris, they lined up for jeans and leather jackets just like those worn by the rebellious movie star James Dean. In Berlin, they spent their pocket money on burgers and Cokes. And in Liverpool, England, a teenage boy named Paul McCartney hooked up a radio antenna to tune in a German station, straining through the static to hear the foot-tapping beat of the latest American craze — rock and roll.

During the postwar years, American music and movies helped establish an international pop culture. Chuck Berry (left) was one of the pioneers of rock and roll music, which gained fans around the world. Actor James Dean (below) became an international star with movies like *Rebel Without a Cause*.

Rock and roll! It was like nothing anyone had heard before. John Lennon was 14 and Paul was 12 when the music hit Britain with Bill Haley and His Comets. Rock and roll didn't just start in America; it *was* America. From Chuck Berry singing "Roll Over, Beethoven" to Elvis Presley swiveling his hips to "Hound Dog," nobody could do rock and roll like the Americans.

Which, in 1964, made the Beatles wonder as their plane touched down in New York — would fans in the United States really embrace their music? What kind of reception would they get?

At first, they thought the roar they heard outside their windows came from the other jets taking off. Then, as they peered out and saw the surging crowd, they wondered what was going on—surely it had nothing to do with them? Only when they stepped out of the airplane, and the screams reached a pitch they had never heard in Europe, and the police lines nearly gave way under the pressure of thousands of shoving fans, did the full realization hit. "On a scale of one to ten," Paul later commented, "that was about a hundred in terms of the shock of it."

America was ready for the Beatles. Their new song, "I Want to Hold Your Hand," had already hit number 1 on the pop charts. *The Ed Sullivan Show* had received 50,000 requests for seats in an auditorium that held just 728. One clever marketer with an eye for the latest teenage trends had even come out with a Beatles wig in imitation of their shaggy, bowl-shaped, mop-top haircuts. (Though when he called stores to sell his product, merchants responded in bewilderment, "Why do you want to put wigs on beetles?")

With radio play, advertising, and press coverage, the Beatles had a big head start. But the real breakthrough was TV. At a time when American television had three commercial networks and not much else, *everybody* knew about Ed Sullivan's variety show. More than 73 million Americans were watching that night when he took the stage and said, "Ladies and gentlemen…the Beatles!"

The British band's conquest of America was swift and total. By April 1964, the top five singles on the Billboard Hot 100 chart were all Beatles songs. Fans flocked to buy not just Beatles records but souvenir memorabilia of all kinds, from inflatable dolls to Beatles bubble bath. Baskin-Robbins put out a new ice cream flavor, "Beatle Nut." Boys grew their hair long, and girls plastered their bedroom walls with pictures of the group. Letters poured in:

Dear Beatles, I am a loyal fan. I have every one of your records and I don't even have a record player.

Dear Beatles, I want to come and see you in London. Please tell me what is the quickest way from Cleveland by bike.

To think that I live on the same planet with the Beatles, breathe the same air as the Beatles, see the same sun, moon, and stars as the Beatles. Oh! It's just too much!

On February 9, 1964, millions of Americans watched the Beatles perform on *The Ed Sullivan Show*. They loved the way the British band had transformed rock and roll—a sign that pop cultural influences were traveling both ways across oceans.

The Beatles' success opened the door to other British groups such as the Rolling Stones, the Who, the Kinks, the Animals, the Moody Blues, and Herman's Hermits. Newspapers called it "The British Invasion." Later commentators called it "splashback" — British bands taking American rock and roll, turning it into something new, and reintroducing it to the United States. Rather than one country simply exporting its culture, a complex system of cultural exchange was developing.

That back-and-forth continued. In 1965, when Beatle George Harrison got interested in the sitar music of India, so did his fans. Harrison's new mentor, classical Indian musician Ravi Shankar, suddenly leaped to fame in the West. Fans also watched closely when the Beatles headed to India in 1968 to practice yoga. Soon yoga schools in New York, London, Paris, and Rio de Janeiro were thriving, as Westerners explored Eastern customs. Even styles of clothing rippled across the globe. The loose and beaded tunics of India appeared on the streets of San Francisco. Nehru jackets, named for the Indian prime minister, were everywhere.

The world was shrinking, and a new global pop culture was beginning to emerge. Teenagers in Tokyo and Toronto, in Los Angeles and London, in Bombay and Buenos Aires wore the same hairstyles, listened to the same music on their transistor radios, peppered their speech with the same slang words—*groovy, cool,* and *wow*. Increasingly, they shared the same attitudes, too—questioning authority, rebelling against traditional beliefs, embracing the "latest thing."

In places far from America and England, parents wondered if their children would soon forget their own country's traditions, their uniquely local ways of life, in their rush to embrace Hollywood movies and rock and roll music. People in non-Western countries, in particular, worried that these new influences would force Western values and lifestyles on the rest of the world. Would everybody everywhere soon be the same, wearing T-shirts and gulping Coca-Cola? Were local cultures doomed to be swallowed by a universal pop culture?

Yes, they were, claimed a Canadian writer named Marshall McLuhan. Thanks to electronic communications, he argued, "'Time' has ceased, 'space' has vanished. We now live in a global village...a simultaneous happening." McLuhan believed that humanity would have to give up thinking on an individual, local, or even national level, and instead join a worldwide common culture.

So far, McLuhan has proven only partially correct. Local and national cultures have proven to be strong and resilient. But a new international popular culture did indeed develop, and it knit together nations and peoples in new and often helpful ways.

For example, in 1970, the people of Bangladesh suffered from war, a cyclone, and devastating floods. Millions fled to India. There, the refugees lived in miserable conditions, with little shelter or food. In the wake of this disaster, George Harrison organized the first benefit concert for humanitarian aid. The concert raised money through ticket sales to help the disaster victims.

The 1971 Concert for Bangladesh brought Harrison, fellow Beatle Ringo Starr, Ravi Shankar, guitarist Eric Clapton, folk singer Bob Dylan, and others together in New York's Madison Square Garden. Forty thousand fans listened to Harrison sing "While My Guitar Gently Weeps" and tell them about the plight of Bangladesh. Millions more bought the live album and learned a little bit more about a very distant reality. Through an international pop culture, the world was growing smaller.

Indian citizens celebrate in Calcutta in August 1947 after India won independence from Great Britain. During the quarter century following World War II, scores of countries in Asia and Africa gained independence from old European empires. This decolonization brought freedom to millions, but it also brought new challenges for young nations.

The End of Empire: Former Colonies Gain Independence

Before World War II, more than a third of the globe lived under colonial rule. People in India, Indochina, North Africa, and elsewhere were ruled by a handful of mostly European nations. Great Britain controlled the largest empire, but other European nations, such as France, Belgium, and Portugal, also directed the destinies of their colonies far across the seas.

During the twenty-five years after the Second World War, however, the rising tide of nationalism quickly eroded the vast European empires of the late nineteenth and early twentieth centuries. In Asia, Africa, and the Middle East, scores of new nations achieved independence.

Historians use the term *decolonization* to refer to the achievement of independence by these Asian and African colonies after World War II. Decolonization happened much more quickly than almost anyone expected. In this chapter, we'll examine how imperial powers were compelled to recognize the independence of their former colonies, and how the new nations struggled to create stable governments and thriving economies in a world polarized by the Cold War.

Colonialism Rejected

It was Western powers — and mainly European ones — that colonized much of Africa and Asia. But by the early twentieth century, some of the strongest voices urging decolonization came from the West.

After World War I, when President Woodrow Wilson issued his Fourteen Points, he stressed self-determination — the idea that people have the right to determine their own fate and choose their own governments. Two decades later, President Franklin D. Roosevelt affirmed this principle when he met with the British prime minister, Winston Churchill, to forge an alliance against Hitler. The two leaders signed a document called the Atlantic Charter, in which they pledged, among other things, to "respect the right of all peoples to choose the form of government under which they will live." Churchill, a proud believer in the British Empire, believed that this statement only applied to people liberated from Nazi rule. But nationalists in the colonized world saw the Atlantic Charter as legitimizing their own struggles to gain independence.

After World War II, both the United Nations Charter and the Universal Declaration of Human Rights upheld the right of people to choose their own form of government. By that time, Europeans were beginning to lose their enthusiasm for ruling faraway colonies. The war had left much of Europe in ruins. The victorious nations, such as Britain and France, had sustained millions of casualties. Their government treasuries were almost broke. Their remaining armies and navies were exhausted. The old imperial powers of Europe could no longer enforce their rule of distant territories.

Meanwhile, in these overseas colonies, nationalists stirred the desire for independence. Some nationalist leaders argued that independence was their rightful reward for helping defeat the Axis Powers. In India, for example, colonists had taken up arms and died to beat back Nazi tyranny. Now that the war was over, Indians wanted to be free of British rule.

After the war, many colonies did indeed become new nations, but the process of decolonization unfolded differently in different places. Here we'll focus on what happened in India, Indochina, and parts of Africa. Let's start with what was once the world's largest colony, India.

India's Advocate: Mohandas Gandhi

To understand how decolonization proceeded in India, we need to step back to the time before World War I, a time when, as the saying went, "the sun never set on the British Empire."

Britain had a complex relationship with India. In the nineteenth and early twentieth centuries, people often described India as "the jewel in the crown" of the British Empire. The British government and British companies built schools, railroads, and highways across the Indian subcontinent. A British-designed civil service, staffed mostly by Indians, ran the colony. Indian taxes paid for soldiers and policemen, most of them Indians, who worked to keep the British in power.

The Indian subcontinent is a huge peninsula jutting from the southern part of Asia. The modern-day country of India covers most of the subcontinent.

Many native-born Indians from prosperous families traveled to Great Britain to receive an elite education. That was the case with Mohandas Gandhi (MOH-huhn-DAS GAHN-dee), who was born in western India in 1869. If you've read Volume 2 of *The Human Odyssey*, you know that Gandhi's family raised him in the traditions of his native land, including India's main religion, Hinduism. As a young man, Gandhi traveled to England to continue his education and, eventually, study law. In London, he learned much about Western ideals of liberty, equality, and human rights.

After he became a lawyer, Gandhi accepted a job with a law firm in South Africa, which was also part of the British Empire. About 100,000 Indians worked in South Africa, many on farms and sugarcane plantations. Gandhi saw that Indians in South Africa were treated poorly and had few rights. They could not vote or ride in the same train cars with whites. They could even be arrested for walking on the same sidewalks as white people. Gandhi spent 20 years leading peaceful protests, trying to convince the South African government to change unjust laws.

In 1914, Gandhi returned to India, where he was celebrated as a champion of the downtrodden. Many Indians called him *Mahatma*, which means "Great Soul." By this time, he had abandoned his European-style clothing in favor of the plain cotton robes and sandals worn by many poor Indians. In his homeland, he saw that most British rulers and white settlers looked down on Indians. He witnessed many of the same injustices that he had seen in South Africa. He realized that as long as India remained a British colony, these injustices would continue. Now Gandhi had a new cause — gaining independence for India.

Gandhi's Nonviolent Resistance

Gandhi tried to change laws and attitudes in India the same way he had brought change to South Africa — by peaceful means. He organized rallies against laws that treated Indians unfairly. He encouraged people to protest colonial rule by closing their shops for a day, boycotting British-made products, or refusing to work. He said that the Indian people should disobey unjust laws, but peacefully.

Sometimes the British used force against the protesters. But when faced with violence, Gandhi and his supporters did not respond with more violence. Their strategy became known as nonviolent resistance, or civil disobedience. Even when facing guns and bayonets, they did not fight back. They went to jail or suffered beatings, but they would not use force.

Nonviolent resistance, said Gandhi, demanded "the strength and courage to suffer without retaliation, to receive blows without returning any." If enough people resisted peacefully, he said, others would see their suffering and eventually be moved to correct the injustice. Gandhi himself spent several years in prison for disobeying colonial laws.

At times, despite Gandhi's efforts, the movement for independence turned bloody. In 1919, in the city of Amritsar, Indians killed three Europeans, looted and burned buildings, and beat a British missionary and left her for dead on the street. Two days later a British general ordered his troops to fire on a largely unarmed crowd of Indians. In ten minutes, hundreds were dead and many more wounded. The Amritsar Massacre, as it came to be known, increased many Indians' determination to bring an end to British rule.

Eleven years later, in 1930, Gandhi commemorated the massacre with a dramatic act of nonviolent resistance. According to British colonial law, Indians were prohibited from making their own salt. They had to buy salt from British sources and pay a tax on it. Gandhi led a 241-mile march to the sea where, with newspaper reporters watching, he scooped up a muddy lump of salt that had been left by the waves on the beach. It was a signal for thousands to gather salt in pans and let it sit on their rooftops to dry, thus producing illegal salt. British officials had no choice but to arrest Gandhi, which brought worldwide attention to an unjust law.

Indian Nationalists United, Then Divided

Gandhi's nonviolent resistance inspired other nationalists to work for Indian independence. One was Jawaharlal Nehru (jah-WAH-hahr-lahl NAY-roo). Like Gandhi, Nehru was born to a prosperous Hindu family and attended school in Britain. He cruised through Cambridge University, where his good looks won him easy popularity. After graduation, back home in India, he began a lackluster career as a lawyer — but his life took a dramatic turn when he met Mohandas Gandhi.

Inspired by Gandhi, Nehru entered politics and soon discovered a powerful gift for leadership. Over the next two decades, he went to jail many times for acts of nonviolent resistance. He spent more than nine years in prison. His dignified willingness to stand up for his beliefs inspired growing resistance to British rule.

In India, various nationalist leaders were united in their opposition to British rule, but other issues divided them. In part they were divided by religion. About 100 million Muslims lived on the Indian subcontinent, compared to 300 million Hindus. The two groups distrusted each other. Many Muslims feared that once India gained independence, Hindus would not share power or respect Muslims' rights. A brilliant lawyer named Mohammed Ali Jinnah (ah-LEE JIH-nuh) headed a group known as the Muslim League. Although Nehru and Gandhi claimed that their party represented all Indians, including Muslims, Jinnah claimed to speak for the Muslim minority.

A *viceroy* is a governor who rules a colony or country on behalf of a king. The word comes from an old French term meaning "in place of the king."

When World War II broke out, the British viceroy declared war on the Axis Powers and sent Indian soldiers off to fight for the empire in which

In 1930, Mohandas Gandhi (left) led a 241-mile march to the sea to protest a British law that forced Indians to buy salt from British sources.

they were second-class subjects. Some resentful Indians protested. Nehru called on Britain to "quit India" — to give up rule of the subcontinent or face mass rebellion. British authorities responded by throwing him into prison.

With Nehru and many of his allies in jail, the Muslim League gained more power. Jinnah and his followers demanded an end to British rule in India, but they also wanted to create *two* new countries on the subcontinent — one mostly Hindu, and one mostly Muslim. Bloody riots broke out between Muslims and Hindus. Great Britain, tired and weakened by war, lacked the resources to end the violence. The once-prized colony now seemed a heavy burden; the jewel in the crown had lost its luster.

Britain Gives Up Its Jewel

Less than two years after World War II ended, the British announced they would "quit India" after all. They said that at exactly midnight August 15, 1947, they would hand over the reins of power. Nationalist leaders in India rejoiced. "At the stroke of the midnight hour," said Nehru, "when the world sleeps, India will awake to life and freedom."

But the British also declared their intention to divide the subcontinent into two countries, India and Pakistan. Pakistan, a homeland for Muslims, would consist of two separate territories, one east and one west of India. British officials, not Indians, decided where the new national borders would run. Gandhi protested that India should be a single land where people of all faiths lived in harmony. Others did not agree.

With the partition came more bloodshed and chaos as millions of Hindus and Muslims scrambled to get to "their" side of the border. Riots broke out and villages burned. Old hostilities and frustrations boiled over. Perhaps a million people were massacred, and more than ten million became refugees.

India, troubled but independent, adopted a constitution that made the new nation the largest democracy in the world. By this time Gandhi

Millions of Hindus, Muslims, and others became refugees when Britain partitioned the Indian subcontinent into two new countries, India and Pakistan. Ancient hostilities between different groups erupted, and an estimated million people died.

was 78 years old. Nehru, 20 years his junior, became India's first prime minister. He began the long work of trying to turn a poor country where millions lived in poverty into a modern, prosperous nation.

Nehru believed that socialism could help solve India's economic policies. His government oversaw much of the country's farming efforts and managed many of its industries, such as mining and electrical production. Their efforts met with some success. Still, India often faced food shortages, and government plans for industry often failed. India remained an impoverished nation.

In foreign affairs, Nehru avoided aligning India with either the United States or the Soviet Union. He believed that the best course for his country was to stay out of the Cold War. In pursuing this policy of *nonalignment*, as he called it, he gained a reputation as a spokesman for nations that did not want to form an alliance with either of the two opposing superpowers.

The one-time leader of the Muslim League, Mohammed Ali Jinnah, became the first governor-general (head of state) of Pakistan, but he died just over a year later. A series of generals then ruled the country, with brief periods of democracy between military coups. The government declared Islam to be Pakistan's official religion, and clerics began pressing for laws based on the Islamic legal code.

Less than a year after gaining independence, India suffered a tragic loss. In January 1948, Mohandas Gandhi was on his way to a prayer meeting for peace between Hindus, Muslims, and Indians of all faiths. A young man walked up to him, pulled out a gun, and fired three shots. Minutes later, India's *Mahatma* was dead. The assassin was a Hindu fanatic angry at some of Gandhi's messages, including his call for greater cooperation with Muslims. The shocking murder reminded Indians that although they had achieved statehood, they were far from becoming the peaceful, prosperous nation Gandhi had envisioned.

Nationalist Fervor in Indochina

Like Great Britain, France ruled colonies around the world, though the French empire was smaller than the British. France held parts of Africa, Asia, and the Americas. During the nineteenth

Jawaharlal Nehru, India's first prime minister, tried to steer his impoverished nation toward prosperity. He hoped to keep India out of the Cold War through nonalignment.

The Nehru Dynasty

The Nehru family, which helped establish democracy in India, became a political dynasty that remains powerful to this day. Jawaharlal Nehru, India's first prime minister, died in 1964 after nearly 17 years in office. Two years later, his daughter Indira Gandhi became prime minister. (She became a Gandhi by marriage, but was not related to Mohandas Gandhi.) She governed until 1977, and again from 1980 until 1984, when she was assassinated. Her son Rajiv Gandhi then became prime minister and held that office until 1989. In 1991, he was assassinated while campaigning in parliamentary elections.

Ho Chi Minh (right) sits with Chairman Mao Zedong of China. Ho led a fight that brought Vietnam independence from French rule, but the former colony was divided into two countries, North Vietnam and South Vietnam. In 1955, Ho Chi Minh became the first president of North Vietnam, a communist nation with close ties to China.

century, the French gained control of Indochina, the eastern part of the long peninsula that extends from southeastern Asia into the South China Sea. French Indochina, as the area came to be called, included what are now the countries of Vietnam, Cambodia, and Laos.

In the early 1900s, a strong nationalist movement took root in Vietnam. A man born with the name Nguyen Sinh Cung but known to the world as Ho Chi Minh (hoh chee min) helped lead the struggle for Vietnamese independence.

The son of a Confucian scholar, Ho left Vietnam at age 21 and did not set foot in his homeland again for 30 years. During that time, he roamed the world. His travels took him to Europe, Africa, India, the Middle East, and America. He worked as a kitchen helper in a London hotel and as a domestic servant in New York. In Paris, he made his living retouching photos.

During his travels, Ho gained fluency in six languages and read the great philosophers of the West. He was drawn to French culture and Enlightenment ideas, but he was most interested in the works of Karl Marx, which led him to embrace communism. In 1920, he became a founding member of the French Communist Party. Later he traveled to the Soviet Union and China, where he founded the Indochinese Communist Party.

In 1941, Ho returned to his native country. By that time, World War II was underway, and the Japanese had invaded Vietnam. Ho founded an organization called the Viet Minh (vee-et MIN) to fight both the Japanese occupation and French colonial rule. It was during this time that he adopted the name for which he is known, Ho Chi Minh, which means "illuminator."

Ho Chi Minh's followers used guerilla warfare to fight the Japanese, striking in small groups where least expected and vanishing before the enemy could respond. As World War II wound down, the Japanese retreated from Vietnam, and the Viet Minh moved into the territories they had abandoned. By the time peace was declared, Ho Chi Minh was in control of the country.

Vietnam—Independent but Divided

In 1945, Ho proclaimed Vietnam an independent republic, using words borrowed from the U.S. Declaration of Independence, in part because he hoped the United States would support Vietnamese independence. American military commanders in the Pacific agreed that Vietnam should be free from colonial rule, but they offered no help because their British allies had different ideas. Britain, as an imperial power, took the view that Indochina rightfully belonged to France. British military commanders, using captured Japanese troops, even fought Vietnamese nationalists to restore French rule.

Soon France began sending its own soldiers to Vietnam, and an eight-year war began. At the outset, Ho warned the French, "You can kill ten of my men for every one I kill of yours, yet... you will lose." France poured troops into Vietnam, but by 1954 the French had suffered 172,000 casualties. That spring, Ho's Viet Minh succeeded in destroying a large French force at Dien Bien Phu and broke France's grip on Vietnam.

At a peace conference in Geneva, Switzerland, Ho found himself bargaining with a new adversary — the United States. American leaders were opposed to imperialism, but they were also committed to the containment of communism. They realized that Ho was a dedicated Marxist, and they worried about a communist regime in Southeast Asia.

The conference agreed to divide French Indochina into three countries — Cambodia, Laos, and Vietnam. It also decided that Vietnam would be temporarily partitioned, with Ho Chi Minh ruling the north, and a fervent anticommunist named Ngo Dinh Diem (en-GO din dyem) in charge of the south. An election was to be held two years later to unify Vietnam and name its president.

So in 1954, Vietnam gained its independence from France. But as in India and Korea, the former colonists found their homeland divided into two countries: the Democratic Republic of Vietnam, also known as North Vietnam, and the Republic of Vietnam, known as South Vietnam.

Ho Chi Minh ruled North Vietnam as a communist dictator with ties to the Soviet Union and China. As in other communist nations, the North Vietnamese had fewer freedoms than citizens of Western democracies. Ho's government controlled the nation's economy, elections, newspapers, and factories.

In South Vietnam, Ngo Dinh Diem also maintained tight control of the government. Diem, who was Catholic, often dealt harshly with the country's Buddhist majority. Diem believed his countrymen were not ready for Western-style democracy. But his government was anticommunist, so the United States was willing to give it aid.

The election that was supposed to unify north and south under one president never took place. Ho was sure he could win such an election, since he was wildly popular in Vietnam as a hero of national liberation — indeed, many Vietnamese called him "Uncle Ho." Diem and many others, including U.S. government officials, feared the same outcome. They also feared that, if elected, Ho would turn all of Vietnam into a communist dictatorship. So Diem and his U.S. backers never allowed the planned election to take place in the south.

Colonialism had ended in Indochina, but the Cold War had arrived, with communists and anticommunists staring at each other across an increasingly hostile border. The years ahead would bring a final showdown in this ongoing struggle.

Nasser and the Suez Canal Crisis

We shift now from Asia to Africa where, in the years after World War II, a group of army officers in Egypt were plotting to end British control of their country. Officially, Egypt was already an independent country — Britain had recognized it as a sovereign nation in 1922. But the British still maintained a great deal of control over the country. Thousands of British troops remained in Egypt to protect British interests in the Suez Canal. When British officials wanted something done in Egypt, the Egyptian prime minister and king usually made sure the British got what they wanted.

This situation angered a young army officer named Gamal Abdul Nasser. In 1949, he became the leader of the Free Officers, a group dedicated to overthrowing Egypt's king, whom Nasser regarded as little more than a British puppet. The revolutionaries plotted for three years in such secrecy that even Nasser's wife didn't know his purpose when he left for mysterious evening meetings. In 1952, the Free Officers staged a bloodless coup d'etat and sent the Egyptian king into exile.

Nasser became Egypt's prime minister and then its president. Like many other leaders of former colonies, he believed that socialism offered a way to relieve poverty and transform his country into a modern nation. His government redistributed land to farmers and exerted a greater control over industry. He also pressured the British to withdraw their troops from Egypt.

Because he hoped to rid Egypt of foreign domination, Nasser steered a course of nonalignment, avoiding close alliances with either of the world's two superpowers. He was determined to build up his country's military, so he asked U.S. officials to sell arms to Egypt. When the United States said no, he bought the equipment from the Soviets instead.

Egyptian leader Gamal Abdul Nasser nationalized the Suez Canal in 1956, prompting Britain, France, and Israel to attack Egypt. Nasser responded by sinking ships in the canal, closing it to shipping until early 1957. Above, shipwrecks block the entrance to the canal.

Alarmed by this turn of events, the United States and Britain offered to lend Egypt money to build an enormous dam, the Aswan High Dam, on the Nile River in southern Egypt. Nasser wanted to build the Aswan High Dam to generate badly needed electricity, and to help control flooding along the Nile. But Egypt and the two Western nations could not reach an agreement about the terms of the loan, so the offer of aid fell through.

Nasser saw another obvious source of revenue that could help build the dam and fund many other projects in Egypt — the Suez Canal. Traffic streamed through the canal, from the Red Sea to the Mediterranean, including tankers bringing oil to the nations of Europe thirsty for fuel. The canal lay entirely within Egyptian territory, but it was operated by a private European firm. This European company took in millions of dollars every year but gave Egypt only a small percentage of the profits.

In July 1956, Nasser told a cheering crowd in Alexandria that he was nationalizing the canal — taking control of it for Egypt. Even as he spoke, his military forces were moving in. By nightfall, the Suez Canal was in Egyptian hands.

The British were outraged. Their leaders cried that Nasser was no better than a thief. The *Times of London* declared Egyptians too primitive to run such a complex waterway. British and French jets started bombing Egypt, hoping to topple Nasser and take back the canal. Israeli troops joined the attack.

By this time, Dwight D. Eisenhower, hero of the D-day invasion, had succeeded Harry Truman as president of the United States. He was furious that Britain, France, and Israel had not consulted the United States before launching the attack on Egypt. He feared the attack would drive the entire Middle East into the Soviet camp. The United States quickly took the issue to the United Nations, which called for a cease-fire and the reopening of the canal. American pressure forced the invaders to withdraw.

Arabs saw Nasser's seizing of the Suez Canal as a tremendous nationalist victory. In their view, Egypt had finally become its own master by getting rid of the last remnants of

A jubilant crowd carries Egyptian Prime Minister Gamal Abdul Nasser through the streets of Port Said, Egypt, in 1956. British troops had just withdrawn from the country, leaving the Suez Canal in Egyptian hands.

British control. Throughout the Arab world, Nasser was cheered as a hero for standing up to the old imperial powers.

The End of Colonialism in Africa

Other Africans shared the same nationalist feelings that led the Egyptians to cast off British control. In the nineteenth and early twentieth centuries, most of the continent had been carved up and colonized by European powers. During World War II, European colonial governments enlisted many African soldiers to fight against the Axis Powers. In the decades following World War II, one colony after another proclaimed independence. In most cases, independence brought new challenges. Many of the new African nations struggled to establish stable governments and economies. Some were torn by fighting between ethnic and tribal groups.

In some parts of Africa, the old imperial powers let their colonies go without much resistance. Partly, Europeans were willing to give up control because they realized it was time to practice, not just preach, the ideal of self-determination for all peoples. Partly, they believed that the costs of maintaining overseas territories and battling nationalists were not worth the benefits that the colonies' resources might bring.

After World War II, in the colony called the Gold Coast, the British allowed more Africans to take part in government. A nationalist leader named Kwame Nkrumah (KWAH-mee uhn-KROO-muh) led boycotts and strikes to pressure the British to grant independence. In 1957, Britain granted independence to the Gold Coast. The former colony renamed itself Ghana, after a great medieval West African kingdom. As president, Nkrumah tried to modernize the country by building new schools, roads, and hospitals but the army opposed him and eventually seized control of the country. In recent times, Ghana has witnessed struggles for control between civilian and military rulers.

Some African colonies had to fight for their independence. For example, Algeria, a large French colony in north Africa, suffered through

Africa from Colonization to Independence

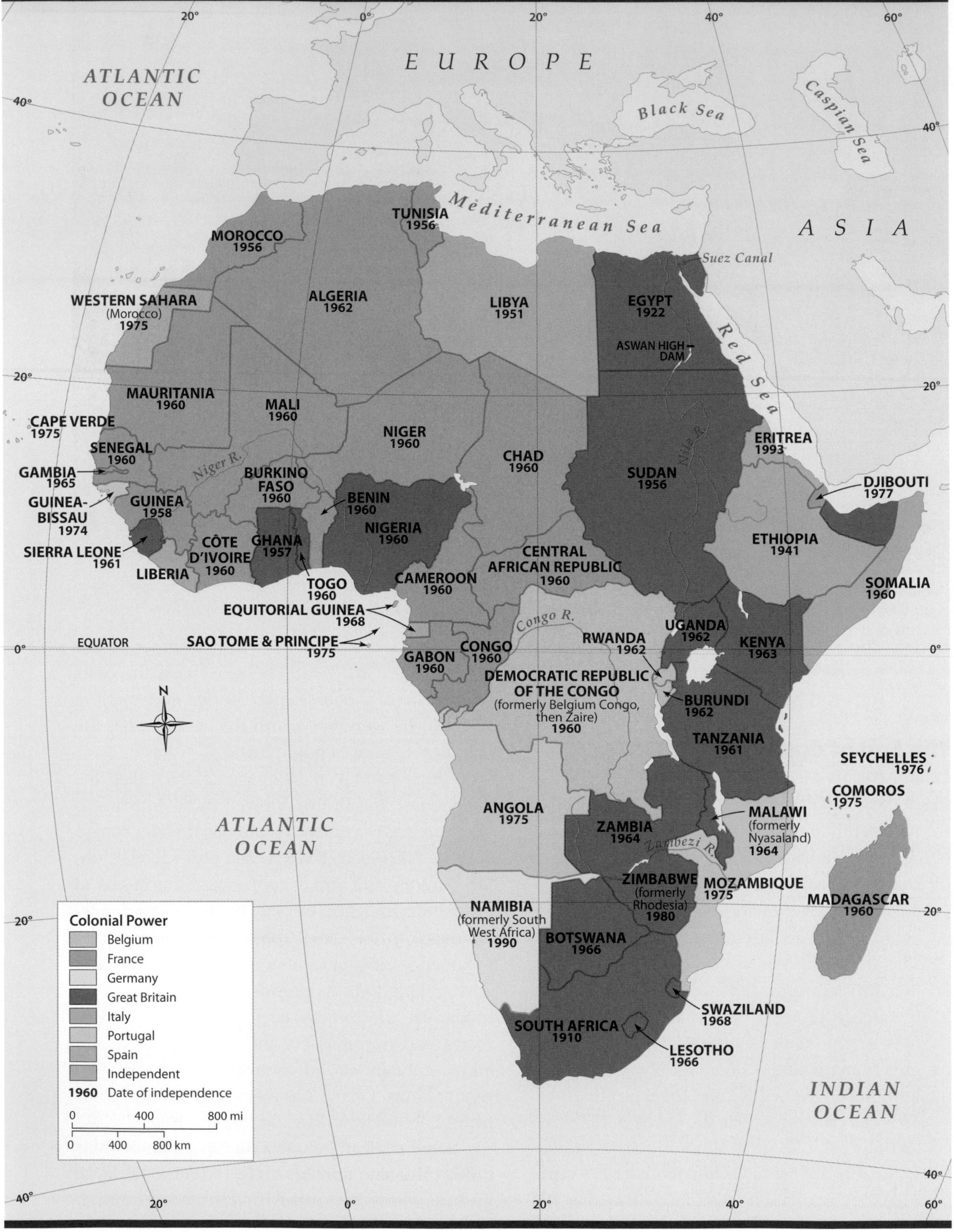

EUROPE
ATLANTIC OCEAN
Black Sea
Caspian Sea
Mediterranean Sea
ASIA
Suez Canal
Red Sea
TUNISIA 1956
MOROCCO 1956
ALGERIA 1962
LIBYA 1951
EGYPT 1922
ASWAN HIGH DAM
WESTERN SAHARA (Morocco) 1975
MAURITANIA 1960
MALI 1960
NIGER 1960
CHAD 1960
SUDAN 1956
Nile R.
ERITREA 1993
DJIBOUTI 1977
CAPE VERDE 1975
SENEGAL 1960
GAMBIA 1965
GUINEA-BISSAU 1974
GUINEA 1958
SIERRA LEONE 1961
LIBERIA
CÔTE D'IVOIRE 1960
GHANA 1957
BURKINO FASO 1960
Niger R.
BENIN 1960
NIGERIA 1960
TOGO 1960
CAMEROON 1960
CENTRAL AFRICAN REPUBLIC 1960
ETHIOPIA 1941
SOMALIA 1960
EQUITORIAL GUINEA 1968
SAO TOME & PRINCIPE 1975
EQUATOR
GABON 1960
CONGO 1960
Congo R.
RWANDA 1962
UGANDA 1962
KENYA 1963
DEMOCRATIC REPUBLIC OF THE CONGO (formerly Belgium Congo, then Zaire) 1960
BURUNDI 1962
TANZANIA 1961
SEYCHELLES 1976
COMOROS 1975
ANGOLA 1975
ZAMBIA 1964
Zambezi R.
MALAWI (formerly Nyasaland) 1964
ATLANTIC OCEAN
ZIMBABWE (formerly Rhodesia) 1980
MOZAMBIQUE 1975
MADAGASCAR 1960
NAMIBIA (formerly South West Africa) 1990
BOTSWANA 1966
SWAZILAND 1968
SOUTH AFRICA 1910
LESOTHO 1966
INDIAN OCEAN
N
Colonial Power
Belgium
France
Germany
Great Britain
Italy
Portugal
Spain
Independent
1960 Date of independence
0 400 800 mi
0 400 800 km
20° 0° 20° 40° 60°
40° 20° 0° 20° 40°

Demonstrators for and against independence from France pack a street in the Algerian capital of Algiers in 1961. France had controlled Algeria for decades. After World War II, native Algerian rebels launched a guerilla war against French troops and civilians, and the French army responded with equally brutal force. In 1962, France granted Algeria independence.

a bloody revolution. More than a million French people lived in Algeria, and the French government considered it part of France. In 1954, Algerian rebels launched a guerrilla war that included bombing and killing European civilians living in Algeria. The French army responded by burning farmlands and forcing millions of native Algerians into concentration camps. Perhaps a million people died before France gave in and granted independence to Algeria in 1962. Later, the new nation lapsed into civil war. On one side were government officials intent on modernizing the nation. On the other side were Islamic militants seeking to make Algeria an Islamic state.

In east Africa, Kenya also had to fight for its independence. British settlers did not want to give up their hold on the rich farmlands of Kenya. The British met resistance from two groups. One was a nationalist movement led by Jomo Kenyatta. The other was a secret band of guerrilla warriors known as the Mau Mau (mow

Harambee—*Pulling Together*

You've seen that when some colonies gained independence, their new leaders—Nehru in India, Nasser in Egypt—established socialist economies. They thought government control of the economy was necessary to transform their countries into modern nations. But when Kenya gained independence, Jomo Kenyatta encouraged individual entrepreneurs and foreign investment in a free-market, capitalist economy. He adopted the motto of *Harambee*, a Swahili word for "pulling together." Kenya's economy grew rapidly, though much of the wealth remained concentrated in the hands of a few leading families and government officials.

mow). In 1952, the Mau Mau started a rebellion, using tactics of sabotage and assassination against the British. British troops struck back, killing thousands of the Mau Mau and locking thousands more into detention camps.

The British also jailed Jomo Kenyatta, whom they accused of leading the Mau Mau rebellion. He responded that his nationalist party had nothing to do with the violent tactics of the Mau Mau. Still, he was sentenced to seven years in prison. After his release in 1961, he traveled to London, where he helped negotiate the terms for Kenya's independence, which the British finally granted late in 1963. Kenyatta became prime minister, and later the new nation's first president.

Civil War in Congo and Angola

As you've seen, when some African colonies gained independence, the end of colonial rule was followed not by peace and prosperity but by violence and bloodshed. Such was the case in Congo and Angola.

In 1960, Belgium granted independence to Congo, a colony the Belgians had ruled for almost a century. The country was rich in ivory, timber, copper, and especially rubber. In the late 1800s, Belgium's King Leopold forced Africans to collect rubber. Belgian troops used mass murder and other tactics of terror to compel labor from the people of the so-called Congo Free State, which was anything but free. In the novel *Heart of Darkness*, the writer Joseph Conrad summed up the situation in the colony in a phrase spoken by a dying character — "The horror! The horror!"

The Belgians stopped some of their most horrific practices, but they continued to exploit the colony and rule with a heavy hand. They

Congolese shout for joy in celebration of their country's newly won independence from Belgium in 1960. But such celebrations were short-lived. It was not long before Congo fell into chaos and civil war as rival groups of Congolese began fighting each other.

did nothing to prepare the people of Congo, brutalized for almost a century, for independence and self-rule. Thus it is little surprise that when the Belgians left in 1960, old hatreds and suppressed tensions exploded. Rival groups of Congolese began fighting with each other, and the new nation fell into chaos. The United States and USSR soon took sides, making Congo a battlefield of the Cold War. The civil war left the country's economy in ruins and caused deep divisions among its people.

South of Congo lies Angola, long a colony of Portugal. Portugal, the first European country to acquire colonies in Africa, was the last to give up territory. And it did not grant independence peacefully.

When World War II ended, Portugal tried to strengthen its hold on Angola by encouraging many more Portuguese to settle in the colony. Many new settlers arrived, drawn by the lure of profits from coffee plantations, mining, and petroleum. Wealthy white landowners used forced African labor on farms growing coffee and cotton. European businessmen profited while barely paying their African workers.

In 1961, fighting broke out in Angola as various nationalist rebel groups launched uprisings against the Portuguese. Portugal struck back forcefully. By the mid-1960s, more than seventy thousand Portuguese troops were in Angola. The Portuguese also enlisted Africans to fight against the rebels.

Soon, the burden of the war became too much for Portugal, consuming about 40 percent of the European country's national budget. In 1974, an army coup toppled the Portuguese government in Angola. By 1975, the Portuguese had withdrawn from Angola.

One of the rebel groups — the MPLA (Popular Movement for the Liberation of Angola) — took over the government of the newly independent nation. Other groups fought to seize power. The communist-leaning MPLA received support from the Soviet Union and Cuba. The United States and South Africa stepped in to support the noncommunist rebels opposing the MPLA. Civil war tore Angola for decades, until an uneasy peace was reached in 2002.

The Legacy of Imperialism

When, in 1975, Portugal accepted the independence of Angola and another of its colonies, Mozambique, European colonization of Africa came to an end. Even though colonialism all but disappeared in the decades following World War II, its effects did not vanish. Decades of imperial rule planted the seeds of much future trouble. In southern Africa, independent countries like Rhodesia (later named Zimbabwe) and South Africa still faced a long struggle between a white ruling class and native Africans. In Southeast Asia, warring regimes battled for the power given up by imperial masters.

Many new nations with no history of self-government fell prey to brutal dictators. Many sank into grinding poverty and exploitation by outside powers. Others became pawns in the Cold War competition between the two superpowers. National borders drawn by outside powers often created antagonism by dividing people who felt they belonged together, or by grouping people who felt no common bond.

It would take decades for new countries to recover from the wounds of imperialism. Indeed, some of the problems left behind by colonization still remain unhealed.

Soldiers of the Popular Movement for the Liberation of Angola (MPLA) pose for a photograph in Luanda, Angola's capital, in 1975.

Nelson Mandela Fights Apartheid

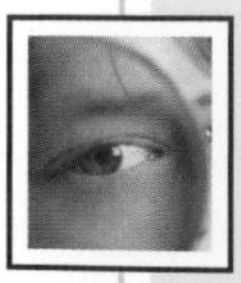

Historical Close-up

Like much of the vast African continent, the region known as South Africa was colonized by Europeans — Dutch, French, and British settlers — who ruled the native peoples. In the late nineteenth century, when Britain controlled the colony, gold and diamond mines brought riches to many of those settlers and their descendants. In 1910, the colony attained self-government. But the years of imperialism left a society in which whites held most of the country's wealth and political power, while most blacks lived in poverty and had few rights. Nelson Mandela (man-DEHL-uh), who led his country to a better future, was born into this post-colonial world.

"We are slaves in our own country. We are tenants on our own soil. We have no strength, no power, no control over our own destiny in the land of our birth."

A 16-year-old boy stood on the bank of the Mbashe River and listened to those words, spoken by a tribal chief. He knew exactly what the chief meant. In South Africa, the country's population was divided into four categories: Europeans (or Whites), Indians, Coloreds (people of mixed races), and Africans. People of European descent — then about 20 percent of the population — lived in the best houses, ate in the best restaurants, sat on the best park benches, and sent their children to the best schools. Anything designated for "non-European" use was clearly inferior. Africans, who composed the large majority of the population, were considered the lowest of the non-Europeans.

The boy standing and listening on the bank of the river was one of those Africans. He had been born in 1918 with the name Rolihlahla Mandela. (*Rolihlahla* means, roughly translated, "troublemaker.") It seemed that even his name was not good enough for the Whites. On his first day at a one-room school run by English missionaries, his teacher decided he needed a new name, one that sounded more British. So Rolihlahla became Nelson Mandela.

He learned many valuable things from his teachers, such as how to read and write. He also learned about Western culture, including the rights and freedoms that many people in the Western world enjoyed. Mandela thought hard about those rights, and about how Africans had no control over their own destiny in the land of their birth. He made up his mind to become a lawyer so he could fight more effectively for his people's rights.

In 1941, Mandela moved to Johannesburg (joh-HAH-nuhs-burg), the largest city in South Africa. There he saw, more than ever before, the stark difference between the way white people of European descent and dark-skinned Africans lived. Even though Johannesburg — known as the "City of Gold" because of nearby gold mines — was one of the richest cities in the world, people with dark skin were forced to live in poor, crowded neighborhoods, with no electricity, plumbing, or heat. On the streets of Johannesburg, Mandela experienced what he later remembered as "a steady accumulation of a thousand slights and a thousand indignities [that] produced in me an anger, a desire to fight the system that imprisoned my people."

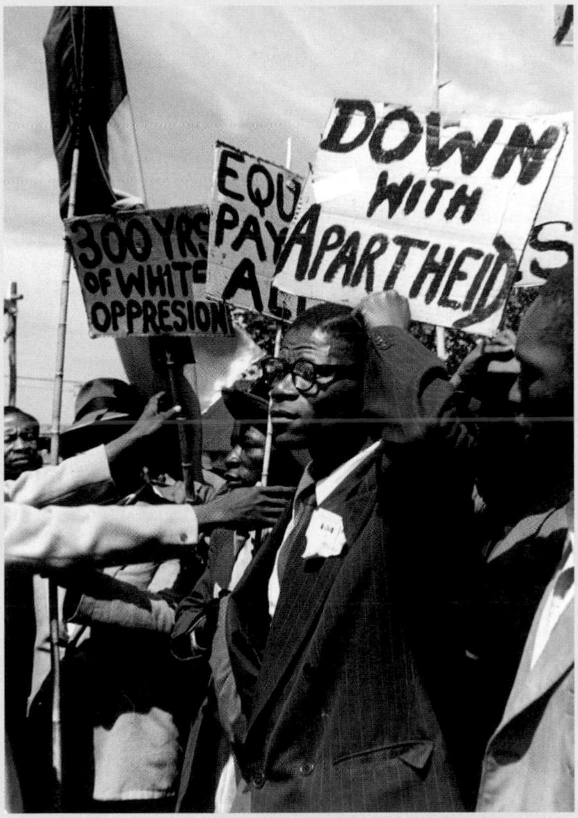

South Africans gather in Johannesburg in 1952 to protest against apartheid.

Mandela joined the African National Congress (ANC), the oldest national organization of Africans in the country. He helped organize strikes, rallies, and peaceful protests against unjust racial laws. Some white people sympathized with the ANC's objectives, but most thought the ANC threatened their way of life. The 1948 elections — in which only people of European ancestry could vote — brought to power a political party that promised to keep the races separated.

The country's new leaders, who were all white, established a policy called

Afrikaans, one of the languages spoken in South Africa, is related to Dutch. It also contains elements of French, German, and native African languages.

apartheid (uh-PAHR-tiyd), a word in the Afrikaans language that means "separateness." Apartheid laws kept people of color separate from whites. Neighborhoods, offices, businesses, schools, churches, hospitals, restaurants, theaters, and sports fields—all were segregated.

Apartheid laws required Africans to carry passbooks identifying them wherever they went. If they forgot their passbooks, they could be thrown in jail.

Many white South Africans did not approve of apartheid. One law firm that opposed it hired Mandela as a clerk while he finished college and law school. But when strangers visited the law office, Mandela had to pretend he was an errand boy.

The grip of apartheid tightened. Whites imposed, as Mandela later recalled, "a grim program of mass evictions, political persecution, and police terror." Mandela organized more protest marches, boycotts, and strikes, and emerged as a leader in the ANC.

In 1960, during a protest against the passbook laws, several thousand black people surrounded a police station in Sharpeville, near Johannesburg. The South African police opened fire on the crowd. Sixty-nine people were killed. Outraged, Mandela publicly burned his own passbook. He believed that "the state had given us no alternative to violence." He and other ANC members began to plan bombings of power plants, South African military installations, and other targets.

The government banned the ANC, but Mandela continued his anti-apartheid activities. For a while he managed to elude the police. But one day, as he was driving away from a secret ANC meeting, he was surrounded by three cars filled with government officials. They arrested him and charged him with plotting acts of violence against the government.

The penalty for these crimes was death, and Mandela fully expected to be executed. Appearing at his trial in full tribal dress, he delivered an impassioned speech. "I have cherished the ideal of a democratic and free society in which all persons live together in harmony and with equal opportunities," he said. "It is an ideal which I hope to live for and achieve. But if needs be, it is an ideal for which I am prepared to die."

Mandela was found guilty, but to his surprise, he was not executed. On June 12, 1964, he was sentenced to life in prison.

He spent the next 26 years in prison. For the first 13 years, he hacked away at rocks in a limestone quarry. The sun's glare on the white rocks was so intense that his eyesight was permanently damaged. Meals consisted of porridge made from corn, sometimes with a carrot or piece of cabbage thrown in. He slept in a cell so small that he could touch all four walls from his bed.

During his years in prison, Nelson Mandela became an international symbol of the struggle for human rights in South Africa. Those who opposed apartheid wore buttons such as this one to call attention to Mandela's plight.

Mandela craved communication with the outside world, but it was forbidden. When he was caught with a newspaper he'd picked up from a bench, he was sentenced to three days of solitary confinement. But the small amount of news that seeped into prison convinced him that the world was becoming aware of the injustice of apartheid — and the injustice of his own imprisonment.

Indeed, Mandela's wife and supporters worked tirelessly to tell the world about apartheid and Mandela's imprisonment. Eventually, the publicity worked. Protests against apartheid increased around the world, and Nelson Mandela became an international symbol of the struggle for human rights. World leaders began pressuring the South African government to release Mandela. As criticism mounted, South African leaders quietly offered Mandela his freedom if he would agree to give up his protests against apartheid. Mandela refused.

Outside the prison walls, apartheid was coming under more attack from the international community. Many countries imposed economic sanctions against South Africa — that is, they refused to do business with South Africa, which hurt the South African economy. The country's athletes were banned from participating in the International Olympics.

Finally, after years of protests and violence, the South African government realized that it must bring an end to the system that was tearing the country apart. In 1990, it began abolishing apartheid laws. That same year, South Africa's president, Frederik Willem de Klerk, granted Mandela's release. On February 10, 1990, Nelson Mandela walked away from prison, free at last.

In 1994, South Africa held its first truly democratic election in which citizens of every race were allowed to vote. The ANC, no longer banned, won the largest share of votes, and Nelson Rolihlahla Mandela became the country's new president.

Some people expected President Mandela to arrest white people or exile them from the country, as punishment for the years of apartheid. But he did not. In his inaugural address, he described apartheid as "an extraordinary human disaster that lasted too long," and vowed to build a "society in which all South Africans, both black and white, will be able to

Nelson Mandela greets supporters at a campaign rally in Durban, South Africa, in 1994. In that year, South Africa held its first truly democratic election in which citizens of every race were allowed to vote. Voters gave ANC candidates the largest share of votes, and Mandela became president of South Africa.

walk tall, without any fear in their hearts, assured of their inalienable right to human dignity."

During his five years as president, Mandela began the long process of unifying South Africans, black and white. It was, in many ways, a tense situation. People who were used to thinking of each other as enemies now had to learn to work side-by-side and put a long, bloody past behind them. Mandela assembled a government in which blacks and whites shared power. When tempers between old adversaries flared, he moved to smooth things over. He prodded white business owners to give blacks more opportunities, and reminded blacks that it would take time for society to overcome the effects of racism.

In 1995, the South African national rugby team, the Springboks, hosted the Rugby World Cup. For years many blacks had hated the Springboks — a white team that played a sport brought to Africa by colonial masters. But when the Springboks beat New Zealand in the World Cup finals, Nelson Mandela walked onto the field wearing the green Springbok jersey to present the team captain with the trophy. Millions erupted in cheers at the gesture of reconciliation.

South Africa, once a European colony and then a bastion of white rule, moved to ensure equal rights and opportunities for all its citizens under the leadership of the troublemaker turned statesman, Nelson Mandela.

Palestinian guerrilla fighters patrol the streets of Amman, Jordan, in September 1970 during a period of civil war. Ancient hostilities, widespread poverty, repressive regimes, nationalism, Islamism, Arab resentment toward Israel and the West—all of these factors and more caused conflict in the Middle East during the decades following World War II.

Conflict in the Middle East

We return now to the Middle East, the region that embraces Egypt and the Arabian Peninsula, and swings through Iran and Asia Minor. You've learned that most inhabitants of this region are Arabic speakers, united by a shared religion, Islam, and by the culture based in Islam. In the early twentieth century, the treaties that ended World War I put Britain and France in charge of affairs in much of the region. Stirred by nationalist feelings, many Middle Easterners were determined to free themselves from European rule. Thus a combination of potent forces—nationalism and Islamism—shaped the Middle East, and continued to do so for much of the twentieth century.

Before World War II, Iraq and Egypt managed to win their independence from European rule (though not entirely from European influence). During and after World War II, other countries such as Syria, Lebanon, and Transjordan (later Jordan) became independent nations.

These newly independent nations shared a lingering sense of opposition to Western interference in the Arab world. From this feeling there emerged in the 1950s and 1960s a movement known as *pan-Arabism*. Pan-Arabism promoted the idea that the mostly-Arab states of Egypt, Syria, Iraq, Lebanon, Jordan, and Saudi Arabia could act with unity for a common purpose. It was not entirely clear what they were united for. But they knew what they were united against—on one hand, foreign occupiers, and on the other, the Jewish state of Israel, created in 1948 on land set aside by a United Nations decree.

The story of the Middle East in the decades following World War II is a tale of conflicts of various kinds. There was, as news reports call it, "the Arab-Israeli conflict," the ongoing wars between Israel and its Arab neighbors. There were wars between Arab countries. And there was strife between two groups of Arab nationalists—one group that wanted to build secular states, and another group, the Islamists, who wanted to build Islamic states governed by Muslim teachings and law.

As many of these newly independent nations struggled to find workable forms of government, they also dealt with the consequences of a new source of riches — oil. Oil brought great wealth to some Middle Eastern nations. But, with the exception of (oil-less) Israel, none found ways to become developed, democratic nations.

New Nations and an Arab League

After World War I, Western nations redrew the map of the Middle East. They created new countries with national boundaries that sometimes seemed to ignore the realities of Middle Eastern life. Some of the new boundaries stirred up conflicts by combining rival ethnic groups or religious sects into a single nation. Longstanding tensions between some of these groups promised trouble ahead.

Consider, for example, Iraq. After World War I, Iraq was a British mandate, its borders drawn by Western powers. The new boundaries combined diverse groups. In the north were the Kurds, a people who spoke their own language and were largely Sunni Muslim, but not Arabs. In a central region were many Sunni Arabs. And in south-central and eastern regions were many Shi'ite Arabs. These groups were often at odds and sometimes at war with each other. Even after Iraq gained its independence in 1932, the tensions between these groups continued to trouble the nation.

The boundaries drawn by Western powers also led to disputes between the new states in the Middle East. For example, Egypt insisted that its territory included all of Sudan, which it had dominated in ancient times. Egypt did not recognize Sudan as a separate and independent country until 1956. Iraq claimed that neighboring, oil-rich Kuwait was part of its territory. Morocco claimed the Western Sahara, while Syria tried to dominate Lebanon, which had once been part of its territory.

In 1945, prompted by the British, many Arab countries formed an organization called the Arab League. The League's purpose was to help Arab countries cooperate economically and to settle political disputes with talk instead of arms. The League's member nations — originally Egypt, Iraq, Saudi Arabia, Syria, Lebanon, and Jordan — struggled to chart a neutral course in the Cold War, but they found true neutrality hard to achieve. And they had only limited success in preventing disputes and bloodshed among themselves.

The 1948 Arab-Israeli War

One new nation in the Middle East stood apart from the others — Israel. The modern-day state

Sunni and Shi'ite

Early in the history of Islam, not long after the death of the Prophet Muhammad, a disagreement over who should rule split Muslims into two groups.

One group believed that the caliph—Muhammad's successor who would lead the Muslims—should always be someone from Muhammad's family. Muhammad left no son, so this group rallied around his son-in-law, Ali, and Ali's descendents. Ali's supporters were called the Shia Ali ("the party of Ali"), or Shi'ahs (SHE-ahs) for short. They are often referred to as Shi'ites (SHEE-iyts).

Another group disagreed. They said the leadership of Islam should be in the hands of the most capable Muslim, and that he should rule following the Qur'an and the example of Muhammad. In Arabic, "example" is *sunna*, so these Muslims are called Sunnis (SOU-neez).

This split between Shi'ites and Sunnis has caused bitter struggles within Islam. The division persists to this day. Currently there are far more Sunni than Shi'ite Muslims. Sunnis make up roughly 85 percent of the world's Muslim population.

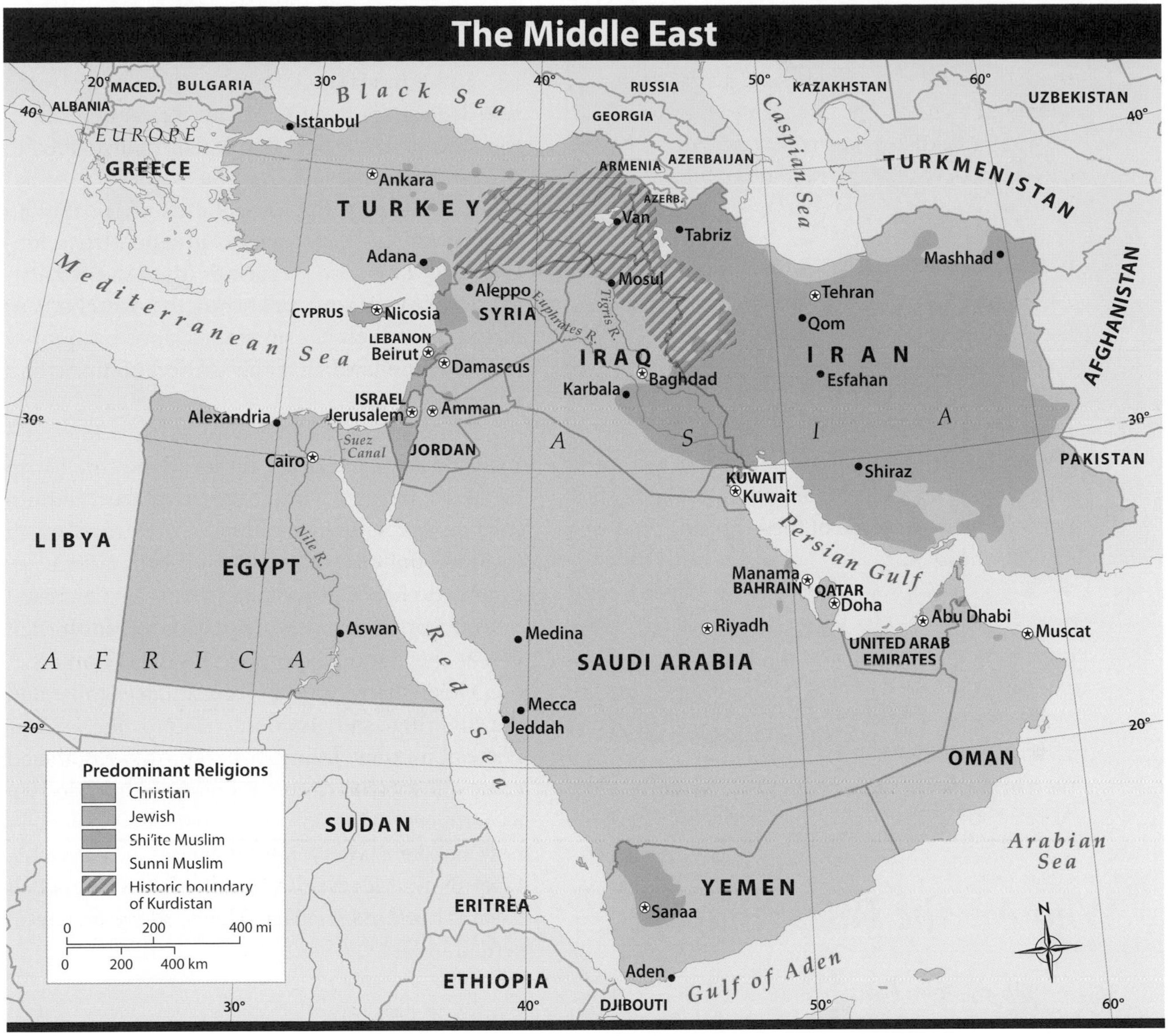

of Israel, as you've read, emerged from the nineteenth-century nationalist movement known as Zionism. Zionists believed the Jewish people deserved a state of their own in Palestine, the small region bordering the eastern shore of the Mediterranean Sea, often called the Holy Land because of its historical importance to Jews, Christians, and Muslims. Many Jews living in Europe and elsewhere considered Palestine their ancestral homeland. It was the "promised land" where Moses had led the Hebrews. In ancient times, a Jewish state had existed in Palestine until the Romans forced most Jews out of the region.

In the late nineteenth and early twentieth centuries, when anti-Jewish sentiment was on the rise in Europe, Zionists began buying land in Palestine and moving there. During World War I, the British government supported the idea of a homeland for Jews in Palestine. After the war, when Palestine was a British mandate, hopeful Zionists encouraged more Jews to move into the area, to the alarm of many Arabs already living there. International support for a Jewish homeland slowly grew, especially near the end of World War II, when the horrors of the Holocaust came to light.

After World War II, the United Nations decided to split Palestine into two parts. One part became the Jewish state of Israel. According to the UN plan, the other part was supposed

The state of Israel proclaimed its existence on May 14, 1948. Jews celebrated in Tel Aviv and other Israeli cities, but Arab states refused to recognize the new nation.

Who Are the Palestinians?

Before 1948, the term *Palestinian* referred to anyone living in the region of Palestine—Arabs, Jews, Muslims, Christians—regardless of religion or ethnic background. After 1948, when Palestine was divided and the nation of Israel came into being, most people living in Israel, who were mainly Jews, began to refer to themselves as Israelis. There are now a little more than seven million Israelis. Arabs from Palestine came to be known as Palestinian Arabs or simply as Palestinians. Today there are some nine million Palestinians. They are mostly Arabic-speaking, and mostly Muslim. Almost half live in the region of Palestine (including more than one million in Israel), and the rest mostly in nearby Arab countries.

to become an Arab state. The city of Jerusalem belonged to neither side and was to be administered by the United Nations. Zionists accepted this decision and rejoiced. But Arabs rejected it, refusing to recognize that Israel had a right to exist in Palestine.

On the day that Israel raised its flag in May 1948, five Arab armies invaded the country. They intended to reclaim the land for Palestinian Arabs and push out the Israelis. But Israel beat back these armies and conquered much of the land that the United Nations had set aside for the Arabs.

During this 1948 war, the Arab armies did make some gains. Egypt captured the small strip of land along the eastern coast of the Mediterranean Sea known as the Gaza Strip, which includes the city of Gaza. The Jordanian army occupied part of Jerusalem. Jordan also annexed a swath of land on the west side of the Jordan River. This became known as the West Bank.

More than 700,000 Palestinian Arabs fled the fighting and suddenly found themselves without a home. Many fled to hastily organized camps in various Arab nations. Others ended up as refugees living in camps just outside Israel's new borders. Many remained in Gaza and the West Bank. Meanwhile, Arab countries expelled several hundred thousand Jews, many of whom settled in Israel.

Homeless Palestinian refugees trek through scorching heat near the shore of the Dead Sea after the 1948 Arab-Israeli War. Their plight proved a great obstacle to peace.

Consequences of the 1948 War

For the Arab world, this defeat by the tiny nation of Israel was humiliating. The 1949 armistice left many issues unresolved. Would Palestinian Arab refugees be able to return to villages in land won by Israel? Israel said no. Would Israel's Arab neighbors recognize the new nation's right to exist? The Arab nations said no. Should Israel give back the land it had won in the war, land that was not originally part of Israel according to the UN charter? Arabs said yes, but Israelis said no.

In the view of many Arabs, the West was to blame for the plight of the Palestinian refugees. It was, they charged, meddling and decisions by outsiders that had thrust a foreign people — the Jews — into their midst. Zionism and Western interference, they said, had caused hundreds of thousands of Arabs to lose their land and homes in Palestine.

By the mid-1950s, some Palestinians in Gaza were taking up arms. They became guerrilla warriors called *fedayeen* (feh-duh-YEEN), and launched commando attacks on Israel. Egypt supported and funded these raids.

A *commando attack* is a hit-and-run raid.

Meanwhile, many Jewish people living in Arab countries suffered such persecution they had to give up their homes and move to Israel. The Jewish communities in countries like Iraq, Libya, Egypt, and Syria effectively disappeared.

The 1948 Arab-Israeli war introduced new strife and complexity into an already troubled region. In the next 25 years, three more wars would break out between these bitter rivals.

Nasser and Pan-Arabism

You've learned that during the 1950s, Gamal Abdul Nasser helped overthrow Egypt's king and became president of Egypt. Nasser emerged as a popular leader in the Arab world because he challenged European imperialism and directly confronted Israel. In a world divided by Cold War tensions, Nasser shrewdly played the Americans and Soviets against each other. He secured Soviet aid to build the Aswan High Dam, then one of the world's biggest hydroelectric facilities. In 1956, the United States led international pressure to force British, French, and Israeli forces to withdraw from Egypt. The three countries had quickly invaded Egypt when Nasser's government took control of the Suez Canal.

To many in the Arab world, Nasser was a hero because he seemed on his way to forging a modern, independent nation. But at home, Nasser had his critics. Struggling Egyptian peasants and urban workers resented their unchanging poverty. And the Muslim Brotherhood considered Nasser too secular because he refused to impose Shari'ah, the Islamic code of law, as the law of the land. Nasser kept a close watch on the Muslim Brotherhood, as the group was willing to use violent tactics, such as assassinations, to overthrow any government that did not accept Islamic law.

Nasser's popularity across the Arab world gave him the prestige to defeat his critics at home. His broad appeal led him to see himself as the leader not just of Egypt but of the whole Arab world. He began to champion pan-Arabism, the idea that Arab nations should be politically united in their actions.

Nasser also began to champion an idea he called Arab socialism. Unlike the European socialism based on the ideas of Karl Marx, Nasser's Arab socialism was based on Islamic

Gamal Abdul Nasser, Egypt's president from 1956 to 1970, championed the ideas of pan-Arabism and Arab socialism.

The Five Pillars of Islam

Islam's sacred book, the Qur'an, explains five religious duties of all Muslims, sometimes called the Five Pillars of Islam:

1. The Declaration of Faith—All Muslims must profess their faith in the one God, Allah, and must affirm their belief in Muhammad as Allah's prophet.

2. Prayer—Five times a day, Muslims are called to stop what they are doing, kneel, turn toward Mecca, and pray.

3. Giving to the Poor—The Qur'an commands Muslims to give alms to the poor and others in need.

4. Fasting—Muslims are required to fast. For one month each year, called Ramadan (RAH-muh-dahn), Muslims cannot eat, drink, or smoke from before sunrise until after sunset.

5. The Pilgrimage to Mecca—At least once before they die, all Muslims who are able must make a pilgrimage—called the Hajj (haj)—to the city of Mecca.

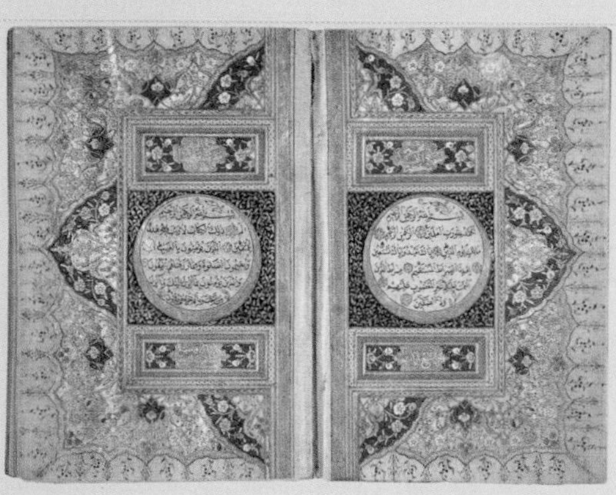

The Qur'an, the holy book of Islam, contains laws that address many aspects of Muslim life.

beliefs. In Nasser's view, the pillars of Islamic faith implied that the state should take responsibility for the welfare of all its citizens. In Arab socialism, he believed, there would be no class warfare. Instead, he hoped the people would work as one to achieve the ideal Islamic society.

Baathists and One Big Arab Nation?

Nasser was not the only one to promote unity among Arabs. In 1940, a Christian Arab educated in Paris, Michel Aflaq (AF-lahk), planted the seeds of the Baath (bath) Party in Syria. Baath is Arabic for "rebirth." Aflaq borrowed an idea from nineteenth-century German philosophers, who envisioned a nation as a *volk*, a people held together by a shared history and destiny. According to this philosophy, the character of such a people could be embodied in one leader or political party.

A similar idea had inspired European Fascists and Nazis to create repressive states under charismatic totalitarian rulers such as Adolf Hitler. But unlike the Nazis, who put race at the core of their nationalism, Aflaq built his vision of Arab identity from shared cultural and historic experience. He said this shared experience derived from Islamic history but did not belong to Muslims alone. Aflaq himself was a Christian.

During World War II, the Nazis found willing allies in the Baathists, who wanted the British and French out of their land. After World War II, the Baath Party gained followers. By the 1950s, they were winning seats in the Syrian parliament, and their influence was spreading to other Arab countries, especially Iraq.

The Baathists proposed that Arabs forge a single, large nation — a secular, socialist state in which the government would run the economy, build industry, and unite all its people in the name of progress. The Baath Party program resembled the pan-Arabism of Nasser.

Inspired by such ideas about Arab unity, Syrian leaders sent an unusual proposal to Nasser in Egypt. They suggested that Egypt and Syria merge into one new country. Nasser, who always saw himself as head of the Arab world, gladly accepted. So in 1958, the United Arab Republic was born, with Nasser as its first president and Cairo as its capital.

Syrian leaders soon discovered that forming one nation really meant that Egypt would rule Syria, and that Egyptian officers would command Syrian troops. After just three years, disgruntled army officers staged a coup that pulled Syria out of the union, leaving Egypt as the only country in the "United" Arab Republic. Other attempts to unify Arab nations also failed.

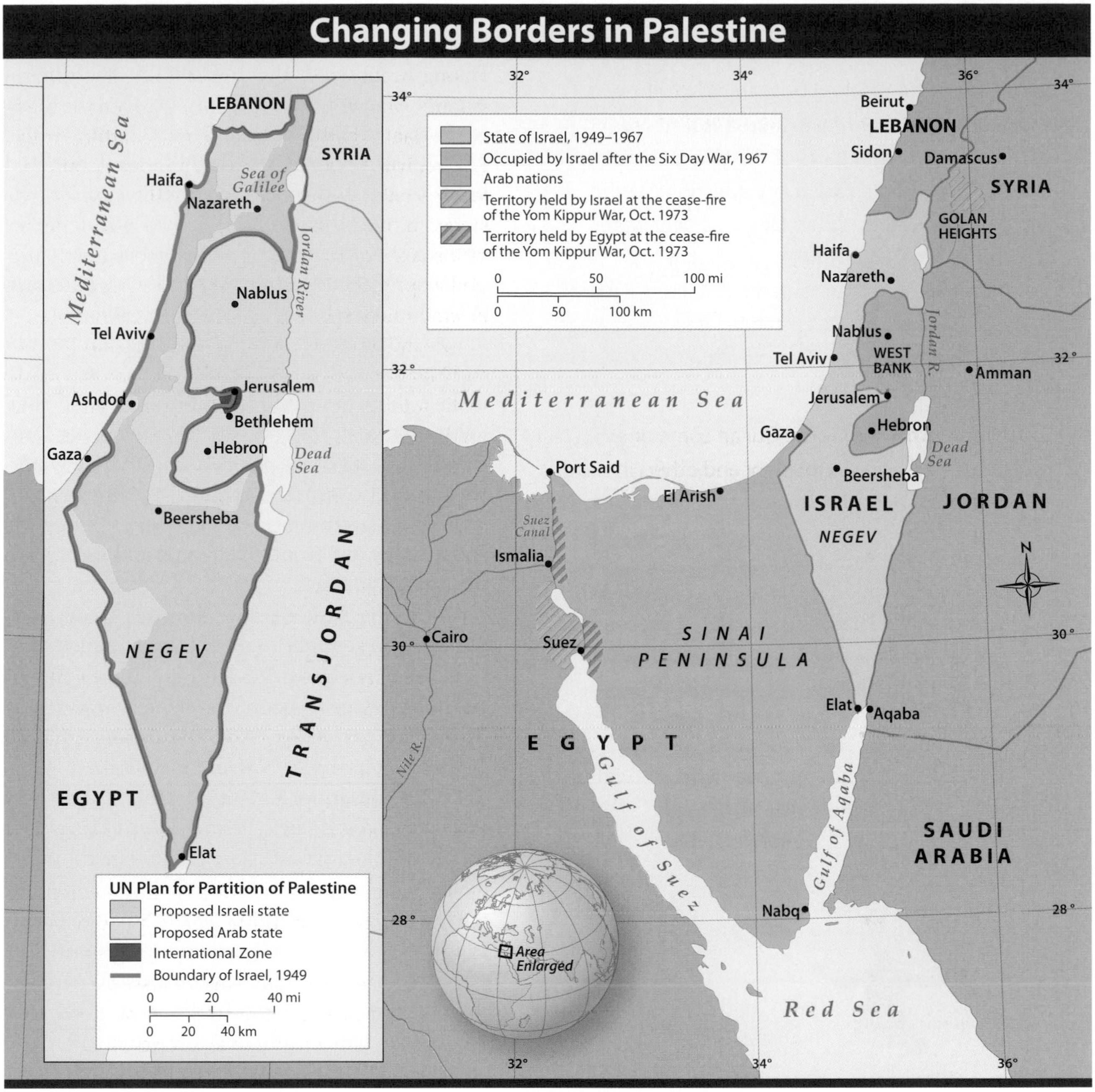

Syria's defiance damaged Nasser's prestige. He tried to restore his image by sending troops to support revolutionaries who were aiming to establish a republic in Yemen, a little region just south of Saudi Arabia. But Saudi Arabia's king sent troops to help Yemen's ruling family resist the revolutionaries. Now one Arab country was battling another Arab country on the soil of a third Arab country. The Arab League stood by, powerless, as the dream of Arab unity dissolved into fighting and bloodshed.

Forming the PLO and Fighting the Six Day War

As Nasser's prestige sank in the 1960s, he saw a way to restore his heroic stature by championing the cause of the stateless Palestinian refugees. Many of these refugees had been living in miserable camps since the end of the 1948 Arab-Israeli War. In the 1950s, Egypt had funded Palestinian commando attacks on Israel. But those raids declined when the United Nations sent a peacekeeping force to the Gaza Strip in 1956.

Fighting for Water

Water, taken for granted by many in the West as a cheap and plentiful resource, is a scarce commodity in other parts of the world. In many areas of the Middle East, a key question is: Who controls the water supply? Disputes over water are ongoing between Turkey, Syria, and Iraq. Control of water resources remains a crucial issue in much of India, Africa, and Asia.

In 1964, after years of work by Nasser, the Arab League established an organization to represent the Palestinians and coordinate their struggle for a return to the lands they had lost in 1948 when Israel was created. The goal of this new group, called the Palestine Liberation Organization (PLO), was to ensure "the liberation of Palestine." How did the PLO hope to achieve that goal? By destroying the state of Israel.

Over the next three years, tension mounted between Israel and its Arab neighbors. Nasser demanded the withdrawal of the UN peacekeeping force from the Gaza Strip. The Baathists, who had seized power in Syria, funded more Palestinian guerrilla attacks. Israel aggravated the tension by building a canal to divert water from the Jordan River to farms in the Negev Desert. Since water was a scarce resource, Israel's canal angered both Jordan and Syria. Syria attacked Israelis constructing the canal. In retaliation, Israel bombed targets in Syria and Jordan.

Palestine Liberation Organization training camps, such as this one photographed in Jordan in 1968, trained young men and boys to wage guerrilla war against Israel.

By 1967, many Arabs were criticizing Nasser. Why, they asked, do you not rush to defend your fellow Arabs under attack? As the champion of Arab pride and unity, Nasser felt pressured to make a show of force. He sent troops to the Sinai Peninsula, just west of the Israeli border, and closed the Gulf of Aqaba (AH-kah-buh), a waterway crucial to Israeli shipping. "We are so eager for battle," he announced, "in order to force the enemy to awake from his dreams and meet Arab reality face to face."

Now the Israeli prime minister faced troubles with *his* public. Some Israelis called him weak and indecisive for letting Nasser's moves go unchallenged. Soon the Israeli army was mobilizing for action. And the action came so swiftly that it caught Nasser by surprise.

Early on June 5, 1967, Israeli fighter jets streaked toward airfields in Egypt. In a few hours of blazing efficiency, the Israeli pilots destroyed hundreds of Egypt's war planes, mostly built and supplied by the Soviets. Israeli jets also launched air strikes on bases in Jordan, Syria, and Iraq, who quickly joined the fighting on Egypt's side. By the end of the first day, Israel had eliminated the threat of Arab air power. Without warplanes to provide cover from above, Arab tanks and ground troops were vulnerable in the exposed desert.

During the next two days, Israel took the Sinai Peninsula away from Egypt and gained control of the city of Jerusalem. By the fourth day, it had captured the West Bank of the Jordan River. On the fifth and sixth days, it captured the Golan Heights, which had belonged to Syria. All these gains were important to Israel, which viewed them as a buffer to protect them against Arab attacks. The United Nations intervened to obtain a cease-fire. After six days, the war was over.

Israeli tanks rumble across the Gaza Strip in June 1967 during the Six Day War. Israel defeated forces from several Arab countries and captured territories that more than tripled Israel's size. The war created thousands more Palestinian refugees and was a severe blow to Arab pride.

The Six Day War of 1967 had profound consequences. It more than tripled the size of Israel and caused thousands of Palestinian refugees to flee the West Bank for Jordan. It also brought at least a million Arabs under direct Israeli rule. Finally, it shattered Nasser's prestige and discredited the secular government he was trying to build. Nasser died in 1970, a broken man.

New Realities and a Militant PLO

Israel hoped to use the land it captured in the Six Day War to bargain with the Arabs. Israel would be willing to give back the land in exchange for agreements that would lay the foundation for a lasting peace.

First, Israel wanted its Arab neighbors to recognize that it had a right to exist. It also wanted its borders secured against raids and attacks. The Arabs, however, demanded that Israel withdraw from territories it had gained and allow Palestinian refugees to return to the land they had fled—not just the land they had recently fled during the Six Day War, but the land Israel had gained nearly twenty years before during the 1948 war. The Israelis refused to agree to these demands since they believed that to give up so much would threaten Israel's security, and even its existence. So the two sides remained at odds.

Meanwhile, the Baath Party had taken advantage of Nasser's weakness to build its own strength. One branch of the Baathists took power in Syria under Hafez al-Assad (hah-FEZ al-ah-SAHD). Another branch, eventually led by the ruthless Saddam Hussein (sah-DAHM hoo-SAYN), tightened its grip on Iraq. Both countries developed into totalitarian states in which the government controlled the economy, censored the media, and severely punished dissenters.

The devastating Arab defeat in the Six Day War also convinced Palestinians they could expect no help from Arab governments. Instead, they looked to the PLO for help.

For leadership the PLO turned to Yasser Arafat (YAH-sihr AIR-uh-fat), the head of a major

In 1969, Yasser Arafat (with dark glasses) became leader of the Palestine Liberation Organization, which used guerrilla warfare against Israeli soldiers and civilians.

A Palestinian terrorist stands guard on a balcony at the Olympic Village in Munich. In 1972, the terrorist group Black September killed 11 Israeli Olympic team members.

guerrilla group. Arafat, who was of Palestinian descent, had joined the Muslim Brotherhood when he was a young man at the University of Cairo. In 1956, he fought against Britain, France, and Israel when they invaded Egypt. He then helped found a group called Fatah (FAHT-ah), which means "Victory." The commandos in Fatah launched guerrilla raids on Israel.

After the Six Day War of 1967, Arafat took over as leader of the PLO. He emphasized the use of guerrilla warfare, not only against Israeli soldiers and military targets, but also against civilian targets such as schools and buses in Israel.

The growing militancy of the PLO troubled not just Israel but also Jordan. Jordan had struggled to absorb the thousands of Palestinian refugees who fled the West Bank when Israel captured it in the 1967 war. The PLO established its headquarters in Jordan. As they continued their attacks against Israel, Palestinian guerrillas formed a rival, though unofficial, government in Jordan itself. They talked openly of overthrowing Jordan's King Hussein. Fearful for the safety of his monarchy, King Hussein launched an attack on the Palestinian guerrillas.

In September 1970—"Black September," as Palestinians later called it—a civil war erupted in Jordan. Jordanian troops stormed Palestinian guerrilla camps. Syria entered the war on the side of the Palestinians. Jordan called for American and British aid, and even secretly sought Israeli assistance. King Hussein ultimately succeeded in driving the PLO and thousands of Palestinian refugees out of his country. This mass of homeless Palestinians moved into Lebanon, where the PLO set up new headquarters. From Lebanon, the PLO stepped up its attacks on Israel.

Two years later, the bitter Arab-Israeli conflict erupted in a place where people least expected it and in a way that shocked the world. During the 1972 Olympics in Munich, Germany, a band of Palestinian militants calling themselves Black September broke into the Olympic Village and killed 11 Israeli Olympic team members. From this time on, in their struggle with Israel, Palestinians increasingly used a tactic called terrorism—the planned use of violence to strike fear into a people or government in order to obtain political goals.

Oil: Blessing and Curse

The largest oil fields in the world are in the Middle East, with perhaps two-thirds of the world's known oil located under and around the Persian Gulf. For the Middle East, oil has proven both a blessing and a curse. It brought great wealth, but that wealth long remained in the hands of a few. Oil has also fueled intense clashes between modernizers sympathetic to the West and supporters of traditional Islamic culture.

By the 1940s, the industrial nations had come to depend on petroleum for their energy needs. It was the fuel that powered millions of new automobiles rolling off assembly lines. It heated homes and powered factories. With oil in increasing demand, several countries in the Middle East began to understand the power that their vast reserves of petroleum gave them.

Before World War II, Western oil companies had signed leases that gave them rights to the Middle Eastern oil fields in exchange for modest payments. In 1960, oil-producing nations organized to gain stronger bargaining power with the big oil companies. Iran, Iraq, Kuwait, and Saudi Arabia, along with the South American nation of Venezuela, banded together to form a cartel — a group of business interests joined together to fix prices and limit competition. This cartel was called the Organization of the Petroleum Exporting Countries (OPEC).

Over the years, other oil-producing countries joined OPEC. Through OPEC, these countries sought greater control over the supply and price of oil. OPEC enabled the oil-producing nations of the Middle East to keep more of the profits generated by their vast oil fields.

In the OPEC nations, a few powerful families and individuals began amassing huge fortunes. Instead of using it to help develop their countries, they often indulged in spectacular consumption or invested their wealth abroad. Wealthy Iranians became international jet-setters. Grandiose palaces went up in Iraq. Saudi aristocrats bought real estate around the globe. The rich got richer — and, as for the poor, while their lives may have improved slightly, tensions heightened as the gap between the haves and have-nots grew ever larger.

These tensions, combined with the humiliating Arab defeat of 1967, energized Islamist groups such as the Muslim Brotherhood. They despised what they saw as the Western decadence of the oil-rich ruling families. Not only did these Islamists oppose all things Western, they also rejected the pan-Arab socialism of Nasser and the Baath Party. It was not enough, these Islamists said, to form a political union of Arabs. Instead, they wanted to topple secular governments and bring the whole Islamic world under the sway of Shari'ah, the Islamic law. The Muslim Brotherhood expanded its ranks and spread its message throughout the Middle East and beyond.

A New Leader in Egypt and Another War

Now let's turn back to the situation in Egypt. Egypt was a country with little oil in a region with a great deal of oil. Nevertheless, it remained a leader among Middle Eastern nations. After Nasser's death in 1970, Anwar Sadat (AHN-wahr suh-DAHT) became Egypt's president. Sadat had lived in Nasser's shadow for so long that many expected little of him. But once he took charge, he asserted himself quickly.

First, Sadat reversed a key aspect of Nasser's foreign policy. Under Nasser, Egypt had been officially a non-aligned nation — it had refused to take sides in the Cold War. That was Egypt's official status, but in fact Nasser had leaned toward the Soviets, from whom he got most of his military supplies and economic aid. Sadat put an end to that strategy. He kept the military equipment but sent the Soviet advisors home and began seeking closer ties to the United States.

At the same time, Sadat laid plans to do what Nasser had never accomplished — defeat Israel. In 1973, on Yom Kippur (yom kih-POUR) — "the day of atonement," the holiest of Jewish holidays — Sadat launched an Egyptian-led invasion of Israel. Several other Arab countries either contributed aid or entered this fourth Arab-Israeli war, sometimes called the Yom Kippur War. Arab forces caught the Israelis by surprise and regained some of the territory lost to Israel in the Six Day War of 1967.

A proud Egyptian soldier holds a portrait of Egypt's president, Anwar Sadat, just before the outbreak of the Yom Kippur War. Sadat launched the war against Israel in 1973.

The Oil Embargo of 1973

In the last days of the Yom Kippur War, the Arab nations sent the world a new kind of warning. Through OPEC, they declared an oil embargo that quadrupled the price of oil within months. (An embargo is a government order to stop trade in certain goods or to impose barriers to trade.) Through this embargo, the oil-producing nations meant to punish the United States and other Western nations for helping Israel.

In nations targeted by the oil embargo, the result was an energy crisis. In the United States, drivers needing to fill their gas tanks waited in lines that stretched for blocks. The federal government imposed a national maximum speed limit of 55 miles per hour. Some schools and offices closed to save heating oil. Factories laid off workers. In some nations, such as France, high fuel prices had ripple effects that led to decreased economic development and increased unemployment. The embargo sent a shiver throughout the Western world, since petroleum was the lifeblood of industrial civilization.

Egyptian President Anwar Sadat (left), U.S. President Jimmy Carter (center), and Israeli Prime Minister Menachem Begin at a historic White House peace treaty ceremony in 1979.

Israel's prime minister, Golda Meir (GOHL-duh may-EER), appealed to the United States for help. President Richard Nixon hesitated at first, but once it became clear that the Soviets were supplying Egypt and Syria, the United States rushed fresh supplies and military equipment to Israel. The tide of battle turned, and Israel took back most of the land it had just lost.

After 16 days of fighting, the war ended with a cease-fire agreement, and with borders largely unchanged. Even though the 1973 Arab-Israeli war ended in a stalemate, many Arabs saw it as a victory. They felt it proved that Arabs could go head-to-head with Israelis in battle.

Egypt and Israel Try for Peace

Egypt's Anwar Sadat emerged from the war with some of the heroic prestige Nasser had once enjoyed. But Sadat came to the conclusion that fighting was not the answer to long-standing disagreements with Israel. Four years after the 1973 Yom Kippur War, he astounded the Middle East by announcing, "I am willing to go to the ends of the earth for peace." A few days later, Sadat flew to Israel, shook hands with Israeli Prime Minister Menachem Begin (muh-NAH-kuhm BAY-gin), and addressed the Israeli parliament. Millions of television viewers around the world watched reports of the visit and wondered — could peace between Israelis and Arabs finally be at hand?

In 1978, at the invitation of U.S. President Jimmy Carter, Sadat and Begin met at the presidential retreat of Camp David in Maryland. After almost two weeks of negotiations, the Egyptian and Israeli leaders signed an agreement known as the Camp David Accords. Under the accords, Egypt recognized Israel's right to exist. In return, Israel agreed to give up parts of the Sinai Peninsula it still occupied, and to recognize the need for self-government for the Palestinians.

The Camp David Accords also called for a peace treaty between Israel and Egypt. The following year, Sadat and Begin flew to Washington, D.C. They signed the peace treaty at the White House. Again millions watched televised reports of the ceremony and were filled with hope when the two old enemies embraced.

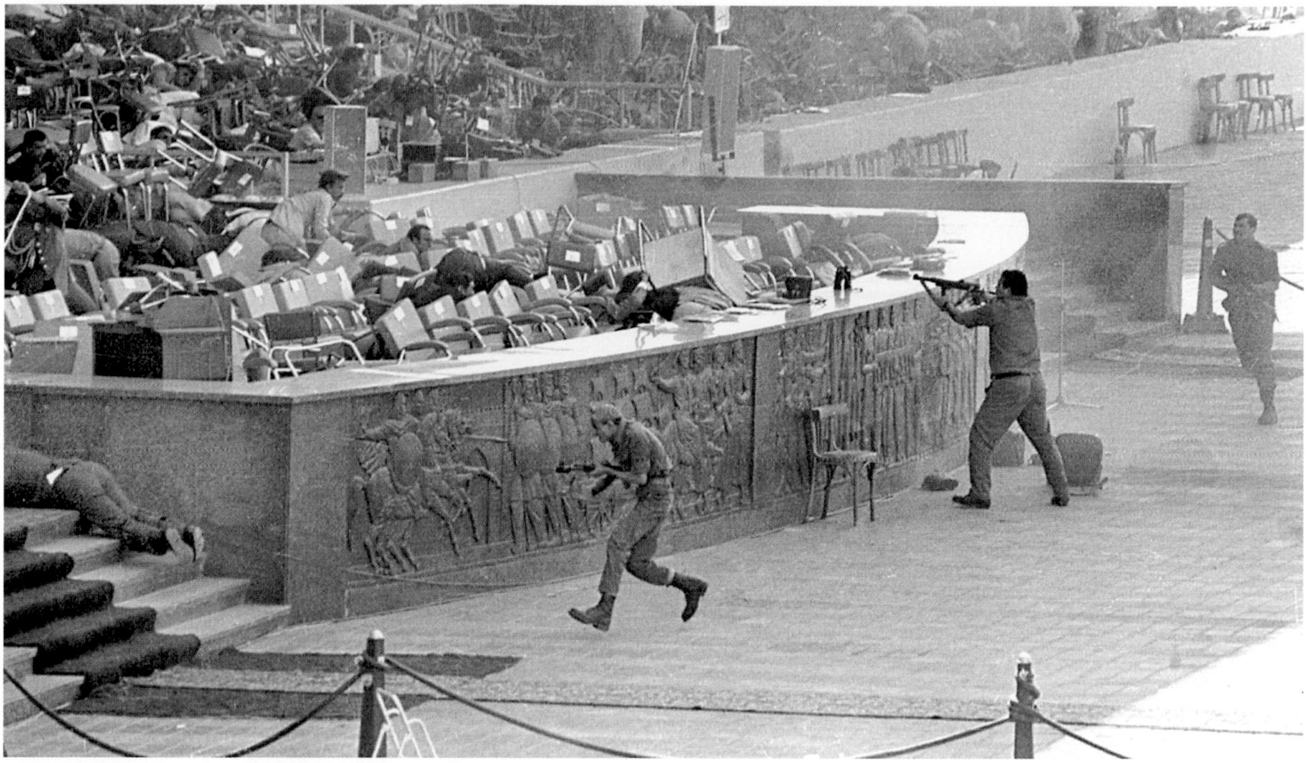

Islamic extremists fire at a reviewing stand in Cairo where Egyptian President Anwar Sadat had been observing a military parade. The gunmen killed Sadat and several others. Sadat's efforts to make peace with Israel had made him a hero in the West, but many Arabs felt betrayed.

But peace in the Middle East remained elusive. No other Arab countries agreed to join the Camp David Accords. And not long after the agreements were signed, tensions rose as the Israeli government allowed Jews to build settlements in the territories it had captured in the 1967 Six Day War—land that the Palestinians considered their own.

Hostilities between Israel and the PLO continued. Israel continued to fear for its existence. In 1981, Israeli bombers destroyed a nuclear reactor that Iraq was building near Baghdad. Prime Minister Begin was convinced that the Iraqis were planning to build a nuclear bomb.

Sadat's peace treaty with Israel infuriated many Arabs. They grew even angrier when Sadat ordered the arrest of some 1,600 political opponents in Egypt.

In October 1981, while Sadat was attending a parade in Cairo, a military truck pulled up in front of his presidential reviewing stand. A small group of militant Islamists who had joined the Egyptian army leapt out of the truck and ran toward the stand, hurling grenades and firing rifles. Anwar Sadat and several others were shot dead.

A Troubled Legacy

As the twentieth century moved into its final decades, the Middle East continued to be a troubled region.

With the exception of Israel, the region's governments were far from democratic. Authoritarian family monarchies ruled in Saudi Arabia, Jordan, and Kuwait. Repressive one-party states dominated Iraq, Syria, Egypt, Libya, and Algeria. In both cases, governments denied their citizens basic human rights such as freedom of speech, freedom of religion, and participation in the political process.

Masses of people living under repressive government control. Millions living in poverty. The simmering anger of the still homeless Palestinians. Resentment toward Israel and the West. The growing influence of a militant Islamism. All of these persist as ongoing sources of strife in the Middle East.

U.S. troops leap to the ground from a helicopter that hovers above the stumps of bomb-shattered trees in 1966, during the Vietnam War. The war was one of several "hot spots" of the Cold War—places in which the United States and Soviet Union sent aid or troops to support their allies in fights between communist and noncommunist forces.

Hot Spots in the Cold War

During the Cold War, the United States and the Soviet Union remained in a tense standoff, like duelists, each with a pistol aimed at the other's heart. Yet neither shot first. The closest the two superpowers came to armed conflict with each other was in the Cuban Missile Crisis of 1962. That crisis was resolved, but each side remained poised, wary, and fearful as the Cold War continued.

At times, the Cold War did turn hot, though the two superpowers did not directly fight each other. Instead, throughout the 1960s and 1970s, each superpower carefully watched over countries it considered its allies. In countries where the struggle between communist and noncommunist forces seemed to hang in the balance, the superpowers often sent aid or troops to assist a friendly government, or to topple a government allied with the other side.

Both the United States and USSR worried that if one country fell to the other side, then neighboring countries might follow. As early as 1954, U.S. President Dwight Eisenhower expressed this anxiety in terms of a familiar image—a line of dominoes knocking each other down. "You have a row of dominoes set up," he said. "You knock over the first one, and what will happen to the last one is the certainty that it will go over very quickly."

This so-called domino theory shaped many events during the Cold War, particularly in Southeast Asia. We'll turn first to Southeast Asia as we examine several hot spots of the Cold War, countries where fighting or revolution erupted as the superpowers took action to curb each other's influence.

Vietnam: America Plunges In

In 1961, few Americans had ever heard of Vietnam. Four years later the name was on everyone's lips. Why did this small country in Southeast Asia become so important to Americans?

You've learned that Vietnam is part of the region known as Indochina, and was once a colony of the French. After the Second World War, the nationalist leader Ho Chi Minh led his country's struggle for independence from France. Many Vietnamese revered Ho as a heroic freedom fighter, but U.S. leaders distrusted him because he was a devoted communist.

In 1954, as part of the negotiations to end Vietnam's war against the French colonizers, Vietnam was divided into northern and southern halves. North Vietnam was ruled by Ho Chi Minh. Since it was a communist nation, the Soviets gave it aid. South Vietnam was ruled

Ngo Dinh Diem, president of South Vietnam, casts a ballot in Saigon in 1961. Diem rigged elections to stay in power.

A MAD Arms Race

Throughout the 1960s and 1970s, the superpowers engaged in an arms race, building enormous arsenals of nuclear weapons that could destroy not just each other, but the planet many times over. Ironically, from this buildup of nuclear arms emerged a strategy for preventing a horrible war between the two superpowers. According to this strategy of Mutual Assured Destruction (MAD), each superpower understood that to launch a nuclear attack would be to sign its own death warrant, because the other superpower would respond with its own devastating nuclear attack.

American and Soviet leaders hoped that the prospect of mutual annihilation would keep them from plunging the world into nuclear catastrophe. The problem with this MAD strategy, however, was that each superpower felt it could be safe only if its military was as powerful or more powerful than the other's. So each side raced to build larger and larger stockpiles of weapons.

by Ngo Dinh Diem, who was backed by the United States.

U.S. leaders hoped that South Vietnam would contain communism and keep it from spreading throughout Southeast Asia. They worried that if they did not help Diem's government, South Vietnam itself might become the next domino to fall to communism.

In February 1955, President Eisenhower sent American military advisors to South Vietnam to train Diem's army. Diem, a thoroughly corrupt power-monger, seemed an unlikely ally of democracy. He rigged elections, ruthlessly controlled key government posts, and jailed critics without trial. But Eisenhower and the U.S. government were willing to ignore Diem's many faults because the South Vietnamese leader was firmly anticommunist.

It soon became clear to U.S. leaders that Ho Chi Minh was trying to bring South Vietnam under communist rule. Communist guerrilla fighters known as the Viet Cong began launching attacks and trying to overthrow Diem's government. They received equipment and advice from the Soviet Union and China. Ho Chi Minh and the Viet Cong regarded Diem's regime as a puppet government controlled by the United States—in their view, yet another foreign power trying to rule Vietnam.

Diem responded to the guerrilla attacks by turning his brutal secret police loose on the Vietnamese people to root out suspected enemies. His harsh methods made him an unpopular ruler. Still, the United States continued to support Diem's regime.

When John F. Kennedy was elected president of the United States, he decided to increase the American presence in South Vietnam. In late 1961, while the Soviets and East Germans were building the Berlin Wall, Kennedy sent 3,000 military advisors—four times the previous total—to help Diem's regime. The U.S. advisors did not usually fight in combat, but they trained and organized South Vietnamese soldiers, supplied weapons, and helped plan the fight against Ho Chi Minh's forces. Kennedy also sent helicopters and American pilots to help the South Vietnamese fight the Viet Cong. Despite U.S. efforts, the Viet Cong continued to attack South Vietnam and gain support among the population.

Two years later, Kennedy decided that Diem's corrupt regime was incapable of containing communism. He concluded that the United States must take steps to overthrow Diem's government. So he authorized a group of South Vietnamese army officers to stage a *coup d'etat*. The president and his aides were shocked when the participants not only removed Diem from power, but also murdered him. Not long after, the American role in Vietnam took a dramatic turn when President Kennedy was assassinated.

Johnson Widens the War

When Kennedy's vice president, Lyndon Johnson, assumed the presidency, he inherited a difficult situation in Vietnam. The United States had spent millions on the war and kept sending

Kennedy Assassinated

On November 22, 1963, U.S. President John F. Kennedy was assassinated in Dallas, Texas, as he rode through the city in an open limousine. Police arrested a man named Lee Harvey Oswald and charged him with Kennedy's murder. Two days later, while being transferred to a county jail, Oswald himself was shot and killed by Jack Ruby, a Dallas nightclub owner. Oswald's motives for assassinating Kennedy remain unclear.

The Vietnam War, 1957–1975

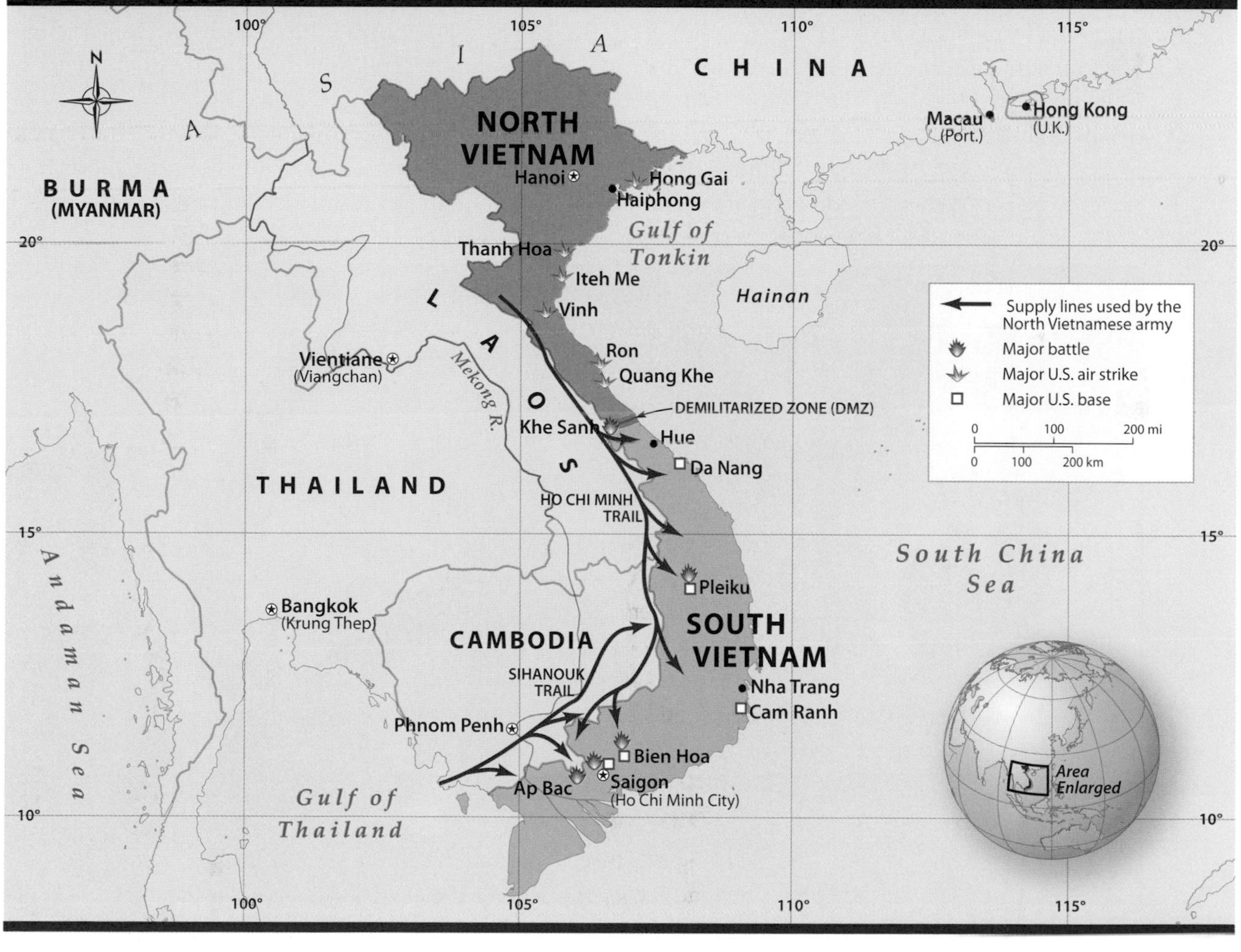

military advisers—about 16,000 by the time Johnson took office. But the communists still seemed to be winning.

Johnson was a firm believer in the domino theory. In 1961, when he was still vice president, after visiting South Vietnam he remarked, "The battle against communism must be joined in Southeast Asia with strength and determination...or the United States, inevitably, must surrender the Pacific and take up our defenses on our own shores."

In August 1964, an incident occurred that gave Johnson the opportunity to confront the communist threat head-on. American naval vessels operating in the Gulf of Tonkin reported torpedo attacks by North Vietnamese patrol boats. Details were sketchy. The American ships suffered no damage or casualties, and some participants later questioned the accuracy of the report. Nevertheless, Johnson convinced Congress to pass the Gulf of Tonkin Resolution, which authorized the president to use military force in Southeast Asia without a formal declaration of war.

Johnson sent more American soldiers to Vietnam—by the end of 1965, some 184,000 U.S. troops, and by 1966, some 385,000. This buildup of troops, however, brought the United States no closer to victory. When faced with overwhelming American firepower, Viet Cong and North Vietnamese units simply melted away into the jungle or fled across the border into neighboring Laos and Cambodia, only to return and take charge once the Americans left an area.

Americans Oppose the War

In the early years of American involvement in Vietnam, most Americans supported President Johnson and the war. First, they believed that stopping the spread of communism was a just cause. And second, they thought that the United States could win the war. As the fighting dragged on, however, many Americans began to have doubts.

Every day, as Americans opened their newspapers or turned on their TVs, they learned that more and more U.S. soldiers were dying in Vietnam. Johnson and his generals kept insisting that with more troops in place, they could turn the tide and win the war. But by early 1968, hundreds of Americans were dying every month. Newscasts reported the steadily increasing casualty figures: "The American death toll in Vietnam is 16,000...17,000...18,000...."

An antiwar movement gained strength in the United States. Across the country, thousands gathered in protests to demand an end to the

As the Vietnam War dragged on, many Americans turned against it. Above, antiwar protesters hold a large peace symbol.

fighting. College students, horrified at the number of young people being killed, often led the protests. Some young men risked prison sentences by burning their draft cards. Others fled to Canada to avoid the draft and escape being sent to Vietnam. Protestors sang songs like "Give Peace a Chance," written by the Beatles' John Lennon, or chanted slogans like "Hell no, we won't go!" Some burned U.S. flags to show their anger at America's role in the war.

Communist Victory in Southeast Asia

In January 1968, the tide of the war turned, but not in the way that President Johnson and his generals hoped. Almost 70,000 Viet Cong and North Vietnamese soldiers launched a series of attacks known as the Tet Offensive because it began during Tet, the Vietnamese New Year celebration. More than a hundred cities and towns all over South Vietnam came under attack. Viet Cong guerrillas even stormed the U.S. Embassy in Saigon, the capital of South Vietnam.

American and South Vietnamese forces soon counterattacked. Within weeks, they recaptured most of the lost territory and killed 37,000 Viet Cong. In strictly military terms, the Tet Offensive was a devastating defeat for the communists. But in a more important sense, they had won a major victory. When Americans saw news reports of the Tet Offensive, they saw more fighting, more bloodshed, more U.S. soldiers dying. Public opinion turned decisively against the war. Americans wanted out of Vietnam.

Faced by overwhelming public opposition to the war, Richard Nixon, who succeeded Lyndon Johnson as president in 1969, believed he had no choice but to begin withdrawing U.S. troops. He hoped to find a way to bring the troops home while keeping the communists from overrunning South Vietnam. He also wanted to avoid the appearance of defeat. "I will not," he vowed, "become the first president of the United States to lose a war."

Nixon planned to turn most of the fighting over to the South Vietnamese army, a plan he called "Vietnamization." South Vietnamese forces soon numbered one million men. The number of U.S. troops in South Vietnam fell from a previous high of 540,000 to about 140,000 in 1972.

Vietnam: The First Television War

The Vietnam War has been called the first "television war" and the first "living room war." That's because, for the first time, millions of people could see daily televised reports from the front lines, showing vivid images of a war as it was being fought. At first, American news coverage of the war was upbeat, with reports of victories and progress. But as the fighting continued, many TV reports questioned whether the United States could win this war. Day after day, scenes of dead and wounded soldiers, burned villages, and bomb-blasted landscapes discouraged many.

Did TV coverage actually cause many Americans to turn against the Vietnam War, or did it simply reflect declining public support? Historians still debate that question. But there is no doubt that by bringing images of fighting directly into homes, television increased people's awareness of the human costs of war.

While the fighting continued, diplomats from the warring sides held peace negotiations in Paris. In early 1973, the United States, South Vietnam, North Vietnam, and the Viet Cong signed a cease-fire agreement. It called for the United States to withdraw its troops from Vietnam, and for the South Vietnamese to hold elections to choose their own government. Nixon claimed he had achieved "peace with honor."

But as the last U.S. ground forces departed, leaving South Vietnam to fend for itself, the North Vietnamese abandoned the cease-fire agreement. With the Americans mostly out of the war, Communist forces overran the south. In the spring of 1975, they reached Saigon. South Vietnam's government quickly surrendered. The capital soon had a new name — Ho Chi Minh City.

The South Vietnamese people never got to hold their elections. The North Vietnamese reunited north and south into a single communist

Americans and selected Vietnamese climb to the roof of a building in Saigon, South Vietnam, to board a helicopter and fly to safety as North Vietnamese troops approach the city in April 1975. Soon after the U.S. evacuation, Saigon fell to the communist forces, bringing an end to the Vietnam War.

nation, the Socialist Republic of Vietnam. Communist leaders imprisoned thousands they considered allies of the United States. Over the next several years, more than a million Vietnamese fled the country, wrecked by war and mired in poverty.

With U.S. troops out of Southeast Asia, Vietnam's neighbors turned communist. In 1975, the same year South Vietnam surrendered, communist forces called the Khmer Rouge (kuh-MEHR roozh) took control of Cambodia. The government outlawed religion, seized land and businesses, and forced most people living in cities to move to farms in the countryside. During a four-year reign of terror, the Khmer Rouge executed, starved, or worked to death some 1.5 million people. Communists also took control of Laos, seizing property and persecuting the country's Buddhists.

To many in the West, it seemed as though the dominoes were indeed falling.

Prague Spring

During the late 1960s, while U.S. troops were bogged down in Vietnam, Soviet leaders faced a different kind of hot spot much closer to their own borders. Their attention was focused on one of the countries behind the Iron Curtain, Czechoslovakia, and its leader, Alexander Dubcek (DOOB-chek).

In January 1968, Dubcek was elected to the most powerful position in his country, first secretary of the Communist Party of Czechoslovakia (the KSC). He seemed well prepared to lead a nation firmly allied with the Soviet Union. His father had been a founding member of the KSC. As a young man during World War II, Dubcek had been wounded while fighting the Nazis. He later studied at a prestigious university in Moscow.

But Dubcek represented a new generation of European communists, a departure from the hard-line Stalinists of the past. Almost immediately after taking control, he began a program of reforms that he called "socialism with a human face." These changes were meant to loosen government censorship of the press and popular culture. He also wanted to increase citizens' participation in party politics.

To Western observers, Dubcek's reforms appeared mild. He never challenged the KSC's grip on political power. He did not propose to abandon the government-planned economy, a cornerstone of communist philosophy. Nor did he at any time question Czechoslovakia's position as a satellite of the Soviet Union.

Nevertheless, his measures had an electrifying effect at home and abroad. In the Czech capital, Prague, and in other cities, students and intellectuals rejoiced when the Czech Communist Party announced its reforms. It would no longer censor newspapers. There would be more freedom of speech on radio and television. People would have the freedom to assemble peacefully.

Citizens engaged in lively public debates about matters once only whispered, such as the best way to run the country. Word spread that the Party would now allow Czechs to travel outside the country — even to the West. The general air of excitement and optimism that swept Czechoslovakia at this time became known as the Prague Spring.

Outside of Czechoslovakia, the Prague Spring caused communist officials to grow uneasy. They did not share Dubcek's vision of "socialism with a human face." They worried that their own citizens might get a whiff of democracy blowing across the Czech border.

Most alarmed of all were the leaders of the Soviet Union. In their view, undisputed Soviet control over Eastern Europe was essential to their national security. Like the United States, the Soviets were operating by the domino theory — the countries behind the Iron Curtain represented Moscow's dominoes. Soviet leaders worried that if one of these countries began to experiment with democracy, the communist government there might eventually fall, and then neighboring countries might follow. "If we let Czechoslovakia go," the Soviet foreign minister warned, "others might be tempted, too."

The Soviets Invade Czechoslovakia

At the time of the Prague Spring, Nikita Khrushchev was no longer in power in the Soviet Union.

Alexander Dubcek (front row, third from right), first secretary of the Czechoslovakian Communist Party, marches with other Czech officials before enthusiastic crowds in Prague in the spring of 1968. Dubcek and his government had abolished censorship, promised freedom of speech, and committed to other bold changes to ensure "socialism with a human face." But the reforms of the Prague Spring caused grave alarm among the leaders of the Soviet Union.

The communist superpower was led by Leonid Brezhnev (LEE-uh-nid BREZH-nef), who had no intention of loosening his grip on Czechoslovakia. Dubcek tried to assure Brezhnev that Czechoslovakia remained a loyal Soviet ally, but Brezhnev was skeptical. In his view, the Prague Spring reforms were "a bad program, opening up possibilities for the restoration of capitalism in Czechoslovakia."

A few weeks later, the democracy movement in Czechoslovakia took on new life when a group of writers and intellectuals published a manifesto called "The Two Thousand Words." The manifesto went far beyond Dubcek's limited reforms. It called for an end to the KSC's domination of Czech politics and asserted that "no gratitude is due the Communist Party."

Dubcek had lost control of the movement that he had started. The rest of the Eastern Bloc—the Soviet Union and its allies—reacted harshly to "The Two Thousand Words." The Moscow newspaper *Pravda*, the mouthpiece of the Soviet leadership, condemned the manifesto as "an overt attack against the Czechoslovak Communist Party and the socialist state."

Dubcek was powerless to prevent what happened next. At midnight on August 20, 1968, half a million Soviet and other Warsaw Pact troops crossed the Czech border. Miles-long columns of tanks headed for Prague, while paratroopers swooped in to secure Czech airfields.

The *Warsaw Pact* was the Cold War military alliance between the USSR and its Eastern European satellite nations.

The Czech army did not put up a fight—which would have been hopeless—but civilians offered resistance in various ways. They removed road markers along the route of the Soviet advance and changed the signposts in many villages to read *Dubcekovo*, which means "belonging to Dubcek." They refused to give the invaders food, gasoline, or directions. The Czech people demonstrated their independent spirit to the end, but the outcome was never in doubt.

Czech students stand on an overturned truck and wave their nation's flag as citizens of Prague surround Soviet soldiers and tanks. The Soviet army invaded Czechoslovakia in August 1968 to end Alexander Dubcek's Prague Spring reforms. The Czechs realized that fighting the Soviets would be useless but they insisted on showing their independent spirit.

A Soviet tank crashes into a building before horrified Czechs. The 1968 invasion of Czechoslovakia sent a clear message: Soviet leaders would tolerate no changes that might threaten their communist empire.

The Red Army occupied Prague and arrested Dubcek. He was flown to Moscow and forced to give in to Soviet demands. Returning to Prague, Dubcek gave a tearful speech confirming that all his reforms, all the progress made during the Prague Spring, were lost.

During the next several months, Soviet leaders replaced reform-minded Czech officials with men obedient to Moscow. Thousands who had taken part in the democratic reforms of the Prague Spring were removed from Czechoslovakia's Communist Party. Dubcek was eventually expelled from the KSC and demoted to an unimportant position in the forestry service. Freedom of speech disappeared as the government tightened censorship of newspapers and magazines. Czechoslovakia's brief experiment with political freedom ended, crushed under the heel of Soviet military might.

East-West Rivalry in Latin America

It would not be accurate to compare the Soviet Union's domination of Eastern Europe to the role of the United States in Latin America. Nevertheless, when it felt American interests were at risk, the United States sometimes intervened in Latin American affairs.

Latin America is a name used to refer to a vast area in the Western Hemisphere south of the United States, including Mexico, Central America, South America, and some of the islands

Youth Makes Its Voice Heard

In the years following World War II, birthrates soared in many countries. Many of those born during this postwar "baby boom" were, by the late 1960s, in their late teens and early twenties, and they began to make their voices heard.

In 1968, during Czechoslovakia's brief Prague Spring, young people led protests for greater political freedom. At the same time, young people in the United States staged frequent protests to challenge authority on many issues, from demanding an end to the Vietnam War to calling for greater civil rights. In West Berlin, a city defended from communism by the United States, students took to the streets to condemn America's involvement in Vietnam. In France, a massive strike led by students forced President Charles de Gaulle to flee Paris.

Young people were restless in China, as well, but there the story was much more violent as Mao Zedong's Cultural Revolution spun out of control. In 1967, thousands of Red Guards rioted in Beijing. Mao responded by banishing several million young people to the countryside for "re-education" through labor. "They just don't listen to me," Mao complained.

in the Caribbean Sea. Ever since the Monroe Doctrine (1823), American presidents had asserted that the U.S. would use military force, if necessary, to keep non-American powers out of the region. During the Cold War, they aggressively pursued this policy. American leaders regarded Latin America as vital to U.S. security. In their view, the Soviet Union had no business meddling in countries so close to the United States. Fidel Castro's revolution in Cuba, only 90 miles from American shores, convinced American officials that they must take active steps to contain communism in the Western Hemisphere.

One example of how far the United States was prepared to go to contain communism is the case of the Dominican Republic, a small country in the Caribbean Sea. In 1961, a group of Dominican army officers assassinated Rafael Trujillo (troo-HEE-yoh), a brutal dictator who had controlled the country for three decades. The next year, Dominicans elected a poet-turned-politician named Juan Bosch to be president. Bosch was not a communist, but he was a socialist who proposed taking land from wealthy landowners and distributing it among the people. His program alarmed U.S. officials, who had dealt with the Cuban missile crisis just two months earlier.

For the next few years, the Dominican Republic was in turmoil. Bosch lost power in a coup, but his supporters mounted a countercoup. Fighting broke out in the capital, Santo Domingo, endangering civilians there, including some U.S. citizens.

In April 1965, President Lyndon Johnson decided to send U.S. troops to the Dominican Republic. At first, their goal was to protect and evacuate American citizens. But Johnson became convinced that Fidel Castro's communist agents were behind much of the trouble in the Dominican Republic. Even though there was little evidence of Castro's involvement, Johnson was determined that the country would not become "another Cuba."

A few days later, Johnson addressed the nation in a televised speech. He claimed that in the Dominican Republic, "what began as a popular democratic revolution, committed to democracy and social justice, very shortly ... was taken over ... and placed into the hands of a band of Communist conspirators."

Johnson stationed warships off the Dominican coast and increased the number of troops ashore. Their goal was no longer simply to protect American citizens; now their job was to make sure that no communist regime came to power. America and its allies, said Johnson, "cannot, must not, and will not permit the establishment of another Communist government in the Western Hemisphere."

Ultimately, a force of more than 23,000 U.S. soldiers and Marines brought an end to the fighting in the Dominican Republic. In elections held several months later, Juan Bosch lost the race for the presidency to Joaquín Balaguer (bah-lah-GAIR), a candidate backed by the United States. For the next several years, Balaguer ruled the Dominican Republic as a strongman—he used military force to control the country, and he cared nothing about democratic practices. Still, the United States supported him because he was anticommunist—and in the Cold War, the United States was willing to accept many compromises in order to contain communism.

East-West Intervention in Chile

The United States made no attempt to hide the fact that it was sending troops to the Dominican Republic to contain communism. Likewise, when Soviet tanks rolled into Czechoslovakia in 1968, the whole world knew what had happened. Both superpowers were sending a strong public message: We will not allow our enemies to gain a foothold near our own borders.

But in some countries, the superpowers worked behind the scenes to influence governments and promote their own interests. One such example is Chile, the nearly 3,000-mile-long nation on South America's Pacific coast. During the 1960s and 1970s, Chile became a stage on which the superpowers played out their rivalries.

Unlike many Latin American countries, Chile had a history of democratic government and free elections—the kind of political system that U.S. leaders supported. And yet one Chilean leader troubled American leaders in much the same way that Alexander Dubcek had worried the Soviets.

Salvador Allende (ahl-YEN-day) was a founder of the Socialist Party of Chile. Allende was a Marxist, but he did not advocate violent revolution. He worked within Chile's constitutional system as an elected member of the Chilean parliament. But his policies and his friendship with Fidel Castro made U.S. leaders deeply suspicious.

In 1970, Allende was elected president of Chile in a three-way race in which he won only 36 percent of the vote. The Soviets secretly spent millions of dollars to help him win, and the United States spent millions to aid his opponents. American leaders kept a careful eye on the new Marxist president. They didn't want another Castro in the Western Hemisphere.

Some wondered if the Americans would assist a coup, as they had in the Dominican Republic. President Richard Nixon announced that the United States had no intention of interfering with the results of a free election. Two days after Allende's inauguration, however, Nixon secretly told his top advisors that the U.S. goal was to bring about the Chilean president's downfall.

Allende moved swiftly to change Chile's free market economy to a socialist state. He nationalized — that is, he had the state take control of — the country's foreign-owned copper mines, banks, and other industries. His government also confiscated private property and gave it to landless peasants.

Although Allende was popular among peasants and some urban workers, many wealthy and middle class Chileans disliked him. American companies resented the fact that he had nationalized their businesses in Chile. The United States cut off aid and blocked international loans to Chile. It did, however, continue to supply military equipment to the Chilean military, whose officers were uneasy under Allende's rule.

Meanwhile, the Soviet Union, China, and Cuba were not idle. They issued loans and credits to Allende's government. Cuban soldiers trained Chilean paramilitary units and smuggled weapons into the country for what they imagined would be a civil war.

Fidel Castro himself paid a three-week visit to Chile. He made speeches calling for a complete communist takeover. Castro's speeches alarmed many Chileans, who bought weapons to defend their homes. The country edged toward civil war.

Cuban leader Fidel Castro greets admirers in Santiago, Chile, in 1971 as Chilean President Salvador Allende (right) looks on. Castro paid a three-week visit to Chile, where he encouraged the country to embrace communism.

With U.S. backing, General Augusto Pinochet (center) seized power in Chile in 1973. He instituted a brutal, anticommunist dictatorship.

By 1973, the Chilean economy was in tatters. Food shortages and a 350 percent inflation rate plagued the nation. Thousands of angry women marched to protest the food shortages. The U.S. Central Intelligence Agency (CIA), hoping to bring down Allende's government, helped engineer a truck driver's strike that paralyzed the sprawling nation. The CIA also urged the Chilean military to take action.

On September 11, 1973, the Chilean army surrounded the presidential palace of Salvador Allende with tanks while Chilean air force jets dropped bombs. Allende refused to surrender and died inside the building.

This coup and its aftermath turned into a very bloody affair. Acting on orders from General Augusto Pinochet (pee-noh-CHET or pee-noh-SHAY), the military rounded up tens of thousands of Allende supporters, tortured many, and executed many on the spot. At least 3,200 people died during the violence. Thousands of citizens were driven into exile.

Because of their democratic past, many Chileans expected a relatively short period of military rule. But General Pinochet proved a brutal, repressive leader. For nearly two decades, Chileans lost liberties they had long enjoyed. Pinochet's regime imprisoned, tortured, and murdered thousands whom the dictator regarded as enemies.

The United States had helped turn a democracy into a dictatorship. But it was an anticommunist dictatorship, so for years the United States looked the other way.

What Is Inflation?

Inflation is a term economists use to describe a situation in which the prices of most goods and services rise. During a time of inflation, prices rise faster than people's incomes, so people cannot afford to buy as much as before. For example, if prices of most goods rise 10 percent in a year, but most people's paychecks rise only 5 percent, then they will not be able to buy the same amount of goods as in the year before.

Détente—Easing Tensions

By the early 1970s, the strains of the Cold War weighed on the world's two superpowers. Leaders in the United States and USSR began to look for ways to ease tensions between their two countries. This effort to establish better relations was known as détente (day-TAHNT), a French word meaning "easing" or "relaxation."

The Soviet leader, Leonid Brezhnev, was interested in détente because his nation's economy was suffering from the costs of the Cold War. The race between the superpowers to build up their armies and nuclear arms had proven terribly expensive. Brezhnev saw that the USSR could not afford to build weapons as quickly as the United States. While the USSR was spending, by some estimates, nearly 30 percent of its resources on its military, the United States was spending 8 percent. Brezhnev hoped that better relations would relieve the burden of the arms race and lead to more trade with the West, which would help the Soviet economy.

The American economy, too, had been strained by the arms race and the fighting in Vietnam. President Nixon believed that détente with the Soviets might be a way to reduce military spending and lessen the likelihood of more wars.

As part of détente, the superpowers tried to slow the buildup of nuclear arms. Beginning in 1969, the United States and USSR began negotiations known as the Strategic Arms Limitation Talks, or SALT for short. Three years later, the two sides signed SALT treaties that placed limits on the numbers and kinds of nuclear missiles each country was building. Critics on each side worried that the other side would not stick to its promises. But supporters of détente viewed the SALT treaties as a good step in thawing Cold War tensions.

In 1975, representatives of the two superpowers and several other nations met in Helsinki, Finland, and signed the Helsinki Accords, another agreement aimed at reducing Cold War tensions. In the Helsinki Accords, Brezhnev achieved a long-cherished Soviet goal — Western recognition of the Soviet Union's claim to Eastern Europe. But the West also got something it wanted. The Helsinki Accords included a clause that required nations to honor the principles and freedoms outlined in the Universal Declaration of Human Rights.

Leonid Brezhnev signed the Helsinki Accords knowing full well that the USSR had no intention of respecting human rights behind the Iron Curtain. "We are masters in our own house," his foreign minister assured him. In the following years, Soviet leaders continued to silence and imprison many who dared challenge their authority.

Still, there was something powerful in the fact that the Soviet leader *had* signed an international agreement guaranteeing rights to freedom of thought, speech, and religion. Although such agreements could easily be ignored, millions behind the Iron Curtain took heart from the Helsinki Accords. As you'll read in the next chapter, they saw the document as an admission by Soviet rulers that citizens in communist countries were, after all, entitled to basic human rights that Westerners enjoyed. They took hope that perhaps the tyranny of communist dictatorships would not last forever.

U.S. President Richard Nixon (left) shakes hands with Soviet General Secretary Leonid Brezhnev in Moscow in 1972 after signing the SALT treaty to limit nuclear arms. The treaty was part of détente, an effort to ease Cold War tensions and improve relations between the world's two superpowers.

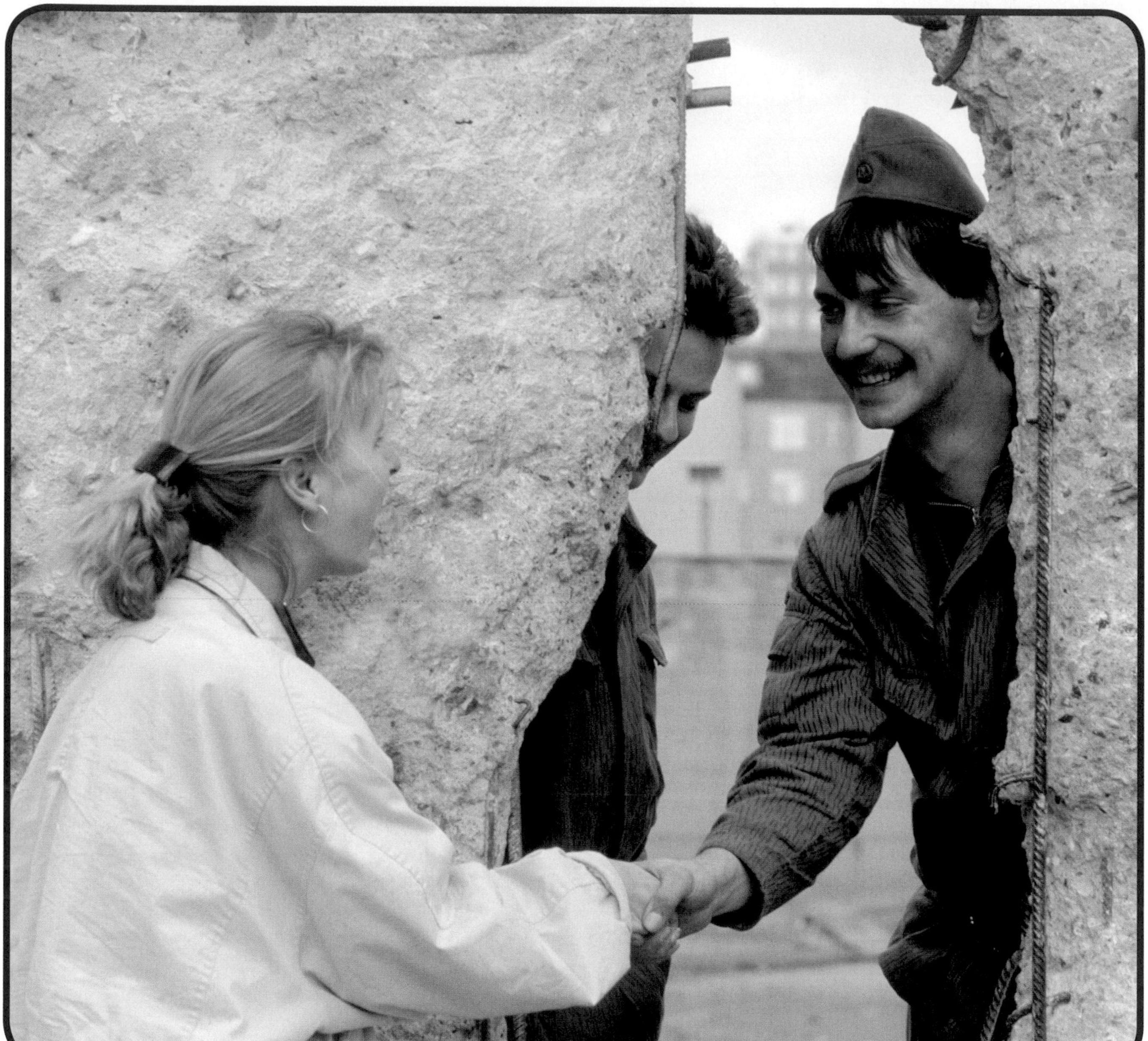

A West German woman and East German soldier shake hands through a gaping hole in the Berlin Wall in 1990—a scene that would have been all but unimaginable just a few years before. After nearly three decades of dividing Berlin into communist and noncommunist parts, the Berlin Wall fell in 1989, an event that symbolized the end of the Cold War.

The Wall Comes Tumbling Down: The End of the Cold War

"A wall is a hell of a lot better than a war." That's what President John F. Kennedy said in 1961 when soldiers rolled out barbwire and erected concrete barriers that trapped East Berliners in their communist-dominated half of the city. While the Berlin Wall might have been the lesser of two evils, it was an evil. Over the next two decades, the Berlin Wall came to symbolize not only the plight of Berliners but also the fate of people living under communist regimes around the globe.

But by the late 1980s, a series of events gave rise to the possibility that such tyranny was about to end. "This wall must fall!" So read a message scrawled on the west side of the Berlin Wall's concrete surface.

This chapter recounts the story of how the Berlin Wall did indeed fall, along with the Soviet Union and its communist empire.

Communism's Failed Promise

Most East Germans lived in modest homes that had few modern conveniences. But many had family members on the other side of the Berlin Wall. East Germans knew that on the other side, large numbers of West Germans were living in comfortable homes, shopping in busy stores, and driving the latest automobiles.

Day by day, it became increasingly clear to people living behind the Iron Curtain that the communist revolution had failed in its promise to improve workers' lives. In Poland, for example, many workers resented that they labored long hours in coal mines and shipyards, but in return received only modest ration cards, which they could use to purchase few consumer goods. In the Soviet Union itself, a huge portion of the Soviet budget went to military spending while most other parts of the economy suffered. In Moscow, as lavish parades showed off the latest missiles, long lines of people waited to buy food and clutched government coupons to buy clothes.

In most communist-controlled nations, far worse than the lack of food or consumer goods was the lack of freedom. Governments in these nations ruled with an iron fist. Secret police hauled people to prison camps on the slightest suspicion of disloyalty. The people enjoyed little freedom of movement—in the Soviet Union and its satellite states, emigration to the West was against the law. Freedom of speech and freedom of the press were distant dreams. A Romanian professor described her nation's government as crushing "people's innermost being, humiliating their aspirations and their legitimate claims, humiliating their conscience, and compelling them under pressure of terror, to accept the lie as truth, and the truth as a lie."

Dissident Voices

Despite all the restrictions, powerful voices of protest emerged inside the Soviet Union during the 1960s and 1970s. The two most prominent dissidents were Alexander Solzhenitsyn (sohl-zhuh-NEET-suhn) and Andrei Sakharov (SAH-kuh-rov).

Russian novelist Alexander Solzhenitsyn wrote books that exposed the brutality of Soviet totalitarianism. In 1974, the USSR expelled him for his outspokenness.

Solzhenitsyn, a gifted novelist, had served in the Soviet army during World War II. Before the war's end, he was arrested for criticizing Stalin in a private letter, and sentenced to eight years in a Siberian labor camp. There he learned all too well the horrors of a Soviet system built on ruthless power. After his release from prison, he began to write books that shocked the world by describing atrocities in the Soviet Union, including torture and slave labor camps.

Solzhenitsyn's first novel, *One Day in the Life of Ivan Denisovich* (1962), chronicled 24 agonizing hours in the life of an inmate at a Stalinist labor camp. Later, in *The Gulag Archipelago* (1973), Solzhenitsyn exposed the Soviet police state in compelling detail. He estimated that during the time of Stalin's rule after World War II, the Soviets held in prison twelve million people per year. The Stalinist state, as Solzhenitsyn described it, was a grinding mill of death: "As some departed beneath the sod," he wrote, "the 'machine' kept bringing in replacements."

Eventually, Soviet authorities exiled Solzhenitsyn for his disloyalty. He lived first in Switzerland, and then in the United States for 18 years. His writings were smuggled into many countries behind the Iron Curtain. There, huddled in secret, people read his works, and told themselves that such a cruel system had to end.

A prominent Soviet physicist, Andrei Sakharov, also fueled unrest. He had helped develop atomic weapons for the Soviet Union, and was known as "the father of the Soviet hydrogen bomb." But he came to believe that the arms race threatened the survival of the planet. After he began campaigning for disarmament and human rights in the communist world, the Soviets ended his career as a physicist and eventually banned his writings. Nevertheless, his essays were smuggled out of the Soviet Union and, like the writings of Solzhenitsyn, they found readers around the world.

In an essay published in the *New York Times* in 1968, Sakharov condemned the Soviet government and its buildup of nuclear arms. He argued for a "democratic, pluralistic society . . . a humanitarian society

A *pluralistic* society is one that welcomes people of different backgrounds, races, ethnic groups, religions, and political views.

The Czech band Plastic People of the Universe earned the enmity of hard-line communists by playing Western-style rock and roll music. The band members insisted that they weren't trying to make a pro-Western statement—they just wanted to play music they liked. But communist officials banned them from playing and even arrested them.

which would care for the Earth and its future." In a letter to Soviet premier Brezhnev, he wrote that "Our society is infected...the Party apparatus of the government and the highest, most successful levels of the intelligentsia...are profoundly indifferent to violations of human rights, the interests of progress, the security and future of mankind."

The *intelligentsia* are the leading intellectuals—such as writers, scholars, and artists—who help shape the culture of a society.

Inspired by the courage of men such as Sakharov and Solzhenitsyn, the drive against communism gained force.

From Détente to Human Rights

By the early 1970s, the United States and the Soviet Union — faced with the possibility of mutual nuclear destruction, and strained by a long military buildup — tried to ease tensions and establish better relations through an effort known as *détente*. In 1975, representatives of the two superpowers and several other nations signed the Helsinki Accords. While those agreements recognized the Soviet Union's control in Eastern Europe, they also contained language that required the signing nations to respect "the universal significance of human rights and fundamental freedoms."

When Leonid Brezhnev signed the Helsinki Accords, he imagined that the human rights clauses would not really apply to people in the Eastern Bloc. But people in those nations seized on the language about freedom in the agreements. Those words pledged to guarantee the very rights that the Soviet Union had long denied. In many Eastern European countries, people began to form "Helsinki Groups," which demanded that the Soviet Union live up to the promises of the Helsinki agreements.

Some reformers behind the Iron Curtain found another cause to rally around — not a signed document, but a rock and roll band. The band, called the Plastic People of the Universe, had formed just after the Soviets invaded Czechoslovakia in 1968. The musicians were young, rebellious, long-haired youths who liked Western-style music and attracted large, rowdy crowds. In 1976, Czech police arrested the band members and hauled them off to jail for "organized disturbance of the peace." The arrests dramatized the lack of freedom in communist regimes — people could not even play the kind of music they liked.

The arrest of the Plastics angered a Czech writer and playwright, Vaclav Havel (VAHT-slahf

HAH-vehl). Havel and fellow writers, artists, and intellectuals soon drafted a manifesto, which they signed on January 1, 1977. The document, called *Charter 77*, insisted that the Czech government honor the rights of free expression spelled out in the Helsinki Accords.

For their challenge to the government, Havel and several others went to prison. But their efforts made the world aware that Soviet-dominated governments were flagrantly violating rights guaranteed in the Helsinki Accords.

In the United States, President Jimmy Carter was sympathetic to the plight of Havel and other dissidents. He repeatedly denounced the Soviet Union for robbing people of basic freedoms. He declared that the United States would not ignore "global questions of justice, equity, and human rights." Such criticisms angered the Soviets and put strains on détente.

The Soviets in Afghanistan

In the late 1970s, détente was threatened by events in Afghanistan, a country bordering the Soviet empire. Communists in Afghanistan, with aid and support from the USSR, launched a coup and took over Afghanistan's government. The new Marxist regime adopted atheism as its official policy and imprisoned many religious leaders. Many Afghan Muslims opposed the communist government's atheistic policies, and they resented the Soviet Union's domination of the new government. Some Afghan Muslims believed that the country's laws should be based on Islamic law. Nationalist Muslim rebels known as *mujahideen* (moo-ja-hih-DEEN) took up arms against the Afghan communists.

In 1979, the leaders of the Soviet Union decided to make sure that communism gained the upper hand in Afghanistan. They dispatched an army to occupy the country and battle the mujahideen.

The war became a nightmare and embarrassment for the powerful Soviet military. The Afghan rebels — supplied with weapons and money from the United States and other nations opposed to

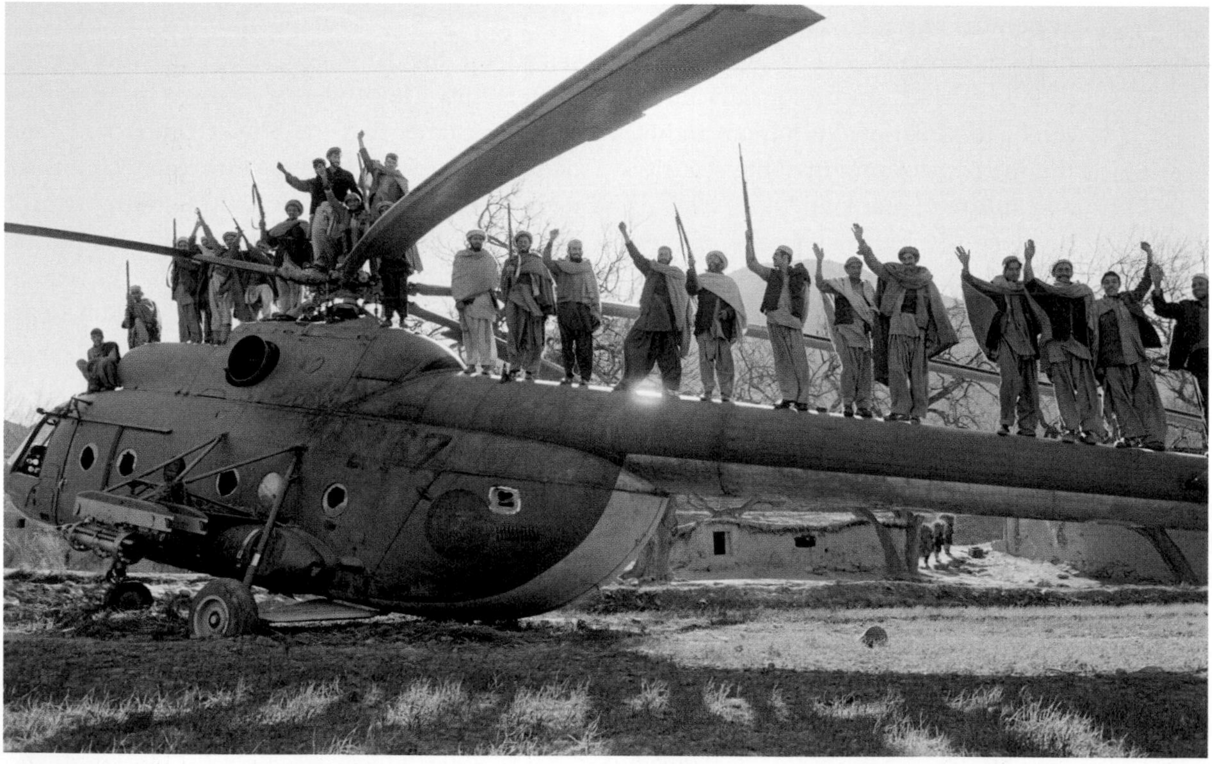

Afghan rebels known as mujahideen stand atop a destroyed Soviet helicopter. The mujahideen spent years fighting a guerrilla war against the Soviet army, which invaded Afghanistan in 1979 to support a communist government. The United States and other Western governments opposed to communism supplied the mujahideen with weapons and aid.

communism — used guerrilla tactics against the Soviet invaders. Striking from hideouts in vast, mountainous regions, they ambushed Soviet troops and bombed Soviet garrisons. The Soviets lost more and more men. People began to refer to the Russian involvement in Afghanistan as the Soviet Union's Vietnam.

President Carter denounced the Soviet invasion of Afghanistan as a glaring violation of human rights. The United States cut back on trade with the Soviet Union and refused to allow U.S. athletes to take part in the 1980 Olympic Games in Moscow. Cold War tensions between the two superpowers increased.

Enter a Polish Pope

In 1978, a new leader joined the Cold War struggle when the Roman Catholic Church chose Karol Jozef Wojtyla (voy-TEE-wah), an archbishop from Poland, to be its pope. Wojtyla was the first non-Italian pope in more than 400 years, and the first Polish pope ever — a fact that would prove important at this key time in the Cold War.

As a young man growing up in Poland, Karol Wojtyla had studied Polish literature and linguistics. A brilliant student with a deep love of language and philosophy, he was also deeply committed to his Catholic faith. He decided to study to become a priest.

During the German occupation of Poland, the Nazis suspected Catholic priests of trying to help Jews escape persecution. The Nazis rounded up priests, executed some, and took others off to concentration camps. So Wojtyla studied for the priesthood in secret, taking a job as a stonecutter in a quarry, where he labored for five years.

After World War II, Wojtyla became a priest and then a bishop. He watched with sorrow as his nation fell under Soviet control. While the Soviets had tried to eliminate all religion in the USSR, they realized they could not do that in Poland, where so many people were devoutly Catholic. Instead the Soviets tried to bring Poland's Catholic Church under communist control. Communist authorities demanded the right to approve the appointments of all bishops in Poland. They also discouraged many religious activities, and often prohibited the building of new churches.

In 1963, when the Vatican in Rome proposed that Wojtyla become archbishop of Krakow, Poland's communist authorities stepped in to take a close look at the candidate. They saw that he was an outgoing man who spoke 12 languages and had published poetry and plays. Nothing that he had said or written gave them reason to think he would cause them much trouble. So the communist officials decided to approve his selection as archbishop. In the years to come, they learned to regret it. As archbishop, Wojtyla urged Poles to hold on to their religious beliefs, and to distrust any regime that tried to take away their freedom to worship.

Wojtyla was 58 years old in 1978 when the Catholic Church chose him to be its new pope. Custom dictated that as pope he must take a new name. He chose the name John Paul II. He stood on the balcony of his new papal apartment at the Vatican and delivered a message of hope in this time of Cold War: "Be not afraid!"

Stirrings of Freedom in Poland

Soon after becoming pope, John Paul expressed his desire to visit his native Poland. Communist Party officials in Poland and the Soviet Union wrestled with a problem. Should they allow him to enter Poland? Soviet officials warned against it. They feared the enthusiasm that the pope's visit might create among the people.

Yet, in this age of détente, Polish officials could see no way to tell the pope that he could not return to his native land. They feared that if they forbid the pope's visit, the Polish people would riot in the streets.

So, instead, Communist Party officials tried to blunt the effects of his visit. For example, they issued a secret directive to schoolteachers. It declared that "the pope is our enemy. He is dangerous...because he charms everyone...shakes all hands, kisses children...." Worried that the pope's visit would increase interest in religion, communist officials declared that "our activities designed to atheize the youth not only cannot diminish but must intensely develop."

The communists' strategy did not work. On his arrival in Warsaw in June 1979, the pope knelt and kissed the ground. People lined the

An Attempt on the Pope's Life

In 1981, a Turkish gunman shot John Paul II as his vehicle entered St. Peter's Square in the Vatican in Rome. Though seriously wounded, the pope survived. In 1996, an investigation ordered by the Italian parliament concluded that the Soviet Union had organized the attempted assassination in order to stop the pope's efforts to bring greater freedom to Eastern Europe. Soviet officials denied any involvement in the shooting.

streets and highways outside the city. Inside Warsaw, hundreds of thousands cheered and threw flowers.

In Victory Square in downtown Warsaw—often the scene of army parades and pro-communist rallies organized by the government—the pope addressed a huge gathering of fellow Poles while Communist Party officials stared from nearby windows. John Paul told his countrymen that God had given them the right to worship. The crowd answered with a thunderous eruption of applause, along with chants of "We want God!" Clearly, the Polish people wanted the same freedom to practice their faith that so many in the West enjoyed.

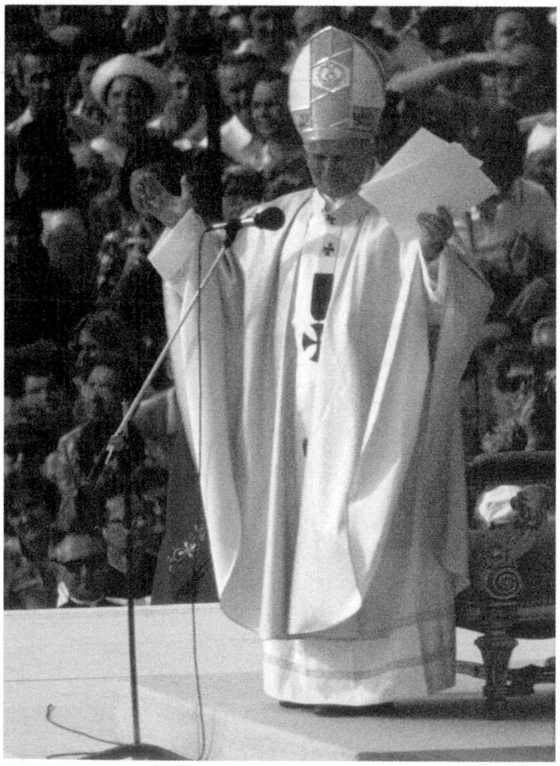

Pope John Paul II addresses fellow Poles at Victory Square in Warsaw, Poland, in 1979. The pope's message of freedom and faith shook Poland's communist regime.

Communist Party officials looked on in chagrin. Although the pope had not directly challenged their authority, throughout his nine-day visit he had firmly insisted that communism should not take away people's basic rights, including the freedom to worship. The pope's message of freedom inspired millions living behind the Iron Curtain.

Solidarity Against Communism in Poland

A year after Pope John Paul II's visit to his homeland, another event shook Poland's communist regime. In the summer of 1980, the government announced that it was raising the price of meat by as much as 100 percent. Across the country, angry workers went on strike to protest the increase. At the Lenin Shipyard in the port city of Gdansk (guh-DAHNSK), workers joined the strike, and then went one step further. A young unemployed electrician named Lech Walesa (lehk va-WEN-suh) stood outside the locked gates of the shipyard, flanked by many supporters carrying photos of the pope, and announced the formation of a trade union. They called it Solidarity.

Solidarity was the first self-governing union to take root in the Soviet empire. The significance was monumental—a worker's union had formed in opposition to the government of what was supposed to be a worker's state. The very existence of Solidarity was a slap in the face of communist regimes that claimed to rule on behalf of workers.

Solidarity presented the Polish government with demands for increased pay and better working conditions. It also called for political changes, such as greater freedom of worship and an end to censorship. The union began to attract attention and enlist new members, eventually signing up ten million members. As it grew, Solidarity evolved from a trade union into a home

Cheering shipyard workers at Gdansk, Poland, carry Lech Walesa, leader of the trade union Solidarity. The 1980 founding of the workers' union was yet another blow to the communist system, which claimed to be run by and for the workers.

for all of those who hated Poland's communist regime. Lech Walesa emerged as the spokesman for a nation of Poles eager for freedom.

As Soviet officials in Moscow watched these developments, they wondered if they had another Prague Spring on their hands. They considered sending troops into Poland, as they had done in Czechoslovakia in 1968, but decided to wait and see. When Solidarity demanded a national vote on the future of the Communist Party in Poland, the Polish government cracked down and proclaimed martial law. Solidarity was banned. Lech Walesa and thousands of others were arrested.

While Poland's communist government could throw people into jail, it could do nothing to change the minds of millions of Poles sick of Soviet domination and desperate for freedom. "This is the moment of your defeat," Walesa told the officials who arrested him. "You just hammered the last nails into the coffin of communism."

Reagan Takes Aim at an "Evil Empire"

In 1980, less than two months after Lech Walesa and other Polish workers founded the Solidarity trade union, voters in the United States elected a new president. By the time he reached the White House, Ronald Wilson Reagan had enjoyed a long and varied career. He had been a movie and television actor and, for a time, president of the Screen Actors Guild in Hollywood. Eventually he entered politics and became a firm anticommunist. His skill as a public speaker helped him win two terms as governor of California. When he was inaugurated as the nation's 40th president, Reagan was nearly 70 years old, the oldest man ever elected to the office. He was determined to change the way the United States engaged in the Cold War.

Reagan did not disappoint those who had applauded his speeches against Soviet aggression. He thought the policy of détente had failed in many ways. In his view, détente had done nothing to halt the nuclear arms race, and it had allowed communism to grow. Reagan made it clear that he would do more to prevent the spread of communism, and that he would build up the military strength of the United States. He confided to an advisor, "My idea of American policy toward the Soviet Union is simple. It is this: We win and they lose."

In an address to the British Parliament in 1982, Reagan declared that the Soviet Union could not survive because its totalitarian

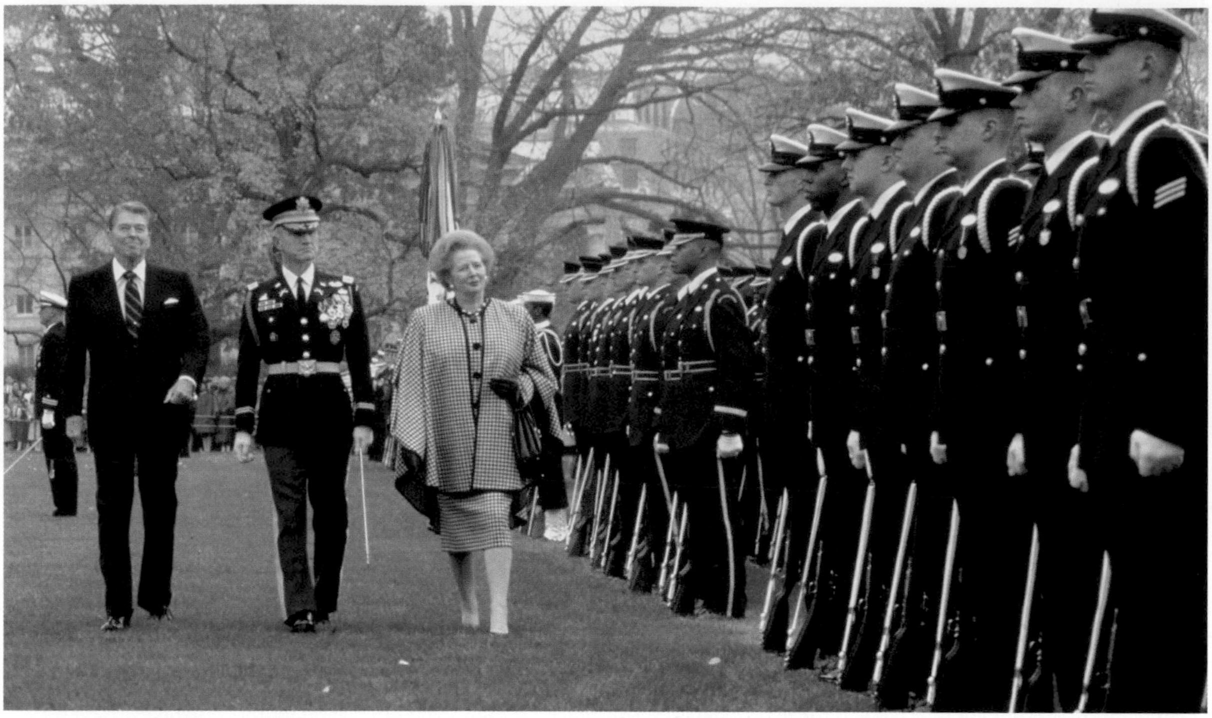

U.S. President Ronald Reagan (left) and British Prime Minister Margaret Thatcher review an honor guard on the White House lawn in Washington, D.C., in 1988. The two leaders became fast friends during the Cold War. Both viewed the Soviet Union as a corrupt, repressive regime, and believed that the West must take a firm stand against totalitarianism.

Margaret Thatcher, the "Iron Lady"

In 1979, Great Britain elected its first female prime minister. Margaret Thatcher, like Ronald Reagan, was a tough critic of the Soviet Union. "The Russians are bent on world dominance," she believed. A no-nonsense leader, she thought Europeans should take a firmer stance against the spread of totalitarianism. Thatcher viewed détente as a ruse or trick used by the Soviets to exploit Western weakness. When the Soviet press called her the "Iron Lady" for her unbending opposition to communism, Thatcher gladly embraced the label.

Reagan and Thatcher became strong allies who worked closely during the final years of the Cold War. When Reagan introduced his Strategic Defense Initiative plan for a missile defense shield, Thatcher stood firmly at his side.

government was crushing its own people's spirit by robbing them of their basic rights and freedoms. Moreover, said Reagan, the Soviet's government-planned economy was such a failure that the country could not even feed its own people. "The march of freedom and democracy . . . will leave Marxism-Leninism on the ash heap of history," Reagan predicted.

Such talk alarmed Soviet authorities. Several months later, speaking in Florida, Reagan went further. He described the Cold War as a battle between good and evil, freedom and tyranny, truth and lies. On one side, said the president, stood the United States, representing democracy and freedom. On the other side stood the Soviet Union, representing totalitarianism and tyranny. The Soviet Union, said Reagan, was nothing less than an "evil empire."

Reagan followed such talk by proposing a new system to help the United States defend itself and its allies from a missile attack. Rejecting the theory of Mutual Assured Destruction, Reagan instead proposed the Strategic Defense Initiative (SDI). As Reagan described it, SDI would eventually allow the United States to use lasers and other new technologies to create a defensive shield to destroy incoming missiles. He offered to share SDI technology, once it was developed, with other countries — including the Soviet Union — so that all nations could be safe from nuclear attack.

Critics called SDI "Star Wars" — the whole idea, they said, was, like the popular movie, science fiction fantasy. They charged that trying to build a missile defense shield would only heighten Cold War tensions. Soviet leaders pointed out that building SDI would violate certain treaties. And despite Reagan's promises, Soviet leaders did not believe the United States would really share such technology. Still the president pushed ahead with SDI research.

Gorbachev Takes a New Soviet Path

In 1985, a new and younger leader, Mikhail Gorbachev (mih-kah-EEL gawr-buh-CHAWF), took the helm in the Soviet Union. Born in 1931, Gorbachev rose from the obscurity of a peasant family to become General Secretary, the head of the Communist Party. Along the way, he built a reputation for being an energetic, quick-witted idealist, and an enemy of corruption and inefficiency. He was the opposite of the aging, business-as-usual men who had led the Soviet Union since the death of Khrushchev.

Unlike Brezhnev, Gorbachev recognized a simple fact — the clumsy, government-controlled Soviet economy was in shambles. By the late 1980s, the Soviet economy was efficient only in producing weapons. And even in military technology, the Soviets were falling behind the United States. Worse, the ongoing war in Afghanistan continued to drain resources. The new General Secretary realized that his country must either reform or collapse.

Gorbachev advocated changes to make the Soviet system work more efficiently. He called for *perestroika* (pehr-uh-STROY-kuh), a Russian word that means "restructuring." He wanted to restructure the Soviet economy so that the Communist Party would have less power over production decisions. Under perestroika, for example, officials in local factories, rather than bureaucrats in Moscow, would have more power to run their own affairs.

Even bolder than perestroika was Gorbachev's call for *glasnost* (GLAZ-nohst), a Russian term that means "openness, candor, transparency." In Gorbachev's view, Soviet citizens should be allowed to speak more openly about their society's problems. He believed that the government needed to stop trying to control ideas and speech. He called for an end to such practices as banning books, jamming foreign radio broadcasts, and throwing dissidents into prison.

The policies of perestroika and glasnost led to drastic changes in a country where, for seven decades, Communist Party rulers had kept a tight grip on almost every aspect of people's lives. The Soviet Union did not transform overnight — people still enjoyed only limited freedoms. But as Gorbachev's reforms rippled through the Soviet Union, people who lived in Soviet satellite states took notice. Dissidents in Eastern European nations increased their demands for more freedom from Communist Party rule.

Reform-minded Soviet leader Mikhail Gorbachev—his famous birthmark clearly showing on his forehead—waves to crowds.

In 1986, Reagan and Gorbachev held a summit in Reykjavik, Iceland. Their meeting ended without an agreement, but they realized they shared a vision of abolishing nuclear arms.

Looking Over the Horizon

When Gorbachev took office in 1985, more than forty years had passed since the United States dropped two atomic bombs to end World War II. The arms race following the war made the world a far more dangerous place. Both superpowers agreed that a nuclear war could not be won and should never be fought. Both sides wanted to put an end to the massive buildup of nuclear arsenals. But Gorbachev had an extra incentive — the arms race was bankrupting his country. Reagan knew the Soviet leader's plight.

A *summit* is a meeting between the top leaders of nations.

In 1986, Reagan and Gorbachev held a summit at Reykjavik, Iceland. Gorbachev was desperate to cut back his nation's military spending. He offered to make major weapons cutbacks if the United States would do the same. Reagan responded with a breathtaking proposal — that both sides eliminate *all* nuclear weapons in ten years. It was a possibility hardly to be dreamed of — perhaps a chance to end the arms race.

Gorbachev countered by requiring one condition — Reagan must give up his Strategic Defense Initiative. In the Soviets' view, SDI was part of the arms race, and it must halt. The Soviets also worried that if the United States developed a system to protect itself from nuclear attack, it would have the upper hand in any confrontation.

Reagan was unwilling to give up SDI. He was determined to make sure the United States could defend itself against missile attack. Besides, he knew the USSR was in a race it could not afford.

The two leaders left Reykjavik without an agreement, but they had looked each other in the eye and realized they shared a vision of abolishing nuclear arms. "Reykjavik is not a failure," Gorbachev said. "It is a breakthrough which for the first time enabled us to look over the horizon."

Reagan believed that Gorbachev sincerely wanted to reform the Soviet Union. But the American president also realized that, despite perestroika and glasnost, the Soviet Union continued to deny basic human rights to millions. In June 1987, Reagan decided to issue a public challenge to his Soviet counterpart. He traveled to West Berlin, a city surrounded by the communist dictatorship of East Germany. Standing near the hated Berlin Wall, the president gave a speech that was broadcast across Western Europe. "General Secretary Gorbachev," said Reagan, "if you seek peace, if you seek prosperity for the Soviet Union and Eastern Europe, if you seek liberalization: Come here to this gate! Mr. Gorbachev, open this gate! Mr. Gorbachev, tear down this wall!"

Reagan knew that his words would be heard on the east side of the Berlin Wall. He was speaking not just to Mikhail Gorbachev but to the millions of people trapped in the Soviet system. Despite Soviet oppression, these people knew that, since World War II, democracy had made advances in much of the world. From the Helsinki Accords, to the words of Pope John Paul II, to the Solidarity movement and perestroika, there were signs of change that inspired hope in those living under communist rule. In his speech at the Berlin Wall, President Reagan was sending an encouraging message to those longing for freedom, a message affirming that the United States was on their side.

"Mr. Gorbachev, tear down this wall!"

In June 1987, President Ronald Reagan traveled to West Berlin to take part in the city's 750th anniversary. In a speech at the Brandenburg Gate, Reagan offered a direct challenge to Soviet leader Mikhail Gorbachev. Reagan knew that his words would reach millions behind the Berlin Wall and Iron Curtain.

A Page from the Past

Twenty-four years ago, President John F. Kennedy visited Berlin, speaking to the people of this city and the world at the City Hall. Well, since then two other presidents have come, each in his turn, to Berlin. And today I, myself, make my second visit to your city. We come to Berlin, we American presidents, because it's our duty to speak, in this place, of freedom....

Behind me stands a wall that encircles the free sectors of this city, part of a vast system of barriers that divides the entire continent of Europe.... Standing before the Brandenburg Gate, every man is a German, separated from his fellow men. Every man is a Berliner, forced to look upon a scar....

We hear much from Moscow about a new policy of reform and openness. Some political prisoners have been released. Certain foreign news broadcasts are no longer being jammed. Some economic enterprises have been permitted to operate with greater freedom from state control.

Are these the beginnings of profound changes in the Soviet state? Or are they token gestures, intended to raise false hopes in the West, or to strengthen the Soviet system without changing it? We welcome change and openness; for we believe that freedom and security go together, that the advance of human liberty can only strengthen the cause of world peace. There is one sign the Soviets can make that would be unmistakable, that would advance dramatically the cause of freedom and peace.

General Secretary Gorbachev, if you seek peace, if you seek prosperity for the Soviet Union and Eastern Europe, if you seek liberalization: Come here to this gate! Mr. Gorbachev, open this gate! Mr. Gorbachev, tear down this wall!

The Soviets Signal Change

Gorbachev did not tear down the Berlin Wall. But he continued on the path of reform, and he kept talking with Reagan.

In his drive to reform his country, Gorbachev was not looking to overthrow the Soviet regime or attack socialism. He hoped to re-energize the system, to make it more effective in a modern setting. He realized that it was becoming impossible for Moscow to maintain control over so many millions of unwilling people. Gorbachev also recognized that totalitarian regimes robbed their subjects of basic human dignity. He wanted, he later said, to change the Soviet regime "so a human being can feel normal, can feel good, in a socialist state. So that he will feel above all like a human being."

In late 1987, Gorbachev and Reagan signed an important treaty. For the first time during the arms race, Americans and Soviets agreed to eliminate a whole class of weapons. The Intermediate-Range Nuclear Forces (INF) Treaty eliminated ground-launched missiles with ranges of 300 to 3,400 miles.

A year later, Gorbachev went further — much further. In December 1988, he addressed the United Nations General Assembly and delivered a stunning announcement. The Soviet Union had decided to cut its troops in Eastern Europe by a half-million men. While the move would loosen the Soviet grip on its satellite states, it would also bring economic relief because, as Gorbachev saw it, the USSR was being drained by its domination of Eastern Europe.

Out of Afghanistan

In 1988, the Soviet Union decided to give up its decade-long fight in Afghanistan. Islamic rebels, the mujahideen, had waged a successful guerrilla war against the communist superpower. The USSR decided it could no longer afford the war, which had become increasingly unpopular among the Soviet people.

In his address to the United Nations, Gorbachev came close to telling the communist nations that they could make their own decisions regarding their future governments. It was an astonishing historical moment. Reflecting on the history of nations engaging in endless wars, Gorbachev looked to a new day ahead — the emergence of a "mutually connected" world community. He spoke of the right of all people to choose their governments. He talked about the great changes in his own country, a "revolutionary upsurge" toward democratic principles in all areas of life.

After this extraordinary speech, people wondered: Is Gorbachev serious? Can this enormous change in Soviet policy actually be happening? What will happen if the people of a communist-controlled nation begin to tear down their repressive governments?

Hungary Tests the USSR

The first country to test Gorbachev's spirit of openness was Hungary, a nation with a long history of confrontation with the Soviets. In 1956, when Hungarians had marched in the streets of their cities to demand more freedom, the Soviets had responded by sending tanks to crush the rebellion. Now, in January 1989, Hungary's parliament voted to allow independent political parties. Such a change would bring an end to the Communist Party's lock on power. This time, the Soviet response was very different. No tanks appeared. Instead, Soviet troops began to leave the country.

Next the Hungarians did something that, just a few short years before, Moscow would never have allowed. They held a memorial service for the 20,000 people who had lost their lives in the 1956 uprising against the Soviets. They reburied the Hungarian premier who had led that uprising, and whom the Soviets had executed. Two hundred thousand Hungarians attended the overdue funeral. It was a stirring reminder of the pain and suffering endured by the people of Hungary for more than three decades.

The Hungarians proceeded to write a new constitution allowing free elections. They also opened their border with Austria. Suddenly a new way was open to the West and the free world. Thousands of East Germans began traveling to Hungary, then crossed the border into Austria, and from there made their way to West Germany.

This was no mere trickle of people—it was, almost immediately, a stampede through a widening rip in the Iron Curtain.

The Wall Comes Down

In October 1989, thousands of East Germans in the city of Leipzig marched for reform. Protestors shouted at the once-feared East German state police, who stood tensely in their gray-and-blue jackets and stared back, unsure how to react. In other parts of East Germany, dissidents spoke openly of ending communist rule. On both sides of the Iron Curtain, people waited, anxiously wondering whether communist authorities would lash back and try to reassert their power. What followed was a misunderstanding that triggered one of the most significant events of the twentieth century.

On November 9, 1989, the East German government decided to try to relieve tensions by relaxing travel restrictions to the West. At a late afternoon press conference, an official read a hastily written decree announcing the changes. When surprised reporters asked when the new rules were to take effect, the spokesman, who didn't really know, stammered, "immediately." When asked if the new rules applied to travel to West Berlin, the official shrugged, looked through his papers, and replied that "permanent exit can take place via all border crossings." Before almost anyone knew what was happening, word spread that the Berlin Wall was open, even though it was not.

Throngs of East Berliners rushed to the Berlin Wall. Unsuspecting border guards, bewildered by the turn of events and the huge crowd, opened the gates.

Soon thousands of East Berliners stood on the west side of the wall, many for the first time in their lives. West Berliners rushed to embrace them in delirious celebration. People grabbed picks, chisels, and hammers, and began to knock away small pieces of the wall. East German officials realized that there was no turning back. In a matter of days, bulldozers were dismantling the hated symbol of totalitarian oppression.

Around the world, people watched dramatic televised reports from Berlin. Thousands of Europeans flocked to the city to see the wall come down. Thousands reunited with once-trapped friends and relatives. Some handed out flowers to those who were crossing from East Germany. A British student in Berlin later recalled, "I remember one woman, crying her eyes out and hugging us all, saying something in German. When our German teacher translated, we understood why she was crying. Her son had been killed trying to escape East Germany just a year previously."

And suddenly, the wall was gone. No more guards with their dogs and machine guns. No more barbwire. No more forced separation from loved ones. No more degrading feeling of being trapped. It was all over.

Totalitarianism in East Germany crumbled along with the wall. On March 18, 1990, East Germans voted the Communists out of office. Soviet troops began to depart. The Cold War was over.

Berliners line up to pass through the newly opened Berlin Wall. The wall, built by communists in 1961 to keep East Germans from escaping to the West, finally opened in 1989.

Austrian and Czech officials cut the "Iron Curtain" between their countries in 1989 at the Cold War's end.

The Fall of Communism in Eastern Europe

The fall of the Berlin Wall was the single most dramatic symbol of the end of the Cold War. But it was only one in a series of remarkable events that swept the Soviet empire. Anticommunist revolutions, mostly peaceful, broke out across Eastern Europe. It was as if all the pent-up Cold War tensions had been released in a frenzy of change, driving out dictatorships and opening up a new world.

- In 1989, Bulgaria's Communist Party leader resigned, and the country headed toward free elections.
- That same year, the communist government in Czechoslovakia gave up power in a peaceful transition. Vaclav Havel, the playwright who had gone to prison for demanding free

Demonstrators in Bucharest, Romania, burn the flag of the Romanian Communist Party, which for years had run the country as a corrupt and repressive police state that kept strict control over citizens' lives. In 1989, Romanians overthrew the country's communist dictator and began the work of building a democratic government.

expression, became the country's democratically elected president.

- In Romania, crowds stormed government buildings and overthrew the communist regime.
- In Poland, the communist government fell. In 1990, Lech Walesa, the electrician who had founded the Solidarity movement, became president.
- Also in 1990, East Germany and West Germany reunited under democratic rule into a single country, the Federal Republic of Germany, with a unified Berlin as its capital.
- By late summer 1991, Lithuania, Estonia, and Latvia were completely independent of the Soviet Union.

Since the end of World War II, for nearly a half a century, the Soviet Union had dominated the eastern part of Europe. But less than two years after the fall of the Berlin Wall, the Eastern Bloc was gone.

The USSR Dissolves

In most of the countries that Moscow had once dominated, Mikhail Gorbachev gained immense popularity. But in the Soviet Union itself, many viewed Gorbachev as a failure. Perestroika, his attempt at economic reform, had not created prosperity. On the contrary, the Soviet economy was in ruins as the Soviet empire fell apart.

In 1990, when Gorbachev attended the annual May Day parade in Red Square in Moscow, some in the crowd jeered and heckled him — something no Soviet citizen would have dared to do in years past. Banners read "Down with Gorbachev!" and "Down with Lenin's Party!" The Russians were exercising their new freedoms of speech.

The next year, Gorbachev's political opponents staged a coup and placed him under house arrest. He was released after three days, but he had lost much of his power. Moscow was dominated by a new figure, Boris Yeltsin, president of the state of Russia. And Yeltsin had his own goals—to abolish the Communist Party, dissolve the Soviet Union, and turn Russia into an independent, capitalist state.

By the end of the year, the Soviet Union was indeed dissolving. Regions such as Ukraine, Georgia, Armenia, and Kazakhstan broke away to become new republics, free to form their own governments.

On Christmas Day 1991, 74 years after the Russian Revolution brought communism to the world stage, Mikhail Gorbachev signed the decree that officially brought an end to the Union of Soviet Socialist Republics. In his farewell address, the last leader of the Soviet Union said, "An end has been put to the 'Cold War,' the arms race, and insane militarization of our country, which crippled our economy, distorted our thinking and undermined our morals. The threat of a world war is no more."

The statue of Vladimir Ilyich Lenin, founder of the Soviet Union, is toppled in Vilnius, Lithuania, in 1991. Lithuania had been an unwilling part of the Soviet empire.

A Moment of Hope

The year 1989, when the Berlin Wall fell, has taken its place as a landmark date for liberty, alongside 1689 (the year of the English Bill of Rights), 1776 (the American Declaration of Independence), and 1789 (the French Declaration of the Rights of Man and of the Citizen).

For nearly half a century, the two superpowers had maneuvered against each other, using the threat of terrible destruction to keep each other at bay. The Cold War could have turned into World War III and nuclear apocalypse. Instead, after four decades of confrontation that threatened global disaster, the arc of history curved toward freedom and peace. The United States and former Soviet states dismantled many of their nuclear missiles. For the first time in many years, the world did not have to live in the shadow of two nuclear superpowers taking aim at each other, ready to fire at a moment's notice.

But the nuclear threat remained. More countries than ever possessed nuclear weapons. And with the disintegration of the Soviet Union, there was the possibility that some of its missiles might fall into the hands of individuals or governments that would use them recklessly. In that sense, the end of the Cold War made the world a *more* dangerous place.

As nations emerged from the totalitarian rule of communist regimes, they began to experiment with democracy. Many people wondered if these experiments would succeed. Would these nations become stable democracies with prosperous economies? Or would they descend into chaos and poverty, with different factions fighting for control of their governments?

Some people worried about what kind of place the world would become now that it had only *one* military and economic superpower. With its chief rival gone, how would the United States act?

Despite those questions, the end of the Cold War brought a sigh of relief and a moment of hope to people around the globe. The world had survived the threat of Mutual Assured Destruction. And there was at least

Russians in Moscow shout their joy at the changes sweeping the Soviet Union in the summer of 1991. By the end of the year, the Union of Soviet Socialist Republics was no more. The fall of the communist empire left many problems to be resolved, but for those who had lived for so long under the totalitarian regime, it was a moment of high hope.

a chance that millions could enjoy more freedom and better lives.

More than a decade after his triumphant visit to Poland, Pope John Paul II reflected on the Cold War's outcome. "Warsaw, Moscow, Budapest, Berlin, Prague, Sofia, and Bucharest have become stages in a long pilgrimage toward liberty," he said. "It is admirable that in these events, entire peoples spoke out — women, young people, men, overcoming fears; their irrepressible thirst for liberty speeded up developments, made walls tumble down and opened gates."

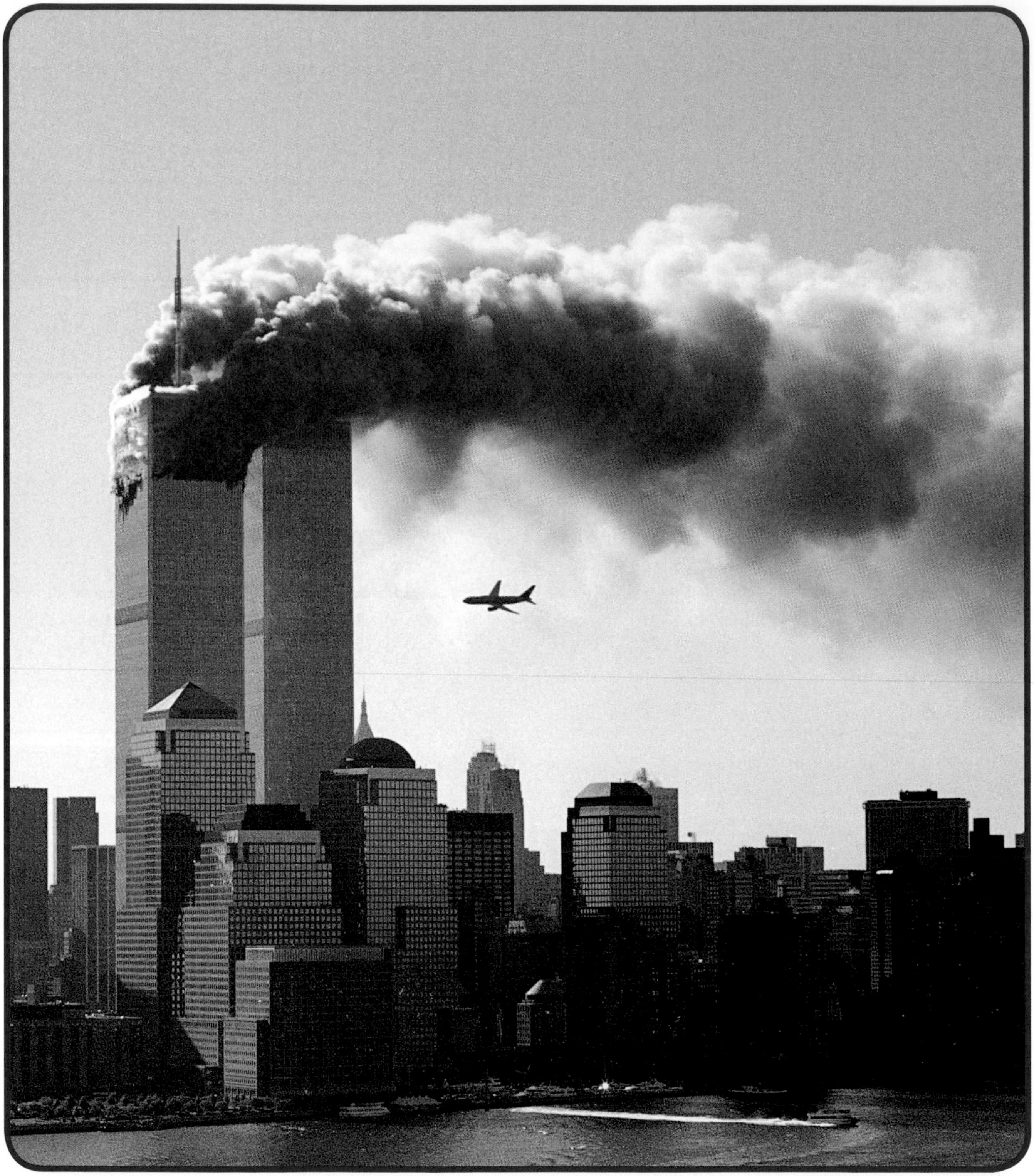

On September 11, 2001, nineteen Islamic extremists hijacked four jets in order to crash them into high-profile targets in the United States. One plane struck the north tower of the World Trade Center in New York City (above, with billowing smoke). A second plane (seen above) struck the south tower. Both towers collapsed, killing more than 2,700 people.

Terrorism: The New Threat

The end of the Cold War and fall of the Berlin Wall brought hopes for a more peaceful, prosperous world. The United States—the sole remaining superpower—rode toward the end of the twentieth century on a wave of economic growth, which in turn helped fuel economic growth around the world.

Of course, in many places, people still faced enormous challenges. In states once dominated by the Soviet Union, bitter struggles broke out between different ethnic groups. In the Middle East, violence continued between Arabs and Israelis, and between Arabs and Arabs. Famine and civil war plagued parts of Africa.

Still, in much of the world the mood was one of optimism. Some statesmen talked of a "peace dividend" — now that the Cold War was over, they hoped that money once spent on armies and missiles could be invested in schools, roads, and public health. Some journalists even described the new post–Cold War period as a "holiday from history."

A little more than a year into the twenty-first century, that illusion was shattered. On September 11, 2001, nineteen radical Islamists hijacked four passenger airliners departing Boston, New York, and Washington, D.C. They flew two of the planes into the twin skyscrapers of the World Trade Center in New York City, destroying the structures and killing more than 2,700 people. Another plane sliced into the side of the Pentagon, the headquarters of the U.S. military just outside Washington, D.C. The fourth plane was also headed toward Washington but crashed in a field in Pennsylvania, killing all on board.

The attack on the United States shocked many in the Western world into realizing that they faced an increasingly ominous and deadly threat — terrorism.

Terror: An Old Tactic in a Modern World

Terrorism is the planned use of violence to strike fear into people or governments in order to obtain political goals. It is a cruel, merciless tactic. Terrorists often choose innocent people to be the victims of their attacks. For example, they may set off bombs in crowded markets, hoping to kill and wound as many people as they can.

Terrorists use such methods because they want the horror of their attacks to draw attention to their cause. They also want people in the societies they are attacking to live in fear. They believe that if they can spread enough terror, their opponents will give in to their demands.

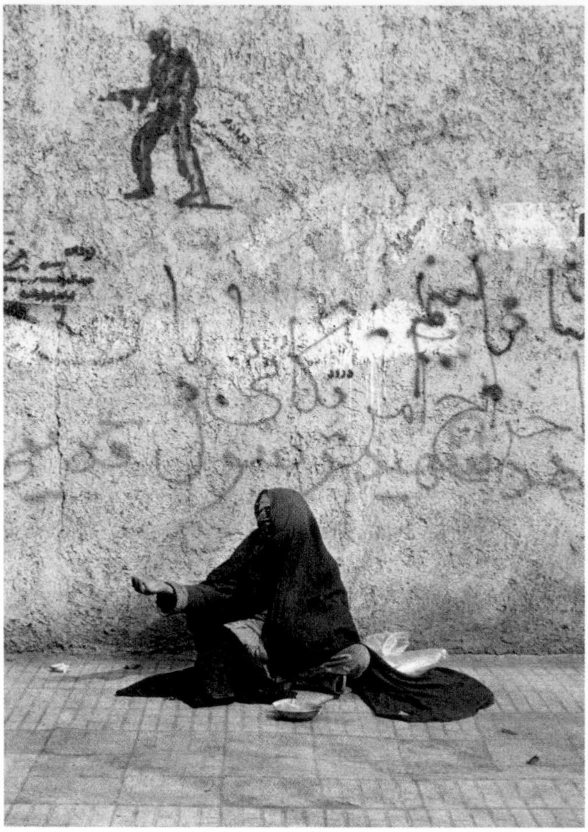

A woman begs in Tehran, Iran. Widespread poverty is one problem that has caused bitterness in the Middle East.

The systematic use of terror to obtain political goals is not new in human history. The ancient Romans used it to discourage rebellion in their empire. They publicly crucified those who tried to incite revolt. During the French Revolution, Robespierre led a "Reign of Terror." Under his leadership, French revolutionaries in the 1790s used the guillotine to kill tens of thousands they considered "enemies of the revolution." The word "terrorism" was even coined during the French Revolution. In the 1930s and 1940s, Germany's Nazis imprisoned, tortured, and executed people by the millions to create a climate of fear and maintain control. Stalin and other Soviet leaders used labor camps in the USSR for the same purpose.

After World War II, a growing number of political movements used terror to obtain their goals. For example, members of a group known as the Irish Republican Army used sniper attacks, bombings, and assassinations to fight against British control of Northern Ireland. In an area of northern Spain inhabited by a people called the Basques (basks), a separatist group has used bombings, sniper attacks, and kidnappings in their quest for Basque independence. Taking advantage of technological innovations such as automatic weapons and miniature explosive devices, these terrorist groups became a growing threat in parts of Europe, Asia, and Latin America.

In the Middle East, terrorism became increasingly common in the 1970s. For example, members of the Palestine Liberation Organization hijacked airlines, attacked buses and cars, and took hostages in an effort to undermine Israel and call attention to the plight of the Palestinian people. You've learned that a Palestinian terrorist group called Black September killed 11 Israeli Olympic team members at the 1972 Olympics in Munich. After the attack, Black September spokesmen declared that "a bomb in the White House…could not have echoed through the consciousness of every man in the world like the operation at Munich."

Deep-Rooted Problems in the Middle East

During the 1970s, a new kind of terrorism began to emerge, one based in the Middle East and rooted in militant Islamism. It was new because it crossed not just national boundaries but also oceans and continents. It emerged in part as a response to deep-rooted problems in the mainly Muslim nations of the Middle East.

By the last decades of the twentieth century, some Muslims felt bitter and angry over the state of affairs in the Middle East. Looking back on their past, they could see a long decline of Islamic civilization from its former greatness. Centuries earlier, Islamic empires had dominated vast portions of northern Africa, Asia, and Europe. Cities such as Baghdad, Damascus, and Cairo stood as unrivaled centers of art and learning. But by the late seventeenth century, the once-glorious Islamic empires were in decline. During the next two hundred years, the industrialized nations of the West surpassed Muslim nations in scientific and technological achievements. Citizens in Western nations enjoyed higher average incomes and generally better standards of living. In the late nineteenth and early twentieth centuries,

European nations used their strength to colonize and rule parts of the old Islamic empires.

By the mid-twentieth century, most Muslim lands in the Middle East had managed to throw off European rule, but they did not achieve their dream of pan-Arabism — the idea that Arab states should act with unity to regain their former stature. Although some Middle Eastern nations grew wealthy from oil, the wealth stayed in the hands of a few. Some Arab states tried to use socialism to improve the welfare of all citizens, but their efforts largely failed. In Islamic lands across much of the Middle East, millions lived in poverty under repressive regimes, with little hope for a better future.

Militant Islamists Blame the West

As you know, during the early twentieth century some Muslims in the Middle East embraced Islamism, the conviction that Islamic teaching and Islamic law — *Shari'ah* — should guide all parts of society, from government to people's daily lives. Islamists came to believe that Middle Eastern nations were in decline because they had failed to follow such teaching and law. Islamists largely blamed this failure on a foreign influence that they believed had contaminated the Islamic world — the West.

It was, after all, the example of modern Western nations that had persuaded leaders such as Ataturk in Turkey to separate church and state. In the twentieth century, Turkey, Egypt, and Iran all adopted constitutions that placed secular leaders in power. In these mostly Muslim nations, Islamic law was not the law of the land.

Islamists had long been bitter toward Britain and other European nations for colonizing the Middle East and stripping the region of valuable resources. In the view of many Islamists, European imperialism had kept Muslim lands from developing into strong, prosperous nations.

In the 1950s, many Islamists began to focus their hatred on the new superpower — the United States. They accused the U.S. government of meddling in Arab affairs, supporting the Jewish state of Israel, trying to control oil supplies, and aiding tyrannical regimes (as in Iran) friendly to American interests.

Increasingly, these Islamists saw Western culture, including American popular culture, as a source of evil. They condemned what they perceived as signs of shamelessly sinful activities — American rock and roll music, American advertisements that showed scantily dressed women, or "decadent" Hollywood movies and television shows.

Many Islamists blamed such influences for corrupting Middle Eastern rulers and businessmen who, although they were Muslims, had adopted tastes and ideas of the West. This small group lived well and liked to show off their riches. They were often educated in secular universities. They wore American and European-style clothing. They owned modern conveniences and luxuries associated with Western nations, such as televisions, flashy cars, stereo systems, and huge yachts. In this mostly upper- class group, more and more women were being educated at universities. Many abandoned wearing the veil and instead preferred "international dress," as Ataturk had called it.

Some Islamists resolved to rid their nations of what they saw as Western contamination. The only hope, they said, was to overthrow secular regimes in Muslim lands and replace them with true Islamic regimes, even if it took violence to reach that goal. These "militant Islamists," as they have come to be known, began to gain followers in parts of the Middle East. Their first major coup was in Iran.

The Iranian Revolution

To understand how militant Islamists came to overthrow the secular government of Iran, we need to go back a few decades and set the background.

You've learned about Reza Khan, the nationalist leader who, in the wake of World War I, modernized and westernized Iran. He became the shah, or king, and as Reza Shah Pahlavi he ruled with an iron hand.

Early in World War II, Allied troops occupied Iran and forced the shah to give up his throne because they feared he would cooperate with Nazi Germany. The Allies agreed to let his eldest son, Mohammad Reza Pahlavi, become the new shah. It was understood that the new

Mohammad Reza Shah Pahlavi and his wife ride through the streets of Tehran, Iran, in their carriage in 1967. Many Islamists were angered by the shah's luxurious lifestyle, repressive regime, and openness to Western influences.

shah would rule as a constitutional monarch, working with a prime minister and an elected parliament. The son thus became Mohammad Reza Shah Pahlavi.

After World War II, the new shah readily cooperated with Western governments and businesses, including Western oil companies. But he was opposed by fervent Iranian nationalists in his government, especially the prime minister, Mohammad Mosaddeq (moh-sah-DEK). With the support of the Iranian Communist Party, Mosaddeq managed to seize the holdings of a big British oil company in Iran, claiming they should belong solely to Iran.

In the next couple of years, Mosaddeq gained a big enough following to force Mohammad Reza Shah Pahlavi to flee the country. That's when, urged on by the British, the United States stepped in. Fearful of Soviet influence in this oil-rich region, the U.S. Central Intelligence Agency supported a military coup that restored the shah to power in Iran.

With the United States backing him, the shah once again opened Iran's oil resources to Western businesses. Oil funded the shah's efforts to modernize and westernize Iran. In the capital city, Tehran, modern factories and skyscrapers dotted the landscape. New cinemas, nightclubs, casinos, and bars lined the streets. The shah funded programs to build roads, railways, and irrigation projects. He made sure that telephones were available throughout much of Iran. He improved rural health care and education services. He tried to increase land ownership among the people. Despite these improvements, many Iranians continued to live in poverty, as wealth from oil remained in the hands of a few.

The gap between rich and poor widened. Many Iranians resented the shah's luxurious ways, though few dared to say so in public. That's because the shah had trained a branch of his police to keep close watch on dissidents. The shah turned these agents into a secret police force that brutally suppressed those who disagreed with him or opposed his rule.

Perhaps the strongest opposition to the shah came from religious leaders called ayatollahs (iy-uh-TOH-luhs) — in Shi'ite Islam, the title *ayatollah* indicates a religious leader who is very learned in Islamic law and other subjects. These ayatollahs objected to all Western influences. They opposed many of the shah's reforms, such as increased women's rights and equality of citizens regardless of religion. Such practices, the ayatollahs said, went against Islamic teaching. The ayatollahs also resented other actions by the shah that had diminished the political power of the Muslim clerics.

The religious opposition to the shah found a leader in the Ayatollah Khomeini (koh-MAY-nee). Khomeini taught Islamic philosophy and law, and he was eager to see Iran become an Islamic republic. In 1963, he spoke out against the shah's secular reforms. The shah responded by sending government troops to attack the ayatollah's school. Several students were killed, and the ayatollah himself was captured and banished from Iran.

In exile, Khomeini moved first to Turkey, then to Iraq, where he lived for years, and eventually to Paris. He kept in touch with his followers by telephone and used cassette tapes to distribute his speeches back in his homeland. In these speeches, he sounded the message of militant Islamism. He called for an Islamic revolution and the overthrow of the shah. Partly because of the shah's repressive and corrupt rule, Khomeini's words found many willing listeners in Iran. The ayatollah's message became increasingly simple: "Down with the shah" and "Death to America."

Ayatollah Khomeini greets a crowd in Iran in 1979, the year he led an Islamic revolution that overthrew the shah.

What Is Jihad?

The Arabic word *jihad* means "struggle." In Islam, the word refers to internal moral striving or the struggle for goodness. But some militants use the term to mean "holy war" against "infidels," nonbelievers in the Muslim faith.

In the fall of 1978, Khomeini's supporters launched massive riots and demonstrations in Iran, which forced the once all-powerful shah to flee his nation. Ayatollah Khomeini, now nearly 80 years old, boarded a plane and flew from Paris to Tehran. He proclaimed the formation of an Islamic republic and announced the beginning of *jihad*, by which he meant a "holy war" against the West.

Upon assuming power, Khomeini's government began a crackdown that rivaled if not surpassed the shah's repressive regime. Islamic revolutionary forces imprisoned and executed thousands who did not support them. Newspapers showed "before" and "after" pictures of accused enemies who had been executed. Iranians gathered around their radios to find out if their loved ones locked in prison had been hauled out to face a firing squad.

Islamic revolutionaries killed many Jews, Christians, and others whose religion they found offensive, including Muslims whose faith they deemed impure or unacceptable. When asked about such treatment, Khomeini replied, "If your finger suffers from gangrene, what do you do? Do you let the whole hand, and then the body, become filled with gangrene, or do you cut the finger off?"

The Iranian Hostage Crisis

American President Jimmy Carter had criticized the shah for his human rights abuses in Iran. Even though the Ayatollah Khomeini was proving no better, the U.S. government hoped to improve relations with the new Iranian regime. In the fall of 1979, the Iranian prime minister met with a top U.S. official. When a photograph of the two men shaking hands reached Iran, militant Islamists were furious. They were determined to make sure that Iran did not grow close to the United States.

In November 1979, a group of Iranian students broke into the U.S. embassy in Tehran and took more than sixty American hostages. They announced that the hostages would be released only when the U.S. government sent the exiled shah, who had traveled to the United States for medical treatment, back to Iran to stand trial. The students' real goals, however, were to destroy any chances of improved relations between Iran and the United States, and to push any moderates out of the new Iranian government. In both they succeeded.

Militant Iranian students display a blindfolded American hostage to a crowd in Tehran. The students seized more than sixty hostages at the U.S. embassy in late 1979.

The students soon released the women and African American hostages. The Iranian government announced that the remaining 53 hostages would be tried as spies. The U.S. government responded by stopping oil imports from Iran and freezing Iranian assets in the United States. The shah left the United States to live in exile in Panama. The Iranian students, urged on by Ayatollah Khomeini, continued to hold the hostages. Khomeini gave speeches denouncing the United States as "the Great Satan." Crowds gathered outside the embassy in Tehran and shouted "Death to America!"

When a government *freezes an asset*, such as property or money, it forbids that asset from being used.

Day after day, Americans watched the news on television, hoping to hear that the hostages had been released or rescued. Instead, their frustration mounted as news reports could do little more than tally the number of days the hostages had spent in captivity: "Today is Day 120 of the Iran hostage crisis... Day 121... Day 122...."

Five and a half months into the crisis, President Carter ordered a secret, high-risk rescue mission. The plan was for 90 commandos to fly into Tehran in eight helicopters, storm the embassy, and bring the hostages out. But at a refueling spot in the desert, two of the helicopters broke down in a sandstorm. A third crashed into an American transport plane, killing eight servicemen. The mission was a complete failure. Americans grew ever more frustrated.

The hostage situation dragged on for 444 days. Not surprisingly, in the fall of 1980, President Carter lost a reelection bid to his challenger, Ronald Reagan. On the day of Reagan's inauguration, Iran finally freed the hostages.

The stand-off with Iran caused many Americans to feel humiliated and bewildered. They wondered why the Iranians had taken such actions. They could not understand how a great superpower could be rendered helpless by a comparatively small and distant nation. In Iran, the effect was the opposite. Militant Islamists felt triumphant. They hailed Khomeini and the hostage-takers as heroes. In their view, the Iranian revolutionaries had successfully used terrorism to challenge the "Great Satan," as they labeled the United States.

Hezbollah's Campaign of Violence

The success of the Iranian Revolution energized Islamic terrorist groups in other parts of the Middle East. In 1981, radicals affiliated with the Muslim Brotherhood gunned down Egypt's president, Anwar Sadat, who had attempted to make peace with Israel. The next year, radical Shi'ite Muslims in Lebanon formed a group called *Hezbollah* (hehz-boh-LAH), a name that means "Party of God." The formation of Hezbollah was partly a response to an invasion of Lebanon by Israeli troops. The Israelis had invaded to try to stop attacks by the Palestine Liberation Organization, which was headquartered in Lebanon.

Members of Hezbollah began a campaign of violence and terror against Israel. Many of the group's leaders were young, militant clerics who had been educated and trained in Iran. They embraced the ideas of Ayatollah Khomeini. They envisioned a revolutionary Shi'ite Muslim state in Lebanon, much like the government that controlled Iran under Khomeini. Israel, they said, was an "infidel" power and therefore an enemy of Islam. Hezbollah radicals also regarded the United States as an infidel nation, dangerous because of its support of Israel.

Hezbollah employed terrorist methods against Israelis occupying Lebanon—kidnappings, bombings, and hit-and-run attacks with rocket launchers. Hezbollah leaders set up a number of hostage-taking teams with names such as "The Revolutionary Justice Organization" and the "Organization of the Oppressed on Earth."

Hezbollah also recruited young volunteers to engage in a new form of terror, one almost impossible to stop—suicide bombers. Suicide bombers strap explosives to their bodies or load their vehicles with bombs, and then get as close as they can to their target, whether a crowded marketplace or military base. They are willing to kill themselves, along with innocent bystanders, in order to generate terror.

Although the Qur'an condemns those who take their own lives, some militant Islamic clerics teach that killing oneself to kill enemies of Islam is a noble act, and that the bomber will be richly rewarded in an afterlife paradise. Groups such as Hezbollah also encourage suicide bombers by making payments to their families after they have completed their missions—a powerful incentive in a poverty-stricken region.

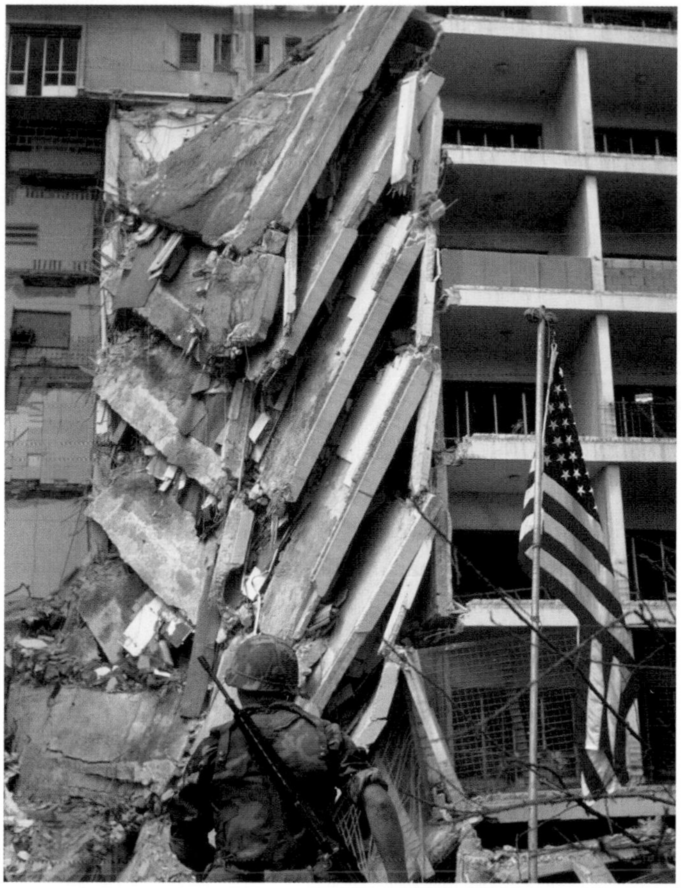

A marine assesses the U.S. embassy in Beirut, Lebanon, shortly after it was attacked in April 1983 by a suicide bomber who was a member of the terrorist group Hezbollah.

Suicide bombings became a fact of life in the Middle East. Hezbollah and other Islamist groups used the deadly tactic against Israelis and Westerners in the region. In April 1983, a member of Hezbollah rammed a van loaded with explosives into the U.S. embassy in Beirut, Lebanon. Sixty-three people died in the explosion. In October 1983, Hezbollah attacked U.S. and French troops stationed in Lebanon as part of an international peacekeeping force. A suicide bomber drove a large truck through a gate at a U.S. Marine compound in Beirut. He plowed into the lobby of the headquarters, setting off the equivalent of more than 12,000 pounds of TNT, and killing 241 U.S. servicemen. At the same time, another suicide bomber attacked barracks housing French troops, killing 58 soldiers.

Hezbollah continued its terrorist activities in the mid-1980s, kidnapping more than forty Westerners over a ten-year period. Some of the prisoners survived their captivity, while others died or were killed by the terrorists.

Hamas Turns to Terror

In 1987, yet another group of militant Islamists formed a terrorist organization called *Hamas* (hah-MAHS), an Arabic name that means "zeal." Hamas was created by members of the Muslim Brotherhood, the movement that rejected Western values and called for government based on strict Islamic law. The founders of Hamas began from two fundamental beliefs. All of Palestine, they claimed, belongs to the Arab Palestinian people. And, they asserted, the existence of the state of Israel is an offense against Islam. Hamas's founders were angry that hundreds of thousands of Arabs had lost their homes in Palestine since the creation of Israel in 1948. They resolved to "raise the banner of Allah over every inch of Palestine" by destroying Israel.

Members of Hamas were impatient with Yasser Arafat and the Palestine Liberation Organization, which they viewed as too secular. Instead they wanted to create an Islamist state in Palestine. In their view, violence was the only way to drive out their enemies, who included not only the Jews but "the imperialistic forces in the Capitalist West and Communist East." In their founding charter, leaders of Hamas flatly stated their belief that "there is no solution for the Palestinian question except through jihad."

Hamas members began a campaign of terror. They launched homemade missiles into Israel. They ambushed Israeli soldiers. They sent suicide bombers against Israeli citizens. They tortured and killed Palestinians whom they believed had been cooperating with Israel.

But Hamas had another side. The organization also acted as a social services agency on the West Bank and Gaza Strip. It spread funds donated by Saudi Arabia and other Arab countries among schools, orphanages, mosques, and health care clinics. In this way, Hamas gained support and popularity among the Palestinian people, though its political methods, like those of Hezbollah, were those of terror.

The Taliban Takes Over Afghanistan

Soon after Hamas began operating in Palestine, Muslim rebels in Afghanistan achieved a surprising victory. As you read in the last chapter, these rebels, called the mujahideen, took up arms against Soviet forces occupying Afghanistan. They were determined to overthrow Afghanistan's communist government. Supplied with weapons and money from the United States and other nations opposed to communism, the mujahideen fought a decade-long guerrilla war against Soviet troops. In 1988, the Soviet Union decided it could no longer afford the fight and called its troops home. Throughout the Middle East and beyond, Islamists rejoiced. As they saw it, their brothers in arms had defeated one of the world's two great "infidel" superpowers.

After the Soviets pulled out, civil war followed in Afghanistan. Within a few years, an Islamist regime called the Taliban (TAL-uh-ban) gained control of the country. The Persian word *taliban* means "students." Many of the Taliban's first members were Muslim students.

The Taliban demanded strict adherence to Islamic law. They forbade activities they considered offensive — a long list, including flying kites, playing chess, and dancing at weddings. They banned satellite dishes, computers, televisions, VCRs, any equipment that produced the "joy of music," wine, statues, sewing catalogs, pictures, and Christmas cards. The Taliban destroyed many works of art and museum artifacts that they deemed anti-Islamic. For example, they demolished two huge ancient statues of Buddha that had been carved into a mountainside cliff thousands of year before, and had not offended other Islamic rulers.

The Taliban dictated how people should dress. Men were required to wear beards longer than the grip of a hand. Violators were imprisoned until their whiskers grew long enough. Jackets, jeans, and other articles of Western-style clothing were prohibited. In public, a woman had to wear a *burqa,* a long cloak that hid her everyday clothing and covered her from head to toe. If a woman did not wear a burqa, then, said the Taliban, "her home will be marked and her husband punished."

Women's rights disappeared under the Taliban. Laws prohibited females over age eight from going to school. Women met in secret schools, but if they were caught, they and their teachers faced possible execution. Women were also forbidden to work outside the home — a law that ruined the country's health care system, civil service, and elementary schools, since a large percentage of doctors, government workers, and teachers had been women. Even women's daily movements were restricted. Women were permitted to go out in public only when accompanied by male relatives. Women who broke Taliban laws could be flogged, stoned to death, or subjected to public amputation or execution.

Western governments and most Muslim nations were appalled by a Taliban regime that grew ever more repressive and violent. These same governments, including that of the United States, had once celebrated the Afghans who resisted communism as freedom fighters. Now Afghanistan seemed to be stuck with a regime more brutal than the old Soviet empire. Most people in the West, however, paid little attention. They were relieved that the Cold War was over, and occasional news reports of Taliban violence struck them as the work of distant madmen.

Saddam Hussein became dictator of Iraq in 1979.

Saddam Hussein's Iraq

In the last decades of the twentieth century, the Middle Eastern nation of Iraq was ruled by the tyrant Saddam Hussein. Hussein had risen to power in the Baath Party, the party that urged Arabs to forge a single, large nation with a secular,

The Tallban, a repressive Islamic regime that ruled Afghanistan after the Soviet withdrawal, required Afghans to conform to its interpretation of Islamic law. When in public, women had to wear burqas, long cloaks that hid their entire body.

socialist government. He became dictator of Iraq in 1979 when he forced the country's ailing president to resign. He then gathered Baath Party leaders in a meeting. There, he announced the names of nearly seventy attendees whom he accused of being disloyal. One by one, the accused were led away for trial and, in many cases, execution.

Saddam Hussein led a secular government that, to the disappointment of many Islamists, did not rely on Islamic law. He saw himself as a modernizer. He used Iraq's oil revenues to build schools, hospitals, and roads. His regime promoted industry in Iraq and brought electricity to much of the country. He worked to increase farm production. He also allowed women more freedom than they enjoyed in some Muslim nations.

Despite these programs and policies, Hussein was also a power-mad egomaniac. Like the dictators Stalin and Mao before him, he plastered buildings and walls throughout Iraq with posters of his image. Hussein gained popularity in much of the Arab world by denouncing the West and threatening to "burn half of Israel" with chemical weapons. His special police units tortured and murdered tens of thousands.

The Iran-Iraq War

In 1980, Saddam Hussein ordered his army to invade Iraq's neighbor, Iran. His goal was to expand Iraq's borders and control Iranian oil. He also wanted to bring down Ayatollah Khomeini's government in Iran. Hussein believed that Khomeini's Islamic regime, which was led by Shi'ite Muslims, posed a threat to Iraq, which was controlled by Sunni Muslims.

Khomeini, in turn, despised Saddam Hussein's secular government and the way it discriminated against Shi'ite Muslims in Iraq, who made up a majority of the country's population. Khomeini urged Shi'ites in Iraq to begin an Islamic revolution and overthrow Saddam Hussein.

The two nations fought an eight-year war that ended in a draw while crippling both countries' economies and leaving perhaps a million dead. During the Iran-Iraq War, the United States and other Western nations sold arms to Iraq and gave it economic aid, in hopes of preventing the spread of Ayatollah Khomeini's Islamic revolution from Iran. Both Iraq and Iran employed heinous tactics, such as launching chemical gas attacks and ordering children and older people to walk through mine fields to clear the way for advancing troops.

Saddam Hussein even used chemical weapons to kill tens of thousands of Kurds in his own country. The Kurds, who lived in northern Iraq, hated Hussein's repressive regime and wanted political independence.

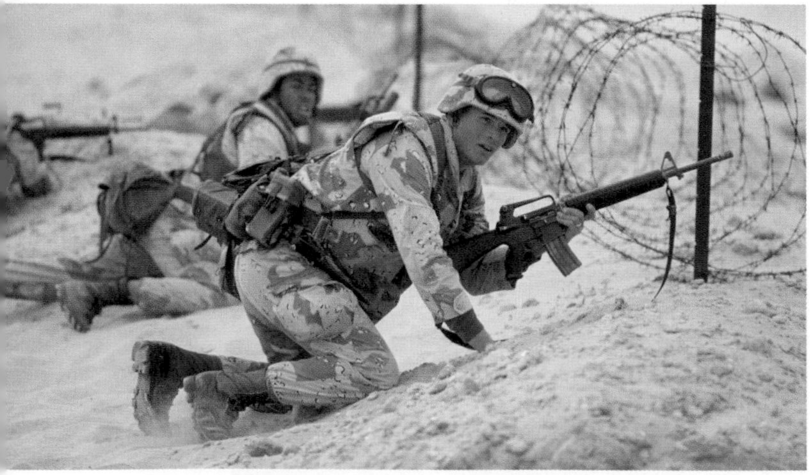

In 1990, after Saddam Hussein invaded Kuwait, the United States sent troops to the Middle East to halt the Iraqi aggression.

The Persian Gulf War

During the Iran-Iraq War, Iraq's neighbor, the small but oil-rich nation of Kuwait, came to Iraq's aid by providing billions of dollars in loans. How did Saddam Hussein repay this aid? By turning around and invading Kuwait.

In August 1990, Hussein sent Iraqi troops into Kuwait. He justified his aggressive action by claiming that Kuwait had once been a part of Iraq, and thus, as Hussein reasoned, should be again. After the invasion, he amassed large numbers of troops on the border between Kuwait and Saudi Arabia.

The Saudis were alarmed. The United States and other Western nations feared that Hussein would attack Saudi Arabia, a move that would severely disrupt the flow of oil from the Middle East, a vital resource to the industrialized West.

At the request of the Saudi government, and with United Nations approval, the United States forged an international coalition of 39 countries to confront Iraq if it refused to withdraw from Kuwait. The coalition included such Middle

Destroyed vehicles line a Kuwaiti highway which U.S.-led coalition forces bombed as Iraqi forces retreated.

Eastern neighbors as Pakistan, Egypt, Syria, and Saudi Arabia. King Fahd of Saudi Arabia asked the United States to station ground and air forces in his country. The United States, eager to protect Saudi oil, sent troops and gave the Saudis assurances that they would leave when asked.

Saddam Hussein stubbornly refused to remove his troops from Kuwait. And so, in January 1991, the Persian Gulf War began, with the United States leading a multinational coalition of troops. It took just a little over six weeks for coalition aircraft and troops to crush Iraq's military.

With the threat to Kuwait removed, George H.W. Bush, president of the United States, chose not to push the war into the Iraqi capital of Baghdad to remove Saddam Hussein from power. President Bush's caution was in part a response to a clear message from several Middle Eastern governments. They welcomed the help of coalition troops in punishing Hussein for invading Kuwait, but they firmly opposed the idea of Western forces occupying Baghdad and overthrowing the Iraqi government. So Saddam Hussein remained in power.

The Persian Gulf War caused widespread destruction in Iraq. Coalition bombs and missiles fell on roads, bridges, and power plants, as well as on Baghdad and other cities. Before they retreated from Kuwait, Iraqi troops set fire to Kuwaiti oil fields, causing both a great loss of oil and a serious air pollution problem in the region. No one is certain how many Iraqi troops and civilians were killed during the war—certainly the number reached the tens of thousands. Many more were wounded or became refugees. Coalition forces suffered fewer than 400 deaths.

Operation Desert Storm

Operation Desert Storm was the name the U.S. government gave the coalition attack against Iraq during the 1991 Persian Gulf War. The campaign began with an air attack designed to destroy Saddam Hussein's ability to fight back. Coalition aircraft dropped thousands of bombs on Baghdad and other targets, including military posts, power stations, communications centers, and biological and chemical weapon sites. U.S. ships also launched missiles from the Persian Gulf. In late February, coalition ground forces swept into Iraq, easily overrunning Hussein's crippled army. About one hundred hours after the ground attack started, U.S. President George H.W. Bush declared victory in the Persian Gulf War.

F-117 Nighthawk

During the Persian Gulf War of 1991, Iraqi forces set Kuwaiti oil fields afire as they retreated. Many Islamists blamed Western interference in the Middle East as much as Saddam Hussein for such destruction.

Osama bin Laden Organizes al-Qaeda

Many people in the Middle East were glad that Saddam Hussein had been pushed back. But others, including some militant Islamists, felt humiliated that it took Western armies to do it. Even worse, they said, was the fact that "infidel" powers had established bases in Saudi Arabia, home of the holiest Islamic sites.

One of the militant Islamists infuriated by the Persian Gulf War was Osama bin Laden (oh-SAH-muh bin LAH-duhn). In his mind, troops from the United States and other Western nations were like locusts descending upon sacred lands in the Middle East, "crowding its soil, eating its fruits, and destroying its verdure." He resolved to strike back at the West by using terrorism.

Bin Laden might seem like an unlikely terrorist. He was born in Saudi Arabia to a wealthy, privileged family. His father had amassed a vast fortune in the construction business, and bin Laden grew up in luxury. As a teenager, he became increasingly devoted to Islam. In high school he joined the Muslim Brotherhood. In college he studied economics, but he was more interested in campus religious activities. He became convinced of the need for jihad against those whom he perceived as threats to Islam. These included not only foreign "infidel" powers but also Muslims who had accepted Western ideas.

In 1979, bin Laden left Saudi Arabia to join the mujahideen, the Muslim rebels who were battling Soviet troops in Afghanistan. He spent much of his time raising money and recruiting fighters from around the Muslim world for the Afghan resistance. Young men from Egypt,

Osama bin Laden formed the terrorist group al-Qaeda and declared jihad on the United States and other Western nations.

Saudi Arabia, Algeria, Lebanon, and other countries rallied to bin Laden's call.

In the late 1980s, bin Laden helped found an organization called al-Qaeda (al-KIY-duh), which is Arabic for "the base." The group's original goal was to set up a base where young men could train to fight the Soviets in Afghanistan. When the USSR withdrew in 1988, bin Laden believed that his forces of jihad had defeated one of the world's two superpowers. One of his fellow warriors gave him an assault rifle taken from a dead Russian soldier. From that moment, he often carried it proudly on his shoulder.

After the Persian Gulf War of 1991, bin Laden came to perceive the United States as the greatest threat to Islamic nations. In his view, Americans were trying to dominate the Middle East in their greedy pursuit of oil. He resented the U.S. government's support of Israel. Above all, he hated the United States for stationing troops in Saudi Arabia — the holiest of Muslim lands, the land of Mecca and Medina, the birthplace of the Prophet Muhammad. In the minds of militant Islamists, the presence of Western troops on Saudi soil was an unforgivable offense against Islam.

Outraged by the Gulf War, bin Laden enlarged al-Qaeda's goals. The major objectives, he said, were to drive Americans and their "Satanic culture" out of all Islamic nations, to destroy Israel, and to topple pro-Western governments in the Middle East. From a cave hideout in Afghanistan, bin Laden declared war on America. Addressing the United States, he proclaimed, "Terrorizing you, while you are carrying arms in our land, is a legitimate right and a moral obligation."

On February 23, 1998, an Arabic newspaper in London published a "Declaration of the World Islamic Front for Jihad against the Jews and the Crusaders," a statement signed by Osama bin Laden and leaders of other terrorist groups. The declaration called for war against America and its allies, including Israel. The statement explicitly urged the use of violence: "We — with God's help — call on every Muslim who believes in God and wishes to be rewarded to comply with God's order to kill the Americans and plunder their money wherever and whenever they find it. We also call on Muslim… leaders, youths, and soldiers to launch the raid on Satan's U.S. troops and the devil's supporters allying with them."

From secret locations in Taliban-controlled Afghanistan, bin Laden and al-Qaeda masterminded several attacks. In 1998, terrorists linked to al-Qaeda simultaneously set off bombs in the U.S. embassies in Tanzania and Kenya, taking the lives of 224 people, including 12 Americans, and injuring more than 4,500. In 2000, al-Qaeda suicide bombers launched a raid against the USS *Cole*, a U.S. Navy destroyer harbored in Yemen. The assault killed 17 American sailors.

The American people were outraged by such attacks, but most were puzzled about the reasons behind them. They seemed to be random acts of terrorism committed by distant fanatics. Very few people in the United States knew who Osama bin Laden was. Most had never heard the word "Islamist." Even U.S. intelligence experts were having a difficult time figuring out exactly what this shadowy figure was up to. No one was prepared for what happened next.

Rescue workers aid a victim of a 1998 bombing of the U.S. embassy in Kenya by terrorists linked to al-Qaeda.

September 11, 2001

Tuesday, September 11, 2001, dawned a glorious day in both Washington, D.C., and New York City — sunny, breezy, a pleasant relief from the long summer. On that morning, as commuters approached the two cities — reading their newspapers while riding trains and buses, or listening to their car radios — they learned about a weakening economy and the recent disappointing defeats of their pro football teams, the Redskins, Giants, and Jets. Readers of the *New York Times* pondered a front-page story about the efforts to impose dress codes on high school students because of a decline in good taste.

At 8 a.m., many people in eastern airports were boarding planes destined for California. Two of those planes left Logan Airport in Boston, another left Newark International Airport in New Jersey, and a fourth left Dulles International Airport outside Washington. Among the passengers on each flight were 4 or 5 Islamic extremists from the Middle East — of the 19 men, 15 were from Saudi Arabia, 2 from the United Arab Emirates, 1 from Egypt, and 1 from Lebanon. All were young, between the ages of 20 and 33, and all were filled

In these photos taken on September 11, 2001, a plane hijacked by Islamic terrorists flies into the south tower of the World Trade Center. A huge hole in the north tower marks the place where another plane struck some 15 minutes earlier.

with hateful and distorted ideas. They had been in the United States taking flight lessons. As they boarded their flights on September 11, they had no intention of traveling to California.

A short while into each flight, the men rose from their seats, pulled out knives and box cutters, and announced that they were hijacking the planes. They rushed the cockpits, assaulted the flight crews, and took control of the jets.

The men were on a suicide mission—not in cars filled with explosives, but in airliners carrying thousands of gallons of highly explosive jet fuel. At 8:46 a.m., one of the hijacked planes slammed into the north tower of the World Trade Center in New York City at nearly 500 miles per hour. An explosion ripped through the upper floors of the 110-story skyscraper, instantly killing hundreds and trapping hundreds more in the floors above.

On the streets below, stunned commuters looked up in disbelief. The World Trade Center's twin towers, two of the tallest buildings in the world, were among New York City's most famous landmarks. Some 50,000 people worked in the World Trade Center complex, which housed businesses related to finance and international trade, as well as offices of several government agencies. Firemen and police officers rushed to the scene, wondering how such a terrible accident could have happened.

Network news shows immediately began broadcasting live reports of the disaster. Just after 9 a.m., millions of Americans watched in horror as a second jet crashed into the World Trade Center's south tower, setting off another huge explosion. At once the country realized that this was no accident.

Black smoke poured from the two skyscrapers. As the fires raged, people were burning to death and suffocating. Many, unable to find a way out, panicked and jumped to their deaths.

At about 9:40 a.m., a third hijacked plane tore into the side of the Pentagon, the gigantic headquarters of the U.S. military just outside of Washington, D.C. A section of the building collapsed, killing dozens.

Just after 10 a.m. came reports of a fourth plane crash, this one in rural Pennsylvania. United Flight 93 had been off course and heading toward

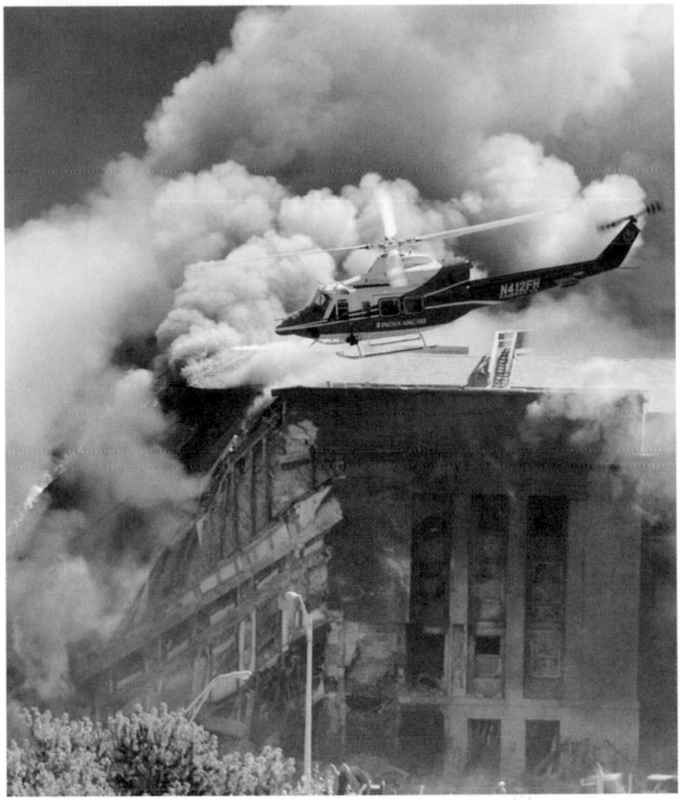

A rescue helicopter flies over the Pentagon, the U.S. military's headquarters outside Washington, D.C., after terrorists flew a jet into the building on September 11, 2001.

United 93: "Let's Roll"

When terrorists seized control of United Flight 93, desperate passengers began calling for help on their cell phones. They quickly learned that other planes had crashed in suicide missions, and realized that their own plane must be headed for a high-profile target. Passenger Tod Beamer told a telephone operator that he and some others had decided to stop the hijackers. "Are you guys ready?" the operator heard him say. "Okay. Let's roll!" Minutes later, Flight 93 crashed near Shanksville, Pennsylvania, killing all aboard. Investigators believe that the terrorists intended to crash the jet into the U.S. Capitol Building or the White House in Washington, D.C. But their plans were apparently thwarted by the passengers who rose up to stop them.

Washington when it went down in a field. All 44 people aboard were killed.

Back in New York, the unimaginable happened. The south tower of the World Trade Center suddenly collapsed, imploding into the streets below, and unleashing a blizzard of dust and debris. Within the hour, the second tower also came down, burying thousands in an enormous pile of mangled steel and concrete.

The events of September 11, 2001, were by far the worst terrorist attack in United States history. Before the morning was over, nearly 3,000 people had died, including many of the firemen and police officers who were trying to evacuate the World Trade Center. It was the largest loss of life in an enemy attack on American territory since Pearl Harbor in 1941.

Freedom at What Price?

"Those who would give up essential liberty to purchase a little temporary safety deserve neither liberty nor safety." Those words of Benjamin Franklin are inscribed at the Statue of Liberty in New York Harbor, not far from the site of September 11, 2001, attack on the World Trade Center.

How much liberty must citizens sacrifice in order to preserve their own security? The question was asked by many Americans when the U.S. Congress passed the Patriot Act as part of the war on terror. Critics argue that portions of the Patriot Act threaten civil rights. For example, the act allows investigators to examine people's library records under certain circumstances. Some say this violates constitutional protections against unreasonable searches and seizures. In response, supporters of the Patriot Act argue that the dangers posed by terrorism are so extreme and the stakes so high that Americans must compromise on some individual liberties in order to protect themselves.

Around the world, people watched reports of the tragedy in bewilderment, outrage, and grief. Across the United States, Americans were stunned, horrified, and desperate to learn who was behind the carnage.

Mobilizing for a War on Terror

Over the next few days, U.S. intelligence agencies determined that Osama bin Laden and al-Qaeda were behind the September 11 attacks. In a televised address before a joint session of the U.S. Congress, President George W. Bush declared that America would wage a "war on terror…until every terrorist group of global reach has been found, stopped and defeated." Bush called the terrorist hijackers "traitors to their own faith" and distinguished them from Muslims in general: "The enemy of America is not our many Muslim friends," he said; "Our enemy is a radical network of terrorists, and every government that supports them."

In 2001, George W. Bush, son of former president George H.W. Bush, became the 43rd president of the United States.

"From this day forward," Bush declared, "any nation that continues to harbor or support terrorism will be regarded by the United States as a hostile regime." U.S. intelligence reports indicated that Osama bin Laden was in Afghanistan, where al-Qaeda's training grounds were located. Bush called on the Taliban to turn over bin Laden and other al-Qaeda leaders. When the Taliban refused, the United States, Great Britain, and several other nations joined forces to invade Afghanistan.

The U.S.-led forces helped Afghan rebels overthrow the Taliban government. Many Taliban and al-Qaeda members fled to mountainous regions they knew well. Osama bin Laden eluded his pursuers and went into hiding, probably somewhere in Afghanistan or Pakistan.

The U.S. government took steps to strengthen its ability to combat terrorism, both at home and abroad. Some of these steps proved controversial, such as the Patriot Act, passed into law in late October 2001. This legislation gave the federal government specific powers to monitor e-mail traffic and phone conversations, search people's homes and cars, detain non-citizens suspected of posing a threat to national security, and take other steps to gather information about possible terrorist activities. In 2003, the U.S. government created a new cabinet agency, the Department of Homeland Security, to coordinate efforts to prevent terrorist attacks.

The Iraq War

Osama bin Laden had promised ongoing jihad against the West. Where would the next terrorist threat come from? This question worried many world leaders soon after the September 11 attacks. President Bush, along with Britain's prime minister, Tony Blair, focused on Iraq.

Intelligence reports indicated that Iraqi dictator Saddam Hussein had aided and harbored terrorist groups, and that Hussein was stockpiling biological and other weapons of mass destruction. In the past, Saddam Hussein had used chemical weapons against the Iranians and against Kurds living in Iraq. After Iraq's defeat in the 1991 Persian Gulf War, the United Nations had banned Iraq from producing or possessing weapons of mass destruction. But Saddam Hussein had often refused to let United Nations inspectors examine sites where they suspected he might be producing such weapons.

The United Nations and United States demanded that Saddam Hussein produce any banned weapons and allow inspectors access to all suspected weapons sites. Hussein stalled and refused to comply. In March 2003, after months of diplomatic efforts, the U.S. government announced that it would use force to disarm Hussein.

It was a controversial decision, because the United States seemed to be edging toward a "preemptive" war—a war in which a nation strikes first to overcome a perceived threat before the threat grows even worse. Some people argued that recent history justified a preemptive war—after all, they said, if Britain and France had launched

In March 2003, the United States and Great Britain led an invasion of Iraq, launching a controversial war. The war began with a bombing of Baghdad, Iraq's capital.

a preemptive war against Hitler, they might have stopped him before he had the chance to overrun much of Europe. Others argued that modern warfare is so potentially catastrophic, no nation should initiate a pre-emptive war, but should only go to war in response to direct acts of aggression. Iraq had not attacked the United States.

In 2003, some nations, such as France and Germany, argued that the United States should not attack Iraq, but instead should give diplomacy more time. The United Nations refused to approve an invasion of Iraq. But President Bush pushed ahead.

On March 20, 2003, the United States and Great Britain led an invasion of Iraq. While the invading force was supported by a coalition of nearly fifty countries, most contributed only a small number of troops or supplies, while the vast majority of troops and equipment came from the United States and Britain. The invasion was called "Operation Iraqi Freedom." Once again, Iraqi forces were no match for Western firepower. In early April, U.S. tanks rolled into Baghdad. Hussein's brutal regime quickly disintegrated. Saddam Hussein himself went into hiding. He was later captured, tried on charges of mass murder, and executed.

Within two and a half years, the Iraqi people had approved a new constitution and elected a parliament. President Bush hoped that Iraq would become a stable democracy capable of defending itself. But invading the country and capturing Saddam Hussein turned out to be far easier than establishing a peaceful Iraq.

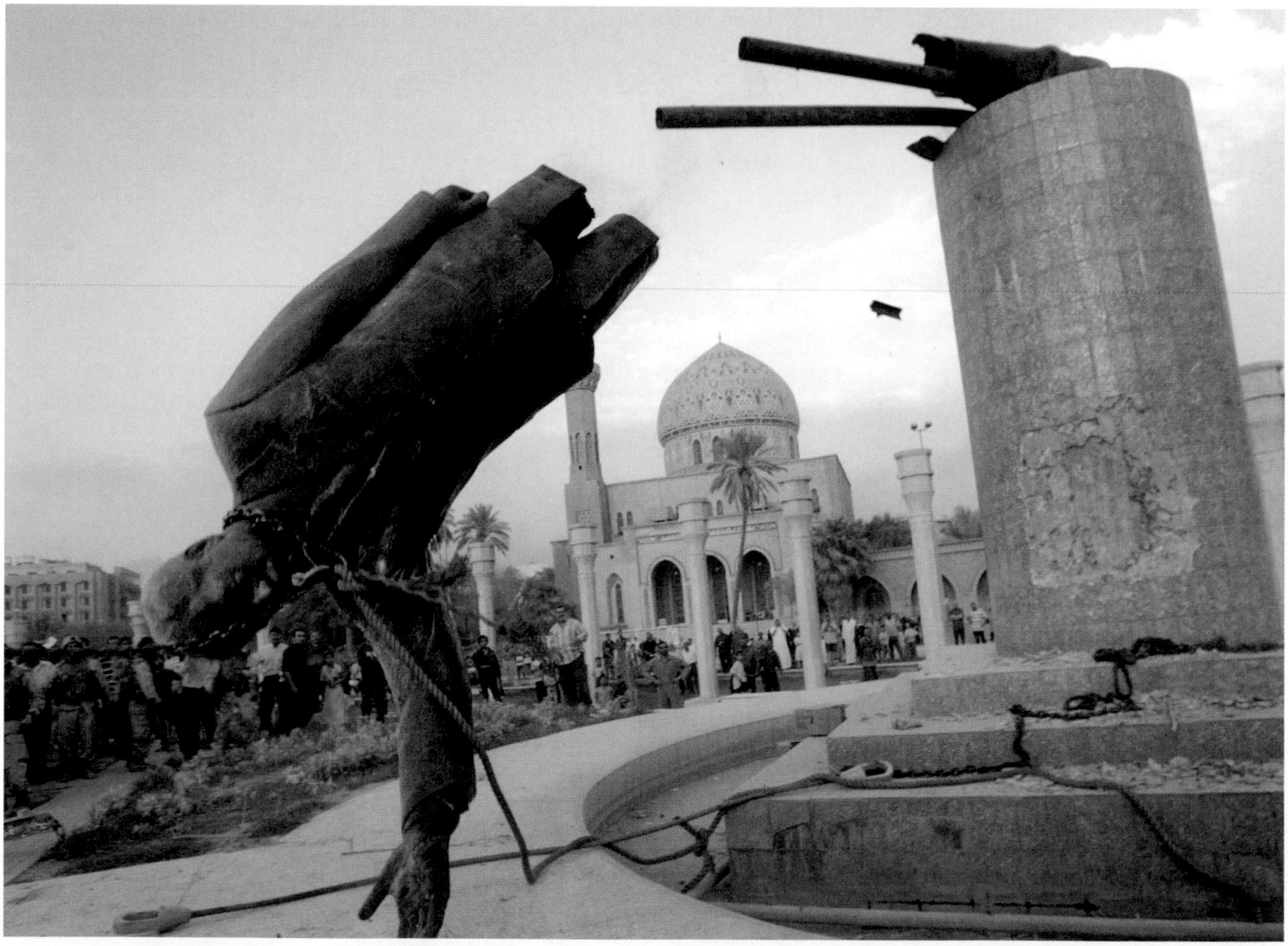

A statue of Saddam Hussein falls in Baghdad in April 2003 after Iraqis placed a noose around its neck, and then attached the rope to a U.S. armored vehicle, which pulled it down. Most Iraqis were glad to see the dictator gone, but the following years turned violent as various factions warred for control of Iraq and militant Islamists mounted suicide attacks.

Soon after the invasion, parts of Iraq—including many neighborhoods in the capital city of Baghdad—descended into chaos and sectarian violence. Even as Hussein's government fell, mobs of Iraqis looted palaces, museums, and other buildings, stealing artwork and historical treasures. In the following months, ancient hatreds between Sunni and Shi'ite Muslims surfaced, with both groups raising militias to fight each other. Militant Islamists, furious at the thought of U.S. and other Western troops on Iraqi soil, mounted suicide bombings against coalition soldiers and Iraqi citizens alike. Tens of thousands of Iraqis died in the violence, and casualties among U.S. troops mounted into the thousands.

Sectarian violence is violence between different religious or political groups.

To make matters worse, no weapons of mass destruction were found in Iraq. It became apparent that U.S., British, and other intelligence agencies had misjudged Saddam Hussein's possession of such weapons. The revelation tarnished the U.S. reputation abroad and led to charges that the U.S. government had used insufficient and inaccurate information to justify a pre-emptive war.

A Long Struggle Ahead?

As the suicide bombings and guerrilla attacks continued, many Americans grew discouraged over the prospects of success in Iraq. People debated the best course. Some insisted that despite all the setbacks, American interests in the Middle East were so vital and so connected to national security that the United States must maintain its military commitment in Iraq. Others wondered if the country had made the right decision in going to war. Yes, the United States had removed a ruthless dictator who had butchered hundreds of thousands of his own people, and who had vowed to rain destruction on America. But in doing so, had the United States become bogged down in what some characterized as "another Vietnam"? Was the American presence in Iraq inciting even more terrorism against the West? The answers were not clear.

Meanwhile, terrorist attacks continued around the world. For example, in 2004, several bombs exploded aboard commuter trains in Madrid, Spain, killing nearly 200 people and wounding more than 1,500. Spanish officials determined that Islamic extremists were responsible. In 2005, four suicide bombers set off blasts in London subway trains and a bus, killing 52 commuters and injuring 700. Again, officials determined that militant Islamists with links to al-Qaeda and Osama bin Laden had carried out the attack.

Intelligence agencies in Western nations worked feverishly to disrupt terrorists' plans. Investigators in Britain, France, the United States, and other nations managed to stop several plots, most engineered by militant Islamists. Still, as the first decade of the twenty-first century unfolded, millions around the world faced the grim reality that the fight against terrorism was likely to be a long and bloody struggle.

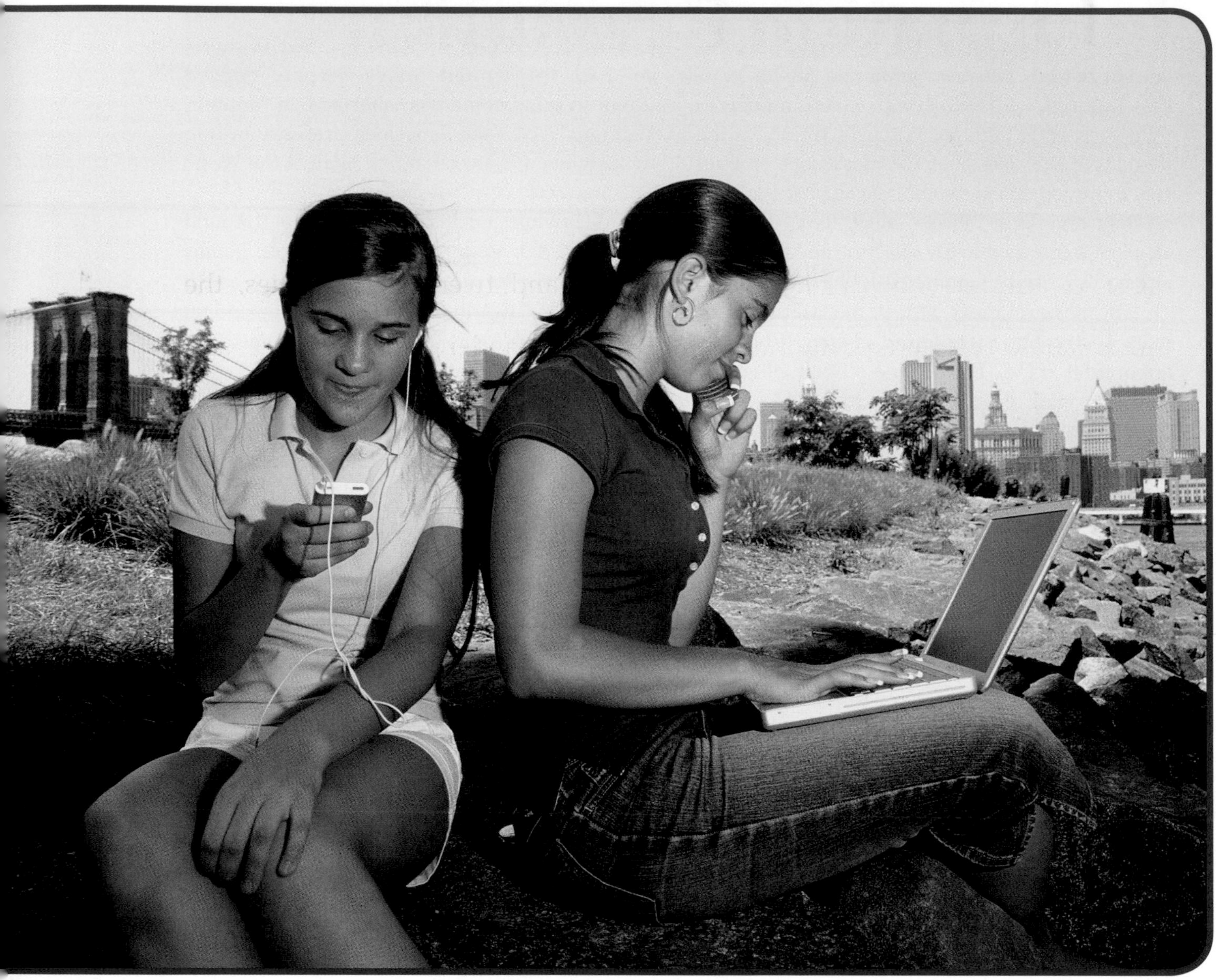

Two teenage girls enjoy the benefits of the Information Revolution as they listen to music, talk to a friend, and surf the Web simultaneously. In the late twentieth century, the development of digital audio players, cell phones, and laptops made it possible to work and play almost anywhere—even outside, far from electrical outlets.

An Electronically Charged Information Revolution

You've learned that during the nineteenth and twentieth centuries, the Industrial Revolution profoundly changed the modern world. More and more people moved from the countryside to cities for new jobs in factories. In these factories, power-driven machinery quickly turned out everything from cloth and buttons to bullets. The Industrial Revolution dramatically increased the speed of transportation (think of steamships, railroads, and eventually automobiles and airplanes) and communication (think of the telegraph, telephones, and radio).

In the late twentieth century, we have witnessed another technological revolution — indeed, we are living in it. This new revolution has been propelled by advances in electronics, a branch of applied physics that finds ways to make electric signals perform useful purposes. These purposes include communicating, calculating, and controlling in devices ranging from elevators to cars to microwave ovens to toys to hearing aids to satellites.

In *applied physics*, scientists conduct research and apply the laws of physics with a practical aim in mind, such as improving a manufacturing process.

This new technological revolution is sometimes called the Information Revolution. Like the Industrial Revolution, the Information Revolution has had far-reaching consequences, especially as innovations in communications and computing have transformed the way many people live and work.

Personal computers, fax machines, cell phones, the Internet, electronic mail, the World Wide Web — these and other electronic developments have made information instantly accessible and as easy to communicate as the click of a mouse. The very phrase, "click of a mouse," would have sounded like nonsense only a few decades ago. Like other terms — for example, *log on, download, IM, broadband*, and *google it* — it has become, for many people, part of everyday speech.

How did this come to be? That is the story this chapter tells.

Thinking Big: ENIAC

We think of computers as devices of our time, and indeed they are. But as with most innovations, pioneers cleared the path for later developments. There have been many pioneers in the Information Revolution. Here we spotlight a few.

In the 1830s, Charles Babbage, an English mathematician, drew up plans for a device he called the Analytical Engine. This machine, controlled by punch cards and driven by a series of steam-powered wheels, levers, and gears, was designed to carry out complex arithmetical calculations with speed and accuracy. In its basic principles, Babbage's machine was the first digital computer. Although Babbage never built a complete Analytical Engine, British scientists in the 1990s, working from plans in Babbage's notebooks, did build such a device. It calculated accurately with numbers up to 31 digits.

In the 1930s, another brilliant English mathematician, Alan Turing, described what has come to be called a Turing Machine. The device he imagined would perform enormously complex processes, beyond arithmetical calculations. While Turing did not build such a device, he explained the complex mathematics behind the processes of modern-day computers, as well as the enormous potential of such machines.

ENIAC's operators programmed the enormous machine by plugging and unplugging cables, and adjusting switches. In the 1940s, six of ENIAC's computer operators were women.

By World War II, scientists and engineers had developed the first computers. These gigantic machines were intended mainly for code-breaking and calculating. (Alan Turing was a key member of the British team that developed a machine to crack the Nazi's Enigma code during World War II.)

Just after the war's end, on Valentine's Day in 1946, two engineers at the University of Pennsylvania, John Mauchly and J. Presper Eckert, exhibited a machine they had been working on for three years. It was called ENIAC, which stood for "Electronic Numerical Indicator And Computer." The U.S. Department of Defense had funded the ENIAC project to develop a machine to predict the trajectory of rapid-fire artillery shells.

When ENIAC was unveiled, it was a daunting sight—a wildly wired contraption that weighed 30 tons, was 8 feet tall, and required as much space as a ballroom. It was made up of tens of thousands of parts, including 18,000 vacuum tubes—hot, glowing, nearly airless glass tubes enclosing filaments to control the flow of electricity. ENIAC required 150 kilowatts of electrical power to make it work, but it could carry out what seemed an amazing 5,000 calculations per second.

This early computer was a dazzling scientific achievement. But would computers ever prove useful to anyone besides military planners? ENIAC was expensive, massive, and finicky. And while it could rapidly solve complex mathematical problems, it was, in effect, just a fabulous adding machine.

Smaller, Faster, Smarter

The professors who designed ENIAC, as well as other scientists in labs and universities around the world, worked day and night to make computers do more. They wondered: How can we tell a computer what to do and when to do it? How can we program a computer—that is, give it a series of instructions—to make it go beyond a single operation to perform a variety of tasks? How can we replace punch cards and other mechanical forms of storage with data stored in instantaneously accessible electronic form?

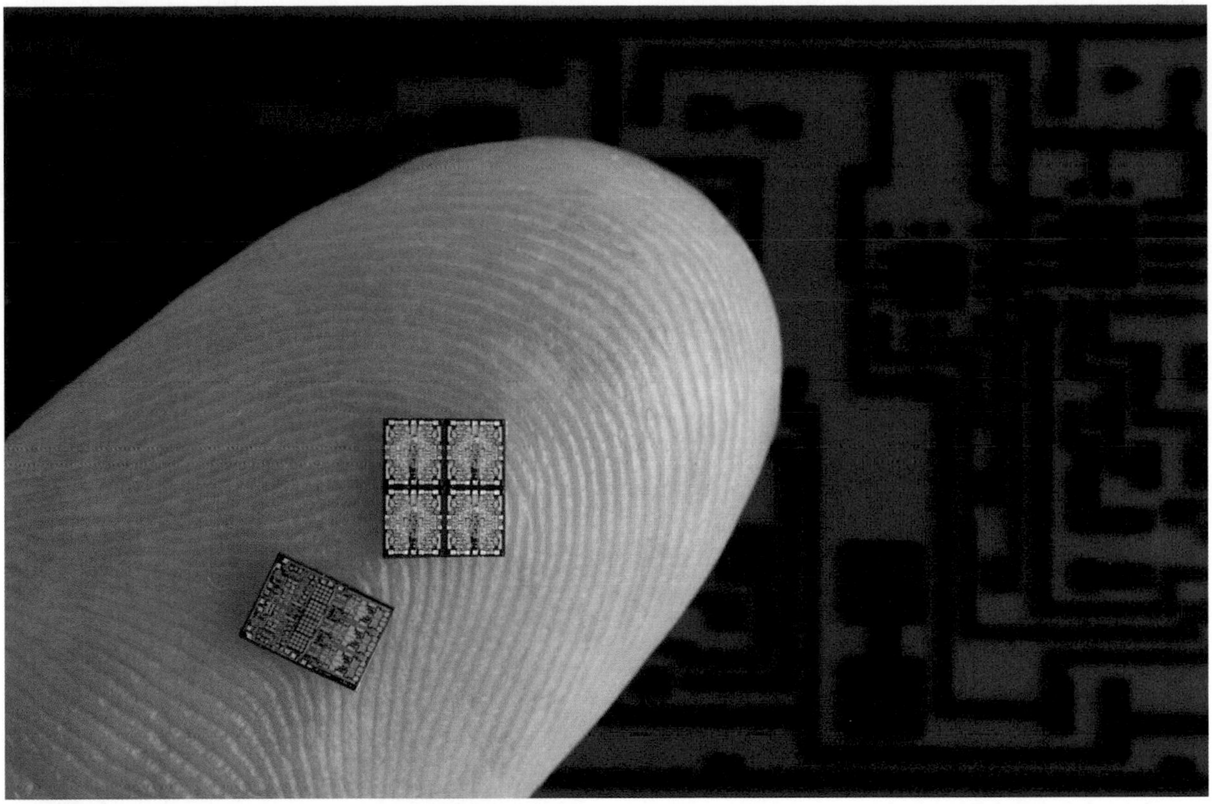

Computer microchips, also called integrated circuits, hold a complex electronic circuit on a very small piece of silicon. Integrated circuits like these were essential for shrinking computers from room-sized machines to desktop devices. They also vastly improved computing capability.

These and other questions were addressed in a brilliant paper published in 1946, whose chief author was John von Neumann of the Institute for Advanced Study at Princeton. Von Neumann set out his ideas for, as the paper's title announced, the "Logical Design of an Electronic Computing Instrument." One of his main ideas has come to be known as the "stored-program concept" — electronically storing instructions in a computer to enable it to perform a variety of tasks in a given sequence. The concept, advancing Turing's theories from a decade earlier, was critical to the development of computers as we have come to know them.

Another big step in computer design — indeed, in modern electronics in general — was made possible by scientists at Bell Laboratories, a research and development lab that sprang from Alexander Graham Bell's company, Bell Telephone. The Bell Labs scientists invented transistors, tiny devices to control the flow of electric current. Compared to vacuum tubes — which were bulky, fragile, and hot — transistors were small, stable, and cooler in operation. Transistors reduced the size of computers and other electronic devices, and decreased the amount of energy required to run them. They also brought down the price.

Even transistors needed to be wired together on circuit boards. In the late 1950s, however, engineers at Texas Instruments developed a way to integrate an entire circuit on a single chip of solid material. Within years, integrated circuits — called ICs for short — compressed hundreds of thousands of transistors on a single microchip smaller than a fingernail. Not only did ICs make computers smaller, they also enabled many of the technologies of the Information Revolution.

By the 1960s, engineers at IBM — International Business Machines, a big corporation — were designing computers small enough to fit in an elevator. The Apollo Space Program relied on some of the new machines. NASA encouraged computer scientists to keep shrinking the computer. In the 1970s, one company introduced a fairly compact PET computer for business use — PET stood for "Personal Electronic Transactor." Other companies began marketing "microcomputer" kits that hobbyists could assemble in their homes.

New programs, called compilers, enabled people to program computers easily and quickly. Computers were programmed to perform tasks unimagined only a couple of decades earlier, from tracking a company's sales figures to guiding the *Apollo 11* spacecraft safely to the moon and back. Scientists and engineers worked with new productivity, relying on the fabulous machines to do millions of calculations that could not have been made a generation before.

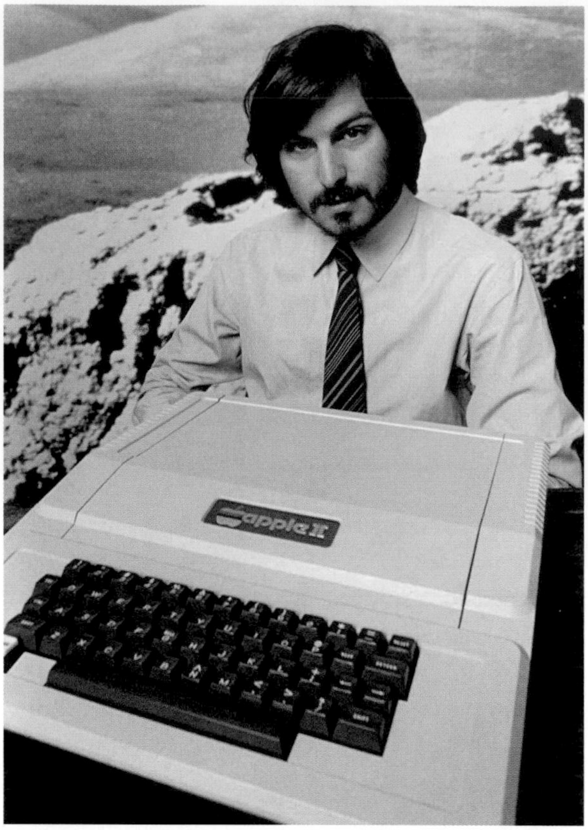

Steve Jobs, founder of Apple Computer Incorporated, introduces the sleek, new Apple II computer in 1977.

PCs—Personal Computers

In the mid-1970s, many new companies sprang up devoted to writing computer programs or "software" to guide the new machines. Two very bright high school friends from Seattle, Bill Gates and Paul Allen, started a little company they called Micro-Soft. Gates left Harvard to devote all his time to his new company. With Allen, Gates developed a clever software program for small computers. They trademarked their company's name as Microsoft in November 1976, by which time they were licensing their software program, called Microsoft BASIC, to several customers, including General Electric, Citibank, and a new little company called Apple.

Microsoft founders Bill Gates (left) and Paul Allen in 1983. High school friends, they formed their company in 1976, and sold key software to IBM and its competitors.

Apple was the brainchild of a 21-year-old hobbyist in California, Steve Jobs, and his friend Stephen Wozniak. They wanted to build their own small, practical computers. To fund their efforts, Jobs sold his Volkswagen minibus. In the garage of his parents' home, Jobs, along with Wozniak, built a small computer they dubbed the Apple I. For $666.66, anyone — but mostly hobbyists — could purchase this little wonder. A local computer hobby store quickly sold 200 of these machines. In 1977, the little firm introduced the Apple II. This computer was housed in a sleek plastic case. Wozniak soon found ways to enhance the Apple II's speed and reliability, and sales took off.

Meanwhile, industry giant IBM decided not to leave the field of small computers to hobbyists. IBM wanted to build a "personal computer" — soon to be called a PC, a small affordable machine that people could use in their homes. IBM wanted to get its product on the market fast. So in 1980, instead of writing its own programming, IBM hired Microsoft to provide the software to run IBM's PCs.

Young Bill Gates and his handful of employees bought a program they thought would work, improved it, and quickly delivered their DOS (disk operating system) software to IBM. Gates then sold the program to other companies that sprang up to compete with IBM. These IBM "clones" were soon selling faster than IBM's own PCs. In a very short time, Bill Gates and Paul Allen, owners of the operating system installed on every IBM PC and every IBM clone, became multimillionaires and then billionaires.

By 1982, store owners proudly displayed the new personal computers in mall windows. In short order, PCs rendered electric typewriters and adding machines obsolete. College students and young professors liked the fact that personal computers could "process words," which made it easy to insert footnotes and revise papers. Businesses and some families took advantage of software that efficiently performed accounting functions that once took a lot of time and paper.

Despite their high price tag and, by modern standards, slow speed, the first generation of PCs was a quantum leap from the dinosaur-like computers of a mere three decades past. Typically, each tiny microchip could perform close to five million operations per second, compared to ENIAC's five thousand. The speed, power, and memory capacity of these chips continued to double every two years or less, as their price and size steadily decreased. New companies competed to supply parts like hard drives and memory chips, all rapidly evolving as scientists pushed the boundaries of physics and materials science.

Engineers continued to make computers faster and smarter. In 1984, Apple introduced an innovative model called the Macintosh. With the "Mac," as it was called, users no longer had to type a complex string of keystrokes to give the computer commands. Instead, using a device

Making Money and Using It Well

Microsoft cofounder Bill Gates showed a knack for making money early on. When he was 14, he and his friend Paul Allen started a company to make traffic counters using computers. In their first year of business they made some $20,000. When clients found out the owners of Traf-o-Data were high school students, business dropped off. Gates—whose net worth in 2007 amounted to more than $50 billion dollars, making him the richest man in the world—has channeled some of his wealth into the philanthropic projects of the Bill and Melinda Gates Foundation. The foundation has funded programs to improve health care and reduce poverty in developing nations. It also sponsors efforts to improve education, in part through the use of computers and other technology.

IBM president John Opel (seated) demonstrates his company's new personal computer in 1981. *Time* magazine named the personal computer "Machine of the Year" for 1982.

The Apple Macintosh rolled off the company's California assembly lines in 1984. It had a powerful new microprocessor, a built-in three-and-a-half-inch disk drive, a nine-inch display, and the then-impressive memory of 128k RAM. It sold for $2,495.

Apple vs. IBM

Apple, the company cofounded by California entrepreneur Steve Jobs, abandoned the early Microsoft software and developed its own operating system. Building a reputation for free-spirited independence, Apple even developed much of its own hardware, in contrast to the manufacturers of IBM "clone" computers, who mixed and matched readily available components. Over the years, despite intense competition, Apple grew into a worldwide corporation. It has held on to its niche of zealously dedicated owners in the personal computer market. Users have benefited from the innovations spurred by the competition between Apple and the PC makers that opt for the Microsoft operating system.

called a mouse, users pointed to icons — little pictures — on a computer monitor screen organized as a series of windows. The Mac might have been ahead of its time — at first it did not sell well. But it would not be long before most personal computers embraced the Mac's innovations.

Computers not only got faster but also smaller. In 1990, a brand new 14-pound "laptop" model came on the market — about like having a fat cat or a small Thanksgiving turkey on your lap. Only a year later, Steve Jobs's company produced an Apple laptop that weighed just five pounds. Journalists loved these portable computers. Executives could tote them to important meetings and work while traveling on airplanes.

The use of computers rapidly spread throughout businesses, schools, government agencies, and the military. Engineering firms, of course, leapt on the new tool since computers so dramatically increased problem-solving abilities. As companies introduced new computers that could do more and yet cost less, many families began to think of the PC as an appliance as essential as a refrigerator or oven. Software developers introduced games that made computers not only useful but also fun.

The stage was set for the next big breakthrough, which came in the early 1990s — finding a way to allow all these computers to talk to each other.

The Internet and the Web: A World Brain?

The British novelist H.G. Wells, who lived from the mid-nineteenth to the mid-twentieth century, is most famous today as the author of such science fiction classics as *The War of the Worlds* and *The Time Machine*. But he also deserves credit for proposing a project that he envisioned as fact, not fiction. Wells feared that as a result of the Industrial Revolution, most jobs — and, indeed, most fields of science — had become too narrow and specialized. Although human knowledge had increased greatly, Wells believed that people either had no access to it or were too focused on their own narrow sphere to benefit from it.

In the 1930s, in lectures across the United States, Wells campaigned for the creation of a sort of World Encyclopedia, not "as a row of volumes printed once for all, but as a...depot where knowledge and ideas are received, sorted, summarized, digested, clarified, and compared." Even though the Electronic Revolution had not yet begun, Wells believed that this depot "need not be concentrated now in one place; it might have the form of a network [that] would constitute the material beginning of a real World Brain." If Wells were still alive he would undoubtedly recognize that much of his dream exists today in the Internet and the World Wide Web.

The Internet began in the 1960s during the Cold War. At a time when tensions ran highest between the United States and the Soviet Union, J.C.R. Licklider, a professor at the Massachusetts Institute of Technology, was conducting research for the U.S. Defense Department's Advanced Research Projects Agency, or ARPA. ARPA wanted to find a way to transfer large amounts of data from government computers to the computers at universities and research labs doing government-sponsored work. Licklider had even bigger ideas.

With access to technology that Wells could not have imagined, Licklider dreamed of building, as he described it, "a 'thinking center' that will incorporate the functions of present-day libraries together with...advances in information storage and retrieval." He envisioned what he called an "Intergalactic Computer Network," a vast interconnected array of computers that would make it possible for almost anyone to have access to the information stored on the computers linked to the network.

In the early 1960s, Licklider took the first steps to link ARPA's computers in a system he called ARPANET. Within a few years, other scientists expanded ARPANET so that the network linked computers in geographically distant locations in California and Utah. Every computer linked to the system could access every other computer on the network, thus allowing users to share files, programs, and computer resources.

As ARPANET grew, it increased computer efficiency and productivity while lowering overall cost. But because the agency's defense-related work was secret, private institutions had very limited access to this network. By the 1980s, however, some businesses, government agencies, and universities had built further networks, not for military use. The university-based networks provided a fast, inexpensive way for researchers across the country to exchange ideas. Soon, several networks in Europe were linked to the North American networks.

The ongoing effort to link these research networks in the United States and Europe led to the development of what we know as the Internet — an *inter*connected *net*work of networks. Scientists established standards to allow the various networks to work with each other. With the explosion in popularity of the personal computer during the 1980s, private companies such as CompuServe, Prodigy, and America Online filled the demand from businesses and individuals for access to other computers. The need to move information rapidly encouraged

TCP/IP—Communicating in Packets

A key innovation that made the Internet possible was the development of certain protocols—in computer science, protocols are rules for the format and transmission of data. In the 1970s, Vincent Cerf of Stanford University and Robert Kahn at ARPA designed the Transmission Control Protocol/Internet Protocol, or TCP/IP for short. These protocols made it possible for various computers on different networks to communicate with each other.

For one thing, the protocols defined how to break large data files into smaller files called packets. Each packet—that is, each piece of the larger data file—is assigned information that identifies the Internet address the packet is coming from and going to. Each packet also carries data to tell the receiving computer how to reassemble the packets in the right order. It's like putting a paper letter through a shredder, then jotting a code on each shredded piece, then following the codes to reassemble the pieces into a whole letter again, with no tears or seams showing.

The protocols also work to guide the packets along many possible routes on the Internet. For example, say a lab in Los Angeles sends a message to an office in Paris. The message is broken into packets, and the various packets might go through New York; Washington, D.C.; Hong Kong; and London before being received in Paris. If a packet encounters a problem along the way, the protocols work to send the packet around the problem along another possible route—and it all happens almost instantaneously. This feature was especially important to the Defense Department, which wanted to be able to send messages even if part of a network was damaged or destroyed.

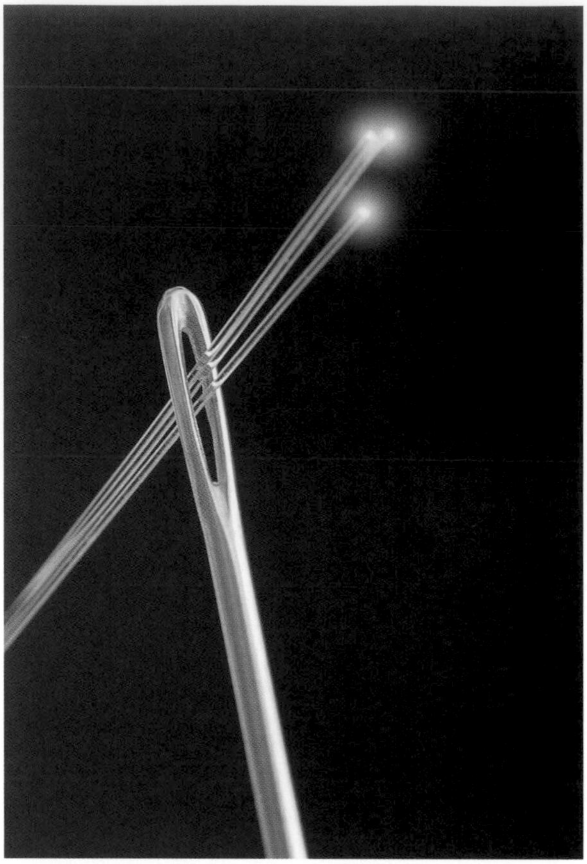

Thin, transparent fiber optic threads like these are bundled together to form fiber optic cables. The glass or plastic threads transmit information through light pulses.

other companies to build networks of fiber optic cables that use pulses of light to transmit data in greater quantity and at much higher speed than was possible with copper telephone wires. The U.S. government also provided funding to help broaden and strengthen the infrastructure of the Internet.

Infrastructure refers to the underlying framework of a system or organization.

The Internet is now established as a publicly available network of many different computer networks run by businesses, academic institutions, governments, nonprofit organizations, and more. It is not run by any single government or company. Instead, a number of agencies and voluntary groups cooperate to set standards and keep the Internet free, open, and working. As one of these groups, the Internet Society, explains, "The Internet is as much a collection of communities as a collection of technologies."

Weaving the Web

Into the 1980s, the Internet, while growing, was still limited to government agencies, universities, and a handful of businesses. Could the information on the Internet be presented in such a way that everyone — teachers, students, workers — could easily access and understand it, and even add to it? Many people doubted it, but a young British physicist named Tim Berners-Lee thought otherwise.

In his spare time while working at a European research laboratory for particle physics, Berners-Lee began to tinker with a program he called Enquire. He was convinced that the right software programs, called *browsers*, joined to the right standards for the display of information, could effectively organize the billions of pieces of data on the Internet.

Not long after the Berlin Wall fell, a technical wall came down, too. Berners-Lee called his creation the World Wide Web, or WWW. The Web is composed of a highly flexible, easy-to-change, interconnected system of computer files linked to each other on the Internet. The system allows data on the Internet to appear as "pages" of text and images on a computer screen. Anyone with a computer, the right software, and a connection to the Internet can view those pages, move from page to page and, with a little technical know-how, create and add new pages of content to the Web.

Berners-Lee realized that for the Web to succeed there would have to be certain rules, just as any language has. He devised a standard for addresses at which Web pages can be found. Through his work, abbreviations such as URL (Universal Resource Locator), HTML (Hypertext Markup Language), and HTTP (Hypertext Transfer Protocol) have become familiar to computer users.

During the 1990s, Berners-Lee's World Wide Web helped transform the Internet into an information superhighway. New Web standards made electronic mail a convenient and attractive mode of communication for everyday computer users. Simple text e-mail had been around since the

In the late 1990s, Internet cafés, like this one in Thailand, sprang up worldwide. The cafés offered access to an Internet-ready computer for a time-based fee. They became very popular in countries where people could not afford PCs.

Tim Berners-Lee, inventor of the World Wide Web

early days of ARPANET, but the new standards allowed users to go beyond plain text and add colors, images, links, and even sounds to their messages. Businesses and many private users quickly embraced e-mail and its power of almost instantaneous communication, and began referring to old-fashioned paper letters as "snail mail."

The Web made new kinds of interaction possible. On different continents around the globe, people with a shared interest, perhaps in the game of chess, could meet — not physically but virtually — and play together. Some colleges began offering online courses, giving students the opportunity to earn a degree without ever setting foot on campus. Online schooling soon extended into high school and even into elementary school. Businesses began advertising and selling products over the Internet. Individuals began posting their thoughts and opinions in "web logs," familiarly known as "blogs."

By 2004, the number of pages on the Web, containing (for better or worse) every type of content imaginable, exceeded eight billion. By this time, Tim Berners-Lee was directing a major computer laboratory at the Massachusetts Institute of Technology. In that year, the British monarch conferred upon Berners-Lee an honor that, centuries earlier, had been given to Isaac Newton. At Buckingham Palace, the queen bestowed a knighthood on the inventor of the Web.

Googling the Web

In the 1990s, one of the biggest challenges facing users of the World Wide Web was sifting among the millions of pages to find the information they wanted, and finding it quickly. (The Web has a way of making people impatient for instant results.) Researchers worked on developing a search engine, a kind of computer-generated map of the Web to guide people efficiently through the maze of available content.

Two Stanford graduate students, Larry Page and Sergey Brin, worked on such an engine, and by 1998 they had invented something they called Google. The name came from a misspelling of the word *googol*, which is a very large number — the digit 1 followed by 100 zeros. Originally, their Google search engine ran on a dozen computers in Page's dorm room. Page and Brin saved money by building the housings for some of their computers out of Lego toy bricks.

They showed their invention to one of the founders of a major company in the computer industry, Sun Microsystems. He was so impressed that he immediately wrote a check for $100,000 to Google, Incorporated, to help the company make progress. Page and Brin were delighted, except that there was no Google, Incorporated — they had not yet formed a company.

In the next few weeks, the two young men put their company together. Like Steve Jobs at Apple, they started in a garage. During the next few years, various search engines were offered to users of the Web, but Google became the leading search engine. Its inventors devised a method of calculating what they called PageRank, a way to rank Web pages in order of their relevance to the search request submitted by a user. The math was sophisticated — as Brin and Page summed it up, "PageRank or *PR(A)* can be calculated using a simple iterative algorithm, and corresponds to the principal eigenvector of the normalized link matrix of the web" — but the results were transparent to users, who turned to Google to help them sort quickly and easily through an immense amount of online information.

Brin and Page offered their service free to anyone with access to the Internet. They made money by selling space on their website to

Stanford buddies Sergey Brin (left) and Larry Page developed Google while in graduate school. Brin had emigrated to the United States from the Soviet Union; Page came from Lansing, Michigan. They stand in front of corporate headquarters in 2004.

advertisers who, in turn, hoped Google users would be drawn to their websites.

The Google site now responds to hundreds of millions of search requests every day. It has become such a popular destination on the Web that Merriam-Webster has added the verb "to google" to its dictionary.

From Telephone to Cell Phone

The Internet and the World Wide Web connected people in new ways and made the world a little smaller. The world shrank a bit more when the telephone went wireless.

Alexander Graham Bell's telephone made it possible for people to communicate instantly over great distances, but for decades one drawback remained—phones had to be connected by a series of wires. At the dawn of the twentieth century, Marconi's radio paved the way for wireless communication. By World War II, soldiers communicated with portable but bulky two-way radios. These "walkie-talkies" held a key to wireless communications, but they were much too large and expensive for ordinary folks.

By the 1970s, engineers at Motorola Corporation were trying to make an integrated circuit small enough to fit in a handheld telephone that could communicate without wires to a regular phone. A Motorola engineer named Martin Cooper made it all work. On April 3, 1973, he stood on a busy sidewalk in Manhattan and punched a telephone number into a handset. The handset sent a signal to a base station, or cell, on a nearby building and then through the regular telephone network. Cooper recalls that, as curious passersby looked on, "I called my counterpart at Bell Labs, Joel Engel, and told him: 'Joel, I'm calling you from a "real" cellular telephone. A portable handheld telephone.'"

Martin Cooper displays the first cell phone.

Cooper's first cell phone was larger than a brick, weighed two-and-a-half pounds, and took 10 hours to recharge. He wanted to make it smaller, cheaper, and easier to recharge. He envisioned millions of people using little handheld phones. His company liked the idea.

Motorola put out the first commercial cellular phones in 1983. The weight was down to 28 ounces, but they cost $3,995. Still, in the communications industry, wireless was the new way to go. In a flurry of activity, companies began putting up cell towers to receive signals. And, as with computers, engineers used ever more compact electronics to make the new devices smaller and more affordable. "Given a choice," Cooper observed, "people will demand the freedom to communicate wherever they are, unfettered by the infamous copper wire."

By 1990, more than four million people in the United States had their own cell phones. By the first decade of the twenty-first century, more people were using cell phones than traditional phones worldwide.

All in the Palm of Your Hand

In the twenty-first century, one tendency in consumer electronics is for devices to get smaller and do more. Several companies introduced a line of small, handheld devices, called personal digital assistants. These PDAs, such as the popular BlackBerry, employed wireless technology to allow users to check e-mail, browse the Web, or perform other computer functions without being tied to a desk in the office.

It didn't take long to figure out how to integrate that technology into a cell phone. For example, in 2007 the Apple Corporation introduced the iPhone. Announcing "Apple reinvents the phone," Steve Jobs unveiled a device weighing less than five ounces and small enough to fit easily in the hand. It let users send and receive e-mail, listen to music, watch TV shows or movies, play video games, search the Web, find the quickest route to a friend's house, get stock quotes, read the *New York Times*, do Internet research for a report, and type it right on the screen. And, yes, they could also phone home on it.

Apple had by this time used the power of electronics, coupled with innovative user design, to create a wildly popular line of handheld music devices, called iPods, as well as an online music distribution company, iTunes. These drove further innovations, such as "podcasting," which allows users to download files from the Internet—for example, a news report, or a recorded concert or lecture—onto their handheld devices (whether iPods or the new competitors) for playback later at the user's convenience.

Combining mobile phone, e-mail, and Web access, handheld devices like these BlackBerrys made it easy to access all kinds of information.

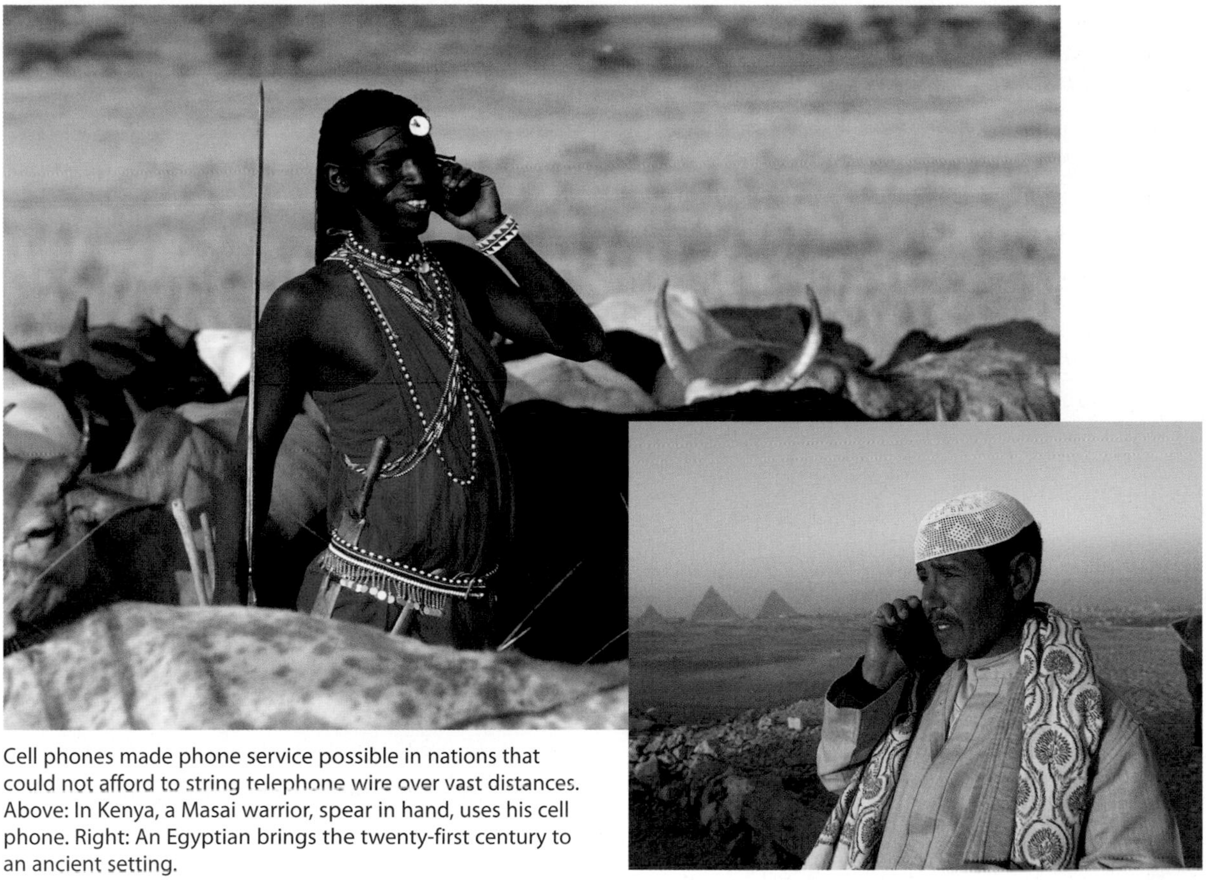

Cell phones made phone service possible in nations that could not afford to string telephone wire over vast distances. Above: In Kenya, a Masai warrior, spear in hand, uses his cell phone. Right: An Egyptian brings the twenty-first century to an ancient setting.

The cell phone brought instant communications to people in poor and undeveloped regions. It was easier and cheaper to build a cell phone tower than to string wires across vast expanses. By 2005, Masai cattlemen in the Serengeti grasslands of East Africa and goat herders in Afghanistan were all chatting on their cell phones. They were connected to family, friends, and businesses as never before.

Business Goes Global

Like the Industrial Revolution, the Information Revolution has dramatically changed the way many people live and work. The Industrial Revolution forced people to move to increasingly crowded cities to find jobs in factories. In contrast, the electronically charged Information Revolution is making it possible for many people to work almost anywhere — from their homes or from offices in a state or country far from their employer. Businesses can bring together teams of people around the globe who would never have been united before.

The term *globalization* has come to describe this trend toward interconnectedness and interdependence in many areas of life, but especially in business. With computers, the Internet, the World Wide Web, and cell phones, many corporations find they can work easily almost anywhere in the world. Businesses now make use of an international labor force.

Some American computer firms have cut costs by moving parts of their operations to India, where there is a well-educated, English-speaking labor force, and where wages are much lower than in the United States. The Web allows these workers to be inexpensively connected to the United States.

Outsourcing is the practice of using overseas labor to accomplish something once done locally.

A computer manufacturer in Texas, for example, might "outsource" its customer service operations by setting up a call center in New Delhi to respond to user questions. The firm hires English-speaking Indian technicians and pays them a far lower salary than their American counterparts would receive, but

Terrorism and the Information Revolution

The Information Revolution has improved billions of lives, but as with most technological advances, its potential can be a curse as well as a blessing. For example, it has given terrorists new tools for destruction. Terrorists all over the world use laptop computers, cell phones, and e-mail to communicate with each other and plan their attacks. They use the Internet to find information about how to build bombs and about potential targets. They even use the Internet to spread terror by posting videos of their cruel acts.

a far higher salary than their Indian compatriots receive. The Indian employees are trained to speak in different English accents (Australian, British, and several varieties of American) and choose English versions of their Indian names. A puzzled computer user in Ohio might call customer service and speak to a technician in New Delhi.

Old Problems in the Brave New World

We have been looking at some of the more dazzling manifestations of the brave new world of technology — computers, the Internet, cell phones, and other electronic innovations that have fueled the Information Revolution. Technology continues to advance in leaps and bounds, but sometimes it leaps right over parts of the world, where people still live in conditions closer to the Middle Ages than the twenty-first century — communicating face-to-face rather than by e-mail or text messaging, riding in horse-drawn carts rather than sports cars, farming with oxen rather than tractors, drawing water from wells rather than turning on a faucet or pouring it cool and sparkling from a pale green bottle.

A sometimes startling phenomenon of our times is the side-by-side coexistence of the old and new. Regions that fell behind in the Industrial Revolution are reaping some fruits of the Information Revolution, but still living with grave deficiencies. Consider, for example, the crowded city of New Delhi in India, the site of our imagined customer service call center for a United States–based computer company. New Delhi is in fact home to many young, well-educated people

Old and new combine as men in Western dress and women in traditional garb work on developing twenty-first-century software programs at this outsourcing center in Kashmir, a region north of India.

A study in contrasts, the Indian city of Mumbai (formerly Bombay) is a thriving center for business, banking, film, and high-tech industries. But in nearby slums, people struggle to find necessities.

who perform high-tech jobs — often outsourced by Western companies — such as website design, computer support, or software programming. While they receive salaries lower than the pay for similar tasks in the United States, their pay goes further in India. They live relatively comfortable lives in modern apartments, and they own high-tech luxuries such as flat-screen televisions and laptop computers and cell phones.

In the same city, however, not far from the modern apartments, there is a slum where, every morning at dawn, women gather in a line. They are carrying buckets and plastic jugs. They wait, sometimes an hour, sometimes all day. They are waiting for the tanker truck carrying fresh water. They have no running water. The wells are polluted or have run dry. Even in the middle-class apartments of New Delhi where the high-tech workers live, running water is available only a few hours per day. Sleepy residents wake before dawn to turn on their taps and stockpile water — often brown and muddy — for use later in the day when the water supply is cut off.

In this city, new and old exist in jarring juxtaposition. Even as members of the high-tech middle-class workforce are writing computer code or designing digital graphics, they, like the women in the slums carrying plastic jugs, still struggle to get enough water, one of life's most basic needs.

An Indian professor offers these eloquent reflections on the situation in his land: "We speak of our information technology and the advances we have made in our society with justifiable pride.... We take seriously the discussion of Indians going to the moon. We have very big dreams. Yet here we are, a deeply backward country peering at modernity from the threshold."

We live in a time in which many people are still "peering at modernity from the threshold," while many others are peering at the colorful glowing screens of their iPods.

The words of Shakespeare echo across the centuries to describe our present day: "O brave new world that has such people in it."

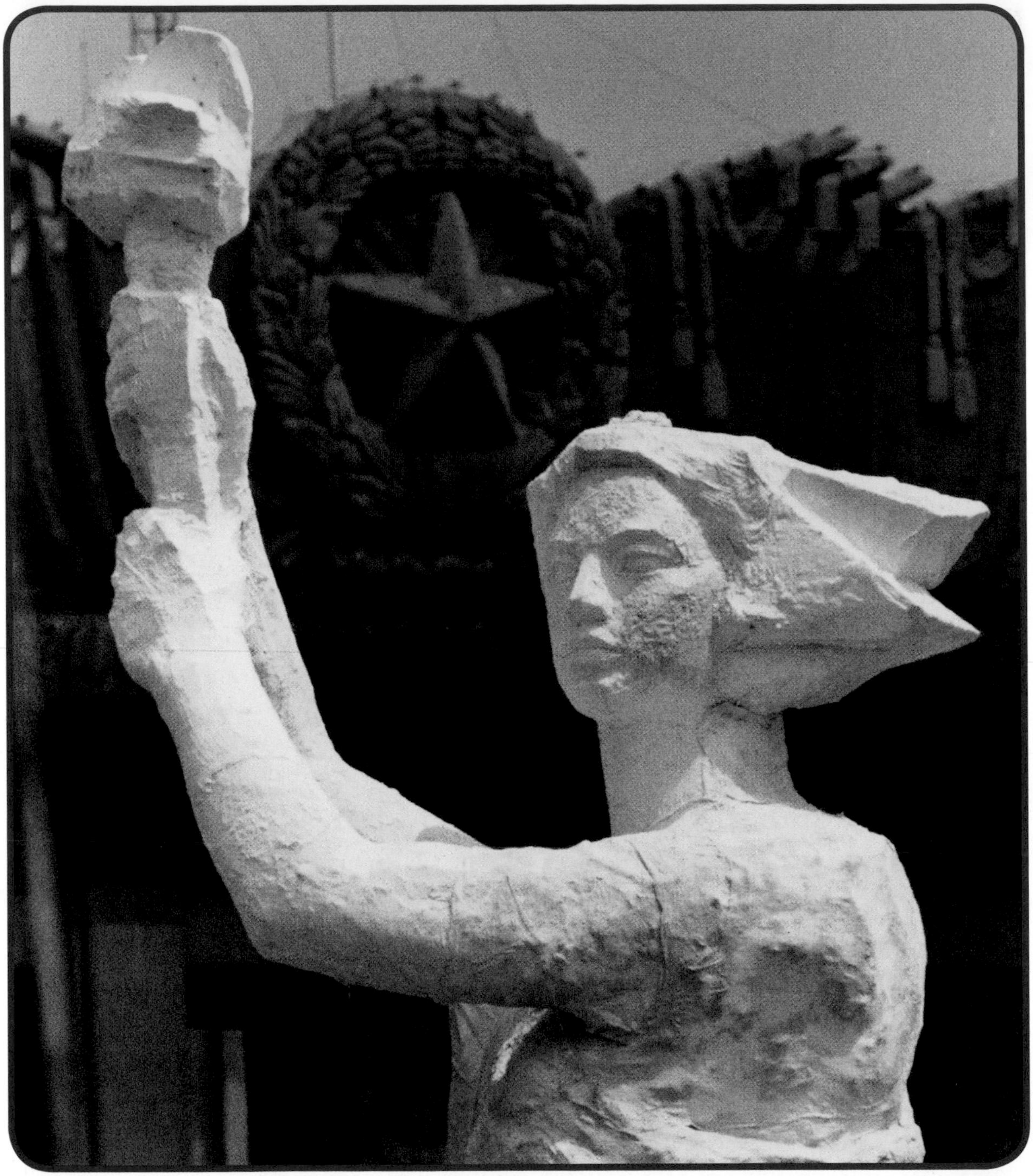

The *Goddess of Democracy,* modeled on the American *Statue of Liberty,* was erected by Chinese students in Tiananmen Square in Beijing in 1989. Thousands of Chinese demonstrated for democratic change. Their protest was brutally suppressed, but this symbol of democratic revolution was seen around the world. Democratic stirrings elsewhere proved more successful.

Ongoing Democratic Revolutions

The Information Revolution has brought people around the world closer together. In recent years, many people have begun to speak of a new "global community." But in what sense is our world a "community"? Do the nearly two hundred countries have any common goals or uniting principles?

At the close of World War II, world leaders at the United Nations proclaimed their shared belief in the principles of human rights and self-determination as stated in the Universal Declaration of Human Rights. The Universal Declaration affirmed that the ideals of the American and French Revolutions — natural rights, human dignity, equality of persons, liberty, and self-rule — applied not just to a fortunate few in the West but to all humankind.

Many nations failed to live up to the lofty standards of the Universal Declaration of Human Rights. Communist governments called themselves democracies or republics, but in fact tyrants like Stalin and Mao Zedong ruled with an iron fist. Some nations newly liberated from colonial rule succumbed to military dictatorships or power-mad strongmen.

But the human desire for liberty remained strong and vital. The belief that all individuals have basic human rights — a belief that brought down Louis XVI in eighteenth-century France — brought down the Berlin Wall in 1989.

In this chapter, we look at ongoing revolutions motivated by democratic principles and ideals. Some involve the quest for basic human rights and self-government. Others have been social revolutions, including the one we examine first, the Women's Movement.

Women's Roles in the Workplace

As a growing number of nations affirmed the principles of equality and self-determination, many women asked how those principles applied to them. In the early twentieth century, women in many Western nations had won the right to vote and other political rights. Woman suffrage — the right to vote — was a triumph achieved only after long struggle. But it was, as many women realized in the decades following World War II, only a partial victory.

In World War II, as many men were called to fight, millions of women took on jobs once done by men. They welded, soldered, and riveted parts for weapons and aircraft. They staffed banks and ran businesses. Many women liked their jobs (and the money they earned). When the war ended, however, they were often dismissed to make room for the returning male veterans.

At a California aircraft plant in 1942, this woman ratchets a part into place. During World War II, three million American women took jobs in the defense industry.

Most women left their jobs quietly. Millions got married and concentrated on raising their children, caring for their homes, and volunteering in their communities. Others found lower-paying secretarial jobs. Many women were happy with their return to homemaking and raising their families. They enjoyed the challenges and rewards of being a mother. But others found that driving kids to school, mopping floors, and shopping for groceries did not provide the same satisfaction as assembling a B-17 bomber.

Betty Friedan Moves Beyond Mystique

In 1949, the French writer Simone de Beauvoir (see-MOHN deh bohv-WAHR) expressed the dissatisfaction felt by many women in a book titled *The Second Sex*. She said male-dominated society had condemned women to an inferior status by defining the ideal woman as a submissive creature, "frivolous, infantile, [and] irresponsible." De Beauvoir's book was translated into more than a dozen languages and set off a worldwide discussion about the role of women in society.

One of the leaders in that discussion was an American named Betty Friedan (free-DAN). A writer and mother of three, Friedan sent a questionnaire to her Smith College classmates asking how satisfied they were with their lives 15 years after graduation. In 1963, their responses led to her book called *The Feminine Mystique*.

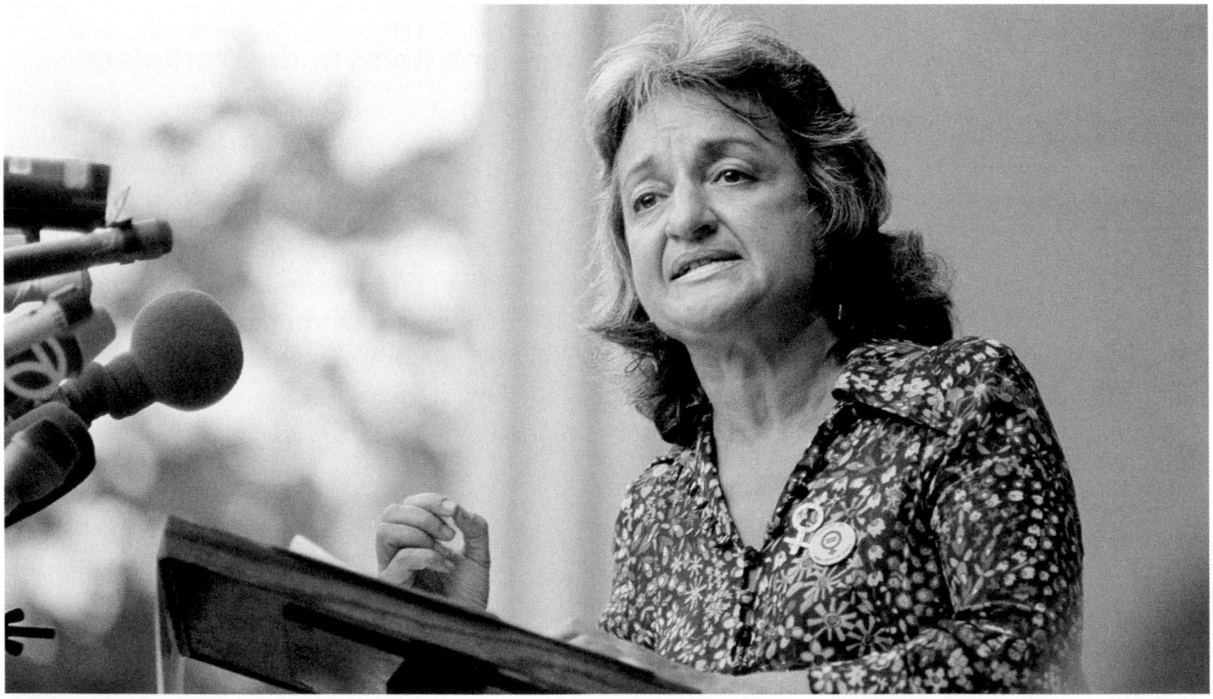

Writer Betty Friedan energized the new women's movement in 1963 with her book *The Feminine Mystique*. She urged women to seek higher education and careers outside the home. Above, she addresses a Women's Strike for Equality in 1970.

In *The Feminine Mystique*, Friedan described the "nameless, aching dissatisfaction" that many American women felt, particularly educated suburban housewives. Many women said they loved their husbands and their children, but still felt a sense of deep longing. As one woman put it, "I begin to feel I have no personality. I'm a server of food and a putter on of pants and a bedmaker, somebody who can be called on when you want something, but who am I?"

Friedan argued that in the years since World War II, Western culture had created a "feminine mystique," an idea that women were truly feminine only to the extent that they devoted themselves to their husbands, children, and homes. Young women, she said, were being "taught to pity the neurotic, unfeminine, unhappy women who wanted to be poets or physicists or presidents." They were, said Friedan, deluded into thinking that higher education and a career "masculinized" women.

In the mid-twentieth century, Friedan observed, women were equal to men in that they were "free to choose automobiles, clothes, appliances, [and] supermarkets." In other words, women were free to be consumers. But this, said Friedan, was hardly enough — and many women agreed with her.

The Feminine Mystique quickly became a manifesto for feminism—the conviction that women are in every way the political, economic, and social equals of men. In the 1960s, the feminist movement began to grow in the United States and Europe. Its leaders encouraged women to pursue higher education and careers outside the home.

American marine biologist Rachel Carson examines a specimen of sea life. Her 1962 book *Silent Spring* warned of the environmental dangers of excessive pesticide use.

Leading by Example

Feminist leaders could point with pride to some contemporary women as inspiring examples of moving beyond the "feminine mystique." In the United States, for example, many admired Eleanor Roosevelt, who had been a champion of civil rights in the United States and had led the UN effort to draft the Universal Declaration of Human Rights.

An *anthropologist* studies human beings and their cultures, seeking to understand patterns in human behavior.

Other notable American women included the anthropologist Margaret Mead, who had been writing influential and widely read books since the 1920s. In 1938, Pearl Buck received the Nobel Prize for literature for her novels about China. In 1962, Rachel Carson, a marine biologist, gripped the world's attention with the publication of *Silent Spring*, a book that warned of the dire environmental hazards of pesticides.

In England in the 1950s, a microbiologist named Rosalind Franklin was a key member of a team of scientists that discovered the structure of DNA, though the men she worked with tried to hide the fact that they had benefited from her research. In Kenya, Austrian-born conservationist Joy Adamson pioneered a movement to preserve African wildlife. In the United Kingdom, astrophysicist S. Jocelyn Bell Burnell

In 1963, Valentina Tereshkova of the USSR became the first woman in space. Orbiting the earth once every 88 minutes, she used manual controls to guide her spacecraft.

A *radio pulsar* is a rapidly rotating neutron star from which pulses of electromagnetic radiation are detected on earth.

first discovered radio pulsars. And in 1963, Soviet cosmonaut Valentina Tereshkova orbited the earth 48 times over a three-day period.

These women often had to work harder, and make greater sacrifices, than men in similar positions. German-born Maria Goeppert-Mayer, for instance, shared the 1963 Nobel Prize in physics with two men, but she was the only one who had done most of her research as an unpaid volunteer. For many years, the University of Chicago granted her laboratory space and a great deal of respect, but no salary.

Women in the Ivies

Many of the world's most prestigious universities, such as the famous Ivy League schools in the northeastern United States, did not admit women until the 1960s and 1970s, when Harvard, Yale, Dartmouth, and Princeton began to accept women. Columbia did not decide to do so until 1983.

Riding the Second Wave

As the message of feminism spread, women in the United States and Europe began to push for greater access to all sorts of jobs. They wanted equal pay, maternity leave, and child-care centers.

Feminists called these economic and social issues the "second wave" of feminism — a follow-up to the first wave about fifty years before that had established women's right to vote in most Western countries.

By the 1970s, young women were entering professions that had once been limited to men. In the United States, Europe, Canada, and many parts of South America, many more women enrolled in colleges and earned their degrees. In the United States, for example, the percentage of women in law school rose from less than 4 percent in 1963 to 47 percent in 2006. The percentage of women in medical schools shot up from 6 percent in 1961 to 50 percent in 2006. The number of women in the workforce continued to rise, from 18.4 million in 1950 to 65.7 million in 2005 — from 29 percent of the workforce to 46 percent.

New questions faced families with wives and mothers working outside the home: Who will care for the children? Who will make dinner? Who will do the laundry? Although many husbands and fathers took on more housework and child-rearing tasks, most wives carried the double burden of being their family's primary homemaker while holding down a job outside the home.

The second wave of feminism met with a backlash. Some people blamed the new feminists for rising divorce rates. They worried that children were being raised in day-care centers instead of by caring parents. But feminists dismissed these concerns. Betty Friedan said, "Some people think I'm saying, 'Women of the world unite — you have nothing to lose but your men.' It's not true. You have nothing to lose but your vacuum cleaners."

Women in Government

As more women entered the workforce, some rose to positions of leadership that their mothers and grandmothers could never have imagined.

One of the first women to lead a democratic country was Golda Meir (GOHL-duh may-IR), who devoted much of her life to making a homeland for the Jewish people. When she was a child, her family fled religious persecution in Russia for freedom in the United States. After she grew up, she moved to Palestine, where she first lived on a *kibbutz* — a commune where all shared the work — with her husband and children. But the politics of establishing a Jewish state kept calling her away from home.

Meir was one of the signers of the document that founded the country of Israel in 1948. "After I signed," she later recalled, "I cried. When I studied American history as a schoolgirl and I read about those who signed the Declaration of Independence, I couldn't imagine these were real people doing something real. And there I was sitting down and signing a declaration of independence."

Meir served her new country as ambassador to Russia, where she ran the embassy like a kibbutz, with everyone pitching in with chores. Later, she was a member of the Israeli parliament, a cabinet member, and finally prime minister from 1969 to 1974.

Near the end of her life, Meir looked back on her decision to leave the kibbutz and spend so much time away from her family. "There is a type of woman who cannot remain at home," she said.

An Israeli honor guard welcomes Prime Minister Golda Meir to the Sinai front in 1970. Israel requires military service of nearly all 18-year-old men and women.

Ride, Sally Ride

Sally Ride, a scientist and astronaut from California, was cheered by millions in 1983 when she blasted off aboard the Space Shuttle *Challenger* and became the first American woman to travel into space. Ride was a physicist from Stanford University and had helped develop the Space Shuttle's robot arm. On that 1983 flight, she and her fellow astronauts became the first crew to use the robot arm to release and retrieve a satellite. Sally Ride was not the first woman to go into space. That honor was won 20 years earlier by Soviet cosmonaut Valentina Tereshkova.

From the Space Shuttle *Challenger*, physicist Sally Ride communicates with the Johnson Space Center in Houston in 1983.

Indira Gandhi, India's first woman prime minister, held office from 1966 to 1977, and from 1980 to 1984, when she was assassinated. She was the daughter of Jawaharlal Nehru.

"In spite of the place her children and family fill in her life, her nature demands something more."

Since the 1960s, dozens of women have been chosen to head democratic governments around the globe. Indira Gandhi twice led India as the country's prime minister. Margaret Thatcher was the longest serving British prime minister of the twentieth century. In recent years, Germany's Angela Merkel, Liberia's Ellen Johnson-Sirleaf, and Chile's Michele Bachelet have headed their country's now democratic governments. In the United States, which led the world in the second wave of feminism, women have served in the highest levels of government, including two women—Madeleine Albright and Condoleezza Rice—who have held the key position of secretary of state.

Left Behind?

While many Western women broke free of the "feminine mystique," millions of women in other parts of the world have remained "the second sex." In the 1990s, for instance, women in China and India were valued so little that millions of baby girls were abandoned or even killed shortly after their births.

Another large group of women left behind in the progress toward women's rights were those living under strict Islamic regimes. You've read about the repression and cruelty women endured under the Taliban regime in Afghanistan, which was overthrown in 2001. There a woman could be beaten for leaving home without wearing her burqa, the long cloak that covers the body from head to toe.

In Iran, when Ayatollah Khomeini and his followers threw out the shah and set up Iran's Islamic Republic, they also threw out many rights that Iranian women had enjoyed for decades under the shah's westernized rule. On International Women's Day in 2006, Iranian police attacked hundreds of women and men who had peacefully assembled with placards stating "discrimination against women is an abuse of human rights." The police dumped cans of garbage on the heads of women, then beat and kicked those assembled.

In Saudi Arabia with its Wahabbi-inspired regime, women cannot hold driver's licenses or vote. Moreover, when they go out in public, they must wear a veil and robe.

Democracy Gains Ground After World War II

The women's movement was strongest in the West where democracy had the deepest roots. Since World War II, democracy has spread to several countries around the world, and democratic revolutions are ongoing. The continuing spread of democracy is remarkable, because throughout much of recorded human history, most people had little if any say in the way they were ruled. Representative government existed only in small geographic pockets and for brief periods of time. But democracy gained ground after the American and French Revolutions in the eighteenth century, and after the Industrial Revolutions of the nineteenth and twentieth centuries.

By 1948, the Universal Declaration of Human Rights proclaimed that "everyone has the right to take part in the government of his country." The Declaration went on to say that governments should also protect other fundamental rights, like the right to free speech, the right to freedom of worship, and the right to be treated equally under the law. Putting those ideals into practice has involved a long struggle — one that continues today.

By 2007, just under half of the world's people lived in countries with representative forms of government that respect human rights. That number may seem surprisingly small, but it is a significant increase compared to three decades before. In 1976, only 26 percent of the world's people lived in countries with democratic forms of government. But since the end of European colonial rule in the 1960s and 1970s, and the end of the Cold War in 1989, more nations and peoples have embraced representative government and taken steps to protect human rights.

In many places, the spread of representative government has brought greater freedom. The map below divides the nations of the world into three broad categories: Free, Partly free, and Not free. In countries categorized as "free," people enjoy representative government and a broad range of human rights, freedom of the press, and free elections. In "partly free" nations, governments have limited respect for such rights and liberties; these countries may also suffer from frequent corruption in government, fighting among ethnic or religious groups, and the domination of one political party over others. In nations described as "not free," people generally lack basic political rights and civil liberties.

As the map indicates, people in Europe, Australia, and most of the Americas enjoy significant freedom. In many parts of Africa and Asia, however, freedom is still an elusive goal. Some countries have emerged from colonialism or communism only to lapse into civil war or fall prey to new forms of dictatorship.

Democracy Stumbles in Africa

In the late twentieth century, new African nations, many of which were former British and French

The Ongoing Struggle for Freedom

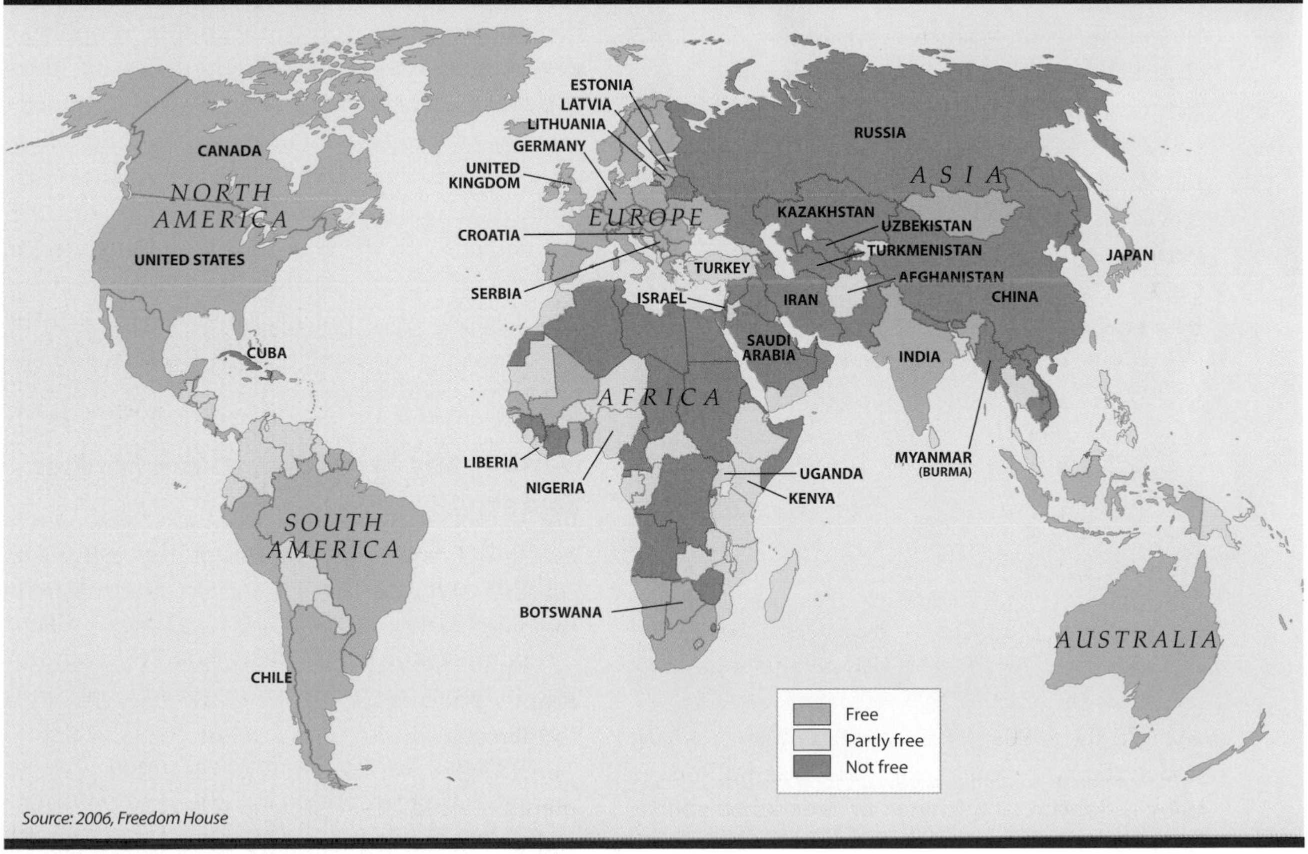

Source: 2006, Freedom House

colonies, struggled to establish democratic governments and protect human rights.

Nigeria, Africa's most populous nation, illustrates how great that challenge could be. A former British colony, Nigeria gained independence in 1960. At that time, it seemed poised for successful self-rule and prosperity. Nigerians chose a parliamentary government with a prime minister. Nigeria's farms were productive, and the nation could feed itself. Geologists located oil and gas reserves.

But the new nation was torn by rivalries among various ethnic groups competing for power. These rivalries eventually erupted in civil war. Eight military dictatorships followed, one after another, most utterly corrupt. The generals did begin to pump Nigeria's vast reserves of oil, but they looted the treasury. Despite the fact that Nigeria was the sixth largest oil producer in the world, the people's standard of living fell by more than two-thirds between 1980 and 1999.

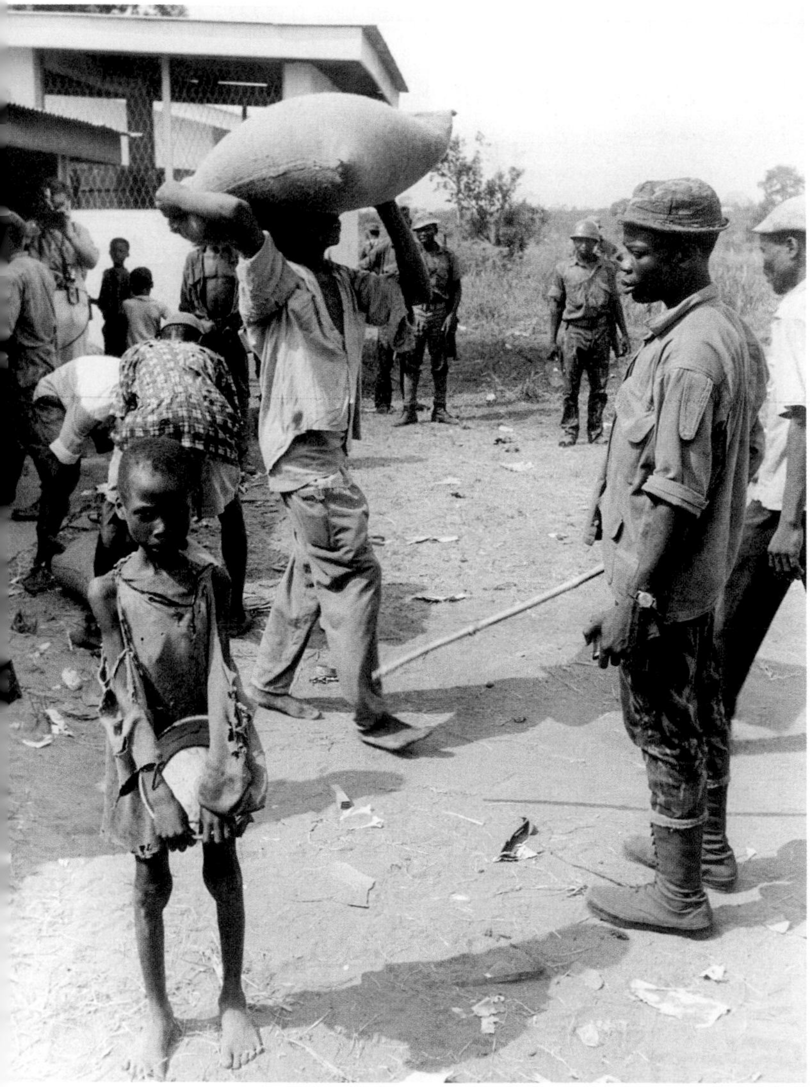
A young refugee holding a pan awaits food at a distribution center in Nigeria in 1970. Civil war ravaged the former British colony after it gained independence.

Another example of the challenges facing democracy in Africa is the country of Uganda. In 1962, the densely populated East African nation gained independence from the British. But there was turmoil from the start. The nation had three different constitutions in its first nine years, and in 1971 a crazed and brutal military strongman, Idi Amin Dada (EE-dee ah-MEEN DAH-dah), gained control. He executed many thousands of his fellow countrymen, and held on to power for eight dark years. Since 1980, the nation has struggled to maintain representative government and civilian rule, experiencing periods of military rule and civil war.

In contrast, Botswana is an African nation that, while poor, seems to have made a peaceful and successful transition to self-government and democracy. A former British colony, Botswana has maintained a fully functioning republican government since 1966. Its population includes two major ethnic groups, along with a significant number of people of European descent. These groups have managed to live in relative harmony. Economic growth between 1960 and 1995 has helped with the transition to independence, though a rising standard of living is no guarantee of stable government. There is much to be celebrated in the young nation's four-decade history of peaceful self-rule.

Democratic Struggles in the Former Eastern Bloc

When the Cold War ended and communist regimes collapsed, people danced in the streets and celebrated. But during the 1990s, in several countries that had been ruled by communist dictators, the celebration gave way to cries of anguish.

A tragic case is the former Yugoslavia, an Eastern European nation on the Balkan Peninsula. After Yugoslavia's communist government

Two women grieve over the loss of loved ones after Serbian troops massacred some seven thousand Muslim men and boys in an "ethnic cleansing" at Srebrenica, Bosnia, in 1995.

fell in 1990, civil war broke out between the three main groups living in the country — the Serbs, the Croats, and the Muslims — groups deeply divided by religion and ethnicity.

Wherever one group was in the majority, it tried to drive out members of the other groups. At its worst, these actions of "ethnic cleansing," as they were called, amounted to mass murder. In 1995, at a place called Srebrenica (sreh-breh-NEET-sah), Serbian troops massacred more than seven thousand Muslim men and boys — some of them as young as 13. This crime — one of the worst atrocities in Europe since World War II — shocked the world, though no other nations intervened to stop the "ethnic cleansing."

The bloody civil war finally came to an end in the late 1990s, leaving the former Yugoslavia fractured into five separate nations. Violence in the region has continued into the twenty-first century. Each of these nations has achieved some form of representative government — but at a terrible price. The future of democracy in the region is far from certain.

The year 1991 saw the breakup not only of Yugoslavia but also of the Soviet Union. Today, the territory of the former Soviet Union contains 15 separate nations. All call themselves democracies, but some are democratic only in name. Russia, the heart of the old Soviet Union, has seen continual shifts in power since the fall of the Soviet empire. The Russian people vote in parliamentary and local elections. But in the early 2000s, the government of President Vladimir Putin (POO-tihn) increasingly cracked down on critics, discouraged freedom of the press, and controlled elections by restricting the ability of reformers to run for office.

Among former Eastern Bloc countries, the most successful transitions to democracy have

Chile Returns to Democracy

In 1989, as many formerly communist nations reached for freedom, Chileans left behind their military dictatorship. Chile was a country with a long history of democratic institutions prior to the military takeover in 1973. In 1980, the military itself proposed a new constitution and a transition to elected government. Since 1989, Chileans have revised their constitution and chosen their presidents in free elections. In 2006, they elected as president Michele Bachelet, a physician and a former prisoner of the Pinochet regime.

Michele Bachelet was elected president of Chile in 2006.

In 1989, one million people formed a human chain that stretched across Estonia, Latvia, and Lithuania in a show of Baltic solidarity. Such cooperation helped make a successful transition to democracy in the Baltic States.

been made by Latvia, Estonia, and Lithuania. These European countries had enjoyed democratic institutions before they were conquered by the Soviet Union at the close of World War II. In contrast, Central Asian countries like Kazakhstan, Uzbekistan, and Turkmenistan had no experience of popular decision making or respect for human rights. In those nations, former communist leaders have persecuted their political opponents and rigged elections to keep themselves in power.

Communism Holds On in Cuba

Like gigantic China, the small island nation of Cuba remained a communist stronghold after the Cold War. The Soviet Union had provided Cuba with aid and cheap oil, as well as markets for Cuban sugar. The fall of the USSR dealt an economic blow to Fidel Castro's regime. While other nations around the world abandoned communism, Castro held on. At the outset of the twenty-first century, Cuba was the only communist country in the Americas, and its government continued to limit people's freedom.

China: The Last Big Communist Stronghold?

China, the world's most populous nation, has been ruled by the Communist Party since 1949. In the late 1980s, as communist rule weakened in the Soviet Union and Eastern Europe, China's communist leaders faced a dramatic challenge. In June 1989, thousands of college students gathered to demonstrate in Tiananmen Square in the capital city of Beijing. They called on the communist government to listen to the people, and grant basic rights like freedom of speech. In the middle of the square, the students set up a giant statue of a woman holding a torch, modeled on the *Statue of Liberty*. They called the woman the *Goddess of Democracy*. (See page 354.)

The world tuned in to watch television reports on the courageous students. The Chinese government reacted brutally. Late one night, troops and tanks poured into Tiananmen Square. Tanks crushed the statue of *Democracy*. Soldiers with automatic weapons opened fire on the unarmed students. Hundreds of demonstrators were killed; the rest fled the square. The number of dead is not known because Chinese authorities banished cameras and reporters. For the time being, the Chinese government had succeeded in crushing the democracy movement.

Although China remained under communist rule, the democracy movement worried the nation's leaders. To divert the people from their lack of *political* freedom, the government decided to allow much greater *economic* freedom. A communist government usually keeps its nation's economy under tight control. But the Chinese government changed its old policies and encouraged people to go into business for themselves. They could become as wealthy as they wanted, as long as they did not challenge the authority of the Communist Party.

These new economic policies attracted foreign investment and raised the standard of living in China. Today, while the majority of Chinese remain poor, there is a large middle class that dresses in Western clothes, drinks coffee in Starbucks, and eats hamburgers in McDonald's. In some ways, the lives of these Chinese resemble those of people in Europe or America—except that they cannot vote in a free election, criticize their government, or worship as they see fit.

Will the Chinese people remain willing to accept material prosperity at the expense of democratic freedoms? That story remains to be told.

A Chinese man stood up for freedom and caught the world's attention when he dared to block a column of tanks during the Tiananmen Square uprising in Beijing in 1989.

Iran's Struggle

The Middle East has struggled to meet the challenges of modern times while remaining faithful to its traditions and its predominant faith, Islam. Except for the Jewish state of Israel, no Middle Eastern nation in the early twenty-first century could claim to be a functioning, multiparty democracy.

Turkey, which is a predominantly Muslim nation, comes the closest. Its parliamentary regime, established under Ataturk, maintains separation of church and state, and has a functioning court system. But it forbids criticism of state institutions and restricts other basic rights. Still, Turkey is a free nation compared to many other Middle Eastern lands, which are ruled by monarchs, strongmen, and, increasingly, clerics.

Iran's history shows some of the struggles faced by Muslim nations in modern times. In 1978, Iranians overthrew the shah and established a *theocracy*—rule by religious leaders. Iran calls itself an "Islamic Republic." The country does have some representative institutions, including an elected president and parliament. But the ultimate power in the country rests with an Islamic religious figure known as the Supreme Leader. The first Supreme Leader was Ayatollah Khomeini, who led the 1979 revolution that deposed the shah. The Supreme Leader commands the armed forces, appoints judges, and oversees the parliament. The parliament itself can pass no law unless the religious leaders decide it is in accord with traditional Islamic law.

An Iranian citizen who violates Islamic morality can be brutally punished. People caught drinking alcohol may be whipped in a public square. Adulterers have been sentenced to death by stoning. Everywhere, religious police patrol the streets, looking for couples engaging in the forbidden practice of holding hands, or stopping people wearing "immodest" clothing. Women are supposed to wear clothes that completely cover their bodies, as well as a scarf or other covering on their heads.

When in public, Iranian women are required to wear clothes that cover their bodies. Those who violate the Islamic regime's code of morality may be severely punished.

Will things change in Iran? As of mid-2007, well over half the Iranian population was under 30, and many young Iranians are quietly defying the theocracy. In their homes, out of sight of the religious police, they wear Western clothes, watch DVDs from abroad, and listen to American music on their iPods. Above all, they use their computers to surf the Web and get news and information from the rest of the world.

One young Iranian told a journalist, "There are no more borders between countries because of the Internet. Frontiers are breaking down and people are starting to think alike. You cannot sit in government and set the rules and tell people how to react." As a younger generation of Iranians grows to maturity, they may start to challenge the control of their repressive religious leaders.

Democracy's Challenges

A functioning democracy is a difficult thing to achieve. Democracy is not just about holding elections. For representative government to be successful, citizens must be prepared to accept the rule of law, and to abide by the will of the majority while respecting minority rights. They must be educated enough to participate through their elected representatives in the making of policy. And they must insist that their governments respect basic individual rights and the right to freedom of speech.

Today, most of the world's governments claim to agree with the democratic principles spelled out in the Universal Declaration of Human Rights. But many governments still ignore those principles in practice. Especially in countries where the mass of people are poorly educated, divided by ethnic hatreds, or ground down by a long history of oppression, democracy may continue to find tough and rocky soil in which to sink any roots.

"The Lady" Challenges the Military in Burma

In the twenty-first century, democracy remains a precious and vulnerable ideal. Its survival demands vigilance. Its spread demands effort and, in some places, great sacrifice. In Southeast Asia, Myanmar (myan-MAR), also known as Burma, is one of those places of sacrifice.

Historical Close-up

In a New York apartment in 1971, a young woman contemplated one of life's big decisions: Should she marry the man she loved?

In her heart, Aung San Suu Kyi (awn sahn soo chee) — better known as Suu Kyi — knew the answer was yes. But she also knew she must warn her fiancé about what might lie ahead. So she took out pen and paper. "I only ask one thing," she wrote, "that should my people need me, you would help me do my duty by them. Would you mind very much should such a situation ever arise? How probable it is I do not know, but the possibility is there."

Aung San Suu Kyi stands before a poster of her deceased father, whom the Burmese revere as a hero of their nation.

The possibility was indeed real. Suu Kyi was the only daughter and youngest child of Burma's heroic nationalist and freedom fighter, Aung San. Burma had been a British colony until World War II, when it was conquered by Japan. After the war, Aung San led Burma to independence and the promise of democracy. But he was slain by assassins in 1947, just before he was to become the first prime minister of Burma.

Suu Kyi was only two years old when her father died, and she grew up listening to stories of his greatness. She watched how her mother, Khin Kyi, dedicated herself to the ideals of democracy in the years after her husband's death. When she was appointed Burma's ambassador to India in 1960, Khin Kyi took her family to New Delhi. There, 15-year-old Suu Kyi studied Mohandas Gandhi's teachings about nonviolence.

While the family was in India, Burma itself fell on hard times. The country's fledgling democracy was overwhelmed by a military dictatorship. Suu Kyi's mother remained in India as the nation's ambassador, but in 1964 Suu Kyi, at age 19, followed Gandhi's path to England. There she studied political science, economics, and philosophy at Oxford University. Her studies deepened her commitment to liberty and human rights. And while at Oxford she met and fell in love with a British scholar of Asian studies named Michael Aris.

They did not marry immediately. After graduation, Suu Kyi went to New York for almost three years, where she worked for the United Nations and thought about what it would mean to marry a citizen of the country that had so long colonized Burma. After Aris assured Suu Kyi that he understood the people of Burma must always come first, they were married in 1972.

Suu Kyi devoted most of the next several years to raising their two sons in Britain. She sewed the family's clothes and hauled the boys to school on the back of her bicycle. Her mother had returned to Burma and was deeply troubled by the military regime. Visitors from Burma often crowded into the Aris's small London apartment, lamenting how their once-prosperous homeland was turning into one of the poorest, most repressive nations on earth.

In March 1988, Suu Kyi received a telephone call reporting that her mother had suffered a massive stroke. Two days later she was at her mother's bedside in Burma.

She arrived in Burma just as student protestors, fed up with years of military dictatorship and a declining economy, were marching in the streets

As Aung San Suu Kyi watched Burma's military regime grow more and more repressive, she realized that she must join the struggle for democracy. Above, she works on a speech with the flag of the National League for Democracy (NLD) behind her.

of the nation's capital, Rangoon. When the Burmese police brought in tanks and tear gas to break up the crowds, scores of demonstrators died.

At first, preoccupied by her mother's illness, Suu Kyi just watched the protests. Then Burma's military dictator abruptly resigned and was replaced by a police commander known as "the Butcher." As more Burmese took to the streets, thousands of peaceful demonstrators were killed, and hundreds more were wounded.

The international community never actually saw these atrocities because Burmese soldiers had orders to shoot anyone with a camera. But friends flocked to the rundown villa where Suu Kyi's mother lay dying. When they told Suu Kyi what was happening, she knew she could ignore the crisis no longer. "I could not, as my father's daughter, remain indifferent to all that was going on," she later said.

On August 26, 1988, Suu Kyi attended a rally of 500,000 people at the Shwedagon Pagoda, in the city of Rangoon. With her husband and sons standing behind her, she announced she was taking up her father's old fight.

"This national crisis," she said, "could in fact be called the second struggle for national independence."

Suu Kyi knew Burma's government would portray her as a meddlesome outsider because of the years she'd spent in Great Britain. "Some people have been saying that I know nothing of Burmese politics," she said, "but the trouble is that I know too much. My family knows best how complicated and tricky Burmese politics can be and how much my father had to suffer on this account."

She quickly emerged as the leader of a new political party, the National League for Democracy (NLD). Suu Kyi traveled around the country, giving speeches that advocated a peaceful transition to democracy. Even her mother's funeral turned into a rally for democracy, at which Suu Kyi promised thousands of mourners that she would follow her parents' example and devote her life to serving the people of Burma.

Suu Kyi knew this meant she would not return to Britain with her husband and sons, then going on 12 and 16 years old. Burma needed her. The military leaders nervously watched her growing popularity. A group of generals, still loyal to the old dictator, had seized power and established the ominously named State Law and Order Restoration Council (SLORC) to rule the country, which they renamed Myanmar.

SLORC promised free and fair parliamentary elections, but sent military troops to arrest and frighten Suu Kyi's supporters. One officer even ordered his troops to shoot Suu Kyi herself as she walked at the head of a campaign march. But Suu Kyi kept walking until, at the last moment, a higher-ranking officer overruled the order and stopped the soldiers from shooting.

SLORC leaders thought voters would be too frightened to vote for Suu Kyi and her fellow candidates in the National League for Democracy. To be on the safe side, they decided to stop "the Lady," as she was coming to be known, from campaigning. They put her under house arrest and simply ignored outcries from the international community.

A person under *house arrest* is not allowed to leave his or her home. Contacts with the outside world, such as phone conversations, often are limited.

Now the SLORC leaders were ready to let the elections proceed, confident that the results would go their way. After all, the military thugs reasoned,

Suu Kyi was locked away, unable to campaign, and her followers must surely be frightened. But when nationwide elections were held on May 27, 1990, NLD candidates supporting Suu Kyi captured 82 percent of the vote, or 392 parliamentary seats. The military regime won only 10 seats.

Suu Kyi was now the elected leader of the country. But the military leaders did not allow her to take office. They disqualified, arrested, or drove into exile the victorious NLD candidates. They offered to release Suu Kyi from house arrest if she would leave the country immediately. She refused.

Even under house arrest, Suu Kyi continued to oppose SLORC. Her phone wires were cut, but visitors managed to smuggle out of Myanmar tapes and letters with her statements about human rights and democracy. Suu Kyi's husband and children, however, were barred from visiting her for years.

The international community did not forget Aung San Suu Kyi. She was awarded many honors, including the 1991 Nobel Peace Prize. Because she was still under house arrest, she did not attend the ceremony. Her teenage sons accepted the peace prize for her.

Suu Kyi remained under house arrest on and off for more than a decade. SLORC did not allow her husband into the country even when he was dying of cancer and asked to see his wife one last time. Government leaders offered to let Suu Kyi visit him, but she did not go because she feared she would not be allowed back in the country.

For years, Burma's military dictatorship ignored the international community's support of Aung San Suu Kyi. In late 2010, however, she was released from house arrest and returned to politics. A more reform-oriented government came to power in Burma in March, 2011, and in April, 2012, parliamentary elections brought Aung San Suu Kyi and her party into office. As of August 2012, the United States prepared to name an ambassador to Burma for the first time since 1990.

Epilogue

Like astronomers gazing at distant stars, we peer into the unknown future through the lens of the past.

Reflections on the Human Odyssey

From the poetry of ancient Greece, we get our word *odyssey* — a long, adventure-filled voyage. Homer's epic hero, Odysseus, fought bravely on distant shores and then embarked on a journey to his native land — a perilous journey, as it proved, filled with dangers, enemies, and accidents. At times Odysseus lost his way and wandered. But, resourceful and shrewd, he remained resolute and ultimately found his way back home.

This book in your hands, as well as its two predecessors, tell the story of *The Human Odyssey*, the epic adventure of humankind over many thousands of years, a journey that still has far to go. We have focused mainly on recorded history, the roughly five-thousand-year period for which we possess written records that tell us of human thoughts and deeds. This final volume in particular has sharpened that focus even further, devoting most attention to the past hundred years, the contemporary era.

What stands out about the human odyssey in this contemporary era? What is most distinctive about our times?

We must answer cautiously because we can't be sure. As we approach the present, it becomes more difficult to distinguish what matters most. While the writers and editors of this book have striven for accuracy and objectivity, we do not have the distance that helps bring long-ago events into focus. We do not know how things will turn out. We do not have all the evidence in hand. And we have ourselves been part of the recent times whose story we have tried to tell. So we see things from a limited and specific perspective.

The closer we get to the present, the more numerous and variable are the interpretations of events and their significance. When we recount, for example, the story of the American response to September 11, 2001, our account is only one among a clamor of voices. Others who have lived through these events will perhaps disagree with the way we have explained them. As new evidence comes to light, our views may change.

Our contemporary era has been, to borrow the words of Charles Dickens, "the best of times and the worst of times." It has been a period of medical, scientific, and technological wonders; of advancing rights and liberty; of rising wealth and improved standards of living for many. Ours is also an era of instantaneous communication, rapid access to information, and daring space exploration.

But the contemporary era has also been a period of world wars, genocide, totalitarianism, and terrorism. Alongside the great wealth of our age there exists extreme poverty. While the nations of the world sit together at a common assembly in the United Nations, they often confront common problems with different values and opposed interests.

We are in some ways like the mariner Odysseus, struggling to make our way in a sea of contradictions. To help chart the course ahead, let's look back on the most recent leg of our journey. How far have we come in the last hundred years?

Hong Kong harbor, c. 1900

The World in 1900

The world in 1900 was a very different place from the world in the year 2000. In 1900, most of the globe's inhabitants still tilled the earth. They used plows pulled by horses, mules, or oxen. When they needed to move beyond their farms, they traveled by horse-drawn cart or wagon. Birds flew; people didn't. Steamships made it possible to cross the Atlantic in a week, but few people ever made that journey. Most people still lived in homes lit by candlelight or kerosene lanterns, and warmed by fireplaces or coal stoves. They hauled water for cooking and bathing from nearby rivers, streams, or wells. They faced constant threats of famine and disease.

In 1900, the vast majority of the world's population lived in lands ruled by kings, queens, tsars, sultans, or emperors. Many who lived in Asia and Africa were ruled by distant imperial powers. European empires spanned the globe.

In the Western world, there were stirrings of dramatic change. In 1900, the Industrial Revolution was well underway, rapidly changing life in Western nations. Factory jobs drew people from the countryside into towns. Cities in Europe and North America ballooned in size and suffered from a host of problems—overcrowding, contaminated water, filth, and disease.

In 1900, communication was getting easier for those in the West who had access to the new technologies. People in some cities and towns could go to a telegraph office to send a message speedily. Both the telephone and automobile had been recently invented but neither was in widespread use. People in some cities thrilled to the innovation of electric light, and there were high hopes for other uses of electricity in the future.

The Western world in 1900 showed the shaping influence of the American and French Revolutions. In many countries, monarchical governments made way for elected legislatures in which laws were made by the people's representatives. There had been a growing movement for women's rights in the mid to late nineteenth century, but in 1900 no European nation, and not even the democratic United States, allowed women to vote.

Hong Kong harbor, c. 2000

The World in 2000

A little more than a hundred years later, we behold a dramatically different scene. In the first decade of the millennium, a much smaller percentage of the world's people worked the land. In fact, many people today rarely if ever see a farm. They have no idea how to do the tasks that were part of the daily routine a century ago, such as harnessing a horse or splitting firewood. In today's industrialized world, a car zipping along at 70 miles per hour doesn't turn heads, but a horse and buggy does.

People think nothing about flying vast distances; a trip across the ocean takes hours, not days or weeks. In 1969, it took astronauts just four days to make the first voyage to the moon's surface. Travel into space, while still an adventure, has become sufficiently common that the evening news gives only passing mention to the latest flight of the space shuttle to the International Space Station.

Feel like talking with a friend or relative across the country or halfway around the world? Just pull a cell phone from your pocket, which sends signals bouncing off satellites to connect with other phones hundreds or thousands of miles away. Or dash off an e-mail or text message: "hey wut r u doing 2nite?" Have to check some facts for that history paper you're writing? No need to spend hours in the library poring through dusty reference books. Just log on, google it, and download (though be careful about what you get—just because it's on the Web hardly means it's true!). Hungry for a quick meal? No need to light a fire on the stove; just pop it in the microwave.

In many parts of our world, people now live much longer, healthier lives. Before Alexander Fleming and penicillin, an infected scratch on the arm might kill you. Now a quick trip to the doctor and the pharmacist fixes you up. Or, think about this: In 1900, someone born in the United States could expect to live, on average, about 47 years. By the year 2000, average life expectancy had reached almost 77 years. That's an extra 30 years of life, thanks in part to the medical advances of the twentieth century.

In 2003, when scientists working on the Human Genome Project unlocked the human genetic code, they opened the door to further health improvements in the twenty-first century and beyond. As scientists edge toward unprecedented abilities to manipulate human development and perhaps even clone human beings, they are also opening doors to new ethical questions.

A Mongolian nomad stands beside his portable home, known as a yurt, complete with a satellite dish and solar panel. Many people once considered isolated are now much more connected to the rest of the world.

Many parts of the world, however, remain almost untouched by advances in medicine, air travel, or computers. And in some places, such as India and China, developed and undeveloped worlds exist side-by-side.

Just as parts of the world remain untouched by the Industrial Revolution and the Information Revolution, there are parts of the world relatively unaffected by the great political changes that have altered life in many lands over the last century. As we've seen, there are still kings and dictators who wield enormous power over their subjects. There are places such as Burma and China where representative government still struggles to gain a foothold. And there are countries where women are still second-class citizens.

Yet overall the world is a much freer place than it was a century ago. In 1900, the ideal of universal human rights was a distant dream for most people. Today, while many nations still fail to live up to that ideal, more countries than ever before are working hard to achieve it.

In 2000, the old European empires of the late nineteenth and early twentieth centuries were gone. The decolonization that followed World War II and the fall of communism after the Cold War both helped democracy spread around the world. In the Western world, the few remaining kings and queens are now regarded more as celebrities than all-powerful rulers.

In many countries, women are no longer second-class citizens who are denied even the right to vote. Now they are presidents of corporations, senators and congressional representatives, members of parliament, even prime ministers. In the Western world, the twentieth century, more than any other era in history, has helped bring women closer to political, social, and economic equality.

One truly distinctive feature of the past century—and of this there is no doubt—is the pace and scale of change. Scientific, industrial, and electronic revolutions radically accelerated change of many kinds—change in communications, business, politics, and many aspects of daily life around the globe. We're still racing to keep up.

A (Mostly) Rising Standard of Living

Since the Second World War, more people around the world have enjoyed greater wealth. After 1945, the standard of living rose worldwide. The Industrial Revolution and electronic innovations dramatically increased production and expanded global markets. It was, in general, capitalist nations with free market economies that enjoyed greater wealth and higher standards of living. Most nations with government-controlled economies did not thrive. One big exception to the worldwide rise in wealth after World War II was the continent of Africa. There, as various lands became independent of their colonial rulers, economies declined in new nations that fell into civil war or came under the control of despots.

War: The Dreadful Constant

From your study of history, you know that human beings have both creative and destructive impulses. Sometimes human creativity takes the form of an inspiring symphony or beautiful building, sometimes a powerful vaccine or elegant mathematical formula.

You have seen, all too often, how our destructive impulses take shape in war. War has been a grim constant in human history, from ancient Sumer to modern Iraq. Wars have been waged in nearly every decade for which we have records.

Recent wars give the twentieth century the lamentable distinction of being the bloodiest century ever. For the first time ever, advances in communication, transportation, and technology expanded warfare to a global scale. Ever more powerful forms of destruction left widespread physical ruin and hundreds of millions dead. With the development of nuclear weaponry, human beings suddenly had the horrifying potential to destroy not just their enemy, but themselves and much of the planet as well.

During the Cold War the superpowers managed to avoid an all-out nuclear war. Although the Cold War has ended, the nuclear threat remains. In the hands of unscrupulous leaders or terrorist groups, nuclear weapons pose a serious threat for the future.

The Ongoing Odyssey

In our contemporary era, as in ages past, we've seen how beliefs and ideas can shape history — and not always for the better. Nationalism, with its aggressive stance of "my country first," triggered and prolonged the First World War. Communism, grounded in class conflict and committed to state control, took shape as a seven-decade tyranny over millions worldwide. Nazism, rooted in a twisted idea of Aryan racial superiority, led to world war and genocide on a massive scale. Militant Islamism, with its commitment to worldwide jihad, has embarked on a path of destruction and terrorism.

Other beliefs and ideas have moved the world along more constructive paths. Radical ideas introduced in the eighteenth century have been formally recognized and acted on by many nations in the twentieth century. These ideas include universal human rights, self-determination of peoples, representative government, and economic and political liberty.

Not only have powerful ideas shaped history, but so have extraordinary individuals, again for both better and worse. The world has suffered much from the evil actions of Adolph Hitler, Joseph Stalin, and Mao Zedong. But the world has gained much from the lives and works of Mahatma Gandhi, Eleanor Roosevelt, and Pope John Paul II, among many others.

As the pace of change accelerates, we'll need to sprint to keep up. As new global interactions bring together diverse peoples, there is potential for great advancement and great unrest. For the human odyssey ahead, we, like Odysseus, will need to have our wits about us.

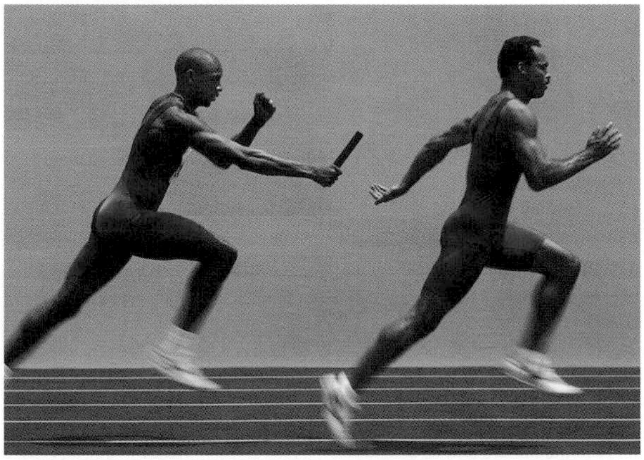

From ancient Greek times to the contemporary era, it seems we have been running to keep up with history. As the pace of change accelerates, we'll need to sprint on the next leg of our human odyssey.

Appendix: Geographic Terms and Concepts

The word *geography* comes from the Greek terms for "description of the earth." *Physical geography* concerns the natural features of the earth such as landforms and climates. *Human geography* focuses on people and how they interact with their environments.

To understand historical events, we often need to understand the related geography. Historians want to know what a place was like long ago. They look for the influence the environment had on the people who lived there. They want to know the significance of location. They make connections between where events took place and why things happened as they did.

Throughout this book, we treat historical and geographic issues hand in hand. Here we offer a brief overview of some specific geographic terms and concepts.

The World in Spatial Terms

Globes, Maps, and Map Projections

Globes and *maps* represent the earth. They are the geographer's most important tools. Since the earth is roughly sphere-shaped, globes are the most accurate way to show it. However, flat maps are more practical. Try putting a globe in your pocket or on the page of a book!

While flat maps are practical, they all share one disadvantage. It's impossible to represent a sphere on a flat surface with complete accuracy. Thus all flat maps distort the earth when they try to show it. Common distortions include distances, direction, and the shapes and sizes of landmasses.

Cartographers, or mapmakers, have developed various *map projections* as a way to minimize inaccuracies. One kind of projection might minimize distortions in the shape of landmasses, while another projection might minimize distortions in distance.

See pages 402–403 for examples of different map projections.

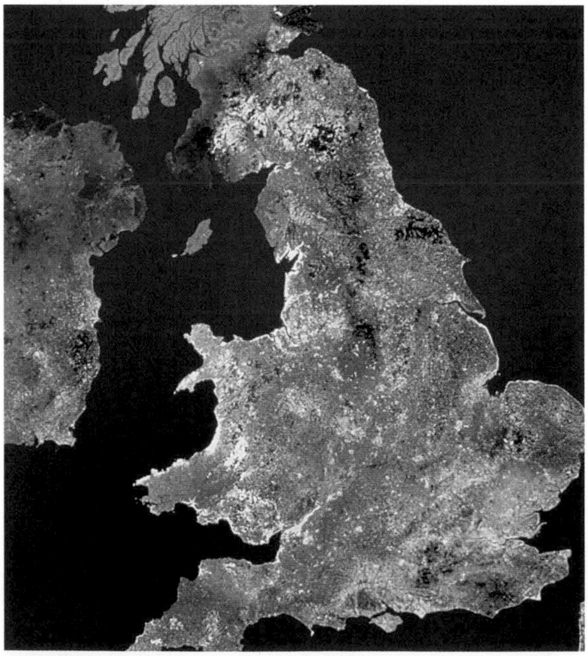

A map generated by a Landsat satellite shows part of the British Isles and the surrounding seas.

Types of Maps

Different kinds of maps provide different kinds of information.

Physical maps use symbols and colors to indicate natural features like mountains and rivers. For example, see pages 386–387. *Political maps* show man-made features such as national boundaries, cities, and roads. For example, see pages 388–389.

Some *general purpose maps* show both political features (such as national boundaries and cities) and physical features (such as rivers and mountains). The maps on pages 390–401 show both physical and political features.

Special purpose maps focus on one type of information such as climate or population. Historical maps might show trade routes or settlements. For examples of special purpose maps, see pages 404–407.

Today, Earth Resources Technology Satellites (ERTS) allow us to make maps from photographs of energy waves. Scientists and geographers use these *Landsat* maps, as they're called, to study the earth's features and resources in greater detail than ever before.

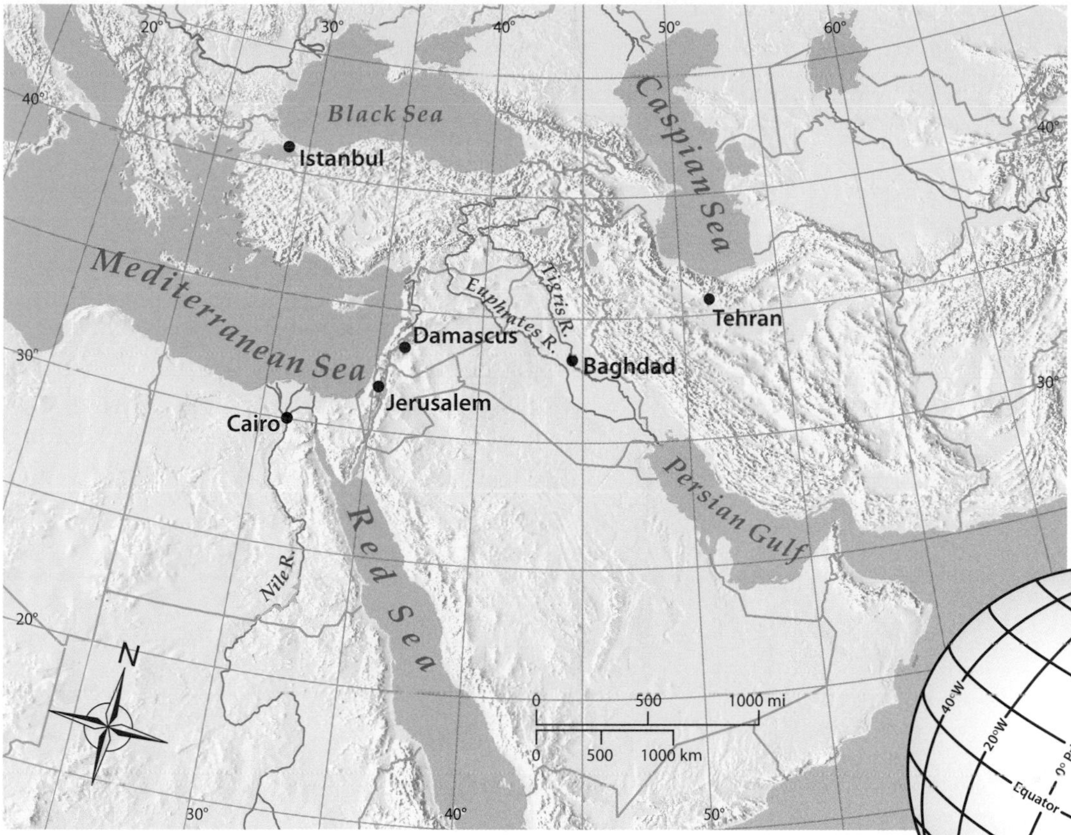

This general purpose map of the Middle East shows both political and physical features. Note the compass rose and scale on the map.

Lines of latitude and longitude

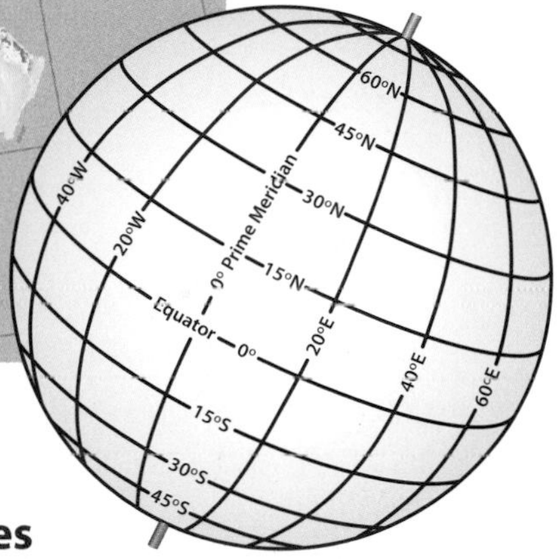

Map Symbols

A *map key* tells you what the symbols on a map mean. For example, a road map might use red lines for two-lane roads and blue lines for highways. Political maps often use a dot to represent cities, and sometimes a circled dot for the capital city.

See the Climate Zones map on page 404. At the bottom right is a map key that explains which color stands for which climate.

Many maps identify the *cardinal directions*—north, south, east, and west—with an arrow pointing north, or in a *compass rose* that shows all four directions.

Scale tells us the ratio between what is on the map and what is in the real world. A large-scale map of the Egyptian city of Cairo might use one inch on the map to represent 1,000 feet in the real world. A small-scale map of Africa might use one inch to represent 500 miles.

Locating Ourselves

Latitude and Longitude

Mapmakers use a grid of imaginary lines to divide the world into sections. This grid lets us locate places on a map or globe.

Running around the middle of the globe is an imaginary line called the *equator*. The equator is halfway between the North Pole and the South Pole.

On a globe you'll see lines running around the globe parallel to the equator. We call these lines of *latitude*, or *parallels*. Latitude lets us identify a location north or south of the equator, measured in units called *degrees*. The latitude of the equator is 0° (zero degrees). Lines of latitude are numbered from 0° (the equator) to 90° north (the North Pole), and 0° (the equator) to 90° south (the South Pole).

On a globe, the lines that run north and south, from pole to pole, are called lines of *longitude,* or *meridians.* You'll notice that meridians are not parallel since they come together at the poles. Meridians are also measured in degrees. An imaginary line called the *prime meridian* is 0°. The prime meridian runs through Greenwich, England, at the original site of the Royal Greenwich Observatory. There are 180 degrees east of the prime meridian, and 180 degrees west.

Hemispheres

The equator and the prime meridian let us divide the earth into halves, called *hemispheres.* North of the equator is the *Northern Hemisphere,* while south of the equator is the *Southern Hemisphere.* To the west of the prime meridian is the *Western Hemisphere,* while to the east of the prime meridian is the *Eastern Hemisphere.*

Degrees, Minutes, Seconds

Lines of latitude and longitude are spaced in units called degrees. The distance between one parallel and the next (one degree of latitude) is approximately 69 miles, or 111 kilometers. The distance between one meridian and the next (one degree of longitude) varies from about 69 miles at the equator to zero at the poles.

To help pinpoint locations more precisely, each degree is divided into smaller units called minutes and seconds. These minutes and seconds are measures of distance, not time. There are 60 minutes in a degree, and 60 seconds in a minute.

You can identify a location by its coordinates—that is, by the intersection of the parallel (latitude) and the meridian (longitude). For example, the coordinates of the Emperor's Palace in Tokyo, Japan, are 35°40'45" N, 139°46'14" E. You say that as "35 degrees, 40 minutes, 45 seconds north; 139 degrees, 46 minutes, 14 seconds east."

Every place on earth is in two hemispheres at once. For example, the city of Chicago, Illinois, is in the Northern and Western Hemispheres. The city of Bombay in India is in the Southern and Eastern Hemispheres.

Absolute and Relative Location

The grid system allows us to identify any place on earth by its specific position, or what geographers call its *absolute location.* Often, however, we use *relative location* — that is, the location of a place compared to another place. For example, if you're driving, knowing that Baltimore is about 35 miles (56 kilometers) northeast of Washington, D.C., can be more useful than knowing that it is at 39° N and 77° W.

Places, Regions, and Landforms

Geographers use concepts of *place* and *region.* One way to describe *place* is to look at natural physical features, including land, water, and climate.

Geographers group places that have similar characteristics into *regions.* Regions may be defined by various characteristics — for example, by a physical characteristic such as climate, or by a cultural characteristic such as language. In the United States, the Pacific Northwest is a mountainous, rainy region. Latin America — which includes Mexico, Central America, South America, and islands in the West Indies — is a vast region where most people speak Spanish or Portuguese, languages that developed from Latin.

Continents

About 30 percent of the earth's surface is land. The largest landmasses are *continents.* Most geographers identify seven continents — Asia, Africa, North America, South America, Antarctica, Europe, and Australia. Europe and Asia are part of the same landmass, called Eurasia, but are usually considered separate continents. On the map on pages 386–387, locate each of the seven continents.

Mountain peaks in the Himalaya, the highest mountain range in the world

Major Landforms

Landforms are natural land features. Major landforms include mountains, plateaus, and plains. We identify landforms by their *relief,* or shape, and their *elevation,* or height above sea level.

Mountains, sometimes called *highlands*, stand well above the surrounding landscape and have distinct relief, including steep slopes and peaks. They range from 2,000 feet (roughly 600 meters) above sea level, like parts of the Appalachians in eastern North America, to a high of about 29,000 feet (8,850 meters). The Himalaya in Asia are the highest mountains in the world.

Plateaus are areas of moderate or high elevation with little relief. They are sometimes called *tablelands*. The surface of a plateau may be flat or have small, rolling hills.

Plains are large areas of flat or almost flat land, usually at low elevations. Coastal plains lie near the shore at sea level.

Canyons and *valleys* are much lower than the land around them. *Islands* are landmasses surrounded by water. A *peninsula* is a landmass almost surrounded by water.

While those are some of the common landforms, there are others as well.

Canyonlands National Park in Utah

One of the Maldive Islands in the Indian Ocean

Bodies of Water

Most of the earth is covered by water. Water continually cycles from ocean to air to ground and back to ocean. Geographers identify bodies of water by their size, shape, and content.

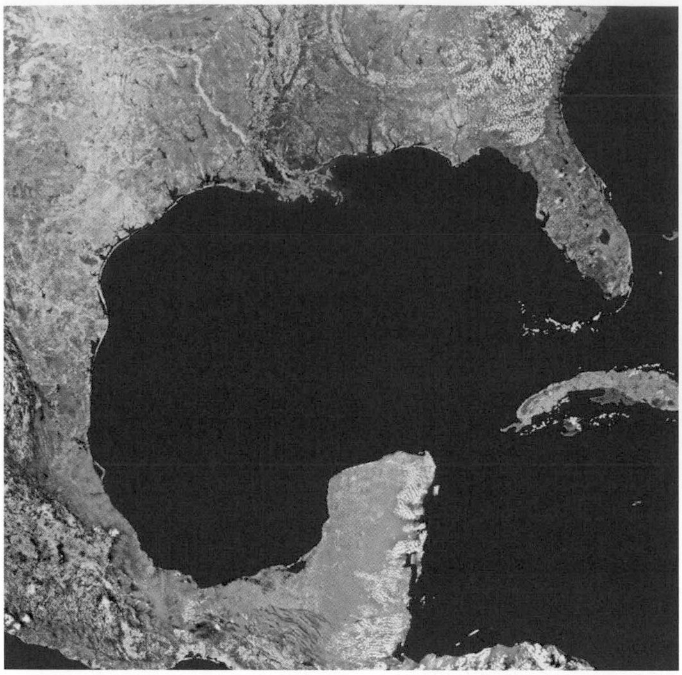

The Atlantic Ocean extends into the Gulf of Mexico. The Gulf is bounded by the coastline of the United States to the north and Mexico to the west.

A River Delta

A *delta* is a triangular piece of land at the mouth of a river. It's usually laden with rich deposits of alluvial soil (that is, soil deposited by flowing water). The term *delta* comes from the fourth letter of the Greek alphabet, which looks like this: Δ.

Oceans and Seas

The enormous body of salt water that surrounds the continents and makes up more than 95 percent of the world's water is divided into four *oceans* — Arctic, Atlantic, Indian, and Pacific. All of the earth's land could fit in the Pacific Ocean alone. If the highest mountain, Mount Everest, were placed in the Pacific at its deepest spot, Everest's peak would lie a mile beneath the ocean's surface.

Seas are smaller bodies of salt water, almost surrounded by land. Where portions of seas or oceans extend into coastlines, we find *gulfs* or *bays*.

Lakes and Rivers

Lakes are bodies of water completely surrounded by land. Most lakes hold fresh water. Many lakes were formed by glaciers that carved deep valleys in the earth where rain and melting ice collected. The largest freshwater lake in the world is Lake Superior, one of the Great Lakes of North America.

Rivers are waterways that flow through land and into larger bodies of water. Rivers usually begin as *streams* at high elevation. Streams join one another to form a river. These rivers often combine to form larger rivers. A *tributary* is a stream or river that feeds into a larger stream, river, or lake. For example, the Ohio River is a tributary of the Mississippi River.

The longest river in the world is the Nile in Africa, which begins as several smaller rivers in the East African Highlands and flows more than 4,100 miles (6,650 kilometers) north to the Mediterranean Sea.

Climate

Weather refers to atmospheric conditions in a particular time and place — "We're having stormy weather today." *Climate* is the general weather pattern that occurs in an area over a long time — "We live in a dry climate." Climate is determined by many factors, including distance from the equator (latitude), elevation, and proximity to water or mountains. Geographers divide the earth's many climates into four major zones. (See page 404 for a detailed climate map.)

Rain forest in northeastern Australia

Tropical Climates

Near the equator there are two types of climate — tropical rain forest and tropical savanna. Because the sun's rays shine directly on the tropics year-round, temperatures there are always warm.

A *tropical rain forest* gets rain almost daily, totaling more than 80 inches (2,000 millimeters) per year. The result is dense vegetation and a remarkable variety of plant and animal life. Tropical rain forests are home to millions of species of plants and animals, more than anywhere else on earth.

Tropical savannas extend farther from the equator than rain forests, but still in latitudes that are warm year-round. They experience dry and wet seasons. Savannas are grasslands with few trees.

Mid-latitude Climates

Farther from the equator are several climate zones grouped as *mid-latitude climates*. While they vary in their temperatures and precipitation, they are all moderate climates that have distinct seasons.

These moderate climates are home to most people. See the map on page 404 to locate some of these mid-latitude climates, including Mediterranean, humid subtropical, humid continental, and marine west coast.

High-latitude Climates

In the polar regions farthest from the equator, climates are so cold that little vegetation can survive. High-latitude climates include the tundra, which supports short grasses during brief summers, and the ice sheet, where nothing grows. High-latitude conditions can also occur at very high elevations, regardless of latitude. For example, mountain peaks at high elevations are snowcapped even in the tropics.

Elephants on an African savanna with Mount Kilimanjaro in the background

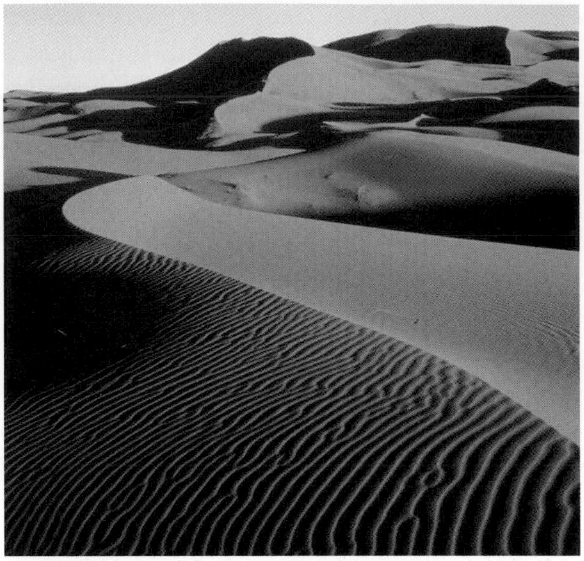

Dunes in the Sahara, the world's largest desert

Dry Climates

Dry climates are those with little or no precipitation. They can be hot year-round, or have bitterly cold winters. Because the air in these regions is so dry, temperatures tend to fall dramatically at night. *Deserts* typically receive less than 10 inches (250 millimeters) of rain per year. Steppes get 10 to 20 inches (250 to 500 millimeters) of rain annually.

Physical Systems: Our Changing Earth

The earth's surface is constantly changing. Forces within the earth and on the surface cause much of this change. But human activity also changes earth's physical systems.

Internal Forces

The part of the earth on which we walk and on which the oceans rest is called the *crust*. The crust varies in thickness, but generally extends about 25 miles (40 kilometers) beneath land surface. Below the crust are the *mantle*, an *outer core*, and an *inner core*.

The crust is made up of *plates*, huge masses of rock that float on the semiliquid material in the mantle. These plates can shift position and bump or rub against each other, causing earthquakes. Earthquakes beneath the ocean cause tidal waves or tsunamis. Plates pushing against each other can also build mountains. When plates pull apart, they can form gorges and valleys.

Deep in the earth flows melted rock called *magma*. When a volcano erupts, magma comes to the surface, where it is called *lava*. Volcanoes can dramatically change the earth's surface.

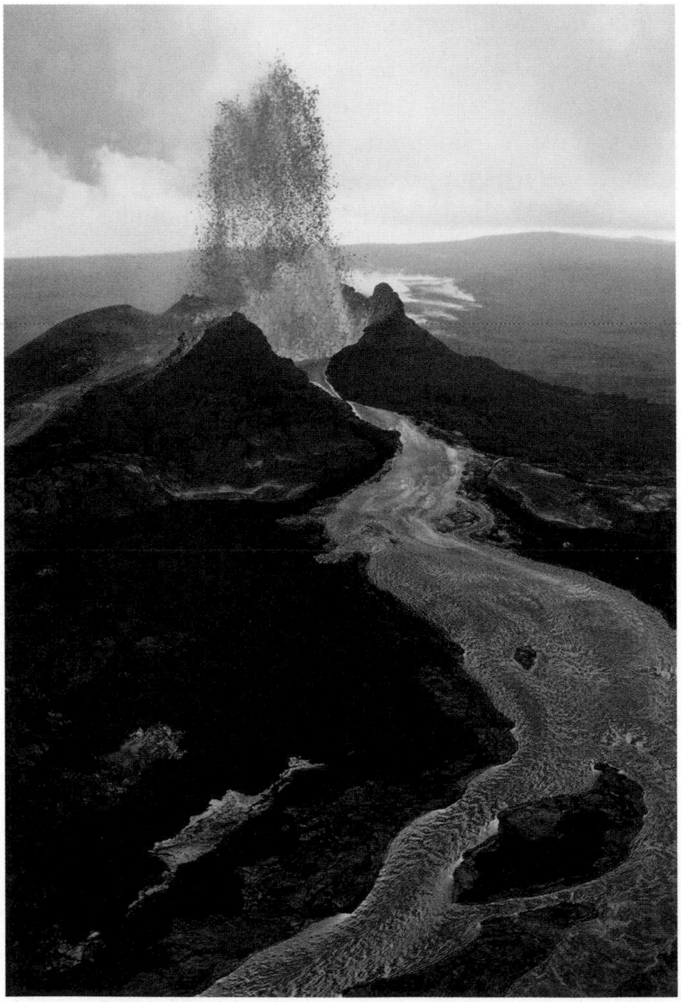

A river of lava flows from an erupting volcano in Hawaii. Lava is melted rock. Beneath the earth's surface, it is called *magma*.

External Forces

Some changes to the earth's surface come from external forces such as wind and water. *Weathering* occurs when water breaks down the chemicals in rocks and they disintegrate. When water freezes and melts, it can split rocks apart.

Flowing water, wind, and the movement of glaciers are some of the causes of *erosion*, the wearing away of the earth's surface.

Ecosystems and Human Systems

Ecosystems

An *ecosystem* is a group of living things and the environment in which they live. Ecosystems can be as small as a tiny pond and the living things it supports, or as large as the tundra.

Small changes in factors such as climate or air quality can alter or even destroy an ecosystem. Humans can change ecosystems when they alter some element of the environment around them. Some human activity, such as digging mines or clearing forests, can have dramatic effects on the environment.

Human Systems

Historians and geographers ask questions about individuals and about groups of people. They study human settlements around the world and across time, and observe the distribution of population. See page 407 for a map of population density. They pay attention to patterns of *migration* — why people move from one place to another, and the results of those moves. They want to know about *culture* — the traditions and customs of a group of people, their ways of life and thought, and how those ways differ from the ways of other groups. Historians and geographers also look for patterns in the way groups of people trade and interact with each other, sometimes peacefully, sometimes not.

Environment and Society

Resources

Geographers examine the resources available in different areas. *Renewable resources* can be replenished by the earth's own processes or, in some cases, by human activity as they are used. These resources include water, forests, and solar power. *Nonrenewable resources* cannot be replenished once they are used. Minerals and fossil fuels like coal and oil are examples of nonrenewable resources. Because nonrenewable resources are limited, their use and distribution affect human interaction.

The specific resources that people use and value vary by place and change over time. For example, petroleum was not valued before the combustion engine was invented.

Human-Environmental Interaction

Humans adapt to their environments and change them. When we put on a winter coat, or jump into the surf to cool off, we are adapting to our environment. We change the environment every time we build a house or fertilize a lawn.

One dramatic historical example of humans adapting to and changing the environment occurred in the early 1500s, soon after Christopher Columbus came in contact with the Americas. The exchange of hundreds of species of plants and animals among continents in the years following his voyages resulted in profound changes in populations, ways of life, and ecosystems.

The geography of an area, in turn, has a huge impact on human activity in that area. People build differently in earthquake or hurricane zones than in the Amazon. Historians look at geography to explain, for example, why people in one part of the world developed farming communities while people elsewhere remained nomads. Geography affects economic, social, and political activity.

Wind turbines convert wind energy into electricity, making wind a clean and renewable source of energy.

World Physical

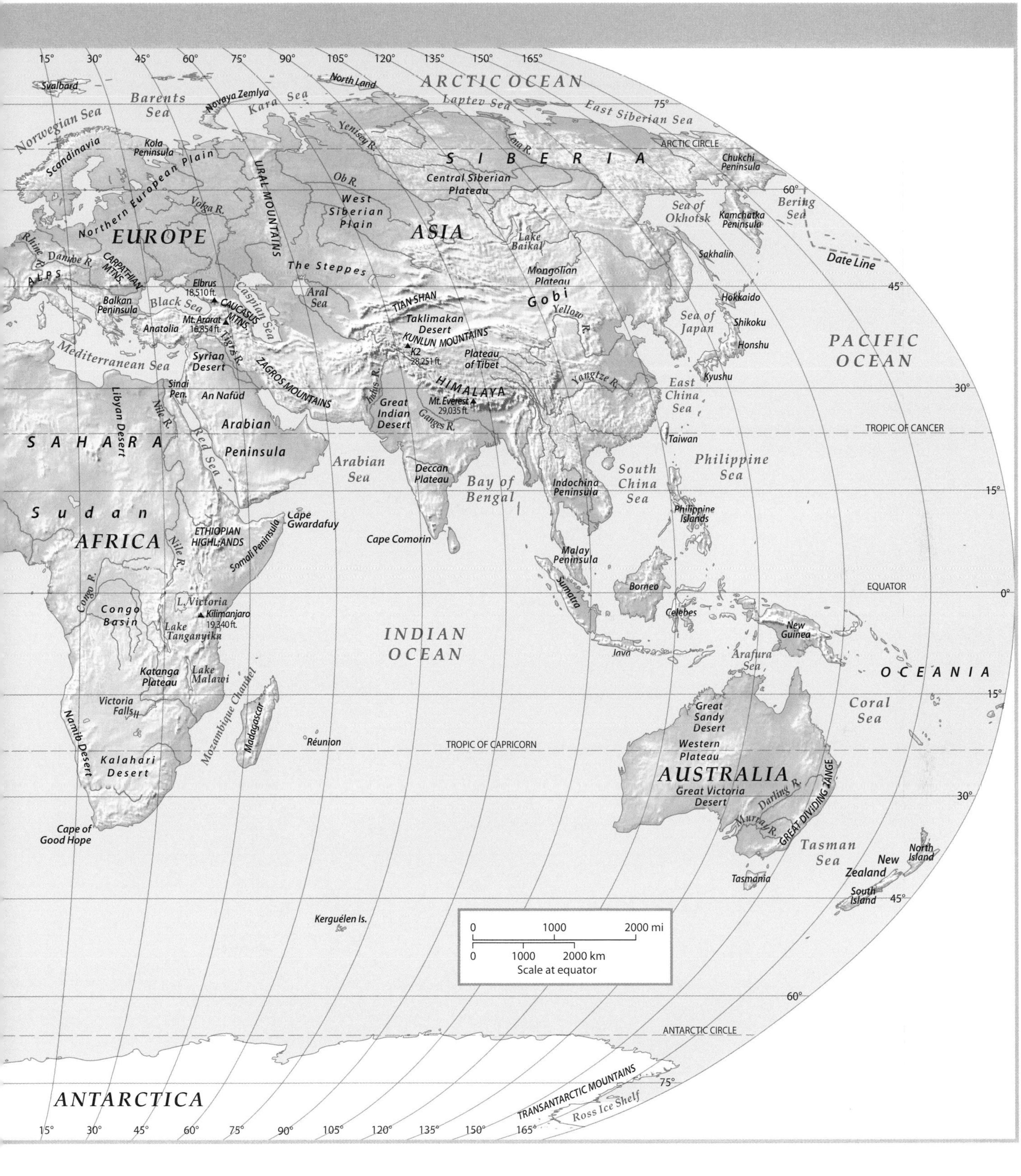
15°
30°
45°
60°
75°
90°
105°
120°
135°
150°
165°
Svalbard
North Land
ARCTIC OCEAN
Barents Sea
Novaya Zemlya
Kara Sea
Laptev Sea
East Siberian Sea
Norwegian Sea
Scandinavia
Kola Peninsula
Yenisey R.
Lena R.
ARCTIC CIRCLE
S I B E R I A
Chukchi Peninsula
Northern European Plain
URAL MOUNTAINS
Ob R.
Central Siberian Plateau
Bering Sea
Volga R.
West Siberian Plain
Sea of Okhotsk
Kamchatka Peninsula
EUROPE
ASIA
Lake Baikal
Rhine R.
Danube R.
CARPATHIAN MTNS.
ALPS
The Steppes
Sakhalin
Date Line
Mongolian Plateau
Elbrus 18,510 ft.
Caspian Sea
Aral Sea
TIAN SHAN
Gobi
Hokkaido
Black Sea
CAUCASUS MTNS.
Balkan Peninsula
Anatolia
Mt. Ararat 16,854 ft.
Taklimakan Desert
Yellow R.
Sea of Japan
Shikoku
KUNLUN MOUNTAINS
Honshu
PACIFIC OCEAN
Mediterranean Sea
Tigris R.
Syrian Desert
K2 28,251 ft.
Plateau of Tibet
Indus R.
ZAGROS MOUNTAINS
HIMALAYA
Yangtze R.
East China Sea
Kyushu
Sinai Pen.
An Nafūd
Mt. Everest 29,035 ft.
Great Indian Desert
Ganges R.
Libyan Desert
Nile R.
Arabian Peninsula
TROPIC OF CANCER
S A H A R A
Red Sea
Taiwan
Arabian Sea
Deccan Plateau
Bay of Bengal
Indochina Peninsula
South China Sea
Philippine Sea
Sudan
Cape Gwardafuy
Philippine Islands
AFRICA
ETHIOPIAN HIGHLANDS
Somali Peninsula
Cape Comorin
Malay Peninsula
Congo R.
Sumatra
Borneo
EQUATOR
0°
Congo Basin
L. Victoria
Kilimanjaro 19,340 ft.
Lake Tanganyika
Celebes
New Guinea
INDIAN OCEAN
Java
Arafura Sea
OCEANIA
Katanga Plateau
Lake Malawi
Mozambique Channel
Madagascar
Victoria Falls
Coral Sea
Great Sandy Desert
Namib Desert
Réunion
TROPIC OF CAPRICORN
Western Plateau
Kalahari Desert
AUSTRALIA
Great Victoria Desert
Darling R.
Murray R.
GREAT DIVIDING RANGE
Cape of Good Hope
Tasman Sea
North Island
New Zealand
Tasmania
South Island
Kerguélen Is.
0 1000 2000 mi
0 1000 2000 km
Scale at equator
ANTARCTIC CIRCLE
TRANSANTARCTIC MOUNTAINS
Ross Ice Shelf
ANTARCTICA

World Political

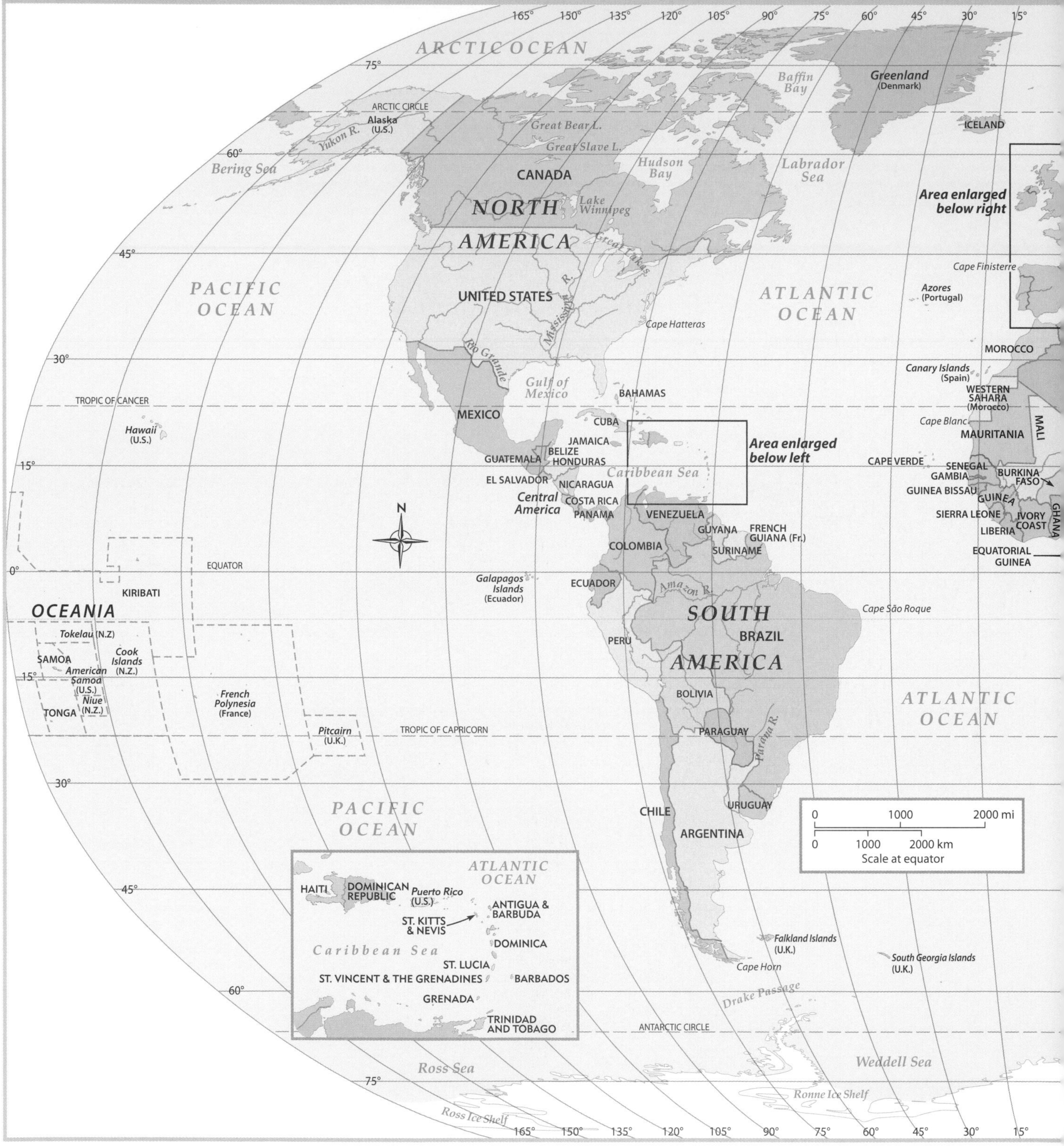

ARCTIC OCEAN
ARCTIC CIRCLE
Alaska (U.S.)
Yukon R.
Bering Sea
Great Bear L.
Great Slave L.
Hudson Bay
Baffin Bay
Greenland (Denmark)
ICELAND
Labrador Sea
CANADA
NORTH AMERICA
Lake Winnipeg
Great Lakes
Area enlarged below right
Cape Finisterre
Azores (Portugal)
PACIFIC OCEAN
UNITED STATES
Mississippi R.
ATLANTIC OCEAN
Cape Hatteras
Rio Grande
MOROCCO
Canary Islands (Spain)
Gulf of Mexico
BAHAMAS
TROPIC OF CANCER
WESTERN SAHARA (Morocco)
MEXICO
CUBA
Hawaii (U.S.)
Cape Blanc
MAURITANIA
MALI
JAMAICA
BELIZE
HONDURAS
GUATEMALA
Area enlarged below left
Caribbean Sea
CAPE VERDE
SENEGAL
GAMBIA
BURKINA FASO
EL SALVADOR
NICARAGUA
GUINEA BISSAU
GUINEA
Central America
COSTA RICA
PANAMA
VENEZUELA
SIERRA LEONE
IVORY COAST
GHANA
LIBERIA
GUYANA
FRENCH GUIANA (Fr.)
SURINAME
COLOMBIA
EQUATORIAL GUINEA
EQUATOR
Galapagos Islands (Ecuador)
ECUADOR
Amazon R.
KIRIBATI
Cape São Roque
OCEANIA
SOUTH AMERICA
Tokelau (N.Z)
PERU
BRAZIL
SAMOA
Cook Islands (N.Z.)
American Samoa (U.S.)
Niue (N.Z.)
TONGA
French Polynesia (France)
BOLIVIA
Pitcairn (U.K.)
TROPIC OF CAPRICORN
PARAGUAY
Paraná R.
PACIFIC OCEAN
CHILE
URUGUAY
ARGENTINA
0 1000 2000 mi
0 1000 2000 km
Scale at equator
ATLANTIC OCEAN
HAITI
DOMINICAN REPUBLIC
Puerto Rico (U.S.)
ANTIGUA & BARBUDA
ST. KITTS & NEVIS
DOMINICA
Caribbean Sea
ST. LUCIA
ST. VINCENT & THE GRENADINES
BARBADOS
GRENADA
TRINIDAD AND TOBAGO
Falkland Islands (U.K.)
South Georgia Islands (U.K.)
Cape Horn
Drake Passage
ANTARCTIC CIRCLE
Ross Sea
Weddell Sea
Ronne Ice Shelf
Ross Ice Shelf
165° 150° 135° 120° 105° 90° 75° 60° 45° 30° 15°
75° 60° 45° 30° 15° 0° 15° 30° 45° 60° 75°
N

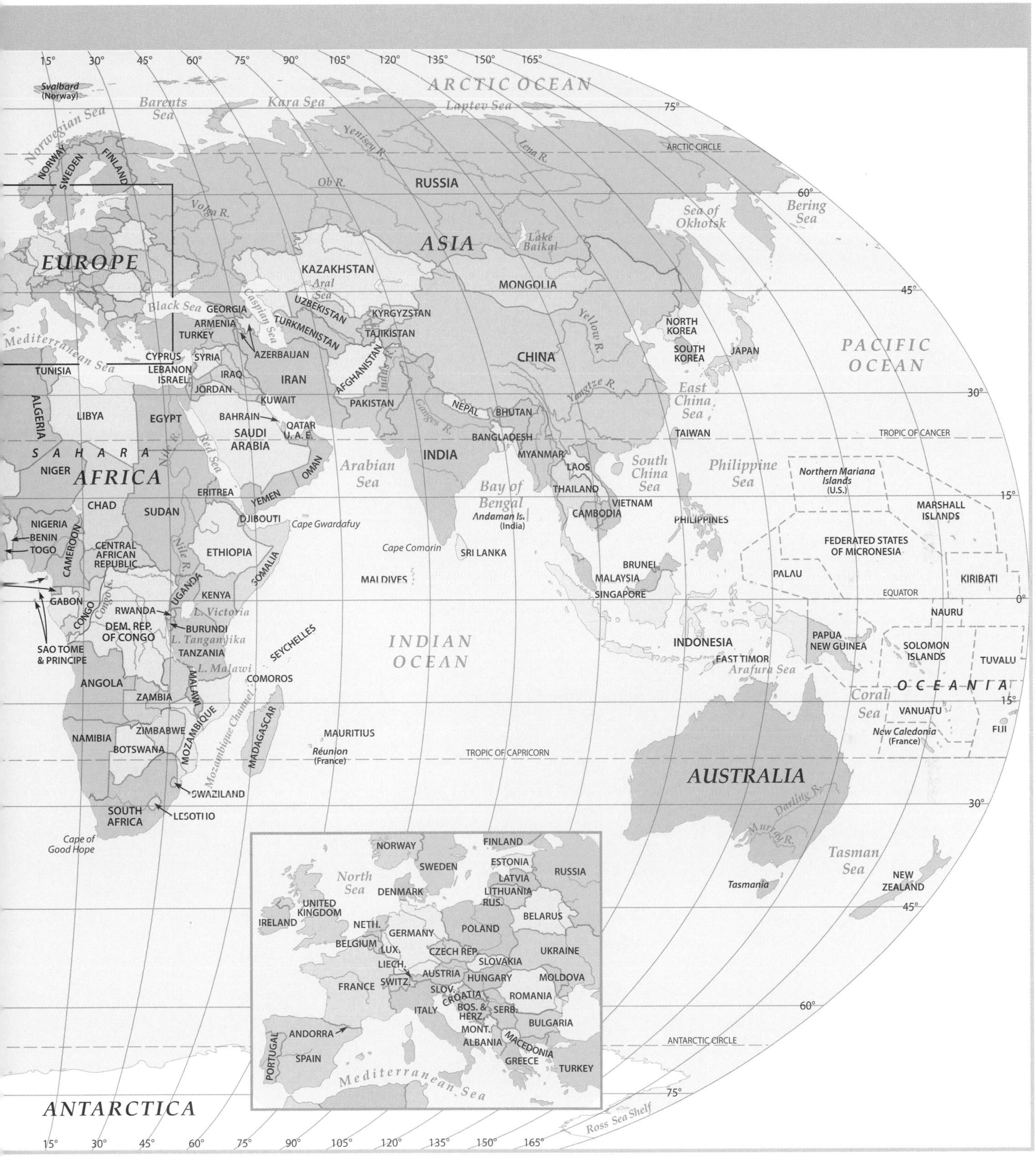
15°
30°
45°
60°
75°
90°
105°
120°
135°
150°
165°
ARCTIC OCEAN
Svalbard (Norway)
Barents Sea
Kara Sea
Laptev Sea
Norwegian Sea
NORWAY
SWEDEN
FINLAND
Yenisey R.
Lena R.
ARCTIC CIRCLE
Ob R.
RUSSIA
Volga R.
Bering Sea
Sea of Okhotsk
Lake Baikal
EUROPE
ASIA
KAZAKHSTAN
Aral Sea
MONGOLIA
Black Sea
GEORGIA
Caspian Sea
UZBEKISTAN
KYRGYZSTAN
ARMENIA
TURKMENISTAN
TAJIKISTAN
TURKEY
Yellow R.
NORTH KOREA
SOUTH KOREA
JAPAN
PACIFIC OCEAN
Mediterranean Sea
CYPRUS
SYRIA
AZERBAIJAN
AFGHANISTAN
CHINA
TUNISIA
LEBANON
ISRAEL
IRAQ
IRAN
JORDAN
KUWAIT
Indus R.
PAKISTAN
NEPAL
BHUTAN
Yangtze R.
East China Sea
ALGERIA
LIBYA
EGYPT
BAHRAIN
QATAR
U. A. E.
SAUDI ARABIA
Ganges R.
BANGLADESH
TAIWAN
TROPIC OF CANCER
SAHARA
Nile R.
Red Sea
OMAN
Arabian Sea
INDIA
MYANMAR
LAOS
South China Sea
Philippine Sea
Northern Mariana Islands (U.S.)
NIGER
AFRICA
ERITREA
YEMEN
Bay of Bengal
THAILAND
VIETNAM
CHAD
SUDAN
DJIBOUTI
Cape Gwardafuy
Andaman Is. (India)
CAMBODIA
PHILIPPINES
MARSHALL ISLANDS
NIGERIA
BENIN
TOGO
CAMEROON
CENTRAL AFRICAN REPUBLIC
ETHIOPIA
SOMALIA
Cape Comorin
SRI LANKA
FEDERATED STATES OF MICRONESIA
BRUNEI
MALAYSIA
PALAU
KIRIBATI
MALDIVES
UGANDA
KENYA
SINGAPORE
EQUATOR
GABON
CONGO
Congo R.
RWANDA
L. Victoria
NAURU
DEM. REP. OF CONGO
BURUNDI
L. Tanganyika
SEYCHELLES
INDIAN OCEAN
INDONESIA
PAPUA NEW GUINEA
SOLOMON ISLANDS
SAO TOME & PRINCIPE
TANZANIA
L. Malawi
EAST TIMOR
Arafura Sea
TUVALU
COMOROS
ANGOLA
ZAMBIA
MALAWI
Coral Sea
OCEANIA
VANUATU
Mozambique Channel
MOZAMBIQUE
NAMIBIA
ZIMBABWE
BOTSWANA
MADAGASCAR
MAURITIUS
Réunion (France)
New Caledonia (France)
FIJI
TROPIC OF CAPRICORN
AUSTRALIA
SWAZILAND
SOUTH AFRICA
LESOTHO
Darling R.
Murray R.
Cape of Good Hope
Tasman Sea
Tasmania
NEW ZEALAND
NORWAY
FINLAND
ESTONIA
SWEDEN
RUSSIA
North Sea
LATVIA
DENMARK
LITHUANIA
RUS.
UNITED KINGDOM
BELARUS
IRELAND
NETH.
GERMANY
POLAND
BELGIUM
LUX.
CZECH REP.
UKRAINE
SLOVAKIA
LIECH.
AUSTRIA
MOLDOVA
HUNGARY
FRANCE
SWITZ.
SLOV.
ROMANIA
CROATIA
ITALY
BOS. & HERZ.
SERB.
BULGARIA
MONT.
ANDORRA
ALBANIA
MACEDONIA
PORTUGAL
SPAIN
GREECE
TURKEY
Mediterranean Sea
ANTARCTIC CIRCLE
ANTARCTICA
Ross Sea Shelf

Pacific Rim

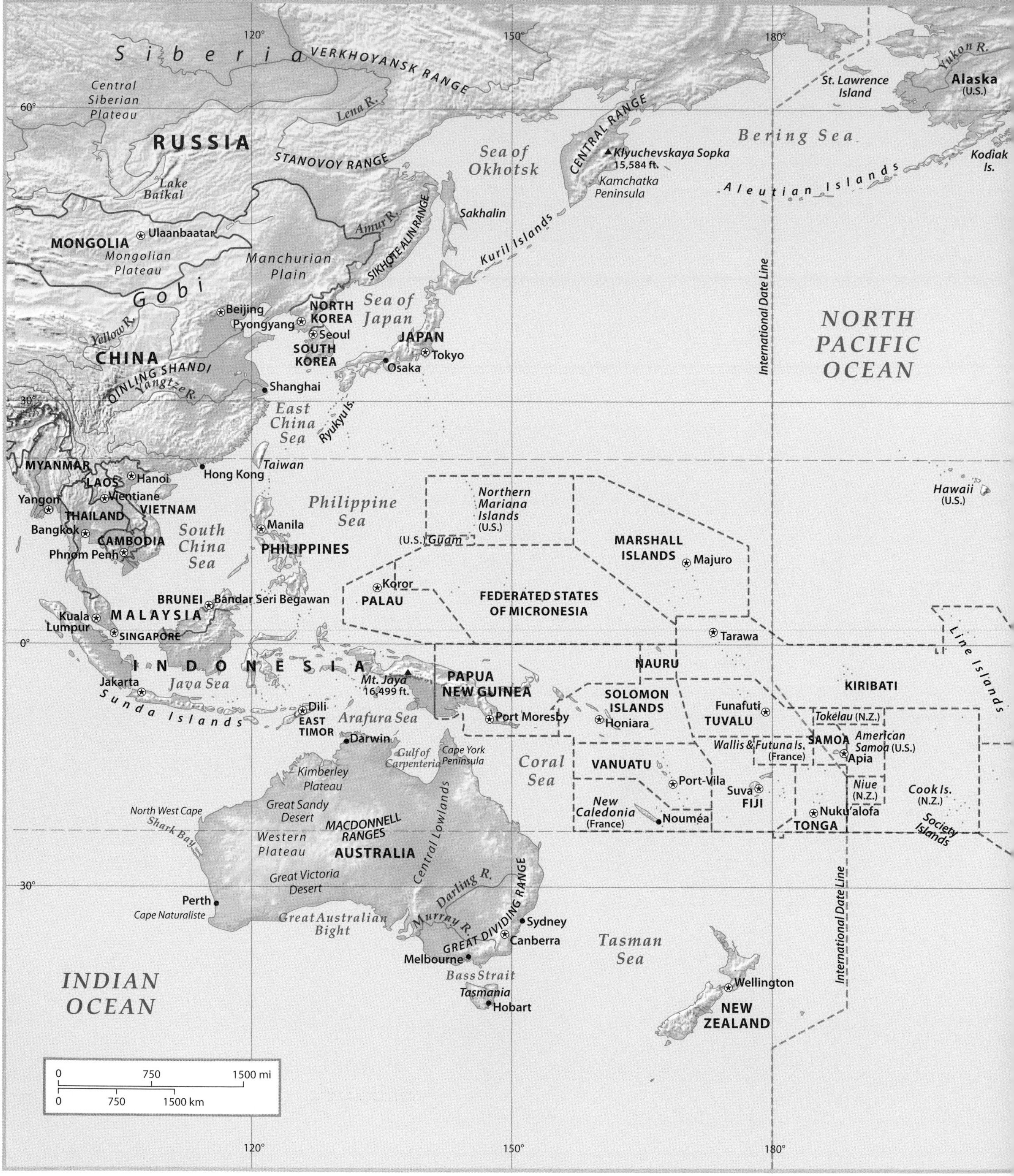

Siberia
Central Siberian Plateau
VERKHOYANSK RANGE
Lena R.
RUSSIA
STANOVOY RANGE
Lake Baikal
Sea of Okhotsk
CENTRAL RANGE
Klyuchevskaya Sopka 15,584 ft.
Kamchatka Peninsula
Bering Sea
St. Lawrence Island
Alaska (U.S.)
Yukon R.
Kodiak Is.
Aleutian Islands
Sakhalin
Kuril Islands
SIKHOTE ALIN RANGE
Amur R.
MONGOLIA
Ulaanbaatar
Mongolian Plateau
Manchurian Plain
Gobi
Beijing
Pyongyang
NORTH KOREA
Seoul
SOUTH KOREA
Sea of Japan
JAPAN
Tokyo
Osaka
Yellow R.
CHINA
QINLING SHANDI
Yangtze R.
Shanghai
East China Sea
Ryukyu Is.
International Date Line
NORTH PACIFIC OCEAN
MYANMAR
LAOS
Hanoi
Vientiane
VIETNAM
Yangon
THAILAND
Bangkok
CAMBODIA
Phnom Penh
Hong Kong
Taiwan
Philippine Sea
South China Sea
Manila
PHILIPPINES
Northern Mariana Islands (U.S.)
(U.S.) Guam
MARSHALL ISLANDS
Majuro
Hawaii (U.S.)
Koror
PALAU
FEDERATED STATES OF MICRONESIA
BRUNEI
Bandar Seri Begawan
Kuala Lumpur
MALAYSIA
SINGAPORE
Tarawa
Line Islands
INDONESIA
Mt. Jaya 16,499 ft.
PAPUA NEW GUINEA
NAURU
KIRIBATI
Jakarta
Java Sea
Sunda Islands
Dili
EAST TIMOR
Arafura Sea
Port Moresby
SOLOMON ISLANDS
Honiara
Funafuti
TUVALU
Tokelau (N.Z.)
Darwin
Gulf of Carpentaria
Cape York Peninsula
Wallis & Futuna Is. (France)
SAMOA
American Samoa (U.S.)
Apia
Kimberley Plateau
Coral Sea
VANUATU
Port-Vila
Suva
FIJI
Niue (N.Z.)
Cook Is. (N.Z.)
Great Sandy Desert
North West Cape
Shark Bay
MACDONNELL RANGES
Western Plateau
Central Lowlands
AUSTRALIA
New Caledonia (France)
Nouméa
Nuku'alofa
TONGA
Society Islands
Great Victoria Desert
Darling R.
GREAT DIVIDING RANGE
Perth
Cape Naturaliste
Great Australian Bight
Murray R.
Sydney
Canberra
Tasman Sea
Melbourne
Bass Strait
Tasmania
Hobart
Wellington
NEW ZEALAND
INDIAN OCEAN
0 750 1500 mi
0 750 1500 km
120°
150°
180°
60°
30°
0°

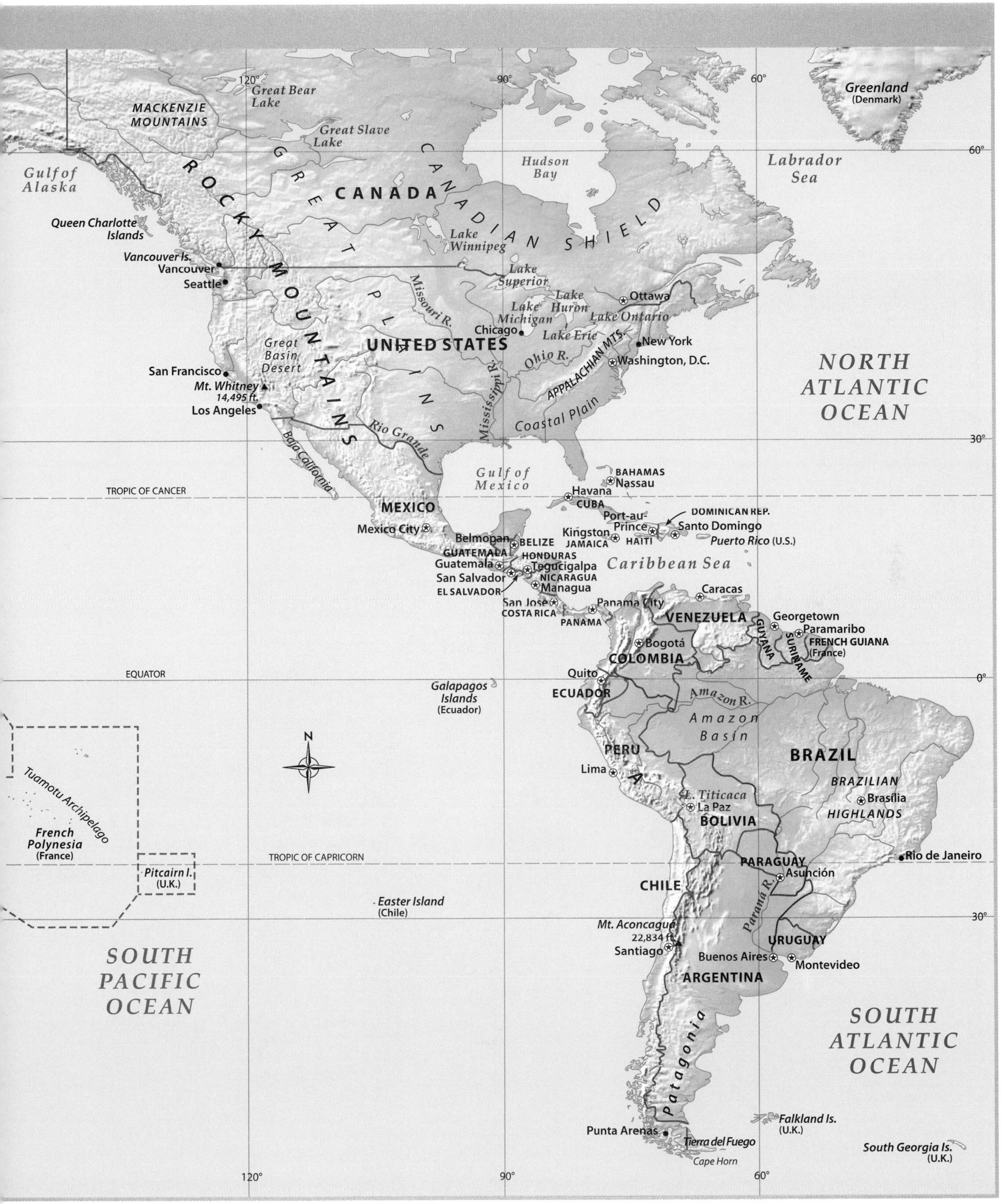
Greenland
(Denmark)
Great Bear Lake
MACKENZIE MOUNTAINS
Great Slave Lake
Gulf of Alaska
ROCKY MOUNTAINS
GREAT PLAINS
CANADA
CANADIAN SHIELD
Hudson Bay
Labrador Sea
Queen Charlotte Islands
Vancouver Is.
Vancouver
Seattle
Lake Winnipeg
Lake Superior
Missouri R.
Lake Michigan
Lake Huron
Ottawa
Lake Ontario
Lake Erie
Chicago
UNITED STATES
New York
Washington, D.C.
Great Basin Desert
San Francisco
Mt. Whitney
14,495 ft.
Los Angeles
Ohio R.
APPALACHIAN MTS.
Mississippi R.
Coastal Plain
Rio Grande
Baja California
NORTH ATLANTIC OCEAN
Gulf of Mexico
BAHAMAS
Nassau
Havana
CUBA
TROPIC OF CANCER
MEXICO
Mexico City
Port-au-Prince
DOMINICAN REP.
Santo Domingo
Kingston
JAMAICA
HAITI
Puerto Rico (U.S.)
Belmopan
BELIZE
GUATEMALA
HONDURAS
Guatemala
Tegucigalpa
San Salvador
NICARAGUA
EL SALVADOR
Managua
Caribbean Sea
San José
COSTA RICA
Panama City
PANAMA
Caracas
VENEZUELA
GUYANA
Georgetown
Paramaribo
SURINAME
FRENCH GUIANA
(France)
Bogotá
COLOMBIA
EQUATOR
Quito
ECUADOR
Galapagos Islands
(Ecuador)
Amazon R.
Amazon Basin
PERU
BRAZIL
Lima
ANDES
BRAZILIAN HIGHLANDS
Brasília
L. Titicaca
La Paz
BOLIVIA
Tuamotu Archipelago
French Polynesia
(France)
TROPIC OF CAPRICORN
Pitcairn I.
(U.K.)
Rio de Janeiro
PARAGUAY
Asunción
CHILE
Paraná R.
Easter Island
(Chile)
Mt. Aconcagua
22,834 ft.
URUGUAY
Santiago
Buenos Aires
Montevideo
SOUTH PACIFIC OCEAN
ARGENTINA
SOUTH ATLANTIC OCEAN
Patagonia
Falkland Is.
(U.K.)
Punta Arenas
Tierra del Fuego
South Georgia Is.
(U.K.)
Cape Horn
120°
90°
60°
30°
0°

North America

South America

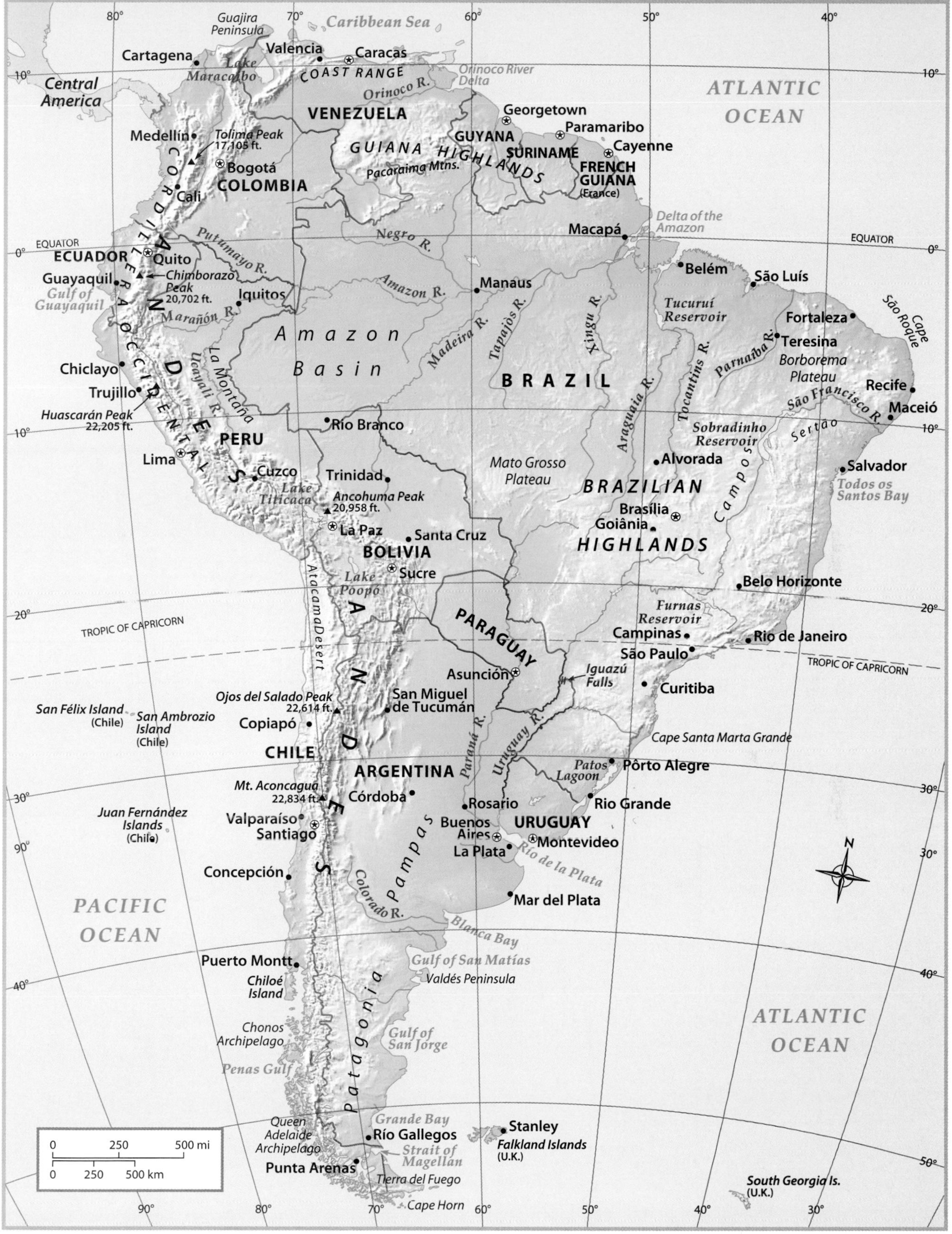

Guajira Peninsula
Caribbean Sea
Cartagena
Valencia
Caracas
Lake Maracaibo
COAST RANGE
Orinoco River Delta
Orinoco R.
Central America
ATLANTIC OCEAN
VENEZUELA
Georgetown
Paramaribo
Medellín
Tolima Peak 17,105 ft.
GUYANA
SURINAME
Cayenne
GUIANA HIGHLANDS
Bogotá
Pacaraima Mtns.
FRENCH GUIANA (France)
COLOMBIA
Cali
CORDILLERA OCCIDENTAL
Delta of the Amazon
Macapá
EQUATOR
Negro R.
Putumayo R.
ECUADOR
Quito
Belém
São Luís
Guayaquil
Chimborazo Peak 20,702 ft.
Manaus
Gulf of Guayaquil
Iquitos
Amazon R.
Marañón R.
Tucuruí Reservoir
Fortaleza
Cape São Roque
Amazon Basin
Madeira R.
Tapajós R.
Xingu R.
Parnaíba R.
Teresina
Borborema Plateau
Chiclayo
La Montaña
Ucayali R.
Tocantins R.
BRAZIL
Recife
Trujillo
ANDES
São Francisco R.
Maceió
Huascarán Peak 22,205 ft.
Rio Branco
Araguaia R.
Sobradinho Reservoir
Sertão
PERU
Lima
Alvorada
Mato Grosso Plateau
Salvador
Cuzco
Trinidad
BRAZILIAN HIGHLANDS
Todos os Santos Bay
Lake Titicaca
Ancohuma Peak 20,958 ft.
Campos
Brasília
Goiânia
La Paz
Santa Cruz
BOLIVIA
Sucre
Atacama Desert
Lake Poopó
Belo Horizonte
Furnas Reservoir
TROPIC OF CAPRICORN
PARAGUAY
Campinas
Rio de Janeiro
São Paulo
Asunción
Iguazú Falls
Curitiba
Ojos del Salado Peak 22,614 ft.
San Miguel de Tucumán
San Félix Island (Chile)
San Ambrozio Island (Chile)
Copiapó
Paraná R.
Uruguay R.
Cape Santa Marta Grande
CHILE
ARGENTINA
Patos Lagoon
Pôrto Alegre
Mt. Aconcagua 22,834 ft.
Córdoba
Rosario
Rio Grande
Juan Fernández Islands (Chile)
Valparaíso
Santiago
Buenos Aires
URUGUAY
Montevideo
La Plata
Rio de la Plata
Pampas
N
Concepción
Colorado R.
Mar del Plata
PACIFIC OCEAN
Blanca Bay
Puerto Montt
Gulf of San Matías
Valdés Peninsula
Chiloé Island
Patagonia
Chonos Archipelago
Gulf of San Jorge
ATLANTIC OCEAN
Penas Gulf
Queen Adelaide Archipelago
Grande Bay
Río Gallegos
Stanley
Falkland Islands (U.K.)
Strait of Magellan
Punta Arenas
Tierra del Fuego
Cape Horn
South Georgia Is. (U.K.)
0 250 500 mi
0 250 500 km
80° 70° 60° 50° 40° 30° 90°
10° 0° 20° 30° 40° 50°

Europe

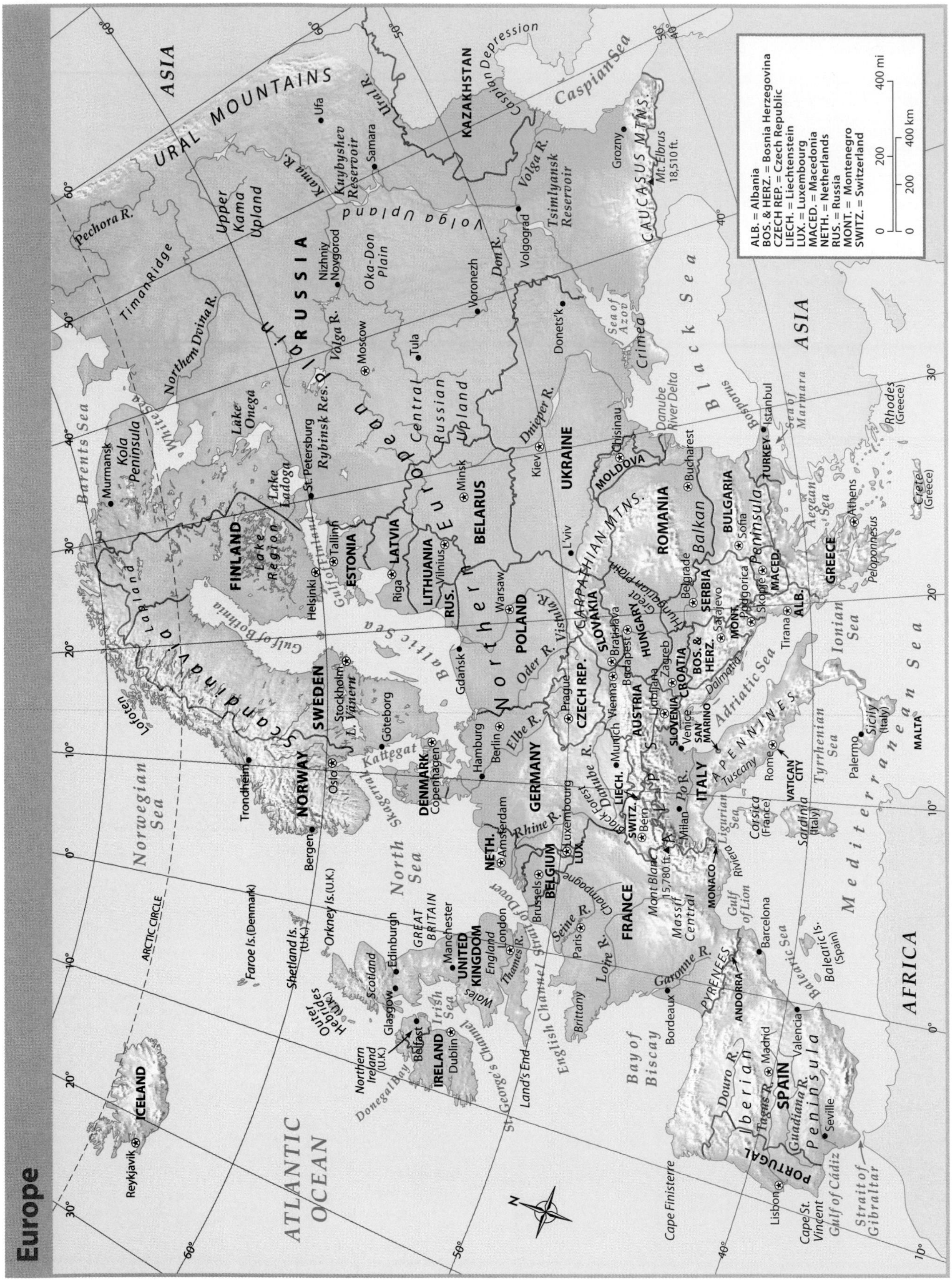
ALB. = Albania
BOS. & HERZ. = Bosnia Herzegovina
CZECH REP. = Czech Republic
LIECH. = Liechtenstein
LUX. = Luxembourg
MACED. = Macedonia
NETH. = Netherlands
RUS. = Russia
MONT. = Montenegro
SWITZ. = Switzerland
0 200 400 mi
0 200 400 km
ATLANTIC OCEAN
ASIA
AFRICA
URAL MOUNTAINS
RUSSIA
UKRAINE
BELARUS
POLAND
GERMANY
FRANCE
SPAIN
PORTUGAL
ITALY
UNITED KINGDOM
IRELAND
ICELAND
NORWAY
SWEDEN
FINLAND
ESTONIA
LATVIA
LITHUANIA
DENMARK
NETH.
BELGIUM
LUX.
SWITZ.
LIECH.
AUSTRIA
CZECH REP.
SLOVAKIA
HUNGARY
SLOVENIA
CROATIA
BOS. & HERZ.
SERBIA
MONT.
ALB.
MACED.
GREECE
BULGARIA
ROMANIA
MOLDOVA
TURKEY
KAZAKHSTAN
Northern European Plain
Scandinavia
Lapland
Iberian Peninsula
Balkan Peninsula
North Sea
Norwegian Sea
Barents Sea
Baltic Sea
Black Sea
Caspian Sea
Mediterranean Sea
Adriatic Sea
Aegean Sea
Ionian Sea
Tyrrhenian Sea
Bay of Biscay
English Channel
ALPS
APENNINES
PYRENEES
CARPATHIAN MTNS.
CAUCASUS MTNS.
Mt. Elbrus 18,510 ft.
Mont Blanc 15,780 ft.
ARCTIC CIRCLE

Africa

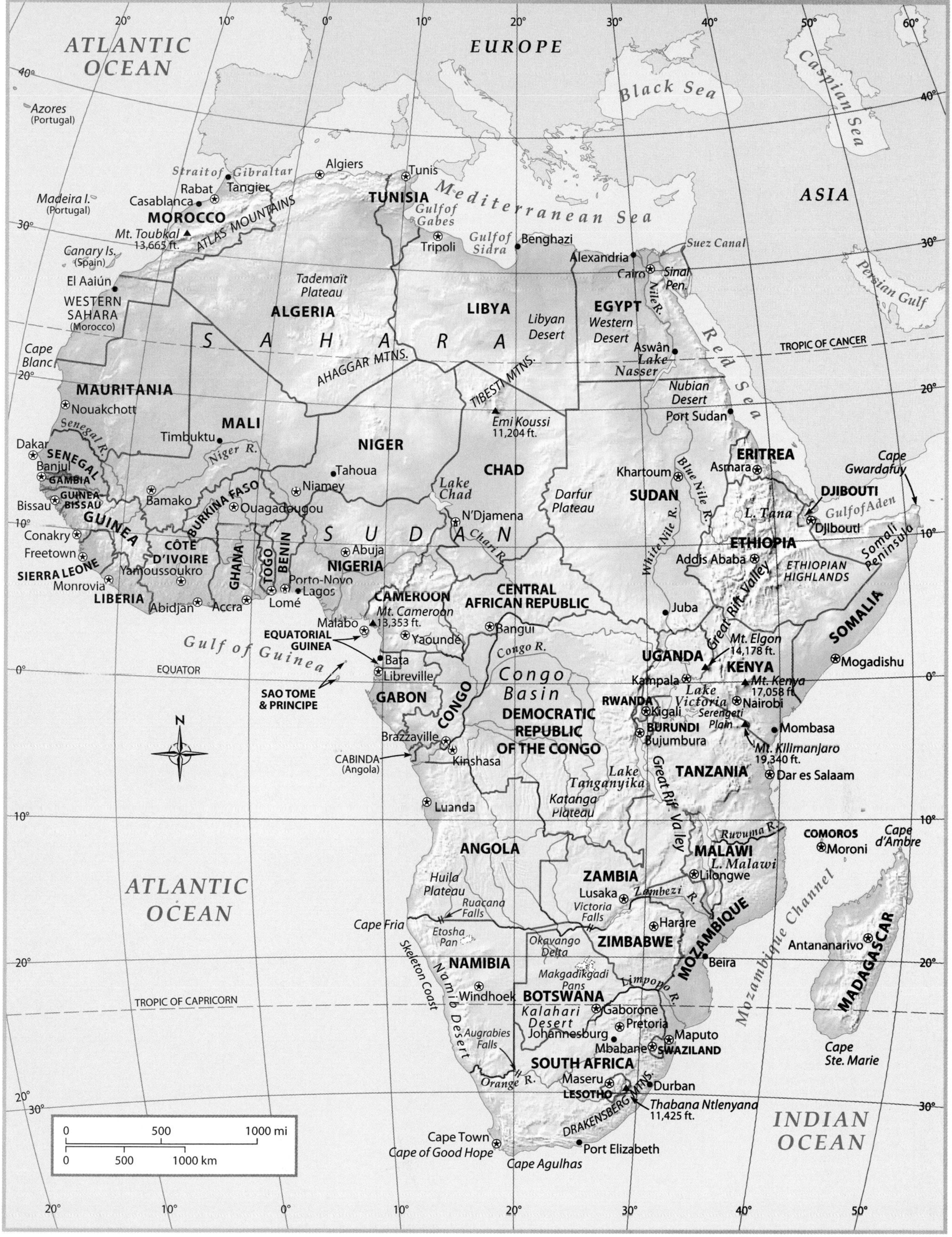

ATLANTIC OCEAN
EUROPE
Black Sea
Caspian Sea
ASIA
Azores (Portugal)
Madeira I. (Portugal)
Canary Is. (Spain)
Strait of Gibraltar
Tangier
Rabat
Casablanca
MOROCCO
Mt. Toubkal 13,665 ft.
ATLAS MOUNTAINS
Algiers
Tunis
TUNISIA
Mediterranean Sea
Gulf of Gabes
Tripoli
Gulf of Sidra
Benghazi
Alexandria
Suez Canal
Cairo
Sinai Pen.
Nile R.
Persian Gulf
El Aaiún
WESTERN SAHARA (Morocco)
Tademaït Plateau
ALGERIA
LIBYA
Libyan Desert
EGYPT
Western Desert
Red Sea
TROPIC OF CANCER
S A H A R A
Cape Blanc
AHAGGAR MTNS.
TIBESTI MTNS.
Aswân
Lake Nasser
MAURITANIA
Nouakchott
Emi Koussi 11,204 ft.
Nubian Desert
Port Sudan
Senegal R.
MALI
Timbuktu
Niger R.
NIGER
CHAD
Dakar
SENEGAL
Banjul
GAMBIA
GUINEA-BISSAU
Bissau
Tahoua
Niamey
Bamako
BURKINA FASO
Ouagadougou
Lake Chad
N'Djamena
Darfur Plateau
Khartoum
SUDAN
Blue Nile R.
ERITREA
Asmara
Cape Gwardafuy
DJIBOUTI
Djibouti
Gulf of Aden
L. Tana
ETHIOPIA
Somali Peninsula
GUINEA
Conakry
Freetown
SIERRA LEONE
CÔTE D'IVOIRE
Yamoussoukro
GHANA
TOGO
BENIN
S U D A N
Abuja
NIGERIA
Chari R.
White Nile R.
Addis Ababa
ETHIOPIAN HIGHLANDS
Monrovia
LIBERIA
Abidjan
Accra
Lomé
Porto-Novo
Lagos
CAMEROON
Mt. Cameroon 13,353 ft.
CENTRAL AFRICAN REPUBLIC
Juba
Great Rift Valley
SOMALIA
Gulf of Guinea
Malabo
EQUATORIAL GUINEA
Yaoundé
Bangui
Congo R.
Mt. Elgon 14,178 ft.
UGANDA
KENYA
Mogadishu
EQUATOR
Bata
Libreville
SAO TOME & PRINCIPE
Congo Basin
Kampala
Mt. Kenya 17,058 ft.
GABON
CONGO
RWANDA
Lake Victoria
Nairobi
Kigali
Serengeti Plain
DEMOCRATIC REPUBLIC OF THE CONGO
BURUNDI
Bujumbura
Mombasa
Brazzaville
Kinshasa
Mt. Kilimanjaro 19,340 ft.
CABINDA (Angola)
Lake Tanganyika
TANZANIA
Dar es Salaam
Great Rift Valley
Katanga Plateau
Luanda
Ruvuma R.
COMOROS
Moroni
Cape d'Ambre
ANGOLA
MALAWI
L. Malawi
ATLANTIC OCEAN
Huila Plateau
ZAMBIA
Lilongwe
Lusaka
Zambezi R.
Ruacana Falls
Victoria Falls
Mozambique Channel
Cape Fria
Harare
MOZAMBIQUE
Etosha Pan
Okavango Delta
ZIMBABWE
MADAGASCAR
Antananarivo
Skeleton Coast
NAMIBIA
Beira
Makgadikgadi Pans
Limpopo R.
Windhoek
BOTSWANA
Namib Desert
TROPIC OF CAPRICORN
Kalahari Desert
Gaborone
Pretoria
Johannesburg
Maputo
Mbabane
SWAZILAND
Augrabies Falls
Cape Ste. Marie
SOUTH AFRICA
Orange R.
Maseru
LESOTHO
Durban
DRAKENSBERG MTNS.
Thabana Ntlenyana 11,425 ft.
INDIAN OCEAN
Cape Town
Cape of Good Hope
Port Elizabeth
Cape Agulhas
0 500 1000 mi
0 500 1000 km
N

Eurasia

ATLANTIC OCEAN
ARCTIC OCEAN
Norwegian Sea
Svalbard (Norway)
Franz Josef Land
IRELAND
Dublin
UNITED KINGDOM
London
North Sea
NORWAY
Oslo
Scandinavia
SWEDEN
Gulf of Bothnia
Stockholm
FINLAND
Helsinki
Barents Sea
Novaya Zemlya
Kara Sea
Kola Peninsula
Yamal Peninsula
Lisbon
PORTUGAL
Iberian Peninsula
Madrid
SPAIN
ANDORRA
PYRENEES
Paris
BELGIUM
NETH.
Amsterdam
Brussels
LUX.
FRANCE
DENMARK
Copenhagen
GERMANY
Berlin
Baltic Sea
Tallinn
Riga
ESTONIA
LATVIA
St. Petersburg
Bern
SWITZ.
Alps
Prague
CZECH REP.
POLAND
Warsaw
RUS.
LITHUANIA
Vilnius
AUSTRIA
Vienna
Bratislava
SLOVAKIA
Ljubljana
SLOV.
CROATIA
Zagreb
Budapest
HUNGARY
Minsk
BELARUS
Northern European Plain
Balearic Is.
Corsica
Sardinia
ITALY
Rome
Sicily
Moscow
Mediterranean Sea
Sarajevo
BOS.
MONT.
Belgrade
SERBIA
Podgorica
Tirana
ALBANIA
MACED.
Skopje
Sofia
BULGARIA
ROMANIA
Bucharest
MOLDOVA
Chisinau
Kiev
Dnieper R.
UKRAINE
Central Russian Upland
Volga R.
URAL MOUNTAINS
Ob R.
West Siberian Plain
Yekaterinburg
Tobol R.
RUSSIA
Yenisey R.
GREECE
Athens
Crimea
Black Sea
Sea of Azov
CAUCASUS MTNS.
Caspian Depression
The Steppes
Astana
KAZAKHSTAN
Kazakh Uplands
Anatolia
Ankara
Crete
TURKEY
GEORGIA
T'bilisi
ARMENIA
Yerevan
AZER.
Baku
Caspian Sea
Aral Sea
Turan Lowland
Syr Darya
UZBEKISTAN
Lake Balkhash
CYPRUS
Nicosia
LEBANON
SYRIA
ISRAEL
Damascus
Jerusalem
Euphrates R.
Tigris R.
ZAGROS MTNS.
TURKMENISTAN
Tashkent
Bishkek
Almaty
KYRGYZSTAN
Sinai Pen.
JORDAN
Syrian Desert
Baghdad
IRAQ
Ashgabat
Tehran
Amu Darya
Dushanbe
Communism Peak 24,590 ft.
TIAN SHAN
Taklimakan Desert
TAJIKISTAN
Kongur Shan 25,324 ft.
An Nafūd
Salt Desert
Plateau of Iran
HINDU KUSH
Kabul
K2 28,251 ft.
KUNLUN MTNS.
KUWAIT
Kuwait
IRAN
AFGHANISTAN
Indus R.
Islamabad
Plateau of Tibet
SAUDI ARABIA
Persian Gulf
Manama
BAHRAIN
QATAR
Doha
Riyadh
HIMALAYA
Red Sea
Arabian Peninsula
Abu Dhabi
U.A.E.
PAKISTAN
Great Indian Desert
New Delhi
Annapurna I 26,545 ft.
Kathmandu
NEPAL
Mount Everest 29,035 ft.
Ganges Plain
Ganges R.
Muscat
Karachi
Indus R. Delta
AFRICA
Sanaa
Rub' al Khali
OMAN
INDIA
Narmada R.
BANGLADESH
YEMEN
Kozhikode
Aden
Gulf of Aden
Arabian Sea
Gulf of Khambhat
Mumbai
Godavari R.
Chota Nagpur Plateau
Hyderabad
WESTERN GHATS
Deccan Plateau
EASTERN GHATS
Bay of Bengal
Chennai
Laccadive Sea
Malabar Coast
INDIAN OCEAN
SRI LANKA
Colombo
Gulf of Mannar
Dondra Head
Male
MALDIVES
AZER. = Azerbaijan
BOS. = Bosnia Herzegovina
CZECH REP. = Czech Republic
LUX. = Luxembourg
MACED. = Macedonia
NETH. = Netherlands
MONT. = Montenegro
SWITZ. = Switzerland
U.A.E. = United Arab Emirates

ARCTIC OCEAN
Wrangel Island
Chukchi Peninsula
Cape Navarin
Bering Sea
North Land
New Siberian Islands
Laptev Sea
Lena R. Delta
Kolyma Lowland
Taymyr Peninsula
Kolyma R.
KOLYMA RANGE
Kamchatka Peninsula
VERKHOYANSK RANGE
Lena R.
Central Siberian Plateau
SIBERIA
Sea of Okhotsk
Sakhalin
Kuril Islands
STANOVOY RANGE
SIKHOTE-ALIN RANGE
Tatar Strait
Amur R.
SAYAN MOUNTAINS
Lake Baikal
Hokkaido
Sapporo
L. Khanka
Manchurian Plain
Ulaanbaatar
Sea of Japan
JAPAN
MONGOLIA
Mongolian Plateau
ALTAY MTNS.
Gobi
Shenyang
NORTH KOREA
Pyongyang
Seoul
Tokyo
Honshu
PACIFIC OCEAN
Yellow R.
Beijing
Bo Hai
SOUTH KOREA
Pusan
Kitakyushu
Kyushu
Mu Us Desert
North China Plain
Yellow Sea
ALTUN SHUN
Qinghai Hu
CHINA
Shanghai
QIN LIN
Yangtze R.
East China Sea
Ryukyu Islands
Naha
Salween R.
Gongga Shan 24,790 ft.
Taipei
Taiwan
BHUTAN
Ayeyarwady R.
WUYI SHAN
Hongshui R.
Guangzhou
Hong Kong
Luzon Strait
Philippine Sea
MYANMAR
Hanoi
Leizhou Bay
Hainan
Luzon
LAOS
Gulf of Tonkin
Vientiane
South China Sea
Manila
Yangon
Indochina Peninsula
THAILAND
Mekong R.
PHILIPPINES
Koror
PALAU
VIETNAM
Bangkok
CAMBODIA
Palawan
Mindanao
Andaman Sea
Phnom Penh
Ho Chi Minh City
Gulf of Thailand
Andaman Islands (India)
Celebes Sea
Bandar Seri Begawan
BRUNEI
BORNEO HIGHLANDS
Halmahera
MAOKE MTNS.
Malay Peninsula
Nicobar Islands (India)
MALAYSIA
Mt. Jaya 16,499 ft.
New Guinea
Medan
Kuala Lumpur
Borneo
INDONESIA
SINGAPORE
Celebes
Sumatra
Banda Sea
Torres Strait
Coral Sea
BARISAN MOUNTAINS
Java Sea
Dili
EAST TIMOR
Jakarta
Java
AUSTRALIA
160°
80°
120°
60°
40°
180°
20°
0°
100°
140°

Middle East

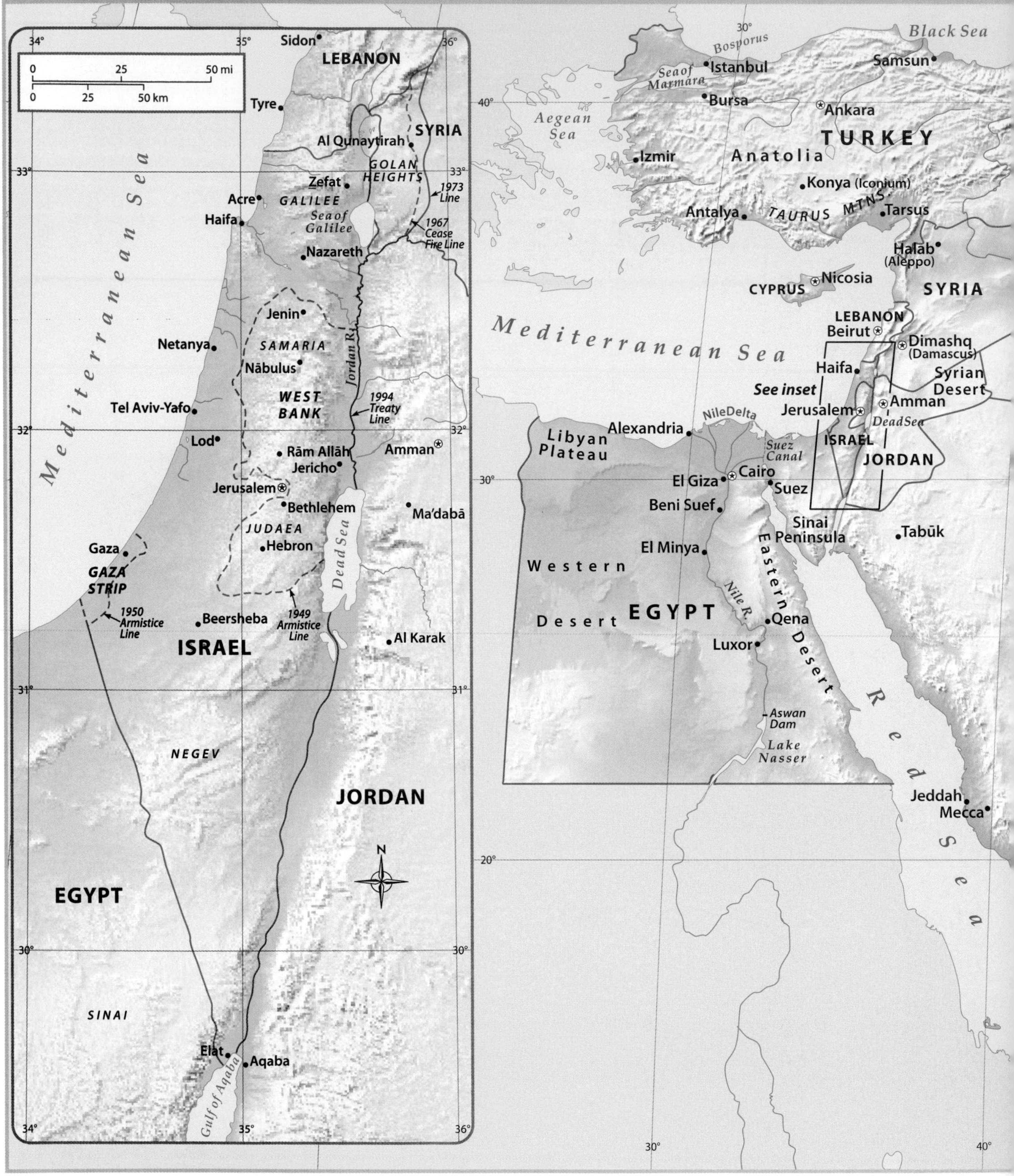

34°
35°
36°
0
25
50 mi
0
25
50 km
Sidon
LEBANON
Tyre
SYRIA
Al Qunaytirah
GOLAN HEIGHTS
33°
Zefat
1973 Line
Acre
GALILEE
Haifa
Sea of Galilee
1967 Cease Fire Line
Nazareth
Mediterranean Sea
Jenin
SAMARIA
Jordan R.
Netanya
Nābulus
WEST BANK
1994 Treaty Line
Tel Aviv-Yafo
32°
Lod
Rām Allāh
Amman
Jericho
Jerusalem
Bethlehem
Ma'dabā
JUDAEA
Hebron
Dead Sea
Gaza
GAZA STRIP
1950 Armistice Line
Beersheba
1949 Armistice Line
Al Karak
ISRAEL
31°
NEGEV
JORDAN
N
EGYPT
30°
SINAI
Elat
Aqaba
Gulf of Aqaba
30°
Black Sea
Bosporus
Sea of Marmara
Istanbul
Samsun
Bursa
40°
Ankara
Aegean Sea
TURKEY
Izmir
Anatolia
Konya (Iconium)
Antalya
TAURUS MTNS.
Tarsus
Halab (Aleppo)
CYPRUS
Nicosia
SYRIA
LEBANON
Mediterranean Sea
Beirut
Dimashq (Damascus)
Haifa
Syrian Desert
See inset
Amman
Jerusalem
Nile Delta
Dead Sea
Alexandria
Libyan Plateau
ISRAEL
Suez Canal
JORDAN
30°
El Giza
Cairo
Suez
Beni Suef
Sinai Peninsula
Tabūk
El Minya
Western Desert
Eastern Desert
Nile R.
EGYPT
Qena
Luxor
Red Sea
Aswan Dam
Lake Nasser
Jeddah
Mecca
20°
30°
40°

Caspian Sea
Erzurum
Mt. Ararat 16,854 ft
Lake Van
Van
Tabrīz
Lake Urmia
ELBURZ MOUNTAINS
Mashhad
Al Mawsil (Mosul)
Tehran
Mt. Damavend 18,934 ft
Mesopotamia
Tigris R.
Euphrates R.
ZAGROS MOUNTAINS
Dasht-e Kavīr (Salt Desert)
Baghdad
Esfahan
IRAQ
IRAN
Dasht-e Lūt
Al Hillah
Lake Helmand
Ābādān
Kermān
Shīrāz
Zāhedān
Kuwait
KUWAIT
An Nafūd
Persian Gulf
Bandar 'Abbās
Manama
BAHRAIN
Strait of Hormuz
OMAN
QATAR
Doha
SAUDI ARABIA
Ad Dah-nā
Hasa Plain
Riyadh
Al Hufūf
Dubayy
Abu Dhabi
Gulf of Oman
Sabkhat Mattī
UNITED ARAB EMIRATES
Muscat
TUWAYQ MTNS.
Şūr
Cape Hadd
Arabian Peninsula
OMAN
Tihama Plain
Rub' Al Khali (Great Sandy Desert)
Arabian Sea
Qmar Bay
Al Ghaydah
Sanaa
YEMEN
Hadramawt
INDIAN OCEAN
Aden
Gulf of Aden
0 250 500 mi
0 250 500 km
N
40°
50°
60°
70°
40°
30°
20°

South Asia

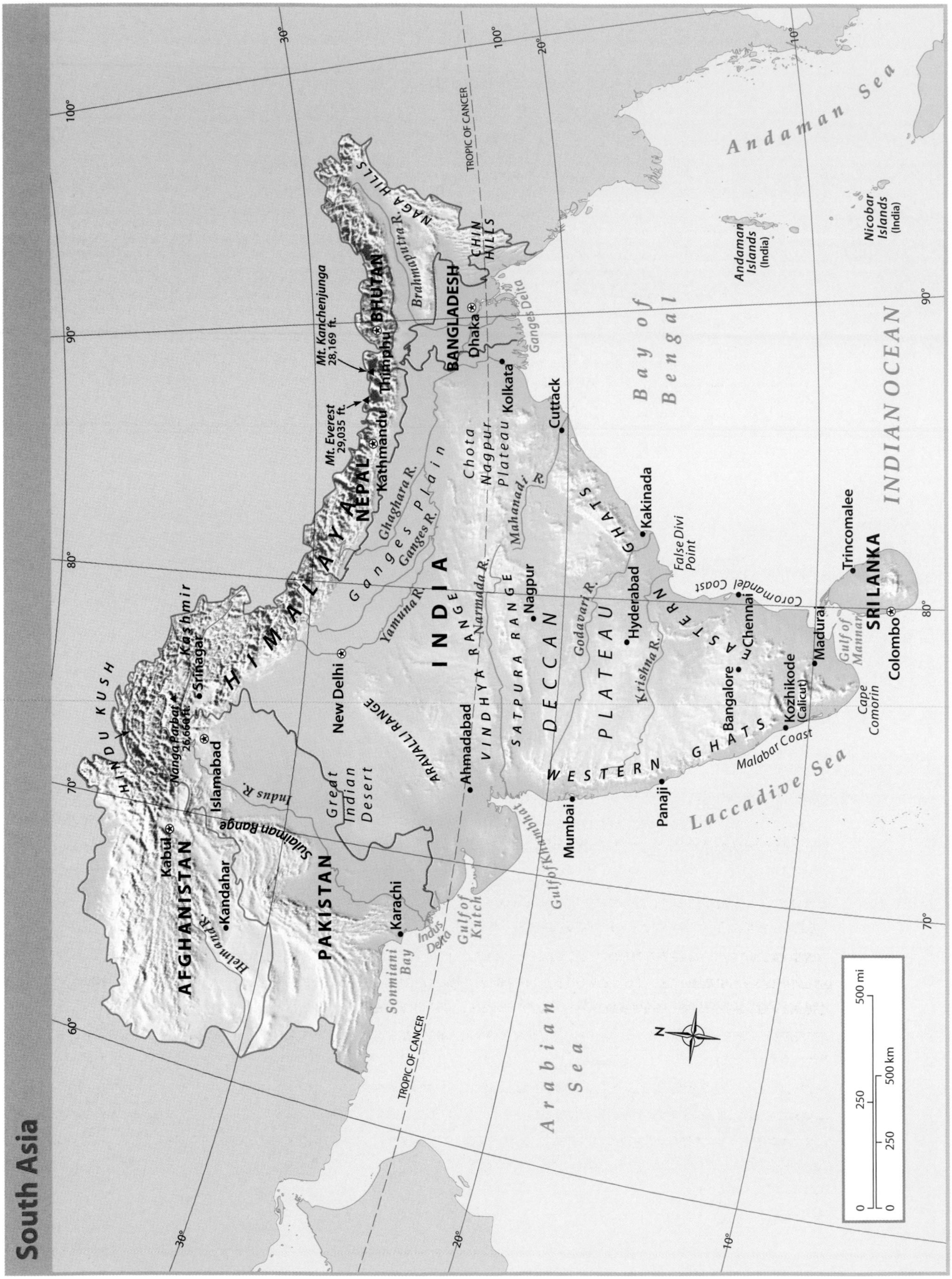

AFGHANISTAN
PAKISTAN
INDIA
NEPAL
BHUTAN
BANGLADESH
SRI LANKA
Kabul
Kandahar
Islamabad
Karachi
Srinagar
Kashmir
New Delhi
Ahmadabad
Mumbai
Panaji
Nagpur
Hyderabad
Bangalore
Chennai
Kozhikode (Calicut)
Madurai
Colombo
Trincomalee
Kakinada
Cuttack
Kolkata
Dhaka
Kathmandu
Thimphu
Mt. Everest 29,035 ft.
Mt. Kanchenjunga 28,169 ft.
Nanga Parbat 26,660 ft.
HINDU KUSH
HIMALAYA
Sulaiman Range
ARAVALLI RANGE
VINDHYA RANGE
SATPURA RANGE
DECCAN PLATEAU
WESTERN GHATS
EASTERN GHATS
NAGA HILLS
CHIN HILLS
Chota Nagpur Plateau
Ganges Plain
Great Indian Desert
Helmand R.
Indus R.
Yamuna R.
Ganges R.
Ghaghara R.
Brahmaputra R.
Narmada R.
Mahanadi R.
Godavari R.
Krishna R.
Ganges Delta
Indus Delta
Sonmiani Bay
Gulf of Kutch
Gulf of Khambhat
Malabar Coast
Coromandel Coast
False Divi Point
Cape Comorin
Gulf of Mannar
Arabian Sea
Laccadive Sea
Bay of Bengal
Andaman Sea
INDIAN OCEAN
Andaman Islands (India)
Nicobar Islands (India)
TROPIC OF CANCER
N
0 250 500 mi
0 250 500 km

North and South Poles

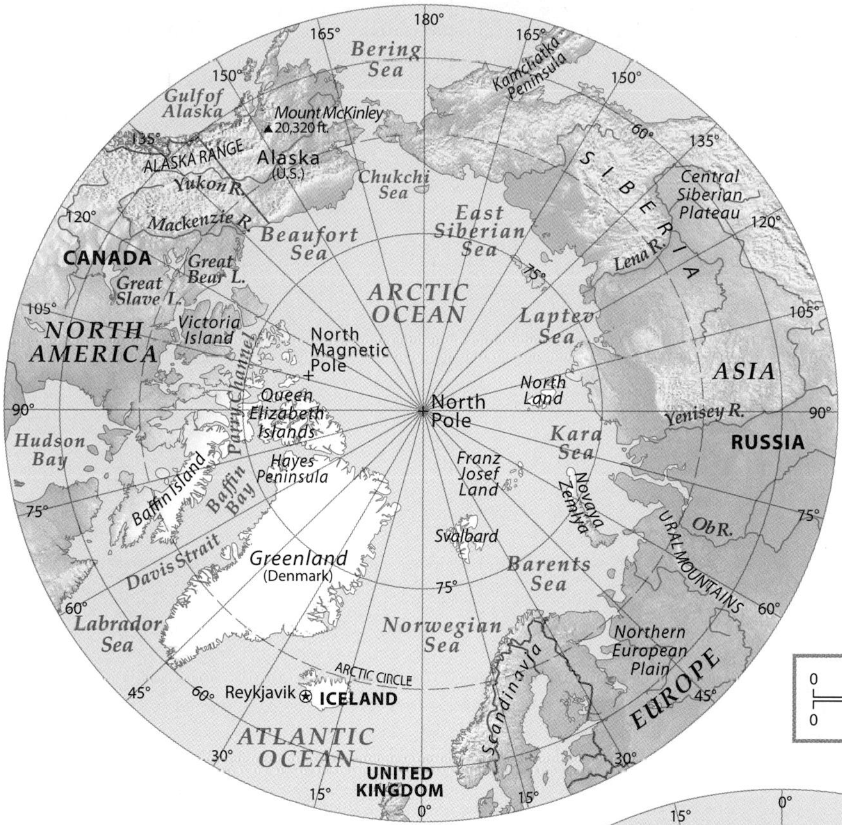
Bering Sea
Gulf of Alaska
Mount McKinley ▲20,320 ft.
ALASKA RANGE
Alaska (U.S.)
Yukon R.
Mackenzie R.
Chukchi Sea
Beaufort Sea
East Siberian Sea
Kamchatka Peninsula
SIBERIA
Central Siberian Plateau
Lena R.
CANADA
Great Bear L.
Great Slave L.
NORTH AMERICA
Victoria Island
ARCTIC OCEAN
North Magnetic Pole
Laptev Sea
ASIA
North Land
North Pole
Queen Elizabeth Islands
Parry Channel
Yenisey R.
RUSSIA
Hudson Bay
Kara Sea
Baffin Island
Baffin Bay
Hayes Peninsula
Franz Josef Land
Novaya Zemlya
URAL MOUNTAINS
Ob R.
Svalbard
Davis Strait
Greenland (Denmark)
Barents Sea
Labrador Sea
Norwegian Sea
Northern European Plain
EUROPE
ARCTIC CIRCLE
Reykjavik
ICELAND
Scandinavia
ATLANTIC OCEAN
UNITED KINGDOM

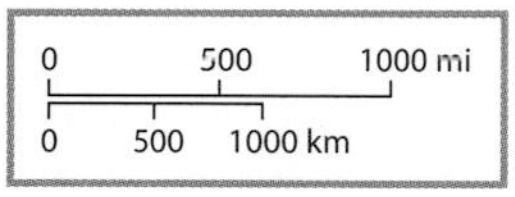
0 500 1000 mi
0 500 1000 km

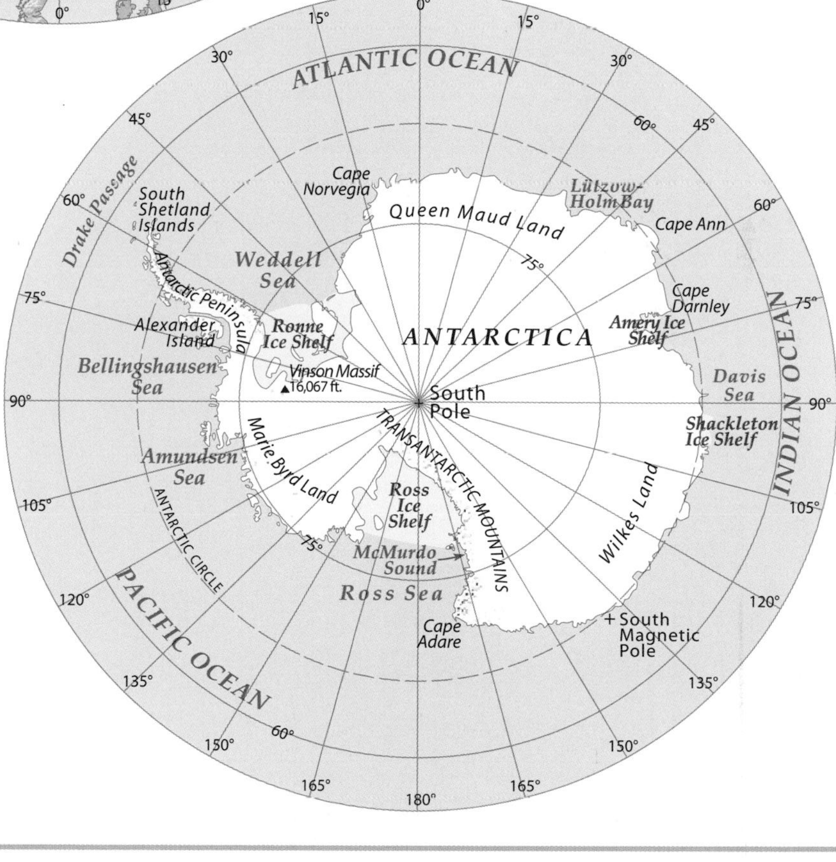
ATLANTIC OCEAN
Drake Passage
South Shetland Islands
Cape Norvegia
Queen Maud Land
Lützow-Holm Bay
Cape Ann
Weddell Sea
Antarctic Peninsula
Alexander Island
Ronne Ice Shelf
ANTARCTICA
Amery Ice Shelf
Cape Darnley
Bellingshausen Sea
Vinson Massif ▲16,067 ft.
South Pole
Davis Sea
INDIAN OCEAN
Shackleton Ice Shelf
TRANSANTARCTIC MOUNTAINS
Marie Byrd Land
Amundsen Sea
Ross Ice Shelf
Wilkes Land
ANTARCTIC CIRCLE
McMurdo Sound
Ross Sea
PACIFIC OCEAN
Cape Adare
South Magnetic Pole

Goode's Interrupted Homoline Projection

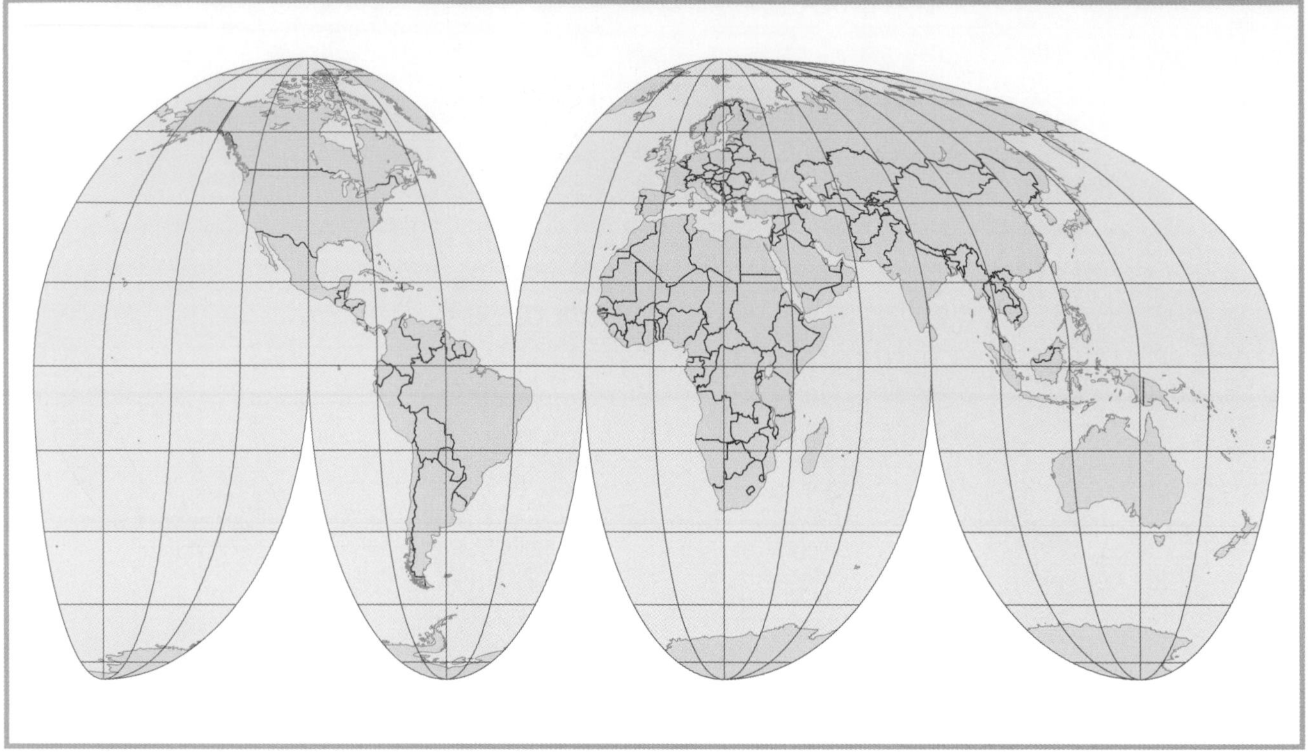

Miller Projection

Mollweide Projection

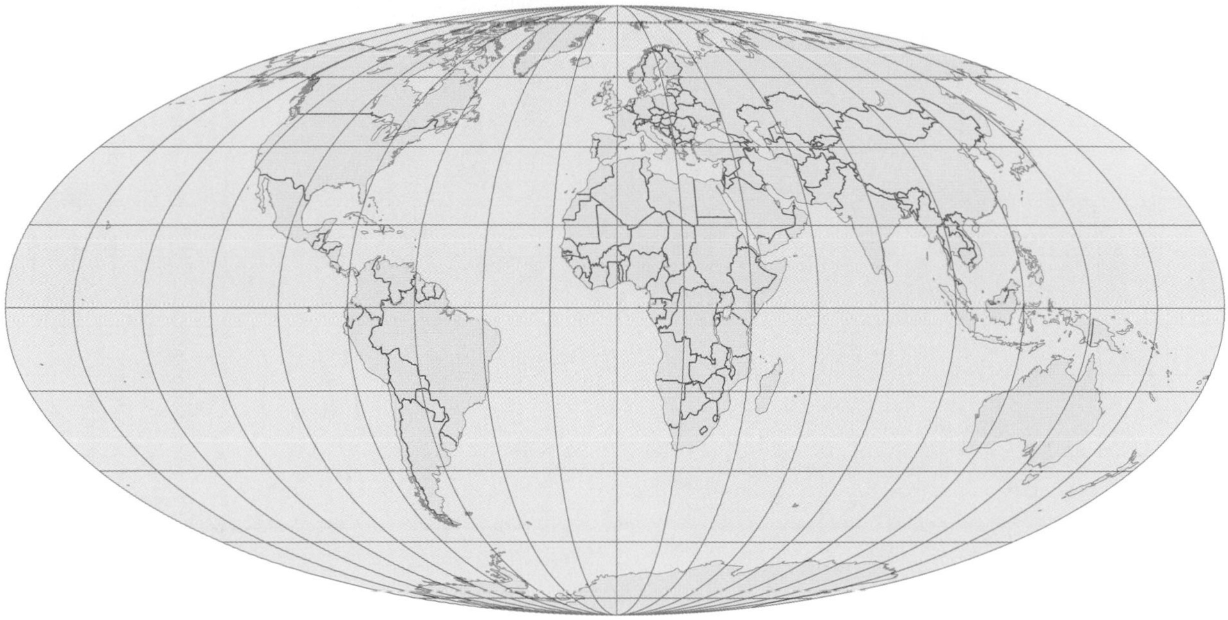

Winkel Tripel Projection

Climate Zones

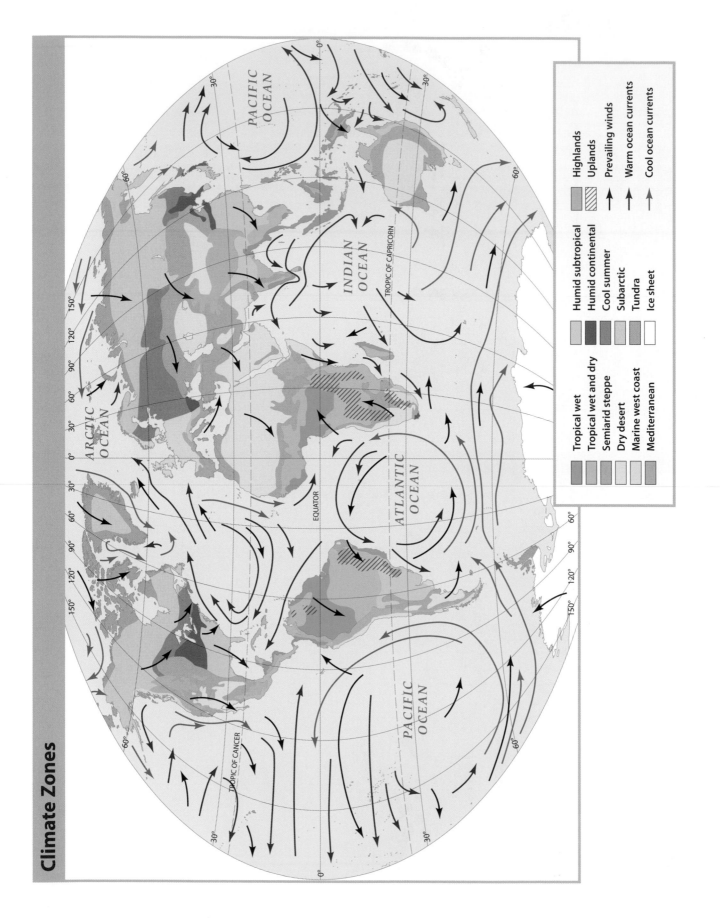

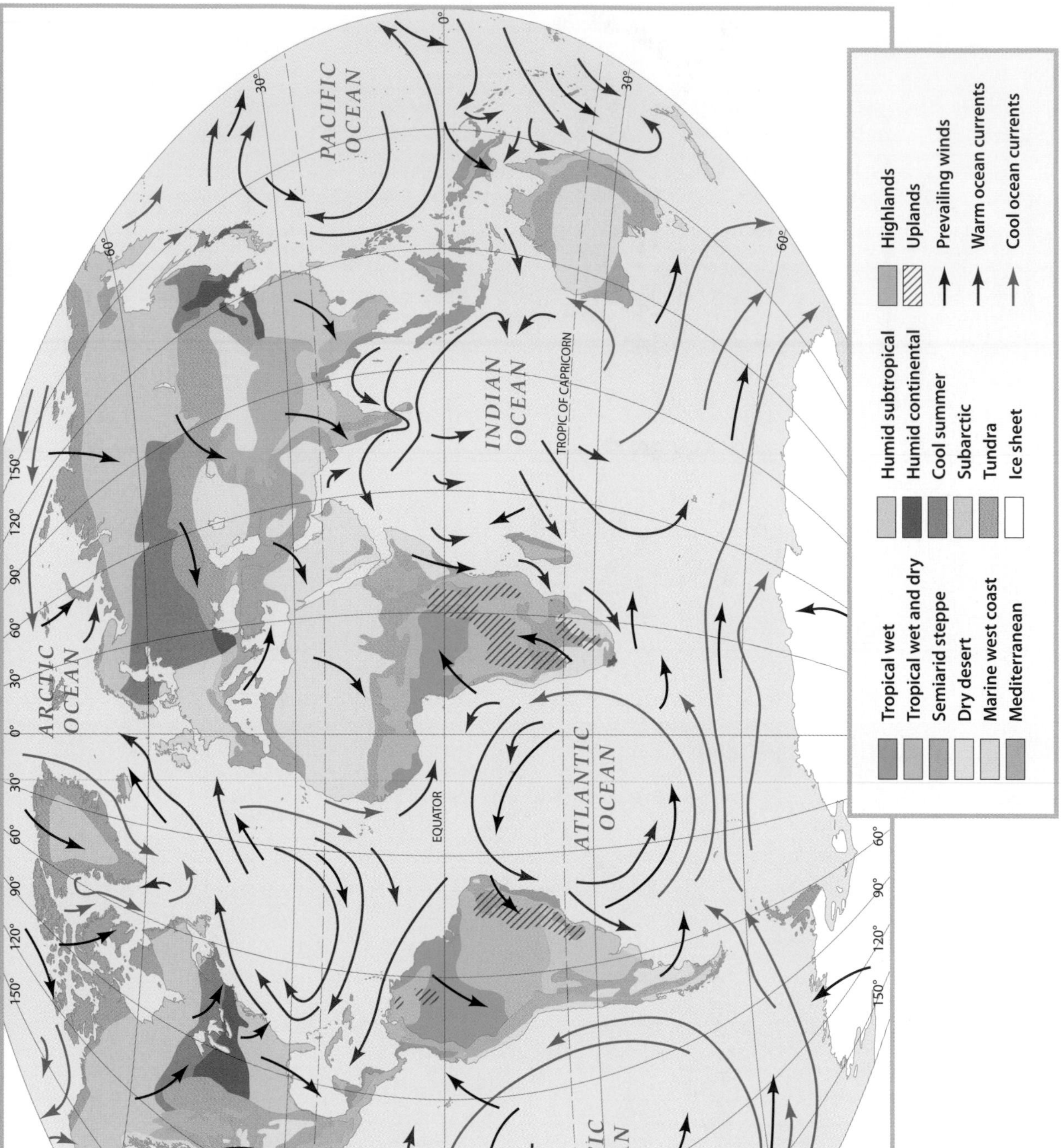

ARCTIC OCEAN
PACIFIC OCEAN
INDIAN OCEAN
ATLANTIC OCEAN
PACIFIC OCEAN
TROPIC OF CANCER
EQUATOR
TROPIC OF CAPRICORN
0°
30°
60°
90°
120°
150°
Tropical wet
Tropical wet and dry
Semiarid steppe
Dry desert
Marine west coast
Mediterranean
Humid subtropical
Humid continental
Cool summer
Subarctic
Tundra
Ice sheet
Highlands
Uplands
Prevailing winds
Warm ocean currents
Cool ocean currents

Terrestrial Biomes

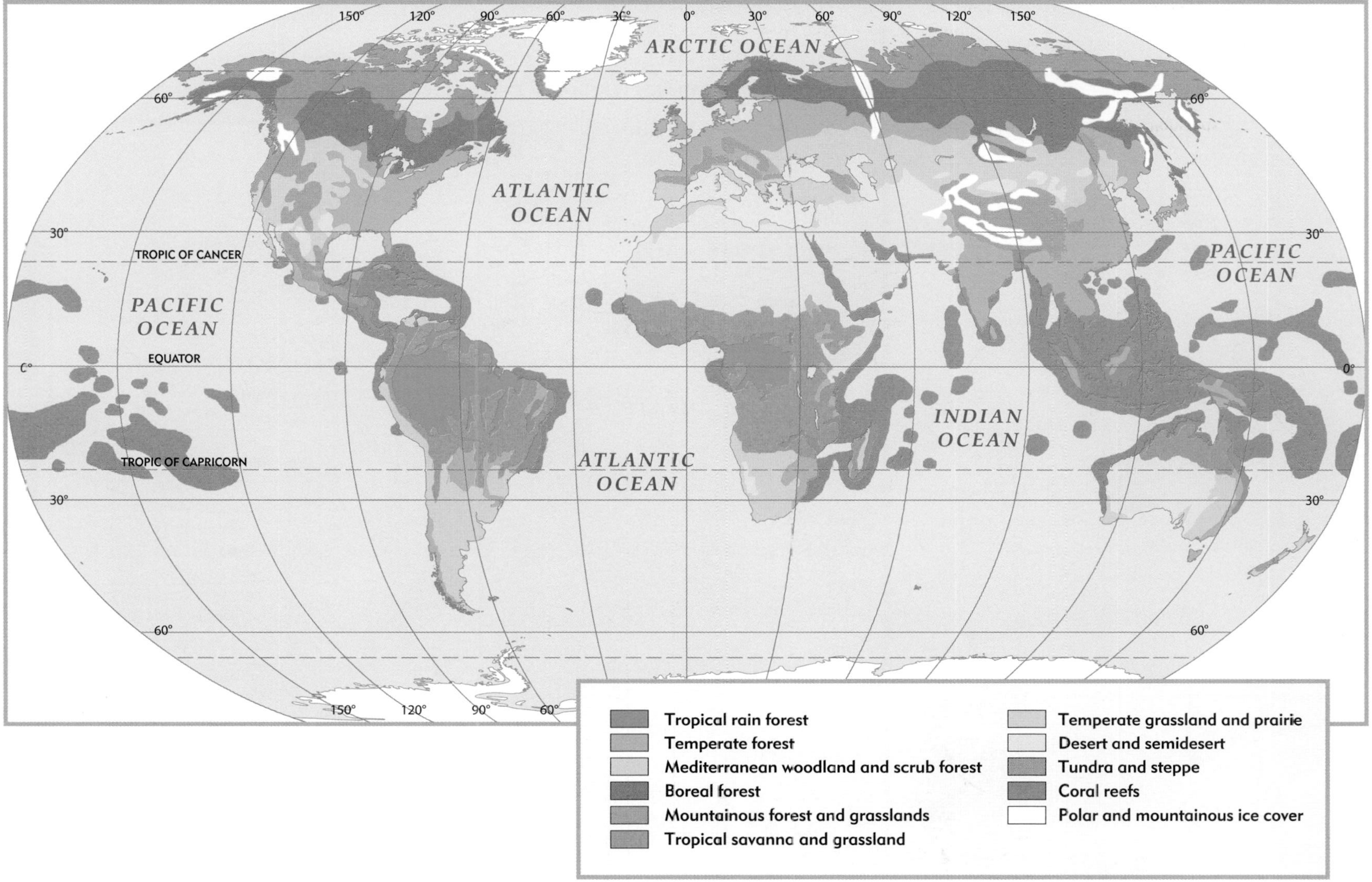

ARCTIC OCEAN
ATLANTIC OCEAN
PACIFIC OCEAN
INDIAN OCEAN
ATLANTIC OCEAN
PACIFIC OCEAN
TROPIC OF CANCER
EQUATOR
TROPIC OF CAPRICORN
150° 120° 90° 60° 30° 0° 30° 60° 90° 120° 150°
60° 30° 0° 30° 60°
Tropical rain forest
Temperate forest
Mediterranean woodland and scrub forest
Boreal forest
Mountainous forest and grasslands
Tropical savanna and grassland
Temperate grassland and prairie
Desert and semidesert
Tundra and steppe
Coral reefs
Polar and mountainous ice cover

GNI (Gross National Income)

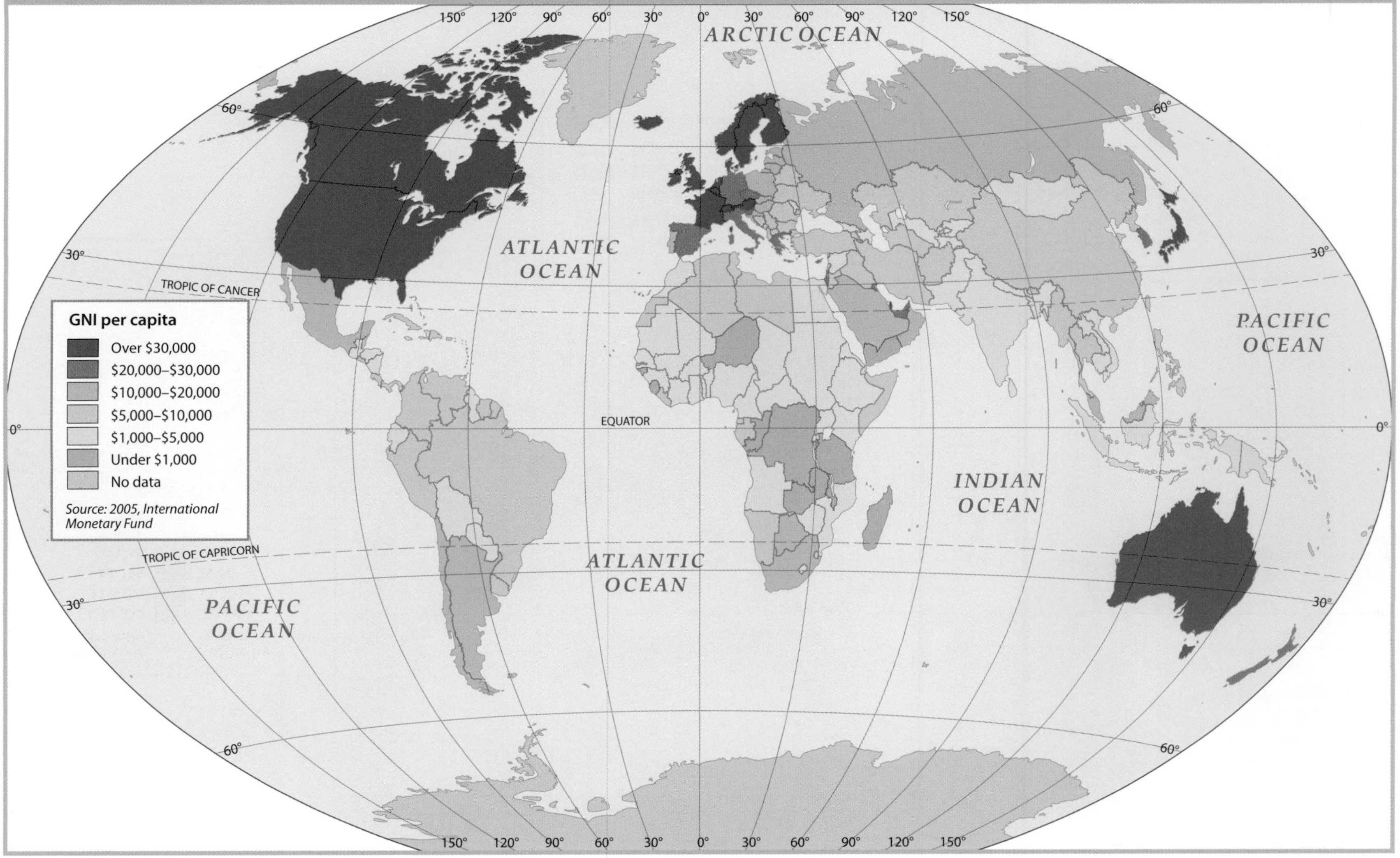

GNI (Gross National Income) is the total value of goods and services produced by a nation in a given period (typically in a year). Per capita is a statistical term meaning per person.

Population Density

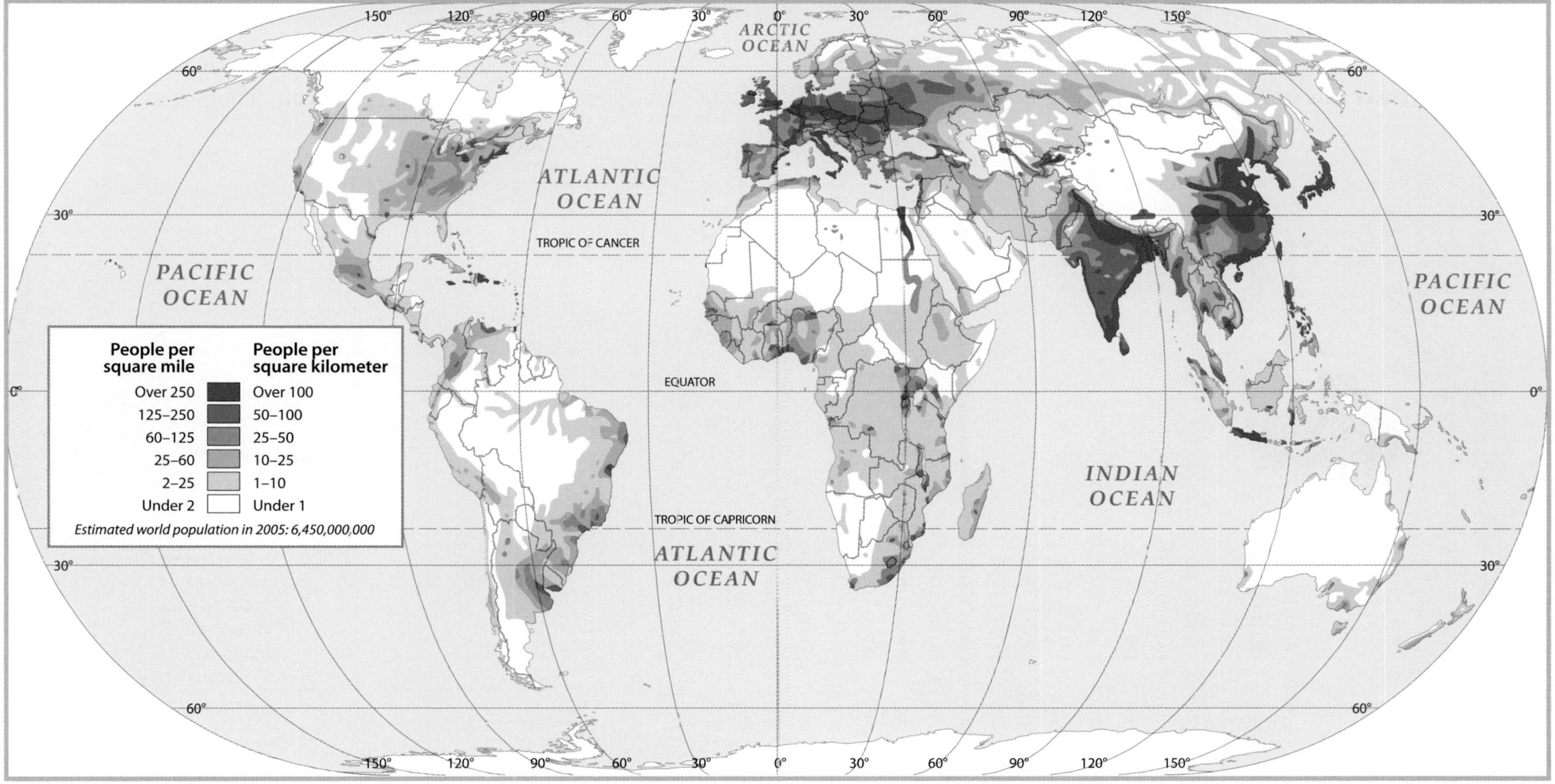
ARCTIC OCEAN
ATLANTIC OCEAN
PACIFIC OCEAN
PACIFIC OCEAN
INDIAN OCEAN
ATLANTIC OCEAN
TROPIC OF CANCER
EQUATOR
TROPIC OF CAPRICORN
150°
120°
90°
60°
30°
0°
30°
60°
90°
120°
150°
60°
30°
0°
30°
60°
People per square mile
Over 250
125–250
60–125
25–60
2–25
Under 2
People per square kilometer
Over 100
50–100
25–50
10–25
1–10
Under 1
Estimated world population in 2005: 6,450,000,000

Pronunciation Guide

The table below provides sample words to explain the sounds associated with specific letters and letter combinations used in the respellings in this book. For example, in the respelling of *Czechoslovakia*—cheh-kuh-sloh-VAH-kee-uh—the letters *AH* represent the vowel sound you hear in *hot* and *father*.

Vowels

a	short a: **a**pple, c**a**t
ay	long a: c**a**ne, d**ay**
e, eh	short e: h**e**n, b**e**d
ee	long e: f**ee**d, t**ea**m
i, ih	short i: l**i**p, act**i**ve
iy	long i: tr**y**, m**igh**t
ah	short o: h**o**t, f**a**ther
oh	long o: h**o**me, thr**ow**
uh	short u: sh**u**t, **o**ther
yoo	long u: **u**nion, c**u**te

Letter combinations

ch	**ch**in, an**c**ient
sh	**sh**ow, mi**ss**ion
zh	vi**s**ion, a**z**ure
th	**th**in, heal**th**
th	**th**en, hea**th**er
ur	b**ir**d, f**ur**ther, w**or**d
us	b**us**, cr**ust**
or	c**our**t, f**or**mal
ehr	**er**ror, c**are**
oo	c**oo**l, tr**ue**, f**ew**, r**u**le
ow	n**ow**, **ou**t
ou	l**oo**k, p**u**ll, w**ou**ld
oy	c**oi**n, t**oy**
aw	s**aw**, m**au**l, f**a**ll
ng	so**ng**, fi**ng**er
air	**Ar**istotle, b**arr**ister
ahr	c**ar**t, m**ar**tyr

Consonants

b	**b**utter, ba**b**y
d	**d**og, cra**d**le
f	**f**un, **ph**one
g	**g**rade, an**g**le
h	**h**at, a**h**ead
j	**j**u**dg**e, gor**g**e
k	**k**ite, **c**ar, bla**ck**
l	**l**i**l**y, mi**l**e
m	**m**o**m**, ca**m**el
n	**n**ext, ca**n**did
p	**p**rice, co**pp**er
r	**r**ubbe**r**, f**r**ee
s	**s**mall, **c**ircle, ha**ss**le
t	**t**on, po**tt**ery
v	**v**ase, **v**i**v**id
w	**w**all, a**w**ay
y	**y**ellow, ka**y**ak
z	**z**ebra, ha**z**e

Glossary

absolute monarch a king or queen who rules with unlimited power

Allied Powers in World War I, the countries that formed an alliance to fight the Central Powers; the principal Allied Powers in World War I were the United Kingdom, Belgium, France, Russia, Italy, and the United States (from 1917 to end); in World War II, the countries that formed an alliance to fight the Axis Powers; the principal Allied Powers in World War II were the United Kingdom, France, the United States, and the USSR

anti-Semitism hatred of or prejudice against Jews

apartheid (up-PAHR-tiyd) policy of strict racial segregation in South Africa pursued from 1948 to 1991

appeasement policy of giving in to an aggressor nation's demands in the hope of preventing war; most frequently applied to the British and French response to Hitler before World War II

Arafat (AIR-uh-fat), Yasser (1929–2004) leader of the Palestine Liberation Organization from 1969–2004

Armenian Massacre the forced deportation and massacre of Armenians by the Ottoman Turkish government during World War I; death toll estimates range from hundreds of thousands to over a million, and many consider it the first genocide in history

Armstrong, Neil (b. 1930) on July 20, 1969, became first person to set foot on the moon

Ataturk, Kemal (1881–1938) Turkish nationalist leader; founder and first president of the Republic of Turkey; he implemented sweeping social, political, and economic reforms to modernize Turkey

Aung San Suu Kyi (awn sahn soo chee) (b. 1945) activist for democracy in Burma (Myanmar); she leads the opposition to military rule in that nation and has been under house arrest frequently since 1989

Axis Powers in World War II, the nations of Germany, Italy, and Japan; they fought the Allied Powers

ayatollah (ih-uh-TOH-luh) in Shi'ite Islam, a religious leader learned in Islamic law and other subjects

Baath (bath) Party an Arab nationalist party founded in Syria in the 1940s that gained followers in Syria, Iraq, and Lebanon; it promotes Arab unity, freedom from Western influence, and economic socialism; it produced two dictators: Saddam Hussein of Iraq and Hafez al-Assad of Syria

Bataan (buh-TAN) Death March the forced march of more than 70,000 American and Filipino prisoners over 60 miles in April 1942 during World War II; prisoners of the Japanese, they endured starvation, physical cruelty and abuse, and many died

Battle of Britain decisive World War II air battle between the British and Germans fought from July to September 1940; having conquered much of Western Europe, Germany attempted to force Britain to surrender by bombing British airbases and London itself, but the British prevailed

Battle of Stalingrad World War II battle between Soviet and German forces from summer 1942 to February 1943; a turning point in World War II and the most deadly battle in human history, leaving almost two million dead

Bay of Pigs site of failed United States–sponsored invasion of Cuba in April 1961; the American intent was to overthrow the island's communist dictator, Fidel Castro

Beauvoir, Simone de (see-MOHN deh bohv-WAHR) (1908–1986) French author who sparked a post–World War II debate on the role of women with her book *The Second Sex*

Berlin Airlift initiative of the United States, the United Kingdom, and France to supply West Berlin by air after Soviets blocked land entries into the city's western sector in 1948; the airlift brought food, fuel, and other supplies to more than two million residents and lasted about a year

Berlin Wall built in 1961 to prevent East Germans from moving to democratic West Germany; it became a symbol of communist oppression and Cold War rivalry

bin Laden, Osama (oh-SAH-muh bin LAH-duhn) (b. 1957) Islamic extremist who founded the terrorist organization al-Qaeda and masterminded the bombing of the World Trade Center in New York City in 2001

Bismarck, Otto von (1815–1898) known as the "Iron Chancellor," he masterminded Germany's unification in the late nineteenth century, and its economic and political development in the late nineteenth and early twentieth century

Black September Palestinian term for September 1970, when Jordanian forces attacked the PLO in Jordan; also the name of a group of Palestinian militants who, during the 1972 Munich Olympics, killed 11 members of the Israeli Olympic team

blitzkrieg (BLIHTZ-kreeg) "lightning war"; a type of warfare employed by Nazi Germany in World War II, with the objective of quickly overwhelming the enemy; it involved surprise air attacks and light, fast-moving tanks followed by foot soldiers; it allowed the Germans rapid conquest early in the war

Bolshevik (BOHL-shuh-vik) Party communist party founded by Vladimir Lenin as a party of professional revolutionaries; the Bolsheviks came to power in Russia in 1917

Borlaug, Norman (b. 1914) American plant geneticist responsible for dramatically improving crop yields in the 1960s; he helped bring about the Green Revolution, which eliminated the threat of starvation for many in the developing world

Boxer Rebellion uprising against the numerous foreigners in China in 1900, led by a secret society known as the Boxers, who resented foreign domination of China; they were crushed by an eight-nation invasion force intent on preserving foreign dominance

Brezhnev, Leonid (LEE-uh-nid BREZH-nef) (1906–1982) Soviet leader from 1964 to 1982; he signed the Helsinki Accords in 1975, which triggered human rights activism in Eastern Europe

Camp David Accords major agreement signed by Egypt and Israel in 1978, in which Egypt recognized Israel's right to exist, while Israel agreed to give up parts of the Sinai Peninsula it still occupied; the Accords called for a peace treaty between Egypt and Israel

capitalism economic system based on private ownership of land and resources, in which individuals and businesses produce goods and services in order to make money; also known as the free enterprise (or free market) system

Castro, Fidel (b. 1926) communist dictator who overthrew U.S.-backed dictator Fulgencio Batista in 1959 and has ruled the island-nation for more than four decades

Central Powers term used in World War I to describe an alliance formed by Germany, Austria-Hungary, and the Ottoman Empire; the Central Powers fought the Allied Powers

Chamberlain, Neville (1869–1940) British prime minister from 1937 to 1940; he attempted to appease Adolf Hitler and was famously wrong in his 1938 proclamation that he had secured "peace in our time"

Churchill, Winston (1874–1965) British prime minister through most of World War II and one of the greatest statesmen in history

Clemenceau, Georges (zhorzh kleh-mahn-SOH) (1841–1929) led France through the close of World War I and presided over the Paris Peace Conference; he was eager to see a severe and punitive peace against Germany

Cold War period of tension and rivalry between communist nations (led by the Soviet Union) and noncommunist nations (led by the United States) lasting from 1947 to 1991; the superpowers did not fight an actual war (a "hot" war), so the rivalry was referred to as the Cold War

communism an economic and political system based on the writings of Karl Marx and Vladimir Lenin; communism assumes class conflict and allegedly pursues social equality and the goal of a worker state; communist governments own and control the means of production, plan all aspects of social and economic life, and, in practice, restrict free expression; they have often become totalitarian regimes led by a dictator

Communist Manifesto 1848 pamphlet written by Karl Marx and Friedrich Engels that predicted class warfare between the proletariat (workers) and bourgeoisie (owners of industry), and the collapse of the capitalist system, to be followed, Marx hoped, by a communist society in which all would share in the society's wealth; it urged working men of all countries to rise in revolt

concentration camp a place where political prisoners and/or members of groups deemed dangerous to the state are imprisoned and sometimes killed; they differ from prisons because those incarcerated receive no trial; Nazi Germany employed concentration camps on a massive scale, mainly for Jews but also for others regarded as "misfits"

constitutional monarchy a form of government in which a king or queen rules in conjunction with a parliament, congress, or some representative body elected by citizens as set forth in a constitution that guarantees certain rights

Cuban Missile Crisis confrontation between the United States and the USSR in October 1962, when the Soviets secretly installed nuclear missiles on the island of Cuba; the United States blockaded the island; the crisis was the closest the world has ever come to nuclear war

Dadaism a sort of anti-art; it was a post–World War I movement in the arts that rejected tradition and convention, mocked certitude, and emphasized absurdity

Darwin, Charles (1809–1882) English scientist who formulated the theory of evolution by natural selection; author of *The Origin of Species*

D-day a military term for the date an operation is to begin; it now generally refers to the massive Allied invasion of the European continent on June 6, 1944, at Normandy; a major turning point in World War II, after which the Allies went on to defeat Hitler

decolonization term referring to the end of (mainly) European empires in the wake of World War II, and the achievement of independence by many former Asian and African colonies

détente (day-TAHNT) an effort to reduce tensions and establish better relations between superpowers in the 1970s; from the French word meaning "easing" or "relaxation"

domino theory Cold War theory expressed by U.S. President Dwight D. Eisenhower; it maintained that in a world of interconnected nations, if one country fell to the communist side, then neighboring countries might follow, like a line of dominoes knocking each other down

Dubcek (DOOB-chek), Alexander (1921–1992) Czech leader who tried to reform communism in his nation, promoting "socialism with a human face"; his program of reforms proposed in the late 1960s reduced government censorship and was intended to increase citizens' participation in party politics (*see* Prague Spring), but resulted in Soviet invasion

Einstein, Albert (1879–1955) greatest physicist of the twentieth century; his theories of matter and energy, space, and time solved hitherto insoluble problems and prompted new understandings and ideas

Eisenhower, Dwight D. (1890–1969) U.S. commander of Allied forces during World War II, and director of the important D-day operation; he served as president of the United States from 1953 to 1961

ENIAC one of the world's first electronic, digital computers, developed during World War II and completed in 1946; filling an entire room, it could carry out 5,000 calculations per second and was considered a marvel

fascism a form of government usually headed by a dictator that controls all aspects of political, social, and economic life (though permits private ownership of industry and property); characterized by extreme patriotism, hatred or persecution of minorities, and often warlike policies; Benito Mussolini introduced the term after World War I

fedayeen (feh-duh-YEEN) Islamic term for those willing to sacrifice themselves to attain a group goal; now generally refers to Palestinian guerrilla fighters who launched raids on Israel, starting in the mid-1950s

feminism the belief that women are in every way the political, economic, and social equals of men

Fleming, Alexander (1881–1955) Scottish physician who studied bacteria and discovered the germ-killing power of penicillin, the first important antibiotic

Fourteen Points Woodrow Wilson's idealistic set of principles for a World War I peace settlement; proposed in 1918, they included self-determination of peoples, removal of barriers to trade among nations, and an international organization to mediate differences; many of the Fourteen Points were opposed by other powers negotiating the peace

Franco, General Francisco (1892–1975) dictator who ruled Spain from 1939–1975; he emerged victorious from Spain's bloody civil war, and was accused of heading a Fascist regime through much of his rule

Franz Josef (1830–1916) emperor of the dual monarchy of Austria-Hungary; he ruled for 68 years but triggered World War I when he declared war on Serbia for the assassination of his nephew and heir

Freud, Sigmund (1856–1939) Austrian physician and psychiatrist who emphasized the role of the unconscious and subconscious in human behavior; his highly influential theories transformed the field of psychiatry and greatly influenced the arts in the first part of the twentieth century

Friedan (free-DAN), Betty (1921–2006) American women's rights activist who sparked the women's movement with her publication of *The Feminine Mystique* in 1963

Fukuzawa Yukichi (fou-kou-ZAH-wah yoo-KEE-chee) (1835–1901) Japanese writer, educator, and intellectual who encouraged the Meiji to abandon Japan's feudal past and modernize, adopting Western science, technology, and industry in order to strengthen Japan

Gagarin (guh-GAHR-in), Yuri (1934–1968) Soviet cosmonaut who became the first person in space on April 12, 1961, when he orbited the earth in a flight that lasted one hour and forty-eight minutes

Gandhi (GAHN-dee), Mohandas Karamchand (1869–1948) Indian activist who used nonviolent resistance to win rights for Indians in South Africa and then to gain India's independence from Great Britain

Gates, Bill (b. 1955) American computer programmer and entrepreneur who cofounded Microsoft, a software company that developed operating systems used by most personal computers; one of the wealthiest individuals in the world and heavily involved in philanthropy

Gaza Strip a small strip of land along the eastern coast of the Mediterranean Sea, where Egypt and Israel meet; fought over since 1948 and densely populated, it has been home to a large Palestinian refugee population; the Palestinian Authority currently governs Gaza

genocide the deliberate and systematic destruction of a racial, political, religious, or cultural group; the term was coined in World War II

glasnost (GLAZ-nohst) Russian word meaning "openness, candor, transparency"; in the 1980s Soviet leader Mikhail Gorbachev made the term common when he called for glasnost in his nation, or an end to such practices as banning books, jamming foreign radio broadcasts, and throwing dissidents into prison

Gorbachev (gur-buh-CHAWF), Mikhail (b. 1931) became general secretary of the Communist Party in 1985; he advocated reform and openness in the Soviet socialist system through the policies of glasnost and perestroika; in 1991, he signed the decree that officially brought an end to the Union of Soviet Socialist Republics

Great Depression severe, worldwide economic decline during the 1930s; it resulted in high unemployment and low business activity, and contributed to political unrest in Europe

Great Leap Forward Mao's program of modernization for China, which was in fact a great leap backward

Great War term used to describe World War I before World War II began; at the time, World War I was rightly regarded as a war of unprecedented magnitude

Green Revolution a sharp increase in crop yields worldwide in the 1960s, owing to use of modern agricultural techniques and plant breeding; it reduced the threat of famine and starvation in the developing world

Hamas (hah-MAHS) Palestinian political party and terrorist organization founded in 1987 by militant Islamists

Helsinki Accords 1975 agreement signed by the United States and the USSR aimed at reducing Cold War tensions; included Western recognition of the Soviet Union's claim to Eastern Europe, but also a requirement for nations to honor the principles and freedoms outlined in the Universal Declaration of Human Rights; it encouraged Eastern European human rights activism, ultimately culminating in Soviet withdrawal

Hezbollah (hehz-boh-LAH) militant Islamist organization formed in Lebanon in 1982 and inspired by the Iranian Revolution; it engages in terrorist activities against many Western targets, and also participates in Lebanese politics

Hirohito (1901–1989) Emperor of Japan during World War II, he oversaw his nation's military buildup and ultimate defeat, personally announcing Japan's surrender in 1945

Hiroshima (heer-uh-SHEE-mah) Japanese city that during World War II became the first city in history to be hit by an atomic bomb; the bomb was dropped by a U.S. Air Force bomber on August 6, 1945, immediately killing more than 70,000 people

Hitler, Adolf (1889–1945) German dictator who founded the Nazi party and ruled Germany from 1933 to 1945; he started World War II and was responsible for the deaths of untold millions

Ho Chi Minh (hoh chee min) (1890–1969) nationalist leader and communist dictator of North Vietnam; he led the Vietnamese to independence from the French, cultivated ties to the Soviet Union and China, and ruled over communist North Vietnam (Democratic Republic of Vietnam) during the Vietnam War

Holocaust, the refers to the Nazis' systematic mass slaughter of Europe's Jews and others during World War II; the Holocaust brought about the deaths of at least six million people, approximately two-thirds of Europe's Jewish population

Hussein, Saddam (sah-DAHM hoo-SAYN) (1937–2006) Iraqi dictator who governed Iraq from 1979 to 2003; he was ousted by a U.S.-led invasion in 2003 and executed in 2006

Ibn Saud, Abd al-Aziz (1880–1953) conquered and united the various kingdoms of the Arabian peninsula after World War I, becoming king of the new state of Saudi Arabia in 1932, which he ruled as an absolute monarch until his death

imperialism the policy by which one nation controls another country or territory, often one that is far away

Industrial Revolution the great changes brought about in the late eighteenth and nineteenth century, when power-driven machinery began to produce many goods, which were assembled in factories

Information Revolution dramatic increase in the availability of information, made possible by enormous advances in electronics in the late twentieth century

Iranian Revolution the 1979 overthrow of Mohammad Reza Shah Pahlavi, a corrupt monarch of Iran who historically had the backing of the United States, in favor of Shi'ite cleric Ayatollah Ruhollah Khomeini, who sought an Islamic Republic

Islamism a political and social movement that insists Islamic law (Shari'ah) and teaching must govern all aspects of life; most Islamists believe in armed struggle, which they call jihad, to attain their goals, which include the overthrow of all secular Middle Eastern regimes; the expulsion of Israel; and the defeat of Western powers, particularly the United States

isolationism a policy of withdrawal from world affairs

jihad literally translated, "struggle"; in Islam, it is sometimes used to describe moral striving or the struggle for goodness; it is also used to refer to armed struggle against nonbelievers in the Muslim faith

Jobs, Steve (b. 1955) one of the pioneers of personal computers, and cofounder of Apple Computer Incorporated

John Paul II (born Karol Jozef Wojtyla) (1920–2005) Polish pope of the Roman Catholic Church from 1978 to 2005; he was instrumental in ending the Cold War

kamikaze Japanese pilots who undertook suicide missions during World War II, often ramming their planes into enemy warships

Kennedy, John F. (1917–1963) U.S. president during the Cuban Missile Crisis; his deft handling of the crisis helped avoid nuclear war

Khomeini (koh-MAY-nee), Ruhollah (1900?–1989) as Ayatollah Khomeini, he led the 1979 Iranian Revolution against the shah and turned Iran into an Islamic republic, governed by strict Islamic law

Khrushchev, Nikita (nih-KEE-tuh kroosh-CHEHF) (1894–1971) Soviet leader from 1953 to 1964, he denounced Stalin and encouraged his nation's space program, but his plan to install nuclear missiles in Cuba provoked the Cuban Missile Crisis

Korean War fought between 1950 and 1953, after troops from communist North Korea invaded noncommunist South Korea; the United Nations, for the first time, played a military role in a war, although the United States provided most of the troops

Lawrence of Arabia (1888–1935) Thomas Edward Lawrence, a British soldier and writer who helped mobilize Arabs against the Ottomans in World War I, led guerrilla raids, and encouraged nationalist hopes in the Middle East

League of Nations international organization formed after World War I to maintain peace among nations; the United States did not join the League, which was unsuccessful in deterring fascist aggression in the 1930s

lebensraum (LAY-bens-rowm) translated as "living space," was Hitler's justification for annexing land beyond German borders

Lenin, Vladimir (VLAD-uh-mihr LEN-in) (1870–1924) founded Russia's Communist Party and established the world's first communist dictatorship; his pamphlet "What Is to Be Done?" built on the ideas of Karl Marx, but called for a professional class of revolutionaries

Lloyd George, David (1863–1945) British statesman responsible for major social welfare legislation; served as prime minister during last half of World War I

Lost Generation generation that fought and survived World War I, many of whom were disillusioned by the war and its aftermath; American writers such as Ernest Hemingway and F. Scott Fitzgerald were part of the Lost Generation

Lusitania luxurious British ocean liner torpedoed and sunk by a German U-boat in 1915 during World War I

MacArthur, Douglas (1880–1964) American general who led forces during World War II and the Korean War, and who oversaw the American occupation of Japan immediately after World War II

Mandela (man-DEHL-uh), Nelson (b. 1918) South African leader who spent almost three decades in prison for anti-apartheid activities; in 1994, he became South Africa's first black president

Manhattan Project secret research program launched by the U.S. government during World War II to develop the first atomic bomb

Mao Zedong (MOW zuh-DOUNG) (1893–1976) dictator who led the struggle to make China a communist nation; ruled the People's Republic of China from 1949 until his death in 1976

Marshall Plan U.S. program that supplied billions of dollars in aid to help rebuild Europe after World War II; named for Secretary of State George Marshall

Marx, Karl (1818–1883) critic of capitalism and author of the *Communist Manifesto* and *Das Kapital*; he predicted a revolution of workers and ultimately a communist state

Meiji (MAY-jee) era period of Japanese history (1868–1912) during which the Meiji emperor reigned, a time when Japan began to modernize and become a world power; means "Enlightened Rule"

Meir, Golda (GOHL-duh may-IR) (1898–1978) Israeli leader who helped found the State of Israel in 1948; served as Israel's prime minister from 1969 to 1974

militarism the glorification of military might

Mohammad Reza Pahlavi (1919–1980) shah of Iran who reigned from 1941 to 1979; he was overthrown during the Islamic Revolution of 1979

mujahideen (moo-ja-hih-DEEN) literally, one who wages jihad; Islamic guerrilla fighters, for example, Muslim rebels who fought against the Soviet invasion of Afghanistan in the 1980s

Muslim Brotherhood an Islamist political and religious organization, founded in Egypt in 1928 by Hasan al-Banna, advocating society and governments based on Islamic law and teaching; historically opposed to secular government, it organized a terrorist arm in the 1940s

Mussolini, (MOO-soh-LEE-nee), Benito (1883–1945) founder of fascism and dictator of Italy from 1925 until 1943

Mutual Assured Destruction (MAD) a Cold War strategy to avoid nuclear war; the United States and the USSR each understood that to launch a nuclear attack on the other would result in a nuclear retaliation, resulting in the destruction of both countries

Nasser, Gamal Abdul (1918–1970) Egyptian nationalist who in 1952 helped overthrow Egypt's king and establish a republic; became Egypt's president and a champion of pan-Arabism; he was frequently a hero to the Arab world until the Six Day War

nationalism a strong sense of attachment or belonging to one's own country; at its worst, nationalism means glorifying one's own nation over all other countries, even at the expense of other countries

NATO North Atlantic Treaty Organization, a Cold War military alliance established by the United States, Britain, and other Western nations in 1949 to deter a Soviet attack on a member nation

Nazi (NAHT-see) Party National Socialist German Workers' Party, the German political party led by Adolf Hitler before and during World War II; Nazi goals included eliminating races they viewed as "inferior," especially the Jews

Nehru (NAY-roo), Jawaharlal (1889–1964) first prime minister of India

Nicholas II (1868–1918) last tsar of Russia, ruling from 1894 to 1917; Nicholas was overthrown and subsequently killed by Bolsheviks during the Russian Revolution

nonalignment policy of avoiding alliance with either of the world's two Cold War superpowers, the United States and the Soviet Union

nuclear weapons weapons of enormous destructive power that produce an explosion by converting matter into energy; atomic bombs and hydrogen bombs are both nuclear weapons

Nuremberg Trials trials held at Nuremberg, Germany, after World War II to judge Nazi officials accused of committing war crimes and other atrocities

OPEC Organization of Petroleum Exporting Countries, a cartel of oil-producing countries, established in 1960, that seeks greater control over the supply and price of oil

Ottoman Empire vast Islamic empire centered in Asia Minor that became one of the world's most powerful empires in the fifteenth and sixteenth centuries; the Ottomans were defeated by the Allies in World War I

Palestine small region bordering the eastern shore of the Mediterranean Sea, often called the Holy Land because of its historical importance to Jews, Christians, and Muslims

Palestine Liberation Organization (PLO) organization established by Arab leaders in 1964 to represent Palestinians and help them regain lands they lost in 1948 with the creation of Israel; has often conducted guerrilla attacks against Israel, although it negotiated for peace with Israel in the 1990s

Palestinians in contemporary usage, an Arabic-speaking people native to the region of Palestine; nearly all Palestinians are Muslims

pan-Arabism movement that promoted the idea that the Arab world could act with unity for a common purpose

Pearl Harbor site of a U.S. naval base in Hawaii; the surprise attack on Pearl Harbor by Japanese planes on December 7, 1941, brought the United States into World War II

perestroika (pehr-uh-STORY-kuh) Russian word meaning "restructuring"; a reform initiated by Mikhail Gorbachev to restructure the Soviet economy so the Communist Party would have less power over production decisions

Persian Gulf War 1991 war in which a coalition of 39 countries led by the U.S. and Britain quickly defeated Iraq, which had invaded the neighboring country of Kuwait

Prague Spring period of political reforms in Czechoslovakia in early 1968 that emphasized greater freedom; it triggered an invasion by the Soviet Union

proletariat (PROH-luh-TEHR-ee-uht) factory laborers and others who work for wages; according to Karl Marx, the huge proletariat class would someday overthrow the wealthy owners of businesses

Qaeda, al Islamist terrorist organization founded by Osama bin Laden in the late 1980s; responsible for destruction of the World Trade Center in New York City on September 11, 2001

Qur'an (kuh-RAN) the sacred book of Islam

Reagan, Ronald (1911–2004) U.S. president from 1981 to 1989; a tough critic of Soviet totalitarianism, Reagan sought to win the Cold War by building up U.S. military strength, but also agreed with the USSR's Mikhail Gorbachev to reduce nuclear arms

Reza Shah Pahlavi (1878–1944) Iranian military officer and nationalist leader who staged a coup, became Iran's shah, or king, and attempted to modernize the country; he ruled from 1921 to 1941

Roaring Twenties term referring to the 1920s, a decade marked by a "roaring" economy, mainly in the United States; a time when many Americans sought fun and amusement (jazz music, ragtime, flappers, talking movies) in the wake of World War I

Roosevelt, Eleanor (1884–1962) wife of President Franklin D. Roosevelt who became a prominent advocate for the poor and minority groups; she chaired the committee that drafted the Universal Declaration of Human Rights for the United Nations

Roosevelt, Franklin D. (1882–1945) U.S. president from 1933 to 1945; helped lead Americans through the Great Depression and most of World War II

Russian Revolution of 1917 overthrew Russia's tsar, Nicholas II, in March 1917 and ended centuries of tsarist rule; it paved the way for Lenin's communist takeover in November of that year

Russo-Japanese War (1904–1905) war in which Japan defeated Russia for control of parts of Manchuria

Sadat (suh-DAHT), Anwar el- (1918–1981) president of Egypt from 1970 until his assassination in 1981; launched a war against Israel in 1973, but in 1978 he signed the Camp David Accords with Israel's Menachem Begin

Sakharov (SAH-kuh-rov), Andrei (1921–1989) Soviet dissident; as a nuclear physicist, he helped develop atomic weapons for the Soviet Union; he later campaigned for disarmament, human rights, and reform in communist countries

Salk, Jonas (1914–1995) American physician and researcher who developed the first effective vaccine for protection against polio

SALT Strategic Arms Limitation Talks, negotiations that began in 1969 between the United States and the Soviet Union to slow the buildup of nuclear arms

Second Industrial Revolution social and economic transformations in late nineteenth and twentieth centuries spurred by the development of steel and electrical power

self-determination the belief that nations should rule themselves; the idea that people have the right to determine their own fate and choose their own government

September 11 date of 2001 terrorist attacks on the United States, in which radical Islamists hijacked four passenger airliners and flew them on suicide missions, destroying the World Trade Center and damaging the Pentagon, and killing approximately three thousand people

Shari'ah (shuh-REE-uh) the Islamic code of law

Shi'ites (SHEE-ites) members of the smaller of the two branches of Islam (*see* Sunnis), also called Shi'ahs (from Shiat Ali, "the party of Ali"); Muslims who believe that the successor to Muhammad should always be a descendant of the Prophet Muhammad's family

Sino-Japanese War (1894–95) war in which the small nation of Japan defeated the forces of China, marking the emergence of Japan as a world power

Six Day War one of a series of Arab-Israeli military conflicts; in this June 1967 clash, Israeli forces, using swift air strikes, shocked the Arabs and made significant gains in territory, including the Sinai Peninsula, the Gaza Strip, and the West Bank; Israel also gained control of all Jerusalem

Social Darwinism the view that applies Charles Darwin's ideas of natural selection to society, seeing human interaction as driven by fierce competition and "survival of the fittest"

socialism an economic and political system emphasizing government control of productive property (such as factories and land) and regulation of the distribution of income; community ownership is preferred to private ownership, and government control often replaces the free play of market forces

Solidarity trade union formed in the summer of 1980 in Poland; the first self-governing worker's union to take root in the Soviet bloc (*see* Walesa, Lech)

Solzhenitsyn (sohl-zhuh-NEET-suhn), Alexander (b. 1918) Russian novelist and dissident who was exiled for writing about oppression in the Soviet Union

Sputnik the first artificial satellite; launched by the Soviet Union in 1957, it orbited the earth for months and spurred a "space race" between the United States and the USSR; further USSR satellites were also named *Sputnik*, including *Sputnik II*, which carried the first living creature into space, a dog named Laika

Stalin, Joseph (1879–1953) totalitarian dictator of the Soviet Union who expanded Soviet territory and built the USSR into a military-industrial superpower, but crushed individual freedom under the rule of a brutal police state

Suez Canal canal across the Isthmus of Suez in Egypt, linking the Red Sea and the Mediterranean; it was built by the French and zealously guarded by the British through the early twentieth century until Nasser nationalized the waterway in 1956

suffrage the right to vote, as in the movement for woman's suffrage

Sunnis (SOU-neez) members of the far larger of the two branches of Islam (*see* Shi'ites); Muslims who believe the caliph (successor to Muhammad) should be the most capable Muslim and not necessarily a descendant of Muhammad's family

Sun Yat-sen (soun yaht-sen) (1866–1925) Chinese nationalist and revolutionary; first president of the Chinese republic

surrealism short for "super realism"; term coined in 1924 by André Breton to describe the exploration by writers and artists of the deep reality of the unconscious mind

Taliban extremist Islamist regime that came to power in Afghanistan in the mid-1990s after the Soviet withdrawal and demanded strict adherence to Islamic law, banned many so-called Western behaviors, and brutally suppressed women's rights

terrorism the planned use of violence to strike fear into people or governments to obtain political goals

Thatcher, Margaret (b. 1925) first woman prime minister of Great Britain, elected in 1979, and the longest-serving British prime minister of the twentieth century

Tiananmen Square a huge plaza in central Beijing where in 1989 student demonstrations in support of democracy were swiftly and brutally suppressed by Chinese soldiers

totalitarianism a form of government that controls almost every aspect of people's lives, including political, economic, cultural, religious, and social activities

trench warfare warfare closely associated with World War I in which enemy forces attack and defend from long trenches

Truman Doctrine specifically, U.S. President Harry Truman's 1947 declaration of aid to Greece and Turkey, both threatened by communist movements; generally, a policy committing the United States to the containment of communism wherever it might spread

United Nations international organization with representatives from almost all countries in the world, established in 1945 to prevent war, promote cooperation among countries, and help settle international disputes

Universal Declaration of Human Rights document written by a United Nations committee led by Eleanor Roosevelt and committing nation-states to key principles of human dignity and rights

USSR abbreviation for Union of Soviet Socialist Republics, former communist empire consisting of Russia and other socialist states; established in 1922, it broke up in 1991

Versailles (vuhr-SIY), Treaty of treaty ending World War I between Germany and the Allied Powers; signed in 1919 at the Palace of Versailles in France, imposing harsh terms on defeated Germany, and establishing the League of Nations

Vietnam War (1957–1975) war in Southeast Asia between the eventually victorious forces of communist North Vietnam with their guerrilla allies, called the Viet Cong, and South Vietnam with its chief ally, the United States

Walesa (vah-WEN-suh), Lech (b. 1943) Polish labor leader who helped found the Solidarity trade union movement in communist Poland; elected president of Poland in 1990

Warsaw Pact Cold War military alliance between the USSR and its eastern European satellite nations, established in 1955 in response to the NATO alliance of noncommunist nations; in 1991, with the dissolution of the USSR, it ceased to exist

Weimar Republic the name given to Germany's government between 1919 and 1933; Weimar is the town where the government's constitution was drafted

West Bank land on the west side of the Jordan River, annexed by Jordan but occupied by Israel in the Six Day War of 1967, and since an area of frequent disputes

Wilhelm II (1859–1941) German kaiser (emperor) who led his nation into the catastrophe of World War I

Wilson, Woodrow (1856–1924) 28th president of the United States, known for his idealism, he reluctantly led the U.S. into World War I and afterward devoted himself to creating the League of Nations

World War I initially called the Great War, fought from 1914 to 1918 mainly between the Allied Powers of France, Russia, and Britain against the Central Powers of Germany, Austria-Hungary, and the empire of the Ottoman Turks; in 1917 the United States entered the war on the side of the Allies; the Allies won but the war left millions dead, empires in ruins, and economies shattered

World War II war fought from 1939 to 1945 mainly between the Axis Powers of Germany, Italy, and Japan, and the Allies, consisting of France, Britain, the Soviet Union, and later the United States; it was the most destructive war in human history, involving massive genocide and the first use of atomic weapons against an enemy

Yalta Conference meeting in February 1945, near the end of World War II, in which U.S. President Franklin Roosevelt, British Prime Minister Winston Churchill, and Soviet Premier Joseph Stalin negotiated agreements regarding the future of European nations and of defeated Germany

Yom Kippur War Arab-Israeli war launched in 1973 on Yom Kippur ("the day of atonement," the holiest of Jewish holidays), starting with surprise attacks by Egypt and Syria that took a heavy toll on Israeli troops; Soviet aid to Egypt and Syria spurred the United States to send aid to Israel; the war ended in a stalemate but, after Israel's swift defeat of Arab forces in the Six Day War of 1967, restored Arab confidence

Zionism Jewish nationalist movement based on the belief that the Jews should have their own nation, and specifically aiming to establish a Jewish state in Palestine (which occurred when the state of Israel was proclaimed in 1948)

Permissions

60 The Encouragement of Learning, excerpt from *The Encouragement of Learning* as translated and reprinted in Fukuzawa Yukichi, THE AUTOBIOGRAPHY OF YUKICHI FUKUZAWA. Translated by Eiichi Kiyooka. New York: Columbia University Press, 1966. Reprinted by permission of the publisher.

70 Lin Zexu Writes to Queen Victoria. Reprinted by permission of the publisher from "Lin Tse-hsü's Moral Advice to Queen Victoria," 1839 in CHINA'S RESPONSE TO THE WEST: A DOCUMENTARY SURVEY, 1839–1923, by Ssu-yü Têng and John King Fairbank, pp. 24–27, Cambridge, Mass.: Harvard University Press, copyright © 1954, 1979 by the President and Fellows of Harvard College, copyright renewed 1982 by Ssu-yü Têng and John King Fairbank.

95 Excerpt from *All Quiet On the Western Front*. Reprinted by permission of the publisher, from ALL QUIET ON THE WESTERN FRONT by Erich Maria Remarque. "Im Westen Nichts Neus," copyright 1928 by Ullstein A.G.; copyright renewed © 1956 by Erich Maria Remarque. *All Quiet On The Western Front*, copyright 1929, 1930 by Little, Brown and Company; copyright renewed © 1957, 1958 by Erich Maria Remarque. All rights reserved.

125 Excerpt from "Soldier's Home." Abridged from "Soldier's Home." Used by permission of Scribner, an imprint of Simon & Schuster Adult Publishing Group, from IN OUR TIME by Ernest Hemingway. Copyright 1925 Charles Scribner's Sons. Copyright renewed 1953 by Ernest Hemingway.

While every care has been taken to trace and acknowledge copyright, the editors tender their apologies for any accidental infringement when copyright has proven untraceable. They would be pleased to include the appropriate acknowledgement in any subsequent edition of this publication.

Illustrations Credits

Key: t=top; b=bottom; c=center; l=left; r=right

Front cover, title page: (t) NASA; (b) © Bettmann/Corbis.

Back cover: (t) © Fox Photos/Getty Images; (b) © Karel Prinsloo/AP Photo.

Prologue

8 © Sekai Bunka/Premium/Panoramic Images (pyramids); © Jupiterimages (airplane). **10** (t) © Gianni Dagli Orti/Corbis; (b) © SuperStock, Inc./SuperStock. **11** © M. Robertson/Robert Harding. **12** © NRM/SSPL/The Image Works. **13** © Index Stock (computer screen); © Masterfile (Parthenon).

Part 1

Chapter 1: 14 © David Noton/Getty Images. **16** National Archives and Records Administration, 69-RH-4L-2. **17** © Hulton Archive/Getty Images.

Chapter 2: 18 © Réunion des Musées Nationaux/Art Resource, NY. **21** © Stock Montage/SuperStock. **23** © Réunion des Musées Nationaux/Art Resource, NY. **24** © Private Collection/The Bridgeman Art Library. **26** © The Art Archive/Bibliothèque des Arts Décoratifs Paris/Dagli Orti. **27** © akg-images, London.

Chapter 3: 30 © Rue des Archives/The Granger Collection, New York. **33** © Corbis. **34** © The Granger Collection, New York. **37** © Hulton-Deutsch Collection/Corbis. **38** © Réunion des Musées Nationaux/Art Resource, NY.

Chapter 4: 40 © akg-images, London. **44** (t) © Interfoto Germany/AAA Collection Ltd.; (b) © Super-Stock, Inc./SuperStock. **46** © Bild-archiv Preussischer Kulturbesitz/Art Resource, NY. **47** © The Art Archive/Eileen Tweedy. **48** © The Art Archive/Imperial War Museum. **51** © The Art Archive/Culver Pictures. **52** © Private Collection/The Stapleton Collection/The Bridgeman Art Library.

Chapter 5: 54 © The Art Archive/Private Collection Paris/Dagli Orti. **57** © The Art Archive/British Museum. **58** Keio University Library. **59** © The Art Archive. **61** © Photo Japan/Alamy. **62** © Philadelphia Museum of Art/Corbis.

Chapter 6: 64 © Mary Evans Picture Library/Alamy. **68** © Hu Weibiao/Panorama/The Image Works. **69** © The Art Archive/Eileen Tweedy. **71** © The Granger Collection, New York. **73** © Hulton Archive/Getty Images. **74** © Hulton Archive/Getty Images. **75** © Hulton Archive/Getty Images.

Part 2

Chapter 1: 76 © Ludwig Meidner-Archiv, Jüdisches Museum der Stadt Frankfurt am Main/akg-images, London. **80** (t) © Bettmann/Corbis; (b) © The Art Archive/Domenica del Corriere/Dagli Orti.

Chapter 2: 82 © Archives Larousse, Paris, France/Giraudon/The Bridgeman Art Library. **86** Courtesy of the Director, National Army Museum, London. **87** © Bettmann/Corbis. **88** © Hulton Archive/Getty Images. **90** © The Image Works. **92** © SEF/Art Resource, NY. **93** © EON Images.

Chapter 3: 96 © The Art Archive/Private Collection/Marc Charmet. **99** © TASS/Sovfoto. **101** © Sovfoto. **103** ullstein bild/The Granger Collection, New York. **104** The Granger Collection, New York.

Chapter 4: 108 Library of Congress, Prints and Photographs Division, LC-USZ62-19271. **111** © Time Life Pictures/Getty Images, Inc. **112** © The Image Works. **113** © F. J. Mortimer/Getty Images, Inc. **114** National Archives and Records Administration, 111-sc-055456. **115** © Collection Kharbine-Tapabor, Paris, France/The Bridgeman Art Library.

Chapter 5: 118 © 2007 Salvador Dali, Gala-Salvador Dali Foundation/Artists Rights Society (ARS), New York/The Museum of Modern Art/Licensed by SCALA /Art Resource, NY. **120** © 2007 Artists Rights Society (ARS), New York/VG Bild-Kunst, Bonn/Bildarchiv Preussischer Kulturbesitz/Art Resource, NY. **122** © 2007 Artists Rights Society (ARS), New York/ADAGP, Paris/akg-images. **123** Library of Congress, Prints and Photographs Division, LC-USZC4-12986. **124** © Frank Driggs Collection/Getty Images, Inc. **125** John F. Kennedy Presidential Library. **128** © Bettmann/Corbis.

Chapter 6: 130 © Topham/The Image Works. **132** © Atlantide Phototravel/Corbis. **134** © Thinkstock.com/Jupiterimages. **135** (t) © Albert Harlingue/Roger-Viollet/The Image Works; (b) © liquidlibrary/Jupiterimages. **137** (t) © Roger-Viollet/The Image Works; (b) © General Photographic Agency/Getty Images. **139** © Topical Press Agency/Getty Images. **140** © Steve Wisbauer/Getty Images. **141** © Hulton-Deutsch Collection/Corbis. **142** The Granger Collection, New York.

Chapter 7: 144 © Hulton Archive/Getty Images. **146** Library of Congress, Prints and Photographs Division, LC-USF34-009058-C. **147** Library of Congress, Prints and Photographs Division, LC-USZ62-127379. **148** © Topham/The Image Works. **150** © Underwood & Underwood/Corbis. **153** © Topical Press Agency/Getty Images. **154** © Private Collection/The Stapleton Collection/The Bridgeman Art Library. **155** © Mary Evans Picture Library/Alamy. **156** Rue des Archives/The Granger Collection, New York. **157** © Bettmann/Corbis.

Chapter 8: 158 ullstein bild/The Granger Collection, New York. **160** © Hulton-Deutsch Collection/ Corbis. **161** © Corbis. **164** National Archives and Records Administration, 535895. **166** © Bettmann/Corbis. **167** © Bettmann/Corbis. **168** ullstein bild/ The Granger Collection, New York. **169** The Granger Collection, New York. **171** © Hulton Archive/Getty Images.

Chapter 9: 174 © Bettmann/ Corbis. **177** © akg-images. **178** © POPPERFOTO/Alamy. **179** (t) National Archives and Records Administration, 778813 28-1178a; (b) Library of Congress, Prints and Photographs Division, LC-USE6-D-006632. **180** © Bettmann/ Corbis. **181** ullstein bild/The Granger Collection, New York. **182** © The Jewish Museum, NY/ Art Resource, NY. **183** USHMM, courtesy of National Archives and Records Administration, College Park. **184** © SuperStock, Inc./ SuperStock. **185** The Granger Collection, New York. **186** (t) © Corbis; (b) © Corbis. **188** National Archives and Records Administration, 28-1378a. **189** (t) © Time Life Pictures/Getty Images; (b) © epa/Corbis. **193** © Popperfoto/Alamy.

Chapter 10: 194 Planting the Tree of Nations, poster for the United Nations, 1947 (colour litho), Eveleigh (fl.1947)/Private Collection, Archives Charmet/ The Bridgeman Art Library. **196** National Archives and Records Administration, 531340. **197** © Bettmann/Corbis. **198** © Topham/ The Image Works. **199** (t) © Helene Rogers/Alamy; (b) The Granger Collection, New York. **202** © AFP/ Getty Images.

Part 3

Chapter 1: 204 ullstein bild/The Granger Collection, New York. **206** © Science Museum/SSPL/The Image Works. **208** Library of Congress, Prints and Photographs Division, LC-3b17497v. **209** The Granger Collection, New York. **210** National Archives and Records Administration, 27-0179a. **211** © Bettmann/Corbis. **213** Library of Congress, Prints and Photographs Division, LC-USZ62-111645. **214** © David Hancock/ Alamy. **215** © Bettmann/Corbis. **216** © AP Images. **217** © Bettmann/ Corbis. **218** © AFP/Getty Images. **219** © Robert Lackenbach/Getty Images.

Chapter 2: 220 (t) © TASS/Sovfoto; (b) © Bettmann/Corbis. **222** (t) © Bettmann/Corbis; (b) © Bettmann/Corbis. **223** ullstein bild/The Granger Collection, New York. **225** © AFP/Getty Images. **226** © Time Life Pictures/Getty Images. **229** © Bettmann/Corbis. **230** © Bettmann/Corbis. **231** © Time Life Pictures/Getty Images. **233** © Berlin-Bild/SV-Bilderdienst/ The Image Works.

Chapter 3: 234 NASA. **236** © Condé Nast Archive/Corbis. **237** Ewing Galloway/Camerique Inc./Classic Stock. **238** © Omni/ omniphoto.com. **239** ullstein bild/ The Granger Collection, New York. **240** © Topham/The Image Works. **241** NASA. **242** NASA. **243** NASA. **244** © Art Rickerby/Getty Images. **245** © Bettmann/Corbis. **246** © Hulton-Deutsch Collection/Corbis. **248** (t) © Frank Driggs/Getty Images; (b) © John Kobal Foundation/Getty Images. **250** © Bettmann/Corbis.

Chapter 4: 252 © Hulton Archive/ Getty Images. **255** © Hulton Archive/Getty Images. **256** © Time Life Pictures/Getty Images. **257** © ullstein bild/Peter Arnold, Inc. **258** © Bettmann/Corbis. **260** ullstein bild/The Granger Collection, New York. **261** © POPPERFOTO/Alamy. **263** © Topham/The Image Works. **264** © Topham/The Image Works. **265** ullstein bild/The Granger Collection, New York. **267** © POPPERFOTO/Alamy. **269** © HIP/Art Resource, NY. **270** © AFP/Getty Images.

Chapter 5: 272 © Central Press/ Getty Images. **276** (t) © AFP/Getty Images; (b) © Charles Hewitt/Getty Images. **277** © Bettmann/Corbis. **278** © Bridgeman-Giraudon/ Art Resource, NY. **280** © Leif Skoogfors/Corbis. **281** (t) ullstein bild/The Granger Collection, New York; (b) © Genevieve Chauvel/Corbis. **282** © W. Schmitt/ SV-Bilderdienst/The Image Works. **283** © Simonpietri Christian/Corbis Sygma. **284** © AP Images. **285** © Makaram Gad Al-kareem/Getty Images.

Chapter 6: 288 © AP Images. **290** Library of Congress, Prints and Photographs Division, LC-USZ62-126863. **292** © Wally McNamee/ Corbis. **294** © POPPERFOTO/ Alamy. **295** © AFP/Getty Images. **296** © Libor Hajsky/Getty Images. **297** © SV-Bilderdienst/The Image Works. **299** © Sovfoto. **300** © Horacio Villalobos/Corbis. **301** © Wally McNamee/Corbis.

Chapter 7: 302 © Peter Turnley/ Corbis. **304** © Hulton-Deutsch Collection/Corbis. **305** © Sovfoto. **306** © Alain DeJean/Sygma/ Corbis. **308** © Corbis. **309** © Alain Keler/Sygma/Corbis. **310** © Diana Walker/Getty Images. **311** © Bernard Bisson & Thierry Orban/ Sygma/Corbis. **312** © Martin Athenstaedt/dpa/Corbis. **315** © Régis Bossu/Sygma/Corbis. **316** © epa/Corbis. **317** © AP Images. **318** © Wojtek Druszcz/Getty Images. **319** © Pascal Le Segretain/ Corbis Sygma.

Chapter 8: 318 © Masatomo Kuriya/Corbis. **320** © Christine Spengler/Sygma/Corbis. **322** © Bettmann/Corbis. **323** © Patrick Chauvel/Sygma/Corbis. **324** © AP Images. **325** © Bill Pierce/Getty Images. **327** (t) © Reuters/Corbis; (b) © Shah Marai/Getty Images. **328** © Peter Turnley/Corbis. **329** (t) © Peter Turnley/Corbis; (b) © Randy Jolly/The Image Works. **330** (t) © Peter Turnley/Corbis; (b) © epa/Corbis. **331** © Khalil Senosi/AP

Images. **332** © Sean Adair/Reuters/Corbis. **333** © Reuters/Corbis. **335** © Jérome Sessini/In Visu/Corbis. **336** © Reuters/Corbis.

Chapter 9: 338 © Andreanna Seymore/Getty Images. **340** © Corbis. **341** © age fotostock/SuperStock. **342** (t) © AP Images; (b) © Doug Wilson/Corbis. **343** © Time Life Pictures/Getty Images. **344** © Paul Sakuma/AP Images. **346** © Tetra Images/Corbis. **347** © Fredrik Renander/Alamy. **348** © Louie Psihoyos/Science Faction. **349** (t) © Ben Margot/AP Images; (b) © Liz Mangelsdorf/San Francisco Chronicle/Corbis. **350** © AP Images. **351** (t) © Joseph Van Os/Getty Images; (b) © Thomas Hartwell/Corbis. **352** © Fayaz Kabli/Reuters/Corbis. **353** © Viviane Moos/Corbis.

Chapter 10: 354 © Reuters/Corbis. **356** (t) The Granger Collection, New York; (b) © AP Images. **357** © Time Life Pictures/Getty Images. **358** © Nowosti/RIA/ullstein bild/Peter Arnold, Inc. **359** (t) © Micha Bar Am/Magnum Photos; (b) © Jack Novak Collection/Mary Evans Picture Library. **360** © Jean-Louis Nou/akg-images. **362** © Bettmann/Corbis. **363** (t) © Tom Stoddart/Getty Images; (b) © Roberto Candia/AP Images. **364** © cbg/str/Robert Tonsing/AP Images. **365** © Reuters/Corbis. **366** © Michele Falzone/Alamy. **367** © Anat Givon/AP Images. **369** © Steve McCurry/Magnum Photos.

Epilogue

372 © Louie Psihoyos/Corbis. **374** © Hulton Archive/Getty Images. **375** © Earl & Nazima Kowall/Corbis. **376** © Alison Wright/Corbis. **377** (l) © Erich Lessing/Art Resource, NY; (r) © CS Productions/Brand X/Jupiterimages.

Appendix: Geographic Terms and Concepts

378 © Maptec International/Photo Researchers, Inc. **381** (t) © Colin Monteath/Minden Pictures; (c) © Daryl Benson/Masterfile; (b) © Corbis. **382** (t) © WorldSat International/Photo Researchers, Inc.; (b) NASA. **383** (t) © Mark Taylor/Warren Photographic/Bruce Coleman USA; (b) © Tim Davis/Corbis. **384** (t) © Noboru Komine/Photo Researchers, Inc.; (b) © Jim Sugar/Corbis. **385** © Lester Lefkowitz/Corbis.

Index

A

B

C

G

H

K

L

M

N

O

P

T